Business and Management

for the IB Diploma

Peter Stimpson and Alex Smith

Cambridge University Press's mission is to advance learning, knowledge and research worldwide.

Our IB Diploma resources aim to:

- encourage learners to explore concepts, ideas and topics that have local and global significance
- help students develop a positive attitude to learning in preparation for higher education
- assist students in approaching complex questions, applying critical-thinking skills and forming reasoned answers.

CAMBRIDGE UNIVERSITY PRESS
Cambridge, New York, Melbourne, Madrid, Cape Town,
Singapore, São Paulo, Delhi, Mexico City

Cambridge University Press
The Edinburgh Building, Cambridge CB2 8RU, UK

www.cambridge.org
Information on this title: www.cambridge.org/9780521147309

First published 2011
Reprinted 2012

Printed in the United Kingdom at the University Press, Cambridge

A catalogue record for this publication is available from the British Library

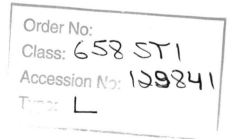

ISBN 978-0-521-14730-9

Contents

Topic 1 Business organisation and environment

Topic 2 Human resources

Topic 3 Accounts and finance

Topic 4 Marketing

Contents

Introduction

Nature of the subject

The IB Diploma Programme Business and Management is designed to develop an understanding of essential business theory and the ability to apply business principles, practices and skills. It encourages students to analyse the diverse range of business organisations and activities and the cultural and economic context in which businesses operate. The emphasis is placed on strategic decision-making and the business functions of marketing, production, human resource management and finance. Business and management is the study of both the way in which individuals and groups interact in an organisation and of the transformation of resources. It is, therefore, perfectly placed within the group 3 subject area (individuals and societies) of the IB Diploma Programme hexagon.

Who is this book for?

This book accurately and comprehensively follows the International Baccalaureate (IB) higher level (HL) and standard level (SL) syllabus for Business and Management.

If you are a student preparing for the assessments based on this syllabus, or a teacher preparing students for the assessments, you can be confident that the book provides comprehensive coverage of the course. Other students of business management courses at equivalent levels could also greatly benefit from the subject content, activities and advice that this book contains.

What are the aims of the book?

Apart from providing the appropriate subject content for the IB Business and Management course, the book aims to:

- introduce business and management as a study of the ways in which individuals and groups interact in an organisation and of how resources are transformed by businesses
- explain that business and management is a rigorous and rewarding subject that examines dynamic decision-making processes and assesses how these decisions impact on and are affected by internal and external environments
- help students to develop an understanding of business theory and the ability to apply business principles, practices and skills
- encourage students to consider the activities of business in a global market and appreciate cultural diversity
- evaluate the diverse range of business organisations and activities
- develop in students an awareness of the cultural and economic context in which businesses operate
- encourage the appreciation of ethical issues and the concept of social responsibility in the global business environment
- enable the development of decision-making skills through the use of case studies that enhance students' ability to make informed business decisions
- make a clear distinction between higher level and standard level content
- help students improve their performance on the internal and external assessments used in the Business and Management syllabus
- show how the Business and Management syllabus relates to the Theory of knowledge part of the IB Programme.

The focus on the higher level topic of business strategy in Chapter 38 also means that the book highlights the following very important aspects of business management:

- Strategic decision-making is holistic and cannot be undertaken effectively by studying a series of disconnected subject areas.
- There is no single perfect solution to a business problem – a variety of strategic solutions might exist that reflect the objectives of the business, the external environment and the cultures of both the organisation and the countries in which it operates.

What are the key features of this book?

- **Learning objectives** – identifying the key syllabus-related topics and concepts covered in each chapter.
- **'Setting the scene' case studies** – raising important areas for discussion on business issues through case studies drawn from many different countries. These provide a context to the business applications of the material to be covered in each chapter.
- **Clearly laid out text** – with easy-to-follow subsections and many tables of data and key advantages and disadvantages.
- **Examiner's tips** – helping to avoid common errors made by candidates in examinations.
- **Activities** – based on business case studies, these give practice at applying learning.
- **Revision checklists** – allowing monitoring of understanding of key issues.
- **Revision case studies and examination practice questions** – testing the skills of application, analysis and evaluation, using international business situations.
- **Theory of knowledge assignments** – these reflect the very close relationship between theory of knowledge and Business and Management.

Skills needed by Business and Management students

The skills acquired and developed by successful students of Business and Management interlink with the IB Learner Profile. In particular, decision-making, risk-taking and thinking skills are needed to weigh up and make judgements on a wide range of business strategies, and options will be transferable both to other disciplines and to higher level undergraduate study at university.

The assessments used in the IB Business and Management course will test the following skills:

- **Knowledge and understanding** of business terminology, concepts, principles and theories.
- **Application** of skills and knowledge learned to hypothetical and real business situations.
- **Analysis and evaluation** of business decisions and business strategies and practices using critical thinking.
- **Decision-making** by identifying the issue(s), selecting and interpreting data, applying appropriate tools and techniques, and recommending suitable solutions.
- **Synthesise** knowledge in order to develop a framework for business decision-making.

Difference between higher and standard levels

The HL course in Business and Management differs from the SL course in a number of important ways. These are reflected in this book by the subject content in Chapter 38 (Business strategy) and in the use of more evaluative questions and strategic decision-based tasks based on the activities and examination practice questions.

IB assessment

The exam practice questions at the end of each chapter are IB-style questions designed to give students practice at answering examination questions. Additional case studies with differentiated Standard and Higher Level questions and markschemes are provided on the Cambridge IB teacher support website (ibdiploma.cambridge.org) along with sample schemes of work for Standard and Higher Level, and revision materials.

The final chapter of the book gives clear guidance on the forms of assessment used at both SL and HL. It explains the requirements for the extended essay coursework, internal assessment and examination papers. Written by a senior IB examiner with many years' experience in preparing students for both levels of the IB Diploma, it is essential reading for all those preparing for the assessment in IB Business and Management.

Peter Stimpson
Alex Smith
February 2011

01 The nature of business activity

This chapter covers syllabus section 1.1

On completing this chapter you should be able to:

- understand what business activity involves
- identify inputs, outputs and processes of a business
- identify and explain the main business functions
- identify and explain the main sectors of industry
- (H) analyse the impact on business activity of changes in economic structure.

SETTING THE SCENE

Dulip starts his business

Dulip lives in a large country which has many natural resources such as coal and timber. He plans to start a business growing and cutting trees to sell as timber. He wants to buy a forest from a farmer and cut down a fixed number of trees each year. As Dulip is concerned about the environment of his country, he will plant two new trees for each one he cuts down.

He has contacted suppliers of saws, tractors and other equipment to check on prices. He plans to employ three workers to help him with much of the manual work. Dulip has also visited several furniture making companies to see if they would be interested in buying wood from him and he has even visited furniture shops to see which types of wood sell best. He has arranged a bank loan for much of the capital that he will need to get started.

Points to think about:

- Why do you think Dulip decided to own and run his own business rather than work for another firm?
- What resources (or inputs) does Dulip need to run his business successfully?
- What do you think are the essential differences between these three businesses: Dulip's forestry business; a furniture manufacturer; a shop selling furniture?

01 The nature of business activity

Introduction

This chapter explains what a business is and what businesses do. It outlines the main business functions (or departments) and explains the differences between primary, secondary and tertiary sectors of industry.

Higher Level additional material analyses the impact on business activity of changes in economic structure.

What is a business?

A business is any organisation that uses resources to meet the needs of customers by providing a product or service that they demand. There are several stages in the production of finished goods. Business activity at all stages involves adding value to resources such as raw materials and semi-finished goods and making them more desirable to – and thus valued by – the final purchaser. Without business activity we would all still be entirely dependent on the goods that we could make or grow ourselves – as people in some communities still are. Business activity uses the scarce resources of our planet to produce goods and services that allow us all to enjoy a much higher standard of living than would be possible if we remained entirely self-sufficient.

What do businesses do?

Businesses identify the needs of consumers or other firms. They then purchase resources, which are the inputs of the business, or factors of production, in order to produce output. The 'outputs' of a business are the goods and services that satisfy consumers' needs, usually with the aim of making a profit. Business activity exists to produce goods or services, which can be classified in several ways: consumer goods, consumer services and capital goods.

KEY TERMS

consumer goods the physical and tangible goods sold to the general public. They include cars and washing machines, which are referred to as durable consumer goods. Non-durable consumer goods include food, drinks and sweets that can only be used once.

consumer services non-tangible products that are sold to the general public and include hotel accommodation, insurance services and train journeys

capital goods physical goods that are used by industry to aid in the production of other goods and services, such as machines and commercial vehicles

What are business 'inputs'?

FACTORS OF PRODUCTION

These are the resources needed by business to produce goods or services. Firms will use different combinations of inputs, depending on the product being produced and the size of the business. There are four main inputs:

- **Land** – this general term not only includes land itself but all of the renewable and non-renewable resources of nature, such as coal, crude oil and timber.
- **Labour** – manual and skilled labour make up the workforce of the business. Some firms are labour intensive, that is they have a high proportion of labour inputs to other factors of production, e.g. house cleaning services.
- **Capital** – this consists of the finance needed to set up a business and pay for its continuing operations as well as all of the man-made resources used in production. These include capital goods such as computers, machines, factories, offices and vehicles. Some firms are capital intensive, that is they have a high proportion of capital to other factors of production, e.g. power stations.
- **Enterprise** – this is the driving force of business, provided by risk-taking individuals, which combines the other factors of production into a unit that is capable of producing goods and services, It provides a managing, decision-making and co-ordinating role. Without this essential input, even very high quality land, labour and capital inputs will fail to provide the goods and services that customers need.

Businesses have many other needs before they can successfully produce the goods and services demanded by customers. Figure 1.1 shows the wide range of these needs.

Business functions

Most businesses have four main functional departments. These will be staffed by people with specific qualifications and experience in the work of the functional areas.

MARKETING

This department is responsible for market research and for analysing the results of such research so that consumer wants can be correctly identified. This information will then be discussed with other departments of the business so that the right product decisions are made. Once a product is available for sale, the marketing function will have to make important decisions concerning its pricing, how and where to promote it and how to sell it and distribute it for sale.

FINANCE

This function has responsibility for monitoring the flow of finance into and out of the business, keeping and analysing accounts and providing financial information to both senior management and other departments. Without adequate finance, no effective decisions can be made within the other functional areas, so finance is a key division of any business.

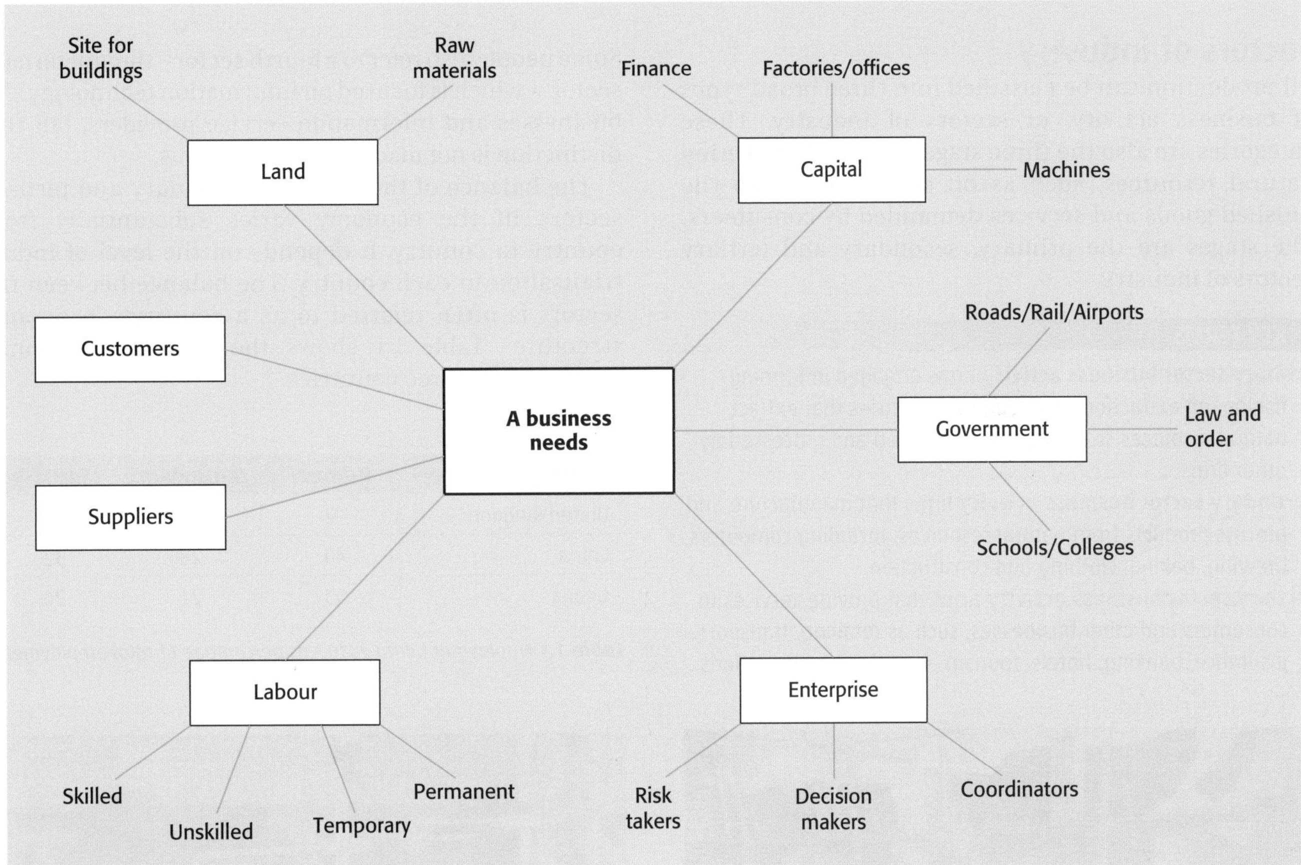

Figure 1.1 *What businesses need*

HUMAN RESOURCE MANAGEMENT

Human resource (HR) management identifies the workforce needs of the business, recruits, selects and trains appropriate staff and provides motivational systems to help retain staff and encourage them to work productively. It also draws up contracts of employment and covers the redundancy or redeployment of staff if these become necessary.

OPERATIONS MANAGEMENT

Once known simply as the 'production function', operations management has responsibility for ensuring adequate resources are available for production, maintaining production and quality levels and achieving high levels of productive efficiency.

INTERRELATIONSHIP OF FUNCTIONS

It should not be assumed that all business decisions taken within these departments are separate and unconnected from the other parts of the business. Nothing could be further from reality! Effective strategic decision-making develops from the functions working closely together. Good communication, co-operation and close interrelationships between functions are essential before major decisions are taken. For example, the decision by Peugeot Citroen in 2010 to launch the world's first hybrid diesel car required interaction between:

- marketing – will consumers be prepared to buy this car and at what price?
- finance – do we have the capital needed to develop and produce it?
- HR management – do we need to recruit additional engineers before this project can be turned into a market-ready car?
- operations management – can we produce this product at a cost which allows the marketing department to set a profitable price level?

Sectors of industry

All production can be classified into three broad types of business activity, or sectors of industry. These categories are also the three stages involved in turning natural resources, such as oil and timber, into the finished goods and services demanded by consumers. The stages are the primary, secondary and tertiary sectors of industry.

KEY TERMS

primary sector business activity firms engaged in farming, fishing, oil extraction and all other industries that extract natural resources so that they can be used and processed by other firms

secondary sector business activity firms that manufacture and process products from natural resources, including computers, brewing, baking, clothing and construction

tertiary sector business activity firms that provide services to consumers and other businesses, such as retailing, transport, insurance, banking, hotels, tourism and telecommunications

Some people also refer to a fourth sector – the 'quaternary sector' – which is focused on information technology (IT) businesses and information service providers, but this distinction is not made in the IB syllabus.

The balance of the primary, secondary and tertiary sectors in the economy varies substantially from country to country. It depends on the level of industrialisation in each country. The balance between the sectors is often referred to as a country's 'economic structure'. Table 1.1 shows the different economic structures of three countries.

Country	Primary	Secondary	Tertiary
United Kingdom	2	17	81
China	40	28	32
Ghana	53	21	26

Table 1.1 *Employment data 2010 – as percentage of total employment*

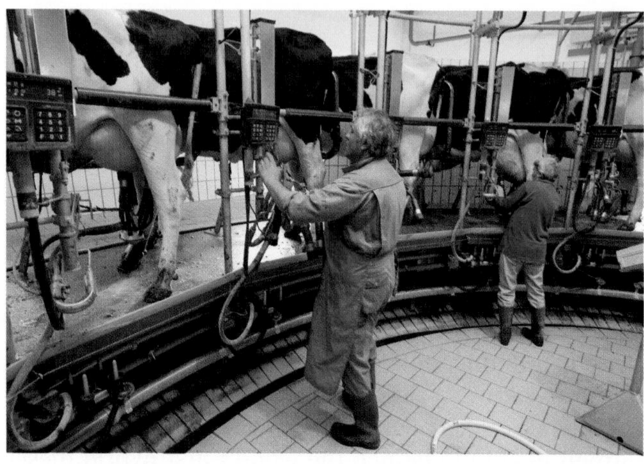

Primary production – dairy cattle following milking

Secondary production – clothing factory in India

Tertiary sector – the breathtaking Burj Al Arab hotel in Dubai

ACTIVITY 1.1

Business	Primary	Secondary	Tertiary	Description of main activities
Coca-Cola				
HSBC				
FAW (China)				
RTZ				
Wyndham Worldwide				
RR plc				

20 marks, research time

1 Copy out this table. Use the internet or other means of research to:
  a identify these well-known international companies
  b identify the **main** sector of industry that they operate in
  c give details of their main activities. [10]

2 Research **five** businesses that operate in your country and identify which sector of industry they **mainly** operate in and what their main activities are. [10]

CHANGES IN ECONOMIC STRUCTURE

It is very important to recognise two features of this classification of business activity:

1 The importance of each sector in a country's economic structure changes over time. **Industrialisation** describes the growing importance of the secondary sector manufacturing industries in developing countries. The relative importance of each sector is measured in terms either of employment levels or output levels as a proportion of the whole economy. In many countries of Africa and Asia, the relative importance of secondary sector activity is increasing. This brings many benefits as well as problems.

Benefits

- Total national output (Gross Domestic Product) increases and this raises average standards of living.
- Increasing output of goods can result in lower imports and higher exports of such products.
- Expanding manufacturing businesses will result in more jobs being created.
- Expanding and profitable firms will pay more tax to the government.
- Value is added to the country's output of raw materials rather than simply exporting these as basic, unprocessed products.

Problems

- The chance of work in manufacturing can encourage a huge movement of people from the country to the towns, which leads to housing and social problems. It may also result in depopulation of rural areas and problems for farmers in recruiting enough workers.
- The expansion of manufacturing industries may make it difficult for a business to recruit and retain sufficient staff.
- Imports of raw materials and components are often needed, which can increase the country's import costs. Business import costs will vary with changes in the exchange rate.
- Pollution from factories will add to the country's environmental problems.
- Much of the growth of manufacturing industry is due to the expansion of multinational companies. The consequences of this are covered in Chapter 9.

In developed economies, the situation is reversed. There is a general decline in the importance of secondary sector activity and an increase in the tertiary sector. This is known as **deindustrialisation.** In the UK, the proportion of total output accounted for by secondary industry has fallen by 15% to 23% in 25 years. The reasons for and possible impact of this change on business include:

- Rising incomes associated with higher living standards have led consumers to spend much of their extra income on services rather than more goods. There has been substantial growth in tourism, hotels and restaurant services, financial services and so on – yet spending on physical goods is rising more slowly.
- As the rest of the world industrialises, so manufacturing businesses in the developed countries face much more competition and these rivals tend to be more efficient and use cheaper labour. Therefore, rising imports of goods are taking market away from the domestic secondary sector firms and many have been forced to close.
- Employment patterns change – manufacturing workers may find it difficult to find employment in other sectors of industry. This is called structural unemployment.

2 The relative importance of each sector varies significantly between different economies. Table 1.1 above gives details of the differences that exist between the economies of different countries and the share of total employment accounted for by each sector of industry.

EXAM TIP

During your IB Business and Management course it is a good idea to read the business section of newspapers regularly. This will help you to apply the work you have done in class to the world outside. What, for example, was the major business story in your country this week?

OVER TO YOU

REVISION CHECKLIST

1 What is a 'business'?
2 What is a 'business input'?
3 Give two examples of primary sector businesses, explaining why they are classified in this sector.
4 Give two examples of secondary sector businesses, explaining why they are classified in this sector.
5 Give two examples of tertiary sector businesses, explaining why they are classified in this sector.
6 Allocate each of these decisions into the appropriate business functional department:
   a deciding on stock levels for an important raw material
   b deciding between using shops or a website to sell a new range of clothing
   c deciding whether to promote a manager from within the business or from another firm
   d deciding on how to raise $3 million for a factory expansion.
7 Explain why, for a recent major business decision of your choice, it was important for all four business functions to work closely together.
(H) 8 Using data from your own country:
   a How has total output or employment in the secondary sector changed over recent years?
   b Consider **two** effects of this change on any business in your country.

THEORY OF KNOWLEDGE

Business and Management is considered to be a human science.

a Explain what you understand by the term human science.
b Outline the reasons why you think Business and Management is a human science.
c Using business examples and examples from the natural science(s) you are studying, examine the differences between ways of knowing in human sciences and natural sciences.

REVISION ACTIVITY

BP operates in all three sectors of industry

BP is the third largest oil company in the world. Here are extracts from three recent newspaper articles about the company:

BP ANNOUNCES GIANT OIL WELL DISCOVERY IN THE GULF OF MEXICO

BP is already the largest producer of crude oil and natural gas in the Gulf of Mexico. This new discovery could double the company's reserves in this region of the world.

BP Kwinana refinery is now the largest refinery in Australia

Significant improvements to this oil refining and processing plant have led to Kwinana becoming one of the most modern in the region, enabling a wide range of fuels to be produced for drivers and for industry, and materials for the plastics and chemical industries.

BP to open 500 more petrol stations in the Jiangsu province of China

A huge new investment by BP in petrol retailing stations will lead to a huge increase in the sales of petrol in China of this large multinational business.

12 marks, 21 minutes

1 Using examples from these articles, explain the statement that 'BP operates in all three sectors of industry'. [6]

2 Explain why the decision to open 500 new petrol stations in China will involve effective cooperation between all four business functions. [6]

(H) **10 marks, 18 minutes**

3 Discuss how changes in the economic structure of Australia could impact on BP's Kwinana refinery. [10]

EXAM PRACTICE QUESTION

Read the case study and then answer the questions that follow.

RECESSION SPARKS NEW BUSINESS IDEAS

Disney, McDonald's, Burger King, Procter & Gamble, Johnson & Johnson, Microsoft – what do they all have in common? They all started during a recession or depression.

The message, delivered to around 40 would-be entrepreneurs at a workshop in Stratford, east London is clear: don't let bad economic headlines put you off. Most of the people at this session are not aiming to create new multinational corporations. But during the coffee break, they seem pretty confident that their ideas can prosper even in the current climate. 'I'm here to find out about starting up a business providing CVs to school leavers,' says Jessica Lyons, wearing a lapel badge with My First CV, the name of the future business, written on it. 'For my particular business idea I think this is the ideal time, because there are more people than ever out there looking for work.'

The recession is causing a spike in interest in setting up small businesses. Another interesting example was from a gym instructor who wants to take his equipment to companies around London, giving people a lunchtime workout without them having to leave their offices. Most of the would-be entrepreneurs in Stratford are looking at potential opportunities in the tertiary sector which don't require large amounts of start-up finance to purchase capital equipment and rely more on their own skills and interests.

Source: Adapted from various sources

25 marks, 45 minutes

1 Explain the following terms in the text:
  a entrepreneur
  b tertiary sector
  c start-up finance
  d capital equipment. [8]

2 Outline the factors of production needed to set up the business providing CVs to school leavers. [5]

3 Using the gym instructor's business as an example, list the business functions involved in this business. [5]

4 Explain the reasons why most of the would-be entrepreneurs were choosing to set up businesses in the tertiary sector. [7]

02 Types of organisation

This chapter covers syllabus section 1.2

On completing this chapter you should be able to:

- distinguish between organisations in the private sector and public sector, applying these distinctions to your own country
- explain reasons for starting a business, how to identify a market opportunity and the problems faced by business start-ups
- distinguish between different types of profit-based organisations: sole traders, partnerships and companies
- evaluate the most appropriate form of legal organisation for different businesses
- compare and contrast the objectives of non-profit and non-governmental organisations and analyse the impact of their actions
- (H) explain the nature of public–private partnerships, analysing the costs and benefits of co-operation between the public and private sectors.

SETTING THE SCENE

Dulip's business is a success

Dulip's business had been operating successfully for two years when he decided to expand it by opening his own furniture making factory. He wanted his business to grow so that he could bring his two sons into the venture.

Dulip realised that he would need more capital to build a furniture making factory. Although his business was profitable it was not making enough of a surplus to pay for the extra costs involved. 'Why don't you ask one of your friends to invest in your business as a partner?' suggested Maria, his wife. 'This would mean that you would not have to borrow so much.'

Dulip replied: 'I could do this and also ask them to help me manage the business. I am not sure that I could carry all of the management responsibilities. I might make my business a legally recognised organisation – a company – because this would be easier to leave to our sons and offers some protection for our savings.'

Forestry businesses in Dulip's country have been criticised by environmental pressure groups for cutting down too many trees. Dulip has responded to this pressure by planting more trees for each one his business cuts down.

Points to think about:

- Do you think it is a good idea for this business, currently only producing timber, to make and sell furniture? Explain your answer.
- Would you advise Dulip to involve one of his friends in the business as a partner? Explain your answer.
- What benefits does Dulip seem to think a 'company' will offer him?
- Why do some businesses change their decisions in response to pressure from environmental and other groups?

Introduction

The first chapter looked at the classification of business into different economic sectors. This chapter further classifies business activity into:

- the private and public sectors
- profit-based and non-profit-based organisations.

Profit-based businesses in the private sector can take different legal forms and the advantages and disadvantages of these are very important. The growing importance of non-profit-based and non-governmental organisations is also analysed in this chapter.

Public and private sector organisations

Industry may be classified by public or private sector and by type of legal organisation. These two types of classification are interlinked as some types of legal structure are only found in the private sector.

The relative importance of the private sector compared to the public sector is not the same in all mixed economies. Those economies that are closest to free-market systems have very small public sectors. Those countries with central planning command economies will have very few businesses in the private sector.

KEY TERMS

private sector comprises businesses owned and controlled by individuals or groups of individuals

public sector comprises organisations accountable to and controlled by central or local government (the state)

mixed economy economic resources are owned and controlled by both private and public sectors

free-market economy economic resources are owned largely by the private sector with very little state intervention

command economy economic resources are owned, planned and controlled by the state

LINKS BETWEEN SECTORS

In most mixed economies, certain important goods and services are provided by state-run organisations – they are in the public sector. It is argued that they are too significant to be left to private sector businesses. They include health and education services, defence and law and order (police force). In some countries, important 'strategic' industries are also state owned and controlled, such as energy, telecommunications and public transport. These public sector organisations therefore provide essential goods and services for individual citizens and organisations in the private sector, and they often have objectives other than profit; for example:

- ensuring supplies of essential goods and services – perhaps free of charge to the user, e.g. health and education services in some countries
- preventing private monopolies – single firms that dominate an industry – from controlling supply
- maintaining employment
- maintaining environmental standards.

In recent years, there has been a trend towards selling some public sector organisations to the private sector – privatisation – and this means that they put profit making as one of their main objectives.

KEY TERM

privatisation the sale of public sector organisations to the private sector

Starting a business

ROLE OF THE ENTREPRENEUR

KEY TERM

entrepreneur someone who takes the financial risk of starting and managing a new venture

New business ventures started by entrepreneurs can be based on a totally new product or customer service idea or a new way of offering a service. People who set up their own new business show skills of 'entrepreneurship'. They have:

- had an idea for a new business
- invested some of their own savings and capital
- accepted the responsibility of managing the business
- accepted the possible risks of failure.

The personal qualities and skills needed to make a success of a new business venture are described below.

Innovative

The entrepreneur may not be a 'product inventor', but they must be able to carve a new niche in the market, attract consumers in innovative ways and present their business as being 'different'. This requires original ideas and an ability to do things innovatively.

Commitment and self-motivation

It is never an easy option to set up and run your own business. It is hard work and may take up many hours of each day. A willingness to work hard, a keen ambition to succeed, energy and focus are all essential qualities of a successful entrepreneur.

Multi-skilled

An entrepreneur will have to make the product or provide the service, promote it, sell it and count the money. These different business tasks require a person with many different qualities such as being keen to learn technical skills, an ability to get on with people and being good at handling money and keeping accounting records.

Leadership skills

An entrepreneur has to lead by example and must have a personality that encourages people in the business to follow them and be motivated by them.

Belief in oneself

Many business start-ups fail, yet this would not discourage a true entrepreneur who would have such self-belief in their abilities and business idea that they would bounce back from any setbacks.

Risk taker

Entrepreneurs must be willing to take risks in order to see results. Often the risk they take involves investing their own savings in a new business.

WHY START A BUSINESS?

Reasons for starting a new business include some or all of the following:

- Losing a job encourages many people to set up in business by themselves, either providing their former employer's product or another product, perhaps based on an interest or skill they have.
- Desire for independence – some people do not like the idea of being told what to do! By creating their own business, they have work flexibility and control over their working lives.
- By talking to friends or family, it might become clear that a business opportunity exists that an entrepreneur could take advantage of.
- A wish to make more money than in the current job – many people setting up their own business believe that they will earn a higher income working for themselves.

START-UP BUSINESSES

New business start-ups can be found in nearly all industries. However, there are some industries and sectors of industry where there is a much greater likelihood of new entrepreneurs becoming established. These include:

- primary sector – fishing, market gardening (producing cash crops to sell at local markets)
- secondary sector – jewellery making, dress making, craft manufacture, e.g. batik cloth, building trades
- tertiary/service sector – hairdressing, car repairs, cafés and restaurants, child minding.

It would be unusual for entrepreneurs to successfully establish themselves in, say, the steel making industry or car manufacturing because of the vast amount of capital equipment and financial investment that would be required.

ACTIVITY 2.1

Read the case study below and then answer the questions that follow.

Bangalore Enterprise Blossoms

Rama Karaturi had the idea for his rose-growing business when he searched the city of Bangalore, without success, for a bouquet of roses for his wife's birthday. The city was a rose-free zone, so he decided to start growing them himself. He had wanted to take decisions for himself for some time and he also wanted to earn much more than his current salary. In 1996, he opened two greenhouses growing just roses. He used his own savings so took a considerable risk, but his confidence in the growth of 'flower giving' at times of major festivals encouraged other investors too. He sold the flowers in India, but his business also became one of the first in India to start exporting flowers on a large scale. Rama worked long hours to make his business a success. The business, called Katuri Networks, has grown at a tremendous rate, helped by Rama's all-round business skills. He recently bought out a large rose grower in Kenya and his business is now the world's largest cultivator of roses – and Rama achieved this in a little over ten years.

Source: business.timesonline.co.uk (adapted)

16 marks, 28 minutes

1. Rama is an example of a 'business entrepreneur'. Explain what is meant by this term. [4]
2. Outline **two** reasons why Rama started his own business. [6]
3. Explain any **two** problems Rama's business might have experienced during the set-up stage. [6]

IDENTIFYING MARKET OPPORTUNITIES

Many people say that they want to work for themselves, but they then do not make the leap into entrepreneurship successfully because they have not been able to identify a **market opportunity** that will generate sufficient demand for their product or service to enable the business to be profitable. The original idea for most new businesses comes from one of several sources including:

- own skills or hobbies, e.g. dress making or car bodywork repairer
- previous employment experience, e.g. learning hairdressing skills with an established business
- franchising conferences and exhibitions offering a wide range of new business start-up ideas, e.g. fast-food restaurants
- small budget market research – the use of the internet allows any user to browse business directories to see how many businesses there are in the local area offering certain goods or services. This low-cost research might indicate gaps in local markets that could be profitably filled by the entrepreneur.

PROBLEMS FACED BY START-UPS

Even if an entrepreneur has all of the qualities listed above, success with a new business can never be guaranteed. Many businesses fail during their first year of operation. The most common reasons for this are discussed below.

Competition

This is nearly always a problem for new enterprises unless the business idea is unique. More generally, a newly created business will experience competition from older, established businesses with more resources and market knowledge. The entrepreneur may have to offer better customer service to overcome the cost and pricing advantages of bigger businesses.

Building a customer base

To survive, a new business must establish itself in the market and build up customer numbers as quickly as possible. The long-term strength of the business will depend on encouraging customers to return to purchase products again and again. Many small businesses try to encourage this by offering a better service than their larger and better-funded competitors. This service might include:

- personal customer service
- knowledgeable pre- and after-sales service
- providing for one-off customer requests that larger firms may be reluctant to offer.

Lack of record keeping

Accurate records are vital to pay taxes and bills and chase up debtors. Many entrepreneurs fail to pay sufficient attention to this as they either believe that it is less important than actually meeting customers' needs or they think they can remember everything, which they could not possibly do after a period of time. For example, how can the owner of a new, busy florist shop remember:

- when the next delivery of fresh flowers was booked for?
- whether the flowers for last week's big wedding have been paid for?
- if the cheque received from an important customer has been paid into the bank yet?
- how many hours the shop assistant worked last week?

Lack of working capital

Running short of capital to run day-to-day business affairs is the single most common reason for the failure of new businesses to survive in the first year. Capital is needed for day-to-day cash, for the holding of stocks and to allow the giving of trade credit to customers, who then become debtors. Without sufficient working capital, the business may be unable to buy more stocks or pay suppliers or offer credit to important customers.

Serious working capital shortages can usually be avoided if businesses take several important steps:

- Construct and update a cash-flow forecast so that the liquidity and working capital needs of the business can be assessed, month by month.
- Inject sufficient capital into the business at start-up for the first few months of operation when cash flow from customers may be slow to build up.
- Establish good relations with the bank so that short-term problems may be, at least temporarily, overcome with an overdraft.
- Use effective credit control over customers' accounts – do not allow a period of credit which is too long, and quickly chase up late payers.

Poor management skills

Most entrepreneurs have had some form of work experience, but not necessarily at a management level. They may not have gained experience of:

- leadership skills
- cash handling and cash management skills
- planning and coordinating skills
- decision-making skills
- communication skills
- marketing, promotion and selling skills.

Entrepreneurs may be very keen, willing to work hard and with undoubted abilities in their chosen field; for example, a new restaurant owner may be an excellent chef but management skills may be lacking. Some learn these skills very quickly once the business is up and running, but this is a risky strategy. Some entrepreneurs buy in the experience by employing staff with management experience, but this is an expensive option.

It is wrong to think, just because a business is new and small, that enthusiasm, a strong personality and hard work will be sufficient to ensure success. This may prove to be the case, but it often is not. Potential entrepreneurs are encouraged to attend training courses to gain some of these skills before putting their capital at risk or seek management experience through employment.

Changes in the business environment

Setting up a new business is risky. Not only are there the problems and challenges referred to above but there is also the risk of change, which can make the original business idea much less successful. New businesses may fail if any of the following changes occur, which turn the venture from a successful one to a loss-making enterprise:

- new competitors
- legal changes, e.g. outlawing the product altogether
- economic changes that leave customers with much less money to spend
- technological changes that make the methods used by the new business old-fashioned and expensive.

This list of changes could, no doubt, be added to, but even these four factors indicate that the business environment is a dynamic one, and this makes owning and running a business enterprise very risky indeed.

EXAM TIP

The reasons for business failure could apply at any stage of the development of a business, but the first few months are the riskiest of all.

ACTIVITY 2.2

Read the case study below and then answer the questions that follow.

Farah branches out on her own

Farah was a well-qualified dress maker. She had worked for two of the biggest dress shops in town, but was keen to set up her own business. Her father agreed to invest $5000 into her business, but she would have to find the rest of the capital needed – about $10 000 she guessed – from her savings and a bank loan.

She investigated the prices of shop premises, and was shocked by how expensive city centre locations were. Her father suggested a cheaper, but less busy, out-of-town location. She contacted an accountant who offered to look after the financial side of the business, but he would charge at least $2000 per year. Farah wondered if she could learn to keep the accounts herself if she attended accounts classes.

She wanted to make her shop very different from all of the competitors in the city, and planned to offer lessons in dress making as well as selling finished dresses. She had been asked many times by customers 'How did you do that?' when they were pleased with her latest dress designs and she was sure this was a great business opportunity. What she had not realised was the amount of paperwork she would have to complete before her business could even start trading.

16 marks, 28 minutes

1 Outline **three** problems that Farah has to deal with in setting up her business. [6]

2 Which of these problems do you think is the **most important** one for Farah to find a good solution to? Explain your answer. [6]

3 Is Farah's business operating in the private or public sector? Explain your answer. [4]

Profit-based organisations

Figure 2.1 shows the main types of profit-based private-sector businesses.

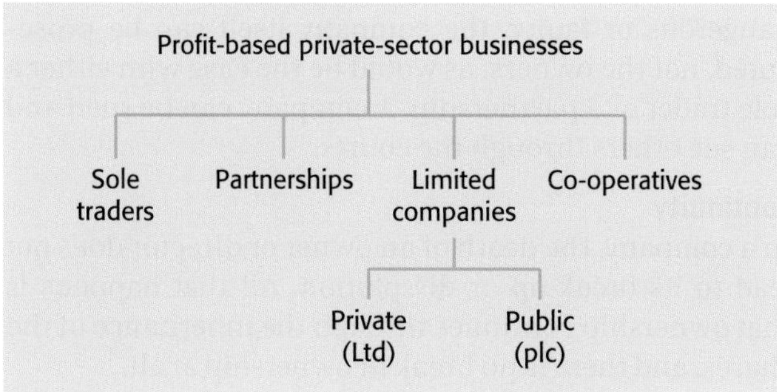

Figure 2.1 Legal structure of profit-based organisations

SOLE TRADER

KEY TERM

sole trader a business in which one person provides the permanent finance and, in return, has full control of the business and is able to keep all of the profits

This is the most common form of business organisation. Although there is a single owner in this business organisation, there may be employees but the firm is likely to remain very small. Although they are great in number, sole traders account for only a small proportion of total business turnover. All sole traders have unlimited liability. This means that the owner's personal possessions and property can be taken to pay off the debts of the business should it fail. This can discourage some potential entrepreneurs from starting their own businesses.

Another problem faced by sole traders involves finance for expansion. Many sole traders remain small because the owner wishes to remain in control of their own business, but another reason is the limitations that they have in raising additional capital. As soon as partners or shareholders are sought in order to raise finance, then the sole trader becomes another form of organisation altogether. In order to remain a sole trader the owner is dependent on own savings, profits made and loans for injections of capital.

This type of business organisation is most commonly established in construction, retailing, hairdressing, car servicing and catering. The advantages and disadvantages of sole traders are summarised in Table 2.1.

Advantages	Disadvantages
• Easy to set up – no legal formalities • Owner has complete control – not answerable to anyone else • Owner keeps all profits • Able to choose times and patterns of working • Able to establish close personal relationships with staff (if any are employed) and customers • The business can be based on the interests or skills of the owner – rather than working as an employee for a larger firm	• Unlimited liability – all of owner's assets are potentially at risk • Often faces intense competition from bigger firms, e.g. food retailing • Owner is unable to specialise in areas of the business that are most interesting – is responsible for all aspects of management • Difficult to raise additional capital • Long hours often necessary to make business pay • Lack of continuity – as the business does not have separate legal status, when the owner dies the business ends too

Table 2.1 Sole traders – advantages and disadvantages

PARTNERSHIP

KEY TERM

partnership a business formed by two or more people to carry on a business together, with shared capital investment and, usually, shared responsibilities

A partnership agreement does not create a separate legal unit; a partnership is just a grouping of individuals. Partnerships are formed in order to overcome some of the drawbacks of a sole trader. When planning to go into partnership it is important to choose business partners carefully – the errors and poor decisions of any one partner are considered to be the responsibility of them all. This also applies to business debts incurred by one partner – in most countries there is unlimited liability for all partners should the business venture fail. In the UK, it is possible to set up limited liability partnerships. It is usual, although not a legal requirement, to draw up a formal Deed of Partnership between all partners. This would provide agreement on issues such as voting rights, the distribution of profits, the management role of each partner and who has authority to sign contracts.

Partnerships are the most common form of business organisation in some professions, such as law and accountancy. Small building firms are often partnerships too. Many other owners of businesses prefer the company form of organisation and these are considered next. The advantages and disadvantages of partnerships are summarised in Table 2.2.

LIMITED COMPANY

There are three important differences between companies and sole traders and partnerships: limited liability, legal personality and continuity.

Advantages	Disadvantages
• Partners may specialise in different areas of business management • Shared decision-making • Additional capital injected by each partner • Business losses shared between partners • Greater privacy and fewer legal formalities than corporate organisations (companies)	• Unlimited liability for all partners (with some exceptions) • Profits are shared • As with sole traders, no continuity and the partnership will have to be reformed in the event of the death of one of the partners • All partners bound by the decisions of any one of them • Not possible to raise capital from selling shares • A sole trader, taking on partners, will lose independence of decision-making

Table 2.2 *Partnerships – advantages and disadvantages*

Limited liability

The ownership of companies is divided into small units called shares. People can buy these and become 'shareholders' – they are part owners of the business. It is possible to buy just one share, but usually these are owned in blocks, and it is possible for one person or organisation to have complete control by owning more than 50% of the shares. Individuals with large blocks of shares often become directors of the business. All shareholders benefit from the advantage of limited liability.

KEY TERMS

limited liability the only liability – or potential loss – a shareholder has if the company fails is the amount invested in the company, not the total wealth of the shareholder

Nobody can make any further claim against shareholders should the company fail. This has two important effects:

- People are prepared to provide finance to enable companies to expand.
- The greater risk of the company failing to pay its debts is now transferred from investors to creditors (those suppliers/lenders who have not been paid). Creditors, as a result, are very interested in both ensuring that the word 'limited' appears in the company name and scrutinising the company's accounts for signs of potential future weakness.

Legal personality

A company is legally recognised as having an identity separate from that of its owners. This means, for example, that if the products sold by a company are found to be dangerous or faulty, the company itself can be prosecuted, not the owners, as would be the case with either a sole trader or a partnership. A company can be sued and can sue others through the courts.

Continuity

In a company, the death of an owner or director does not lead to its break-up or dissolution. All that happens is that ownership continues through the inheritance of the shares, and there is no break in ownership at all.

Private limited companies

The protection that comes from forming a company is therefore substantial. Small firms can gain this protection when the owner(s) create(s) a private limited company.

KEY TERMS

private limited company a small to medium-sized business that is owned by shareholders who are often members of the same family. This company cannot sell shares to the general public

shareholder a person or institution owning shares in a limited company

share a certificate confirming part ownership of a company and entitling the shareholder to dividends and certain shareholder rights

The word 'Limited' or 'Ltd' ('Pte' in some countries) indicates that the business is a private company. Usually, the shares will be owned by the original sole trader (who may hold a majority of the shares to keep control of the company), relatives, friends and employees. New issues of shares cannot be sold on the open market and existing shareholders may only sell their shares with the agreement of the other shareholders.

Legal formalities must be followed in setting up a private limited company and these can be expensive and time consuming in some countries. The advantages and disadvantages of private limited companies are summarised in Table 2.3.

Public limited companies

These can be recognised by the use of 'plc' or 'inc.' (incorporated) after the company name. It is the most common form of legal organisation for really large businesses, for the very good reason that they have access to very substantial funds for expansion. Converting a private limited company to public limited company (plc) status is referred to as a stock market flotation.

Advantages	Disadvantages
• Shareholders have limited liability • Separate legal personality • Continuity in the event of the death of a shareholder • Original owner is still often able to retain control • Able to raise capital from sale of shares to family, friends and employees • Greater status than an unincorporated business	• Legal formalities involved in establishing the business • Capital cannot be raised by sale of shares to the general public • Quite difficult for shareholders to sell shares • End-of-year accounts must be sent to Companies House – available for public inspection there (less secrecy over financial affairs than sole trader or partnership)

Table 2.3 *Private limited companies – advantages and disadvantages*

KEY TERM

public limited company (plc) a limited company, often a large business, with the legal right to sell shares to the general public. Its share price is quoted on the national stock exchange

A plc has all the advantages of private company status plus the right to advertise its shares for sale and have them quoted on the stock exchange. Public limited companies have the potential to raise large sums from public issues of shares. Existing shareholders may quickly sell their shares if they wish to. This flexibility of share buying and selling encourages the public to purchase the shares in the first instance and thus invest in the business.

The other main difference between private and public companies concerns the 'divorce between ownership and control'. The original owners of a business are usually still able to retain a majority of shares and continue to exercise management control when it converts to private company status. This is most unlikely with public limited companies, due to the volume of shares issued and the number of people and institutions as investors. These shareholders own the company, but they appoint, at the annual general meeting, a board of directors who control the management and decision-making of the business.

This clear distinction between ownership and control can lead to conflicts over the objectives to be set and direction to be taken by the business. The shareholders might prefer short-term maximum-profit strategies, but the directors may aim for long-term growth of the business, perhaps in order to increase their own power and status. Many private limited companies convert to plc status to gain the benefits referred to in Table 2.4. It is also possible for the directors or the original owners of a business to convert it back from plc to private limited company status. Richard Branson and the Virgin group are one of the best-known examples. The reasons for doing this are largely to overcome the divorce between ownership and control – in a private limited company it is normal for the senior executives to be the major, majority shareholders. In addition, the owner of a private limited company can take a long-term planning view of the business. It is often said that the major investors in a plc are only interested in short-term gains. 'Short-termism' can be damaging to the long-term investment plans of a business.

A summary of the advantages and disadvantages of public limited companies is given in Table 2.4.

Advantages	Disadvantages
• Limited liability • Separate legal identity • Continuity • Ease of buying and selling of shares for shareholders – this encourages investment in plcs • Access to substantial capital sources due to the ability to issue a prospectus to the public and to offer shares for sale	• Legal formalities in formation • Cost of business consultants and financial advisers when creating a plc • Share prices subject to fluctuation – sometimes for reasons beyond business's control, e.g. state of the economy • Legal requirements concerning disclosure of information to shareholders and the public, e.g. annual publication of detailed report and accounts • Risk of takeover due to the availability of the shares on the stock exchange • Directors influenced by short-term objectives of major investors

Table 2.4 *Public limited companies – advantages and disadvantages*

Legal forms of business organisation

Businesses often change their legal form as they expand and as the objectives of the owners change. Many newly formed businesses are sole traders and then accept partners if the aim of the original owner is to expand and share management responsibilities. Conversion to company status is often caused by owners wishing to protect their personal wealth and encourage new shareholder investors. When further expansion is very expensive, perhaps because of the nature of the business activity as with the development of new technology products, conversion to public limited company status is common. However, much depends on the desire for control of the original owners/shareholders. We have seen above that in some instances, the desire to get back overall control from 'short-term minded' investors can lead the original owners of a business to convert a plc back into a private limited company.

ACTIVITY 2.3

Read the case study below and then answer the questions that follow.

Footie Ltd to stay private after ruling out float

Footie Ltd, the shoemaker and retailer, is to remain a private limited company. The directors received overwhelming advice against converting it to a plc. The company has no need of further capital to fund further expansion, and is now one of the world's largest private limited companies. In 2004, after a decade of declining fortunes, it came within five votes of opting for a takeover by Shoeworks plc. But in April this year, it announced annual profits up from $42.7 million to $50.8 million on sales of $825 million. That was its third year of record profits, reflecting its strategy of reducing its reliance on own manufacture and investing in its brands and shops.

Footie Ltd is now more of a retailer and wholesaler than manufacturer, owning or franchising 650 shops and importing shoes from abroad. Five years ago, 75% of its shoes were manufactured in Footie's European factories. Now it is just 25%, with 40% of the business based in Asia. Jim Parker, chief executive, has claimed that Footie is the largest conventional shoe brand in the world, having sold 48 million pairs last year. He said the business was expanding rapidly in nearly all markets and this growth strategy requires a lot of capital. 'We can continue to build the business with benefits of moving to lower-cost countries and with investment in our brand and retailing operations.'

Despite ruling out a float for now, the company said it would continue to examine 'the most appropriate legal structure to meet shareholders' interests on the basis of its strategy for future growth and the conditions in the footwear market'.

26 marks, 45 minutes

1 Explain **two** differences between a private limited company and a public limited company. [4]

2 Is Footie Ltd in the private sector or public sector? Explain your answer. [3]

3 Which industrial sector(s) does Footie Ltd operate in? Explain your answer. [5]

4 Examine possible reasons for the directors deciding to keep Footie Ltd a private limited company. [6]

5 Analyse the main benefits to the business and to existing shareholders if the company did 'go public'. [8]

Public sector enterprises

EXAM TIP

Public limited companies are in the private sector of industry – but public corporations are not.

The term 'public' is used by business organisations in two different ways, and this often causes confusion. We have already identified public limited companies as being owned by shareholders in the private sector of the economy. Thus, public limited companies are in the private sector. However, in every country there will be some enterprises that are owned by the state – usually central or local government. These organisations are therefore in the public sector and they are referred to as public corporations.

KEY TERM

public corporation a business enterprise owned and controlled by the state – also known as nationalised industry

Public sector organisations do not often have profit as a major objective. In many countries the publicly owned TV channels have as their main priority the quality of public service programmes. State-owned airlines have safety as a priority. Selling off public corporations to the private sector, known as privatisation, often results in changing objectives from socially orientated ones to profit-driven goals. A summary of the potential advantages and disadvantages of public corporations is given in Table 2.5.

Advantages	Disadvantages
• Managed with social objectives rather than solely with profit objectives • Loss-making services might still be kept operating if the social benefit is great enough • Finance raised mainly from the government	• Tendency towards inefficiency due to lack of strict profit targets • Subsidies from government can encourage inefficiencies • Government may interfere in business decisions for political reasons, e.g. by opening a new branch in a certain area to gain popularity

Table 2.5 *Public sector organisations – advantages and disadvantages*

THEORY OF KNOWLEDGE

1 'All countries have organisations that are part of the private sector; they come in the form of business organisations that exist to create a profit for their owners. All countries also have public sector organisations that exist to improve the welfare of all people in society. As a consequence of this, governments should look to expand the proportion of countries' organisations that are owned by the state.'

   a Analyse the evidence you would use to prove or disprove this statement.

   b In the light of this statement, discuss some of the reasons why so many countries have privatised former public sector organisations.

2 'Organisations always run more efficiently when they are free of government control.'

   In groups, discuss to what extent you agree or disagree with this statement.

Non-profit and non-governmental organisations

Not all organisations in the world aim to make profits. There are many thousands of organisations that have objectives other than profit: for example, charities and pressure groups. Many of these are also termed non-governmental organisations (NGOs).

KEY TERMS

non-profit organisation any organisation that has aims other than making and distributing profit and which is usually governed by a voluntary board

non-governmental organisation (NGO) a legally constituted body with no participation or representation of any government

Non-profit organisations include charities and pressure groups. Charities may employ professional managers, but they often depend greatly on the work of unpaid volunteers. Profit is not an objective, but they are still usually trying to increase their income to put more money back into achieving their charitable objectives. For example, the ASHA charity in India has, as its primary objective: 'To provide education for underprivileged children in India.'

Well-known international charities include Oxfam, Red Cross and Red Crescent Societies and Médecins sans Frontières. Apart from raising money to support and promote their work, many charities aim to inform the public, persuade them to support their causes and try to convince governments to give more attention to the problems the charities are trying to solve such as poverty, gender inequality, hardship in old age or protection of wildlife. Many charities have only a national or local presence, but they can still have a significant impact on the people they aim to support.

Non-governmental organisations cover a very wide range of activities, but their common feature is that they are separate from government. They are often charities too and many of them are involved in development, health and humanitarian issues. Their work can support and add to the efforts made by government organisations, for example in disaster or poverty relief. The objectives of NGOs are not profit-based but are specifically focused on social or humanitarian objectives. In Russia, the GLOBUS group aims to 'stimulate an effective national response to the HIV/AIDS epidemic'. Also in the humanitarian field, the International AIDS Alliance in Ukraine aims to 'reduce HIV incidence and death rates from AIDS'.

PRESSURE GROUP

Pressure groups are non-profit-making organisations that aim to change the behaviour and decisions of either organisations or governments.

KEY TERM

pressure group an organisation created by people with a common interest or objective who lobby businesses and governments to change policies so that the objective is reached

Perhaps the best-known international examples are:

- Greenpeace – campaigns for greater environmental protection by both businesses adopting green strategies and governments passing tighter anti-pollution laws.
- Fairtrade Foundation – aims to achieve a better deal for agricultural producers in low-income countries.
- WWF – aims to improve animal welfare, especially protecting and conserving the habitat of wild animals.
- Amnesty International – rigorously opposes anti-human rights policies of governments.
- Jubilee 2000 – campaigns for western governments to reduce or eliminate the debt burden on developing countries.

Pressure groups want changes to be made in three important areas:

- governments to change their policies and to pass laws supporting the aims of the group
- businesses to change policies so that, for example, less damage is caused to the environment

- consumers to change their purchasing habits so that businesses that adopt 'appropriate' policies see an increase in sales, but those that continue to pollute or use unsuitable work practices see sales fall.

Pressure groups try to achieve these goals in a number of ways.

Publicity through media coverage
Effective public relations are crucial to most successful pressure group campaigns. Frequent press releases giving details of undesirable company activity and coverage of 'direct action' events, such as meetings, demonstrations and consumer boycotts will help to constantly keep the campaign in the public eye. The more bad publicity the group can create for the company concerned, then the greater the chance of it succeeding in changing corporate policy. The pressure group may spend money on its own advertising campaign – as Amnesty International does – and the success of this approach will depend upon the financial resources of the group.

Influencing consumer behaviour
If the pressure group is so successful that consumers stop buying a certain company's products for long enough, then the commercial case for changing policy becomes much stronger. The highly successful consumer boycott of Shell petrol stations following a decision to dump an old oil platform in the sea led to a change of strategy. Shell is now aiming to become 'the leading multinational for environmental and social responsibility'. Public sympathy for a pressure group campaign can increase its effectiveness significantly.

Lobbying of government
This means putting the arguments of the pressure group to government members and ministers because they have the power to change the law. If the popularity of the government is likely to be damaged by a pressure group campaign that requires government action, then the legal changes asked for stand a greater chance of being introduced.

SOCIAL ENTERPRISE

Social enterprises are not charities, but they do have objectives that are often different from those of an entrepreneur who is only profit motivated. Making a profit may be one of their objectives, but it will be much less important than the organisation's social objectives.

In other words, a social enterprise is a proper business that makes its money in socially responsible ways and uses most of any surplus made to benefit society. Social entrepreneurs are not running a charity, though – they can and often do keep some of any profit made for themselves.

ACTIVITY 2.4

Read the case study below and then answer the questions that follow.

Tibet protesters target BP over PetroChina stake

The oil giant BP Amoco will face renewed action next week from Tibetan pressure groups to withdraw from PetroChina, the state-run Chinese oil company which is building a gas pipeline through ethnic Tibetan areas. Tibetan activists will coordinate a worldwide series of protests starting next Thursday while the Free Tibet Campaign is planning to disrupt BP's AGM in April. It has tabled a resolution calling on BP to dispose of its PetroChina stake on the grounds that it is against the company's ethical policy on human rights and the environment. The pressure group may also call for a consumer boycott of BP petrol stations. A government minister admitted to reporters in Beijing that BP and PetroChina would face a public relations 'disaster' if the resolution is passed.

17 marks, 35 minutes

1 What change in the strategy of BP and PetroChina is the Tibetan pressure group attempting to bring about? **[3]**
2 Explain what impact a 'public relations disaster' could have on BP. **[6]**
3 Evaluate the factors that will determine whether this pressure group's campaign is successful. **[8]**

Social enterprises compete with other businesses in the same market or industry. They use business principles to achieve social objectives. Most social enterprises have these common features:

- They directly produce goods or provide services.
- They have social aims and use ethical ways of achieving them.
- They need to make a surplus or profit to survive as they cannot rely on donations as charities do.

Objectives of social enterprises

Social enterprises often have three main aims:

- Economic – to make a profit or surplus to reinvest back into the business and provide some return to owners.
- Social – to provide jobs or support for local, often disadvantaged, communities.
- Environmental – to protect the environment and to manage the business in an environmentally sustainable way.

These aims are often referred to as the triple bottom line. This means that profit is not the sole objective of these enterprises.

KEY TERMS

social enterprise a business with mainly social objectives that reinvests most of its profits into benefiting society rather than maximising returns to owners

triple bottom line the three objectives of social enterprises: economic, social and environmental

Below are two examples of social enterprises:

- SELCO in India provides sustainable energy solutions to low-income households and small businesses. In one scheme, solar-powered lighting was provided by SELCO to a silkworm farmer who depended on dangerous and polluting kerosene lamps. The farmer could not afford the upfront cost, so SELCO helped with the finance too.
- The KASHF Foundation in Pakistan provides microfinance (very small loans) and social support services to women entrepreneurs who traditionally find it very difficult to receive help. This enables the women to set up their own businesses in food production, cloth making and other industries. The loans have to be repaid with interest, but the interest rates are much lower than a profit-maximising international bank would charge.

H HIGHER LEVEL

Public–private partnership (PPP)

KEY TERM

public–private partnership (PPP) involvement of the private sector, in the form of management expertise and/or financial investment, in public sector projects aimed at benefiting the public

There are three main types of PPP:

- Government funded – these are privately managed schemes. In this type of venture, the government provides all or part of the funding, but the organisation is managed by a private business that uses private sector methods and techniques to control it as efficiently as possible. For example, the Hope Clinic Lukuli in Kampala, Uganda, receives government funding for its malaria prevention and HIV testing services. These are managed efficiently and successfully by this private sector, but non-profit making, clinic. Analysts believe that the clinic operates the health services more efficiently than a government department would with many officials becoming involved.
- Private sector funded – these are government or state-managed schemes. In this type of venture, which often involves large sums of capital investment, the government is released from the financial burden of finding taxpayers' money to pay for the project. Once the assets have been paid for and constructed, they are then managed and controlled by a government department which pays rent or a leasing charge to the private sector business that constructed the project. This form of PPP started in Australia and the UK and is known as the Private Finance Initiative (PFI).
- Government directed but with private sector finance and management – this type of PPP encourages both private sector funding and some private sector management control of public projects. For example, a new London hospital has been built using private sector finance – it is leased to the state-controlled health authority which manages and controls the hospital's health services; in Australia, the international bank HBOS has invested in several PFI schemes for public sector projects such as new prisons in Victoria and the new toll road into Melbourne city centre.

KEY TERM

Private Finance Initiative (PFI) investment by private sector organisations in public sector projects

The potential costs and benefits of public–private partnerships are shown in Table 2.6.

Costs	Benefits
• The private sector business, if asked to manage the project, could try to increase profits by cutting staff wages and benefits. In effect, workers would no longer have the security of being employed by the public sector. • PFI schemes have been criticised for earning private sector businesses large profits from high rents and leasing charges – these must be paid for by taxpayers. • Private sector organisations may lack the experience needed to operate large public sector projects – such as social housing schemes – and failure of the scheme could leave vulnerable groups in society at risk.	• Many schools, roads, prisons and hospitals have been built through PPP/PFI schemes – it is argued that these would not have been constructed unless the private sector had been involved. • Private sector businesses aim to make profits – their managers will therefore operate services as efficiently as possible. This could mean that costs to the public sector are lower than if the projects were operated by government/public sector managers. • By using private sector business finance, the government can claim that public services are being improved, without an increase in taxes (at least in the short run as the capital cost is not paid for by the government).

Table 2.6 *Potential costs and benefits of PPPs*

H

OVER TO YOU

REVISION CHECKLIST

1 What is the difference between private sector and public sector organisations?

2 State **three** differences between a sole trader and a private limited company.

3 Who (a) owns and who (b) controls a public limited company? Explain why this distinction might lead to conflict.

4 Why might the directors of a public limited company decide to convert the business back into a private limited company by buying a majority of the shares?

5 Explain how legal personality and continuity help businesses and companies to operate effectively.

6 In what way does limited liability make it easier for companies to raise finance?

7 Using the examples of a sole trader business and a public limited company, explain how the relationship between ownership and control differs in these two types of organisations.

8 Using the examples of a partnership and a public limited company, explain how the legal structure of a business affects its ability to raise finance.

9 List **two** organisations in your own country that are in the public sector.

10 Analyse **one** impact of the distinction between ownership and control for:
a shareholders of a plc
b employees of a plc.

H 11 Explain **two** potential advantages to a country when its government uses Private Finance Initiatives to pay for new motorways.

H 12 Explain **two** potential disadvantages to a country when its government uses public–private partnerships to pay for and manage health clinics.

HIGHER LEVEL

REVISION ACTIVITY

Read the case study below and then answer the questions that follow.

Waste – a good case for public–private partnership?

Capital Waste Disposal plc was created 5 years ago when the capital city's rubbish collection service was privatised. As a public sector enterprise, the organisation had been overstaffed and inefficient, but charges for collecting waste were low and the service was popular with local residents. The city government subsidised the waste services and this helped to keep charges down. Shortly after privatisation, the directors announced substantial job cuts to save on costs. The waste collection service was reduced to once a week, yet charges were increased. The city government also announced that the city's rubbish collection services would be opened up to competition.

The business started to make big profits. It invested in new equipment and paid dividends to its shareholders. Last year, for the first time since privatisation, profits fell. This was due to competition from a newly formed waste disposal business. Many of Capital Waste's shareholders wanted the directors to be replaced. The biggest shareholders demanded to be on the board of directors. The chief executive discussed with the bank whether a loan could be obtained to enable him to buy out most of the shares to convert the business into a private limited company. He told the bank manager, 'If I turn the business into a private company, I can run it without any interference from big shareholders and publish less data about the company.'

The government still owns and manages the old and inefficient waste recycling plant in the city. It now wants to involve Capital Waste in a public–private partnership to build a new, environmentally friendly waste recycling plant. The business would be asked to invest capital in the new facility and to use its private sector managers to help manage the new plant. A PPP would help to make sure that it was built quickly. However, some local residents are worried that private sector managers would try to cut costs, and that difficult to recycle waste would simply be dumped in the local river.

36 marks, 65 minutes

1 Explain the terms:
 a public sector
 b public–private partnership
 c public limited company
 d private limited company. [8]

2 Explain two likely reasons why the city government decided to privatise this organisation. [4]

3 Examine the likely impact of this privatisation, in the short run and the long run, on:
 a customers
 b shareholders
 c workers. [6]

4 Examine the advantages and disadvantages of the proposed public–private partnership for the building and operation of a new waste recycling plant. [8]

5 Recommend to the chief executive whether he should aim to convert the business to a private limited company. Justify your answer. [10]

EXAM PRACTICE QUESTION

Read the case study below and then answer the questions that follow.

THE GOOGLE™ PHENOMENON

In 1995, Larry Page and Sergey Brin met at Stanford University. The following year they formed a partnership and began collaborating on a search engine called BackRub. In 1997, they decided to rename BackRub and came up with Google (derived from 'googol' a mathematical term for the number represented by the numeral 1 followed by 100 zeros).

With $100 000 support from a backer, Google Inc was set up in 1998 in a garage in California. Later that year, *PC Magazine* recognised Google's search engine as one of the top 100 websites. In 2000, Google became available in many languages including French, German, Italian and Chinese. By 2004, the Google search index contained 6 billion items, including 4.28 billion web pages and 880 million images. It moved to an office in California called Googleplex with over 800 employees and offices all over the world. In the same year, Google became a public limited company offering for sale 19,605,052 shares at an opening price of $85 a share.

Over the next five years, Google refined and added to its search engines a range of products such as Google News, Google Earth, Google Maps and Google Video. Today, Google is a huge multinational corporation worth around $160 billion and its share price is over $500 a share.

Source: Adapted from various sources

25 marks, 45 minutes

1 Explain the term 'partnership'. [2]

2 Outline two benefits to Larry Page and Sergey Brin of starting Google as a partnership. [4]

3 Examine the difficulties the partners would have encountered when they set up Google. [8]

4 Explain the term 'public limited company' (plc). [2]

5 Discuss the advantages and disadvantages to Google following its conversion to a plc in 2004. [9]

03 Organisational objectives

This chapter covers syllabus section 1.3

On completing this chapter you should be able to:

- explain the importance of setting objectives in managing an organisation
- explain the purpose of mission statements and vision statements
- distinguish between objectives, strategies and tactics and discuss how these interrelate
- analyse the potential conflicts between corporate objectives and why objectives might change over time
- examine the reasons why organisations set ethical objectives and analyse the advantages and disadvantages of ethical objectives
- explain the different views that firms may take of their social responsibility in an international context
- (H) evaluate the need for firms to change objectives over time
- (H) discuss why a firm's view of its social responsibilities and its strategies towards them may change over time.

SETTING THE SCENE

Health and Beauty for You

Since setting up their beauty salon Health and Beauty for You, June Wong, with her brother Will, had managed to keep the business going through three difficult years. They agreed that their initial business objective should be survival. Despite the country's economic difficulties and fierce competition, the business had built up a good customer base and had covered all costs for the first three years.

Now the pair had decided to plan for the next three years, and were keen to focus on a new set of business objectives. June wanted the business to grow. She believed the best way to do this was to buy a beauty salon in another area of the city. 'This will get the business name really well known and will give us the basis for further sales growth of around 20% a year,' she told Will. He was not so sure that he wanted the staffing and marketing problems associated with another salon. 'I think we should aim to make as much profit as we can from the existing salon. We could offer a wider range of services and increase our prices. I think we could aim for a profit of $40 000 per year. After all, we went into business with the intention of becoming rich!' he reminded June.

After much discussion, June and Will agreed that the new business objective should be, in the short term, to open a new salon and to double sales within three years. After this had been achieved, the aim should be to maximise long-term profits from the two locations by improving image and raising prices – Will thought a five-year target of $90 000 per year was realistic.

Points to think about:

- What do you understand by the term 'objective'?
- Do you think it is important that Health and Beauty for You should have clear objectives? Explain your answer.
- Why do you think June and Will are thinking of changing the objectives for their business over time?

Introduction

Businesses of any size can benefit from setting clear objectives. In small businesses, such as sole traders, these objectives are often not written down or formalised in any way, but the owners will often have a clear idea of what they are trying to achieve. In partnerships, it is important for partners to agree on the direction their business should take to avoid future disagreements. Limited companies must state the overall objectives of the business in their Memorandum and Articles of Association, but this often lacks much strategic detail. This chapter focuses on the importance of business objectives, the different forms that these can take, including ethical and social targets, and how they can be used to direct the work of all staff in an organisation.

Importance of objectives

A business aim helps to direct, control and review the success of business activity. In addition, for any aim to be successfully achieved, there has to be an appropriate strategy – or detailed plan of action – in place to ensure that resources are correctly directed towards the final goal. This strategy should be constantly reviewed to check whether the business is on target to achieve its objectives. Both the aims of an organisation and the strategies it adopts will often change over time. Indeed, a change of objective will almost certainly require a change of plan too. A poor plan or strategy will lead to failure to reach the target.

The most effective business objectives usually meet the following SMART criteria:

S – **Specific** Objectives should focus on what the business does and should apply directly to that business. For example, a hotel may set an objective of 75% bed occupancy over the winter period – the objective is specific to this business.

M – **Measurable** Objectives that have a quantitative value are likely to prove to be more effective targets for directors and staff to work towards, for example to increase sales in the south-east region by 15% this year.

A – **Achievable** Objectives must be achievable. Setting objectives that are almost impossible to achieve in a given time will be pointless. They will demotivate staff who have the task of trying to reach these targets.

R – **Realistic and relevant** Objectives should be realistic when compared with the resources of the company, and should be expressed in terms relevant to the people who have to carry them out. For example, informing a factory cleaner about 'increasing market share' is less relevant than a target of reducing usage of cleaning materials by 20%.

T – **Time-specific** A time limit should be set when an objective is established. For example, by when does the business expect to increase profits by 5%? Without a time limit it will be impossible to assess whether the objective has actually been met.

EXAM TIP

Remember the acronym: SMART.

Aims, objectives, plans and strategies

Figure 3.1 shows the links between the different stages in the setting of aims and objectives.

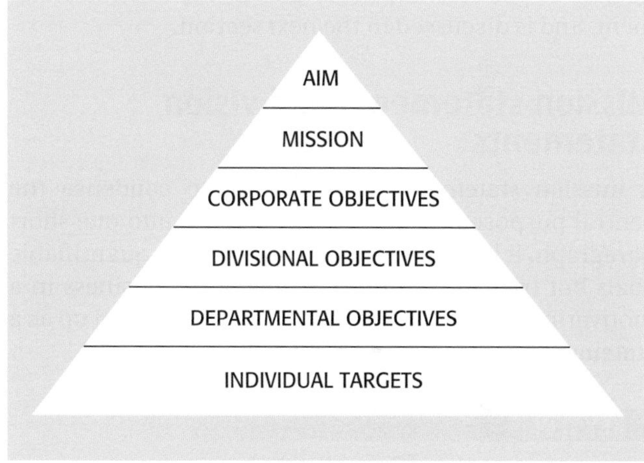

Figure 3.1 *The hierarchy of objectives*

Corporate aims are the long-term goals which a business hopes to achieve. The core of a business's activity is expressed in its corporate aims and plans. A typical corporate aim is: 'To increase shareholder returns each year through business expansion.' This example demonstrates a typical corporate aim. It tells us that the company aims to give shareholders maximum returns on their investment by expanding the business. Other corporate aims tend to concentrate on customer-based goals, such as 'meeting customers' needs', or market-based goals, such as 'becoming the world leader'. Corporate aims are all-embracing, and are designed to provide guidance to the whole organisation, not just a part of it.

Corporate aims have several benefits:

- They become the starting point for departmental objectives on which effective management is based. This is shown by their position at the top of the hierarchy of objectives in Figure 3.1.
- They can help develop a sense of purpose and direction for the whole organisation if they are clearly and unambiguously communicated to the workforce.

- They allow an assessment to be made, at a later date, of how successful the business has been in attaining its goals.
- They provide the framework within which the strategies or plans of the business can be drawn up.

A business without a long-term corporate plan or aim is likely to drift from event to event without a clear sense of purpose. This will become obvious to the workforce and customers, who may respond in adverse ways.

It is becoming increasingly common for businesses to express the corporate aim in one short, sharp 'guiding hand' statement to be made known to as many stakeholders as possible. This is known as the mission statement, and is discussed in the next section.

Mission statements and vision statements

A mission statement is an attempt to condense the central purpose of a business's existence into one short paragraph. It is not concerned with specific, quantifiable goals but tries to sum up the aims of the business in a motivating and appealing way. It can be summed up as a statement about 'who we are and what we do'.

KEY TERMS

mission statement a statement of the business's core aims, phrased in a way to motivate employees and to stimulate interest by outside groups

vision statement a statement of what the organisation would like to achieve or accomplish in the long term

Here are some examples of mission statements:

- College offering IB and A Level qualifications – 'To provide an academic curriculum in a caring and supportive environment'.
- BT – 'To be the most successful worldwide telecommunications group'.
- Nike, Inc. – 'To bring inspiration and innovation to every athlete in the world'.
- Microsoft – 'To enable people and businesses throughout the world to realise their full potential'.
- Google – 'To organise the world's information and make it universally accessible and useful'.
- Merck – 'Provide society with superior products and services by developing innovations and solutions that improve the quality of life and satisfy customer needs, to provide employees with meaningful work and advancement opportunities and investors with a superior rate of return'.

An effective mission statement should answer three key questions:

- What do we do?
- For whom do we do it?
- What is the benefit?

Mission statements outline the overall purpose of the organisation. A vision statement, on the other hand, describes a picture of the 'preferred future' and outlines how the future will look if the organisation achieves its mission. It is a clear statement of the future position that offers the ideal of what owners and directors want their business organisation to become. Table 3.1 compares the mission and vision statements of three organisations.

Organisation	Vision statement	Mission statement
Nokia	Our vision is a world where everyone is connected.	Nokia exists to connect people with each other and the information that is important to them with easy-to-use and innovative products. Nokia aims to provide equipment, solutions and services for consumers, network operators and corporations.
Minnesota Health Department (USA)	Keeping all residents healthy.	To protect, maintain and improve the health of all residents.
McDonald's Restaurants	Where the world buys more McDonald's than any other fast food.	McDonald's aims to be the world's best quick service restaurant experience. Being the best means providing outstanding quality, service, cleanliness and value so that we make every customer in every restaurant smile.

Table 3.1 *Comparing vision and mission statements*
Source: www.samples-help.org.uk

So what is the link between vision statements, mission statements and strategies? It is simple. Without the direction and focus brought to an organisation by vision and mission statements, planning new strategies will be like trying to steer a ship with no idea of either where it is or the direction it is meant to be heading in. Vision and mission statements give the organisation a sense of purpose and can prevent it from drifting between the tides and currents of powerful events.

EVALUATION OF THESE STATEMENTS

Which of the mission and vision statements above do you think is the most effective? Do you agree that some of them are interchangeable, that is, they could apply to any of the businesses? If you do, then this is one of the potential limitations of such statements. In recent years, virtually any organisation of any size has devised a mission statement. Do they perform a useful function or are they just another management fad? Below are some arguments in favour of these statements:

- They quickly inform groups outside the business what the central aim and vision are.
- They help to motivate employees, especially where an organisation is looked upon, as a result of its mission statement, as a caring and environmentally friendly body. Employees will then be associated with these positive qualities.
- Where they include ethical statements, they can help to guide and direct individual employee behaviour at work.
- They help to establish in the eyes of other groups 'what the business is about'.

On the other hand, these statements are often criticised for being:

- too vague and general so that they end up saying little which is specific about the business or its future plans
- based on a public relations exercise to make stakeholder groups 'feel good' about the organisation
- virtually impossible to analyse or disagree with
- rather 'woolly' and lacking in specific detail, so it is common for two completely different businesses to have very similar mission statements.

Communicating mission and vision statements is almost as important as establishing them. There is little point in identifying the central vision for a business and then not letting anyone else know about it. Businesses communicate their mission statements in a number of ways, for example in published accounts, communications to shareholders and the corporate plans of the business. Internal company newsletters and magazines may draw their title from part of the mission statement. Advertising slogans or posters are frequently based around the themes of the mission statements – The Body Shop is most effective in incorporating its mission into its eco-friendly campaigns.

On their own, mission statements are insufficient for operational guidelines. They do not tell managers what decisions to take or how to manage the business. Their role is to provide direction for the future and an overall sense of purpose, and in public relations terms, at least, they can prove very worthwhile. It is important that both vision and mission statements are applicable to the business, understood by employees and convertible into genuine strategic actions.

ACTIVITY 3.1

Read the case study below and then answer the questions that follow.

Corporate aims of Domestic Detergents Inc

- To increase annual sales from $1 billion to $2 billion in five years.
- To enter a new market every 18–24 months.
- To achieve 30% of sales each year from products not in the company's product line five years earlier.
- To be the lowest cost, highest quality producer in the household products industry.
- To achieve a 15% average annual growth in sales, profit and earnings per share.

20 marks, 35 minutes

1 Explain what is meant by the term 'SMART objectives'. [4]

2 To what extent are the corporate objectives for Domestic Detergents SMART objectives? [8]

3 Analyse the benefits and limitations to a company of setting specific and time-limited objectives. [8]

ACTIVITY 3.2

1 Use the website www.samples-help.org.uk/mission-statements to look up more mission statements for well-known corporations.

2 Evaluate the usefulness of any **one** of these mission statements for planning of future strategies for this business.

3 Suggest how the statements might be communicated to **three** different stakeholder groups.

4 Find out if your school or college has a mission statement. By asking staff, students and parents, attempt to establish whether this statement has had any impact on their view of the school.

Corporate objectives

The aims and mission statements of a business share the same problems – they lack specific detail for operational decisions and they are rarely expressed in quantitative terms. Corporate or strategic objectives are much more specific. They are based upon the business's central aim or mission, but they are expressed in terms that provide a much clearer guide for management action or strategy.

KEY TERM

corporate or strategic objectives important, broadly defined targets that a business must reach to achieve its overall aim

COMMON OBJECTIVES

Profit maximisation

Profits are essential for rewarding investors in a business and for financing further growth, and are necessary to persuade business owners and entrepreneurs to take risks. Profit maximisation means producing at the level of output where the greatest positive difference between total revenue and total costs is achieved – see Figure 3.2.

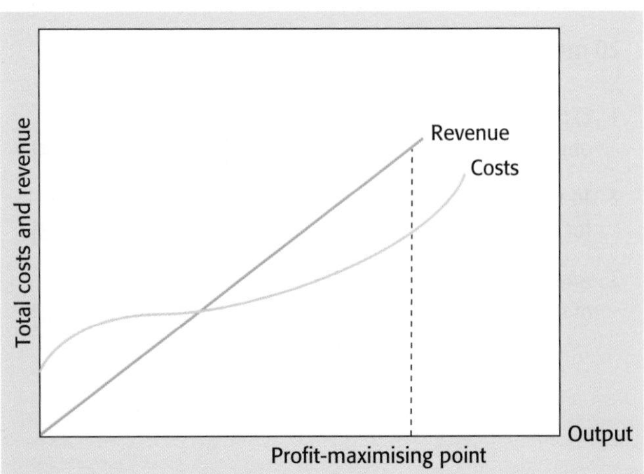

Figure 3.2 Profit maximisation – the greatest possible difference between total revenue and total cost

It seems rational to seek the maximum profit available from a given venture. Not to maximise profit is seen as a missed opportunity, but there are limitations with this corporate objective:

- High short-term profits may lead competitors to enter the market.
- Many businesses seek to maximise sales in order to secure the greatest market share possible, rather than maximise profits. The business would expect to make a target rate of profit from these sales.
- Owners of smaller businesses may be more concerned with issues of independence and keeping control – these may be of more importance than making higher profits.
- Most business analysts assess business performance through return on capital employed – the rate of profit returned on each dollar invested in the business – rather than through total profit.
- Profit maximisation may well be the preferred objective of the owners/shareholders, but other stakeholders will give priority to other issues. Managers cannot ignore these. Hence, the growing concern over job security for the workforce and the environmental concerns of local residents may force profitable business decisions to be modified, giving lower profit levels (see Chapter 4, page 39 for further discussion on stakeholder objectives).
- In practice, it is very difficult to assess whether the point of profit maximisation has been reached, and constant changes to prices or output to attempt to achieve it may well lead to negative consumer reactions.

Profit satisficing

This means aiming to achieve enough profit to keep the owners happy but not aiming to work flat out to make as much profit as possible. This is often the objective of owners of small businesses who wish to live comfortably but do not want to work very long hours in order to earn more profit. Once a 'satisfactory' level of profit has been achieved, the owners consider that other aims take priority, such as more leisure time.

Growth

The growth of a business – in terms of sales or value of output – has many potential benefits for the managers and owners. Larger firms will be less likely to be taken over and should be able to benefit from economies of scale. Managers may gain higher salaries and fringe benefits. Businesses that do not attempt to grow may cease to be competitive and, eventually, will lose their appeal to new investors. Business objectives based on growth have limitations:

- Over-rapid expansion can lead to cash-flow problems.
- Sales growth might be achieved at the expense of lower profit margins.
- Larger businesses can experience diseconomies of scale.
- Using profits to finance growth – retained profits – can lead to lower short-term returns to shareholders.
- Growth into new business areas and activities – away from the firm's 'core' activities – can result in a loss of focus and direction for the whole organisation.

Increasing market share

Closely linked to overall growth of a business is the market share it enjoys within its main market. It is possible for an expanding business to suffer a loss of market share if the market is growing at a faster rate than the business itself. Increasing market share indicates that the marketing mix of the business is proving to be more successful than that of its competitors. Benefits resulting from being the brand leader with the highest market share include:

- Retailers will be keen to stock and promote the best-selling brand.
- Profit margins offered to retailers may be lower than competing brands as the shops are so keen to stock it – this leaves more profit for the producer.
- Effective promotional campaigns are often based on 'buy our product with confidence – it is the brand leader'.

Survival

This is likely to be the key objective of most new business start-ups. The high failure rate of new businesses means that to survive for the first two years of trading is an important aim for entrepreneurs. Once the business has become firmly established, then other longer-term objectives can be established.

Corporate social responsibility (CSR)

KEY TERM

corporate social responsibility this concept applies to those businesses that consider the interests of society by taking responsibility for the impact of their decisions and activities on customers, employees, communities and the environment

Objectives that focus on meeting social responsibilities are increasingly important for most business organisations. The reasons for this and the consequences for businesses are considered below.

Maximising short-term sales revenue

This could benefit managers and staff when salaries and bonuses are dependent on sales revenue levels. However, if increased sales are achieved by reducing prices, the actual profits of the business might fall.

Maximising shareholder value

Management, especially in public limited companies, take decisions that aim to increase the company share price and dividends paid to shareholders. These targets might be achieved by pursuing the goal of profit maximisation. This shareholder value objective puts the interests of shareholders above those of other stakeholders.

ISSUES RELATING TO CORPORATE OBJECTIVES

Some important issues relating to corporate objectives include the following:

- They must be based on the corporate aim and should link in with it.
- They should be achievable and measurable if they are to motivate employees.
- They need to be communicated to employees and investors in the business. Unless staff are informed of the objectives and their own targets that result from these, then the business is unlikely to be successful.
- They form the framework for more specific departmental or strategic objectives – see below.
- They should indicate a time scale for their achievement – remember SMART!

CONFLICTS BETWEEN CORPORATE OBJECTIVES

Conflicts between objectives can often occur. These conflicts will need to be resolved by senior managers and decisions taken on the most significant objective for the next time period. The most common conflicts that can occur are:

- growth versus profit – achieving higher sales by raising promotional expenditure and by reducing prices will be likely to reduce short-term profits

- short term versus long term – lower profits and cash flow may need to be accepted in the short term if managers decide to invest heavily in new technology or the development of new products that might lead to higher profits in the longer term
- stakeholder conflicts – these are covered in detail in Chapter 4, page 40.

ACTIVITY 3.3

Read the case study below and then answer the questions that follow.

Reuters achieving its aims

Reuters, one of the world's largest news agencies, has returned to profitability after several years of losses. It aims to increase value for shareholders and the fact that Reuters shares have risen 7% faster than average share prices suggests that the company is becoming increasingly successful. Profits are being made for two main reasons. Many jobs have been lost in the company in recent years as a result of chief executive Tom Glocer's policy of cutting costs. Secondly, an ambitious growth objective has been established to increase sales and this target is being reached. New products – such as electronic trading – and new markets – such as China, Russia and India – have allowed an increase in sales of over 6% this year. This is above the growth target that was set. Some analysts are predicting a 40% increase in profit for the company next year.

Source: business.timesonline.co.uk (adapted)

18 marks, 32 minutes

1 What evidence is there that Reuters is meeting its objectives? [4]

2 Explain **two** benefits to the managers and other employees of the company from having clearly stated company aims and objectives. [6]

3 To what extent does the policy of increasing shareholder value conflict with other objectives the business might have? [8]

ACTIVITY 3.4

Read the case study below and then answer the questions that follow.

Is STS plc successful?

STS plc collects waste from houses, offices and factories. Most of the waste is burnt to produce heat and electricity for the company's own use. This saves costs and reduces the impact on the environment by not using areas of land to bury the rubbish. A recent increase in customers has meant that not all of the waste can be burnt and the company has dumped it in old quarries where it causes smells and gas emissions. Investment in labour-saving equipment has allowed the business to save on wage costs. The company's new mission statement is 'to become the country's number one waste business and to protect the environment for our children's benefit'. This has been explained to all shareholders in a recent letter to them, but the workers of the company were not involved in helping create the mission statement and they have not been informed of it.

The latest company accounts stated: 'We aim to maximise returns to shareholders through a strategy of aggressive growth. Our objectives are to expand year on year.' These accounts contained the following data.

	2007	2008	2009	2010
Sales revenue ($m)	20	25	35	40
Net profit ($m)	3	8	10	20
Total value of country's waste market ($m)	120	140	160	180
Number of employees	1000	950	900	800

20 marks, 35 minutes

1 How useful is the company's new mission statement? [4]

2 The company's objectives are not completely SMART. Explain the problems that might result from this. [6]

3 Using the information provided, to what extent is the business achieving success? Explain your answer. [10]

FACTORS DETERMINING CORPORATE OBJECTIVES

There are several reasons why firms have different objectives.

Corporate culture

This can be defined as the code of behaviour and attitudes that influence the decision-making style of the managers and other employees of the business. Culture is a way of doing things that is shared by all those in the organisation. According to the Cadbury plc 2007 Annual Report, 'Culture is about people, how they deliver, what they are accountable for, how aggressive they are in the pursuit of objectives and how adaptable they are in the face of change.'

If directors are aggressive in pursuit of their aims, keen to take over rival businesses and care little about social or environmental factors, then the objectives of the business will be very different to those of a business owned and controlled by directors with a more 'people' or 'social' orientated culture.

Size and legal form of the business

Owners of small businesses may be concerned only with a satisficing level of profit. Larger businesses, perhaps controlled by directors rather than owners, such as most public limited companies, might be more concerned with rapid business growth in order to increase the status and power of the managers. This is often a result of the divorce between ownership and control (see Chapter 2, page 15). Directors and managers may be more concerned about their bonuses, salaries and fringe benefits – which often depend on sheer business size – than on maximising returns to shareholders.

Public sector or private sector businesses

State-owned organisations tend not to have profit as a major objective. When the service these organisations provide is not 'charged for', such as education and health services, then a financial target would be inappropriate. Instead, quality of service measures are often used, such as the maximum days for a patient to wait for an operation. Even businesses earning revenue in the public sector, such as the postal service, may have among their objectives the target of maintaining services in non-profitable locations. In contrast are recent branch closures in rural areas by private sector banks in order to raise profits.

Well-established businesses

Newly formed businesses are likely to be driven by the desire to survive at all costs – the failure rate of new firms in the first year of operation is very high. Later, once well established, the business may pursue other objectives such as growth and profit.

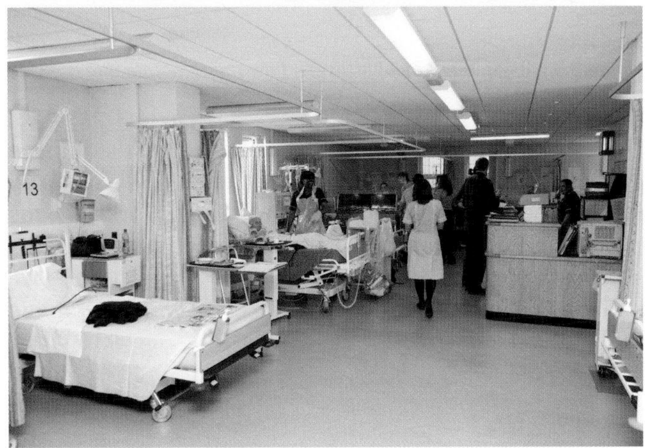

The objectives of these two organisations will be very different

Interrelated objectives, strategies and tactics

Corporate objectives relate to the whole organisation. They need to be broken down into specific tactical or operational objectives for separate divisions.

KEY TERM

tactical or operational objectives short- or medium-term goals or targets which must be achieved for an organisation to attain its corporate objectives

Divisional, operational objectives are set by senior managers to ensure:

- co-ordination between all divisions – if they do not work together, the focus of the organisation will appear confused to outsiders and there will be disagreements between departments
- consistency with strategic corporate objectives
- adequate resources are provided to allow for the successful achievement of the objectives.

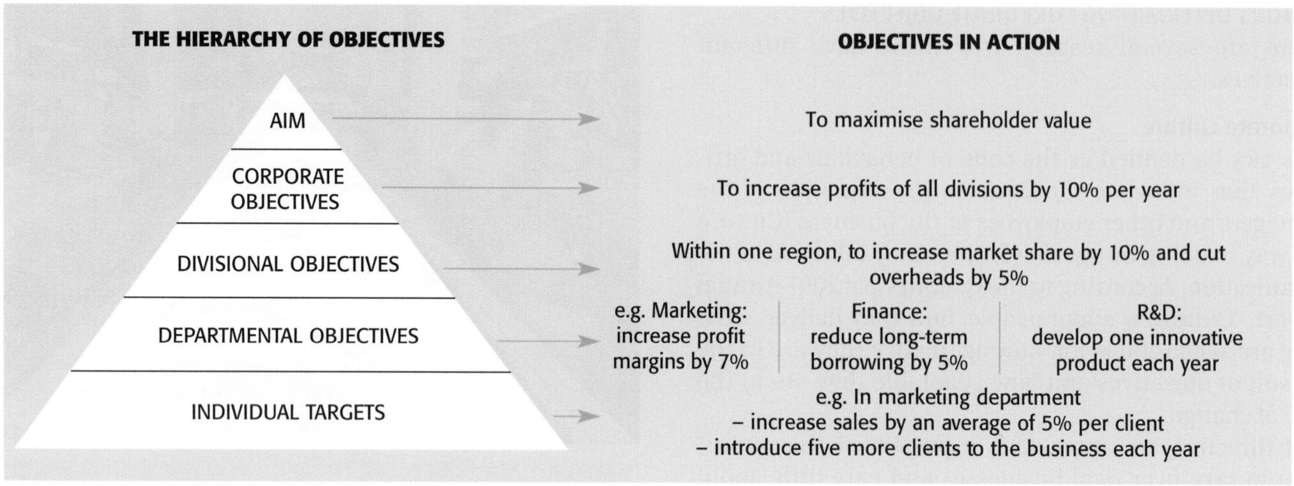

Figure 3.3 *Management by objectives – how the corporate aim is divided at every level of the organisation*

Once divisional objectives have been established, these can be further divided into departmental objectives and finally budgets and targets for individual workers. This process is called management by objectives (MBO), as shown in Figure 3.3.

Table 3.2 looks at the differences between strategic and tactical objectives.

Strategic/corporate	Tactical/divisional
• Set by board of directors or very senior managers • Set long-term goals for the whole organisation • Often high-risk objectives involving many resources • Difficult to reverse or change once established	• Set by senior managers for each department or division • Shorter-term goals • Involve fewer resources than strategic objectives • Often easier to change or reverse

Table 3.2 *Differences between strategic and tactical objectives*

HIGHER LEVEL

Changing business objectives

Businesses can change their corporate objectives over time. These changes will be in response to internal factors, such as resource constraints, or external factors, such as changes in the social and economic environment.

Some of the most significant reasons for businesses changing their objectives include the following:

- A business may have satisfied the survival objective by operating for several years and now the owners wish to pursue objectives of growth or increased profit. The internal resources of the business might have increased which will allow the objective of growth to be realistically established.
- An important senior manager responsible for international expansion might leave the business which leads to focusing on growing the business in domestic markets until an effective replacement can be found.
- The external competitive and economic environment may change. The entry into the market of a powerful rival or an economic recession may lead a firm to switch from growth to survival as its main aim. The UK airline, BA, has responded to the dual impact of increased low-fare competition and the recession by focusing less on its objectives to increase business-class and first-class market share and more on cost cutting and low fares. This has led to serious disputes with trade unions representing BA cabin staff.
- A short-term objective of growth in sales or market share might be replaced by a longer-term objective of maximising profits from the higher level of sales.

Business objectives need to be flexible enough to be adapted to reflect internal and external changes, but they should not be changed too dramatically or frequently as this may result in the loss of many of the benefits of setting SMART targets, including a loss of focus, sense of direction and specific measures to judge present performance. Before making a significant change to objectives, senior managers need to consider:

- Is the internal or external change significant and long-lasting enough to make a change in objectives necessary?
- What would be the risks of not adapting objectives to meet the new situation?

- What would be the cost and other consequences of new business objectives for the business and its staff?
- How can changed objectives – and the strategies needed to achieve them – be effectively managed within the business?

Ethical objectives

Ethical objectives are targets based on a moral code for the business, for example 'doing the right thing'. The growing acceptance of corporate social responsibility has led to businesses adopting an 'ethical code' to influence the way in which decisions are taken.

KEY TERMS

ethics moral guidelines that determine decision-making

ethical code (code of conduct) a document detailing a company's rules and guidelines on staff behaviour that must be followed by all employees

Most decisions have an ethical or moral dimension. For example:

- Should a toy company advertise products to young children so that they 'pester' their parents into buying them?
- Is it acceptable to take bribes in order to place an order with another company?
- Should a bank invest in a company that manufactures weapons or tests new chemicals on animals?
- Is it acceptable to feed genetically modified food to cattle?
- Do we accept lower profits in the short term by purchasing less-polluting production equipment?
- Should directors receive substantial pay rises and bonuses when other workers in the business might be being made redundant?
- Is it acceptable to close a factory to save costs and increase profits even though many jobs will be lost and workers may find it hard to get other jobs?
- If legal controls and inspections are weak in a country, is it acceptable to pay very low wages for long hours of work as this policy will reduce the firm's costs?
- Should a business employ child labour to reduce costs compared with employing adults?
- Should a business continue to produce potentially dangerous goods as long as 'no one finds us out'?

These are all examples of ethical dilemmas. The way in which employees behave and take decisions in these cases should be covered and explained by a company's ethical code of conduct. To what extent should businesses take ethics into consideration when making decisions? There is now considerable evidence that more and more companies are considering the ethical dimension of their actions – not just the impact they might have on profits.

Different people will have different answers to these dilemmas. Some managers will argue that any business decision that reduces costs and increases profits is acceptable as long as it is legal – and some might argue that even illegal actions could be justified too. Other managers will operate their business along strict ethical rules and will argue that, even if certain actions are not illegal, they are not right. Morally, they cannot be justified even if they might cut costs and increase sales.

EVALUATING ETHICAL OBJECTIVES

Adopting and keeping to a strict ethical code in decision-making can be expensive in the short term. For example:

- Using ethical and Fairtrade suppliers can add to a business's costs.
- Not taking bribes to secure business contracts can mean losing out on significant sales.
- Limiting the advertising of toys and other child-related products to an adult audience to reduce 'pester power' may result in lost sales.
- Accepting that it is wrong to fix prices with competitors might lead to lower prices and profits.
- Paying fair wages – even in very low-wage economies – raises costs and may reduce a firm's competitiveness against businesses that exploit workers.

However, in the long term there could be substantial benefits from acting ethically. For example:

- Avoiding potentially expensive court cases can reduce costs of fines.
- While bad publicity from being 'caught' acting unethically can lead to lost consumer loyalty and long-term reductions in sales, ethical policies will lead to good publicity and increased sales.
- Ethical businesses attract ethical customers and, as world pressure grows for corporate social responsibility, this group of consumers is increasing.
- Ethical businesses are more likely to be awarded government contracts.
- Well-qualified staff may be attracted to work for companies that have ethical and socially responsible policies.

Corporate social responsibility

To whom is business answerable? Should business activity be solely concerned with making profits to meet the objectives of shareholders and investors or should business

ACTIVITY 3.5

Read the case study below and then answer the questions that follow.

Siam Cement Group (SCG)

The SCG has a strict ethical code of conduct. Its key features are shown in the table below.

Business ethics	Code of conduct
• Fairness to all who have business relationships with the company, including society and environment. • Making business gains in a proper manner. • No alliances with political parties. • Non-discriminatory treatment of all staff and stakeholder groups.	• Upholding the principles of honesty and fairness. • Protecting the properties and reputation of SCG. • Conducting business in the best interests of SCG and its stakeholders. • Behaving appropriately at all times towards others.

According to a report by Judith Ross, as SCG expanded beyond Thailand managers came under pressure to compromise on its corporate code of ethics. The company's standards on bribes and other improper payments, for example, made it difficult to compete in places where such unethical payments are a way of life. This example demonstrates the classic problem: should firms conform to the standards of the country they operate in or should they try to export their own high moral principles to other lands?

Source: http://hbswk.hbs.edu (adapted)

22 marks, 38 minutes

1 Explain what you understand by the terms:
 a business ethics
 b code of conduct. **[4]**

2 Explain how SCG and its employees might benefit from the clear statement of business ethics and the code of conduct. **[8]**

3 Should a business such as SCG ever use unethical methods in a country where they are the 'norm', for example the giving and accepting of bribes? Justify your answer. **[10]**

decisions also be influenced by the needs of other stakeholders? When a firm fully accepts its legal and moral obligations to stakeholders other than investors, it is said to be accepting corporate social responsibility (CSR).

One important measure of a firm's attitude to its social responsibility is the way in which it deals with environmental issues. Our environment can be greatly affected by business activity. Air and noise pollution from manufacturing processes, road congestion caused by heavy trucks, business expansion into country areas, emissions of gases that can lead to global warming and the use of scarce non-renewable natural resources are all environmental issues that are of increasing concern to people and governments all over the world. How should business managers react to these concerns? Should they respond by adopting environmentally safe or green policies, even if these are expensive, or should they always take the cheapest option no matter what the consequences for the environment might be?

Other issues connected with the concept of CSR cross over into ethical decisions. In fact, the two concepts are closely linked. Examples of recent CSR developments include:

- the growth in the number of firms that promote organic and vegetarian foods
- increasing numbers of retailers emphasising the proportion of their products made from recycled materials
- businesses that refuse to stock goods that have been tested on animals or foods based on genetically modified ingredients.

In these cases, is the action being taken because trade and reputation might be lost if it is not or because such action is increasingly profitable? Might businesses be criticised for paying lip service to CSR rather than praised for their genuine concern for society and the environment? Conceivably, firms are being ethical or environmentally conscious because they have an objective that Peter Drucker, a famous writer on management, calls 'public responsibility', because they want to behave in these ways. However, many consumer groups and pressure groups are still dubious as to whether these objectives are based on genuinely held beliefs.

Table 3.3 looks at the benefits and drawbacks for businesses of adopting CSR policies.

Benefits	Drawbacks
• The image of the business and its products can be improved with a green or socially responsible approach. This could become a major competitive advantage, attracting new customers and loyalty from existing customers. • Attracting the best motivated and most efficient employees may become easier as many workers will prefer to work for and be associated with socially aware businesses. • Bad publicity and pressure group activity resulting from socially irresponsible behaviour should not arise. • The goodwill of other stakeholder groups, resulting from socially responsible behaviour, could lead to better relations with workers, suppliers, customers and the local community. • Higher long-term profitability should result from all of the factors above.	• Short-run costs could increase, e.g. fitting anti-pollution equipment, paying workers above-poverty wage levels, paying suppliers promptly, not exploiting vulnerable groups in advertising. • Shareholders may be reluctant to accept lower short-run profits (even though long-run profitability might increase). • Loss of cost and price competitiveness if rival businesses do not accept social responsibilities and have lower costs as a result. • Consumers may be prepared to pay higher prices for products made in a socially responsible manner, but during an economic recession, they might just prefer low prices and worry less about how products were made. • There could be a considerable social backlash against a business that *claims* to be socially responsible but is discovered to operate in socially irresponsible ways, e.g. a furniture maker claims to use sustainable timber but buys from rainforest suppliers – this is sometimes referred to as 'greenwash'.

Table 3.3 *Benefits and drawbacks of corporate social responsibility*

ACTIVITY 3.6

Read the case study below and then answer the questions that follow.

Virgin's environmental policies – green or just 'greenwash'?

The Virgin Atlantic jumbo jet that flew between London and Amsterdam using a proportion of bio-fuel was a world first. This fuel was derived from Brazilian babassu nuts and coconuts and is much less polluting than ordinary jet kerosene. The airline's boss, Sir Richard Branson, hailed this as a 'vital breakthrough' for the industry. Other well-publicised fuel saving measures used by the airline are the towing of aircraft to the runways for take-off instead of using their own engines and offering first-class passengers train tickets to travel to the airport in place of chauffeur-driven cars. Unfortunately, very few passengers have taken up this last offer, and towing of aircraft has been stopped as it causes damage to the undercarriage.

Greenpeace's chief scientist has labelled these efforts to make air travel more environmentally friendly 'high altitude greenwash' and said that 'less air travel was the only answer to the growing problem of climate changing pollution caused by air travel'. A Friends of the Earth spokesman said that bio-fuels do little to reduce emissions, and large-scale production of them leads to higher food prices.

Source: www.bbc.co.uk, article number 7261214 (adapted)

Air pollution is one way in which business activity can damage the environment – should companies be forced to use cleaner production methods?

18 marks, 32 minutes

1 Analyse why Virgin Atlantic is making efforts to reduce the amount of jet fuel (kerosene) used by its aircraft. [8]

2 To what extent will the company lose or benefit from these well-publicised attempts to reduce air pollution? [10]

ENVIRONMENTAL AUDITS

An audit simply means an independent check. It is most commonly known in connection with the accounts of a company which have to be verified as a true and fair record by an external auditor. Accounts only measure the financial performance of a business. In recent years, some businesses have been using the auditing approach to evaluate their performance in other ways than just profit and loss.

KEY TERM

environmental audit assesses the impact of a business's impact on the environment

Environmental factors are often difficult to measure in monetary terms and they do not, currently, have to be legally included in published accounts. An environmental audit would check the pollution levels, wastage levels, energy use, transport use and recycling rates of the business and compare them with previous years, pre-set targets and possibly other similar businesses. At present, these audits are entirely voluntary. Those firms who undertake them and publish the results nearly always have a very good environmental record – that is why they are published. Firms with a poor reputation or record in this area are unlikely to carry out an audit unless it becomes compulsory.

Those firms that do publish the results of environmental audits expect to gain something from the process. Favourable consumer reaction could lead to increased sales. Positive media coverage will give free publicity. Working towards the common aim of reducing harm to the environment could help to bring workers and managers together as a team.

SOCIAL AUDITS

KEY TERM

social audit an independent report on the impact a business has on society. This can cover pollution levels, health and safety record, sources of supplies, customer satisfaction and contribution to the community

Social audits report on a firm's 'social' performance, that is the impact it has on society and how effectively its ethical behaviour matches up to its ethical objectives. Social audits can include an environmental audit (see above), but they give details of other impacts on society too. These include:

- health and safety record, e.g. number of accidents and fatalities
- contributions to local community events and charities
- proportion of supplies that come from ethical sources, e.g. Fairtrade Foundation suppliers
- employee benefit schemes
- feedback from customers and suppliers on how they perceive the ethical nature of the business's activities.

The social audit will also contain annual targets to be reached to improve a firm's level of social responsibility and details of the policies to be followed to achieve these aims. By researching and publishing these reports, firms are often able to identify potentially anti-social behaviour and take steps to root this out of the company's practices. Publishing detailed and independently verified social and environmental audits can improve a firm's public image, increase consumer loyalty and give the business a clear direction for future improvements in its socially responsibility achievements. The benefits and limitations of social audits are considered in Table 3.4.

Benefits	Limitations
• Identifies what social responsibilities the business is meeting – and what still needs to be achieved. • Sets targets for improvement in social performance by comparing audits with the best-performing firms in the industry. • Gives direction to the action plans a business still needs to put into effect to achieve its social/ethical objectives. • Improves a company's public image and this can be used as a marketing tool to increase sales.	• If the social audit is not independently checked – as published accounts must be – will it be taken seriously by stakeholders? • Time and money must be devoted to producing a detailed social audit – is this really necessary if it is not legally required? • Many consumers may just be interested in cheap goods, not whether the businesses they buy from are socially responsible. • A social audit does not prove that a business is being socially responsible.

Table 3.4 *Benefits and limitations of social audits*

Evaluation of audits

- Until environmental and social audits are made compulsory and there is general agreement about what they should include and how the contents will be verified, some observers will not take them seriously.
- Companies have been accused of using them as a publicity stunt or a 'smokescreen' to hide their true intentions and potentially damaging practices.
- They can be very time consuming and expensive to produce and publish and this may make them of limited value to small businesses or those with very limited finance.

ACTIVITY 3.7

Read the case study below and then answer the questions that follow.

Corporate social responsibility

Corporate social and environmental awareness has become an essential for companies as they realise that they must listen to all stakeholders if they are to achieve their objectives.

The combination of environmental responsibility, ethics and profits is one that is attracting increasing attention. Many chief executive officers of leading companies now disagree with the idea that the interests of shareholders and those of other stakeholders (employees, community, customers and so on) must always conflict. Increasingly, corporations seek to weld these two seemingly opposite forces so that 'doing good' and 'doing good business' become the same thing.

Social and environmental responsibility has moved from a 'nice to do' to a 'need to do'. The importance of the employee has been highlighted by the so-called 'war for talent'. Recruiting the brightest and best has become a key concern, says a human resources manager at PricewaterhouseCoopers: 'There is such a limited number of the right type of graduates, and they are choosy about the type of company they will work for. The cost of recruiting and retaining staff is likely to be higher if you are not seen to be an ethical employer and organisation.' A company's reputation also has significant implications for its financial performance. Analysts believe it is one of the key factors in the valuation of companies. One company could have a higher stock market valuation than another one solely due to its good social and environmental reputation.

Shell, a company with traditionally one of the worst reputations among environmental and social pressure groups, has made enormous efforts to reinvent itself as a socially responsible business. It has stated its aims as nothing less than to become 'the leading multinational in economic, environmental and social responsibility'. Shell's chairman has said that the reason for Shell's conversion to environmental protection is: 'We won't achieve our business goals unless we are listening to and learning from the full range of our stakeholders in society.'

22 marks, 40 minutes

1 Explain the terms:
   a socially responsible business
   b ethics. [4]

2 Analyse **two** factors given in the article which could encourage a business to adopt ethical and socially responsible objectives and strategies. [8]

3 Discuss the likely cost and benefits for Shell of the company working towards being seen as 'the leading multinational in economic, environmental and social responsibility'. [10]

10 marks, 18 minutes

4 Assess whether businesses should change their strategies of corporate responsibility over time. [10]

THEORY OF KNOWLEDGE

OIL LEAK UPDATE

BP's oil leak is now the worst ever oil leak in history and one of the biggest man-made environmental disasters the US has ever faced. According to the Associated Press, the oil leak that began on 20 April 2010, killing eleven men, leaked 4.9 million barrels of crude oil into the Gulf. As a plc, one of BP's key objectives is to maximise its return to its shareholders. Deep-water drilling for oil in the Gulf of Mexico will increase its profits in the future but, as this oil leak demonstrates, at a price to the environment.

Source: Reuters (adapted)

1 Are there ethical obligations for businesses to treat the natural environment in a particular way?

2 Analyse the constraints on businesses that aim to protect the environment.

3 Discuss the view that businesses who claim they have an objective to protect the environment are really just trying to create a positive image in order to increase their sales and profits.

HIGHER LEVEL

Changes in corporate responsibility

Attitudes towards corporate responsibility have changed over time. The standards that companies are expected to reach are determined by societal norms, and in most countries these now focus on stakeholders rather than shareholders.

The main reasons for changing corporate approaches to social responsibility include:

- increasing publicity from international pressure groups that use the internet to communicate, blog, raise funds and organise boycotts
- the United Nations Millennium Development Goals, agreed by more than 120 countries in 2000, which includes 'environmentally sustainable growth' – this has forced many developing nations to insist that new company investment in their economy take environmental concerns into consideration
- global concern over climate change and the impact this could have on social and economic development – this is forcing companies to confront the climatic consequences of their actions and their investments, e.g. the rapid increase in wind-power farms in Germany
- legal changes at local, national and European Union level – these have forced businesses to refrain from certain practices. In most countries, businesses can no longer pay staff very low wages or avoid legal responsibility for their products.

CHANGES IN CORPORATE STRATEGIES

The changing corporate strategies of the world's mining companies are an excellent example of how firms may adopt different strategies towards their social responsibilities in response to pressure. In the 1970s and 1980s, many mining companies signed mineral extraction deals with undemocratic political regimes. Environmental concerns were given very low priority and the interests of the local or indigenous peoples (displaced by the mine workings) ignored. The Grasberg (West Papua) and Bougainville (Papua New Guinea) gold and copper mines are useful case studies.

- In Bougainville, joint owners of the mine, RTZ and Freeport, allowed the government to use force to put down civil unrest caused by the displacement of people by the mine and its environmental damage. The company took a very tough line and military action took place next to the mine. Eventually, the company was forced to close it.
- The Grasberg mine, which opened later than Bougainville, benefited from a very different objective by RTZ towards its social responsibilities as a result of the poor publicity over its policy in Papua New Guinea. A trust fund has been set up to spend 1% of total mine revenue to fund village development. In addition, one quarter of the total workforce is drawn from local communities.
- RTZ went even further with the Jabiluka uranium mine in northern Australia. Publicity by the local Mirrar tribe and their supporters led to an unprecedented extraordinary general meeting of shareholders, which led to the mine being closed – it has never reopened.

OVER TO YOU

REVISION CHECKLIST

1 Differentiate clearly, with examples, between mission statements and vision statements.
2 What are often considered to be the practical limitations of mission statements?
3 State **four** factors that would help to ensure that corporate objectives were effective in assisting a business to achieve its aim.
4 Give an example of a SMART objective that could be set for your school or college.
5 Explain, with **two** examples, what corporate objectives a car manufacturing business could establish.
6 Why might short-term profit maximisation not be an appropriate objective for a car manufacturer?
7 Explain the meaning of the corporate objective 'increasing shareholder value'?
8 Why might the owners/directors of a small private limited company set a profit satisficing objective?
9 Why might the objective of increasing shareholder value conflict with corporate social responsibility?
10 Why should departmental objectives be co-ordinated?
11 Why are more companies adopting objectives that include corporate social responsibility?
12 What do you understand by the term 'ethical code of conduct'?
13 Explain the possible benefits to a clothing retailer of strictly observing an ethical code when choosing and checking on its suppliers.
14 Why might some firms decide not to act ethically in a competitive market?
H 15 Using a business example from your own country, explain why its key corporate objectives might change over time.

REVISION ACTIVITY

Read the case study below and then answer the questions that follow.

Peugeot Citroen's road ahead laid out

The chairman of the car maker Peugeot Citroen, Mr Streiff, has set the company the aim of becoming the 'most competitive car maker in Europe by 2015'. This overall aim is supported by more specific and measurable objectives. The profit margin of each car sold is targeted to increase from 2% to 7% by 2015. The overall sales objective is to reach 4 million car sales a year by 2010. One million car sales are aimed for in the emerging markets by 2015. In Europe, one of the most competitive car markets in the world, the target is to increase sales by 300 000 cars a year by the same date.

Departmental operating targets have also been established. For example, the human resources department must prepare for up to 8000 job losses and operations must aim to cut fixed manufacturing costs by 30% and costs of purchasing car parts by 4–6% a year. Marketing must plan to launch 12 new models in the Chinese market.

Mr Streiff also announced his intention to take both car brands upmarket and establish them as premium car brands that increasing numbers of customers will want to own.

Source: www.timesonline.co.uk

24 marks, 42 minutes

1 Analyse whether Peugeot Citroen's objectives fit the SMART criteria. [6]

2 Analyse the importance of the chairman not only setting an overall aim for the company but also establishing departmental objectives. [10]

3 Do you think Peugeot Citroen's shareholders would be pleased by Mr Streiff's new objectives for the company? Explain your answer. [8]

H **10 marks, 18 minutes**

4 To what extent might these objectives have to be changed before the 2015 target date is reached? [10]

EXAM PRACTICE QUESTION

Read the case study below and then answer the questions that follow.

CORPORATE AND SOCIAL RESPONSIBILITY AT NIKE, INC.

The Nike 'Swoosh' logo is one of the most famous corporate symbols in the world. Nike, Inc. is an organisation that people look to as a leading sports brand and a business that encapsulates US corporate power and globalisation.

Nike, Inc.'s mission statement has two elements:

- To bring inspiration and innovation to every athlete in the world.
- If you have a body you are an athlete.

Much of Nike, Inc.'s success is based on the way it focuses on consumers in a sporting context and provides products which strongly support this. In recent years it has, like many multinational companies, suffered from adverse publicity on issues such as working conditions in its factories. It has tried to answer its critics by becoming a socially responsible organisation and communicating this to its stakeholders.

Below is a short extract from Nike, Inc.'s website (www.nikebiz.com) on its corporate social responsibility:

> Nike, Inc. shares the widely held view that climate change is a serious issue requiring immediate and meaningful action across government, industry, consumers and society. Nike, Inc. has made cutting greenhouse gas emissions across our operations, incorporating sustainability into the design of our products and reducing the overall environmental footprint a cornerstone of our environmental efforts.
>
> *Source: www.nike.com (adapted)*

25 marks, 45 minutes

1 Explain the reason for Nike, Inc. having a mission statement. [4]

2 Analyse **two** strategic objectives that Nike, Inc. might try to achieve. [6]

3 Using Nike, Inc. as an example, outline the main components you might expect to see in its environmental audit. [6]

4 Evaluate the advantages and disadvantages to Nike, Inc. of aiming to be a socially responsible organisation. [9]

04 Stakeholders

This chapter covers syllabus section 1.4

On completing this chapter you should be able to:

- explain what is meant by 'stakeholder' and differentiate between internal and external stakeholders
- analyse and comment on business responsibilities to stakeholders
- discuss possible areas of conflict between stakeholders
- (H) evaluate ways in which conflicting stakeholder objectives might be recognised and responded to by business.

SETTING THE SCENE

Tata Nano divides opinions

It is three metres long, seats four, does 100 kilometres an hour and aims to revolutionise travel for millions. The 'People's Car' is also the cheapest in the world at 100 000 rupees (US$2600) – about the same price as a DVD player in a Lexus. Rattan Tata, the company chairman, unveiled the cute, snub-nosed car that will allow millions of Asia's emerging middle classes to buy a car for the first time. 'This will change the way people travel in India and Asia. Most people are denied mobility due to the high prices of cars. This is a car that will be affordable to millions of consumers for the first time,' he said when the car was launched.

The car will be built in a factory in West Bengal. This will offer relatively well-paid factory employment to thousands of workers for the first time. The country will gain export revenue when the car is sold abroad. The steel and other materials used in the car will be purchased from Asian suppliers, which will help to boost local economies and suppliers.

The idea of millions of Nanos on the road alarms environmental groups. Rajendra Pachauri, the UN's chief climate scientist, said that he was 'having nightmares' about it. Delhi, where air pollution levels are more than twice the safe limit, is registering 1000 new cars a day, and this could double when the Nano is in production. Average speed of traffic at rush hour is 10 kilometres an hour and the government might be forced to spend much more on building new roads if Nano ownership became widespread. Bus operators also fear increased competition from private car users.

Source: www.timesonline.co.uk, 11 January 2008 (adapted)

Points to think about:

- List the groups of people who might benefit from Nano car production.
- List the groups who might be badly affected by the use of large numbers of Nano cars.
- Do you think Tata, the manufacturer, has a responsibility to all of these groups?

What makes the Nano so cheap?

Introduction

The traditional view of business is often referred to as the shareholder concept. As the shareholders are the owners of the company, the firm has a legally binding duty to take decisions that will increase shareholder value. Since directors and managers ultimately owe their position to shareholders, it is important to keep them satisfied. In recent times, this limited view of business responsibility has been extended to include the interests not just of the investors/owners but also of suppliers, employees and customers. This approach to business responsibilities does not end with these four groups, however. The stakeholder theory or concept is that there are many other parties involved and interested in business activity and that the interests of these groups – local communities, the public, government and pressure groups such as environmental lobbyists – should be considered by business decision-makers.

KEY TERMS

stakeholders people or groups of people who can be affected by, and therefore have an interest in, any action by an organisation

stakeholder concept the view that businesses and their managers have responsibilities to a wide range of groups, not just shareholders

Who are the stakeholders?

INTERNAL STAKEHOLDERS

There are three main internal stakeholders, each with their own set of interests in the business's activities. They include:

- employees – employment security, wage levels, conditions of employment, participation in the business
- managers – employment security, salary and benefits offered, responsibilities given
- shareholders – annual dividends, share price, security of investment.

EXTERNAL STAKEHOLDERS

The external stakeholders and their interests include:

- suppliers – speed of payment, level and regularity of orders, fairness of treatment
- customers – value for money, product quality, service levels
- government – jobs created, taxes paid, value of output produced, impact on wider society
- special interest groups such as:
  - banks and other creditors – security of their loans and the ability of the business to repay them
  - pressure groups that want to change a business's policy towards pollution or testing of chemicals on animals
  - community action groups concerned about the local impact of business activity
- competitors – fairness of competitive practices, strategic plans of the business.

EXAM TIP

Do not confuse the terms 'stakeholder' and 'shareholder'. Stakeholder is a much broader term that covers many groups, including shareholders.

Business responsibilities to stakeholders

Table 4.1 outlines the responsibilities that businesses could have towards stakeholders and identifies the benefits to businesses of accepting these.

Stakeholder conflicts

Business decisions and activities can have both positive and negative effects on stakeholders, but it is rare for all stakeholders to be either positively or negatively affected by any one business activity. It is also possible for any one stakeholder group to experience both negative and positive effects from the same business decision. This is why conflicts of interest between stakeholder groups, with different objectives and interests, can arise. Table 4.2 outlines some business decisions and the conflict of stakeholder interests that can result.

ACTIVITY 4.1

15 marks, 25 minutes

1 In the three examples in Table 4.2, analyse the likely positive and negative effects on **two** other stakeholder groups. [6]

2 State **two** other examples of business decisions. Try to use actual and recent examples from your own country. Analyse the potential conflict of interests between any **three** stakeholder groups. [9]

EXAM TIP

Many examination questions involve the conflict of stakeholder objectives. Remember that it is difficult for a business to meet all of its responsibilities to all stakeholders at any one time. Compromise might be necessary – meeting as many stakeholder objectives as possible or meeting the needs of the most important group in each situation.

	Business's responsibilities to stakeholders	Benefits of accepting responsibilities
Customers	• Not to break the laws on consumer protection and accurate advertising. • Not taking advantage of vulnerable customers, such as the elderly, and not using high-pressure selling tactics. • Giving customers assurances about quality, delivery dates, service levels and continued supplies of vital components and materials.	• In a world of increasing free trade and international competition, it is essential to satisfy customers' demands in order to stay in business in the long term. • Consumer loyalty and repeat purchases. • Good publicity when customers give 'word of mouth' recommendations; positive customer feedback helps to improve goods and services.
Suppliers	• Establish effective two-way relationships that are of benefit to the business and suppliers. • Avoid excessive pressure on smaller or weaker suppliers to cut prices. • Pay fair prices and pay invoices promptly.	• Supplier loyalty – meeting deadlines and requests for special orders. • More likely to receive supplies of high quality. • Reasonable credit terms more likely to be offered. • 'Payment holidays' may be offered to struggling businesses, if this means keeping them as customers.
Employees	• Adhere to country's laws that outline business responsibilities to workers – such laws are stricter in some countries than others. • Some businesses also provide training, job security, pay more than minimum wages, offer good working conditions, involve staff in some decision-making.	• Employee loyalty and low labour turnover. • Motivated staff more committed to the success of the organisation. • Easier to recruit good employees to fill vacancies – they will be attracted by the responsibility the business shows to its employees.
Shareholders	• Incorporated businesses should be operated in accordance with company law. • Annual accounts presented to shareholders. • Actions taken to increase shareholder value over time.	• Shareholders will be reluctant to sell shares and this will help avoid share price falls. • Shareholders may be willing to buy new issues of shares to invest further capital in the company.
Special interest groups	• Banks: payment of interest and repayment of loans as required. • Pressure groups: recognition of genuine concern over business activity – business may respond by changing decisions or operations. • Local community: avoid pollution and other damaging operations, support for local groups.	• Banks: more willing to provide financial support in the future. • Pressure groups: less likely to engage in practices damaging to the interests of the business such as consumer boycotts. • Local community: more likely to agree to business expansion plans.
Competitors	• To compete fairly and within the law. • It is *not* a responsibility of business to provide details of its strategic plans to competitors.	• Avoid legal action as a consequence of uncompetitive practices. • Opportunities for co-operation and joint ventures – as long as these do not contravene competition laws.
Managers	• Job security. • Competitive salaries and other benefits. • Opportunities for responsibility and career advancement.	• Low turnover of management staff. • Work incentive. • Easier to attract well-qualified managers to the business.

Table 4.1 *Benefits to business of accepting stakeholder responsibilities*

Business decision/ activity	Impact on:		
	Employees	Local community	Customers
Expansion of the business	✓ More job and career opportunities. ✗ More complex lines of communication after expansion.	✓ More jobs for local residents and increased spending in other local businesses. ✗ External costs caused by increased traffic and loss of green fields for amenity use.	✓ Better service provided by bigger business with more staff. ✗ Larger business could be less personal and therefore offer inferior customer service.
Takeover of a competing firm (horizontal integration)	✓ The larger business may be more secure and offer career promotion opportunities. ✗ Rationalisation may occur to avoid waste and cut costs – jobs might be lost.	✓ If the business expands on the existing site, local job vacancies and incomes might increase. ✗ Rationalisation of duplicated offices or factories might lead to closures and job losses.	✓ The larger business may benefit from economies of scale, which could lead to lower prices. ✗ Reduced competition could have the opposite effect – less customer choice and higher prices.
New IT introduced into production methods	✓ Training and promotion opportunities might be offered. ✗ Fewer untrained staff will be required and those unable to learn new skills may be made redundant.	✓ Local businesses providing IT services could benefit from increased orders. ✗ Specialist workers may not be available locally, so more staff may need to commute.	✓ More efficient and flexible production methods might improve quality and offer more product variety. ✗ IT reliability problems could cause supply delays.

Table 4.2 *Potential conflicts of interest between stakeholder groups*

THEORY OF KNOWLEDGE

LLOYDS TO CUT ANOTHER 2100 JOBS

Lloyds Banking Group has announced it is to cut a further 2100 jobs over the next three years. The Unite union was 'astonished' by the scale of the cuts, which it said brought total job losses at the group since January to 7000. The banking giant, which is 43% owned by UK taxpayers, was formed by the merger of Halifax Bank of Scotland and Lloyds TSB late last year. Rob MacGregor of the Unite union said morale at the banking group was 'now truly low. Employees across Lloyds are in a permanent state of anxiety as they see their employer announce hundreds of job losses every week,' he said.

Lloyds share price rose 4.2 per cent today on news of the job cuts.

Source: www.bbc.co.uk/news (adapted)

1 Comment on the conflict in stakeholder interests that arises from the article.
2 Discuss the ethical questions businesses face when they make job cuts.

HIGHER LEVEL

Evaluating stakeholder conflict

One way of reducing conflict is to compromise. For example, a business aiming to reduce costs may close one of its factories in stages rather than immediately to allow workers time to find other jobs but, as a result, business costs will fall more slowly. Plans to build a new chemical plant may have to be adapted to move the main site away from a housing estate to protect the local community, but the new site might be more expensive. The introduction of 24-hour flights at an airport – to the benefit of the airlines and passengers – may only be accepted if local residents are offered sound insulation in their homes, thereby increasing costs for the airport and airlines.

Clearly, senior management must establish its priorities in these situations. They need to decide who the most important stakeholders are in each case, what the extra cost of meeting the needs of each stakeholder group will be, and whether bad publicity resulting from failure to meet the interests of one group will lead to lost revenue – perhaps this will be greater than the cost savings of not satisfying this group.

Table 4.3 considers methods available to businesses to reduce stakeholder conflict, and the potential advantages and disadvantages of each.

Method of conflict resolution	Advantages	Disadvantages
Arbitration – to resolve industrial disputes between workers and managers	An independent arbitrator will hear the arguments from both sides and decide on what they consider to be a fair solution. Both sides can agree beforehand whether this settlement is binding, that is they have to accept it.	Neither stakeholder group will be likely to receive exactly what they wanted. The costs of the business might rise if the arbitrator proposes higher wages or better work conditions than the employer was originally offering.
Worker participation – to improve communication, decision-making and reduce potential conflicts between workers and managers, e.g. works councils, employee directors	Workers have a real contribution to make to many business decisions. Participation can motivate staff to work more effectively.	Some managers believe that participation wastes time and resources, e.g. in meetings that are just 'talking shops', and that the role of the manager is to manage, not the workers. Some information cannot be disclosed to staff other than senior managers, e.g. sensitive details about future product launches.
Profit sharing schemes – to reduce conflict between workers and shareholders over the allocation of profits and to share the benefits of company success.	The workforce is allocated a share of annual profits before these are paid out in dividends to shareholders. Sharing business profits can encourage workers to work in ways that will increase long-term profitability.	Paying workers a share of the profits can reduce retained profits (used for expansion of the business) and/or profits paid out to shareholders, unless the scheme results in higher profits due to increased employee motivation.
Share ownership schemes – to reduce conflict between workers, managers and shareholders	These schemes, including share options (the right to buy shares at a specified price in the future) aim to allow employees (at all levels including directors) to benefit from the success of the business as well as shareholders. Share ownership should help to align the interests of employees with those of shareholders.	Administration costs, negative impact on employee motivation if the share price falls, dilution of ownership – the issue of additional shares means that each owns a smaller share of the company. Employees may have to stay with the company for a certain number of years before they qualify, so the motivation effect on new staff may be limited.

Table 4.3 *Methods to reduce stakeholder conflict – advantages and disadvantages*

OVER TO YOU

REVISION CHECKLIST

1 Distinguish between the shareholder concept and the stakeholder concept.
2 Explain why a business might experience lower profits by meeting its stakeholders' objectives.
3 Explain why a business might experience higher profits by meeting its stakeholders' objectives.
4 Outline the responsibilities a business in the oil industry might have to **two** stakeholder groups.
5 Outline the responsibilities a tertiary sector business might have to **two** stakeholder groups.
6 What do you understand by the term 'conflicts between stakeholder interests'?
7 Explain an example, from your own country, of a business decision that involves a conflict of stakeholder interests.
8 Explain **three** examples of potential stakeholder conflict of interests.

9 Evaluate how each of the conflicts you identified in question 8 might be resolved.

REVISION ACTIVITY

Read the case study below and then answer the questions that follow.

Daily Record: 'Merger results in job losses'

The merger of two of the largest airlines in the country will lead to job losses, reports the *Daily Record*. Special Air and Flights4U have announced a huge merger which will result in a business worth over $2 billion. The long-term plans are to offer more routes and cheaper prices to passengers. The merger has the support of the government as it is expected to keep inflation down and boost tourist numbers into the country.

Non-profitable routes to small regional airports are to be closed, together with Special Air's headquarters in New City. More than 500 staff are expected to lose their jobs, resulting in annual savings of over $10 million. Trade union leaders are threatening to take industrial action to support workers who will lose their jobs. The local governments in the towns which are losing routes are very worried about the impact on local suppliers of fuel and food to the airlines. The chief executive of Flights4U said: 'Sure, there will be losers from this merger, but there will be many more winners as we expand our operations from the major cities.'

22 marks, 45 minutes

1 Are the two airlines focused on shareholder interests or other stakeholder interests? Explain your answer. [10]

2 Why is it difficult in this case for the two merging companies to meet their responsibilities to all stakeholder groups? [6]

3 Why might the negative impact on some stakeholders mean that the merger will not turn out to be as profitable as expected? [6]

(H) **10 marks, 18 minutes**

4 Discuss how the newly merged business could attempt to meet some of its responsibilities to the stakeholder groups worst affected by this decision. [10]

FURY AT BANGLADESH MINE SCHEME

A huge open-cast coal-mining project by a British firm, that would involve moving the homes of up to 130 000 workers in Bangladesh, is at the centre of an international row. The company, GCM, plans to dig up to 570 million tonnes of coal in a project that will displace people from Phulbari, in north-west Bangladesh. A river will also have to be diverted and the mangrove forest, which is a world heritage site, would be destroyed too.

The project has attracted widespread hostility. In protests against the scheme 18 months ago, three people were killed in an area now said to be controlled by the armed forces. Many international campaign groups have written to the Asian Development Bank demanding that it turns down a $200 million loan for the project. The World Development Movement is claiming that the social and environmental damage can never be repaired if the scheme receives government approval. A spokesman for GCM, on the other hand, stressed the importance to one of the world's poorest countries of jobs, incomes and exports.

Protests in Dhaka over the mine project

Source: Observer, *9 March 2008 (adapted)*

EXAM PRACTICE QUESTION

Read the case study and then answer the questions that follow.

25 marks, 45 minutes

1 Using examples from the case study, explain the differences between internal and external stakeholders. [4]

2 Explain the benefits of any **two** stakeholder groups resulting from this mine project. [6]

(H) 3 Explain the disadvantages to any **two** stakeholder groups resulting from this mine project. [6]

4 Discuss the ways in which GCM could reduce the impact of the disadvantages it has created for stakeholder groups negatively affected by the mine. [9]

05 External environment

This chapter covers syllabus section 1.5

On completing this chapter you should be able to:

- prepare a PEST analysis for a given situation
- use PEST analysis to examine the impact of the external environment on a firm
- evaluate the impact on a firm's objectives and strategy of a change in any of the PEST factors
- analyse the impact that external opportunities and threats may have on business objectives and strategy
- explain how external opportunities and threats can impact on business decision-making.

SETTING THE SCENE

Nokia sets good example – but BP is fined

Nokia, the world's leading mobile phone maker, has announced the closure of its Bochum factory in Germany with the loss of 2300 jobs. The company reached an agreement with the workers' trade union leaders. Nokia will pay US$314 million in redundancy pay and will set up a social plan for employees to help them look for other jobs. This sum is much greater than that demanded by German employment law. Nokia is trying to set a good example and is attempting to limit the bad publicity in Germany from the factory closure. Sales of mobile phones in some countries were badly hit by the 2009–10 global economic downturn and Apple's technologically advanced iPhone has taken sales away from Nokia.

BP, the giant oil company, has been fined US$373 million by the US Department of Justice for environment crimes and committing fraud. These huge fines include a penalty for the 2005 Texas refinery fire in which 15 people were killed. The accident also led to environmental damage and resulted from infringements of health and safety laws. BP has denied claims that it gave cost reductions at the refinery a higher priority than safety. The fraud committed by four of BP's employees was an attempt to fix high prices in the gas propane market illegally. This was against consumer protection laws.

Source: www.bbc.co.uk and www.news.yahoo.com (adapted)

Points to think about:

- What external factors have influenced Nokia's sales in recent years?
- In what ways did government laws have an impact on both of these companies?
- Do you think companies such as BP and Nokia might increase their profits if they meet all legal requirements in the countries they operate in?

05 External environment

Introduction

This chapter assesses the importance of external influences on business performance and decision-making. Businesses depend for their survival on understanding and responding to external factors that are beyond their control. Many of the factors are 'constraints' because they may limit the nature of decisions that business managers can take. The legal requirements imposed by governments, on environmental pollution for example, are one of the most obvious constraining influences on business activity. However, external influences can also create opportunities and enable a business to become even more successful – introducing new technology in advance of rival firms is one example.

PEST analysis

KEY TERM

PEST analysis – an acronym standing for political, economic, social, technological that refers to an analytical framework for external environmental factors affecting business objectives and strategies. PEST is sometimes rearranged as STEP and has also been extended to STEEPLE (social, technological, economic, environmental, political, legal and ethical) and PESTLE (same categories as STEEPLE but without ethical considerations)

Managers undertake PEST analysis to assess the importance of the major external influences on their organisation's future activities. This form of analysis will be referred to in later chapters of this book when major strategic decisions are being considered, such as entering new markets or developing new products.

PEST analysis may be conducted regularly to allow a business to review its objectives and strategies in the light of external changes. Some businesses may only do this form of analysis as a one-off when a major decision needs to be taken. This is likely to be less effective than regular PEST reviews which monitor changes to the external environment. It is the responsibility of managers to decide which of the key PEST factors are relevant to their business. The analysis itself can be undertaken by managers alone or with the participation of other staff. Much will depend on the leadership style and the corporate culture of the business.

USING PEST ANALYSIS

Table 5.1 shows a simplified PEST analysis for McDonald's restaurants which the company would carry out when planning to enter a national market for the first time. Other business scenarios may lead to different factors being considered important.

Political (and legal) issues	Economic issues
• Political stability of the country – is civil unrest likely? • Employee and consumer protection laws – how restrictive are these, e.g. health and safety laws? • Trade restrictions or membership of free trade bloc – can food be imported without tariffs? • Environmental regulations – what forms of packaging of fast food are allowed? • Health concerns about fast food – could the government pass new laws about the contents of fast-food products?	• Economic growth – is this slowing or even negative (recession)? • Unemployment – is this rising and reducing consumer incomes? • Interest rates – are these high or low? • Exchange rate – is this likely to appreciate or depreciate? • Is the government's fiscal policy likely to lead to increases or reductions in consumer incomes?
Social issues	**Technological issues**
• Dietary trends are changing and may be different between different countries (cultural and religious factors). • More married couples both work – less time to prepare meals. • Growing health consciousness – demand for healthy foods might be increasing. • Is the population ageing? Do the elderly buy more or fewer fast-food meals than the young? • Is the population growing?	• Can the food production process be automated? Is technical support available? • Online selling – is full internet coverage available? Will customers order online? • Environment – is environmentally friendly packaging technically possible and available in this country?

Table 5.1 *Example of possible PEST analysis for McDonald's*

ACTIVITY 5.1

10 marks, 18 minutes (plus research time)

Prepare a PEST analysis for a foreign fashion retailer planning to set up a chain of shops for the first time in your country. [10]

External opportunities and threats

POLITICAL AND LEGAL CONSTRAINTS

In most countries, political and legal constraints on a business fall into the following main categories:

- employment laws
- consumer protection laws
- business competition laws
- political changes resulting from a new government, e.g. policies towards foreign direct investment by multinationals
- major policy changes such as nationalising some UK banks after the 2008–9 crisis.

Table 5.2 shows the possible impact of some political and legal factors on business objectives and strategies.

ACTIVITY 5.2

Read the case study below and then answer the questions that follow.

Employment rights in your country

In China, current employment rights are governed by the PRC Employment Law of 1995. There are 13 sections to this law which cover almost all aspects of employment relationships. These include working hours, holidays, health and safety, training, social welfare, disputes and discrimination on the grounds of race, sex, disability or age.

24 marks, 45 minutes (plus research time)

1 Why do you think the Chinese government introduced such a wide-ranging law as this, covering all aspects of employer–employee relationships? [4]

2 Do these laws help or damage business interests? Explain your answer. [10]

3 **Research task:** Find out about the main employment laws in your country and the main rights they offer to workers. Do you think that these laws need changing in any way? If so, how and why? [10]

Examples of political/legal factors	Impact on business objectives and strategies
Improved employee legal protection, e.g. better health and safety at work, redundancy pay, protection from discrimination, minimum pay levels, maternity pay	• Increases cost of employing staff – may be reluctant to expand in this country by taking on extra staff. • Encourages business to increase labour productivity to pay for the cost of these legal improvements. For example, Germany has some of the most rigorous laws protecting workers rights, but labour productivity is one of the highest in the world. • If employers are seen to be positive about these legal changes and accept them fully, they will appear to be a caring business that will encourage well-motivated staff to work for them. Some businesses offer benefits above the legal minimum for this reason (see 'Setting the scene' case study on page 45).
Consumer protection laws that constrain businesses from advertising inaccurately or inappropriately, selling faulty goods or those described incorrectly, high-pressure selling tactics, not allowing consumers to change their minds after signing credit agreements	• Sales staff will need training in the legal rights of consumers – breaking consumer laws will lead to expensive legal claims. • Design and production of new products will have to put customers' safety and product quality as priorities. • Full disclosure of any safety problems to minimise risks to customers. • All of these strategies will add to costs. However, if a business is seen to put customers and customer service first, it may benefit from good publicity, word-of-mouth promotion and customer loyalty.
Competition laws can restrict unfair competition or restrictive practices by businesses, monopoly exploitation of consumers, mergers and takeovers (external growth) that could lead to a monopoly	• No collusive agreements with competitors. • Internal growth is less likely to lead to reports and action by the competition regulators. • Expand into other countries rather than growing in existing country which can lead to monopoly market share.

Table 5.2 *Political and legal factors and their impact on business*

ACTIVITY 5.3

Read the case study below and then answer the questions that follow.

Consumer rights in your country

In Malaysia, the 1999 Consumer Protection Act is an important law protecting the interests of consumers. It has 14 main sections which include outlawing all misleading and deceptive conduct by firms, false advertising claims, guarantees in respect of supply of goods and strict liability for defective and potentially dangerous products.

In India, the 1986 Consumer Protection Act provides for the regulation of all trade and competitive practices, creates national- and state-level consumer protection councils and lists unfair and uncompetitive trade practices.

24 marks, 45 minutes (plus research time)

1 Why do you think governments, as in Malaysia and India, pass laws to protect consumer rights? [4]

2 Do you think that such laws help or damage business interests? [10]

3 **Research task:** Find out the main consumer protection laws in your country (Malaysia and India have others). Give examples of how firms try to break these laws. Are the laws strict enough? If not, why not? [10]

ACTIVITY 5.4

Read the case study below and then answer the questions that follow.

Ryanair – adverts are 'misleading'

Ryanair is one of Europe's most successful low-cost airlines. It risks prosecution and a substantial fine for repeatedly misleading customers about the availability of its cheapest fares. Some customers claim that they are not told when the fares include taxes and charges and when they do not. Also, the cheapest fares have many restrictions placed on them and these are not clear, it is suggested, when a booking is being made. The airline has broken the Advertising Code seven times in recent years. It has failed to heed warnings by the Advertising Standards Authority (ASA). The company is being referred to the Office of Fair Trading, which has the power to prosecute advertisers who make misleading claims about products or prices. Ryanair could face substantial fines. In January 2010, Ryanair refused to withdraw an advert of a woman dressed as a young schoogirl, despite the ASA's ruling that it breached advertising rules on social responsibility and ethics. Ryanair accused the ASA of censorship, saying it was run by 'unelected, self-appointed dimwits'.

Source: www.timesonline.co.uk (adapted)

18 marks, 28 minutes

1 In what ways might Ryanair gain from 'misleading' customers in the ways described? [6]

2 Do you think that advertisers should be controlled over the claims they make and the way they promote their products? Explain your answer. [6]

3 If you were the chief executive officer of Ryanair, how would you respond to this bad publicity and the threat of legal action? Justify your answer. [6]

EXAM TIP

You will not be asked to give details on laws in any specific country, but you may be asked how a business is affected by laws in general.

ECONOMIC INFLUENCES

Changes in the economic environment can have a very significant impact on business objectives and strategies. The global downturn of 2009–10 forced many international businesses to revise their growth and profit targets and adapt their product and marketing strategies to a world in which credit was in short supply and consumers became much less willing to spend, especially on luxury goods. Other economic factors present businesses with opportunities rather than constraints such as the opening up of China's consumer market following its membership of the World Trade Organization in 2001.

Other changes in the economic environment result from changes in government economic policies. These policies – mainly fiscal and monetary – aim to help governments achieve four main macro-economic objectives:

- economic growth and rising living standards
- low levels of inflation
- low levels of unemployment
- balance of payments equilibrium, over time, between the value of imports and exports.

The important economic factors that businesses should monitor and respond to are explained in Table 5.3.

KEY TERMS

fiscal policy changes in government spending levels and tax rates

monetary policy changes in the level of interest rates which make loan capital more or less expensive

economic growth increases in the level of a country's Gross Domestic Product (total value of output)

inflation the rate of change in the average level of prices

unemployment the numbers of people in an economy willing and able to work who cannot find employment

SOCIAL AND CULTURAL INFLUENCES

The structure of society is constantly evolving. The changes occurring in many countries include:

- an ageing population with reduced birth rates and longer life expectancy, although in some nations the average age is falling due to high birth rates
- changing role of women – increasingly seeking employment and posts of responsibility in industry
- improved education facilities – resulting in increasing literacy and more skilled and adaptable workforces
- early retirement in many high-income countries – leading to more leisure time for a growing number of relatively wealthy pensioners
- in some countries, rising divorce rates – creating increasing numbers of single-person households
- job insecurity, often created by the forces of globalisation – forcing more employees to accept temporary and part-time employment (some workers prefer this option)
- increased levels of immigration – resulting in changing and widening consumer tastes.

This list is by no means complete. You could add to it from your knowledge of the changes occurring in your own society. How do these changes impact on business objectives and strategy? We will look at two of these changes – an ageing population and patterns of employment – but the analysis used can be adapted when considering the impact of the many other social changes.

An ageing population

The main effects associated with an ageing population are:

- a larger proportion of the population over the age of retirement
- a smaller proportion of the population in lower age ranges, e.g. 0–16 years old
- a smaller number of workers in the economy but a larger number of dependants, that is below working age or retired – this puts a higher tax burden on the working population.

Business objectives and strategy will need to adapt to:

- changing patterns of demand. There will be more 'grey' consumers than teenagers and they buy different products. Therefore, a construction company might switch from building large apartments for families to smaller units with special facilities for the elderly. Market research will be important for a business that believes the demand for its portfolio of products could change as the population ages.
- a change in the age structure of the workforce. There may be reduced numbers of youthful employees available, and businesses may need to adapt their workforce planning to enable the employment of older workers, or to keep existing workers beyond retirement age. Although younger employees are said to be more adaptable and easier to train in new technologies, older workers may show more loyalty to a business and will have years of experience that could improve customer service.

Changing patterns of employment

The main features of changing patterns of employment include:

- an increase in the number of women in employment and in the range of occupations in which they are employed
- an increase in student employment on a part-time basis – some industries are substantially staffed by students and part-timers, e.g. McDonald's; most other fast-food shops and supermarkets are largely staffed in this way
- an increase in temporary, part-time and flexible employment contracts – these are introduced by employers to reduce the fixed costs of full-time and salaried posts and to allow for flexibility when faced with seasonal demand or uncertainties caused by increasing globalisation
- more women taking maternity leave and then returning to work.

Main economic influences and government economic policies	Impact on business objectives and strategies
Economic growth Recession	• During a period of economic growth, demand for most goods and services will increase as consumers have higher incomes – businesses may plan to expand. However, inferior goods may be rejected by consumers who now have higher incomes. • A recession will have the reverse impact – it can lead to business retrenchment, closures and redundancies. • Business flexibility will be important for survival and profitability in both cases, e.g. aiming to have a product portfolio with a wide range of products to appeal to market segments with different income levels.
Interest rates through the use of monetary policy	• An increase in interest rates will reduce consumer demand for many products bought on credit, e.g. houses and cars. Businesses may offer their own credit deals to customers. • Increased loan capital costs will reduce profits for a business with high debt. Selling assets or new shares to reduce debt may be considered. • Business expansion plans may be delayed or cancelled – the expected profit may be below the interest cost on the loans required. • The country's currency is likely to appreciate as more investment finance from abroad is attracted to the country – see effects below.
Exchange rates – increases (appreciation) and decreases (depreciation) in the value of a currency value against other currencies	• A depreciation of currency (e.g. when 1 euro: $1 changes to 1 euro: $0.80 is a depreciation of the euro) will make imported goods more expensive. It also offers the opportunity for domestic firms to charge less for exports, leading to a possible increase in demand, especially if demand for them is price elastic – i.e. responsive to price changes. • More expensive imports can raise business costs if it has to buy materials or components from other countries – they might try to buy more supplies from domestic suppliers. • Businesses might target foreign markets more and change their strategies towards exporting rather than selling in the domestic market. • Foreign businesses may decide to locate in the country with the depreciating currency – it will avoid the risk of its goods becoming too expensive to import into the country. • The opposite would occur in the event of a appreciation.
Tax changes through the use of fiscal policy	• Higher rates of income tax reduce consumers' disposable incomes – demand for luxury and income elastic products will fall so businesses selling such products may offer lower priced alternatives or be forced to enter other markets. • Higher rates of tax on profits (corporation tax) will reduce the profits after tax of companies. A decision to relocate to a country with lower rates of tax might be made. Poland has recently experienced an increase in foreign investment after reducing its corporation tax rate to 10%.
Unemployment	• Higher numbers of workers without employment will give businesses more choice in staff recruitment. As there are many workers applying for each vacancy, a decision may be taken to reduce wage rates, which will reduce business costs. • Average consumer incomes are likely to fall with extensive unemployment – the demand for budget ranges of cheaper goods, e.g. supermarket own brands, could increase and production of these will have to rise to meet demand.
Inflation (cost-push and demand-pull)	• Higher wage demands from workers to maintain real incomes during inflation and higher costs of materials and components will lead to cost-push inflation. If businesses cannot increase prices for fear of demand falling, profit margins will fall. Businesses might seek cheaper sources of supply or more efficient production methods to help in lowering costs per unit. • Demand-pull inflation will encourage firms to raise prices to increase profit margins. • Substantial increases in inflation will lead to action being taken by the government or country's central bank to increase interest rates – see the effects of these above.

Table 5.3 *Economic factors and their influence on business*

KEY TERMS

recession six months (two quarters) of falling GDP (negative growth)

exchange rate the value of one currency in terms of another currency

cost-push inflation caused by rising costs forcing businesses to increase prices

demand-pull inflation caused by excess demand in an economy, e.g. an economic boom, allowing businesses to raise prices

Many countries are increasingly multicultural and this also has an effect on the pattern of women at work. In the UK, three out of ten women of Pakistani origin and two out of ten women of Bangladeshi origin seek full-time employment. In the UK as a whole, 75% of women seek full-time employment.

Firms can make these changes work to their benefit, while accepting some of the cost implications. Part-time workers can offer a firm much greater flexibility by being available at peak times and this will help to keep down overheads. Yet part-time and temporary staff can be difficult to mould into a team and may not contribute as much as a result.

By employing more females and removing barriers to their progress and promotion, firms can benefit from a wider choice of staff and improved motivation among women workers. However, there will be the increased costs of maternity leave and of providing staff cover for this. As with all other external influences on business behaviour, the most successful firms will be those that adapt to changes the most quickly and attempt to turn them to their own competitive advantage.

Many businesses employ mainly part-time staff – this can be beneficial for both the employer and the workers

ACTIVITY 5.5

Consider Table 5.4 and then answer the questions that follow.

	2000		2010		2020 (estimated)	
	(000s)	**%**	**(000s)**	**%**	**(000s)**	**%**
Total labour force	7042.0		9572.0		12 939.6	
Age distribution		**100.0**		**100.0**		**100.0**
15–24	2014.0	28.6	2498.3	26.1	3112.2	24.1
25–34	2204.1	31.3	2,979.2	31.1	4118.9	31.8
35–54	2436.5	34.6	3,611.3	37.7	4995.5	38.6
55–64	387.4	5.5	483.7	5.1	713.1	5.5
Educational structure		**100.0**		**100.0**		**100.0**
Primary only	2380.2	33.8	2604.3	27.2	1643.3	12.7
Lower and middle secondary	4042.1	57.4	5624.5	58.8	6,767.4	52.3
Tertiary (university)	619.7	8.8	1343.7	14.0	4528.9	35.0
Labour force participation rate		**65.3**		**65.5**		**68.1**
Male		85.6		85.4		86.4
Female		44.1		44.5		49.0

Table 5.4 *Profile of a country's labour force, 2000–2020 (in 000s)*

22 marks, 42 minutes

1 Calculate the forecasted percentage increase in the labour force between 2000 and 2020. [2]

2 Identify **two** changes to the structure of the labour workforce forecast over this period. Explain how these changes might have an impact on the human resources strategy of a business. [10]

3 Evaluate whether a business should provide more than the basic legal minimum in terms of conditions of employment and health and safety at work. [10]

Impact of technology

In its simplest form, technology means the use of tools, machines and science in industry. This section assesses the impact on businesses of the relatively recent introduction of high-technology machines and processes that are based on information technology (IT).

KEY TERM

information technology the use of electronic technology to gather, store, process and communicate information

Technological change is affecting all businesses and all departments within business. Table 5.5 explains some of the most common business applications of IT, the departments likely to benefit most from them and the potential advantages to be gained.

KEY TERMS

computer-aided design using computers and IT when designing products

computer-aided manufacturing the use of computers and computer-controlled machinery to speed up the production process and make it more flexible

internet the worldwide web of communication links between computers

In addition to these uses of technology, advances in technical knowledge are opening up new product markets, such as hydrogen-powered cars and 'flexible' mobile phones. The use of technology to develop new products is part of the research and development function of businesses (see Chapter 35, page 365).

EXAM TIP

It is wrong to assume that a business must always use the latest technology in all circumstances. There are substantial costs to be paid and some businesses thrive on using old-fashioned methods. For example, hand-made designer furniture will sell because each piece is unique and computer-controlled robots might be completely impractical.

The use of computer-controlled robots has increased productivity in this Mini factory

IMPACT ON OBJECTIVES AND STRATEGIES

Costs

Capital costs can be substantial, labour training costs will be necessary and will recur regularly with further technological development. Redundancy costs will be incurred – existing staff may be replaced by the technology. However, the use of technology may achieve higher profits in the future.

Labour relations

These can be damaged if technological change is not explained and presented to workers in a positive way with the reasons for it fully justified. If many jobs are being lost during the process of change, then remaining workers may suffer from reduced job security, and this

Information technology application	Common business applications	Impact on business
Spreadsheet programs	• Financial and management accounting records can be updated and amended. • Cash-flow forecasts and budgets can be updated in the light of new information. • Changes in expected performance can be inputted to the spreadsheet and changes in total figures made automatically. • Income statements and balance sheets can be drawn up frequently.	• Flexibility and speed – changes to accounting records can be made quickly and the impact of these on total figures can be demonstrated instantly. • 'What if' scenarios in budgeting and sales forecasting can be demonstrated, e.g. what would happen to forecasted profits if sales rose by 10% following a 5% cut in price?
Computer-aided design (CAD)	• Nearly all design and architectural firms now use these programs for making and displaying designs, e.g. cars, house plans, furniture, garden designs. • Designs can be shown in 3-D and 'turned around' to show effect from all angles.	• Saves on expensive designer salaries as work can be done more quickly. • More flexibility of design as each customer's special requirements can be easily added. Can be linked to other programs to obtain product costings and to prepare for ordering of required supplies.
Computer-aided manufacturing (CAM)	• Programs are used to operate robotic equipment that replaces many labour-intensive production systems. • Used in operations management in manufacturing businesses.	• Labour costs are reduced as machines replace many workers. • Productivity is increased and variable costs per unit are lower than in non-computerised processes. • Accuracy is improved – less scope for human error. • Flexibility of production is increased – modern computer-controlled machinery can usually be adapted to make a number of different variations of a standard product, and this helps to meet consumers' needs for some individual features. • All of these benefits can add to a firm's competitive advantage.
Internet/intranet	• Marketing department – for promoting to a large market and taking orders online (see Chapter 29, page 311, for discussion of e-commerce). • Operations management – business-to-business (B2B) communication via the internet is used to search the market for the cheapest suppliers. • Human resources uses these systems for communicating within the organisation. • Intranets allow all staff to be internally connected via computers.	• Cost savings from cheap internal and external communications. • Access to a much larger potential market than could be gained through non-IT methods. • Web pages project a worldwide image of the business. • Online ordering cheaper than paper-based systems. • B2B communications can obtain supplies at lower costs. • Internal communication is quicker than traditional methods.

Table 5.5 *Impact of applications of technology on business*

could damage their motivation levels. Trade unions can oppose technological change if it puts members' jobs at risk. However, if the issue is handled sensitively, including effective communication with and participation of staff, introducing technology in the right way can improve industrial relations.

Management

Some managers fear change as much as their workforce, especially if they are not very computer literate themselves. In addition, recognising the need for change and managing the technological change process require a great deal of management skill. However, IT can improve productivity greatly and lead to improved company efficiency: for example, the use of database programs to control stock ordering to achieve just-in-time advantages. Technology has other benefits too:

- Managers can obtain data frequently from all departments and regional divisions of the business.
- Computers can be used to analyse and process the data rapidly so that managers can interpret them and take decisions quickly on the basis of them.
- It accelerates the process of communicating decisions to other managers and staff.

Information gives managers the opportunity to review and control the operations of the business. IT-based management information systems provide substantial power to centralised managers. Although this could be used for improving the performance of a business, there are potential drawbacks:

- The ease of transferring data electronically can lead to so many messages and communications that 'information overload' occurs. This is when the sheer volume of information prevents decision-makers from identifying the most important information and decisions.
- The power which information brings to central managers could be abused and could lead to a reduction in the authority and empowerment extended to work teams and middle managers. Information used for central control in an oppressive way could reduce job enrichment and hence motivation levels.

Effective managers will apply the information provided by the modern IT systems to improve and speed up decision-making. They should not allow it to change their style of leadership to a centralised or authoritarian one, using data to control all aspects of the organisation.

THEORY OF KNOWLEDGE

'The last two years have seen seismic shifts in the environment within which businesses have to trade. The growth of the internet, mobile communications, globalisation and social responsibility have confronted CEOs and shareholders with new challenges that have given rise to innovative, exciting corporations like Apple and Microsoft but have seen old giants like General Motors teeter on the edge of collapse. Organisations that don't react to changes in their environment will eventually fail.'

Prepare a presentation with the title 'Organisations that don't react to changes in their environment will eventually fail'.

ACTIVITY 5.6

Read the following case study and then answer the questions that follow.

More chips please?

The major European supermarkets have been putting IT at the front of their drive for lower costs, improved customer service and more information about their customers. Bar codes, check-out scanners, automatic product re-ordering systems, automated stock control programs, robot-controlled transport systems in warehouses, chip and pin machines for payment, loyalty cards that record each individual shopper's purchases and internet shopping for customers – the list of IT applications employed by the large supermarkets is almost endless.

Some of these systems have been controversial. For example, centralised ordering and delivery of products reduced the independence and control of individual store managers. The rapid growth of internet shopping left some companies with a shortage of stock and delivery vehicles, which led to poor service. Some smaller suppliers who have been unable to cope with the cost of introducing compatible IT systems to take orders from the huge retailers have been dropped.

The latest development is causing further controversy. RFID or radio frequency ID tagging involves putting a small chip and coiled antenna, at the initial point of production, into every item sold through the supermarkets. Unlike bar codes that are manually scanned, the RFID simply broadcasts its presence and data, such as sell-by date, to electronic receivers or readers. German supermarket chain Metro already uses RFID and claims that food can be easily traced back to the farm where it is produced, queues at tills no longer exist as customer's bills are calculated instantly as they pass by a receiver and all products are tracked at each stage of the supply chain – 'We know where everything is!'

Consumer groups are concerned that shoppers will be tracked and traceable too – not just the goods they have bought. Is this an invasion of privacy? Unions are opposed to it as it could lead to many redundancies due to its non-manual operation. Some supermarket managers fear yet another IT initiative that will mean even more central control over them and they fear breakdowns in the system and lack of training in dealing with problems.

24 marks, 45 minutes

1 What do you understand by the term 'information technology'? [2]

2 Outline how any **two** of the IT systems mentioned in the case study are likely to benefit customers. [6]

3 Analyse the likely benefits of supermarkets using RFID to trace and collect data from every product they sell. [6]

4 Discuss whether all supermarkets should have the adoption of RFID technology as a major strategy. [10]

5 **Research task**: Use the internet to research **one** of the following and write a report explaining the potential impact on objectives and strategy of any **one** well-known business in your country: CAD; CAM; RFID.

OVER TO YOU

REVISION CHECKLIST

1 Why is PEST important to a business planning a major change in strategy?
2 Give **one** example of how a business strategy might be affected by a consumer protection law.
3 Give **one** example of how a business strategy might be affected by an employment law.
4 Explain how an increase in interest rates might lead to a change of business strategy.
5 Explain how a depreciation of your country's currency might lead to a business in your country changing one of its strategies.
6 Do you think an economic recession in your country would lead to the soft drinks manufacturer Coca-Cola changing the strategies used to sell its products in your country?
7 Identify **two** recent social changes in your country that could have an impact on a business's objectives and strategy.
8 Give **one** example of how technology has changed production methods in an industry that you have studied.
9 Give **one** example of how technology has led to a recently introduced innovative product.

REVISION ACTIVITY

Read the case study below and then answer the questions that follow.

China to take action against inflation

The Chinese government is becoming increasingly concerned about higher rates of inflation. Rising oil and petrol prices have increased costs to industry and firms are being forced to raise their prices to cover these higher costs. In addition, rising demand for food from a wealthier population, together with supply problems resulting in excess demand, have led to the price of pork rising by 63% and fresh vegetable prices by 46%.

The People's Bank of China has just increased interest rates by a further 0.27%. This is the third increase in less than a year. A spokesman from Goldman Sachs, the investment bank, reported that the increase shows that the central bank is now much more prepared to use interest rates to manage the economy and tighten monetary policy at the first signs of the booming economy overheating. China's GDP increased by 10.7% in 2007, and the prime minister has said that this rate of growth is becoming 'unsustainable'. Chinese leaders face conflicting pressures in balancing the top priority of maintaining high-speed economic growth to create millions of new jobs each year, with managing growing environmental problems and rising cost-push pressures causing higher inflation.

33 marks, 58 minutes

1 State **two** reasons for the increase in inflation in China. [2]

2 Are these causes of inflation cost-push or demand-pull pressures? Explain your answer. [4]

3 If the Chinese government increased interest rates again, explain what impact this could have on:
   a consumer spending on luxury goods
   b spending on new expansion projects by Chinese businesses
   c the exchange rate of China's currency. [9]

4 Examine possible changes to the long-term objectives set by Chinese businesses if inflation is not brought under control. [8]

5 China has experienced rapid economic growth in recent years. Discuss the likely effects of this on the strategies adopted by Chinese car manufacturers. [10]

EXAM PRACTICE QUESTION

Read the case study below and then answer the questions that follow.

CARREFOUR EXPANDS IN CHINA

Carrefour, the French supermarket chain, is one of Europe's biggest public limited companies. In world terms, it is right up there with Walmart and Tesco as a major multinational retailer. The general manager of Central and Western China has announced that the supermarket will open two more stores in Chengdu this year and more in 2011.

A company statement said: 'Chengdu's sound administrative environment and huge market potential attract a large number of foreign-funded enterprises to settle in and Carrefour regards entering Chengdu as an important strategic development in China.'

Carrefour has developed close relations with over 400 suppliers locally and has spent a great deal of time researching the local market. It has also worked closely with local government agencies to ensure its entry into the region goes smoothly. Carrefour's directors believe that growing popularity and acceptance of western brand names are a genuine sales opportunity in China. Technological advances in their stores have given them the ability to monitor and manage their stores globally.

Rapid economic growth in China is bringing huge potential revenue to North American and European businesses and many are looking to China as a country in which to expand.

25 marks, 45 minutes

1 Explain the following terms from the text:
   a public limited company
   b multinational retailer
   c technological advances. **[6]**

2 Explain how rapid economic growth in China might impact on one aspect of Carrefour's business strategy. **[5]**

3 Analyse the social changes that may be taking place in China which could influence Carrefour's activities in China. **[6]**

4 Produce a PEST analysis for Carrefour as it plans to open new stores in western China. **[8]**

06 Organisational planning tools

This chapter covers syllabus section 1.6

On completing this chapter you should be able to:

- analyse the importance of business plans to stakeholders
- apply a formal decision-making framework to a business situation
- prepare a SWOT analysis for a business situation
- analyse an organisation's position using a SWOT analysis
- (H) analyse and interpret business plans
- (H) apply decision-making processes and planning tools
- (H) compare and contrast scientific and intuitive decision-making processes
- (H) construct and interpret decision trees and evaluate this technique.

SETTING THE SCENE

SanaSana business plan gives business healthy start

Setting up a new business with no clear plan is like sailing across an ocean with no charts or compass. The business plan of SanaSana is an excellent example of how new business entrepreneurs can increase their chances of success, and gain acceptance from stakeholders, with a clear explanation of:

- who the business owners are, their strengths and experiences
- the central purpose of the business and the intended market
- benefits to consumers of using the business
- the market research undertaken
- financial forecasts and the borrowings required
- the main risks likely to be faced by the business.

SanaSana was set up by five friends, 'who share one another's dreams and passions', to provide a health care information service for Hispanic (Spanish) speakers in the USA. Three of the partners are Hispanic and the other two are qualified doctors. Collectively, they have 50 years' experience in management, e-commerce, finance and medicine. The financial projections forecast a net profit of over $18 million by the fifth year of operation.

Source: MOOT CORP® Competition sample business plan

Points to think about:

- Why would you advise new entrepreneurs to write a detailed business plan?
- Which stakeholders would find such a plan useful, and why?
- Do you think SanaSana stands a good chance of being successful? Explain your reasons, referring to the details of the business plan given above.

Introduction

Planning for the future and taking effective decisions are two very important management functions that are linked. Planning means establishing the future direction the business should take and setting overall objectives and targets. Strategic decision-making focuses on making choices between different strategies so that the objectives of the business are more likely to be achieved.

Business plans

KEY TERM

business plan a written document that describes a business, its objectives and its strategies, the market it is in and its financial forecasts

The contents of a typical business plan are:

- the executive summary – an overview of the new business and its strategies
- description of the business opportunity – details of the entrepreneur; what is going to be sold, why and to whom
- marketing and sales strategy – details of why the entrepreneur thinks customers will buy what the business plans to sell and how the business plans to sell to them
- management team and personnel – the skills and experience of the entrepreneur and the staff he/she intends to recruit
- operations – premises to be used, production facilities, IT systems
- financial forecasts – the future projections of sales, profit and cash flow – for at least one year ahead.

IMPORTANCE OF BUSINESS PLANS

- Business plans are most important when setting up a new business, but they should be referred to and updated when important strategic choices are being made too. The main purpose of a business plan for a new business is to obtain finance for the start-up. Potential investors or creditors will not provide finance unless clear details about the business proposal have been written down clearly.
- The planning process is very important too. If an entrepreneur went into a new business – even if no external finance was required – without a clear sense of purpose, direction, marketing strategies and what employees to recruit, the chances of success would be much reduced.
- The financial and other forecasts contained in the plan can be used as the targets that the business should aim for. The benefits of SMART objectives were explained in Chapter 3, page 23.

STAKEHOLDERS AS USERS OF BUSINESS PLANS

Business plans may be of real benefit to the stakeholders of both new and existing businesses. All organisations must plan for the future – this is often referred to as 'corporate planning'.

- Corporate planning for existing organisations can involve adapting the original business plan to accommodate new or revised strategies, such as expansion projects. If a major expansion is being considered, bankers and other creditors will almost certainly ask to see a business's corporate plan before agreeing to finance the expansion. This will help these stakeholders to assess the risk and rewards from investing in the expansion.
- The financial forecasts in a business plan can act as budgets and control benchmarks for the internal stakeholders such as business managers.
- Updated versions of the plan can be used to apply for additional funding, to attract additional partners or to supply data for the experts if a stock market flotation becomes an option. Potential shareholders will not invest without seeing a plan first.
- Employees will find that planning helps identify specific objectives and targets and gives focus to their work, which aids motivation.
- Suppliers may be able to tell from the parts of the business plan that are communicated externally whether it is worthwhile establishing a long-term trading relationship with the business.

Decision-making framework

Effective decision-making is one of the key roles of management at all levels of seniority within an organisation. Making choices between different options is potentially risky as the future success of a course of action can never be assessed with great accuracy. Managers have a range of techniques and tools available to reduce the element of risk and increase the chances of them taking effective decisions.

DIFFERENT APPROACHES TO DECISION-MAKING

There are two distinct ways in which managers can take decisions: through the use of intuition or by the scientific analysis of data.

KEY TERMS

intuitive decision-making involves making decisions based on instinct or 'gut feeling' (perhaps based on the manager's experience) for a situation and the options available

scientific decision-making involves basing decisions on a formal framework and a data analysis of both the problem and the options available

In reality, the two extremes often become blurred and most decisions will be taken by managers after some consideration using both their instinct and analysis of the data available (see also 'Decision-making approaches and techniques', page 60.)

THE FRAMEWORK

Figure 6.1 shows a formal decision-making framework that could be used by managers who adopt a scientific approach to decision taking.

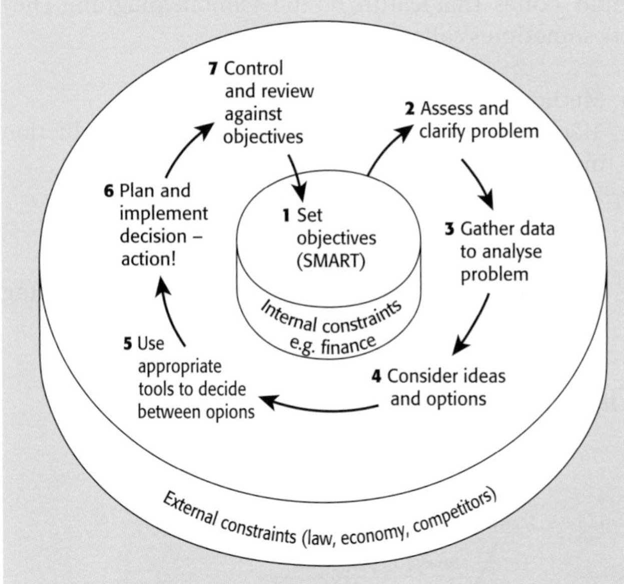

Figure 6.1 The decision-making framework

Stages in the decision-making framework include:

1 **Set objectives.** These will define what the organisation is trying to achieve and will be used to assess the final success of the decision.
2 **Assess the problem or situation.** Why does a decision have to be taken? Are sales or profits declining? Is there an opportunity to take over a rival business? The problem or situation that requires a decision to be made must be analysed carefully using, for example, the fishbone diagram (see Figure 6.2, page 60).
3 **Gather data to analyse both the extent of the 'problem' and the information needed to assess the options available.** This data could be primary and secondary market research data or cost data.
4 **Consider all the options available** – perhaps by brainstorming or using past experience of similar situations. However, original or innovative ideas might be more successful than using options that have been decided on previously.
5 **Decide between the alternative ideas or options using decision-making tools** such as decision trees (see page 61) and investment appraisal methods (see page 185).
6 **Plan and implement the decision.** Making the decision is just one step; putting it into effect is just as important. Resources must be prepared, staff trained, budgets set and managers given authority to carry out the decision successfully.
7 **Control and review.** Progress of the strategy must be monitored against targets and budgets and at the end of the time period set for the decision to take effect, the achievements of the option chosen should be checked against the original objectives set for it.

INTERNAL AND EXTERNAL CONSTRAINTS

Other issues to be taken into account include internal and external constraints.

KEY TERMS

internal constraints limiting factors in decision-making that can be controlled by the organisation

external constraints limiting factors in decision-making that are beyond the organisation's control

Internal constraints include:

- organisational structure – this might limit the authority given to managers to put decisions into effect
- financial constraints – these might prevent 'expensive' decisions from being taken
- labour and other resource constraints – more of these may need to be acquired
- attitude of the workforce to change – will they be likely to accept or resist change?

External constraints would be identified through PEST analysis and include:

- changes in the business cycle that may make raising finance difficult or expensive, e.g. higher interest rates during an economic boom
- changes in legal constraints that could influence demand for new products manufactured as a result of a strategic business decision, e.g. controls on the use of polluting cars in cities.

Decision-making in most organisations is a continuous process, not a series of discrete steps. This means that experience gained from taking a recent decision will assist in the next decision-making cycle and could mean that intuition becomes more important than the scientific data-based decision-making framework.

HIGHER LEVEL

Decision-making approaches and techniques

Table 6.1 compares the benefits of scientific and intuitive decision-making.

Intuitive decision-making	Scientific decision-making
• Less time consuming than a scientific approach – could be an advantage in a fast-changing market situation where a rapid decision is needed. • Less costly than a scientific approach – no expense of collecting and analysing data, use of expert consultants, etc. This might be a particular advantage to a small business with limited resources. • Innovative or non-standard situations, e.g. technology advances, may not have relevant data available on which to base a 'scientific' solution.	• Based on a formal structure – less likely that important points will be missed in gathering data and assessing options. • Based on analysis of data, e.g. market research, costings, future returns. The final decision is likely to have a greater chance of success than one based purely on intuition. • When risks are high or cost is substantial it might be considered irresponsible for a senior manager to base decisions on 'gut feelings'.

◂ ***Table 6.1*** *Benefits of intuitive and scientific decision-making*

THE FISHBONE DIAGRAM

KEY TERM

fishbone diagram a visual identification of many potential causes of a problem

The fishbone diagram – also known as a cause-and-effect diagram or an Ishikawa diagram – may be used to analyse a problem or situation. An example is given in Figure 6.2, and is based on a brainstorming session where a team is attempting to establish all of the possible causes of iron contaminating a food product.

In this example, six main causes of the problem of iron in the product were identified. These are the most common main 'bones' that feature on the fishbone diagram. They are sometimes called the 6Ms:

- Methods – are the bottles used clean?
- Machines – are there rusty pipes in the production machines?
- Manpower – is it skilled enough?
- Materials – are the raw materials to blame?
- Measurement – is the calibration incorrect?
- 'Mother nature' (the environment) – is the working environment contaminated?

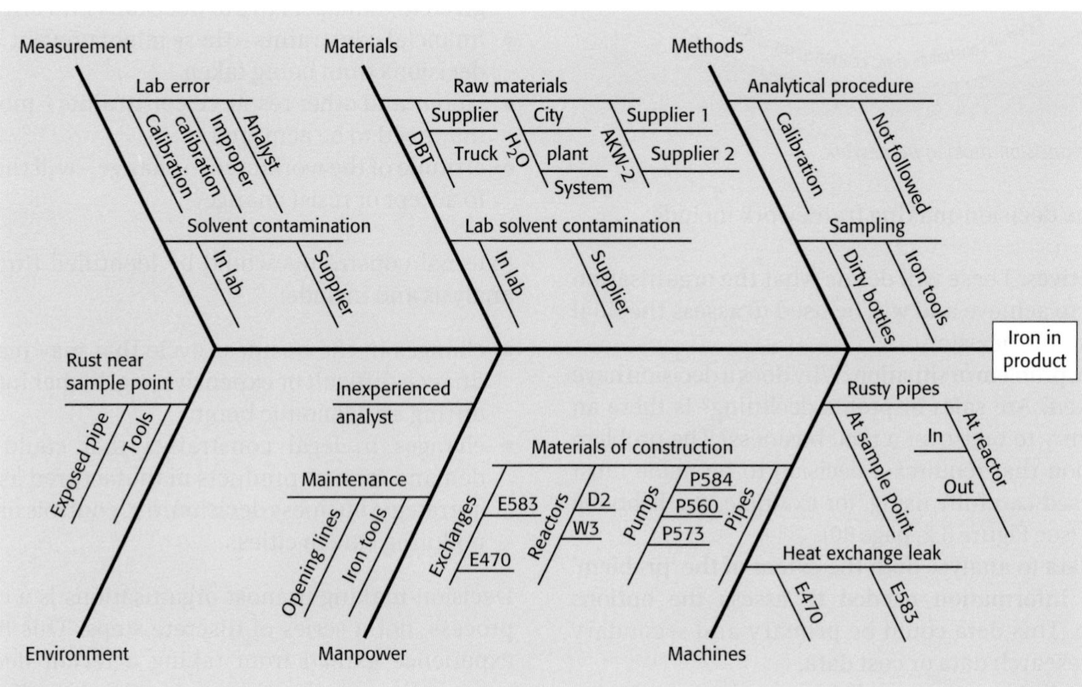

Figure 6.2 *Example of a fishbone diagram*
Source: Nancy R. Tague (2004) The Quality Toolbox *(ASR Quality Press, 2nd edition)*

More detailed discussion of each of these causes led to the factors laid out in the form of the 'smaller bones' of the fish.

Stages in the fishbone process include:

1 Agree on the problem statement and write this in the centre of the whiteboard or screen.
2 Brainstorm the main categories of the causes of the problem, or use the common generic ones (the 6Ms). These become the six main bones of the fish.
3 Brainstorm all of the detailed reasons why problems might occur under each of these headings – the small fish bones.
4 Analyse the findings of the group as shown on the diagram. Investigate the most likely causes of the problem – more research might now be necessary.

Once this process has been completed the business can put strategies in place to remove the most likely causes of the problem, perhaps by adopting different quality assurance systems.

DECISION TREES

This is a technique that considers the value of the options available and the chances of them occurring.

KEY TERM

decision tree a diagram that sets out the options connected with a decision and the outcomes and economic returns that may result

This technique is based on a diagram that is drawn to represent four main features of a business decision:

- all of the options open to a manager
- the different possible outcomes resulting from these options
- the chances of these outcomes occurring
- the economic returns from these outcomes.

By comparing the likely financial results from each option, the manager can minimise the risks involved and maximise the potential returns.

Constructing decision trees

The tree is a diagram, which has the following features:

- It is constructed from left to right.
- Each branch of the tree represents an option together with a range of consequences or outcomes and the chances of these occurring.
- Decision points are denoted by a square – these are decision nodes.
- A circle shows that a range of outcomes may result from a decision – a chance node.
- Probabilities are shown alongside each of these possible outcomes. These probabilities are the numerical values of an event occurring – they measure the 'chance' of an outcome occurring.
- The economic returns are the expected financial gains or losses of a particular outcome – the 'pay-offs'.

Working out 'expected values'

KEY TERM

expected value the likely financial result of an outcome obtained by multiplying the probability of an event occurring by the forecast economic return if it does occur

Therefore, the expected value of tossing a coin and winning \$5 if it comes down heads is 0.5 × \$5 = \$2.50. In effect, the average return, if you repeated this a number of times, would be to win \$2.50 – this is the expected value. The purpose of a decision tree is to show that option which gives the most beneficial expected value.

For example, the manager of an events-organising business has to decide between holding a fund-raising auction indoors or outdoors. The financial success of the event depends not only on the weather, but also on the decision to hold it indoors or outdoors.

Table 6.2 shows the expected net financial returns or 'economic returns' from the event for each of these different circumstances. From past weather records for August, there is a 60% chance of fine weather and a 40% chance of it being poor. The indoor event will cost \$2000 to arrange and the outdoor event will cost \$3000.

Weather	Indoors	Outdoors
Fine	\$5 000	\$10 000
Poor	\$7 000	\$4 000

Table 6.2 *The possible economic returns from the alternative options*

The decision tree of the event is shown in Figure 6.3. This diagram demonstrates the main advantages of decision trees:

- They force the decision-maker to consider all of the options and variables related to a decision.
- They put these on an easy-to-follow diagram, which allows for numerical considerations of risk and economic returns to be included.
- The approach encourages logical thinking and discussion among managers.

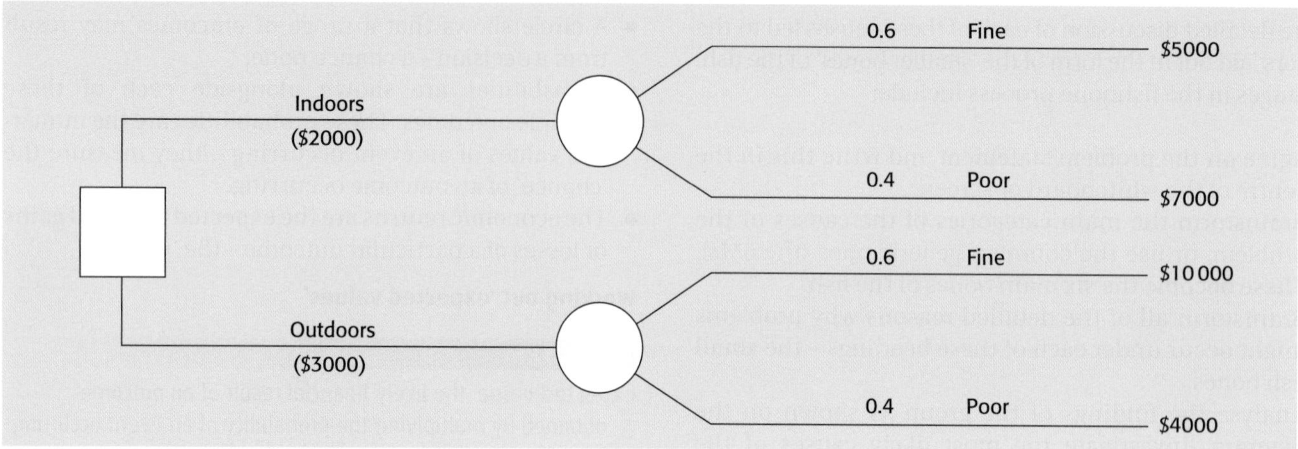

Figure 6.3 Decision tree for the fund-raising auction

Using the tree diagram in Figure 6.3, which option would give the highest expected value – holding the event indoors or outdoors? The answer is gained by calculating the expected value at each of the chance nodes. This is done by multiplying the probability by the economic return of both outcomes and adding the results. The cost of each option is then subtracted from this expected value to find the net return.

This is done by working through the tree from right to left, as follows (see Figure 6.4):

- The expected value at node 1 is $5800.
- The expected value at node 2 is $7600.
- Subtract the cost of holding the event either indoors or outdoors.
- Indoors = $5800 – $2000 = $3800
- Outdoors = $7600 – $3000 = $4600

Therefore, the events manager would be advised to hold the event outdoors as, on average, this will give the highest expected value. The other option is 'blocked off' with a double line in the figure to indicate that this decision will not be taken.

Decision trees – an evaluation

The primary limitation concerns the accuracy of the data used. Estimated economic returns may be quite accurate when they concern projects where experience has been gained from similar decisions. In other cases, they may be based on forecasts of market demand or 'guestimates' of the most likely financial outcome. In these cases, the scope for inaccuracy of the data makes the results of decision-tree analysis a useful guide, but no more. In addition, the probabilities of events occurring may be based on past data, but circumstances may change. What

ACTIVITY 6.1

Read the case study below and then answer the questions that follow.

Expansion decision

The owner of a service station is planning to expand the business. The two options are to build a forecourt to sell petrol or to construct a showroom to sell cars. The estimated building costs are: petrol forecourt – $100 000; car showroom – $150 000. The forecast economic consequences or pay-offs during the expected lives of these investments will depend on the level of demand in the economy, as shown in the table below. The probability of demand being low during the life span of these investments is 0.2 and the probability of high demand is 0.8.

Demand	Petrol forecourt	Car showroom
High	$500 000	$800 000
Low	$400 000	$200 000

The economic returns from the two options

15 marks, 28 minutes

1 Show these options on a decision tree, adding the pay-offs and probabilities. [6]

2 Calculate the expected value of **both** investments and recommend which option should be taken. [6]

3 State **three** other factors that you consider might influence the business owner's final decision. [3]

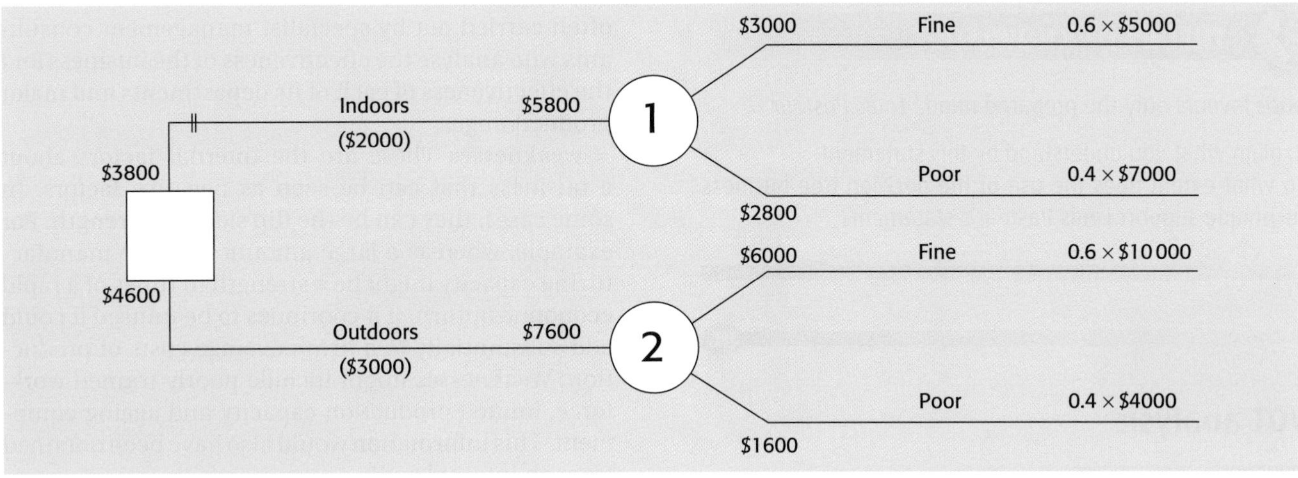

Figure 6.4 Calculating expected values – working from right to left

was a successful launch of a new store last year may not be repeated in another location if the competition has opened a shop there first.

The conclusion is that decision trees aid the decision-making process, but they cannot replace either the consideration of risk or the impact of qualitative factors on a decision. The latter could include the impact on the environment, the attitude of the workforce and the approach to risk taken by the managers and owners of the business. There may well be a preference for fairly certain but low returns, rather than taking risks to earn much greater rewards.

Finally, remember that the expected values are average returns, assuming that the outcomes occur more than once. With any single, one-off decision, the average will not, in fact, be the final result. Decision trees allow a quantitative consideration of future risks to be made – they do not eliminate those risks.

ACTIVITY 6.2

Read the case study below and then answer the questions that follow.

Which market?

Joe Keenan had an important decision to take. He operated a mobile market stall selling cooking pans and kitchen equipment. He has to decide which market to visit next Saturday. There are four options but, of course, he can only go to one town. He has estimated the revenues he could earn from each location by using past records and by consulting with other stall-holders. His estimates in dollars ($), together with the chances of earning them, are given below:

22 marks, 35 minutes

1 Using the data above draw a decision tree of the options Joe has and add the probabilities and forecasted economic returns. [6]

2 Calculate the expected values of the **four** options that Joe has. Which town market should Joe visit on Saturday on the basis of quantitative data alone? [10]

3 Explain **three** factors that could influence the accuracy of Joe's forecasts. [6]

Town A		Town B		Town C		Town D	
Probability	**Revenue ($)**	**Probability**	**Revenue ($)**	**Probability**	**Revenue ($)**	**Probability**	**Revenue ($)**
0.4	5 000	0.3	3 000	0.4	3 000	0.3	5 000
0.6	8 000	0.5	4 000	0.5	6 000	0.3	6 000
		0.2	8 000	0.1	10 000	0.4	9 000

THEORY OF KNOWLEDGE

'Chance favours only the prepared mind.' *Louis Pasteur*

1 Explain what you understand by this statement.
2 To what extent does the use of the decision tree business technique support Louis Pasteur's statement?

SWOT analysis

KEY TERM

SWOT analysis a form of strategic analysis that identifies and analyses the main internal strengths and weaknesses and external opportunities and threats that will influence the future direction and success of a business

A SWOT analysis provides information that can be helpful in matching the firm's resources and strengths to the competitive environment in which it operates. It is, therefore, useful in strategy formulation and selection. It comprises:

S = **strengths** These are the internal factors about a business that can be looked upon as real advantages. They could be used as a basis for developing a competitive advantage. They might include experienced management, product patents, loyal workforce and good product range. These factors are identified by undertaking an internal audit of the firm. This is often carried out by specialist management consultants who analyse the effectiveness of the business and the effectiveness of each of its departments and major product ranges.

W = **weaknesses** These are the internal factors about a business that can be seen as negative factors. In some cases, they can be the flip side of a strength. For example, whereas a large amount of spare manufacturing capacity might be a strength in times of a rapid economic upturn, if it continues to be unused it could add substantially to a firm's average costs of production. Weaknesses might include poorly trained workforce, limited production capacity and ageing equipment. This information would also have been obtained from an internal audit.

O = **opportunities** These are the potential areas for expansion of the business and future profits. These factors are obtained by an external audit of the market the firm operates in and its major competitors. Examples include new technologies, export markets expanding faster than domestic markets and lower rates of interest increasing consumer demand.

T = **threats** These are also external factors, gained from an external audit. This audit analyses the business and economic environment, market conditions and the strength of competitors. Examples of threats are new competitors entering the market, globalisation driving down prices, changes in the law regarding the sale of the firm's product and changes in government economic policy.

This information is usually presented in the form of a four-box grid as shown in Table 6.3.

	Strengths	**Weaknesses**
Internal	• Specialist marketing expertise. • A new, innovative product. • Location of the business. • Quality processes and processes. • Any other aspect of the business that adds value to the product or service.	• Lack of marketing expertise. • Undifferentiated products or services (i.e. in relation to competitors). • Location of the business. • Poor-quality goods or services. • Damaged reputation.
	Opportunities	**Threats**
External	• A developing market such as the internet. • Mergers, joint ventures or strategic alliances. • Moving into new market segments that offer improved profits. • A new international market. • A market vacated by an ineffective competitor.	• A new competitor in the home market. • Price wars with competitors. • A competitor has a new, innovative product or service. • Competitors have superior access to channels of distribution. • Taxation is increased on the product or service.

Table 6.3 *SWOT analysis – possible factors to consider*

SWOT AND STRATEGIC OBJECTIVES

The SWOT diagram focuses on the key issues under each heading. A brief outline of each of these could then accompany the diagram to make it more useful to the managers responsible for strategic planning. This approach helps managers assess the most likely successful future strategies and the constraints on them. A business should not necessarily pursue the most profitable opportunities. It may stand a better chance of developing a competitive advantage by identifying a good 'fit' between the firm's strengths and potential opportunities. In many cases, a business may need to overcome a perceived weakness in order to take advantage of a potential opportunity. SWOT is a common starting point for developing new corporate strategies, but it is rarely sufficient. Further analysis and planning are usually needed before strategic choices can be made.

SWOT EVALUATION

Subjectivity is often a limitation of a SWOT analysis as no two managers would necessarily arrive at the same assessment of the company they work for. It is not a quantitative form of assessment so the 'cost' of correcting a weakness cannot be compared with the potential 'profit' from pursuing an opportunity. SWOT should be used as a management guide for future strategies, not a prescription. Part of the value of the process of SWOT analysis is the clarification and mutual understanding that senior managers gain by the focus that SWOT analysis provides.

ACTIVITY 6.3

Read the case study below and then answer the questions that follow.

Strategic Analysis of LVM Ltd

LVM owns an assembly plant for laptop computers. It supplies products to some of the major brand names in the computer industry, but it does not sell any under its own name. Every six months the managers hold a key strategic review meeting to consider the current position of the business and the long-term plans. The following are extracts from the most recent of these meetings:

Imran Khan – marketing director: 'Sales of our latest large screen models have exceeded expectations and the switch towards laptops from desktop PCs is expected to continue. The chance for computer companies to break into the expanding Asian market when trade barriers are lifted should lead to increased orders too. We need to undertake some market research in Asia as this market has higher growth potential than Europe, where most of our computers are marketed. The development of the newest mobile phone technology and links with the internet remain a concern for us. We decided two years ago not to develop this technology, and, if our competitors succeed in getting a major breakthrough, then sales of laptops will dive in some markets.'

Liz Collins – operations manager: 'The automation of the screen assembly section is now complete. We managed to push this through while maintaining excellent staff relationships. This was helped by our continued expansion, which meant that no jobs were lost. We had to turn down a big order from a big name brand last month due to too little factory capacity and shortages of skilled labour. I do urge you to agree to my plan to extend the factory space by 35% and to train more new recruits. Research into the lighter, faster computer that was agreed on last year is making excellent progress and we will soon have to decide whether to proceed to the production stage.'

Lukas Klimas – finance director: 'Our profits are holding steady, but cash flow remains a concern due to the expenditure on automated machines and research costs. We would need to borrow substantially to finance a factory extension. We would be in trouble if interest rates increased – there is already some government concern about inflation rising. There is a new range of grants available for businesses relocating into high unemployment areas. We must stay aware of exchange rate movements too – the recent depreciation helped our international competitiveness.'

20 marks, 36 minutes

1 Prepare a SWOT analysis based on your assessment of the internal and external factors that influence LVM's success. **[10]**

2 Identify and evaluate two potential strategic options available for LVM Ltd by using the SWOT diagram prepared in question 1. **[10]**

OVER TO YOU

REVISION CHECKLIST

1 Why is planning essential for a new business?
2 Can an existing successful business stop planning for the future? Explain your answer.
3 Identify and explain **four** key features of a typical business plan.
4 In 2009, General Motors decided against selling off its Opel and Vauxhall car manufacturing operations in Europe. Why would GM stakeholders gain from having access to the GM business plan for these operations?
5 Explain the key differences between scientific decision-making and intuitive decision-making.
6 Identify two factors under each of the SWOT headings for any business in your own country.
(H) 7 Explain two advantages of using decision trees.
(H) 8 Explain two limitations of using decision trees.

REVISION ACTIVITY

Read the case study below and then answer the questions that follow.

The Great Walmart of China

Before moving into China, America's biggest and most successful retailer had to learn its business all over again. 'China will be as big and as successful a market for Walmart as the United States,' said a Deutsche Bank retail analyst. However, this will not be easy as China's retail market is dominated by domestic retailers and other foreign retailers have gained ground quickly. Carrefour, the French group, had sales in China in 2008 nearly 50% bigger than Walmart's. Success is not guaranteed, despite the careful analysis that Walmart did before making the big strategic move into China.

The company identified its strengths – such as huge economies of scale – and possible weaknesses – such as being seen mainly as a US retailer. It also identified the great opportunities offered by the retail market in China – with the world's largest population and fastest-growing economy. There were obvious threats to success too – such as Carrefour's expansion plans.

The management then focused their attention on the wider issues that would be important in China. These included political and legal differences with the USA, economic factors such as the yuan exchange rate, social and cultural factors that could determine demand for certain goods and the impact of technological change on retailing practices and consumer buying habits.

Despite all of this strategic analysis, according to Strategic Resource Group, 'Walmart is being outmanoeuvred by Carrefour because its executives have taken too long to understand the Chinese market and add stores.' Perhaps one of the problems for retailers, even giant ones such as Walmart, is the possible lack of a core competence, other than substantial economies of scale, that could allow them to differentiate what they offer to retail consumers.

24 marks, 44 minutes

1 Why do you think it is important to analyse the existing strengths and weaknesses of a business before taking a major strategic decision? [8]
2 Explain, from Walmart's point of view, the strengths, weaknesses, opportunities and threats in the case of its expansion in China. [8]
3 Explain why it would have been important to consider the major differences between China and the USA before going ahead with this expansion. [8]

EXAM PRACTICE QUESTION

Read the case study below and then answer the questions that follow.

FOUR SEASONS LEISURE

After a period of consolidation in 2008–9, when the Four Seasons leisure group saw a big contraction in demand due to the world economic slowdown, the company is looking to increase its share of the upmarket, all-inclusive holiday resort market. Thirty years of providing holidays to high-income European and North American consumers make Four Seasons Leisure one of the most prestigious brands in the Caribbean.

Despite the recession, the company performed fairly well in 2009. Profits fell 5%, but this compared favourably with an industry average profit decline of 9%. Four Seasons has attributed the group's relative success to effective management from a team of people that have considerable knowledge and expertise in the market.

The management team is not complacent, however. The chief executive officer, Austin Walsh, thinks the company's concentration in the Caribbean is a weakness because of competition from new holiday destinations such as Dubai. Austin believes the company needs to expand into some of the new destinations that its customers are interested in visiting. The directors are considering three options for 2013:

			Projected profits based on economic conditions ($m)		
		Initial cost ($m)	**Fast growth**	**Normal growth**	**Recession**
Option 1	Open new resort in Dubai	120	400	200	−100
Option 2	Open new resort in Thailand	150	500	300	-50
Option3	Upgrade existing resorts in Caribbean	80	150	120	100

The consultancy that produced the projected costs and profit data believe that there is a 20% chance of fast economic growth, 50% chance of normal economic growth and a 30% chance of a recession.

25 marks, 45 minutes

1 Produce a SWOT analysis for Four Seasons Leisure's current position. **[8]**

(H) 2 a Construct a fully labelled decision tree showing Four Seasons' options. **[5]**

b Calculate the expected values for each option. **[6]**

c On financial grounds state which option Four Seasons should choose. **[2]**

d Analyse **one** weakness for Four Seasons of using decision tress as a basis for making this business decisions. **[4]**

07 Growth and evolution

This chapter covers syllabus section 1.7

On completing this chapter you should be able to:

- analyse the main types of economies and diseconomies of scale and apply these concepts to business decisions
- evaluate the relative merits of small versus large organisations
- recommend an appropriate scale of operation
- explain the difference between internal and external growth
- evaluate joint ventures, strategic alliances, mergers and takeovers
- analyse the advantages and disadvantages of franchising and evaluate it as a growth strategy
- explain and apply Ansoff's matrix as a decision-making tool
- (H) evaluate internal and external growth strategies as methods of expansion
- (H) examine how Porter's generic strategies provide a framework for building competitive advantage.

SETTING THE SCENE

Tale of two industries

The size of the average Indian steel plant compared to the size of the average Indian retail shop could not be more different.Steel plants employ thousands of workers, have millions of dollars of capital invested in advanced equipment and produce annual output valued in the millions too. Tata, one of the largest steel makers in the world, has recently grown by taking over European steel giant Corus. Contrast this with typical Indian retail outlets. The small shopkeepers and street hawkers that presently account for over 95% of Indian retail sales often employ just a few workers with little investment in modern technology. But all this could be about to change. There is a growing trend of mergers and takeovers in the retail sector. Large retail groups, such as Reliance and Walmart, are becoming established. It is claimed that the market share of this organised sector will be 25% by 2015. A pressure group of small retailers, the National Movement for Retail Democracy, is organising demonstrations to demand that big corporations leave the retail industry.

Points to think about:

- Why is the average steel plant so much larger than the average shop?
- Would Indian consumers benefit from more small shops or more shops owned by large corporations?
- How might consumers of steel, such as car makers, benefit from a takeover of Corus by Tata?
- Why might average costs of production fall as a business increases its scale of operations?

Tata steel plant, India

Introduction

There is a huge difference between the scale of operations of a small business – perhaps operated by just one person – and the largest companies in the world. Some of the latter have total annual sales exceeding the GDP of small countries! In 2009, ExxonMobil recorded sales of over $375 billion, yet the GDP of Thailand, for example, was $260 billion.

KEY TERM

scale of operation the maximum output that can be achieved using the available inputs (resources) – this scale can only be increased in the long term by employing more of all inputs

Increasing the scale of operations

There are risks and costs involved in increasing the scale of production – purchasing land, buildings, equipment, employing more staff – and the capital used for this will always have alternative uses. Firms expand capacity by increasing the scale of production to avoid turning business away and to increase market share, but they also benefit from the advantages of large-scale production – these are called economies of scale.

EXAM TIP

Do not confuse 'producing more' with increasing the scale of operation. More can be produced from existing resources by increasing capacity utilisation. Changing the scale of operation means using more (or less) of all resources, for example opening a new factory with additional machines and workers.

ECONOMIES OF SCALE

KEY TERM

economies of scale reductions in a firm's unit (average) costs of production that result from an increase in the scale of operations

These cost benefits can be so substantial in some industries that smaller firms will be unlikely to survive due to lack of competitiveness, such as in oil refining or soft drink production. The cost benefits arise for five main reasons.

1 Purchasing economies

These economies are often known as bulk-buying economies. Suppliers often offer substantial discounts for large orders. This is because it is cheaper for them to process and deliver one large order rather than several smaller ones.

2 Technical economies

There are two main sources of technical economies. Large firms are more likely to be able to justify the cost of flow production lines. If these are worked at a high capacity level, then they offer lower unit costs than other production methods. The latest and most advanced technical equipment – such as computer systems – is often expensive and can usually only be afforded by big firms. Such expense can only be justified by larger firms with high output levels – so that average fixed costs can be reduced.

3 Financial economies

Large organisations have two cost advantages when it comes to raising finance. First, banks often show preference for lending to a big business with a proven track record and

ACTIVITY 7.1

Read the case study below and then answer the questions that follow.

Operating at full capacity

Ben Rishi is operations manager for a factory making saucepans. The weekly maximum capacity of the factory is 3000 units. The main limit on capacity is the old-fashioned machine for stamping out the metal pans from sheet metal. Purchasing another machine would be expensive – and would require an extension to the building. Workers are working very long shifts. Ben has also been working long days to ensure that all the factory works at full capacity. For the last three months, demand has been high and last week there were orders for 3100 pots. Ben is under pressure from his managing director to see that this number is produced. Ben is unsure whether to recommend purchasing the new machine or to buy in components from another firm in the city that has spare capacity.

20 marks, 42 minutes

1 Outline the problems facing Ben because his factory is operating at full capacity. [6]

2 Analyse the advantages and disadvantages of the two methods suggested for solving the problem. [8]

3 Outline **three** cost advantages Ben's business might gain if it expands the scale of production. [6]

a diversified range of products. Interest rates charged to these firms are often lower than the rate charged to small, especially newly formed, businesses. Secondly, raising finance by 'going public' or by further public issues of shares for existing public limited companies is very expensive. Therefore, the average cost of raising the finance will be lower for larger firms selling many millions of dollars' worth of shares.

4 Marketing economies

Marketing costs obviously rise with the size of a business, but not at the same rate. Even a small firm will need a sales force to cover the whole of the sales area. It may employ an advertising agency to design adverts and arrange a promotional campaign. These costs can be spread over a higher level of sales for a big firm and this offers a substantial economy of scale.

5 Managerial economies

Small firms often employ general managers who have a range of management functions to perform. As a firm expands, it should be able to afford to attract specialist functional managers who should operate more efficiently than general managers, helping to reduce average costs.

EXAM TIP

When answering IB questions about economies of scale, make sure your answer is applied to the business in the question.

DISECONOMIES OF SCALE

KEY TERM

diseconomies of scale factors that cause average costs of production to rise when the scale of operation is increased

If there were no disadvantages to large-scale operations, nearly all industries would be dominated by huge corporations. Some are, of course, as with oil exploration, refining and retailing – the benefits of large-scale production are so substantial that smaller firms find it increasingly difficult to operate profitably. In other industries, the impact of 'diseconomies of scale' prevents one or just a few firms from being able to completely dominate. Diseconomies of scale are those factors that increase unit costs as a firm's scale of operation increases beyond a certain size. These diseconomies are related to the management problems of trying to control and direct an organisation with many thousands of workers, in many separate divisions, often operating in several different countries. There are three main causes of management problems.

1 Communication problems

Large-scale operations will often lead to poor feedback to workers, excessive use of non-personal communication media, communication overload with the volume of messages being sent, and distortion of messages caused by the long chain of command. Poor feedback reduces worker incentives.

These problems may lead to poor decisions being made, due to inadequate or delayed information, and management inefficiency.

2 Alienation of the workforce

The bigger the organisation, the more difficult it is to directly involve every worker and to give them a sense of purpose and achievement. They may feel insignificant in the overall business plan and become demotivated, failing to do their best. Larger manufacturing firms are the ones most likely to adopt flow-line production and workforce alienation is a real problem due to repetitive and boring tasks.

3 Poor co-ordination and slow decision-making

Business expansion often leads to many departments, divisions and products. The number of countries a firm operates in often increases too. The problems for senior management are to co-ordinate these operations and take rapid decisions in such a complex organisation. Smaller businesses with much tighter control over operations and much quicker and more flexible decision-making may benefit from lower average production costs as a result.

LARGE-SCALE PRODUCTION – UNIT COSTS

The combined effect of economies of scale and diseconomies of scale on unit (average) costs of production is shown in Figure 7.1. There is not a particular point of operation at which economies of scale cease and diseconomies begin. The process is more difficult to measure than this, as certain economies of scale may continue to be received as scale increases, but the growing significance of diseconomies gradually begins to take over and average costs may rise. It is often impossible to state at what level of output this process occurs, which is why many managers may continue to expand their business unaware that the forces causing diseconomies are building up significantly.

Merits of small and large organisations

SIGNIFICANCE OF SMALL AND MICRO-BUSINESSES

There is no universally agreed definition of small firms. However, they usually employ few people and have a low turnover compared to other firms. It is now common to make a further distinction for very small businesses known as 'micro-enterprises'. The European Union definitions are shown in Table 7.1.

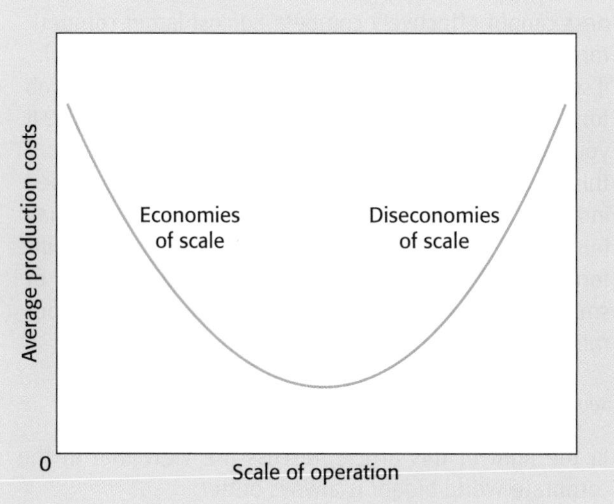

Figure 7.1 *The impact of economies and diseconomies of scale on average costs*

Business category	Employees	Sales turnover	Capital employed
Medium	51–250	over €10 million to €50 million	over €10 million to €34 million
Small	11–50	over €2 million to €10million	over €2 million to €10million
Micro	10 or fewer	up to €2 million	up to €2 million

Table 7.1 *EU classifications of business size*

Small firms (including micro-enterprises) are very important to all economies:

- Many jobs are created by small firms and the small business sector employs a very significant proportion of the working population in most countries.
- Small businesses are often run by dynamic entrepreneurs, with new ideas for consumer goods and services leading to wider consumer choice.
- Small firms create competition for larger businesses. Without this competition, larger firms could exploit consumers with high prices and poor service. For example, the cost of air travel has fallen in recent years due to the establishment of small airlines competing with the large, established companies.
- Small firms often supply specialist goods and services to important industries, e.g. car manufacturing, allowing them to specialise in large-scale assembly.
- All great businesses were small at one time. The Body Shop, for example, began in one small rented store in 1976. The large firms of the future are the small firms today. The more small firms are encouraged to become established and expand, the greater the chances that an economy will benefit from large-scale organisations in the future.
- Small firms may have lower average costs than larger ones and this benefit could be passed on to the consumer too. Costs could be lower because of lower wage rates paid, or the cost of the administration and management of bigger enterprises may increase their average costs dramatically.

The Body Shop opened its first shop in Brighton, England, in 1976

SMALL VERSUS LARGE ORGANISATIONS

The advantages and disadvantages of small and large business organisations are summarised in Tables 7.2 and 7.3.

Recommending an appropriate scale of operation

It is easy just to focus on the benefits of small businesses in certain industries, for example in service industries such as hairdressing. However, large businesses supply most of the world's consumer goods and they do so with increasing efficiency and, in most cases, improving levels of quality. There is no rule that can be applied when deciding on the most appropriate scale of operation. Business owners must weigh up and assess:

- owners' objectives – they may wish to keep the business small and easy to manage
- capital available – if limited, growth is less likely

Small businesses	Large businesses
• Can be managed and controlled by the owner(s). • Often able to adapt quickly to meet changing customer needs. • Offer personal service to customers. • Find it easier to know each worker, and many staff prefer to work for a smaller, more 'human' business. • Average costs may be low due to no diseconomies of scale and low overheads. • Easier communication with workers and customers.	• Can afford to employ specialist professional managers. • Benefit from cost reductions associated with large-scale production. • May be able to set prices that other firms have to follow. • Have access to several different sources of finance. • May be diversified in several markets and products, so risks are spread. • More likely to be able to afford research and development into new products and processes.

Table 7.2 *Potential advantages of small and large businesses*

Small businesses	Large businesses
• May have limited access to sources of finance. • May find the owner(s) has to carry a large burden of responsibility if unable to afford to employ specialist managers. • May not be diversified, so there are greater risks of negative impact of external change. • Unlikely to benefit from economies of scale.	• May be difficult to manage, especially if geographically spread. • May have potential cost increases associated with large-scale production. • May suffer from slow decision-making and poor communication due to the structure of the large organisation. • May often suffer from a divorce between ownership and control that can lead to conflicting objectives.

Table 7.3 *Potential disadvantages of small and large businesses*

- size of the market the firm operates in – very small markets do not need large-scale production
- number of competitors – the market share of each firm may be small if there are many rivals
- scope for scale economies – if these are substantial, as in water supply, each business is likely to operate on a large scale.

EXAM TIP

If an examination question asks you to consider the most appropriate scale of production in a given situation, you will need to assess these five factors.

THEORY OF KNOWLEDGE

Some people have the erroneous idea that a small business cannot effectively compete against larger competitors. This concept is quite far from the truth. For example, if someone were to ask you, 'What is a major source of job formations in America today?' what would you answer? If you said small business, you would be right. How about this question: 'What is the major source of newly formed individual wealth in this country today?' Again, the small business is the answer. Why, then, is there such misinformation about the strength, versatility and wealth of small businesses? The answer is that usually large corporations get the lion's share of publicity.

Source: e-commerce times

In the light of this article, discuss the view that in the corporate world bigger is always better.

Business growth

The owners of many businesses do not want the firm to remain small – although some do for reasons of remaining in control, avoiding taking too many risks and preventing workloads from becoming too heavy. Why do other business owners and directors of companies seek growth for their business? There are a number of possible reasons including:

- increased profits
- increased market share
- increased economies of scale
- increased power and status of the owners and directors
- reduced risk of being a takeover target.

INTERNAL GROWTH

Business growth can be achieved in a number of ways and these forms of growth can lead to differing effects on stakeholder groups, such as customers, workers and competitors. The different forms of growth can be grouped into internal and external growth, as shown in Figure 7.2.

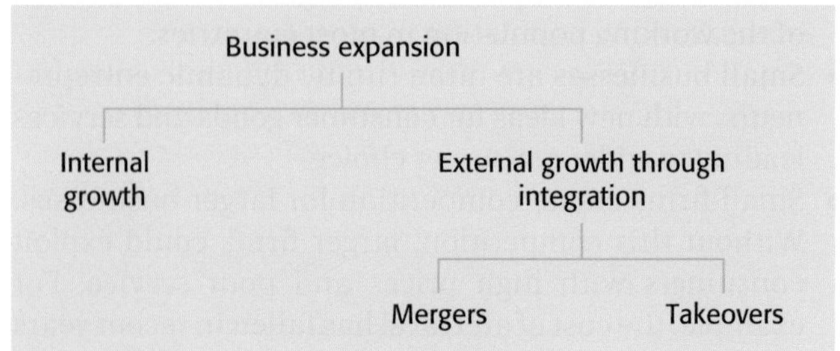

Figure 7.2 *Different forms of growth*

KEY TERM

internal growth expansion of a business by means of opening new branches, shops or factories (also known as organic growth)

An example of internal growth would be a retailing business opening more shops in towns and cities where it previously had none.

EXTERNAL GROWTH

KEY TERM

external growth business expansion achieved by means of merging with or taking over another business, from either the same or a different industry

The different forms of external growth are shown in Figure 7.3.

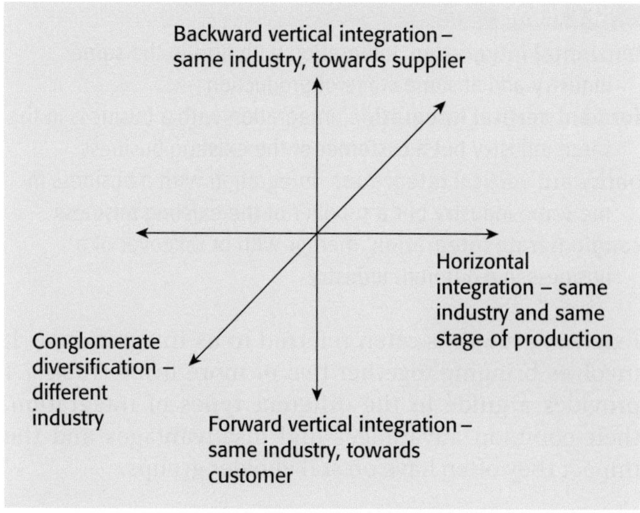

Figure 7.3 *Forms of external growth*

ACTIVITY 7.2

Starbucks confirms rapid growth strategy

Howard Schultz, the chairman of Starbucks, confirmed growth plans for the world's largest chain of coffee shops. The business will open at least 10 000 new cafes over the next four years by using internal growth. Schultz said that he planned to double the size of the business in five years. At the end of 2009, there were over 16 600 stores worldwide.

China will be the main focus of this growth strategy. The US giant opened its first Chinese branch in 1999 and now has over 200 branches. 'No market potentially has the opportunities for us as China hopefully will,' said Schultz. Like many western retailers, Starbucks sees China as its key growth area due to its fast-growing economy, lack of strong local competitors and sheer size of population. The business is also expanding its network of branches in Russia and Brazil.

There are plans to increase sales of non-coffee products to reduce reliance on hot drinks. It has expanded its sale of audio books and music, and Sir Paul McCartney will be the first artist to release an album on Starbucks' 'Hear Music' label.

This rapid internal expansion has not been without problems. *Consumer Reports* magazine recently ranked McDonald's coffee ahead of Starbucks saying it tasted better and costs less. This could be due to the time-saving equipment that has been added to new Starbucks branches that use automatic espresso machines instead of extracting espresso shots in the traditional way. The chairman has also criticised the time-saving policy of designing stores uniformly rather than with some local decoration.

Source: www.iht.com and www.bbc.co.uk

30 marks, 52 minutes

1 Why would you describe Starbuck's growth strategy as being an example of 'internal growth'? [2]

2 Suggest **two** reasons why Starbucks has adopted a rapid expansion strategy. [6]

3 Analyse the possible advantages of focusing growth in China. [8]

4 Explain why Starbucks is planning to reduce its reliance on just selling coffee. [4]

5 Discuss the potential economies and diseconomies of scale that Starbucks might experience from further expansion. [10]

KEY TERMS

horizontal integration integration with firm in the same industry and at same stage of production

forward vertical integration integration with a business in the same industry but a customer of the existing business

backward vertical integration integration with a business in the same industry but a supplier of the existing business

conglomerate integration merger with or takeover of a business in a different industry

External growth is often referred to as integration as it involves bringing together two or more firms. Table 7.4 provides a guide to the different types of integration, their common advantages and disadvantages and the impact they often have on stakeholder groups.

KEY TERMS

merger an agreement by shareholders and managers of two businesses to bring both firms together under a common board of directors with shareholders in both businesses owning shares in the newly merged business

takeover when a company buys over 50% of the shares of another company and becomes the controlling owner – often referred to as 'acquisition'

EXAM TIP

If an examination question refers to a merger or takeover, you should start by identifying what type it is. Do not forget that mergers and takeovers often cause businesses as many problems as they solve.

Type of integration	Advantages	Disadvantages	Impact on stakeholders
Horizontal integration	• Eliminates one competitor. • Possible economies of scale. • Scope for rationalising production, e.g. concentrating output on one site instead of two. • Increased power over suppliers.	• Rationalisation may bring bad publicity. • May lead to monopoly investigation if the combined business exceeds certain size limits.	• Consumers have less choice. • Workers may lose job security as a result of rationalisation.
Forward vertical integration	• Business is able to control the promotion and pricing of its own products. • Secures an outlet for the firm's products – may now exclude competitors' products.	• Consumers may suspect uncompetitive activity and react negatively. • Lack of experience in this sector of the industry – a successful manufacturer does not necessarily make a good retailer.	• Workers may have greater job security because the business has secure outlets. • There may be more varied career opportunities. • Consumers may resent lack of competition in the retail outlet because of the withdrawal of competitor products.
Backward vertical integration	• Gives control over quality, price and delivery times of supplies. • Encourages joint research and development into improved quality of supplies of components. • Business may control supplies of materials to competitors.	• May lack experience of managing a supplying company – a successful steel producer will not necessarily make a good manager of a coal mine. • Supplying business may become complacent having a guaranteed customer.	• Possibility of greater career opportunities for workers. • Consumers may obtain improved quality and more innovative products. • Control over supplies to competitors may limit competition and choice for consumers.
Conglomerate integration	• Diversifies the business away from its original industry and markets. • This should spread risk and may take the business into a faster-growing market.	• Lack of management experience in the acquired business sector. • There could be a lack of clear focus and direction now that the business is spread across more than one industry.	• Greater career opportunities for workers. • More job security because risks are spread across more than one industry.

Table 7.4 *Types of business integration*

ACTIVITY 7.3

Read the case studies below and then answer the questions that follow.

Jet Airways takes over Air Sahara

India's largest private airline, Jet Airways, says it has agreed to buy out its smaller rival, Air Sahara, for $140 million. The takeover gives the airline a combined market share of 32%. Jet Airways acquires the aircraft, equipment and landing and take-off rights at the airports Air Sahara had. 'This deal is definitely going to be good news for Jet Airways shareholders,' Jet Airways founder and chairman, Naresh Goyal, said. Some analysts are predicting substantial synergy (cost reductions and other benefits) from this takeover. Better deals from aircraft manufacturers are expected. Streamlining the two head offices into one unit should reduce fixed costs. The interlinking of the different air routes should allow more passengers to be offered connecting flights with the new enlarged airline.

Before the takeover could go ahead, it had to be approved by the Indian Ministry of Company Affairs. There was some concern that the takeover could lead to a monopolistic position, as Jet Airways will now enjoy a dominant position on many domestic air routes.

Source: www.bbc.co.uk

Daimler sells Chrysler after failed merger

After nine years of trying to make the merger of two large car makers work successfully, Mercedes Benz has at last admitted defeat and sold its 80% stake in the US-based operator, Chrysler. The merger never increased returns to shareholders and it failed in its original aim of creating a global motor company to compete effectively with General Motors, Ford and Toyota.

Management problems in controlling the merged businesses were huge. Distance between Germany (Mercedes Benz) and the USA (Chrysler) made communication difficult. The car ranges of the two companies had very little in common so there were few shared components, and economies of scale were less than expected. Culture clashes between the two management approaches led to top-level director disputes over the direction the merged business should take.

Source: www.timesonline.co.uk

35 marks, 58 minutes

1 Classify the type of integration used in both of these case studies. Explain your answer. [6]

2 If Jet Airways were now to merge with an aircraft manufacturer:
   a how would this merger be classified? Explain your answer. [3]
   b analyse **two** potential benefits to Jet Airways of this merger. [6]

3 Assess the likely impact of the Jet Airways takeover of Air Sahara on any **two** stakeholder groups. [10]

4 Using the DaimlerChrysler case study and any other researched examples, e.g. AOL and Time Warner, discuss why many mergers and takeovers fail to give shareholders the benefits originally predicted. [10]

Joint ventures, strategic alliances, franchising

JOINT VENTURES

KEY TERM

joint venture two or more businesses agree to work closely together on a particular project and create a separate business division to do so

A joint venture is not the same as a merger, but it may lead to a merger of the businesses if their joint interests coincide and if the joint venture is successful. The reasons for joint ventures are:

- costs and risks of a new business venture are shared – this is a major consideration when the cost of developing new products is rising rapidly
- different companies might have different strengths and experiences and they, therefore, fit well together
- they might have their major markets in different countries and they could exploit these with the new product more effectively than if they both decided to 'go it alone'.

Such agreements are not without their risks:

- Styles of management and culture might be so different that the two teams do not blend well together.

- Errors and mistakes might lead to one blaming the other.
- The business failure of one of the partners would put the whole project at risk.

STRATEGIC ALLIANCES

KEY TERM

strategic alliances agreements between firms in which each agrees to commit resources to achieve an agreed set of objectives

These alliances can be made with a wide variety of stakeholders, for example:

- with a university – finance provided by the business to allow new specialist training courses that will increase the supply of suitable staff for the firm
- with a supplier – to join forces in order to design and produce components and materials that will be used in a new range of products. This may help to reduce the total development time for getting the new products to market, gaining competitive advantage
- with a competitor – to reduce risks of entering a market that neither firm currently operates in. Care must be taken that, in these cases, the actions are not seen as being 'anti-competitive' and, as a result, against the laws of the country whose market is being entered.

FRANCHISING

KEY TERM

franchise a business that uses the name, logo and trading systems of an existing successful business

A franchise contract allows the franchisee to use the name, logo and marketing methods of the franchiser. The franchisee can, separately, then decide which form of legal structure to adopt. Franchises are a rapidly expanding form of business operation. They have allowed certain multinational businesses, for example McDonald's and The Body Shop, to expand much more rapidly than they could otherwise have done. Why would a business entrepreneur want to use the name, style and products of another firm? Consider Activity 7.4, which includes all of the main features of a typical franchise contract.

Table 7.5 summarises the benefits and disadvantages of a franchised business for the franchisee.

Benefits	Possible limitations
• Fewer chances of new business failing as an established brand and product are being used. • Advice and training offered by the franchisor. • National advertising paid for by franchisor. • Supplies obtained from established and quality-checked suppliers. • Franchisor agrees not to open another branch in the local area.	• Share of profits or sales revenue has to be paid to franchisor each year. • Initial franchise licence fee can be expensive. • Local promotions may still have to be paid for by franchisee. • No choice of supplies or suppliers to be used. • Strict rules over pricing and layout of the outlet reduce owners' control over own business.

Table 7.5 *Franchises – benefits and disadvantages to the franchisee*

Many McDonald's restaurants are franchised outlets

Ansoff's matrix

This tool is commonly used to portray alternative corporate growth strategies.

KEY TERM

Ansoff's matrix a model used to show the degree of risk associated with the four growth strategies of market penetration, market development, product development and diversification

Ansoff popularised the idea that long-term business success was dependent upon establishing business strategies and planning for their introduction. His best-known contribution to strategic planning was the development of the Ansoff matrix, which represented the different

ACTIVITY 7.4

Read the case study below and then answer the questions that follow.

Harry goes it alone

Harry no longer enjoyed his job as second chef in a famous hotel. He never liked taking orders from the head chef and always hoped to use his talents preparing food for customers in his own restaurant. The main problem was his lack of business experience. Harry had just been to a business conference and had been interested in the franchising exhibition there. One of the businesses offering to sell franchises was Pizza Delight. This firm sold a new type of pizza recipe to franchisees and provided all ingredients, marketing support and help with staff training. They had already opened 100 restaurants in other countries and offered to sell new franchises for a one-off payment of $100 000. If Harry signed one of these franchising contracts, then he would have to agree to:

- only buying materials from Pizza Delight
- fitting out the restaurant in exactly the way the franchisor wanted
- making an annual payment to Pizza Delight of a percentage of total turnover.

In addition, he would have to find and pay for suitable premises and recruit and motivate staff. Pizza Delight claimed that its brand and products were so well known that 'success was guaranteed'. Since the product had already been tested, there should be little consumer resistance, and Pizza Delight would pay for national advertising campaigns.

Harry was promised that no other Pizza Delight restaurant would be permitted to open within five kilometres of his. Harry was almost convinced that this was the business for him. He had inherited money from a relative. However, several things still bothered him – for example,would it give him the independence he so wanted?

24 marks, 45 minutes

1 What is meant by a 'franchise agreement'? [4]

2 Explain **three** potential drawbacks to Harry of agreeing to the terms of the franchise contract. [6]

3 If he decided to open his own restaurant but under his own name, why might the risks of failure be greater than for a Pizza Delight franchise? [4]

4 Using all of the evidence, would you advise Harry to take out a franchise with Pizza Delight? Justify your answer. [10]

options open to a marketing manager when considering new opportunities for sales growth.

He considered that the two main variables in a strategic marketing decision were:

- the market in which the firm was going to operate
- the product(s) intended for sale.

In terms of the market, managers have two options:

- to remain in the existing market
- to enter new ones.

In terms of the product, the two options are:

- selling existing products
- developing new ones.

When put on a matrix, these options can be presented as shown in Figure 7.4.

As there are two options each for markets and for products, this gives a total of four distinct strategies that businesses can adopt when planning to increase sales. These are shown on the matrix and can be summarised as follows.

Market penetration

KEY TERM

market penetration the objective of achieving higher market shares in existing markets with existing products

In 2009, Aer Lingus reduced some of the fares on its European air routes – some even to as little as $15. The directors of the company were attempting to aggressively increase market share by taking passengers away from other low-cost airlines. This is the least risky of all the four possible strategies in that there are fewer 'unknowns' – the market and product parameters remain the same. However, it is

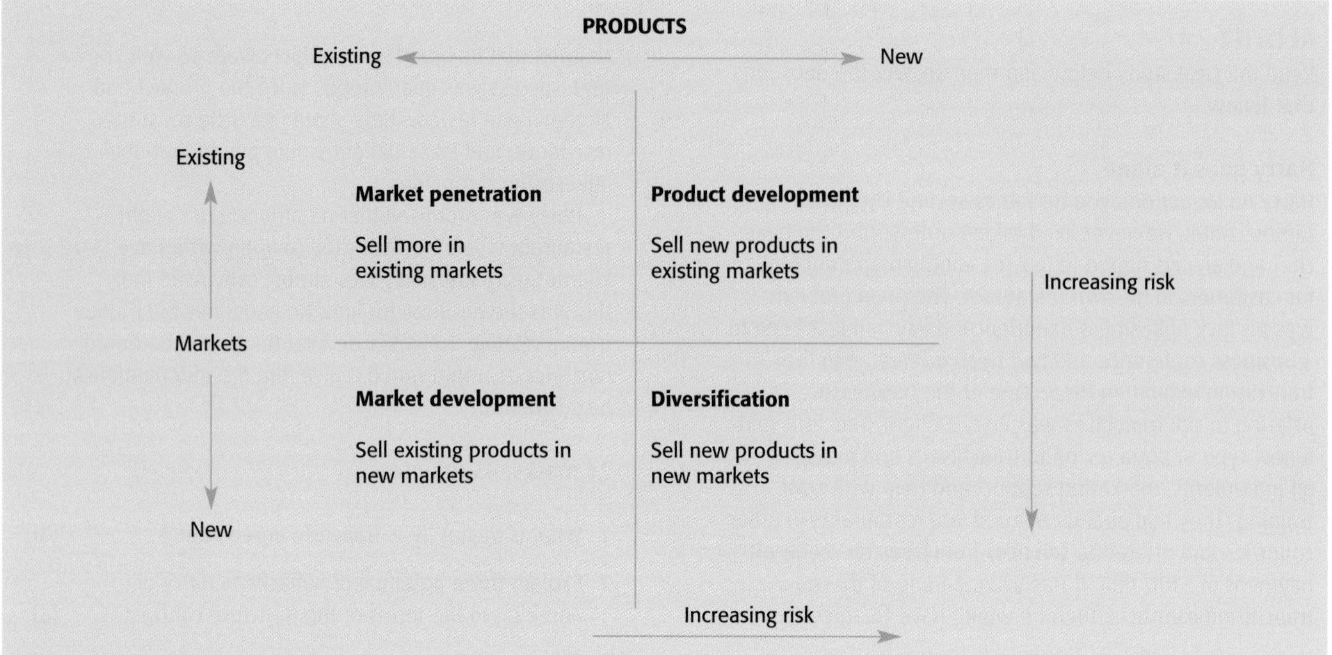

Figure 7.4 *Ansoff's matrix*

not risk free as if low prices are the method used to penetrate the market, it could lead to a potentially damaging price war that reduces the profit margins of all firms in the industry.

Product development

KEY TERM

product development the development and sale of new products or new developments of existing products in existing markets

The launch of Diet Pepsi took an existing product, developed it into a slightly different version and sold it in the soft drinks market where Pepsi was already available. Product development often involves innovation – as with 4G mobile phones – and these brand new products can offer a distinctive identity to the business.

Market development

KEY TERM

market development the strategy of selling existing products in new markets

This could include exporting goods to overseas markets or selling to a new market segment. Lucozade used to be promoted as a health tonic for people with colds and flu. It was successfully repositioned into the sports drink market, appealing to a new, younger range of consumers. Dell or HP can use existing business computer systems and re-package them for sale to consumer markets.

Diversification

KEY TERM

diversification the process of selling different, unrelated goods or services in new markets

The Virgin Group is constantly seeking new areas for growth. Its expansion from a media empire to an airline and then a train operator, then into finance, is a classic example of diversification. Tata Industries in India is another good example of a very diversified business, making a huge range of products – from steel to tea bags.

As the diversification strategy involves new challenges in both markets and products, it is the most risky of the four strategies. It may also be a strategy that is outside the core competencies of the firm. However, diversification may be a possible option if the high risk is balanced out by the chance of a high profit. Other advantages of diversification include the potential to gain a foothold in an expanding industry and the reduction of overall business portfolio risk.

EVALUATION OF ANSOFF'S MATRIX

The risks involved in these four strategies differ substantially. By opening up these options, Ansoff's matrix does not direct a business towards one particular future strategy. However, by identifying the different ways in which a business could expand, the matrix allows managers to analyse the degree of risk associated with each strategy. Managers can then apply decision-making techniques to assess the costs, potential gains and risks associated with all options. In practice, in today's fiercely competitive world, it is common for large businesses to adopt multiple strategies for growth at the same time.

While Ansoff's analysis helps to map the strategic business options, it has limitations too. It only considers two main factors in the strategic analysis of a business's options – it is important to consider SWOT and PEST analysis too in order to give a more complete picture. Recommendations based purely on Ansoff would tend to lack depth and hard environmental evidence.

Management judgement, especially based on experience of the risks and returns from the four options, may be just as important as any one analytical tool for making the final choice.

The matrix does not suggest detailed marketing options. For instance, market development may seem to be the best option, but which market/country and with which of the existing products produced by the business? Further research and analysis will be needed to supply answers to these questions.

Evaluation of growth strategies

Internal growth can be quite slow with, perhaps, only a few branches or shops opening each year. However, it can avoid problems of external growth such as the need to finance expensive takeovers, offer new share issues or expensive additional loans. Also, management problems associated with bringing together very different businesses with their own attitudes and cultures are avoided.

External growth can lead to rapid expansion, which might be vital in a competitive and expanding market. However, takeovers can be very expensive and may result in management problems caused by the need for different management systems to deal with a bigger organisation. There can also be conflict between the two teams of managers – who will get the top jobs? – and conflicts of culture and business ethics.

Porter's generic strategies

FRAMEWORK FOR BUILDING COMPETITIVE ADVANTAGE

Michael Porter, a famous management researcher, argues that a firm's strengths ultimately fall under one of two headings: cost advantage or differentiation (or product uniqueness). By applying these strengths in either a broad way (industry wide) or in a narrow way (a market segment) three generic strategies result.

Cost leadership strategy

Being the lowest-cost producer in the industry for a certain level of product quality will allow the firm to make higher profits than rivals or, if it lowers its prices below the average of competitors, to increase market share. Ryanair, one of Europe's largest and most profitable airlines, is also the lowest average cost airline. Businesses adopting this strategy either sell products at average industry prices to earn higher profit than rivals or below industry average prices to gain market share. Ryanair adopts the second of these pricing strategies. The cost leadership strategy usually targets a broad rather than a niche market.

Cost leadership often stems from the following internal strengths:

- high levels of investment in advanced production methods, requiring access to much capital
- efficient production methods, e.g. low stock levels and low numbers of components used to shorten the production process
- efficient distribution channels, e.g. Ryanair only uses the internet for selling tickets and communicating with customers.

Differentiation strategy

This strategy involves developing a product or service that offers unique features valued by customers. The value added to the product or service by these features may allow the firm to charge a premium price for it. Apple's constant research into innovative products allows it to charge high prices for its differentiated products.

A differentiation strategy often results from the following internal strengths:

- excellent research and development facilities and a track record in developing unique products
- corporate reputation for innovation and quality
- strong sales team able to promote the perceived strengths of the brand and the products.

Focus strategy

This concentrates on a narrow market segment, aiming to achieve either a cost advantage or differentiation. This can lead to a high degree of customer loyalty within the market segment. For example, Princess Boats has a loyal consumer following for its uniquely designed luxury motor boats – some models costing millions of dollars. Discount retailers, on the other hand, focus on low-income market segments through a strategy of low costs leading to low prices. As the focus strategy can lead to imitation by rivals, continued success will depend on continuing to tailor a broad range of products to a relatively narrow market segment that the business knows very well.

Porter's strategies are shown in Table 7.6.

	Advantage	
Target scope	**Low cost**	**Product uniqueness**
Broad (industry wide)	Cost leadership strategy	Differentiation strategy
Narrow (market segment)	Focus strategy (low cost)	Focus strategy (differentiation)

Table 7.6 *Porter's generic strategies*

OVER TO YOU

REVISION CHECKLIST

1 List **four** benefits to the economy of your country that would result from the growth of the number of small firms.

2 A computer manufacturer is planning to expand. Explain to its management the difference between internal and external growth.

3 A producer of fruit drinks in your country has asked you to explain the difference between vertical forward and backward integration. Give examples of each that would be relevant for this business.

4 Two large banks in your country plan to merge. Examine the advantages and disadvantages to the businesses that could result from this integration.

5 In the example used in question 4 identify **two** stakeholder groups that could be affected by this planned merger.

6 In the example in question 4 explain the possible advantages and disadvantages to these **two** groups from the proposed merger.

H 7 Examine briefly **three** reasons why the owner of a small business might decide **not** to expand the business.

H 8 Explain how a clothing design/manufacturing business could use Porter's generic strategies to expand.

REVISION ACTIVITY

Read the case study below and then answer the questions that follow.

Caffè Nero and Asda – contrasting growth strategies

Although both companies have similar objectives – sales growth, leading to profitability – Asda and Caffè Nero present an interesting contrast in business strategy. The coffee bar operator is going for market development. Gerry Ford, Caffè Nero's chairman who led the management buy-out of the business in 2007, has set a target of 100 branches to be opened in Turkey. He said that he was 'also looking around Europe and scouting out China'. He is confident of success in Turkey. He has appointed Isik Asur, a Harvard Business School graduate, who used to run the Starbucks operation in the country. He knows all about the changing consumer tastes in the country as well as the political, social and economic environment there.

Asda – number two supermarket chain in the UK – has decided on the strategies of market penetration and product development to build sales growth. New food stores will be opened in the next few years in an attempt to gain ground on Tesco. It aims to be the lowest-price supermarket to increase food sales futher. In addition, it is expanding rapidly into non-food retailing. It plans to open ten new Asda Living stores, selling a huge range of items for the home, but not food.

Different businesses in different markets will often decide on different strategies for the future – even though overall objectives may be similar.

36 marks, 58 minutes

1 Explain why companies like these need long-term plans to help achieve their objectives. [6]

2 Suggest **five** facts about the Turkish consumer market and economy that Caffè Nero would have found useful before taking this strategic decision. Briefly explain why each one is important. [10]

3 Using Ansoff's matrix, compare and contrast the different strategies being adopted by these two companies and comment on possible reasons why these were decided upon. [10]

4 Discuss the factors that might influence the long-term plans or strategies adopted by a business. [10]

EXAM PRACTICE QUESTION

Read the case study below and then answer the questions that follow.

GROWTH STRATEGY IN DISPUTE AT TRAFFIC CLOTHING PLC

Traffic Clothing plc produces suits and dresses and sells them to major retailers in several countries. Sales turnover has grown by around 15% each year for the last decade – a slower rate than some competitors. Traffic's low prices have been possible due to the opening of low-cost factories in developing countries. This internal growth strategy was supported by most of the directors. They believed that it had been achieved without excessive external borrowing. There were some real causes for concern, however. Sales revenue was increasing, but profits were unchanged for the last three years. This was due to several factors. First, new competitors were entering the clothing market and driving down prices. Secondly, raw material prices for both natural and 'man-made' inputs were rising. Lastly, the number of mergers between large clothing retailers had increased their bargaining power when dealing with producers like Traffic.

Major shareholders in Traffic were not happy with the directors' growth strategy. At the last board meeting, the finance director proposed a policy of rapid external growth. He argued that this could be achieved by aggressive takeovers of either other clothing producers or material suppliers to achieve cost leadership. The marketing director suggested focusing on a smaller, higher-income market segment. This could be reinforced with a merger with a prestige clothing retailer. 'Our own shops will give us real power in the high street as we will be able to offer customers a top quality shopping experience – this will allow differentiation in a crowded market.' The chief executive suggested that both directors prepare a detailed report on these proposals.

25 marks, 45 minutes

1 Use the case study to explain the difference between 'internal' and 'external' growth. [4]

2 Explain how the business increased sales revenue, yet gained no increase in profits for the last three years. [5]

3 Assess the likely advantages and disadvantages of a cost leadership strategy for this business. [8]

4 Assess the likely advantages and disadvantages of a differentiation or a focused strategy for this business. [8]

08 Change and the management of change

This chapter covers syllabus section 1.8 (Higher level only)

On completing this chapter you should be able to:

- (H) explain the causes of change and the factors causing resistance to change
- (H) examine the use of Lewin's force-field analysis and the relative importance of driving and restraining forces
- (H) evaluate different strategies for reducing the impact of change and the resistance to change.

SETTING THE SCENE

IT drives business change at Volkswagen (VW)

Radical changes to the way the IT department supports departments within VW have led to significant cost reductions and quality improvements. VW operates in the world's most competitive car markets. It faces twin threats of changing consumer tastes and Asian rivals who operate with much lower labour costs. Constant change is needed to maintain competitiveness. VW has a clear vision for all major changes it introduces – to reduce costs, improve quality and reduce product development times. These will combine to increase sales. The number of different IT programs has been reduced from 4000 to just 300 and the company is to cut thousands of jobs across all departments over the next two years.

Following the complete redesign of the IT division, it now has a 'horizontal' IT team that connects different parts of the business together into processes rather than departments. For example, the IT team will bridge the gap between market research, designers who know how to design a new car and the production team who know best the process of building it. Chief technology officer Stefan Ostrowski explained that 'we want to design quality cars that are easy to build – IT acts as the link between the different departments that are involved in this process'.

VW trained 400 IT staff in business processes and in how to mediate between different departments. IT staff are rotated to different business areas every four years to give staff new skills. 'Communication was also a key part of this change as if IT does not explain its new role in clear business language you will not change anything,' said Ostrowski.

Source: www.computerworlduk.com/management

Points to think about:

- Why did VW realise that constant change is necessary?
- Why do you think a 'clear vision' or objective is important before making changes?
- Explain why improved communication and training were key features of the successful changes to the work of VW's IT department.
- Do you think important business changes could take place without the support of staff?

Introduction

Change is the continuous adoption of business strategies and structures in response to internal pressures or external forces. Change happens whether we encourage and welcome it or not. To take control of change and to ensure it is a positive process, businesses must have a vision, a strategy and a proven and adaptable process for managing change.

KEY TERM

change management planning, implementing, controlling and reviewing the movement of an organisation from its current state to a new one

Causes of change

EXTERNAL CAUSES

Today, change in business is not the exception but the rule – it has become an accelerating and ongoing process. 'Business as usual' will become increasingly rare as global, economic and technological upheavals necessitate a business response. Change management requires firms to be able to cope with dramatic one-off changes as well as more gradual evolutionary change. Table 8.1 identifies some common external causes of change and strategies for managing them.

Incremental change

Evolutionary or incremental change occurs slowly over time. The trend towards more fuel-efficient cars has been gradually taking place over the last few years. Such change can be either anticipated or unexpected. The decision to increase the London congestion charge was announced months in advance, but a sudden oil price increase may not have been expected. Incremental changes that are expected tend to be the easiest to manage.

Dramatic change

Dramatic or revolutionary change, especially if unanticipated, causes many more problems. Civil conflict in Kenya in 2008 forced many safari holiday companies to re-establish themselves in other countries or markets. In extreme cases, dramatic change might lead to a total rethink of the operation of an organisation – this is called business process re-engineering.

KEY TERM

business process re-engineering fundamentally rethinking and redesigning the processes of a business to achieve a dramatic improvement in performance

EXAM TIP

When discussing how change will affect a business and its strategies, try to analyse whether the change was incremental or dramatic, anticipated or unanticipated.

ACTIVITY 8.1

8 marks, 12 minutes

1 Identify some recent changes in the external business environment that have an incremental impact on business. [4]

2 Identify other recent changes that have had a dramatic impact on business. [4]

ACTIVITY 8.2

Demographic, social and cultural changes can have an impact on business decisions. Research the most significant social or cultural factors that have occurred in your country in recent years, for example migration, employment of women or population changes such as an ageing population.

Analyse how any one business in your country has responded to the changes you have identified.

INTERNAL CAUSES

Table 8.2 identifies some common internal causes of change and strategies for managing them.

Factors causing resistance to change

This is one of the biggest problems faced by organisations when they attempt to introduce change. The managers and workforce of a business may resent and resist change for any of the following reasons:

- Fear of the unknown – change means uncertainty, which worries some people. Not knowing what may happen to your job or the future of the business leads to increased anxiety – this results in resistance.
- Fear of failure – change may require new skills and abilities that, despite training, may be beyond a worker's capabilities. People know how the current system works, but will they be able to cope with the new one?
- Losing something of value – workers could lose income, status or job security as a result of change and they will want to know precisely how the change will affect them.
- False beliefs about the need for change – to allay their fears and to avoid the risks of change, some people fool themselves into believing that the existing system will continue to work without the need for radical change.

Nature of change	Examples	Strategies for management
Globalisation – increasing interdependence of countries' economies through free trade and multinational company investment	• New opportunities to sell products in other countries. • Increased competition from products made more cheaply in other countries – often by multinationals.	• Use either pan-global marketing or localisation strategies. • Achieve and try to maintain a competitive advantage.
Technological advances – leading to new products and new processes	• Products: new computer games, iPods and iPhones, hybrid-powered cars. • Processes: robots in production; computer-assisted design (CAD) in design offices and computer systems for stock control.	• Staff retraining. • Purchase of new equipment. • Additions to product portfolio – other products may be dropped. • Need for quicker product development which may require new organisational structures and teams.
Macro-economic changes – fiscal policy, interest rates, business cycle	• Changes in consumers' disposable incomes – and demand patterns that result from this. • Boom or recession conditions – need for extra capacity or rationalisation.	• Need for flexible production systems – including staff flexibility – to cope with demand changes. • Explain need for extra capacity or the need to rationalise. • Deal with staff cutbacks in a way that encourages staff who remain to accept change.
Legal changes	• Changes to what can be sold (e.g. raising age of buying cigarettes). • Changes to working hours and conditions.	• Staff training on company policy (e.g. on sale of cigarettes). • Flexible working hours and practices.
Competitors' actions	• New products. • Lower prices – based on higher competitiveness/lower costs. • Higher promotional budgets.	• Encourage new ideas from staff. • Increase efficiency by staff accepting the need to change production methods. • Ensure resources are available to meet the challenge.
Environmental factors	• Increasing 'green consumerism'. • Growing concern about climate change and industry's contribution to it.	• Social and environmental audits supported by strategic changes, e.g. Marks and Spencer's 'Plan A', which includes the aim to recycle all packaging.

Table 8.1 *Major external causes of change and possible strategies for managing them*

Nature of change	Examples	Strategies for management
Organisational changes	• Delayering. • Hierarchical structure replaced by matrix structure (see Chapter 11, page 114).	• Retraining of less senior staff to accept more responsibility. • Reassurances on job security. • Retraining of staff in teamwork and project management.
Relocation	• Moving operations to another region or country.	• Redundancy schemes for workers who lose their job. • Relocation grants for those willing to move.
Cost cutting to improve competitiveness	• Capital-intensive rather than labour-intensive methods. • Rationalisation of operations, e.g. closing some operations.	• Retraining of staff to operate advanced equipment. • Redundancy schemes for workers who lose their jobs. • Flexible employment contracts and working practices.

Table 8.2 *Major internal causes of change and possible strategies for managing them*

- Lack of trust – perhaps because of past experiences, there may be a lack of trust between workers and managers who are introducing the change. Workers may not believe the reasons given to them for change or the reassurances from managers about the impact of it.
- Inertia – many people suffer from inertia or reluctance to change and try to maintain the status quo. Since change often requires considerable effort, the fear of having to work harder to introduce it may cause resistance.

The importance of resistance factors will vary from business to business. In those firms where previous change has gone well, where workers are kept informed and even consulted about change and where managers offer support and training to the staff involved, resistance to change is likely to be low. Resistance to change is likely to be greatest in businesses where there is a lack of trust and little communication.

EXAM TIP

When discussing possible resistance to changes proposed by management, try to think of the leadership style being used to implement the change. This could be a major contributory factor in determining the degree of resistance.

Strategies to reduce impact of, and resistance to, change

CHANGE MANAGEMENT

Managing and leading change successfully is the mark of a good manager. Before setting the change process in motion, managers need to ask four questions:

- Is the change anticipated or unexpected?
- Is the change likely to have a dramatic or less significant impact on the business?
- Have managers planned for change?
- To what extent can management control the change process?

EXAM TIP

The IB Business and Management syllabus puts business change at the core of much business decision-making. Many evaluative questions are set on this topic. When answering an evaluative question on change and the management of change, you could start by asking yourself, in the context of the case study, the four questions above.

Key stages in successful change management

Here is a checklist of essential points that managers should consider before attempting to introduce significant changes in an organisation:

1. Where are we now and why is change necessary? It is important to recognise why a business needs to introduce change from the situation it currently finds itself in.
2. New vision and objectives. For substantial changes a new vision for the business may be needed – and this must be communicated to those affected by the change.
3. Ensure resources are in place to enable change to happen. Starting a change and then finding there is too little finance to complete it could be disastrous.
4. Give maximum warning of the change. Staff in particular should not be taken by surprise by change – this will increase their resistance to it (see section above on 'Factors causing resistance to change').
5. Involve staff in the plan for change and its implementation. This will encourage them to accept change and lead to proposals from them to improve the change process.
6. Communicate. The vital importance of communicating effectively with the workforce is a feature of all the stages.
7. Introduce initial changes that bring quick results. This will help all involved in the change to see the point of it.
8. Focus on training. This will allow staff to feel that they are able to make a real contribution to the changed organisation.
9. Sell the benefits. Staff and other stakeholders may benefit directly from changes – these need to be explained to them.
10. Always remember the effects on individuals. A 'soft' human resource approach will often bring future rewards in terms of staff loyalty when they have been supported and communicated with during the change process.
11. Check on how individuals are coping and remember to support them. Some people will need more support than others – a 'sink or swim' philosophy will damage the business if it leads to low quality output or poor customer service because staff were poorly supported during the change period.

EXAM TIP

Your understanding of communication from studying Chapter 12 will allow you to assess the importance of two-way communication in motivating staff to accept change.

LEWIN'S FORCE-FIELD ANALYSIS

Force-field analysis, first developed by Kurt Lewin, provides a framework for looking at the factors (forces) that influence change. These forces can either be 'driving forces for change' that help the organisation towards a goal or 'restraining forces against change' that might prevent an organisation reaching its goal.

KEY TERM

force-field analysis an analytical process used to map the opposing forces within an environment (such as a business) where change is taking place

Steps in force-field analysis

1. Outline the proposal for change – insert in the middle of a force-field diagram, as shown in Figure 8.1.
2. List forces for change in one column and forces against change in the other.
3. Assign an estimated score for each force, with 1 being weak and 5 being strong.

Figure 8.1 shows a proposal for installing IT-controlled manufacturing equipment in a factory.

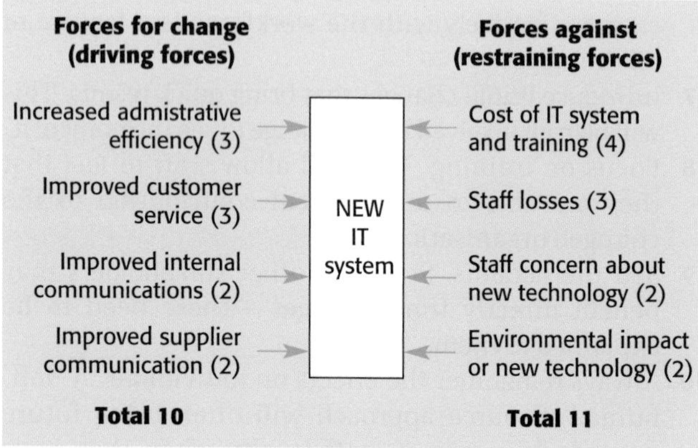

Figure 8.1 *Force-field analysis of an IT-controlled machinery proposal*

The numerical scores indicate whether the forces are weak (e.g. 1) or strong (e.g. 5).

Once the analysis has been carried out, the process can help management improve the probability of success of this major change. For example, by training staff (which might increase cost by +1) their concern about new technology could be reduced (reducing staff concern by –2).

Using Lewin's model

- The force-field diagram helps managers weigh up the importance of these two types of forces.
- It helps identify the people most likely to be affected by the change.
- It encourages an examination of how to strengthen the forces supporting the decision and reduce the forces opposed to it.
- The use of a leadership style that reduces opposition and resistance to change is highlighted as being more effective than forcing through unpopular changes in an autocratic manner.

PROJECT CHAMPIONS

A project champion may be appointed by senior management to help drive a programme of change though a business.

KEY TERM

project champion a person assigned to support and drive a project forward. Their role is to explain the benefits of change and assist and support the team putting change into practice

They will be appointed from within the organisation and will be either a middle or senior manager as they must have sufficient influence within the organisation to smooth the path of the project team investigating and planning the change. The project champion will represent the project at board level or other meetings of senior managers and will try to ensure sufficient resources are put in place to

ACTIVITY 8.3

Read the case study below and then answer the questions that follow.

Project champion, Compass Group

Jane Moger is human resources (HR) director at the restaurant business, Compass Group. She has acted as project champion for the implementation of an e-recruitment system within the organisation. 'Being a project champion in HR gives you an opportunity to get involved in complex, long-term and high value-added activities. Project champions get a new project off the ground and give the team momentum to see the change through,' she said.

Source: www.personneltoday.com

6 marks, 12 minutes

A business is planning to adopt a new IT system that will allow many staff to work from home several days a week. Some senior managers are against this as it will 'reduce control over workers'. The IT manager in charge of implementing the strategy decides to appoint a project champion to smooth the change. Explain what are likely to be the key qualities of this project champion. **[6]**

enable its implementation, but they will not necessarily be involved in day-to-day planning.

PROJECT GROUPS OR TEAMS

Problem solving through team building is a structured way to make a breakthrough in a difficult change situation. It uses the power of a team.

KEY TERM

project groups created by an organisation to address a problem that requires input from different specialists

When a difficult problem arises during implementation of a major change in a business's strategy or structure, a project group may be set up to analyse it and recommend solutions. Project groups work with the manager responsible for introducing the change. A team meeting of experts should involve a rigorous exchange of views leading to the development of an appropriate action. The responsibility for carrying out the plan lies with the original manager, but he or she will be better equipped to solve the problem that was preventing change from being implemented effectively.

PROMOTING CHANGE

Promoting change is an important function of management. Acceptance of change – both by the workforce and other stakeholders – is more likely to lead to a positive outcome rather than imposing change on unwilling groups, which could increase resistance to change and ultimately lead to failure. According to John Kotter, a leading writer on organisational change, the best way to promote change is to follow an eight-stage process:

1. Establish a sense of urgency.
2. Create an effective project team to lead the change.
3. Develop a vision and a strategy for change.
4. Communicate this change vision.
5. Empower people to take action.
6. Generate short-term gains from change that benefit as many people as possible.
7. Consolidate these gains and produce even more change.
8. Build change into the culture of the organisation so that it becomes a natural process.

EXAM TIP

When discussing effective management of change, focus on the positive benefits of change to the stakeholders most affected by it. It is very easy to be too negative about change.

THEORY OF KNOWLEDGE

Organisations are constantly facing change, whether because of developments in the external environment or new managers taking the organisation in a different direction.

How would a manager know whether change taking place within an organisation was having a positive effect?

OVER TO YOU

REVISION CHECKLIST

1. Explain the difference between incremental and revolutionary business change, using recent examples.
2. Outline **two** likely causes of change for a business making cameras.
3. Why is communication an important part of the change process?
4. Explain the role of a project champion to a team of people who are worried about technological change affecting their work practices.
5. Explain how a project group could help a manager with the task of introducing important changes to the business.
6. a Explain any **two** causes of resistance to change that might occur in your school or college after the head teacher or principal has announced a major reorganisation of the departmental/faculty structure.
   b For each of these causes of resistance, explain how staff might be reassured.
7. Land Rover has been sold to the Indian company Tata. If the new management plan involves opening a Land Rover factory in India making the current models, but keeping the existing Solihull plant in the UK open, how might any resistance to this change among existing UK workers be reduced?

REVISION ACTIVITY

Read the case study below and then answer the questions that follow.

Constant change a feature of modern industry

Britax has undergone many changes in recent years. The business grew out of a diverse group of companies. The Britax name and brand were adopted at the end of the 1990s when the business decided to concentrate its efforts and sold off some of its activities. It now focuses on child safety seats and designing and building aircraft interiors. Sales of child safety seats have been boosted by recent changes in the law, while aircraft interiors are a niche market with four international competitors. Overall, turnover of Britax's aerospace division has grown from £20 million to £150 million in six years despite intense competition and an aircraft building industry that fears a fall in aircraft orders.

Britax has just introduced a complex and expensive computer system to manage its production resource planning. Stock levels have fallen dramatically and productivity has improved. But the change involved changes in many people's work practices and skills. As with all changes of this nature the crucial key to success lies not with the product but with those who have to use it. 'People react in different ways to change,' said the company's business systems manager. 'How people approach change is a critical factor. A big factor in managing this is to build a strong project team. The right people need to be involved from the start. The next step is training and communicating the need for change. We spent a great deal of time and effort in this area and it was well worth it.'

32 marks, 55 minutes

1 Why is almost constant change likely to occur within businesses such as Britax? [6]

2 Outline **two** ways in which Britax reduced resistance to change. [6]

3 Analyse how force-field analysis and project champions could have helped during this change. [10]

4 Evaluate the most important stages in the process of implementing and managing large-scale changes within a business. [10]

HMV BUYS MAMA GROUP IN LIVE MUSIC TAKEOVER DEAL

Entertainment firm HMV is expanding its presence in the live music market by buying venue owner MAMA Group for £46 million. HMV's move comes nearly a year after it took a 9.9% stake in MAMA, which runs 11 concert venues including the Hammersmith Apollo in London. MAMA also owns other interests including an artist management business representing bands such as Franz Ferdinand and the Kaiser Chiefs.

The deal marks the latest stage in a three-year 'transformation plan' unveiled by the company in March 2007 in response to falling sales of CDs and the growth of illegal music downloads. Other moves have included introducing the Pure HMV loyalty card scheme, taking a 50% stake in online music store 7digital and even opening a pilot HMV Curzon-branded, three-screen digital cinema in Wimbledon.

HMV's takeover offer for MAMA is subject to approval from shareholders, who are concerned about HMV moving into the market where it has limited direct experience, along with the prospects of raising the finance to fund the takeover. This contrasts with the enthusiastic view of HMV's management who are keen to explore the prospects of live music as a new market.

The takeover of MAMA Group by HMV represents a significant change in direction for the organisation and it is important this change is managed effectively.

Source: http://news.bbc.co.uk (adapted)

EXAM PRACTICE QUESTION

Read the case study and then answer the questions that follow.

20 marks, 35 minutes

1 Define the term 'change management'. [2]

2 Explain the role a project team might have in changing the direction of HMV. [4]

3 Analyse **two** driving forces and **two** restraining forces which are influencing HMV's 'transformation plan' as it tries to change the direction of the organisation. [8]

4 Using an appropriate business model, analyse how HMV's proposed takeover of the MAMA Group will give it a competitive advantage in the music industry. [6]

09 Globalisation

This chapter covers syllabus section 1.9

On completing this chapter you should be able to:

- understand the meaning of globalisation and the factors contributing to it
- analyse the role played by multinationals in the global business environment
- evaluate the impact of multinational companies on the host country
- explain what regional trading blocs are and their impact on a business of a country that is a member of a regional economic group/bloc.

SETTING THE SCENE

Coca-Cola's globalised marketing – India doesn't buy it

Coca-Cola employs nearly 100 000 people producing and selling over 300 brands in over 200 countries. It is a classic example of a large multinational business. It creates jobs and contributes output to many economies across the globe. However, its multinational operations do not always meet with success and they often face serious criticism. Despite spending $1 billion on promotion in India, Coca-Cola sales in this country account for under 1% of its total global sales. The world's most valuable multinational brand – according to Brand Republic – has failed to make any inroads into the Indian market. Per capita consumption of soft drinks is among the lowest in the world, even though both of the USA's giant cola groups – Pepsi and Coca-Cola – have invested millions of dollars in breaking into this market.

What is wrong? Coca-Cola has a serious image problem in many parts of the country. It was thrown out of India in the 1970s for failing to release details of its secret formula and it has been fighting court cases recently against claims that it is causing droughts in some regions due to heavy water use and that its soft drinks contain 25 times the permitted level of pesticides. But perhaps the real problem is cultural. Traditionalists in India fear the erosion of long-standing culture by the importation of western products, advertisements and methods of selling. In addition, tea is still widely drunk in India and Coca-Cola's failure to adapt its global products to local tastes is another major factor. Finally, most Indian retailing is still through informal street and market traders – and Coca-Cola is reluctant to see its products sold in this way. Perhaps this is one reason why it has recently set up a branded university in India to teach modern retailing techniques to millions of small shop and stall owners. Even this has met with opposition from traditional sellers, who fear the growing dominance of foreign products and retailers in India.

Source: www.timesonline.co.uk (adapted)

09 Globalisation

Points to think about:

- What advantages might Coca-Cola have from producing and selling products in many countries?
- Assess the potential benefits and drawbacks to India of Coca-Cola expanding its operations in that country.
- Examine how Coca-Cola might achieve more sales success in India than it does at present.

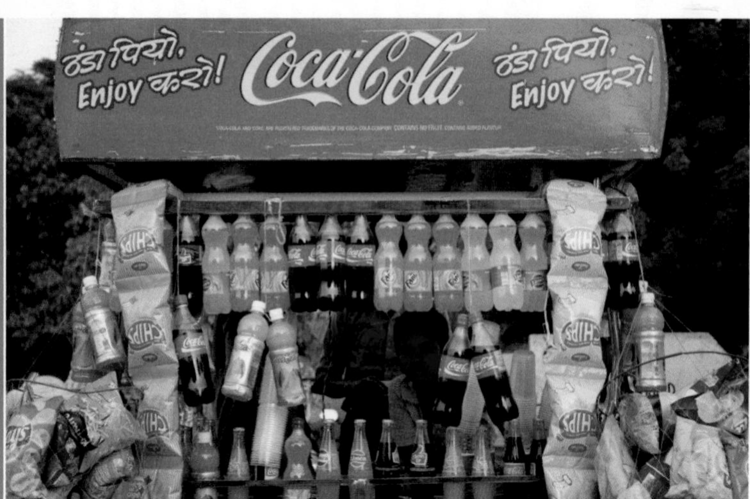

Introduction

KEY TERMS

globalisation the growing trend towards worldwide markets in products, capital and labour, unrestricted by barriers

multinational companies business organisations that have their headquarters in one country, but with operating branches, factories and assembly plants in other countries

free international trade international trade that is allowed to take place without restrictions such as 'protectionist' tariffs and quotas

tariff tax imposed on an imported product

quota a physical limit placed on the quantity of imports of certain products

Globalisation is not a new process, but it has accelerated in recent years with the rapid growth of multinational companies, the expansion of free international trade with fewer tariffs and quotas on imports and the growth of regional trading blocs. The key features of globalisation that have an impact on business strategy are:

- increased international trade as barriers to trade are reduced
- growth of multinational businesses in all countries as there is greater freedom for capital to be invested from one country to another
- freer movement of workers between countries.

Multinational businesses

EXAM TIP

When defining a multinational business, it is not enough to state that such businesses 'sell products in more than one country'.

These firms have benefited greatly from the freedoms offered by globalisation. They are more than just importers and exporters; they actually produce goods and services in more than one country. The biggest multinationals have annual sales turnovers exceeding the size of many countries' entire economies. This sheer size – and the power and influence it can bring – can lead to many problems for nations that deal with such firms. This point is made more obvious by the fact that many of the largest multinationals have their head offices in western European countries or in the USA, yet have many of their operating bases in less-developed countries with much smaller economies. If the companies need to save costs by reducing the size of their workforces, often the *last* countries to lose jobs will be the ones where the head offices are based. Interestingly, there is now the significant development of large companies from emerging markets – such as Tata from India – opening operations in more developed countries.

WHY BECOME A MULTINATIONAL?

There are several reasons why businesses start to operate in countries other than their main base.

1. Closer to main markets – this will have a number of advantages:
   - lower transport costs for the finished goods
   - better market information regarding consumer tastes as a result of closeness to them
   - may be looked upon as a local company and gain customer loyalty as a consequence.
2. Lower costs of production – apart from lower transport costs of the completed items, there are likely to be other cost savings:

- lower labour rates due to much lower demand for local labour compared to developed economies
- cheaper rent and site costs, again resulting from lower demand for commercial property – these cost savings can make the 'local' production very efficient in terms of the market in the rest of the world and can lead to substantial exports
- government grants and tax incentives designed to encourage the industrialisation of such countries.

3 Avoid import restrictions – by producing in the local country there will be no import duties to pay and no other import restrictions.
4 Access to local natural resources – these might not be available in the company's main operating country (see the case study on South Africa in Activity 9.1).
5 Take advantage of expanding markets in other countries which will lead to increased sales and profits.

ACTIVITY 9.1

South Africa accelerates its car production

South Africa is emerging as a profitable production and export base for some of the world's big auto manufacturers, despite the country's remoteness, its reputation for labour militancy and political uncertainties. South Africa has also become a key supplier of motor industry components. With massive platinum and palladium deposits, South Africa has emerged from nowhere to take nearly 10% of the world's production of catalytic converters, which is set to increase to 25%. This did not happen by accident. It is the result of a deliberate strategy by the government to draw the world's best car manufacturers into South Africa, and drag the domestic industry from behind protectionist barriers into the highly competitive global market for cars and components.

'When we started, the South African auto industry was in ruins,' an economist from the government's Motor Industry Development Programme (MIDP), said. 'Domestic production could not even compete with imports, which faced duties in excess of 115%,' he adds. MIDP has kick-started South Africa's ailing motor industry by attracting the world's big car makers with many financial incentives. The new factories have had the benefit of generating thousands of new jobs and forcing hundreds of small and medium-sized local suppliers to improve quality and productivity or face extinction.

Exports of fully built cars have increased to 5 billion rand, and are expected to double within two years. At the same time, exports of components have trebled to 12 billion rand. German car manufacturers have been the first to take advantage of MIDP's export credits and investment allowances, although Italian and French companies, such as Fiat and Renault are rapidly following. DaimlerChrysler has just announced that it is switching its entire production of right-hand drive C-class Mercedes-Benz cars from Bremen in Germany to the Eastern Cape in an investment project worth 1.3 billion rand, which will create 800 new jobs at the plant and 3000 new jobs in the supply industry. Mercedes' East London factory in South Africa is now exporting C-class models to the USA, the biggest car market in the world.

BMW has invested 1 billion rand upgrading its Rosslyn plant near Pretoria, which will export 75% of the 40 000 3-series cars produced each year to Britain, Germany, Japan, America, Australia, Hong Kong, Singapore, New Zealand, Taiwan and Iran. Daily output has increased five-fold since creating 900 new jobs at the Rosslyn plant, and an estimated 18 000 jobs in the car component industry.

The Eastern Cape remains one of the poorest regions in the country. Average black disposable income stands at a low 5000 rand a year, compared with the white population's 45 000 rand a year. When Volkswagen were looking for 1300 workers to replace those who were sacked for participating in an illegal strike, 23 000 turned up outside the factory gates in the hope of being chosen. The extra incomes created by the industry help to boost other local industries such as retailing and house construction. The success of MIDP 'has been a huge confidence booster for us,' the MIDP spokesperson says. 'It has enabled us to bring about big productivity improvements, stabilise employment, reduce the real cost of new vehicles, and give consumers more choice.'

28 marks, 52 minutes

1 List **four** examples of multinational companies that have invested in South Africa. [4]

2 Using the case study as well as your own knowledge, explain **three** reasons for these manufacturers setting up factories in South Africa. [6]

3 Analyse the benefits South Africa appears to be gaining from such investment. [8]

4 Evaluate whether the government of South Africa should continue to support investment by multinational businesses in its economy. [10]

POTENTIAL PROBLEMS FOR MULTINATIONALS

Setting up operating plants in foreign countries is not without risks. Communication links with headquarters may be poor. Language, legal and culture differences with local workers and government officials could lead to misunderstandings. Co-ordination with other plants in the multinational group will need to be carefully monitored to ensure that products that might compete with each other on world markets are not produced or that conflicting policies are not adopted. Finally, it is likely that the skills levels of the local employees will be low and this could require substantial investment in training programmes.

EVALUATION OF IMPACT OF MULTINATIONAL OPERATIONS ON 'HOST' COUNTRIES

There are a range of potential benefits:

- The investment will bring in foreign currency and, if output from the plant is exported, further foreign exchange can be earned.
- Employment opportunities will be created and training programmes will improve the quality and efficiency of local people.
- Local firms are likely to benefit from supplying services and components to the new factory and this will generate additional jobs and incomes.
- Local firms will be forced to bring their quality and productivity up to international standards either to compete with the multinational or to supply to it.
- Tax revenues to the government will be boosted from any profits made by the multinational.
- Management expertise in the community will slowly improve when and if the 'foreign' supervisors and managers are replaced by local staff, once they are suitably qualified.
- The total output of the economy will be increased and this will raise Gross Domestic Product (GDP).

The expansion of multinational corporations into a country could lead to these drawbacks:

- Exploitation of the local workforce might take place. Due to the absence of strict labour and health and safety rules in some countries, multinationals can employ cheap labour for long hours with few of the benefits that the staff in their base country would demand. Recent poor publicity has forced the Gap and Nike clothing companies to improve their monitoring of the employment of illegal child workers at factories that produce their clothes in Thailand. How many large businesses would not care about these practices, especially as the factories are so far removed from western media investigation?
- Pollution from plants might be at higher levels than allowed in other countries. Either this could be because of slack rules or because the host government is afraid of driving the multinational away if it insists on environmentally acceptable practices. This is a sign of the great influence multinationals can have. The worst example of this was the Bhopal gas leakage from the US-owned Union Carbide plant in 1984 which killed thousands of workers and residents.
- Local competing firms may be squeezed out of business due to inferior equipment and much smaller resources than the large multinational.
- Some large western-based businesses, such as McDonald's and Coca-Cola, have been accused of imposing western culture on other societies by the power of advertising and promotion. This could lead to a reduction in cultural identity.
- Profits may be sent back to the country where the head office of the company is based, rather than kept for reinvestment in the host nation.
- Extensive depletion of the limited natural resources of some countries has been blamed on some large multinational corporations. The argument is that they have little incentive to conserve these resources, as they are able to relocate quickly to other countries once they have run out.

EXAM TIP

In questions on multinational business activity, you can often use examples from your own country as well as from the case study to support your answers.

Globalisation is not just about trade and multinational companies. Increased migration to and from most countries of the world is occurring. Many economists argue that increased migration of young workers from eastern Europe is a benefit to the UK economy and that the USA benefits from immigration from South America.

THEORY OF KNOWLEDGE

The later part of the 20th century and beginning of the 21st century have seen globalisation of all aspects of people's lives. Indian people eat in McDonald's, Chinese people drive BMWs, the Vietnamese work for Nike, British people get customer support from offices in India and Malaysia's favourite football team is Manchester United.

Prepare a presentation on the following theme: To what extent is increased globalisation a threat to national culture?

Globalisation and the growth in international trade

World trade – international trade between countries – has grown rapidly in recent years. This has been a sign of increased globalisation resulting from the work of the World Trade Organization (WTO) and its free trade agreements, and the growth of regional free trade blocs or areas that allow no trade barriers between member states.

THE WORLD TRADE ORGANIZATION (WTO)

Averaging 7% growth per year in the decade to 2007, the rate of growth of world trade fell considerably in 2008 and 2009 as a consequence of the world's financial and banking problems. Since 2001, Asian economies, led by China and India, have contributed 40% of total world trade expansion. China's membership of the WTO, which negotiates regular reductions in world trade barriers, was one of the major factors behind this rapid growth. Exports accounted for around 37% of China's GDP in 2009 (at the official exchange rate; source: World Bank). Figures 9.1, 9.2 and 9.3 show the rapid growth of world exports by value and the rapid growth in the volume of world trade compared to world GDP growth.

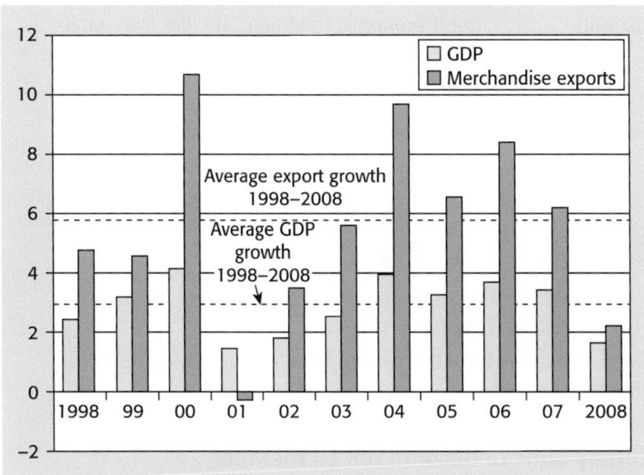

Figure 9.1 Volume of world merchandise trade and GDP 1998–2008 (% annual changes)
Source: WTO Secretariat, 23.3.2009

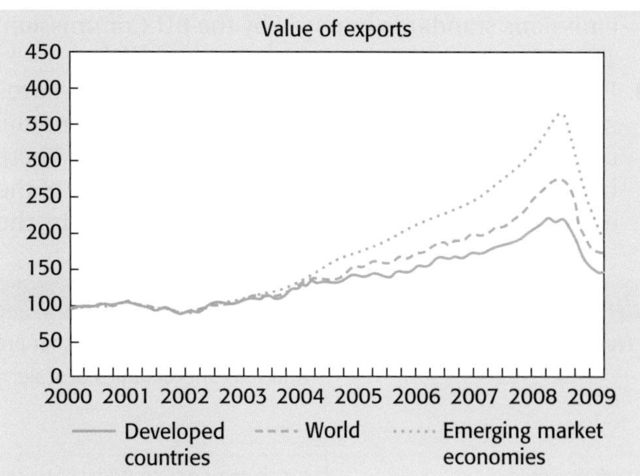

Figure 9.2 Value of world exports (index: 2000 = 100)
Source: UNCTAD secretariat calculations, based on the CPB Netherlands Bureau of Economic Policy Analysis, World Trade database

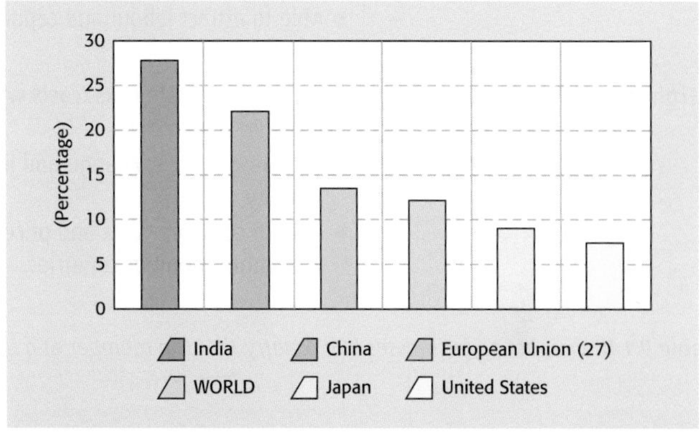

Figure 9.3 Leading exporters of commercial services, growth 2000–7

REGIONAL TRADE BLOCS

There are four main types of trading agreements between nations:

1 Free trade areas, e.g. the North American Free Trade Area (NAFTA), comprising the USA, Canada and Mexico. These exist where countries agree to trade with each other with no tariffs, quotas or other restrictions. Each member country is still allowed to decide its own level of import controls on goods coming from non-member states.
2 Customs unions, e.g. Mercosur, comprising Argentina, Brazil, Paraguay, Uruguay and Venzuela. These are free trade areas, but all member countries agree to set the same level of restrictions – known as common external barriers – on imports from non-member countries. The barriers aim to prevent individual free trade area member countries from gaining a competitive advantage over other member countries by importing important resources with very low levels of tariffs and restrictions.
3 Common markets, e.g. the European Union (EU). These are an extended version of a customs union as they aim to create the trading conditions that would exist within just one country – a 'common market'. They do this by allowing the free movement of capital and people between member states and also imposing common product standards throughout the area. For example, all cars produced in the EU must meet the same strict

emissions standards imposed by the EU Commission. The EU is the world's largest common market.

4 Economic and monetary unions (EMU), e.g the eurozone. These attempt to create many of the economic conditions that exist within just one country. There will be a common currency (the euro in the case of the eurozone), one single interest rate determined by the EMU's central bank (European Central Bank in the case of the eurozone) and agreed limits on individual governments' fiscal deficits. In 2010, the EU had 27 members, 16 of which were members of the eurozone.

Table 9.1 summarises the impact on businesses in countries that are members of a regional economic group/bloc.

Trade bloc	Benefits	Drawbacks
Free trade area	• Access to larger markets for products. • Increased economies of scale.	• Increased competition from other members' industries. • May be no protection for special cases such as strategic or infant industries.
Customs union	• Can compete on equal basis with businesses from other member states in terms of import costs.	• No advantages gained from cheaper imports than other member states' businesses can purchase.
Common market	• Common product/health/safety regulations prevent unfair competition from 'below standard' imports. • Able to attract labour and capital from other member states.	• Increased cost and bureaucracy associated with additional standards and regulations. • May lose quality labour and capital to other member states.
Economic and monetary union	• No exchange rate risks/costs when trading with other EMU members. • May be greater exchange and interest rate stability. • Able to compare costs and prices transparently with other member countries.	• The conversion to a common currency may have been at an uncompetitively high exchange rate. • Common interest rate and fiscal rules assume the same economic conditions in all member states, but if economic conditions are less favourable in any member country, then businesses in that country will suffer.

Table 9.1 *The impact on businesses in a country that is a member of a regional economic trade bloc – potential benefits and drawbacks*

OVER TO YOU

REVISION CHECKLIST

1 Why is globalisation not a recent development?
2 Identify **four** factors that have contributed to globalisation in recent years.
3 Explain **four** benefits to your country from receiving additional investment from multinational companies.
4 Explain **four** potential drawbacks to your country from receiving additional investment from multinational companies.
5 Select one well-known multinational company and explain **four** benefits that this business gains from operating multinationally.
6 ASEAN is an example of a trading bloc. Carry out research into what type of trading bloc it is.
7 Explain the benefits and potential drawbacks to a business in Russia were the country to gain admission to the EU.
8 Would the UK business sector benefit from the UK joining the eurozone? Explain your answer.

REVISION ACTIVITY

Read the case study below and then answer the questions that follow.

Turkey aims to become full EU member

Turkey has plans to become a full member of the EU and gain the substantial economic benefits that it believes will follow from this. Its business sector, including companies such as Tekel and Firat Plastik, would then have free trade access to 500 million people in the existing 27 EU members. The business sector in Turkey would gain from its relatively low cost base compared to most of other EU members. However, there would also be increased competition for Turkish companies within their home market of 72 million consumers, especially in the financial, insurance and business services sectors.

Since Turkey is a relatively poor country, there will be costs to the EU if Turkey joins. In 2009, GDP per head was US$11 900 compared with the average EU figure of US$33 000 (source: CIA World Factbook). Regional assistance to some areas in Turkey will add to the EU's budget expenditure.

The opportunities for increased investment in and exports to Turkey are very appealing to existing EU businesses. Shell, BP and Kraft are well established in Turkey, but EU membership will lead to an increase in multinational operations, currently based in EU member states, in Turkey. They must tread with caution however. Cultural and language differences, relatively poor transport infrastructure and the Turkish lira currency exchange rate fluctuations all present considerable obstacles to business investment within the country.

20 marks, 35 minutes

1 What type of trading bloc is the EU? [2]

2 Outline the main characteristics of this type of trading bloc. [4]

3 Explain **two** reasons why the Turkish government wants Turkey to join the EU. [4]

4 Discuss the advantages and disadvantages Turkish companies would expect to experience from the country's membership of the EU. [10]

EXAM PRACTICE QUESTION

Read the case study below and then answer the questions that follow.

STRONG RUMOURS THAT KRAFT IS LOOKING TO TAKE OVER CADBURY

UK confectionery company Cadbury is facing a £10bn hostile takeover bid from one of the US's leading food manufacturers, Kraft Foods. British citizens ate £3.5bn worth of chocolate last year, which makes the UK one of the world's biggest consumers of chocolate. Historically, the UK has always been a nation of chocolate eaters and Cadbury is one of the country's leading brands. The possible takeover of Cadbury is another sign that food manufacturing is becoming increasingly globalised.

Chocolate produced in the UK has a very different taste to that produced in the US. Kraft's brand, Hershey chocolate, has a more bitter taste and a 'grittier' texture than Cadbury's chocolate. In the UK, chocolate has to contain at least 20% cocoa solids. In the US, however, cocoa need only make up 10% of the product. A Cadbury's Dairy Milk bar contains 23% cocoa solids, whereas a Hershey bar contains just 11%. In Europe, many chocolate bars have an even higher cocoa content of 40% or more.

As the Kraft takeover of Cadbury becomes an increasing possibility, could we see the Hershey bar start to appear in UK retailers?

20 marks, 35 minutes

1 Define the term 'globalisation'. [2]

2 Explain two potential advantages to Kraft of taking over Cadbury. [4]

3 Analyse the problems Kraft might experience as it tries to enter the European chocolate market. [6]

4 Discuss how Ansoff's matrix model might have been useful to Kraft in making the decision to take over Cadbury. [8]

10 Human resource planning

This chapter covers syllabus section 2.1

On completing this chapter you should be able to:

- identify the constraints and opportunities presented by demographic change
- discuss the significance of labour mobility
- analyse the workforce planning process
- evaluate strategies for developing future human resources
- discuss different methods of recruitment, training, appraisal and dismissal
- describe reasons for and consequences of changing work patterns and practices
- (H) analyse the impact on business of legal employment rights
- (H) examine how recruitment, training and appraisal can help achieve workforce planning targets
- (H) analyse the consequences of changing work patterns and practices on business
- (H) apply Handy's Shamrock organisation theory.

SETTING THE SCENE

Human resource planning in China and Australia

Before 1978 in China, all industry was state owned and workers were state employees. Industries were inefficient and over-staffed – jobs were given for life. There was no human resource management (HRM) because firms had no control over staffing or recruitment. Since privately owned companies have been allowed and many state industries bought by the private sector, the need to improve efficiency and productivity has become very great. Nearly all firms of any size now have professional human resource (HR) managers. They recruit, select and train the best workers for their firms and – unheard of in communist times – they can 'hire and fire' in response to changing demand for products. Many posts of responsibility are given to internal staff – it is often said that the cultural links in each firm, or 'guanxi' (interpersonal relationships), are so strong that it is difficult for external recruits to break into the business structure.

Australian businesses have used 'western-style' HRM for many years. This is based on the view that good management of people has a direct impact on a firm's future profitability and success. Advertising job vacancies in papers and even on TV and radio is common. Internal promotions are often given – not for cultural reasons, but because firms do not want to lose their training investment in staff by not promoting and retaining them. Interviews are the most widely used selection procedure, but references from past employers are also important. For senior management jobs, it is common for the husband or wife to be interviewed too. Unlike China, there is a huge private recruitment industry with over 300 agencies giving workers mobility to seek jobs easily in other parts of the country – moving from one region to another in China is still unusual for most workers.

Source: http://marketing/byu/edu

Points to think about:

- From the case study, list as many HRM responsibilities as you can.
- Do you think recruitment, selection and training of staff are important to a firm's success? Explain your answer.
- What HR problems might an Australian business experience if it tried to open a base in China?

Introduction

KEY TERMS

human resource management (HRM) the strategic approach to the effective management of an organisation's workers so that they help the business gain a competitive advantage

human resource or workforce planning analysing and forecasting the numbers of workers and the skills of those workers that will be required by the organisation to achieve its objectives

HRM aims to recruit capable, flexible and committed people, managing and rewarding their performance and developing their key skills to the benefit of the organisation. Human resource planning aims to get the right number of people with the right skills, experience and competencies in the right jobs at the right time at the right cost.

Demographic change

The potential supply of labour to any organisation is affected by demographic changes. Table 10.1 summarises three of these changes and their potential opportunities and constraints.

Labour mobility

KEY TERMS

occupational mobility of labour extent to which workers are willing and able to move to different jobs requiring different skills

geographical mobility of labour extent to which workers are willing and able to move geographical region to take up new jobs

Example of demographic change	Opportunities	Constraints
Natural population growth (or decline) – birth rate exceeds death rate (or vice versa)	• May be easier to recruit good staff as the working population increases.	• Increased birth rates may take years before they impact on the *working* population.
Net migration (immigration compared with emigration)	• May be easier to recruit good staff at lower rates of pay. • Highly qualified staff might be recruited from other countries.	• 'Brain drain' of qualified and experienced staff to other countries will reduce competitiveness. • Immigrants may need more training, e.g. in language and cultural issues.
Ageing population (the average age of the population increases as a result of rising life expectancy)	• It is often claimed that older staff are more loyal and reliable than younger workers – what do you think?	• Older staff may be less flexible and adaptable, e.g. to the introduction of new workplace technologies.

Table 10.1 *The effect of demographic change on labour supply*

High labour mobility helps a country achieve economic efficiency. A mobile workforce means that if jobs are lost in one industry or region, workers are willing and able to move to other jobs and/or other occupations. This helps to keep structural unemployment low.

In developed economies, labour tends to be relatively immobile because:

- high levels of home ownership mean that workers are reluctant to pay the cost in time and money of arranging a house sale and purchase in another region
- high skill levels in one occupation may mean that workers are not equipped to deal with machines, processes and technologies in other industries and occupations.

In emerging market countries, despite strong family or ethnic ties to one area, mobility tends to be higher because:

- home ownership is low
- low skill levels mean that workers can undertake low-skilled jobs in many different industries.

However, a high degree of geographical mobility, especially between rural and urban areas, can lead to overcrowding and very poor living conditions in towns and cities.

Many governments pursue policies to attempt to increase labour mobility. These include:

- relocation grants for key public sector workers
- job centres and other government offices to advertise job vacancies nationally
- training and retraining programmes for the unemployed.

Workforce planning

HR departments need to calculate the future staffing needs of the business to try to avoid having too few or too many staff or staff with the wrong skills. HR departments must respond to the corporate plan of the business and the objectives this contains. If the overall business plan is to expand production and develop products for foreign markets, then this must be reflected in the workforce plan. The starting point for workforce planning is always a workforce audit.

KEY TERMS

workforce audit a check on the skills and qualifications of all existing employees

workforce plan thinking ahead and establishing the number and skills of the workforce required by the business to meet its objectives

Workforce planning involves two main stages.

ACTIVITY 10.1

Global labour mobility

One of the consequences of globalisation has been a shift in the global demand for labour. In recent years, many richer economies have suffered declining birth rates and shifts in types of industry creating new work opportunities. At the same time, development and increasingly open borders in emerging economies have created a labour force more eager to migrate to take advantage of these opportunities. The result has been a significant expansion of global labour mobility. Governments in both origin and destination countries have encouraged this trend. Recently introduced temporary work visas in both the USA and Germany have opened the door to increasing numbers of skilled non-permanent residents. Several origin countries in Asia, including India and the Philippines, actively seek labour markets for their workers overseas.

The benefits of these policies to businesses and to the world economy are becoming clearer. A recent World Bank report estimated that an increase of 3% in the workforce in high-income countries through migration by 2025 could increase global real income by US$356 billion.

Source: http://www.migrationdrc.org

22 marks, 40 minutes

1 Analyse the benefits of increased immigration to any **two** developed country businesses operating in different sectors. [6]

2 Explain how a developed country government might attract immigrants with appropriate skills. [6]

3 Assess the benefits and drawbacks to a country such as the Philippines of encouraging many of its workers to seek employment abroad. [10]

1 Forecasting the *number* of staff required
This will depend on several factors:

- Forecasting demand for the firm's product – this will be influenced by market conditions, seasonal factors, competitors' actions and trends in consumer tastes. It could be a mistake to replace a worker who decides to leave the firm if consumer demand is falling or if there is likely to be a seasonal downturn in demand. Demand forecasts may be necessary to help establish workforce planning needs.
- The productivity levels of staff – if productivity (output per worker) is forecast to increase, perhaps as a result of more efficient machinery, then fewer staff will be needed to produce the same level of output.
- The objectives of the business – these could influence future workforce numbers in two main ways. First, if the business plans to expand over the coming years, then staffing numbers will have to rise to accommodate this growth. Secondly, if the firm intends to increase customer service levels, possibly at the expense of short-term profits, then more workers might need to be recruited. A workforce plan cannot be devised without consideration of business objectives.
- Changes in the law regarding workers' rights – if the government of a country decides to pass laws which establish a shorter maximum working week or introduces a minimum wage level, then there will be a considerable impact on the workforce plan. A shorter working week might lead to a greater demand for staff to ensure that all the available work is completed on time. A minimum wage might encourage firms to employ fewer workers and to substitute them with machines.
- Labour turnover and absenteeism rate – the higher the rate at which staff leave a business, the greater will be the firm's need to recruit replacement staff. The higher the level of staff absenteeism, the greater will be the firm's need for higher staffing levels to ensure adequate numbers are available at any one time.

2 Forecasting the *skills* required
The need for better-qualified staff or for staff with different skills is a constant factor in the minds of HR managers. The importance of these issues will depend upon on the following:

- The pace of technological change in the industry, e.g. production methods and the complexity of the machinery used. The application of IT in offices has meant that traditional typists or clerks are now rarely required – skilled computer operators and web designers are in greater demand than ever.
- The need for flexible or multi-skilled staff. Workers can become over-specialised, finding it difficult to adapt when demand conditions change. Most businesses need to recruit staff or train them with more than one skill that can be applied in a variety of different ways. This gives the firm greater adaptability to changing market conditions – and makes the workers' jobs more rewarding too.

ACTIVITY 10.2

Economic downturn results in Electrolux job losses

Electrolux, a world-leading kitchen appliance maker, made a loss in the first three months of 2008. The company was forced to cut staff costs because demand for its products was falling, especially in the USA. 'Demand for our products has been lower than our forecasts and this has hit our profits,' said Electrolux boss Hans Stralberg. The company planned to cut 400 jobs in its European factories to save $72 million.

12 marks, 23 minutes

1 Explain why HR planning is important to a business such as Electrolux. [6]

2 Apart from a global downturn in demand, explain **three** factors that could influence the numbers of workers required by Electrolux. [6]

Electrolux required fewer workers because of falling demand for kitchen appliances

EXAM TIP

When discussing workforce planning in examination answers it is important to make clear that it can only be effective if it is linked in closely with the firm's long-term objectives.

Recruitment

KEY TERM

recruitment the process of identifying the need for a new employee, defining the job to be filled and the type of person needed to fill it, attracting suitable candidates for the job and selecting the best one

Organisations need to obtain the best workforce available if they are to meet their objectives and be competitive. Workers need to be chosen so that they meet exactly the needs of the organisation in order to reduce the risk of conflict between their personal objectives and those of the business. The recruitment and selection process involves the following steps.

1 Establish the exact nature of the job vacancy and draw up a job description

KEY TERM

job description a detailed list of the key points about the job to be filled, stating all the key tasks and responsibilities of it

This provides a complete picture of the job and includes (i) job title, (ii) details of the tasks to be performed, (iii) responsibilities involved, (iv) place in the hierarchical structure, (v) working conditions and (vi) how the job will be assessed and performance measured. The advantage of the job description is that it should attract the right type of people to apply for the job, as potential recruits will have an idea of whether they are suited to the position or not.

2 Draw up a person specification

KEY TERM

person specification a detailed list of the qualities, skills and qualifications that a successful applicant will need to have

This analyses the qualities and skills being looked for in suitable applicants. It is clearly based on the job description because these skills can only be assessed once the nature and complexity of the job have been identified. The person specification is like a 'person profile' and helps in the selection process by eliminating applicants who do not match up to the necessary requirements.

EXAM TIP

Don't confuse the job description and the person specification.

3 Prepare a job advertisement reflecting the requirements of the job and the personal qualities looked for

The job advertisement can be displayed within the business premises – particularly if an internal appointment is looked for – on the firm's website or in government job centres, recruitment agencies and/or newspapers. Care must be taken to ensure that there is no element of discrimination implied by the advertisement as nearly all countries outlaw unfair selection on the basis of race, gender or religion. Table 10.2 looks at the advantages of internal and external recruitment.

Internal recruitment	External recruitment
• Applicants may already be well known to the selection team. • Applicant will already know the organisation and its internal methods – no need for induction training. • Culture of the organisation will be well understood by the applicant. • Often quicker than external recruitment. • Likely to be cheaper than using external advertising and recruitment agencies. • Gives internal staff a career structure and a chance to progress. • Staff will not have to get used to new style of management approach if vacancy is a senior post.	• External applicant will bring new ideas and practices to the business – this helps to keep existing staff focused on the future rather than 'the ways things have always been done'. • Should be a wide choice of potential applicants – not limited to internal staff. • Avoids resentment sometimes felt by existing staff if one of their former colleagues is promoted above them. • Standard of applicants could be higher than if limited to internal staff applicants.

Table 10.2 *Advantages of internal and external recruitment*

EXAM TIP

The disadvantages of each method of recruitment are the reverse of the advantages of the other method. For example, a drawback of external recruitment is that it *does not* give internal staff a career structure or a chance to progress.

4 Draw up a short list of applicants

A few applicants are chosen based on their application forms and personal details, often contained in a CV (curriculum vitae). References may have been obtained in order to check on the character and previous work performance of the applicants.

5 Conduct interviews
Interviews are designed to question the applicant on their skills, experience and character to see if they are likely to perform well and fit into the organisation. Some interviewers use a seven-point plan to carry out a methodical interview. Candidates are assessed according to achievements, intelligence, skills, interests, personal manner, physical appearance and personal circumstances.

ACTIVITY 10.3

30 marks, 52 minutes

1 Draw up a job description for the head teacher's or principal's post at your school or college. [10]
2 Draw up a detailed person specification for this post. [10]
3 Produce an eye-catching and effective newspaper advertisement for this post (use IT if you can) including key features from the job description and person specification. [10]

THEORY OF KNOWLEDGE

Selecting the right senior managers is a critical decision for many organisations. Businesses use online application form screening, isometric tests, panel interviews and in-tray exercises, as well as interviews.

The board of directors of a company are hiring a new finance director. Discuss the role of evidence, logic and intuition when choosing between candidates.

Training

Having recruited and selected the right staff, the HR department must ensure that they are well equipped to perform the duties and undertake the responsibilities expected of them. This will nearly always involve training in order to develop the full abilities of the worker.

There are three main types of training:

1 Induction training is given to all new recruits. It has the objective of introducing them to the people that they will be working with most closely, explaining the internal organisational structure, outlining the layout of the premises and making clear essential health and safety issues, such as procedures during a fire emergency.
2 On-the-job training involves instruction at the place of work. This is often conducted either by the HR managers or departmental training officers. Watching or working closely with existing experienced members of staff is a frequent component of this form of training. It is cheaper than sending recruits on external training courses and the content is controlled by the business itself.
3 Off-the-job training entails any course of instruction away from the place of work. This could be a specialist training centre belonging to the firm itself or a course organised by an outside body, such as a university or computer manufacturer, to introduce new ideas that no one in the firm currently has knowledge of. These courses can be expensive, yet they may be indispensable if the firm lacks anyone with this degree of technical knowledge.

Training can be expensive. It can also lead to well-qualified staff leaving for a better-paid job once they have gained qualifications from a business with a good training structure. This is sometimes referred to as 'poaching' of well-trained staff and it can discourage some businesses from setting up expensive training programmes.

The costs of not training are also substantial. Untrained staff will be less productive, less able to do a variety of tasks (inflexible) and will give less satisfactory customer service. Without being pushed to achieve a higher standard or other skills, workers may become bored and demotivated. Training and the sense of achievement can lead to what were identified by both Maslow and Herzberg as important motivators. Finally, accidents are likely to result from staff untrained on safety matters.

EXAM TIP

When discussing the costs and benefits of training remember that the risk of 'poaching' is a reason often given by firms for *not* training their staff well. Perhaps they ought to do more to keep their well-trained staff instead.

Appraisal and development of staff

This should be a continuous process. Development might take the form of new challenges and opportunities, additional training courses to learn new skills, promotion with additional delegated authority and chances for job enrichment. To enable a worker to continually achieve a sense of self-fulfilment, the HR department should work closely with the worker's functional department to establish a career plan that the individual feels is relevant and realistic and in line with corporate objectives. In this way, an individual's progress and improvement can also be geared to the needs of the firm.

Appraisal is often undertaken annually. It is an essential component of a staff development programme. The analysis of performance against pre-set and agreed targets combined with the setting of new targets allows the future performance of the worker to be linked to the objectives of the business. Both appraisal and staff development are important features of Herzberg's motivators (see Chapter 14, page 144) – those intrinsic factors that can provide the conditions for effective motivation at work. An appraisal form is often used which will comment on the worker's ability to meet certain criteria and may suggest areas for action and improvement or recommendations for training or promotion. Figure 10.1 shows some examples of questions from appraisal forms.

A1 Score your own capability or knowledge in the following areas in terms of your current role requirements (1–3 = poor, 4–6 = satisfactory, 7–9 = good, 10 = excellent). If appropriate, bring evidence with you to the appraisal to support your assessment. The second section can be used if working towards new role requirements.

1 commercial judgement ☐
2 product/technical knowledge ☐
3 time management ☐
4 planning, budgeting and forecasting ☐
5 reporting and administration ☐
6 communication skills ☐
7 delegation skills ☐
8 IT/equipment/machinery skills ☐
9 meeting deadlines/commitments ☐
10 creativity ☐
11 problem-solving and decision-making ☐
12 team-working and developing others ☐
13 energy, determination and work rate ☐
14 steadiness under pressure ☐
15 leadership and integrity ☐
16 adaptability, flexibility, and mobility ☐
17 personal appearance and image ☐

A2 In light of your current capabilities, your performance against past objectives, and your future personal growth and/or job aspirations, what activities and tasks would you like to focus on during the next year? Again, also think of development and experiences outside job skills – related to personal aims, fulfilment, passions.

Figure 10.1 *Examples of questions from appraisal forms*

KEY TERMS

training work-related education to increase workforce skills and efficiency

on-the-job training instruction at the place of work on how a job should be carried out

off-the-job training all training undertaken away from the business, e.g. work-related college courses

induction training introductory training programme to familiarise new recruits with the systems used in the business and the layout of the business site

staff appraisal the process of assessing the effectiveness of an employee judged against pre-set objectives

Dismissal of employees

It may be necessary for an HR manager to discipline an employee for continued failure to meet the obligations laid down by the contract of employment. Dismissing a worker is not to be taken lightly. Not only does it withdraw a worker's immediate means of financial support and social status, but if the conditions of the dismissal are not fully in accordance with company policy or with the law, then civil court action might result. This can lead to substantial damages being awarded against the firm. Dismissal could result from the employee being unable to do the job to the standard that the organisation requires. It may also be that the employee has broken one of the crucial conditions of employment. Before dismissal can happen, the HR department must be seen to have done all that it can to help the employee reach the required standard or stay within the conditions of employment. Support and training for the person should be offered. The organisation must not leave itself open to allegations of unfair dismissal.

KEY TERMS

dismissal being removed or 'sacked' from a job due to incompetence or breach of discipline

contract of employment a legal document that sets out the terms and conditions governing a worker's job

unfair dismissal ending a worker's employment contract for a reason that the law regards as being unfair

Redundancies

KEY TERM

redundancy when a job is no longer required so the employee doing this job becomes redundant through no fault of his or her own

This is not the same as dismissal. Redundancy occurs when workers' jobs are no longer required, perhaps because of a fall in demand or a change in technology. Often, this is part of a company policy of retrenchment to save on costs to remain competitive. In 2009, General Motors in the USA made thousands of workers redundant as it tried to reduce massive losses. Directors argued that unless these jobs were cut, the company would continue to make losses which could easily result in further redundancies – or the failure of the entire business.

The way these announcements are made can have a very serious effect on the staff who remain – loss of job security – and on the wider community. If a firm is seen to be acting in an uncaring or unethical manner, then external stakeholders may react negatively to the business.

Redundancy can happen if a job that someone has been doing is no longer required and there is no possibility of that person being re-employed somewhere else in the organisation. Redundancy may also happen if, due to budget cuts, the firm needs to reduce its workforce.

Contracts of employment

Employment contracts are legally binding documents. Care must be taken to ensure that they are fair and accord with current employment laws where the worker is employed. The contract details the employee's responsibilities, working hours, rate of pay and holiday entitlement, the number of days notice that must be given by the worker (if they wish to leave) or the employer (if they want to make the worker redundant). The contract imposes responsibilities on both the employer – to provide the conditions of employment laid down – and the employee – to work the hours specified to the standards expected in the contract.

In most countries, it is illegal for an employer to employ workers without offering the protection of a written employment contract. In some states, for example China, a verbal agreement between worker and employer can also be legally binding if there is evidence to prove that both sides intended a contract to be formed.

EXAM TIP

The precise legal requirements of employment contracts are likely to vary slightly between different countries. It would be useful for you to research what these legal requirements are in your country – but you will not be examined directly on them.

ACTIVITY 10.4

Read the case study below and then answer the questions that follow.

India wants more flexible labour contracts

The Indian government has approved a proposal that would allow employers to shut down businesses with less than 100 employees without seeking government permission. This change to the law will allow employers to end employment contracts when economic conditions are bad. This greater flexibility will allow employers to save on labour costs when the economy takes a downturn. Trade unions have criticised the decision. However, some economists say the decision will encourage employers to increase jobs when conditions are favourable.

16 marks, 28 minutes (plus research time)

1 Explain the impact on **(a)** employers and **(b)** workers of this change in employment contract law. **[6]**

2 Research the employment laws in your country. What rights do workers have, if any, when managers want to close a business or a factory? **[10]**

Employment patterns and practices

In developed economies in recent years there has been a move away from traditional work patterns and practices. Traditionally, these were characterised by:

- full-time employment contracts
- permanent employment contracts for most workers
- regular working hours each week
- working at the employer's place of work.

A large proportion of the working population is now faced with very different patterns of work such as:

- part-time and temporary employment contracts
- teleworking from home
- flexible hours contracts

- portfolio working – Charles Handy, the business writer, has argued that portfolio working is becoming an increasing trend and full-time working for one employer for one's working life is a thing of the past.

The main reasons for these changes are:

- focus on competitiveness, driven by competitive pressures from globalisation, by cutting overhead labour costs
- need for greater labour flexibility with the rapid pace of technological change
- greater opportunities for outsourcing, especially in low-wage economies
- changing social and demographic patterns, e.g. increasing number of single parents for whom full-time employment might be difficult to fit in with their lifestyles.

KEY TERMS

temporary employment contract employment contract that lasts for a fixed time period, e.g. six months

part-time employment contract employment contract that is for less than the normal full working week of, say, 40 hours, e.g. eight hours per week

flexi-time contract employment contract that allows staff to be called in at times most convenient to employers and employees, e.g. at busy times of day

outsourcing not employing staff directly, but using an outside agency or organisation to carry out some business functions

teleworking staff working from home but keeping contact with the office by means of modern IT communications

portfolio working the working pattern of following several simultaneous employments at any one time

CONSEQUENCES OF CHANGING WORK PATTERNS AND PRACTICES

Assume that, as part of its workforce plan, an insurance company has decided that ten telephone customer service advisers should be employed. Should the firm's future need for these ten additional workers be met by:

- recruiting ten full-time staff on permanent contracts?
- recruiting 20 part-time staff on 'half-time' or 'flexi-time' permanent contracts?
- employing workers on temporary contracts that can be terminated at short notice?
- not adding to employed staffing levels at all, but offering outsourcing contracts to other firms or self-employed people? These will then supply a specific service or product, but will not be directly employed. This is used increasingly by businesses that want to reduce overhead employment costs.

Recent trends in labour recruitment have been towards employing more part-time staff on temporary contracts and using outsourcing and teleworking. The claimed advantages of a part-time and flexible employment contract are as follows.

For the firm

1. Staff can be required to work at particularly busy periods of the day but not during the slack times, e.g. banking staff needed at lunchtimes or theatre and cinema receptionists needed mainly in the evening. This will reduce overhead costs to a business. This flexibility offers firms real competitive advantages, as they can give good customer service without substantial cost increases.
2. More staff are available to be called upon should there be sickness or other causes of absenteeism.
3. The efficiency of staff can be measured before they are offered a full-time contract.
4. By using teleworking from home for some groups of workers, even further savings in overhead costs can be made, such as smaller office buildings.

For the workers with part-time and flexible contracts

1. This contract could be ideal for certain types of workers, e.g. students, parents with young children or elderly people who do not wish to work a full week and those wishing to improve their work–life balance.
2. They may be able to combine two jobs with different firms, giving greater variety to their working lives.
3. Teleworking allows workers to organise their own working day at home, while meeting pre-set targets and deadlines and keeping in contact with head office via the internet.

There are potential drawbacks of part-time and flexible contracts too.

For the firm

1. There will be more staff to 'manage' than if they were all full time.
2. Effective communication will become much more difficult, not just because there will be more staff in total but also because it may be impossible to hold meetings with all the staff at any one time. There could be greater reliance on written communication methods because of this.
3. Motivation levels may be adversely affected because part-time staff may feel less involved and committed to the business compared to full-time workers. It will be much more difficult to establish a team work culture if all the staff never actually meet each other because of their different working hours.
4. Some managers fear that teleworking will lead to lower productivity as workers cannot be monitored so easily as when they are present in the office.

For the workers

1. They will be earning less than full-time workers.
2. They may be paid at a lower rate than full-time workers.
3. The security of employment and other working conditions are often inferior to those of full-time workers. This is now changing in some countries. In all European Union member states, for example, the law now gives as many employment rights to part-time as to full-time workers. This is still not the case in other regions of the world.
4. Teleworking and temporary/flexi-time contracts can lead to much less social contact with fellow workers – social interaction is an important human need.

Offering temporary employment contracts is a way firms use to reduce the overhead costs of employing staff. Lower levels of job security can mean that 'safety' needs as identified by Maslow may not be satisfied and this will have a negative effect on motivation (see Chapter 14, page 143). Temporary contracts can be either full time or part time. They are contracts for fixed periods of time as opposed to permanent contracts. Permanent contracts only end when a worker is sacked, for example for poor discipline, made redundant or leaves of their own accord. The advantages and disadvantages of temporary contracts are similar to those of part-time contracts, especially the benefit of flexibility offered to employers. Such flexibility is particularly important to seasonal business activities, such as fruit picking.

The combination of part-time and temporary contracts gives firms the chance to create a small team of full-time staff – core workers – and combine this with a number of flexible workers, who are only employed when necessary. This is further enhanced by the increasing trend towards outsourcing, that is using outside self-employed contractors to perform specific jobs within the business rather than employing staff directly. These three types of contracts are termed 'peripheral' workers as they are not part of the central core of full-time employees (see Figure 10.2).

Peripheral
Temporary
Part-time
Self-employed

Core
Full-time
Permanent

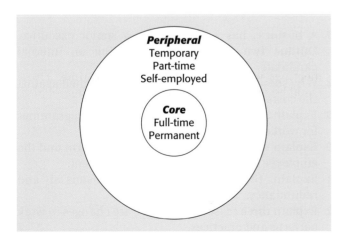

Figure 10.2 The differences between core and peripheral workers

Handy's Shamrock organisation

Another way of representing this trend towards fewer core staff on permanent and salaried contracts was devised by the famous business writer, Charles Handy. He first used the term the 'Shamrock organisation' (see Figure 10.3) with the three leaves made up of:

- core managerial and technical staff, who must be offered full-time, permanent contracts with competitive salaries and benefits. These workers are central to the survival and growth of the organisation. In return for high rewards they are expected to be loyal and work long hours when needed. As core workers are expensive, their numbers are being reduced in most organisations.
- outsourced functions by independent providers, who may once have been employed by the company. Also known as the 'contractual fringe', these workers provide specific services that do not have to be kept within the core. These may include payroll services, transport, catering and IT.
- flexible workers on temporary and part-time contracts, who are called on when the situation demands their labour. As the organisation demonstrates little concern or loyalty towards these workers, they often respond in kind. These workers are most likely to lose their jobs in an economic downturn.

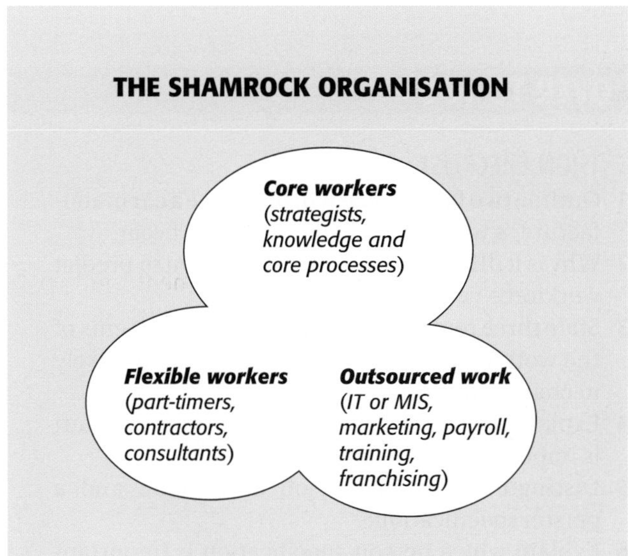

Figure 10.3 Charles Handy's Shamrock organisation

ACTIVITY 10.5

Look at the data opposite, which illustrate one of the most significant changes in the pattern of UK employment, and then answer the questions that follow.

26 marks, 45 minutes

1 Why might employees prefer part-time to full-time employment? [6]

2 What benefits could a business gain from employing:
   a more staff on part-time contracts? [6]
   b more staff on temporary contracts? [6]

3 What disadvantages might these trends in employment patterns have for (a) workers and (b) employers? [8]

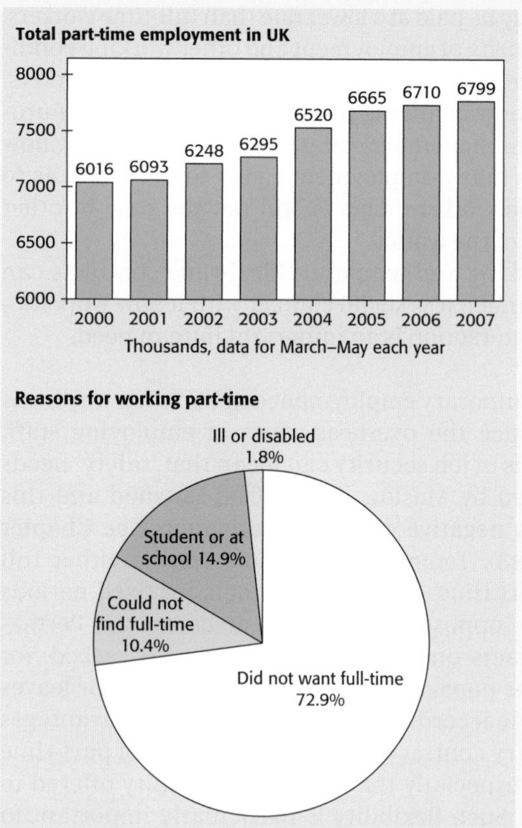

Source: Office for National Statistics

OVER TO YOU

REVISION CHECKLIST

1 Outline **two** factors that will influence a car manufacturer's workforce needs for the next year.
2 Why is it difficult for an HR department to predict workforce needs for the future?
3 State **three** reasons why the skills requirements of the workforce of a manufacturing firm are likely to change over time.
4 Explain why the recruitment of appropriate staff is important to a business.
5 Distinguish between a job description and a person specification.
6 Explain why a person specification is important to the selection process.
7 A business has a vacancy for a senior executive. Outline **two** reasons for appointing an internal candidate.
8 Why should the costs of training be weighed against the costs of not training staff?
9 Explain the importance of staff appraisal programmes for worker motivation.
10 Explain why it is important to both the firm and the employee to have a contract of employment.
11 Explain the difference between dismissal and redundancy.
12 Explain **three** reasons why there are changes in work patterns and practices.
13 Outline the **three** groups of workers identified by Charles Handy.

REVISION ACTIVITY

Read the case study below and then answer the questions that follow.

British Airways (BA) – has outsourcing gone too far?

BA has outsourced more of its operations than any other major world airline. All of its ticketing and internet operations are designed and managed through Indian IT companies. BA now employs relatively few IT staff directly and these are all employed on key strategic projects. The development of the 'shopping basket' feature on ba.com is an example of BA's tactical use of Indian IT companies. BA's overhead cost per passenger is one of the lowest in the industry.

The strike at Gate Gourmet caused chaos on BA flights in 2005. The airline could not serve food on thousands of its flights due to the strike at its only outsourced producer of in-flight catering. This was a low-cost, high-risk strategy that backfired – BA employed no catering staff itself and other catering firms were unable to produce the quantity of meals that the airline needed during the lengthy strike.

Source: www.silicon.com and www.personneltoday.com

17 marks, 32 minutes

1 Explain **two** benefits to BA from outsourcing many of its operations. [8]

2 Analyse **three** possible problems to a business of reducing its core staff to an absolute minimum and using flexible workers and outsourced suppliers. [9]

STAFF VACANCIES AT SELECT COLLEGE

Select College specialises in offering IGCSE and IB courses for students over 16 years old. The college is expanding rapidly. The deputy principal has responsibility for human resource management including recruitment. She has identified that the college will need three more administration workers and ten more lecturers. The lecturers are needed to set up the science and geography departments. The office workers are required to cope with the enrolment of the increasing numbers of students.

The type of employment contracts to be offered to these new workers needs to be decided. The principal is keen to see costs kept as low as possible. He is paid a share of the college profits each year. He believes that part-time and temporary contracts should be given to the office workers. The lecturers, he believes, should be offered full-time, temporary contracts. This would allow the college to let staff go at the end of the year if either they were poor performers or student numbers were lower than anticipated. 'We should pay a specialist recruitment agency to recruit and select all of the college's new staff. We would only need their services for about six weeks each year and we would not have to do any of the interviews,' he told the deputy principal.

However, she does not believe this proposal will work and responded to the principal, 'It would seem unfair to these new office workers and teachers if we offered them shorter-term contracts than our existing staff. Also, there is a national shortage of good science teachers and we need to motivate and keep good staff. We should also have full control over how new teachers are recruited and selected – we have to work with them, after all.'

EXAM PRACTICE QUESTION

Read the case study and then answer the questions that follow.

25 marks, 45 minutes

1 Explain the following terms from the text:
  a human resource management
  b recruitment
  c part-time and temporary contract. [6]

2 Explain the benefits to the college of workforce planning. [5]

3 Analyse the arguments against offering full-time and permanent employment contracts to the new office staff and lecturers. [6]

4 Evaluate the best ways for Select College to recruit and select new lecturers. [8]

11 Organisational structure

This chapter covers syllabus section 2.2

On completing this chapter you should be able to:

- analyse the main features of an organisational chart including levels of hierarchy, chain of command, span of control, flat and tall organisations
- identify why firms need to organise employees and analyse ways in which this is done
- (H) analyse delegation and accountability
- (H) understand the meaning of bureaucracy
- (H) understand the difference between centralised and decentralised structures and the factors that influence the degree of centralisation/decentralisation
- (H) analyse the matrix form of organisation, flexible structures and the informal organisation
- (H) understand some of the organisational theories of Peters and Mintzberg
- (H) analyse outsourcing of HR functions and evaluate whether firms benefit from this.

SETTING THE SCENE

What is happening to organisational structures?

Traditionally, head offices housed all key personnel taking all important decisions. Now, more and more firms are using 'flatter' and more decentralised structures where decisions are taken anywhere else but head office! Instead of all power being focused at the top of an organisation there is now much more involvement and collaboration in decision-making. Why are these changes happening?

- Employees are becoming better qualified and more knowledgeable – they do not want to work in formal hierarchies.
- Multinational organisations find that taking decisions centrally means they are not taking local factors into account.
- Communication systems are becoming quicker and more mobile.
- The old world was one of rigid and formal hierarchies. Today's world needs organisations that encourage and promote leaders who can push, convince and lead people to work in collaborative teams.

Source: www.timesonline.co.uk

Points to think about:

- Has your school or college got an organisational structure? Describe its main features.
- Why would taking all decisions at head office be a 'safe' but inflexible type of organisation?
- Do you think that businesses might need to change the structure of their organisation due to business growth and the need to cut costs and be more flexible? Explain your answer.

Fewer decisions are taken at head office when an organisation is decentralised

Introduction

A sole trader with no employees needs no organisational structure. Even if this sole owner were to take on just one worker or one partner, a sense of formal structure would become necessary. Who is to do what job? Who is responsible to whom and for which decisions? If the business expanded further, with more workers, including supervisory staff, different departments or divisions, then the need for a structure would be even greater. This would allow the division of tasks and responsibilities to be made clear to all. So what is meant by organisational structure? What would happen if it was confused or misunderstood? How does the structure impact on workers and managers? What are the key principles of designing and analysing an organisation's structure? These are the issues that we will look at in this chapter.

KEY TERM

organisational structure the internal, formal framework of a business that shows the way in which management is organised and linked together and how authority is passed through the organisation

The formal structure

A typical business structure is one that is based on functional departmental lines. Structures can be illustrated by means of an organisation chart. A traditional one, showing functional structure, is shown in Figure 11.1 This chart displays a number of important points about the formal organisation of this business. It indicates:

- who has overall responsibility for decision-making
- the formal relationships between people and departments – workers can identify their position in the business and who is their immediate 'line' manager
- how accountability and authority are passed down the organisation – the chain of command
- the number of subordinates reporting to each more senior manager – the span of control
- formal channels of communication both vertical and horizontal
- identity of the supervisor or manager to whom each worker is answerable and should report is made clear.

THE HIERARCHICAL (OR BUREAUCRATIC) STRUCTURE

This is one where there are different layers of the organisation with fewer and fewer people on each higher level – Figure 11.1 demonstrates this. In general terms, it is often presented as a pyramid, as shown in Figure 11.2.

Advantages

Many businesses are still organised in this way as decision-making power starts at the top but may be passed down to lower levels. The vertical divisions do not have to be based on functional departments – they could be based on region or country or product category, for example consumer goods and industrial goods. The rungs on the career ladder for an ambitious employee are illustrated by the different levels of hierarchy. The role of each individual will be clear and well defined, and there is a clearly identifiable chain of command. This traditional hierarchy is most frequently used by organisations based on a 'role culture', where the importance of the role determines the position in the hierarchy.

Disadvantages

Such a structure tends to suggest that one-way (top downwards) communication is the norm – this is rarely the most efficient form. There are few horizontal links

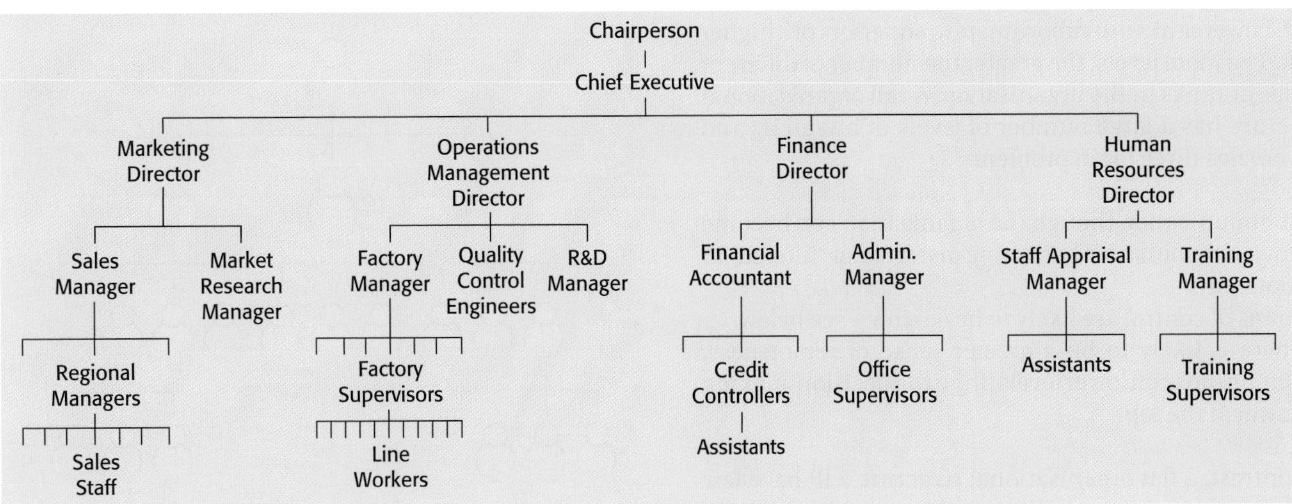

Figure 11.1 An example of an organisation structure

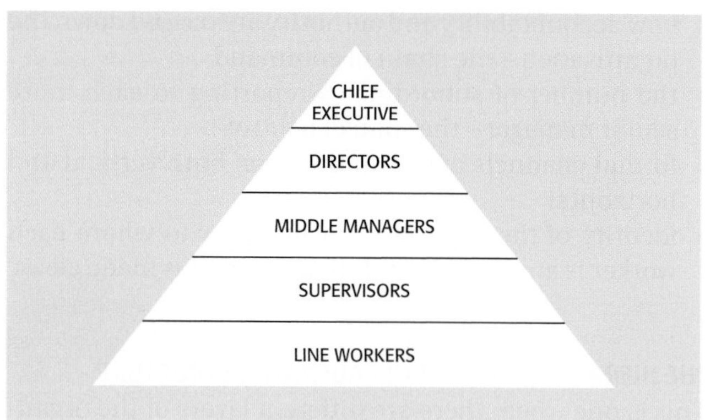

Figure 11.2 A typical hierarchical pyramid

between the departments or the separate divisions, and this can lead to lack of co-ordination between them. Managers are often accused of tunnel vision because they are not encouraged to look at problems in any way other than through the eyes of their own department. This type of structure is very inflexible and often leads to change resistance. This is because all managers tend to be defending both their own position in the hierarchy and the importance of their own department.

Key principles of organisational structure

LEVELS OF HIERARCHY

KEY TERM

level of hierarchy a stage of the organisational structure at which the personnel on it have equal status and authority

Each level in the hierarchy represents a grade or rank of staff. Lower ranks are subordinate to superiors of a higher rank. The more levels, the greater the number of different grades or ranks in the organisation. A tall organisational structure has a large number of levels of hierarchy and this creates three main problems:

- Communication though the organisation can become slow with messages becoming distorted or 'filtered' in some way.
- Spans of control are likely to be narrow – see below.
- There is likely to be a greater sense of remoteness, among those on lower levels, from the decision-making power at the top.

In contrast, a flat organisational structure will have few levels of hierarchy but will tend to have wider spans of control.

KEY TERMS

chain of command this is the route through which authority is passed down an organisation – from the chief executive and the board of directors

span of control the number of subordinates reporting directly to a manager

Chain of command

Typically, instructions are passed down the hierarchy; information, for example about sales or output levels, is sent upwards. The taller the organisational structure, the longer will be the chain of command – slowing down communications.

Span of control

Spans of control can be wide – with a manager directly responsible for many subordinates – or narrow – a manager has direct responsibility for a few subordinates. This difference would be illustrated on an organisation chart, as shown in Figures 11.3 and 11.4.

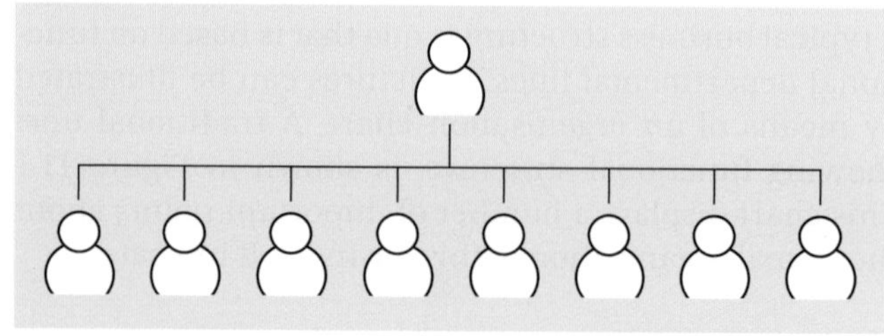

Figure 11.3 Flat structure with a wide span of control of eight

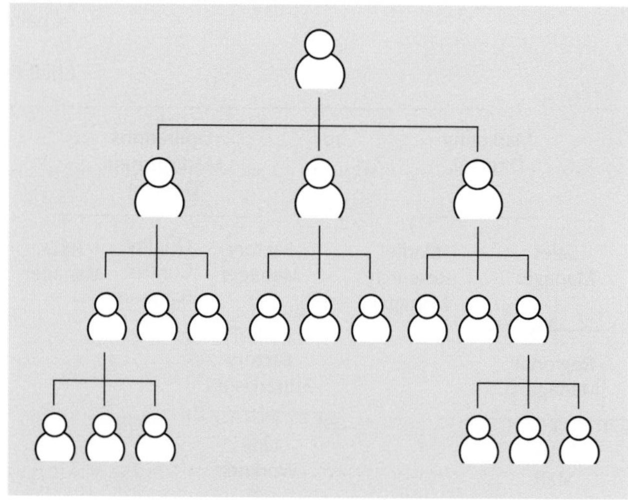

Figure 11.4 Tall structure with a narrow span of control of three

Factors influencing organisational structure

A range of factors will determine the internal structure of the organisation:

1 The size of the business and the number of employees.
2 The style of leadership and culture of management. If senior managers adopted an autocratic style, then narrow spans of control would be adopted in a hierarchical structure. A democratic leader would tend to adopt very few levels of hierarchy and delegate extensively. (See Chapter 13 on leadership styles.)
3 Retrenchment caused by economic recession or increased competition might lead to delayering to reduce overhead costs – this would reduce levels of hierarchy and shorten the chain of command.
4 Corporate objectives. For example, if one of the long-term objectives of the business is to expand in other countries, then the organisational structure must be adapted to allow for some decentralisation.
5 New technologies – especially IT – can lead to a reduced need for certain employee types, e.g. managers sending messages by email rather than by letters typed by secretaries. In addition, central control might be made easier by the flow of information through IT and this could make middle management layers less important.

The organisation of human resources

Firms organise their employees through the human resource (HR) function in different ways. An HR structure should match the business structure. A conglomerate, such as Sabanci Holding (Turkey) and Reliance Industries (India), with interests in many different industries, will have a decentralised and dispersed HR organisation. A single business company, such as a national water company, will have an HR department organised by function (staffing, training, rewards and incentives, organisation design and so on). A multinational business with widely dispersed operations, such as General Motors, will be likely to operate the HR function in geographical divisions. This will give the company a knowledge of local labour markets and employment laws when taking HR decisions.

HIGHER LEVEL

Delegation and accountability

KEY TERMS

delegation passing authority down the organisational hierarchy
accountability the obligation of an individual to account for his or her activities and to disclose results in a transparent way

These are very important principles which can have far-reaching effects on both the organisational structure and the motivation levels of subordinate employees. As Herzberg and other researchers have pointed out, the process of delegation, requiring workers to be accountable for their work, can be very beneficial to motivation. Generally, the wider the span of control, the greater the degree of delegation. Figure 11.3, which shows a wide span of control of eight, is likely to encourage delegation, whereas Figure 11.4, which shows a narrow span of control of three , is likely to lead to close control of subordinates.

Imagine a manager with a span of control of 15 subordinates. It might be impossible to closely supervise the work of each of these every day – the manager would have no time for more important 'strategic' matters. Thus, the manager will delegate authority to his or her staff, and will trust them to perform well. Clearly, the staff are accountable to the manager for good performance; but he or she retains ultimate responsibility for the work done in the department whether it was delegated to others or not. Table 11.1 summarises the advantages and limitations of delegation.

Advantages of delegation	Limitations of delegation
• Gives senior managers more time to focus on important, strategic roles. • Shows trust in subordinates and this can motivate and challenge them. • Develops and trains staff for more senior positions. • Helps staff to achieve fulfilment through their work (self-actualisation). • Encourages staff to be accountable for their work-based activities.	• If the task is not well defined or if inadequate training is given, then delegation will be unlikely to succeed. • Delegation will be unsuccessful if insufficient authority (power) is also given to the subordinate who is performing the tasks. • Managers may only delegate the boring jobs that they do not want to do – this will not be motivating.

Table 11.1 *The advantages and limitations of delegation*

Delayering

KEY TERM

delayering removal of one or more of the levels of hierarchy from an organisational structure

Many businesses aim for a flatter organisational structure to reduce the costs of management salaries. This process is known as delayering (see Table 11.2). It leads to wider spans of control and increased delegation to subordinates. This development in organisational structures has been assisted by improvements in IT and communication technology, which better enable senior managers to communicate with and monitor the performance of junior staff and widely dispersed departments. This has had the effect of diminishing the importance of the role of middle managers.

Advantages of delayering	Disadvantages of delayering
• Reduces business costs. • Shortens the chain of command and should improve communication through the organisation. • Increases spans of control and opportunities for delegation. • May increase workforce motivation due to less remoteness from top management and greater chance of having more responsible work to perform.	• Could be one-off costs of making managers redundant, e.g. redundancy payments. • Increased workloads for managers who remain – this could lead to overwork and stress. • Fear that redundancies might be used to cut costs could reduce the sense of security of the whole workforce – one of Maslow's needs (see chapter 14).

Table 11.2 *The advantages and disadvantages of delayering*

Bureaucracy

KEY TERM

bureaucracy an organisational system with standardised procedures and rules

This system is most commonly found in government organisations. It discourages initiative and enterprise as decisions are taken centrally and then put into effect by staff following set procedures and protocols. Max Weber, the sociologist, identified the main attributes of bureaucracy as rationality and efficiency. However, he also recognised its impersonality and ineffectiveness when a decision needed to be adapted to suit an individual case.

Centralisation and decentralisation

KEY TERMS

centralisation keeping all of the important decision-making powers within head office or the centre of the organisation

decentralisation decision-making powers are passed down the organisation to empower subordinates and regional/product managers

ACTIVITY 11.1

Read the case study below and then answer the questions that follow.

MAS must change strategy, says new boss

Loss-making Malaysia Airlines System (MAS) must raise labour productivity and double services in the region to become profitable, its new boss said in recent remarks. The national carrier's present hierarchical structure was unsuitable as operational costs were far too high, managing director Mohamad Nor Mohamad Yusoff said in an interview with the *Sun* newspaper. Productivity and customer service were also 'disappointing' and had contributed to a decline in overall performance, he said.

'I liken MAS to a house that is supposed to be double-storeyed but instead has five storeys. In such a situation, the position is untenable,' he said. 'We need to reduce the number of storeys. MAS's operational costs are higher than that of the industry and its competitors … each department does not operate according to expectations.' He said MAS aircraft were stationary too long and were under-utilised. He also voiced concern over poor productivity in the catering division. The airline has now reported losses for four straight years and has borrowings totalling 10.34 billion ringgit. On a suggestion that the airline should decentralise and separate its international and domestic operations, Mohamad Nor said this was being studied, but the management found that 'separation is not the best choice'.

Kuala Lumpur International Airport, Malaysia

26 marks, 50 minutes

1 Explain what you understand by:
   a hierarchical structure
   b productivity. [4]

2 Analyse two possible reasons why labour productivity is lower in MAS than other airlines. [6]

3 Evaluate the impact on:
   - MAS staff
   - business efficiency

   of adapting the organisational structure by reducing the number of 'storeys' from five to two (delayering). [8]

4 Assess the likely impact on:
   - the performance of MAS
   - staff motivation

   of a decision to split and operate separately the domestic and international divisions of the airline. [8]

Examples of decentralised businesses are those multinationals that allow regional and cultural differences to be reflected in the products and services they provide. Clothing retailers with operations in several countries often allow local managers to decide on the exact range of clothing to be sold in each country – it could be disastrous for a business to sell European winter clothes in Singapore, for example. Centralised businesses will want to maintain exactly the same image and product range in all areas – perhaps because of cost savings or to retain a carefully created business identity in all markets. See Table 11.3 for the advantages of centralisation and decentralisation.

ACTIVITY 11.2

Read the case study below and then answer the questions that follow.

Tata Steel reorganises structure

India's Tata Steel has reorganised its management structure to realise its corporate goal of becoming a leading player in the global steel industry. The company has formed a centralised body to create common strategies across the whole group, which has steelworks in the UK, Thailand and the Netherlands as well as India. The functions that will be centralised will be technology, finance, corporate strategy and corporate communications.

Source: http://uk.biz/yahoo.com

Carry out research into Tata's business. Find out what different industries and markets it operates in. Write a report recommending whether Tata should be organised with a centralised structure or a decentralised one.

Advantages of centralisation	Advantages of decentralisation
• A fixed set of rules and procedures in all areas of the firm should lead to rapid decision-making – there is little scope for discussion. • The business has consistent policies throughout the organisation. This prevents any conflicts between the divisions and avoids confusion in the minds of consumers. • Senior managers take decisions in the interest of the whole business – not just one division of it. • Central buying should allow for greater economies of scale. • Senior managers at central office will be experienced decision-makers.	• More local decisions can be made which reflect different conditions – the managers who take the decisions will have local knowledge and are likely to have closer contact with consumers. • More junior managers can develop skills and this prepares them for more challenging roles. • Delegation and empowerment are made easier and these will have positive effects on motivation. • Decision-making in response to changes, e.g. in local market conditions, should be quicker and more flexible as head office will not have to be involved every time.

Table 11.3 *The advantages and disadvantages of centralisation*

The matrix structure

KEY TERM

matrix structure an organisational structure that creates project teams that cut across traditional functional departments

This approach to organising businesses aims to eliminate many of the problems associated with the hierarchical structure. This type of structure cuts across the

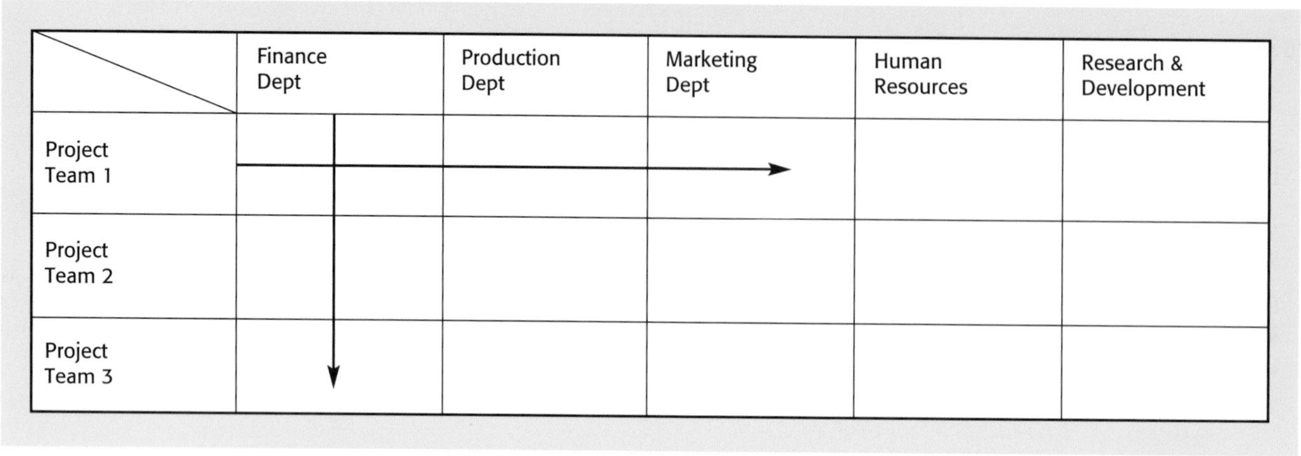

	Finance Dept	Production Dept	Marketing Dept	Human Resources	Research & Development
Project Team 1					
Project Team 2					
Project Team 3					

Figure 11.5 *A matrix organisational structure*

departmental lines of a hierarchical chart and creates project teams made up of people from all departments or divisions. The basic idea is shown in Figure 11.5.

This method of organising a business is task- or project-focused. Instead of highlighting the role or status of individuals it gathers together a team of specialists with the objective of completing a task or a project successfully. Emphasis is placed on an individual's ability to contribute to the team rather than their position in the hierarchy. The use of matrix project teams has been championed by Tom Peters, one of the best-known writers on organisational structure. In his book *In Search of Excellence* (1982) he suggested that:

- organisations need flexible structures that remove as much bureaucracy as possible by getting rid of as many rigid rules and regulations as possible
- the use of project teams should lead to more innovative and creative ideas as staff will be more motivated to contribute.

Advantages

It allows total communication between all members of the team, cutting across traditional boundaries between departments in a hierarchy where only senior managers are designed to link with and talk to each other. There is less chance of people focusing on just what is good for their department. This is replaced with a feeling of what is good for the project and the business as a whole. The cross-over of ideas between people with specialist knowledge in different areas tends to create more successful solutions. As new project teams can be created quickly, this system is well designed to respond to changing markets or technological conditions.

Disadvantages

There is less direct control from the 'top' as the teams may be empowered to undertake and complete a project. This passing down of authority to more junior staff could be difficult for some managers to come to terms with. The benefit of faster reaction to new situations is, therefore, at the expense of reduced bureaucratic control, and this trend may be resisted by some senior managers. Team members may have, in effect, two leaders if the business retains levels of hierarchy for departments but allows cross-departmental teams to be created. This could cause a conflict of interests.

The flexible future

Over the last 20 years, many large businesses, including most multinationals, have been forced to retrench, rationalise and downsize their organisations. At the same time, the increasing pace of globalisation and technological change means that huge organisational structures with many levels of hierarchy and slow bureaucratic systems have had to change. For example, if communication takes a long time to go up and down the hierarchy, then business is lost and the organisation gets a bad reputation for being unresponsive to customer needs.

So, in the current environment, businesses need a flexible and fluid organisational structure. More businesses are moving away from a traditional 'command' structure to one based around team-based problem-solving. This involves removing horizontal boundaries between departments altogether and reducing middle management layers to the absolute minimum. Future success will depend greatly on being able to respond rapidly to the changing business environment and this almost certainly means that the days of the traditional pyramid hierarchy are numbered.

ACTIVITY 11.3

Read the case study below and then answer the questions that follow.

Penang Valley Cars Ltd

Jim Mah founded the Penang Valley car-hire business six years ago. He started out as a sole trader with just three vehicles. His business now employs 33 people and it has a fleet of 2000 vehicles. Jim is chief executive. He has four fellow directors. They are in charge of finance, vehicle repairs, marketing and administration. The latter role includes dealing with all staffing matters. The finance director has three accounting assistants. The director in charge of vehicle repairs has two supervisors who report to him – one for the day and one for the night shift. They each have six mechanics working under them. The marketing department contains four people – one sales manager and three junior sales assistants. Administration has six office staff who take all the bookings and are responsible to an office supervisor who is under the direct control of the director.

This type of structure has served the business well, but Jim is concerned about the impact of further expansion on the organisation. In particular, he is planning two developments – one would involve renting trucks to other businesses and the other would be setting up a new office in another country.

22 marks, 35 minutes

1 Sketch the current organisational structure of Penang Valley Cars Ltd. Include all staff on your chart. [4]

2 Do you think the current structure is appropriate for the business? Give reasons for your answer. [6]

3 Explain how a matrix structure of project teams could be used by this business for its new developments. [4]

4 Evaluate Penang's decision to use project teams to manage the new developments. [8]

HENRY MINTZBERG

According to this renowned management theorist, an organisation's structure emerges from the interplay of the organisation's strategy and the environmental forces it experiences. When these fit together well with the organisational structure, then the business can perform well. When they fail to fit, the organisation is likely to experience severe problems. Different structures result from the different 'pull factors' operating on them. Mintzberg defined several organisational types that can result from the operation of these forces:

1 Entrepreneurial organisation – this has a flat structure, is relatively informal and there is a lack of standardised procedures, which allows for flexibility.
2 Bureaucracy (or machine organisation) – this is defined by standardisation and formalised work. It will have a tight, inflexible and vertical structure.
3 Professional organisation – this has a high degree of specialisation by experts who demand control of their own work. Decision-making is decentralised. This structure is typical when the organisation contains a high proportion of knowledge workers, such as an IT business.
4 Divisional organisation – this has many different product lines and business units. A central headquarters supports a number of autonomous divisions that make their own decisions and have their own structures.
5 Innovative organisation – in new industries, companies tend to innovate and function on an ad hoc basis. Film-making, consulting and pharmaceutical research are project-based industries that often use this structure. Companies use a team of experts from a variety of areas to form a creative, flexible, fast moving, functional team.

TOM PETERS

The Seven-S model, developed by the business theorist Tom Peters, is based on the theory that an organisation is not just a 'Structure' but is made up of seven elements distinguished by the 'hard S's' and the 'soft S's'. The hard elements are practical and easily identifiable from company documents and plans: Structure, Strategy, Systems. The four soft S's are less tangible and easy to identify: Skills, Staff, Style, Shared values. Continuously evolving and changing, the soft S's are determined by the people at work in the organisation and are therefore

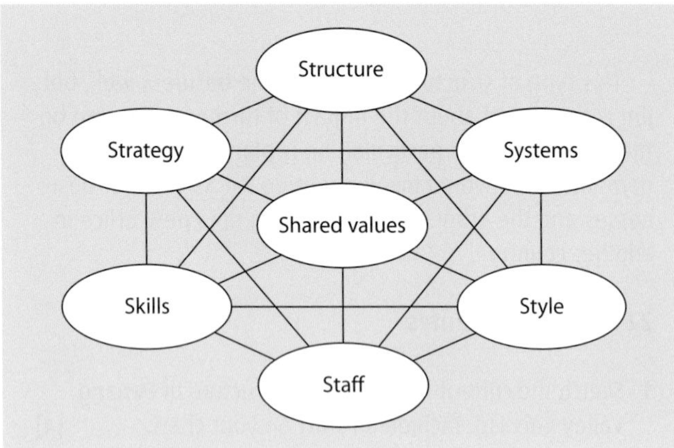

Figure 11.6 Peters's Seven-S model

difficult to anticipate or influence. The Seven-S diagram shows how each of the elements influences and is influenced by all of the other elements (see Figure 11.6).

Peters's Seven-S model helps to increase managers' awareness of the less tangible but critically important factors required for an organisation to be successful.

Informal organisations

Within any business there are two types of organisation – the formal structure and the informal structure. So far, this chapter has focused on the formal structure, but informal structures can also have a considerable impact on the success of a business.

KEY TERM

informal organisation the network of personal and social relations that develop between people within an organisation

The main focus of the informal organisation is the employee as an individual person. Power and influence are obtained from membership of informal groups within the business – and these groups may cross over departmental lines. The conduct of individuals within these groups is governed by 'norms' or normal standards of behaviour. If an individual breaks these norms, then the rest of the group imposes sanctions on them. Informal structures can either be beneficial or harmful to the business.

An individual's effectiveness at work can be greatly affected by the employees around them. A clever manager will try to use informal groups to the benefit of the business, for example by avoiding personality clashes between people in different groups or by basing team-working on informal groups. The problem may arise, however, that the informal group leader has more power and influence over the team than the formal leader – so managers need to choose supervisors carefully.

THEORY OF KNOWLEDGE

The senior management's decision to change working practices at Giant Electronics' Indian plant in Mumbai led to a mass walk-out of production line staff. Everyone knew changes had to be made; poor organisation on the production line meant a low level of productivity and poor-quality finished products. The senior management hadn't, however, understood the power and influence of three long-standing production line supervisors who saw the change in working practices as a threat, not least because they would have to report to a newly appointed senior manager who would reduce their influence. This was the seventh walk-out in three weeks and the disruption to production was causing concern to two of Giant's major customers.

Discuss the view that the informal organisation in a business has more influence over the success of a decision than the formal organisation.

Outsourcing HR functions

Many businesses do not perform all HR functions internally – they outsource some tasks to specialist organisations within the same country or overseas. The functions being outsourced may include:

- payroll management, calculating pay, income tax, other deductions and transfers into workers' bank accounts
- fringe benefits administration
- legal issues relating to employees, e.g. contracts and redundancy
- recruitment
- keeping HR records on training, appraisal and qualifications.

Outsourcing of HR functions is an increasing trend. Table 11.4 outlines the reasons for and benefits and limitations of outsourcing.

Reasons and benefits	Limitations
• Reduces costs. • Increases efficiency by using specialist HR companies. • Provides greater expertise, e.g. in the complex area of employment law. • Aids corporate growth by removing HR resources as a constraining factor. • Remaining internal HR staff able to focus on strategic policy and decisions. • In small businesses, allows owner(s) to focus on gaining new markets and increasing profit.	• Local knowledge, e.g. of the local labour market, and 'ownership' of HR processes may be lost. • The cost savings may not be significant as much new HR management software, payroll and record keeping could be employed, after appropriate training, in-house. • The process of outsourcing may give employees a sense of being controlled, recruited and paid by outside agencies. • Even extensive outsourcing of HR functions can never remove the internal management responsibility of forming good working relationships with employees – this cannot be delegated to other organisations.

Table 11.4 *Reasons for and benefits and limitations of outsourcing HR functions*

H

OVER TO YOU

REVISION CHECKLIST

1 Why do organisations need a formal structure?
2 Identify **three** benefits of a typical hierarchical structure.
3 Explain **two** drawbacks of a typical hierarchical structure.
4 What is meant by a 'long chain of command'?
5 What is meant by a 'wide span of control'?
6 Outline **two** problems associated with a 'long chain of command'.
7 Explain how the organisational structure of a business might change as it expands.
8 State **two** factors that could influence how a business organises its HR function.
H 9 Explain the benefits of a matrix structure.
H 10 Explain why some businesses have a centralised structure.
H 11 Outline the importance of delegation to a business.
H 12 Distinguish between accountability, responsibility and authority.
H 13 Would you advise a multinational furniture retailer to adopt a centralised management structure? Explain your answer.
H 14 Explain the Seven-S model.

REVISION ACTIVITY

Read the case study below and then answer the questions that follow.

HR outsourcing offers real benefits

'Today my company has 47 employees and enjoys a great relationship with CBR, our HR outsourcing firm. They have offered us increasing specialisation in HR functions as the business has grown. I don't worry about HR details; I just focus on targeting new markets and segments. Employee administration is truly the least of my worries each day. New job applicants think we are a much bigger company than we are because of the professional recruitment services CBR offers. They also look after all legal compliance issues.'

– *Roger, landscape garden contractor, Phoenix, USA*

'Since we have used Aussiepay specialists, our payroll problems are a thing of the past. Our HR staff costs are lower and the ICT function of payroll is now the burden of the outsourcing company, not us. Aussiepay facilitates different taxes and pay regulations for my company's five centres in different Australian states and creates individual management reports for each. It quickly and accurately calculates what deductions are needed for each employee and the company's total deductable amount. This used to be one of our biggest headaches.'

– *Amanda Brennan, corporate services manager, Langdon Ingredients, Australia.*

Source: www.outsourcing-hr.com and www.cbri.com (adapted)

16 marks, 28 minutes

1 Explain the following terms from the text:
  a outsourcing
  b HR function. [6]

2 Evaluate the advantages and disadvantages of outsourcing HR functions. [10]

EXAM PRACTICE QUESTION

Read the case study below and then answer the questions that follow.

MITSUBISHI MOTORS REJIG STRUCTURE

Mitsubishi Motors (MMC), the Japanese car maker that is 37 per cent owned by DaimlerChrysler, revealed significant changes to its senior and middle management structure at a shareholders' meeting. The changes reflected underlying tensions between the company's incoming German managers and established Japanese executives who found it difficult adjusting to the new culture. The restructuring aimed to weed out managers whose more traditional mentality could delay the sweeping reforms under way under the new management. Other managers were to be offered early retirement. MMC's chief operating officer and president wanted to dispense with managers at any level who remain locked into the 'length of service' mentality and acted ahead of the shareholders' meeting to weed them out.

Takashi Sonobe, president, demonstrated his commitment to reform when he announced 60 senior staff advisers – who were of an advanced age and made a marginal contribution to the company despite generous remuneration – would be removed.

Soon after he was made chief operating officer Rolf Eckrodt appointed a 'COO Team' comprising about 25 mainly non-Japanese executives from DaimlerChrysler. This team, drawn from different departments, was responsible for overseeing the implementation of the company's restructuring plan. Some long-standing members of MMC's middle and upper management resented the presence and power of the COO Team, all of whom were under 40 years old and who were controlling the strategic direction of the company. The tension between the COO Team and some of MMC's managers was described as stemming from Japanese managers with a 'job for life' attitude. This is not part of German management culture.

25 marks, 45 minutes

1 Explain what is meant by
  a delayering
  b culture conflict. [4]

2 Outline why 'culture conflict' seems to exist in this business. [5]

3 Analyse the possible benefits to MMC of reducing the chain of command through delayering. [7]

4 Discuss the possible consequences for the efficiency of the business of the new management structure described in the case study. [9]

12 Communication

This chapter covers syllabus section 2.3

On completing this chapter you should be able to:

- understand what are meant by effective communication and feedback
- analyse the advantages and disadvantages of different communication media
- evaluate their application in different situations
- understand the barriers to communication and how to overcome them
- analyse the importance of informal communication
- assess the importance of ICT in communication

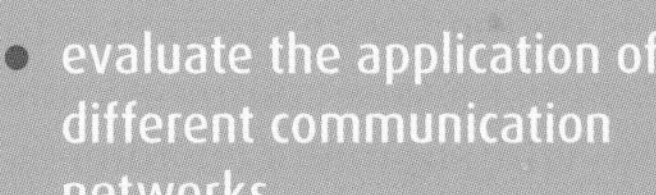

- evaluate the application of different communication networks.

SETTING THE SCENE

Companies use intranet to communicate with staff

Intranets – internal computer networks – are helping drastically to reduce many administrative jobs. Employees can now take training courses, communicate by email with colleagues, find out how much holiday they have left or check out internal job vacancies – all through their company's intranet. Intranets are helping to blur the line between work and leisure. For example, BP, the oil company, is developing a 'Virtual Village', an online shopping mall accessed through the company portal where employees can buy anything from computers to holidays. Companies now regularly use intranets for communicating with employees. When BA announced the closure of its second hub at London's Gatwick airport, the news came out first on BA's intranet. The speed of internet technology means employees can find out about such developments as they take place, rather than from the following day's newspaper.

BP broadcasts live events, such as the launch of its new brand and logo, to its employees worldwide over the intranet. At Anglian Water, a utility company with operations stretching from China to Chile, Chris Mellor, chief executive, uses his personal home page to encourage feedback from any of his company's 6900 workers. At BP, senior executives – often inaccessible to most staff – answer live questions from employees around the globe. Such technology allows employees – particularly those teleworking from home, on the move or in far-flung locations – to feel connected not only to the organisation but also to their colleagues. However, spending large sums of money on an intranet does not guarantee successful internal communications:

- In parts of Asia or Africa, telephone connections can be unreliable, and logging on can be frustrating or impossible.
- Intranet communication is only effective if everyone in the organisation has access to it.
- Employees already overburdened by email and other communications systems can find the intranet is simply another layer adding to their workload.
- Some believe technology cannot create a culture of freer communication and openness unless that culture has first been established by senior staff.

12 Communication

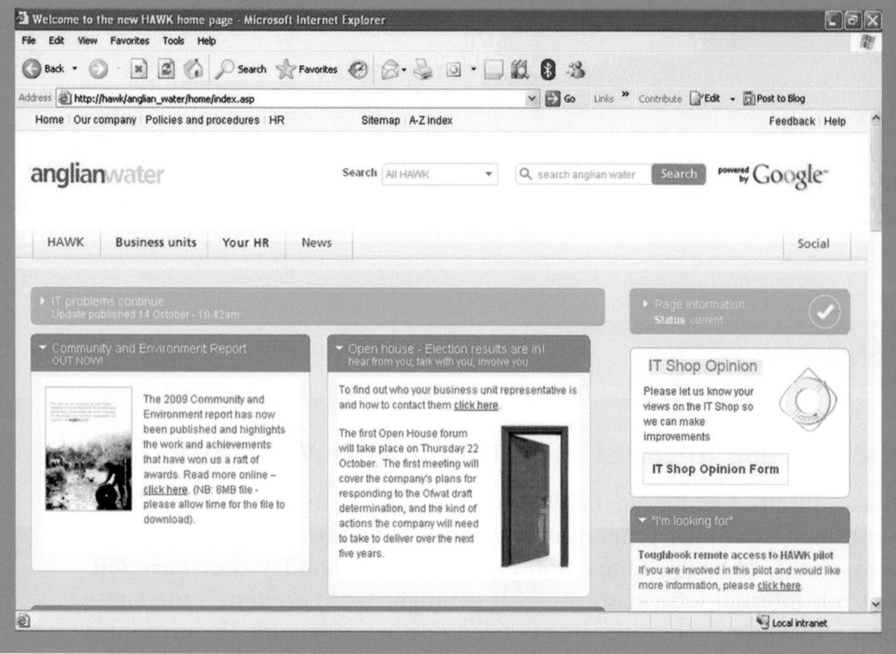

Points to think about:

- Why is it important that there should be effective communication within a business?
- Why is it also important for a business to communicate 'externally'?
- Do you think electronic means of communication are always the best ones to use?

The intranet is an increasingly common way to communicate internally

Introduction

KEY TERM

effective communication the exchange of information between people or groups, with feedback

Communication is only effective if the message has been received and understood by the receiver and the sender knows that it has been understood. Figure 12.1 shows the key features of effective communication:

- sender (or transmitter) of the message
- clear message
- appropriate medium (way in which the message is sent)
- receiver
- feedback to confirm receipt and understanding.

If the message has been sent, but there has been no form of feedback, then the effectiveness of the communication cannot be judged. Feedback is defined as the response to a message by the receiver. All businesses communicate. They communicate externally – with suppliers, customers, shareholders and the government, for example. Internal communication is between different people or groups within the organisation.

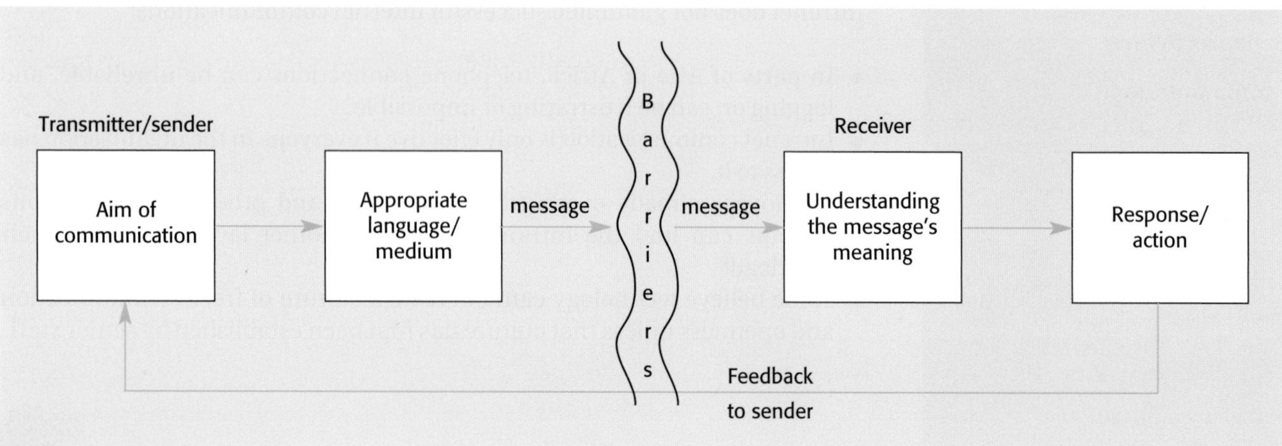

***Figure 12.1** Effective communication – barriers must be reduced or eliminated*

Importance of effective communication

The effectiveness of internal communication can have an impact on many areas of business:

- Staff motivation and labour productivity – if staff are encouraged to participate through group discussion, for example, then effective communication will aid motivation.
- The number and quality of ideas generated by the staff – if staff are asked for their ideas, then this can assist with problem-solving.
- Speed of decision-making – the more people who have to be communicated with, the slower the decision-making system.
- Speed of response to market changes – if changes in consumer tastes take a long time to be communicated to the main decision-makers, then the business will be slow to respond with appropriate products.
- Reduces the risk of errors – incorrect understanding of a poorly expressed message will lead to incorrect responses. This could lead to many internal problems, such as the wrong products being made or incorrect prices being set.
- Effective co-ordination between departments – this will be helped by good communication links between them.

Poor communication will lead to demotivated staff, unco-ordinated departments, poor customer service and a lack of overall direction for the organisation.

Communication media

KEY TERM

communication media the methods used to communicate a message

The range of communication media available can be classified as follows.

Oral communication

This can be one-to-one conversations, interviews, appraisal sessions, group meetings or team briefings. It allows for two-way communication and feedback and this should encourage good motivation. It is instantaneous and evidence of who attended the meeting, and, therefore, of who received the message, can be retained. It allows the sender or the transmitter to reinforce the message with appropriate body language. However, some oral communication can be ambiguous, there may be no written record of what was said, it might not be appropriate for complicated and technical matters and it can be costly in terms of time.

Written communication

Many managers still like everything to be in writing. They will, therefore, tend to use letters, memos, notices on boards, reports, minutes of meetings and diagrams for technical matters, such as house plans. Written messages can be referred to more than once, they should be an accurate record and they allow for the transmission of detailed data. However, they eliminate non-verbal communication, do not allow for immediate feedback and there is often no evidence that the message has been received and/or understood. Reports and research proposals are detailed forms of written communication. A report will contain a cover page, executive summary, main findings, conclusion and recommendations, bibliography and appendices. Research proposals also contain details of the thesis being investigated, theoretical background, research methodology and research methods.

Electronic media

These have the benefit of speed and are often combined with a written record. Internet and email use, intranets, fax messages, video conferencing and mobile telephones (which also allow oral communication) have all revolutionised business communications in recent years. However, these applications of electronic media also have their drawbacks:

- They may require staff to be trained, and the young are usually much more proficient in their use than older employees.
- They reduce social contact and can create a sense of isolation and an important social need may go unsatisfied. Staff may use company time to send personal messages.
- There are security issues with computer technology and hard copies of important messages are often kept in case of a virus.
- Finally, there is increasing evidence that IT can lead to information overload as a result of the speed and low usage cost of these methods. Too many messages – for example, the sheer volume of email messages can take some workers several hours to reply to each day – can prevent the really important communication from being noticed and acted upon. Too much information can also cause stress and a feeling of overwork. The benefits offered by IT and other electronic methods have to be weighed against their actual cost – in terms of equipment and training – and their other potential drawbacks.

ACTIVITY 12.1

EMAILS ARE RUINING MY DAY!

Two million emails are sent every minute in the UK alone. Office staff can spend up to half of each working day going through their inbox. This makes workers tired, frustrated and unproductive. A recent study found that one-third of office workers suffer from email stress caused by both the number they receive, the unnecessary length of some of them and the poor clarity of the language often used.

Now firms are being forced to help staff deal with their avalanche of emails. Some hire email consultants to advise on best email practice, while other firms now insist on an email-free day each week.

- Undertake research within your school or college to discover the average amount of time staff and students spend each day on reading and sending emails. Present your findings in a report. Recommend how the use of IT, to send messages at your school/college, could be made more effective in order to save time but maintain effective communication.

KEY TERMS

information overload so much information and so many messages are received that the most important ones cannot be easily identified and quickly acted on – most likely to occur with electronic media

non-verbal communication messages sent and received without verbal information such as facial expressions, eye contact, tone of voice, body posture and gestures and position within a group

Visual communication

This can be used to accompany and support oral, written or electronic communication. Diagrams, pictures, charts and pages of computer images can be presented by using overhead projection, interactive white boards, data projectors, DVDs and other means. The impact is increased if colour and/or movement are used. This form of communication is particularly useful in training or marketing.

Non-verbal communication

In person-to-person communications our messages are sent on two levels simultaneously. If the non-verbal cues and the spoken messages do not 'match', the flow of communication is hindered. The receiver of the communication tends to base the intentions of the sender on the non-verbal cues received.

Factors influencing choice of media

Managers will consider these factors before deciding on the best communication method:

- the importance of a written record that the message has been sent and received, e.g. an important new legal contract
- the advantages to be gained from staff input or two-way communication, e.g. a new staff shift system proposal could be discussed with workers before implementation
- cost – electronic media often require expensive capital resources but once these are obtained, emails are cost effective. Written memos are cheap, but how many people will see them? The cost of management time in meetings is important – it would be quicker and cheaper, but less effective, to email all those at the meeting instead
- speed – electronic means can be quick, but is this more important than allowing time for opinions to be discussed at a meeting?
- quantity of data to be communicated – the longer and more detailed the message, the less likely it is that oral communication will be adequate
- for clarity and to ensure that the message has been received, it may be better to use more than one method, e.g. a quick telephone call followed up by an official letter or order form will achieve both speed and accuracy
- size and geographical spread of the business – regular and frequent meetings of senior regional managers may be impossible in a multinational business.

Table 12.1 summarises the strengths and weaknesses of each communication method.

Informal communication

KEY TERM

informal communication unofficial channels of communication that exist between informal groups within an organisation

Have you ever heard about important events in, or decisions about, your school or college through the 'grapevine' before any official announcements? There is unofficial communication in every organisation – it takes place in the rest room or over the lunch table, in the queue next to the photocopier or in meetings before the official agenda begins. It may be no more than gossip, but much of it can be well-informed information about the organisation too. In fact, much informal communication is not necessarily about work at all – it might just be social interactive 'chat'. Table 12.2 summarises alternative management views of informal communication.

Method	Strengths	Weaknesses
Oral	• Direct • Can be varied to suit needs of receiver • Easy to understand • Can be questioned quickly	• Need to listen carefully • Affected by noise • Passive • No permanent accurate record • Can be quickly forgotten
Written	• Recorded – permanent record • More structured • Easy to distribute • Cannot be varied • Can be referred to again	• Often difficult to read • Message identical to each receiver • No body language • Feedback slower • No immediate response • May be misinterpreted • Costly and time consuming
Visual	• More interactive • Demands attention • Often easier to remember • Creates greater interest	• Needs close attention • Sometimes too fast • Not always clear • Interpretations by receivers can vary
Electronic	• High speed – virtually instantaneous • Interactive • Creates interest • Encourages response • Ignores boundaries • Good image for external communication	• Cannot always be received • Relies on receiver • Hardware is expensive • Risk of communication overload • Can be intercepted • Diminishes personal contact

Table 12.1 *Strengths and weaknesses of communication methods*

Informal communication is damaging:	Informal communication is useful:
• It wastes valuable working time. • It spreads gossip and rumours which can be unsettling and lead to feelings of insecurity. • It may result in informal groups banding together to resist management decisions – even though they may not have been officially communicated yet.	• It can help create important feelings of belonging and social cohesion. • Management can use the grapevine to 'test out' new ideas and see what the unofficial reaction might be – if it is too negative, they might never make an official announcement. • It can help to clarify official messages by talking them over with colleagues.

Table 12.2 *Alternative views of informal communication*

Barriers to effective communication

KEY TERM

communication barriers reasons why communication fails

Any factor that prevents a message being received or correctly understood is a barrier to communication. These barriers are much more of a problem for large businesses with operations in more than one location and with several levels of hierarchy.

REASONS FOR BARRIERS AND WAYS TO REDUCE THEM

1 Failure in one of the stages of the communication process

- The medium chosen might be inappropriate. If the message contained detailed technical language and flow diagrams, trying to explain these over the phone could lead to incorrect understanding. *Solution:* Select appropriate medium for the message.
- If a receiver forgot part of a long message given to him or her orally, then a written form would have been more appropriate. *Solution:* Use written form when the message is long or complex.
- A misleading or an incomplete message would result in poor understanding – 'send the goods soon' may be interpreted as being tomorrow when in fact the sender meant 'now, or as soon as possible'. *Solution:* Consider the clarity of the message carefully.
- The excessive use of technical language or jargon – terms that are understood by a specific group but not by others – may prevent the receiver from being able to comprehend what is required. Messages sent to branches or staff in another country may not be understood unless they are translated into the local language. *Solution:* Avoid using jargon where possible.
- If there is too much information – perhaps more than is actually necessary for the receiver to respond in the right way – the threat of information overload leads to 'noise', that is unnecessary data, which prevents the receiver from grasping the key elements of the message. *Solution:* Highlight important messages, and consider not sending less important ones.
- If the channel of communication is too long – the channel is the route through which a message is communicated from sender to receiver, as in tall hierarchical organisations – then messages will be slow to reach their intended receiver and they may become distorted or change their meaning on the way. *Solution:* Shorter chains of command (e.g. through delayering) will reduce the risk of distortion.

2 Poor attitudes of either the sender or the receiver

- If the sender is not trusted – perhaps because of previous misleading messages or unpopular decisions – then the receiver may be unwilling to listen to or read the message carefully. In addition, unmotivated or alienated workers make poor receivers. If workers have never been consulted on important issues before, then they may become very suspicious if the management style seems to be changing towards a more participative one. Workers with little interest in their work will not want to take the trouble to ensure that communication is effective. *Solution:* Establish trust between senders and receivers – this could be most easily achieved in a business where all staff are considered to be important with useful contributions to make.

- Intermediaries – those in the communication channel – may decide not to pass on a message, or to change it, if they are poorly motivated. This could occur, for example, if there has been a supplier's query about an order or a customer complaint. *Solution:* Keep the communication channel as short as possible and ensure feedback is built into the system.
- The sender may have such a poor opinion or perception of the receiver that no effort is made to ensure clarity of message or to check on understanding. *Solution:* Train and motivate staff to take an active part in communication process.

ACTIVITY 12.2

Which communication method is best?

Here are eight different examples of communication:

- safety notice on board a cruise ship
- sales order from a customer sent to the production department
- official warning to a staff member about quality of work
- sending of detailed architectural plans from one office to another office abroad
- need to solve a work problem with a team of staff
- 30 members of staff in different regional offices need to be given essential information
- need to check some details of a product order with the customer
- list of emergency telephone numbers in case of accidents in the factory.

24 marks, 42 minutes

1 In each case, explain why it is important that communication is effective. [8]

2 Suggest and justify a suitable method of communication to be used in each case. [16]

ACTIVITY 12.3

Palm Nut Oils Ltd

Managers of this company want workers to share ideas they may have about working processes, so a notice is placed on the canteen noticeboard and a suggestion box is placed in the canteen.

> On and after 1 January a payment of $25 will be given to anyone making suggestions for improving our computer-aided production processes, which we subsequently decide to adopt.
>
> Sabrina Patel
> Managing Director

An incentive is offered and a good response is expected. However, management is not trusted by the workforce, who see this as a worthless gesture, so either they do not make any useful suggestions or they make ones that are unprintable!

The message is written in the wrong language. This often happens when the sender is a specialist such as an accountant or engineer. The tone of the language is not right. This can happen in any form of communication but is most prone to occur when the message is spoken and is particularly true if body language can also be observed. In its layout, the message is formal and unfriendly. The managing director did not even bother to sign it – her name was just printed on the notice.

The wrong medium may have been selected. Some workers may not look at the noticeboard and so never receive the message. The receivers have negative attitudes to the sender and misinterpret the message. They need to be convinced; a more direct and personally involved approach was needed.

25 marks, 43 minutes

1 Outline **four** barriers to effective communication in this case study. [8]

2 Explain **three** other communication media that could have been used in this case. [9]

3 Recommend a more suitable method of communication than the noticeboard for Palm Nut Oils Ltd. Justify your answer. [8]

3 Physical reasons

- Noisy factories are not the best environment for communication. This indicates that the poor quality of the external environment can limit effective communication. *Solution:* Physical conditions should be appropriate for messages to be heard or received in other ways.
- Geographical distance can inhibit effective communication – interpersonal communication in particular will be very difficult. *Solution:* Modern electronic methods, such as video conferencing, are designed to overcome this barrier.

THEORY OF KNOWLEDGE

Antonio Rodriguez is a manager who likes to manage by walking around. He doesn't use the company BlackBerry other managers swear by as a way of keeping their subordinates 'on their toes'. He likes to get out amongst his staff and talk to them, whether it's to keep those who like shopping on the internet on company time on task or to praise those who have made their monthly sales targets. He only uses email to give very basic information to his subordinates and, as a personal rule, never sends any critical e-mails to his staff.

Prepare a presentation on the following theme:
'Electronic communication is never as good as a face-to-face conversation'.

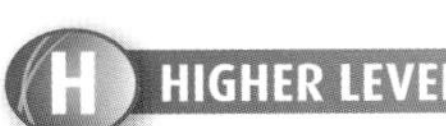

HIGHER LEVEL

Formal communication networks

KEY TERM

formal communication networks the official communication channels and routes used within an organisation

The internal communication structure of a business can be organised in a number of different ways – known as communication networks.

THE CHAIN NETWORK

This is typically used in a hierarchical structure, such as the police, army and civil service. One person, at the top of the chain (A – see Figure 12.2), starts off the communication message and this is passed on to the next person on the lower level (B, C and so on). This is designed for authoritarian leaders.

It has the weaknesses of both long chains of command and one-way communication. It does not encourage either two-way communication or horizontal communication and individuals at the end of the chain can feel isolated and demotivated. However, this method does give the leader control and allows an overview of the communication system.

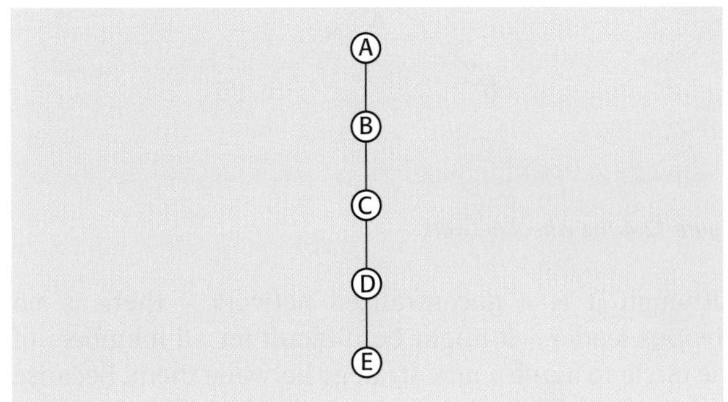

Figure 12.2 The chain network

THE VERTICAL NETWORK

Figure 12.3 illustrates a vertical network, where the leader, probably the owner, has four subordinates and communicates with them directly but individually – there is no group network here. This method could be used in a small department or any situation with a narrow span of control. It suggests only one-way communication and little communication between subordinates.

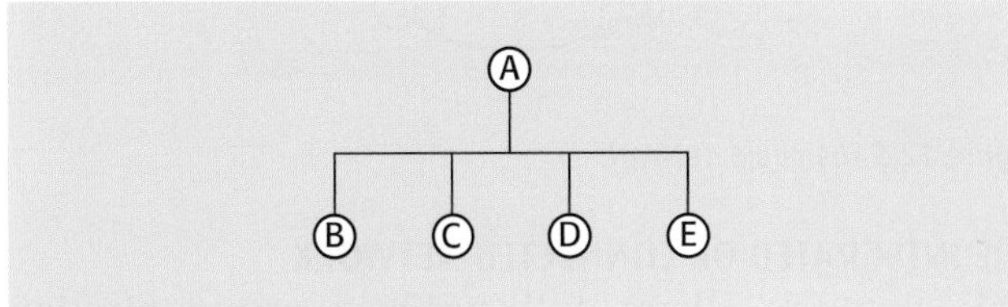

Figure 12.3 The vertical network

THE WHEEL NETWORK

In Figure 12.4, the leader is at the centre – or the person at the centre becomes the leader. There could be two-way communication between the leader and each of the other parts of the wheel, but horizontal communication is poor. The leader is in control and can limit formal contact between the others. This network might represent the situation of a regional manager communicating to each of the branch or site managers.

THE CIRCLE

In this network, shown in Figure 12.5, each person or department can only communicate with two others.

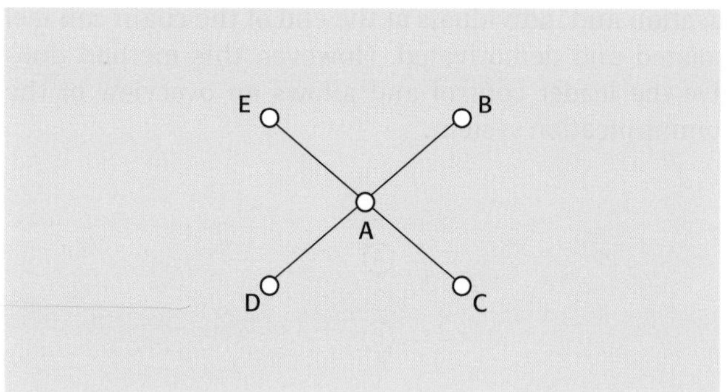

Figure 12.4 The wheel network

Although it is a decentralised network – there is no obvious leader – it might be difficult for all members of the circle to agree a new strategy between them, because of the slow rate of communicating with the whole group. These methods do not allow the receiver to question the message, to ask for further explanation or to discuss it with the sender. There is no assurance for the sender that the message has been received, understood and acted upon.

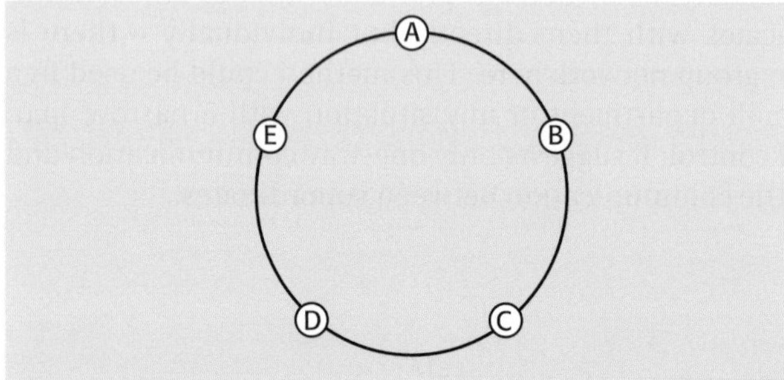

Figure 12.5 The circle network

THE INTEGRATED OR CONNECTED NETWORK

This network allows full two-way communication between any one group member – or with all of them. It is typical of team meetings or 'brainstorming' sessions. It allows a participative style of decision-making. It could assist in solving complex problems where input from all group members is needed.

These five networks featured in research work undertaken by social psychologist Alex Bavelas and his findings are represented in Table 12.3.

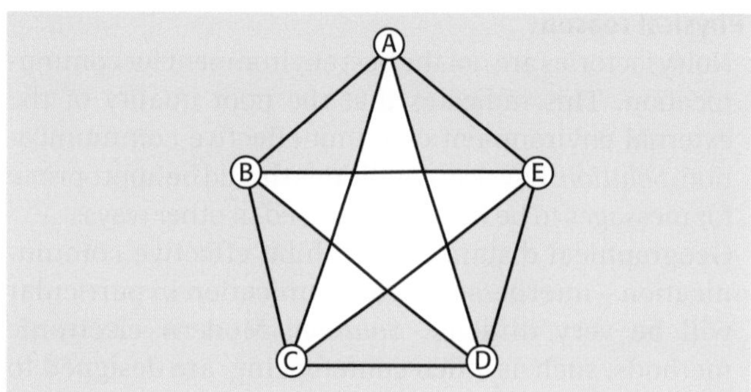

Figure 12.6 *The integrated network*

Table 12.3 summarises the effectiveness of communication networks.

	Centralised networks	Decentralised networks
Speed of learning new procedure	Fast	Slow
Speed of solution with simple problems	Fast	Slow
Speed of solution with complex problems	Slow	Fast
Originality of ideas, e.g. brainstorming	Low	High
Number of messages sent	Few	Many
Satisfaction/ morale	Low	High

Table 12.3 *Effectiveness of communication networks*

EXAM TIP

When discussing suitable communication methods for any business situation, try to assess which formal communication network would be most appropriate.

H

OVER TO YOU

REVISION CHECKLIST

1 Define 'effective communication'.
2 Outline **two** reasons why effective communication is important to a retailing business with branches in different towns.
3 Give **two** examples of communication media.
4 Using your answer to question 3, explain **one** situation for each method in which it could be appropriately used.
5 Explain **three** barriers to effective communication.
6 Using your answer to question 5, explain **one** possible solution for each barrier.
7 Why might staff be opposed to the introduction of a communication system based largely on ICT?
8 What do you understand by 'feedback'?
9 Outline **two** factors that will influence the choice of communication media.
10 Explain the circumstances when two-way communication is likely to be more appropriate than one-way methods.
11 Examine **two** reasons why poor communication might lead to poor staff motivation.
12 Explain **two** reasons why communication might be poorer in large rather than in small firms.
13 Explain **two** reasons why managers would be unwise to try to reduce the amount of informal communication in a business.
H 14 Distinguish between the circle and the connected networks for communication.

REVISION ACTIVITY

Read the case study below and then answer the questions that follow.

We all seem to be working in the dark

Metta Viravong had become completely demotivated by the latest problems in trying to communicate with the sales department. As production supervisor at Asian Lights plc, he was in charge of allocating and managing resources to make sure that sufficient output of light bulbs was available to match demand. The last scribbled note from the south-east sales manager had been the latest in a large number of messages regarding the correct product mix to manufacture. 'How am I meant to read this?' he had shouted. 'It is dated three days ago yet I have only just been handed it by the section head.' Apparently, she had just been handed it by the factory manager, who himself was sent it by the production director. 'I needed to know on Tuesday that sales of the standard bulbs are falling in the south-east due to the increased demand for halogen lamps and energy-saving light bulbs,' he complained to his production staff. 'If we had known that they were planning a big promotion on energy-saving bulbs we could have switched production in time.'

Problems with communication at Asian Lights had become more serious since the major takeover of Bangkok Brightlights ten months ago. The newly formed business was now twice the size. More managers had been employed. More levels of hierarchy had been created. Important internal messages were still checked by each section head or departmental manager before he or she passed them on to the next person who needed to know. The autocratic style of management had not changed with the takeover and the importance of 'keeping everything in writing' was still reinforced at every meeting with senior management.

Metta, being technically minded, was well aware of the latest advancements in IT and he wrote a report to the directors giving the details of all of the systems available with prices and specifications. 'I think I will give this to one of the directors myself rather than one of the section heads who may not pass it on.'

35 marks, 58 minutes

1 Was a report the best way for Metta to communicate to the directors in this case? Explain your answer. [6]

2 Discuss the factors that this business should consider before introducing internal communication based on ICT systems. [10]

3 Analyse three causes of communication problems at Asian Lights. [9]

4 Using the case study and your knowledge of communication media, networks and barriers to communication, examine the internal communication problems and possible solutions within Asian Lights plc. [10]

EXAM PRACTICE QUESTION

Read the case study below and then answer the questions that follow.

SWITCHING OFF IS NO WAY TO HANDLE JOB LOSSES – HOW NOT TO COMMUNICATE BAD NEWS

The voice at the end of the telephone on 16 October was insistent. No, there would be no redundancies among the 2400-strong workforce at the Panasonic factory in Cardiff. No, the informal rumours swirling around the grapevine in south Wales were without foundation. Two days later, Mr Fowler had changed his tune. Yes, there would be job cuts, limited to several hundred. Over the next few days, journalists who left messages at the Panasonic factory were left frustrated when nobody returned their calls. On 22 October the company dropped the bombshell many had feared; 1300 people were to be made redundant.

The company's handling of the affair was a masterclass in bad management practice. The elusive Mr Fowler, who had been asked to deal with press inquiries, is head of personnel at the factory. Mike Emmott, adviser on employee relations at the Chartered Institute of Personnel, says: 'A manager from human resources is not the appropriate man to announce big surprises that affect an entire community. You would have thought it was a task for the most senior person on the ground in the area – or possibly in the UK – to handle.'

Sony, which also announced mass job cuts, took a more common sense approach. Bill Besty, manager of public affairs at the group's corporate headquarters, spent several days at the Welsh factory handling inquiries about the 400 job cuts. 'I would never say to a reporter that we were not laying off people – then on Monday announce a redundancy programme,' he says. 'The idea of staff reading about redundancies in the newspapers before they are told is not an attractive one,' says Mr Besty.

'I was stunned and angry when we found out,' says Tony Harris from the GMB Union, representing the Panasonic workers. 'Although the cuts were voluntary and nobody is twisting anyone's arm, I would have thought they might have had the decency to get us in and talk to us.' Steve Tucker, a Cardiff newspaper reporter says Panasonic has mishandled the affair. 'We were receiving calls from workers who felt totally in the dark,' he says. 'People were panicking, asking: Are we going to lose our jobs? What on earth is going on? For a long time the company was denying anything was happening.'

Most companies would agree that their workers should find out about impending cuts direct, rather than through the media. 'What people fear most is not knowing. It is common sense to inform staff because rumours and insecurity are much worse,' says David Harris, managing director of a firm of business consultants.

20 marks, 35 minutes

1 Define the term 'effective communication.' [2]

2 Outline how this case could harm employer–employee relationships in this factory in the future. [9]

3 Evaluate the different ways in which Panasonic might communicate any future redundancies to staff and the media. Refer to all aspects of effective communication – the appropriate sender and receiver, the clarity of the message, the medium to be used and the opportunity for feedback. [9]

13 Leadership and management

This chapter covers syllabus section 2.4

On completing this chapter you should be able to:

- understand the nature of leadership and recognise the key differences in leadership styles
- evaluate the effectiveness of these styles to different organisational situations
- (H) discuss whether successful leadership results from natural skills or is a consequence of circumstances
- (H) apply the theories of Likert, Fiedler, Blake and Mouton, Tannebaum and Schmidt
- (H) understand the difference between leadership and management
- (H) explain the key functions of management by referring to theories of Fayol, Handy and Drucker.

SETTING THE SCENE

What makes a good leader?

Terry Leahy was until 2011 the chief executive of one of Europe's largest grocery stores – Tesco. It has over 350 000 employees in 2000 stores in 13 countries worldwide. Leahy's views on what makes a good leader are, therefore, important:

- 'Communicate important things simply – avoid management jargon as it is a barrier to understanding.'
- 'Ensure that people in the company know what is expected of them and how they can contribute to the company.'
- 'As leader, the most important thing is what you cause other people to do rather than what you do yourself.'
- 'Believe in people. I believe in the potential of staff. So I've never lost the belief that people are capable of incredible things if you give them the confidence and opportunity.'

Leahy spent a week of each year in a Tesco store doing the work that store workers perform. 'I am reminded how hard people work and how well they work. It's good work and I learn a lot and I bring ideas back here to the office.' His definition of a good leader is 'someone who takes you further than you would go on your own'.

Source: CNN and www.ebfonline.com

Points to think about:

- What seems to make Terry Leahy such an effective leader?
- Why do you think he puts so much emphasis on 'people' in his explanations of leadership?
- Do you think there is a difference between 'leading' people and 'managing' them? Explain your answer.

Introduction

Leadership is a key part of being a successful manager. It involves setting a clear direction and vision for an organisation that others will be prepared to follow. Employees will want to follow a good leader and will respond positively to them. A poor leader will fail to win over staff and will have problems communicating with and organising workers effectively. Most good managers are also good leaders – but some managers are not. Managers who focus on control of people and allocation of resources can fail to provide a sense of purpose or focus that others will understand and be prepared to follow. Without clear and charismatic leadership workers may be very well 'managed', but will they be inspired to help the leader and the business take a fresh direction and achieve new goals?

KEY TERM

leadership the art of motivating a group of people towards achieving a common objective

Leadership styles

There are four distinct leadership (or management) styles (see also Table 13.1):

- autocratic (or authoritarian)
- democratic
- laissez-faire
- situational leadership.

AUTOCRATIC LEADERS

Autocratic leaders will take decisions on their own with no discussion. They set business objectives themselves, issue instructions to workers and check to ensure that they are carried out. Workers can become so accustomed to this style that they are dependent on their leaders for all guidance and will not show any initiative. Motivation levels are likely to be low, so supervision of staff will be essential. Managers using this style are likely only to use one-way communication – that is, they will issue instructions but will not encourage any feedback from the workforce.

This style of management does have some applications. Armed forces and the police are likely to adopt this approach, as orders may need to be issued quickly with immediate response. Also, in crises, such as an oil tanker disaster or a railway accident, leaders may have to take full charge and issue orders to reduce the unfortunate consequences of the incident. It would be inappropriate to discuss these instructions with the staff concerned before they were put into effect.

DEMOCRATIC LEADERS

Democratic leaders will engage in discussion with workers before taking decisions. Communication links will be established on the two-way principle, with every opportunity for staff to respond to and initiate discussion. Managers using this approach need good communication skills themselves to be able to explain issues clearly and to understand responses from the workforce. Full participation in the decision-making process is encouraged. This may lead to better final decisions, as the staff have much to contribute and can offer valuable work experience to new situations. In the light of research by Herzberg, this style of management should improve motivation of staff, as they are being given some responsibility for the objectives and strategy of the business. Workers should feel more committed to ensuring that decisions that they have influenced are put into effect successfully. Employing the democratic approach can be a slow process, however, and this could make it unsuitable in certain situations.

LAISSEZ-FAIRE LEADERSHIP

Laissez-faire literally means 'let them do it' – or allow workers to carry out tasks and take decisions themselves within very broad limits. This is an extreme version of democratic management. There will be very little input from management into the work to be undertaken by subordinates. This style could be particularly effective in the case of research or design teams. Experts in these fields often work best when they are not tightly supervised and when they are given 'free rein' to work on an original project. Many scientific discoveries would have been prevented if the researchers concerned had been restricted in their work by senior management. In other cases, a laissez-faire management style could be a disaster. Leaving workers to their own devices with little direction or supervision might lead to a lack of confidence, poor decisions and poor motivation as they are never sure if what they are doing is 'right'.

SITUATIONAL LEADERS

This type of leader will adapt their style of leadership to the task or job that needs to be undertaken and the skills and experience of the group being led. If the group contains workers who lack specific skills and are unable or unwilling to accept responsibility for the task, then a high level of directive leadership will be needed. If, however, the workers are experienced and willing and able to perform a task and take responsibility for it, then a more participative or democratic style of leadership will be appropriate.

KEY TERMS

autocratic leadership a style of leadership that keeps all decision-making at the centre of the oganisation

laissez-faire leadership a leadership style that leaves much of the business decision-making to the workforce – a 'hands-off' approach and the reverse of the autocratic style

situational leadership effective leadership varies with the task in hand and situational leaders adapt their leadership style to each situation

democratic leadership a leadership style that promotes the active participation of workers in taking decisions

Effectiveness of leadership styles

There is not one leadership style which is best in all circumstances and for all businesses. The style used will depend on many factors including:

- the training and experience of the workforce and the degree of responsibility that they are prepared to take on
- the amount of time available for consultation and participation
- the management culture and business background of the managers, e.g. whether they have always worked in an autocratically run organisation
- personality of managers – do they have the confidence and strength of character to lead by persuading and motivating people to follow them or must they hide behind the authority of their role to 'dictate' what needs to be done?
- the importance of the issue – different styles may be used in the same business in different situations. If there is great risk to the business when a poor or slow decision is taken, then it is more likely that management will make the choice in an autocratic way.

Leadership style	Main features	Drawbacks	Possible applications
Autocratic	• Leader takes all decisions. • Gives little information to staff. • Supervises workers closely. • Only one-way communication. • Workers only given limited information about the business.	• Demotivates staff who want to contribute and accept responsibility. • Decisions do not benefit from staff input.	• Defence forces and police where quick decisions are needed and the scope for 'discussion' must be limited. • In times of crisis when decisive action might be needed to limit damage to the business or danger to others.
Democratic	• Participation encouraged. • Two-way communication used, which allows feedback from staff. • Workers given information about the business to allow full staff involvement.	• Consultation with staff can be time consuming. • On occasions, quick decision-making will be required. • Level of involvement – some issues might be too sensitive, e.g. job losses, or too secret, e.g. development of new products.	• Most likely to be useful in businesses that expect workers to contribute fully to the production and decision-making processes, thereby satisfying their higher-order needs. • An experienced and flexible workforce will be likely to benefit most from this style. • In situations that demand a new way of thinking or a new solution, then staff input can be very valuable.
Laissez-faire	• Managers delegate virtually all authority and decision-making powers. • Very broad criteria or limits might be established for the staff to work within.	• Workers may not appreciate the lack of structure and direction in their work – this could lead to a loss of security. • Lack of feedback – as managers will not be closely monitoring progress – may be demotivating.	• When managers are too busy (or too lazy) to intervene. • May be appropriate in research institutions where experts are more likely to arrive at solutions when not constrained by narrow rules or management controls.
Situational	• Style of leadserhip used will depend on the nature of the task and the work group's skills and willingness to accept responsibility.	• Varying the style of leadership may be difficult for some workers to accept and they may become uncertain of how they will be led in different situations.	• By allowing flexibility of leadership style, different leadership approaches can be used in different situations and with different groups of people.

Table 13.1 *Summary of leadership styles*

ACTIVITY 13.1

Read the following case study and then answer the questions that follow.

Disaster at the bakery

The fire at the bakery was a disaster for T & S Provisions Ltd. Eli Tarranto, the chief executive, had been the first one to be called by the fire services officer, at 3 a.m. 'The whole building is up in flames – we have not been able to save anything,' he had shouted down the phone. The next day, as Eli waited for his staff to turn up for work outside the burnt-out bakery, he was starting to form a plan. He had already contacted his friend who owned a small competing bakery and the estate agent from whom he had bought the land for the bakery four years ago. The bakery owner agreed to allow Eli to use one of his spare ovens if he sent his own workers to operate it. This would give him about 50% of his normal capacity. The estate agent suggested that Eli rent an empty depot on the other side of town for three months. He thought it would take around two weeks to have this equipped as a temporary bakery.

When workers started to arrive, Eli gave them clear instructions. They were shocked by the state of the building, but they seemed willing to help in this crisis. Six of them were sent to the friend's bakery to start organising production. Two were sent to the estate agent to pick up keys for the depot and had instructions to start cleaning the premises. The remaining three workers were to help Eli salvage what he could from the office records of the burnt-out building. Before this could start, Eli telephoned all of his major customers – he did not leave it to his sales manager – to explain the extent of the problem and to promise that some production would be back on stream as soon as possible. He then contacted suppliers to inform them of the disaster, to reduce order sizes and give them the new, temporary address for deliveries.

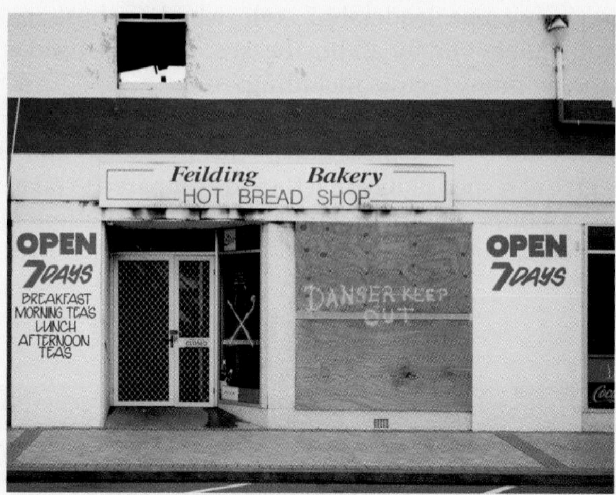

Even the most 'democratic' leader may act in authoritarian ways when dealing with a disaster that requires a quick response

15 marks, 23 minutes

1. Identify the management roles that Eli seems to have demonstrated in this case. [4]
2. What leadership style did Eli seem to be employing in the case? Explain your answer. [3]
3. Discuss whether this was the appropriate style of management to apply in this situation. [8]

Democratic leadership is increasingly common, for a number of reasons. Working people are better educated than ever before and have higher expectations of their experience from work – they expect higher-level needs to be partly satisfied at work. Many managers have realised that the rapid pace of change at work, as a result of technological and other factors, has increased the need to consult and involve workers in the process of change. People find change less threatening and more acceptable if they have been involved in some meaningful way in managing it. Despite these factors many managers will still avoid consultation and staff participation, perhaps because they find it very difficult to adapt to these ways. Others may so doubt their own ability to discuss and persuade that they would rather issue instructions that do not allow for any feedback from staff.

EXAM TIP

When answering a question based on 'the best' or 'most appropriate' leadership style, remember that this will *depend on* the nature of the task being performed, the importance of it and the skills and experience of the workers being led.

ACTIVITY 13.2

12 marks, 21 minutes

Identify what might be the most appropriate leadership style to adopt in each of the following situations. Explain and justify your answer in each case:

- **a** Training of staff in applying the company's ethical code of conduct.
- **b** Trying to find a solution to a long-standing quality problem on a bread production line.
- **c** An oil company responding to an environmental disaster resulting from a spillage involving one of its tankers.
- **d** Teams of IT software designers working on major new IT developments. **[12]**

HIGHER LEVEL

What makes a good leader?

Many studies have been conducted on this point – some argue that leaders are 'born' with natural assets that create an aura or charisma that others will find appealing. This is the essential idea behind trait theory. This theory suggests that effective leaders are in some ways naturally different from other people. A number of personal characteristics have been identified as being common among effective leaders including:

- a desire to succeed and natural self-confidence that they will succeed
- ability to think beyond the obvious – to be creative – and to encourage others to do the same
- multi-talented enabling them to understand discussions about a wide range of issues affecting their business
- incisive mind that enables the heart of an issue to be identified rather than unnecessary details.

Not all leaders or managers will have all of these important characteristics. Other research is more inclined to support the view that leaders can be trained to adopt the key attributes of good leadership. Indeed, critics of trait theory argue that it ignores the impact of life's experiences on the quality of leadership.

Leadership theories

LIKERT'S FOUR LEADERSHIP STYLES

Likert identified the following four main styles of leadership, which focus on how decisions are taken by management and the degree to which people are involved in decision-making:

1. Exploitative authoritative – the leader shows little concern for employees and their views, and adopts threats and other fear-based methods to ensure staff conform with decisions. Communication is almost entirely one-way and downwards through the organisation.
2. Benevolent authoritative – a combination of centralised decision-making with concern for other people. The leader uses rewards to encourage good performance. There is some two-way communication – but perhaps staff will only say what they think the manager wants to hear. There may be some delegation of decision-making, but the leader will take the decisions on all major issues.
3. Consultative – the leader makes genuine efforts to listen to the views of others, but decision-making is done centrally. This style must not be confused with a truly participative style – although employees are consulted, their opinions may be ignored.
4. Participative – the leader makes full use of participative methods of decision-making. There is genuine involvement of people lower down the organisation in decision-making, and there tends to be closer working between people across the organisation.

FIEDLER'S CONTINGENCY THEORY

This theory shows the relationship between a leader's style and group performance under differing situations. It is based on determining the most appropriate and effective leader style (or orientation) as the business situation changes from low to moderate to high control. Fiedler identified two broad types of leader orientation – relationship-orientated and task-orientated. He classified leaders into these categories depending on their 'score' on a sliding numerical scale – known as the LPC (least preferred co-worker) scale – depending on whether the leader is unfriendly (1) or friendly (8), hostile (1) or supportive (8) and so on. A high LPC score indicates a relationship-orientated leader, who is concerned with personal relations, heading off conflict and sensitive to the feelings of others. A low LPC score suggests a task-orientated leader, who is eager and impatient to get on with the job and has a no-nonsense attitude to getting the job done.

BLAKE AND MOUTON MANAGERIAL GRID

Blake and Mouton proposed the notion of a managerial grid containing five management or leadership styles based on the leader's relative concerns for people (e.g. considering the needs of team members) or production (e.g. emphasis on objectives and high productivity):

1 Country club leadership – the leader is concerned about the needs of the team, e.g. are they happy and secure? It results in a relaxed work environment but one where production suffers due to lack of direction and control.
2 Produce or perish leadership – the leader views employee needs as secondary to production targets. Decisions are taken autocratically and fear of punishment is considered to be the best way to motivate workers.
3 Middle of the road leadership – this style is a balance between the two competing concerns of people and production. Neither people nor production needs are fully met, which is typical of a compromise position. Leaders using this style settle for average performance.
4 Impoverished leadership – this leader is the least effective. There is neither a concern for getting the job done or for meeting the needs of team members. The result is dissatisfaction and disorganisation.
5 Team leadership – the Blake/Mouton model defines this as the pinnacle of leadership styles. If workers are involved in understanding organisational purpose and determining objectives, they will be committed to, and have a stake in, the success of the organisation. This creates a team environment which satisfies both people's needs and production targets.

Blake and Mouton's grid is shown in Figure 13.1.

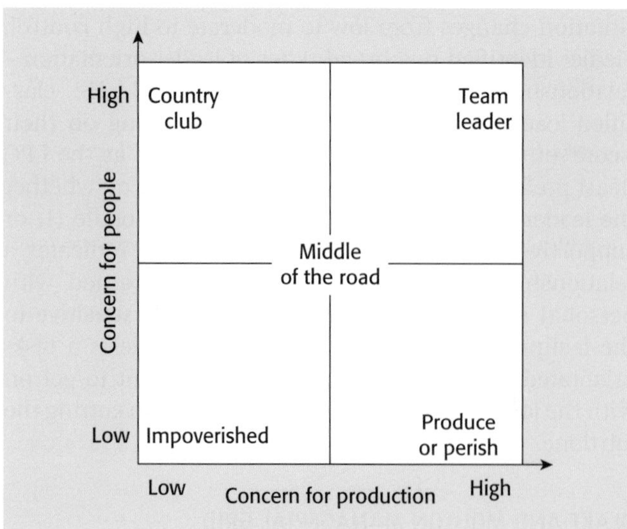

Figure 13.1 Blake and Mouton's managerial grid of leadership styles

TANNENBAUM AND SCHMIDT – A LEADERSHIP CONTINUUM

These two writers developed a continuum of control and decision-making, shared between leader and followers. At one extreme is the use of a leader's authority with little participation; at the other is freedom for subordinates with limited input from the 'boss'. At all points on the continuum both the leader and the followers have some control. The amount of control each party has depends on the leader's assessment of the degree of responsibility that the followers are able and willing to take on. To start with, the leader has most of the control over decision-making but gradually passes this over to the subordinates as they develop their capability, commitment and maturity. Tannenbaum and Schmidt argued that while the general trend is to pass control to followers, leaders can retrieve some if an emergency situation arises for which the subordinates have no experience.

The functions of management

KEY TERM

manager responsible for setting objectives, organising resources and motivating staff so that the organisation's aims are met

Table 13.2 summarises some of the key differences between leaders and managers.

Leadership	Management
Motivating and inspiring others	Directing and monitoring others
Innovators who encourage others to accept change	Problem-solvers
Stems from personal qualities or traits	Official position of responsibility in the organisation
Natural abilities and instincts	Skilled and qualified to perform role
Believes in doing the right thing	Believes in doing things right
Respected and trusted by followers – they want to follow because of leader's personality	Listened to by others because of status – not necessarily because of personality
Creates and develops a culture of change	Accepts and conforms to the 'norms' of the organisation

Table 13.2 *Differences between leaders and managers*

Managers 'get things done' – not by doing all jobs themselves but by working with and delegating to other people. The key functions of management are common to all managers in any size of organisation. These are best explained by reference to some of the best-known management writers, such as Handy, Fayol and Drucker. For example, Henri Fayol suggested the following:

1 Setting objectives and planning – all good managers think ahead. Senior management will establish overall strategic objectives and these will be translated into tactical objectives for the less senior managerial staff. The planning needed to put these objectives into effect is also important. A new production or marketing objective will require the planning and preparation of sufficient resources.
2 Organising resources to meet the objectives – this is not just about giving instructions. People throughout the business need to be carefully recruited and encouraged to take some authority and to accept some accountability via delegation. Senior managers will ensure that the structure of the business allows for a clear division of tasks and that each section or department is organised to allow them to work towards the common objectives.
3 Directing and motivating staff – this involves guiding, leading and overseeing of employees to ensure that organisational goals are met. The significance of developing staff so that they are motivated to employ all of their abilities at work is now widely recognised. This will make it more likely that organisational aims are achieved.
4 Co-ordinating activities – as the average size of business units increases, which is especially true for multinationals, so the need to ensure consistency and

ACTIVITY 13.3

Allstyles department store

Rebecca Allahiq's working day was busy and varied. She had recently been appointed general manager of the Allstyles department store. It had ten departments selling a wide range of products from men's and ladies' clothing to carpets, furniture and electrical goods. A film crew from the local TV company had asked if they could film a typical working day for a programme they were making about different people's working lives. Rebecca agreed and the ten-minute programme used six different clips of film with Rebecca involved in the following activities:

1 Meeting with all departmental managers to explain the store's pricing and promotional strategy for the next 'End of season sale'. At this meeting she expected all managers to inform staff of the agreed price reductions and the way in which goods should be presented in the sale so that consumers would have clear messages about the promotion.
2 Attending a planning meeting with senior executives from head office to agree the 12 monthly sales targets for the store. Rebecca explained that the opening of a competitor's store nearby was a factor that should be taken into account.
3 Presenting three shop workers with 'Reach for the stars' badges for outstanding sales records over the last month. She had her picture taken with them for publication in the store's internal newspaper.
4 Reviewing the poor performance of the electrical products division with the manager. Poor staff absence figures had contributed to this problem and Rebecca suggested that the manager should attend additional training sessions on staff motivation and monitoring of staff performance.
5 Meeting with builders, architects and planners to discuss progress on the new store extension. Rebecca was concerned that they were not working together closely enough and the project could fall behind schedule.
6 Settling a dispute between two departmental managers over which department should be able to stock a new electronic exercise bicycle – sports or electrical goods? It was agreed that it could not appear in both because of lack of space, so sports would stock it for six months next to gym equipment. Sales would be monitored closely and if it did not do well, then relocation might be possible.

(H) **20 marks, 35 minutes**

1 Identify all of the different management functions that Rebecca fulfilled during this busy day. [6]
2 Outline the personal characteristics that you think Rebecca needed to carry out all of these roles successfully. [6]
3 Examine the problems that this store might encounter if Rebecca was not an effective manager. [8]

co-ordination between different parts of the organisation increases. The goals of each branch, division, region and even all staff must be welded together to achieve a common sense of purpose. At a practical level, this may mean avoiding the situation where two divisions of the same company both spend money on research into the same new product, resulting in wasteful duplication of effort.

5 Controlling and measuring performance against targets – management by objectives establishes targets for all groups, divisions and individuals. It is management's responsibility to appraise performance against targets and to take action if underperformance occurs. As Herzberg points out, it is just as important to provide positive feedback when things are going right.

CHARLES HANDY

Charles Handy's views on leadership and the skills needed by good leaders can be summarised by the following extract:

> The word 'leadership' is beginning to replace 'management'. We are not able to use people like other resources. Today's new workers have minds of their own and have to be persuaded rather than told what to do. They have to be led rather than managed and that's very difficult and very different. In the past, management studies concentrated on analytical skills – analysing the future, analysing the market, analysing the cost – and the idea was if the analysis was right, then the plans could be put into action. Now a new set of softer skills are needed, skills to get people committed and excited. I like to talk about the 'e' factors in organisational leadership, 'e' meaning all the words that start with 'e', like excitement, effervescent, enthusiasm, energy. These skills are far more difficult to teach in classrooms.
>
> *Source: From an interview with Charles Handy by Jean-Louis Maxim (http://aurora.icaap.org/index.php/aurora/article/view/52)*

PETER DRUCKER

Peter Drucker is one of the best-known management writers of the twentieth century. He divided the job of manager into five basic tasks:

1 Sets objectives – setting goals for the group and deciding what work needs to be done to achieve them.
2 Organises – managers divide the work into manageable activities and select staff to perform them.
3 Motivates and communicates – managers create a team and communicate with them to achieve integration.
4 Measures – managers set yardsticks and targets and use them to appraise and interpret performance.
5 Develops people – in knowledge-based companies this is of crucial importance as people are the most important asset.

THEORY OF KNOWLEDGE

An almighty row in the workplace could help creative thinking if properly managed, according to new research. So does a consensual attitude strangle what you're trying to achieve? If you are reading this at work, look around you. Is there anyone you really want to shout at? Now could be your chance to do so, safe in the knowledge that it's good for dealing with the task at hand. New research suggests that companies would prosper by encouraging a robust exchange of ideas, even if this descends into a heated argument, because in this way policy and vision are constantly innovated and improved.

Source: www.news.bbc.co.uk

Examine the role emotion plays in the effective management of a business.

Mintzberg's management roles

To carry out these functions managers have to undertake many different roles. In *The Nature of Managerial Work* (1973), Henry Mintzberg identified ten roles common to the work of all managers. These are divided into three groups:

1 interpersonal roles – dealing with and motivating staff at all levels of the organisation
2 informational roles – acting as a source, receiver and transmitter of information
3 decisional roles – taking decisions and allocating resources to meet the organisation's objectives

Mintzberg's managerial roles are set out in Table 13.3.

Role	Description of role activities	Examples of management action to perform the role
Interpersonal		
Figurehead	Symbolic leader of the organisation	Opening new factories/offices Hosting receptions Giving important presentations
Leader	Motivating subordinates Selecting and training other managers/staff	Any management tasks involving subordinate staff
Liaison	Linking with managers and leaders of other divisions and other organisations	Leading and participating in meetings Correspondence with other organisations
Informational		
Monitor (receiver)	Collecting data relevant to the business's operations	Attending seminars, business conferences, research groups, reading research reports
Disseminator	Sending information collected from external and internal sources to the relevant people within the organisation	Communicating with staff within the organisation using appropriate means
Spokesperson	Communicating information about the organisation – its current position and achievements – to external groups	Presenting reports to groups of stakeholders (e.g. annual general meeting) and communicating with the media
Decisional		
Entrepreneur	Looking for new opportunities to develop the business	Encouraging new ideas from within the business and holding meetings to put new ideas into effect
Disturbance handler	Responding to changing situations that may put the business at risk Taking responsibility when threatening factors develop	Taking decisions on how the business should respond to threats, such as new competitors or changes in the economic environment
Resource allocator	Deciding on the allocation of the organisation's financial, human and other resources	Drawing up and approving estimates and budgets Deciding on staffing levels for departments
Negotiator	Representing the organisation in all important negotiations, e.g. with government	Conducting negotiations and building up official links between the business and other organisations

Table 13.3 *Managerial roles according to Mintzberg*

H

OVER TO YOU

REVISION CHECKLIST

1 Explain what you consider to be **three** functions of managers.
2 Outline **two** personality characteristics that you think are important for a successful leader to have.
3 Explain the autocratic (authoritarian) style of management.
4 Under what circumstances might this style of management be necessary?
5 Under what circumstances would the laissez-faire style not be an appropriate style of management?
6 Explain the differences between democratic and laissez-faire leadership styles.
7 Would all workers prefer to operate under democratic management? Explain your answer.
(H) 8 Explain how the manager of a multinational business operating in your country could demonstrate **four** of Mintzberg's roles of management.
(H) 9 Give examples to explain why one manager may need to adopt different styles of management in different circumstances.
(H) 10 Contrast the views on leadership and management of Henri Fayol and Charles Handy.

REVISION ACTIVITY

Read the case study below and then answer the questions that follow.

Leadership styles at McNuggets

McNuggets, one of Asia's largest chains of fast-food restaurants, has established a reputation for cheap meals of consistent quality with rapid customer service. Research surveys suggest that the public appreciate that, no matter which restaurant they are in, they can always depend on buying exactly the same range of dishes, at similar prices with the same quality standards. This reputation is built on a very detailed training programme for staff – failure to pass the end-of-course test or failure to observe the methods and work practices taught would lead to demotion or dismissal. Every single activity of the workers is laid down in company regulations. For example:

- all customers to be greeted with the same welcome
- chicken nuggets to be cooked for exactly two minutes in oil at 100 degrees C
- a portion of French fries to contain 150 grams, to be salted with 10 grams of salt and to be kept for no more than five minutes before sale – they would then have to be disposed of
- staff to be trained to specialise in undertaking two tasks within the restaurant.

The managers at McNuggets believe they have 'thought of everything' and that workers do not have to show initiative – there is a set procedure to deal with any problem. Workers are well looked after. The pay rate per hour is competitive, there are free uniforms and staff meals, and bonus systems are paid to staff who, in the manager's view, have given the best customer service each month. Regular meetings are held at which information about branch performance is discussed with the staff. They are encouraged to air their views but are told that they cannot, under any circumstances, change the method of working laid down by McNuggets head office. Despite what the managers consider to be good working conditions, the staff turnover is very high and absenteeism is a problem.

30 marks, 45 minutes

1 Which style of leadership/management seems to be used at McNuggets? Justify your answer. [4]

2 Using your knowledge of leadership styles, how would you account for the apparent low levels of motivation at McNuggets restaurants? [8]

3 Analyse how a different leadership style might improve motivation of staff within these restaurants. [8]

4 To what extent is the style of leadership used at McNuggets appropriate for a business such as this? [10]

EXAM PRACTICE QUESTION

Read the case study below and then answer the questions that follow.

CATERING AT LE MENU

Le Menu is a catering company, which was founded in 2003 by brothers Oscar and Pierre Decaux. The business specialises in providing high-quality catering for corporate hospitality and private clients. This is a high-pressure operation. A client company will, for example, hire Le Menu to cater for 200 guests at a race meeting. This will involve setting up a mobile kitchen at the racecourse the day before the event and then producing 200 five-course meals, along with canapés and drinks on the day. Apart from Oscar and Pierre the business has four other permanent staff including a head chef, an assistant chef, an administrative assistant and a driver. When Le Menu is catering a large function, such as the racecourse event, it hires temporary staff from an agency. Some of the temporary staff will have regularly worked for Le Menu, but often there will be new staff as well.

Oscar is a tough, direct manager, who tells workers exactly what he wants and then expects them always to meet his high standards. If not, he is quick to let them know; he has a reputation for dismissing temporary workers part way through an event. Pierre is much calmer, preferring to consult with his staff. While Oscar takes the lead during events, Pierre is more involved with strategy. Pierre will, for example, work with Le Menu's chefs on the type of food to prepare for an event.

Le Menu currently faces two major problems:

- It struggles to recruit agency staff because temporary workers do not like Oscar's management.
- The company often overspends on food at its catering events.

20 marks, 35 minutes

1 Explain the types of leadership style Pierre and Oscar most closely represent. [6]

2 Analyse the possible reasons why Le Menu overspends on food. [6]

3 Discuss the advantages and disadvantages to Le Menu of Oscar's style of leadership. [8]

14 Motivation

This chapter covers syllabus section 2.5

On completing this chapter you should be able to:

- understand what motivation is and analyse intrinsic needs and extrinsic needs
- discuss the motivational theories of Taylor, Maslow, McGregor and Herzberg and their relevance to businesses today
- evaluate different forms of financial motivation and their impact on motivation
- assess the role of non-financial methods of motivation and evaluate their impact
- (H) apply the content theories of Mayo and McClelland and the process theories of Vroom and Adams.

SETTING THE SCENE

How important is pay for motivating workers?

Many studies have been undertaken to try to explain what motivates workers. There seems to be some agreement that pay and benefits are important in encouraging staff to work well, but these are not necessarily the most important factors. Work enjoyment, work challenges and recognition for work well done – these are the factors most frequently quoted by employees when asked what keeps them with their current employer. Compared to job satisfaction and pay, benefits (financial and non-financial) have a smaller role in terms of recruitment, retention and motivation.

A recent employee survey led to the following response rate in answer to the question: What increases your morale and motivation?

Increased pay	65%
Increased bonuses	28%
Recognition from managers	22%
Career development through training	20%
Improved career prospects	17%
Option to work flexible hours	17%
Increased benefits: holidays/pensions/discounts	15%
Better work environment	11%
Help with childcare	7%
Option to work from home	6%

Research carried out by the mobile phone company O2 found that 85% of employees would be more loyal to their company if they were praised for their work and 100% suggested that they would stay in their jobs longer if thanked more often. Just under 50% of workers had either never been thanked by their companies or could not remember the last time they were. Finally, managers should take note that 71% of workers would be willing to work harder if they got more recognition for the work they did.

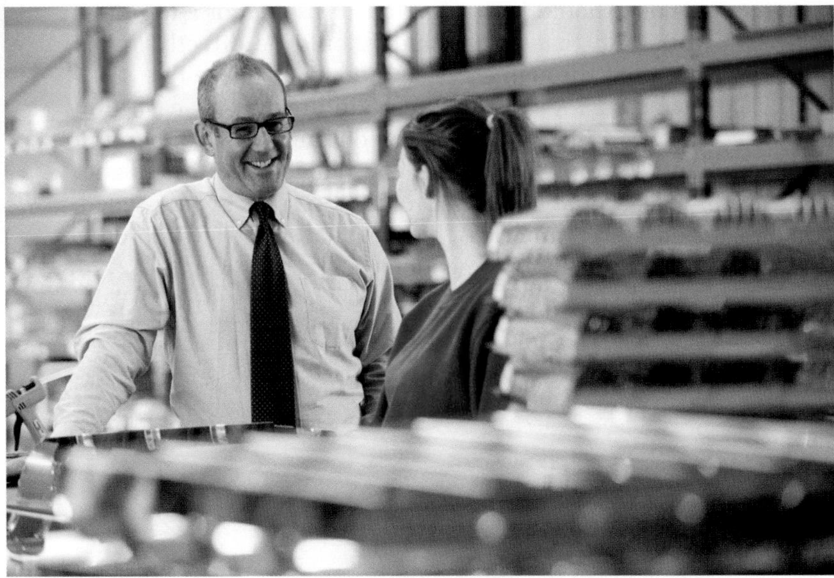

Points to think about:

- Why do you think that pay and bonuses are not the most important factor for *all* workers?
- Explain why 'loyalty' and 'working harder' are important to a business of your choice.
- Why do you think 'recognition' is important to many workers? Is it important to you?

Introduction

Well-motivated workers will help an organisation achieve its objectives as cost effectively as possible. Motivated workers will also be trying to reach their own personal goals by satisfying their own needs. Employers need to be aware of extrinsic needs, such as pay, which can provide motivation even if the job itself does not. Intrinsic motivation stems from the nature of the job itself but this does not mean that employers can pay workers doing interesting work nothing at all! Some rewards will be needed even for workers driven by the fulfilment of intrinsic needs.

Unmotivated or demotivated staff will not perform effectively, offering only the minimum of what is expected. Motivation levels have a direct impact on productivity levels and the competitiveness of the business – highly motivated workers have high productivity and this reduces unit costs. Motivated staff will be keen to stay with the firm, reducing the costs of labour turnover. They will be more likely to offer useful suggestions and to contribute in ways other than their contractual obligations. They will often actively seek promotion and responsibility. In contrast, some indicators of poor staff motivation are shown in Table 14.1.

KEY TERMS

motivation the intrinsic and extrinsic factors that stimulate people to take actions that lead to achieving a goal

intrinsic motivation comes from the satisfaction derived from working on and completing a task

extrinsic motivation comes from external rewards associated with working on a task, for example pay and other benefits

Indicator	Explanation
Absenteeism	Deliberate absence for which there is not a satisfactory explanation; often follows a pattern.
Lateness	Often becomes habitual.
Poor performance	Poor-quality work; low levels of work or greater waste of materials.
Accidents	Poorly motivated workers are often more careless, concentrate less on their work or distract others, and this increases the likelihood of accidents.
Labour turnover	People leave for reasons that are not positive; even if they do not get other jobs, they spend time in trying to do so.
Grievances	There are more of them within the workforce and there might be more union disputes.
Poor response rate	Workers do not respond well to orders or leadership and any response is often slow.

Table 14.1 *Some indicators of poor staff motivation*

Motivation theories

CONTENT THEORIES

These theories are based on the assumption that individuals are motivated by the desire to fulfil their inner needs. They focus on the human needs that energise and direct behaviour and how managers can create conditions that allow workers to satisfy them.

F. W. TAYLOR AND SCIENTIFIC MANAGEMENT

Taylor made the first serious attempt to analyse worker motivation. He aimed to advise management on the best ways to increase worker performance and productivity. The techniques he used – of establishing an idea or hypothesis, studying and recording performance at work, altering working methods and re-recording performance – are still used in modern industry. This approach has become known as 'scientific management' due to the detailed recording and analysis of results that it involves.

Taylor's main aim was to reduce the level of inefficiency that existed in the US manufacturing industry. Any productivity gains could then, he argued, be shared between business owners and workers. The scope for efficiency gains in early twentieth-century manufacturing plants was huge. Most workers were untrained and non-specialised. They were poorly led by supervisors and managers with little or no formal training in dealing with people. There was usually no formal selection or appraisal system of staff and many were recruited on a daily or weekly basis with no security of employment.

How to improve worker productivity

Taylor's scientific approach identified seven steps to improving worker productivity:

1. Select workers to perform a task.
2. Observe them performing the task and note the key elements of it.
3. Record the time taken to do each part of the task.
4. Identify the quickest method recorded.
5. Train all workers in the quickest method and do not allow them to make any changes to it.
6. Supervise workers to ensure that this 'best way' is being carried out and time them to check that the set time is not being exceeded.
7. Pay workers on the basis of results – based on the theory of 'economic man'.

Taylor believed in the theory of 'economic man', which stated that man was driven or motivated by money alone and the only factor that could stimulate further effort was the chance of earning extra money. This formed the basis of Taylor's main motivational suggestion – wage levels based on output. He always maintained that workers should be paid a 'fair day's pay for a fair day's work' and that the amount should be directly linked to output through a system known as 'piece rate'. This means paying workers a certain amount for each unit produced. To encourage high output a low rate per unit can be set for the first units produced and then higher rates become payable if output targets are exceeded. Table 14.2 summarises the relevance of Taylor's approach to modern industry and identifies its limitations.

Ford factory in the 1930s – early mass production manufacturers adopted Taylor's approach

MASLOW'S HIERARCHY OF HUMAN NEEDS

Abraham Maslow's research was not based solely on people in the work environment and his findings have significance for students of psychology and sociology too. He was concerned with trying to identify and classify the main needs that humans have. Our needs determine our actions – we will always try to satisfy them and we will be motivated to do so. If work can be organised so that we can satisfy some or all of our needs at work, then we will become more productive and satisfied. Maslow summarised these human needs in the form of a hierarchy – see Figure 14.1 and Table 14.3.

This hierarchy was interpreted by Maslow as follows:

- Individuals' needs start on the lowest level.
- Once one level of need has been satisfied, humans will strive to achieve the next level.
- Self-actualisation is not reached by many people, but everyone is capable of reaching their potential.
- Once a need has been satisfied, it will no longer motivate individuals to action – thus, when material needs have been satisfied, the offer of more money will not increase productivity.

Taylor's approach	Relevance to modern industry	Limitations
Economic man	Some managers still believe that money is the only way to motivate staff.	A more commonly held view is that workers have a wide range of needs, not just extrinsic needs of money, that can be met, in part at least, from work.
Select the right people for each job	Before Taylor there had been few attempts to identify the principles of staff selection. The importance he gave to this is still reflected in the significance given to careful staff selection in nearly all businesses.	Requires an appropriate selection procedure.
Observe and record the performance of staff	This was widely adopted and became known as 'time and motion study'. It is still employed as a technique but often with the co-operation and involvement of staff.	Taylor's autocratic use of this technique was regarded with suspicion among workers who saw it as a way of making them work harder.
Establish the best method of doing a job – method study	This is still accepted as being important as efficiency depends on the best ways of working being adopted.	The Taylor approach of management, which involved giving instructions to workers with no discussion or feedback, is considered to be undesirable. Worker participation in devising best work practices is now encouraged – see 'Kaizen' (Chapter 33).
Piece-work payment systems – to maximise output through motivating workers to produce more	Of limited relevance as it has become difficult to identify the output of each worker.	This is not now a widely used payment system. Quality may be sacrificed in the search for quantity – workers will vary output according to their financial needs at different times of year and it discourages them from accepting changes at work in case they lose some pay. In most of modern industry, especially service industries, it has become very difficult to identify the output of individual workers.

Table 14.2 *Evaluating how relevant Taylor's views and methods are today*

- Reversion is possible – it is possible for satisfaction at one level to be withdrawn, e.g. a loss of job security, and for individuals to move down a level.

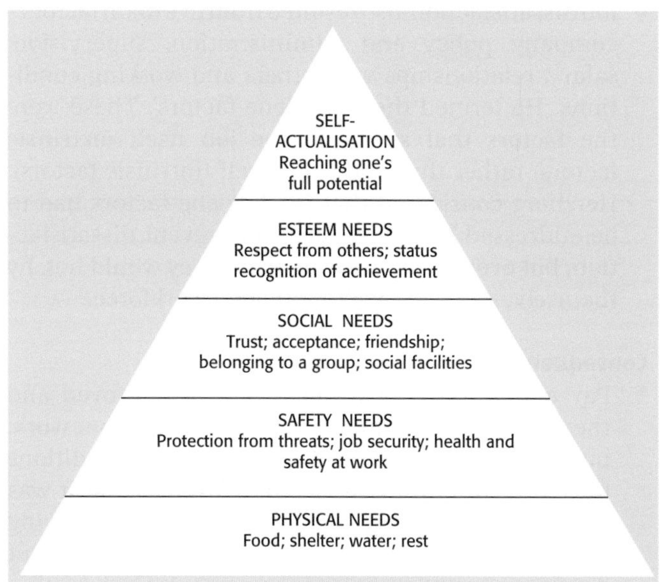

Figure 14.1 *Maslow's hierarchy of needs*

Level of need	Business conditions which could allow for the needs to be met
Self-actualisation – fulfilment of potential	Challenging work that stretches the individual – this will give a sense of achievement. Opportunities to develop and apply new skills will increase potential.
Esteem needs	Recognition for work done well – status, advancement and responsibility will gain the respect of others.
Social needs	Working in teams or groups and ensuring good communication to make workers feel involved.
Safety needs	A contract of employment with some job security – a structured organisation that gives clear lines of authority to reduce uncertainty. Ensuring health and safety conditions are met.
Physical needs	Income from employment high enough to meet essential needs.

Table 14.3 *Significance of the hierarchy of needs to business*

KEY TERM

self-actualisation a sense of self-fulfilment reached by feeling enriched and developed by what one has learned and achieved

Limitations of Maslow's approach

Criticisms of Maslow's hierarchy include:

- Not everyone has the same needs as are assumed by the hierarchy.
- In practice it can be very difficult to identify the degree to which each need has been met and which level a worker is 'on'.
- Money is necessary to satisfy physical needs, yet it might also play a role in satisfying the other levels of needs, such as status and esteem.
- Self-actualisation is never permanently achieved – as some observers of the hierarchy have suggested. Jobs must continually offer challenges and opportunities for fulfilment, otherwise regression will occur.

MCGREGOR'S THEORY X AND THEORY Y

McGregor identified two distinct management views of workers and how they are motivated. He called these Theory X and Theory Y. Theory X managers, according to McGregor, view their workers as lazy, disliking work and unprepared to accept responsibility, needing to be controlled and made to work. Clearly, managers with this view will be likely to adopt an autocratic style of leadership and will focus on extrinsic rewards.

On the other hand, McGregor believed that the managers who held Theory Y views believed that workers did enjoy work and that they found it as natural as rest or play. They would be prepared to accept responsibility, were creative and they would take an active part in contributing ideas and solutions to work-related problems – meeting their intrinsic needs in the process. A very important point to note about McGregor's work is this – he did not suggest that there were two types of workers, X and Y, but that the attitudes of management to workers could, in extreme cases, be described by these two theories. In practice, of course, most managers will have views somewhere between these two extremes.

What is the significance of McGregor's work? The general view is that workers will behave in such a way as a result of the attitudes management have of them. For instance, if a manager believes that all workers behave in a Theory X way, there will be control, close supervision and no delegation of authority. The staff, as a result of this approach, will almost certainly not enjoy their work and may indeed try to avoid it and fail to contribute in any meaningful way. Therefore, they will become like Theory X because of the way they are treated. The exact reverse could be the case for workers treated in a more democratic style, based on the Theory Y view (see Table 14.4).

Theory X managers believe that workers	Theory Y managers believe that workers
• dislike work • will avoid responsibility • are not creative.	• can derive as much enjoyment from work as from rest and play • will accept responsibility • are creative.

Table 14.4 *Summary of Theory X and Theory Y management attitudes*

HERZBERG AND THE 'TWO-FACTOR THEORY'

Despite basing his research on just 200 professionally qualified workers, Herzberg's conclusions and famous two-factor theory have had the greatest impact on motivational practices since Taylor's work almost 60 years earlier. Herzberg used worker questionnaires to discover:

- those factors that led to them having very good feelings about their jobs
- those factors that led to them having very negative feelings about their jobs.

These were his conclusions:

- Job satisfaction resulted from five main factors – achievement, recognition for achievement, the work itself, responsibility and advancement. He called these factors the 'motivators'. He considered the last three to be the most significant.
- Job dissatisfaction also resulted from five main factors – company policy and administration, supervision, salary, relationships with others and working conditions. He termed these 'hygiene factors'. These were the factors that surround the job itself (extrinsic factors) rather than the work itself (intrinsic factors). Herzberg considered that the hygiene factors had to be addressed by management to prevent dissatisfaction, but even if they were in place, they would not, by themselves, create a well-motivated workforce.

Consequences of Herzberg's theory

1 Pay and working conditions can be improved and these will help to remove dissatisfaction about work; but they will not, on their own, provide conditions for motivation to exist. Herzberg argued that it was possible to encourage someone to do a job by paying them – he called this movement. However, movement does not mean that someone wants to do the job – that would require motivation. Motivation to do the job,

and to do it well, would only exist if the motivators were in place. Herzberg did not claim that pay did not matter, but that it moves people to do a job and does not motivate them to do it well.

2 The motivators need to be in place for workers to be prepared to work willingly and to always give of their best. Herzberg suggested that motivators could be provided by adopting the principles of 'job enrichment'. There are three main features of job enrichment:

- Assign workers complete units of work – typical mass-production methods leave workers to assemble one small part of the finished product. This is not rewarding, can be boring and repetitive and prevents the worker from appreciating the importance of what they are doing as part of the overall production system. Herzberg argued that complete and identifiable units of work should be assigned to workers, and that this might involve teams of workers rather than individuals on their own. These complete units of work could be whole sub-assemblies of manufactured goods, such as a complete engine assembly in a car plant. In service industries it could mean that a small team of multi-skilled people, such as waiters, chefs and technicians for IT/video equipment, provide all of the conference facilities in a hotel for a business conference rather than many people doing just one small and relatively unimportant task before moving on to another part of the hotel. 'If you want people motivated to do a good job, give them a good job to do,' said Herzberg.
- Provide feedback on performance – this type of communication could give recognition for work well done and could provide incentives to achieve even more.
- Give workers a range of tasks – to challenge and stretch the individual, a range of tasks should be given, some of which may be, at least initially, beyond the workers' current experience. This, in quite a large measure, ties in with the 'self-actualisation' level in Maslow's hierarchy.

3 A business could offer higher pay, improved working conditions and less heavy-handed supervision of work. These would all help to remove dissatisfaction, but they would all be quickly taken for granted. If work is not interesting, rewarding or challenging, then workers will not be satisfied or will not be motivated to offer their full potential whatever the pay level offered to them.

KEY TERMS

job enrichment aims to use the full capabilities of workers by giving them the opportunity to do more challenging and fulfilling work

hygiene factors aspects of a worker's job that have the potential to cause dissatisfaction such as pay, working conditions, status and over-supervision by managers

motivating factors (motivators) aspects of a worker's job that can lead to positive job satisfaction such as achievement, recognition, meaningful and interesting work and advancement at work

ACTIVITY 14.1

Read the following case study and then answer the questions that follow.

Applying the motivational theories

Corie Jones joined Index Computers after working for IS Computers (ISC) for several years. At ISC, Corie had been paid a high salary, but he did not find the work rewarding. He was given specific programming tasks to perform but was not involved in designing complete software solutions to clients' problems. He worked to tight deadlines. He was not assigned to a team and worked alone on most tasks. He felt that Index offered better career prospects as well as the opportunity to take on more responsibility. He joined Index as a senior programmer on a higher salary – but this was less important to him than the chance to work as a team member. He was appointed to Daveena Davis's five-member team of programmers. Corie had met her already and his team colleagues seemed friendly and were appreciative of Daveena's leadership. She recognised talent and achievement and wanted colleagues to reach their full potential. She allowed team members to take control of complete software solutions – not just a small section of them.

22 marks, 35 minutes

1 Explain which level of Maslow's hierarchy Corie seemed to be on:
   a at ISC
   b at Index Computers. [6]
2 Explain why team working might be important to Corie's motivation. [6]
3 Evaluate, using this case study as a starting point, how Herzberg's research on 'hygiene and motivating factors' can be effectively applied within a work environment. [10]

Evaluation of Herzberg's work

- Team working is now much more widespread as a consequences of his findings, with whole units of work being delegated to these groups.
- Workers tend to be made much more responsible for the quality of their own work rather than being closely supervised by a quality-controlling inspectorate.
- Most firms are continually looking for ways to improve effective communication, and group meetings allowing two-way communication are often favoured.

HIGHER LEVEL

MAYO AND THE HUMAN RELATIONS THEORIES

Elton Mayo is best known for his 'Hawthorne effect' conclusions. These were based on a series of experiments he conducted at the Hawthorne factory of Western Electric Co. in Chicago, USA. His work was initially based on the assumption that working conditions – lighting, heating, rest periods and so on – had a significant effect on workers' productivity. Experiments were undertaken to establish the optimum working conditions and, as in all good scientific practice, the output of a control group was also recorded – this group experienced no changes in working conditions at all. The results surprised the observers – as lighting and other conditions were changed, both improved and worsened, so productivity rose in all groups including the control group. This forced Mayo to accept that:

- working conditions in themselves were not that important in determining productivity levels
- other motivational factors needed to be investigated further before conclusions could be drawn.

Subsequent experiments were carried out with a group of assembly-line workers. Changes to rest periods, payment systems, assembly-bench layout and canteen food were made at 12-week intervals. Crucially, before every major change, the researchers discussed the new changes with the work group. At the end of the experiments, the working conditions and hours of work were returned to how they had been before the start of the trial. Output rose far above the original level. Clearly, other motivational factors were operating to increase productivity completely separate from the conditions of work.

The Hawthorne effect – the conclusions of Mayo's work

Mayo drew the following conclusions from his work:

- Changes in working conditions and financial rewards have little or no effect on productivity.
- When management consult with workers and take an interest in their work, then motivation is improved.
- Working in teams and developing a team spirit can improve productivity.
- When some control over their own working lives is given to workers, such as deciding when to take breaks, there is a positive motivational effect.
- Groups can establish their own targets or norms and these can be greatly influenced by the informal leaders of the group.

Evaluation of Mayo's research for today's businesses

- Since Mayo's research there has been a trend towards giving workers more of a role in business decision-making – this is called participation.
- Personnel departments, which hardly existed in the early years of the twentieth century, were established to try to put the Hawthorne effect into practice.
- Team working and group working can be applied in many types of modern business organisations and these offer the greatest opportunities for workers and firms to benefit from the Hawthorne effect.
- The idea of involving workers, taking an interest in their welfare and finding out their individual goals has opened up new fields of research for industrial psychologists and this area of study is now regarded as an important component of university business courses.
- This development of the 'people' side of business has taken industry away from the engineer-focused and purely money-motivated views of Taylor.

McCLELLAND AND MOTIVATIONAL NEEDS THEORY

A doctor of psychology, David McClelland, pioneered workplace motivational thinking, developed achievement-based motivational theory and promoted improvements in employee assessment methods. He is best known for describing three types of motivational need, which he identified in his book, *The Achieving Society* (1961).

Achievement motivation (n-ach) A person with the strong motivational need for achievement will seek to reach realistic and challenging goals and job advancement. There is a constant need for feedback regarding progress and achievement and a need for a sense of accomplishment. Research has suggested that this result-driven attitude is almost always a common characteristic of successful business people and entrepreneurs.

Authority/power motivation (n-pow) A person with this dominant need is 'authority motivated'. The desire to control others is a powerful motivating force – the need to be influential, effective and to make an impact. There is a strong leadership instinct and when authority is gained over others, it brings personal status and prestige.

Affiliation motivation (n-affil) The person with need for affiliation as the strongest driver or motivator has a need for friendly relationships and is motivated towards interaction with other people. These people tend to be good team members – there is a need to be liked and popular and to be held in high regard.

McClelland stated that these three needs are found to varying degrees in all workers and managers. The mix of motivational needs characterises a person's or manager's behaviour, both in terms of what motivates them and how they believe other people should be motivated. McClelland firmly believed that 'achievement motivated' people are generally the ones who make things happen and get results. However, they can demand too much of their staff in the achievement of targets and prioritise this above the many and varied needs of their workers.

Process theories

Process theories emphasise how and why people choose certain behaviours in order to meet their personal goals and the thought processes that influence behaviour. Process theories study what people are thinking about when they decide whether or not to put effort into a particular activity. One of the best-known process theorists is Victor Vroom.

VROOM AND EXPECTANCY THEORY

Vroom suggested that individuals chose to behave in ways that they believe will lead to outcomes they value. His expectancy theory states that individuals have different sets of goals and can be motivated if they believe that:

- there is a positive link between effort and performance
- favourable performance will result in a desirable reward
- the reward will satisfy an important need
- the desire to satisfy the need is strong enough to make the work effort worthwhile.

His expectancy theory is based on the following three beliefs:

- 'valence' – the depth of the want of an employee for an extrinsic reward, such as money, or an intrinsic reward such as satisfaction
- 'expectancy' – the degree to which people believe that putting effort into work will lead to a given level of performance
- 'instrumentality' – the confidence of employees that they will actually get what they desire regardless of what has been promised by the manager.

Even if just one of these conditions or beliefs is missing then, Vroom argued, workers will not have the motivation to do the job well. Therefore, according to Vroom, managers should try to ensure that employees believe that increased work effort will improve performance and that this performance will lead to valued rewards.

ADAMS AND EQUITY THEORY

John Adams's equity theory is built on the belief that employees become demotivated towards their jobs and employer if they feel that their inputs are greater than their outputs. Inputs include effort, loyalty, commitment and skill. Outputs include financial rewards, recognition, security and sense of achievement.

While many of these factors cannot be quantified, Adams argued that employers should attempt to achieve a fair balance between what the employee gives an organisation and what they receive in return. If workers consider that their inputs are greater than the outputs received, they will moved to try to redress this imbalance. When a balance is reached, then employees will consider their treatment to be fair and will respond with positive attitudes and high levels of motivation.

ACTIVITY 14.2

What people want from work

'I was asked by the principal of my university to help form a committee of ten lecturers to discuss holiday dates, student enrolment and ways to check on the quality of lectures. He told us it was a very important committee, we would receive recognition for our time and our views would influence future decisions. We had many meetings, agreed and wrote a report and sent it to the principal. We heard nothing back – no feedback, no thanks and no decisions made on our recommendations. I would not do it again if I was asked.' Can you believe how demotivated these lecturers were? They had been misled about the degree to which the extra effort they put in to attending these meetings would be responded to by the principal.

According to Bob Nelson, a reward and motivation guru, giving people what they want from work is quite easy – even though it depends on the type of work situation and depends on the individual person. He thinks that people want:

- some control of their work – job enrichment; responsibility for a well-defined task, recognition for achievement
- to receive feedback and to understand how managers take decisions – good communications from management and some participation opportunities
- the opportunity for growth and development – education, career paths, team working
- leadership – providing clear expectations, structure and appropriate rewards if these expectations are met.

Of course, money is important, but once workers have satisfied their essential needs from money, they look for other things from work – according to Susan Heathfield (http://humanresources.about.com), 'Most people want involvement in decisions that affect their work. People who contribute ideas should be recognised and rewarded. True employee involvement is based on the expectation that people are competent to make decisions about their work every single day on the job.'

22 marks, 40 minutes

1 Analyse how the two sets of views can be applied to the work of Herzberg or Vroom or McClelland. [8]

2 Discuss how the views contained in the case study could be applied in practice to:
a a restaurant
b a food shop
c teaching staff at a school or college. [14]

EXAM TIP

When there is a question about motivational theorists, try to do more than just list their main findings – apply their ideas to the business situation given.

Motivation in practice

PAYMENT OR FINANCIAL REWARD SYSTEMS

The most common payment systems are:

- hourly or time wage rate
- piece rate
- salary
- commission
- performance-related pay and bonuses
- profit-related pay
- employee share-ownership schemes
- fringe benefits.

Hourly wage rate

An hourly wage rate or 'time rate' is set for the job – perhaps by comparing with other firms or similar jobs. The wage level is determined by multiplying this by the number of hours worked and is usually paid weekly. Although there is more income security than with piece rate, speed of work is not rewarded with this payment system – indeed, the opportunity to earn overtime might encourage workers to stretch work out unproductively.

Piece rate

A rate is fixed for the production of each unit, and the workers' wages therefore depend on the quantity of output produced. The piece rate can be adjusted to reflect the difficulty of the job and the 'standard' time needed to complete it. The level of the rate can be very important. If set too low, it could demotivate the workers, but, if too high, it could reduce the incentives – because workers will be able to meet their target wage level by producing relatively few units (see Table 14.5).

Advantages	Disadvantages
• It encourages greater effort and faster working. • The labour cost for each unit is determined in advance and this helps to set a price for the product.	• It requires output to be measurable and standardised – if each product is different, then piece work is inappropriate. • It may lead to falling quality and safety levels as workers rush to complete units. • Workers may settle for a certain pay level and will therefore not be motivated to produce more than a certain level. • It provides little security over pay level, e.g. in the event of a production breakdown.

Table 14.5 *Advantages and disadvantages of the piece rate*

Salary

A salary is the most common form of payment for professional, supervisory and management staff. The salary level is fixed each year and it is not dependent on the number of hours worked or the number of units produced. The fixing of the salary level for each job is a very important process because it helps to determine the status of that post in the whole organisation. Job evaluation techniques may be used to assist in deciding the salary bands and the differences between them. In most organisations, all jobs will be put into one of a number of salary bands and the precise income earned within each band will depend upon experience and progress. It is always possible to gain promotion to another job in a higher salary band. Firms that are interested in creating a 'single status' within their organisation are now increasingly putting all staff – manual and managerial – on to annual salaries to give the benefits of security and status to all employees (see Table 14.6). The advantages and disadvantages of a salary system are outlined in Table 14.7.

Job grade	Salary band (per year)
E, e.g. regional heads	\$50 000–\$75 900
D, e.g. departmental heads	\$30 000–\$49 900
C, e.g. office managers	\$20 000–\$29 900
B, e.g. secretaries	\$10 000–\$19 900
A, e.g. junior clerical staff	\$5000–\$9900

Table 14.6 *Salary bands – typical example*

Advantages	Disadvantages
• Gives security of income. • Gives status compared to time rate or piece rate payment systems. • Aids in costing – the salaries will not vary for one year. • Is suitable for jobs where output is not measurable. • Is suitable for management positions where staff are expected to put in extra time to complete a task or assignment.	• Income is not related to effort levels or productivity. • It may lead to complacency of the salary earner. • Regular appraisal may be needed to assess whether an individual should move up a salary band, although this could be an advantage if this becomes a positive form of worker appraisal.

Table 14.7 *Advantages and disadvantages of a salary*

KEY TERMS

hourly wage rate payment to a worker made for each hour worked

piece rate a payment to a worker for each unit produced

salary annual income that is usually paid on a monthly basis

Commission

Commission can make up 100% of the total income of direct sales staff – it reduces security as there is no 'basic' or flat-rate payment if nothing is sold during a particular period – or it can be paid in addition to a basic salary. It has the same advantages and disadvantages as the piece rate used in production industries, except that the potential drawback of low quality of production may be replaced by the risk of high-pressure selling, where sales staff try so hard to convince a customer to buy a product or service that they simply create a bad impression of the company. Commission-based pay also does not encourage team work – each individual sales person will be keen to hold on to each new customer for themselves to earn more commission!

Performance-related pay (PRP)

Performance-related pay is usually in the form of a bonus payable in addition to the basic salary. It is widely used for those workers whose 'output' is not measurable in quantitative terms, such as management, supervisory and clerical posts. It requires the following procedure:

- regular target setting, establishing specific objectives for the individual
- annual appraisals of the worker's performance against the pre-set targets
- paying each worker a bonus according to the degree to which the targets have been exceeded.

The main aim is to provide further financial incentives and to encourage staff to meet agreed targets. Bonuses are usually paid on an individual basis, but they can also be calculated and awarded on the basis of teams or even whole departments.

There are problems with PRP schemes (see Table 14.8). The main issue is one that Herzberg would recognise – does the chance of additional pay 'motivate' or just temporarily 'move' a worker to perform better? As there is no change in the nature of the work being undertaken most of the 'motivators' recognised by Herzberg would not be satisfied by PRP. In addition, the concentration on individual performance can create divisions within teams and groups, and this can work against the findings of the Hawthorne effect. There is also a widely held view that PRP bonuses are often inadequate, even to achieve short-term productivity gains or improvements in effort. The last problem concerns the style of management that PRP can lead to. By giving senior managers the power to decide which subordinates have achieved performances above target, it can lead to claims of favouritism and the ability to control staff by means of the 'carrot' of extra rewards.

Advantages	Disadvantages
• Staff are motivated to improve performance if they are seeking increases in financial rewards. • Target setting can help to give purpose and direction to the work of an individual. • Annual appraisal offers the opportunity for feedback on the performance of an individual, but as it tends to occur only once a year this is not usually sufficient to achieve a key feature of job enrichment.	• It can fail to motivate if staff are not driven by the need to earn additional financial rewards. • Team spirit can be damaged by the rivalry generated by the competitive nature of PRP. • Claims of manager favouritism can harm manager–subordinate relationships. • It may lead to increased control over staff by managers because of the danger that bonuses may not be awarded if workers do not 'conform'.

Table 14.8 *Advantages and disadvantages of performance-related pay*

KEY TERMS

commission a payment to a sales person for each sale made

performance-related pay a bonus scheme to reward staff for above-average work performance

Profit-related pay

KEY TERMS

profit-related pay a bonus for staff based on the profits of the business – usually paid as a proportion of basic salary

The essential idea behind profit-sharing arrangements is that staff will feel more committed to the success of the business and will strive to achieve higher performances and cost savings (see Table 14.9). Some shareholder groups, however, claim that profits should be the return to the owners of the business and are a reward to them for taking risks with their own capital.

Employee share-ownership schemes

Some profit-sharing schemes do not offer cash but shares in the business to each worker when the firm declares a profit. This is designed to establish the workers as part owners of the business and reduce the conflict that might exist between 'them' (the owners and managers) and 'us' (the workers). In practice, many of the shares in such schemes are quickly sold by the workers, thus reducing the hoped-for long-term impact on motivation (see Table 14.9).

Fringe benefits

These are non-cash forms of reward – and there are many alternatives that can be used. They include company cars, free insurance and pension schemes, private health insurance, discounts on company products and low interest rate loans. They are used by businesses in addition to normal payment systems in order to give status to higher-level employees and to recruit and retain the best staff. Some of these fringe benefits are taxed, but others are not and that gives the employees an added benefit, because to purchase these 'perks' from after-tax income would be very expensive. It is very difficult to assess the impact of these benefits on productivity.

NON-FINANCIAL METHODS OF MOTIVATION

It is now widely recognised that businesses cannot use money alone to create the necessary motivation for employees to complete jobs efficiently. Non-financial motivators include:

- job enlargement
- job enrichment
- team working
- empowerment.

Advantages	Disadvantages
• Potential conflict between owners and workers is reduced as everyone now has an interest in higher profits. • They are designed to lead to higher worker effort levels and a greater preparation to accept cost reduction measures and changes that benefit the business. • The business is likely to attract better recruits drawn by the chance of sharing profits or owning shares in the firm. • As the bonuses are paid out of profits, the scheme does not add to business costs, unlike a normal increase in pay levels. • If successful in increasing motivation, then the schemes could lead to an increase in overall business profitability.	• The reward offered is not closely related to individual effort – why should one worker put in greater effort when everyone will be benefiting? • The schemes can be costly to set up and operate, especially in large firms with many employees. • Small profit shares paid at the end of the financial year are unlikely to promote motivation throughout the year. • Profit-sharing schemes will reduce profits available to be paid to owners (reducing dividends) and to be reinvested in the business (retained profits). • Worker share-ownership schemes can increase the total number of shares issued and 'dilute' the value of existing shares.

Table 14.9 *Advantages and disadvantages of profit sharing and employee share ownership*

ACTIVITY 14.3

Look at the job adverts and then answer the questions that follow.

Different jobs, different pay systems

SIX-FIGURE SALARY (AT LEAST $100,000) + SUBSTANTIAL FRINGE BENEFITS
CAR, INSURANCE, PENSION, HEALTH CARE

Human Resources Director – Singapore

Diverse Portfolio of International Businesses

Our client is an undisputed leader in the private equity market. It has financed the acquisition of a wide variety of businesses with a presence in more than 50 countries, an annual turnover in excess of £3.5 billion and 50,000 employees. Key to the group's success has been its close financial management and the assistance it has given portfolio companies in areas such as human resources and IT.

Due to continuing growth, an HR Director is now sought to add value across the group.

THE POSITION

- Optimise the deployment of HR to add value within the portfolio businesses and support the group's overall objectives.
- Provide business and HR support to operating company management teams. Emphasis on management development, leadership teams and compensation.
- Active involvement in evaluation of potential acquisition targets. Provide critical analysis of management strengths and weaknesses.

QUALIFICATIONS

- Outstanding HR professional with a minimum of 15 years' experience, a demonstrable record at group and divisional levels in an international business.
- Practical understanding of business drivers and HR issues within large and small organisations. Highly influential with outstanding business management tool kit.
- Specific experience in Asia is required, with fluency in an Asian language a distinct advantage.

Please send full CV and current salary details to S. Amm at the address below.
Alternatively email: samm@partnership.com

THE PACIFIC RECRUITMENT AGENCY

DRIVER WANTED

- Must have clean driving licence
- Light removal work
- $5 per hour
- Overalls provided
- Ring: 0837 5108 if interested

12 marks, 21 minutes

1 Explain the different pay systems operated by these two businesses for these jobs. [4]

2 Why do you think that these pay systems are different? [4]

3 Why do you think that the higher-paid post also carries a range of other benefits? [4]

KEY TERMS

job enlargement attempting to increase the scope of a job by broadening or deepening the tasks undertaken

team working production is organised so that groups of workers undertake complete units of work

Job enlargement

This can include both job rotation and job enrichment, but it also refers to increasing the 'loading' of tasks on existing workers, perhaps as a result of shortage of staff or redundancies. It is unlikely to lead to long-term job satisfaction, unless the principles of job enrichment are adopted.

Job enrichment

This involves the principle of organising work so that employees are encouraged and allowed to use their full abilities – not just physical effort. The process often involves a slackening of direct supervision as workers take more responsibility for their own work and are allowed some degree of decision-making authority. Herzberg's findings formed the basis of the job enrichment principle. The three key features of it are not always easy to apply in practice, but employers are increasingly recognising the benefits to be gained by attempting to implement them:

- complete units of work so that the contribution of the worker can be identified and more challenging work offered, e.g. cell production (see Chapter 30, page 319)
- direct feedback on performance to allow each worker to have an awareness of their own progress, e.g. two-way communication (see Chapter 12)
- challenging tasks offered as part of a range of activities, some of which are beyond the worker's recent experience – these tasks will require training and the learning of new skills. Gaining further skills and qualifications is a form of gaining status and recognition – see Maslow's hierarchy of human needs (page 142).

To introduce job enrichment into many traditional businesses, a process known as job redesign is often necessary (see Figures 14.2 and 14.3).

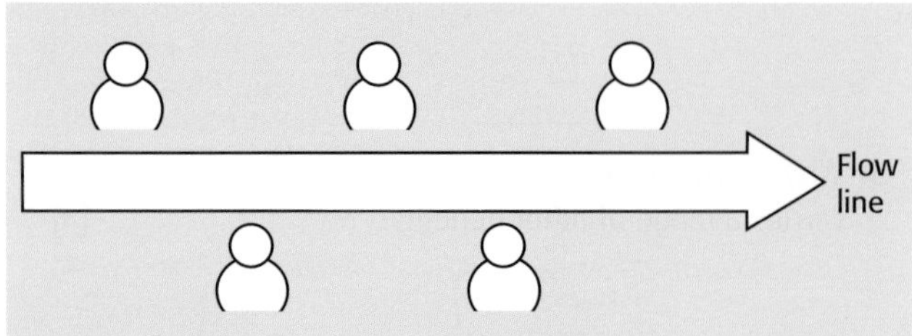

Figure 14.2 Traditional mass production – each worker performs a single task

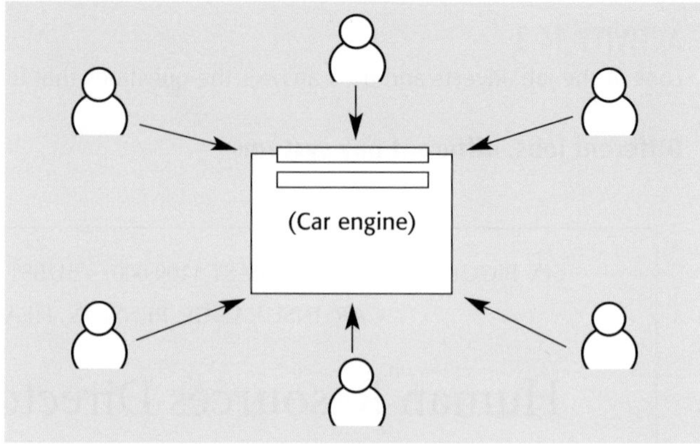

Figure 14.3 Team production allowing for job enrichment – all workers contribute to producing the completed unit

KEY TERM

job redesign involves the restructuring of a job – usually with employees' involvement and agreement – to make work more interesting, satisfying and challenging

EXAM TIP

Do not confuse job enlargement with job enrichment/redesign.

Team working

This approach to work places each member of staff into a small team of employees. Some traditionalists argue that moving away from 'pure division of labour', where one worker performs just one simple task all of the time, will result in lower productivity and time-wasting 'team' meetings. Supporters of job enrichment would respond by claiming that more challenging and interesting work, as allowed by team working or 'cell' production, will lead to:

- lower labour turnover
- more and better ideas from the workforce on improving the product and the manufacturing process
- consistently higher quality, especially when total quality management (TQM) is incorporated (see Chapter 33, page 346).

Table 14.10 summarises the advantages and disadvantages of team working.

There are a number of benefits to the organisation from team working:

- Team spirit should improve motivation of staff.
- Teams are more flexible than hierarchical systems.
- New teams can be formed and redundant teams disbanded as the needs of the organisation change.
- Management costs may be reduced as fewer middle managers and supervisory staff are required.

Advantages	Disadvantages
• Workers are likely to be better motivated as social and esteem needs (see Maslow) are more likely to be met. By empowering workers within teams, job enrichment can be achieved (see Herzberg). • Better-motivated staff should increase productivity and reduce labour turnover – both will help to reduce business costs. • Team working makes fuller use of all of the talents of the workforce. Better solution to problems will be found as those most closely connected with the work participate in suggesting answers. • Team working can reduce management costs as it is often associated with delayering of the organisation – fewer middle managers will be required. • Complete units of work can be given to teams – a key feature of job enrichment.	• Not everyone is a team player – some individuals are more effective working alone. When teams are formed, this point must be considered and training may need to be offered to team members who are not used to working collaboratively in groups. Some workers may feel 'left out' of the team meetings unless efforts are made to involve and encourage all team members. • Teams can develop a set of values and attitudes which may contrast or conflict with those of the organisation itself, particularly if there is a dominant personality in the group. Teams will need clear goals and assessment procedures to ensure that they are working towards the objectives of the organisation at all times. • The introduction of team working will incur training costs and there may be some disruption to production as the teams establish themselves.

Table 14.10 *Advantages and disadvantages of working in teams*

EXAM TIP

Team working might not always be a suitable way of organising a workforce.

Delegation and empowerment

These methods of staff motivation were fully examined in Chapter 11 (see page 111). Delegation involves the passing down of authority to perform tasks to workers. Empowerment goes further, by allowing workers some degree of control over how the task should be undertaken and the resources needed to complete it.

EVALUATION OF FINANCIAL AND NON-FINANCIAL MOTIVATIONAL METHODS

If it is accepted that pay is not the only motivating factor for people to work effectively and to be satisfied in their jobs, then managers need to take a critical look at all of the payment and non-financial methods of motivating staff. What works for some groups of workers will not be effective with others. Managers need to be flexible and adapt the methods and approaches that are available to motivate staff to the particular circumstances of their business and their workforce. The main factors that influence the different degrees of emphasis on pay and non-pay factors include the leadership style of management and the culture of the organisation. If managers have the attitude that workers are naturally lazy and cannot be trusted, then a 'payment by results' system with close supervision will be adopted. If the culture views workers as partners or associates in the business, then production will be organised to give workers a chance to accept responsibility and to participate. A monthly salary payment system is likely under these circumstances. As with so many important decisions made within a business, so much depends on the attitudes and beliefs of senior managers – and the business culture they adopt.

EXAM TIP

You should be able not just to describe and explain different methods of financial and non-financial motivation but to suggest which ones might be most suitable in different business situations – and why.

THEORY OF KNOWLEDGE

The world economy was brought to its knees in 2008 by risk-taking bankers hungry for bonuses that brought them riches beyond the wildest dreams of most normal working people. One American bank paid an average bonus of $500,000 to its staff, with top staff receiving multi-million dollar pay-outs. Striving for such large sums meant bankers took huge risks by making loans to businesses and individuals who were often not in a position to pay them back.

'Organisations like banks should not be allowed to motivate their staff by using large financial rewards.'

In groups, discuss to what extent you agree or disagree with this statement.

OVER TO YOU

REVISION CHECKLIST

1 What do you understand by the term 'motivation'?
2 Why is a 'motivated workforce' important for a manufacturing business?
3 Explain how a high-quality clothing shop might be badly affected by low motivation of sales staff.
4 State **three** features of Taylor's research that might be relevant to manufacturing industries.
5 Explain why studying intrinsic and extrinsic needs is an important part of motivation theory.
6 Give an example of how an individual might revert to a lower level of Maslow's hierarchy of human needs.
7 Consider **two** different levels of Maslow's hierarchy. Explain how these needs could be satisfied at work.
8 Differentiate, using examples, between Herzberg's motivators and hygiene factors.
9 Why did Herzberg consider it important to differentiate between 'movement' and 'motivation'?
10 Outline the **three** key features of job enrichment.
11 Examine **two** problems of using the piece-rate system for each individual in a business that uses a flow line production system.
12 Explain how the payment of a fixed monthly salary could help to satisfy some of the needs identified in Maslow's hierarchy.
13 Assume that you are the manager of a computer shop. Which payment system would you use for your staff: commission only, time-based wage rates or a combination of the two? Justify your choice.
14 Explain to the directors of a private limited company the advantages and disadvantages of introducing a profit-sharing system for the workforce.
15 Do you believe that performance-related pay should be introduced for the teachers in your school or college? Justify your answer.
16 Explain **two** benefits to the firm that might be gained from adopting team work in a factory making computers.
17 Explain **two** benefits to workers from being organised into teams.
18 How might business culture influence the motivational methods adopted by managers?
19 Outline the benefits to a business of using non-financial methods of motivation.
20 Give **two** examples of fringe benefits that might be offered to senior managers in a bank.
21 Analyse the potential benefits of employee empowerment in a busy fast-food restaurant.
(H) 22 Outline the main findings of Mayo's Hawthorne research.
(H) 23 Why did McClelland believe that achievement was so important to motivation?
(H) 24 Outline the differences between content and process motivation theories.

REVISION ACTIVITY

Read the case study below and then answer the questions that follow.

Staff turnover increases at Telemarketing Ltd

The human resources manager at Telemarketing was under pressure to solve the problem caused by so many staff leaving. Recent data gathered about staff are shown below:

	2007	2008	2009
Labour turnover (% of staff leaving each year)	15	20	45
Staff absence (average % of total staff absent)	5	7	9

Recruitment and training costs and covering for absent staff were reducing the profitability of the business. Since it was set up five years ago, Telemarketing has grown rapidly and is now one of the largest telephone direct marketing organisations in the country. It sells insurances and other financial products directly to consumers rather than using banks or insurance brokers as intermediaries.

Seventy-five per cent of staff are telephone sales people. They have two ways of selling the products. Either they 'cold call' potential customers from telephone directories or they receive calls from interested members of the public responding to advertisements. Telephonists work at individual work stations. All of their calls are recorded and monitored by supervisors. Rest time is strictly controlled and excess rest periods lead to pay being reduced. Staff are paid a low basic wage, plus a proportion of the value of sales made. Because of the nature of the job – telephones must be operated 18 hours per day – there is no time for meetings between all of the staff and workers. The main communication is a daily newsletter, pinned to all work stations at the start of every shift, giving details of daily sales targets for the whole business.

32 marks, 58 minutes

1 Explain the drawbacks to the business of high labour turnover and high staff absence. [4]

2 Referring to the work of **two** motivational theorists, explain the likely reasons for the staffing problems at telemarketing. [8]

3 To what extent might the principles of job enrichment be introduced into this business to help staff achieve 'self-actualisation'? [10]

4 Recommend a pay system for staff in Telemarketing that will encourage long-term motivation. Justify your recommendation. [10]

EXAM PRACTICE QUESTION

Read the case study below and then answer the questions that follow.

WHY WOMEN ARE HAPPIER IN THEIR WORK THAN MEN

The world of work is a better experience for women than it is for men, according to a survey. Asked to rate their job satisfaction on a scale of one to seven, they scored an average of 5.56, while males scored 5.22. Experts appear divided over the reasons why women appear to get more out of their work than men. Many women work part time and have job-sharing schemes, which, the survey found, increased job satisfaction as they could pursue other interests too. In addition, older workers get the greatest satisfaction from their jobs, while university graduates are the most dissatisfied of all, according to the survey of 30 000 employees. Employees generally enjoyed their first years at work, but then job satisfaction falls between the ages of 30 and 40. But employees over 60 gained the greatest satisfaction from their work. Professor Andrew Oswald of Warwick University, who conducted the survey, said, 'The young are just happy to have a job. As they grow older they realise that ambitions and needs may not be so easily fulfilled.' It seems that we all begin thinking we will reach the top in our careers, but most of us are forced to adjust. 'The older we get, the more settled and content with our role at work we get,' he added. Graduates are often frustrated by the lack of challenging work on offer. They are often forced to take low-skilled jobs for which they are over-qualified in order to pay off debts. The survey also revealed that long hours at work did not turn people off their jobs.

Employees of small businesses and non-profit-making organisations, such as charities, were more motivated and happier at work than those working for big companies. David Hands, of the Federation of Small Businesses, said, 'There is a greater camaraderie (friendship) in small firms than in big companies.' Workers feel less involved and less secure in bigger firms. He added, 'It is more relaxed in small firms and people enjoy it more. Many also get more responsibility which adds to their satisfaction.'

Source: Adapted from various sources

25 marks, 45 minutes

1 Explain what you understand by the terms:
   a) motivation
   b) responsibility. [4]

2 Identify **two** factors that seem to influence job satisfaction and explain them in terms of Maslow's hierarchy of needs. [6]

3 Explain in terms of the features of job enrichment why it might be easier for small firms to motivate staff than big businesses. [6]

4 Discuss the extent to which it might be possible for large firms to use Herzberg's motivators to improve the level of worker motivation. [9]

15 Organisational and corporate cultures

This chapter covers syllabus section 2.6 (Higher level only)

On completing this chapter you should be able to:

- (H) explain the influences on organisational and corporate culture
- (H) describe different types of culture and analyse their effects on motivation and organisational structures
- (H) analyse the consequences of culture clashes within and between organisations.

SETTING THE SCENE

Culture change to meet increased competition

DLM is a European airline that underwent a spectacular turnaround. Under a new chief executive the company switched from a product- and technology-focused business to one that is market- and customer-service orientated. Under the old organisational culture, pilots, technicians and autocratic managers were the company's heroes. Planning and sales were based on maximising flight hours using the most modern aircraft. With customer numbers and profits falling, the chief executive realised that the rapidly changing and increasingly competitive air-travel market required the company to refocus its approach to concentrate on the needs of current and potential customers. He believed these needs were best understood by front-line staff who had face-to-face contact with customers – the cabin crew and ground staff. However, they had never been asked for their opinions; they were simply a disciplined group of uniformed 'soldiers' trained to follow clear rules and procedures. The new approach required a complete restructuring of the organisation to support front-line staff. Managers now act as advisers, there is regular simulated training in customer relations and staff are given considerable independence in dealing with customers' problems on the spot. They only check with their senior managers after the event – which involves much confidence in employees' judgement with all the risks that this entails. Customer numbers and profits have been on a steady upward flight path since these changes in organisational culture were introduced.

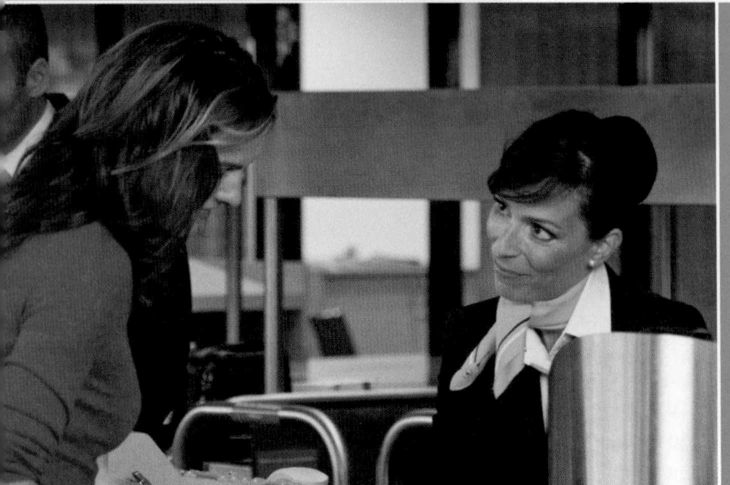

Points to think about:

- What do you understand by the term 'organisational culture' from this case study?
- Explain why the new chief executive officer decided to make changes to the organisational culture.
- Why did these changes seem to have been introduced so successfully?

The culture of an organisation such as an airline will influence its competitiveness

Introduction

A commonly used definition of organisational culture is 'the way we do things around here'. This means how people within the organisation view the world and respond to it in trying to achieve certain goals.

It is widely understood that different organisations have distinctive cultures. This is true of businesses as well as other organisations such as schools and colleges. The culture of a steel company will be very different to that of a nursing home, for example. Similarly, some schools' culture is driven by the need for better examination results while others view that educating the 'complete person' is more important. The culture of an organisation gives it a sense of identity and is based on the values, attitudes and beliefs of the people who work in it, especially senior management.

KEY TERM

organisational culture the values, attitudes and beliefs of the people working in an organisation that control the way they interact with each other and with external stakeholder groups

Values, attitudes and beliefs have a very powerful influence on the way staff in a business will act, take decisions and relate to others in the organisation. They define what is 'normal' in an organisation, so it is possible for the same person to act in different ways in different organisations. What we do and how we behave – in society in general and in business in particular – are largely determined by our culture.

EXAM TIP

Culture is such a powerful force in any organisation that you should take every opportunity in your answers to make reference to it as a factor that helps explain managers' decisions and behaviour.

Influences on organisational culture

Senior management may influence the culture of the organisation through:

- mission and vision statements – these inform staff about what the business is trying to achieve
- the appointment of senior staff – they are likely to share the same values, attitudes and beliefs as the directors of the business
- the organisation's ethical code of conduct – this lists the 'dos' and 'don'ts' that must be observed by staff when dealing with external stakeholders
- strategies on social and environmental issues – these will provide a clear guide to the organisation's social and environmental values and beliefs
- the example they set, e.g. how they treat subordinates and take decisions.

The industry the business operates in will also influence the values and beliefs of the organisation. For instance, the culture of a weapons manufacturer or a tobacco company is likely to be very different to that of a workers' co-operative or a business operating homes for the elderly.

The legal constraints, social norms and cultural values of countries vary markedly and these are likely to be reflected in the culture of organisations that are based there.

Types of organisational culture

Many management writers have used different ways to identify and classify different types of organisational culture. Below are the most widely identified culture types, based on the writings of Charles Handy.

KEY TERMS

power culture concentrating power among a few people

role culture each member of staff has a clearly defined job title and role

task culture based on co-operation and team work

person culture when individuals are given the freedom to express themselves and make decisions

entrepreneurial culture encourages management and workers to take risks, to come up with new ideas and test out new business ventures

POWER CULTURE

Power culture is associated with autocratic leadership. Power is concentrated at the centre of the organisation. Decisions can be made swiftly as so few people are involved in making them. Managers are judged by results rather than the means they used to obtain them. Autocratic leadership and hierarchical structures are features of organisations with a power culture.

Handy uses the analogy of a spider's web – the spider at the centre of the web has all of the power and the web has little purpose without the spider. Motivational methods are likely to focus on financial incentives and bonuses to reward exceptional performance – and this can encourage risky and, in the longer term, inappropriate decisions.

ROLE CULTURE

Role culture is usually associated with bureaucratic organisations. Staff operate within the rules and show little creativity. The structure of the organisation is well

ACTIVITY 15.1

The world 'credit crunch' and resulting economic downturn have been blamed on the 'power culture' and excessive risk taking by some of the world's leading banks. Find out as much as you can about the 2008–9 credit crunch and assess whether you agree that the banks' culture was a major contributing factor.

defined and each individual has clear delegated authority. Power and influence come from a person's position within the organisation. Decision-making is often slow and risk taking is frowned upon.

Tall hierarchical structures are used in organisations with a powerful role culture. Handy uses the image of a substantial building to represent this form of culture – solid and dependable but not going anywhere fast.

TASK CULTURE

Groups are formed to solve particular problems, and lines of communication are similar to a matrix structure (see Chapter 11). Such teams often develop a distinctive culture because they have been empowered to take decisions. Team members are encouraged to be creative and there may be a strong team spirit which can lead to a very motivating environment – based on meeting workers' intrinsic needs.

Handy uses the image of a net to represent task culture – the net's strength is derived from the many strands.

PERSON CULTURE

There may be some conflict between individual goals and those of the whole organisation, but this is the most creative type of culture. There is no emphasis on teamwork as each individual is focused on their own tasks and projects. This type of culture might be found in a scientific research environment or in a professional partnership such as lawyers and architects. Individuals who thrive in this type of environment will often find it difficult to work effectively in a more structured organisation.

Handy depicts this type of culture as a constellation of stars – each person is different from everyone else and they operate alone.

ENTREPRENEURIAL CULTURE

In this culture, success is rewarded, but failure is not necessarily criticised since it is considered a consequence of enterprise and risk taking. Although Handy did not specifically identify entrepreneurial culture, other theorists consider it to be important for certain types of organisations. This type of culture is usually found in flexible organisational structures. Motivation levels are likely to be high among people who enjoy the challenge of innovative risk taking.

ACTIVITY 15.2

For each of the cultures above, suggest **one** business situation where it would be the most appropriate culture to adopt.

15 marks, 25 minutes

EXAM TIP

As with leadership styles, there is no one right or wrong culture for a business. The appropriate culture will depend on the firm's objectives, the type of market it operates in and the values and expectations of managers and employees.

EXAM TIP

Do not expect all departments in a business to have the same culture. It may be very different. A team working with IT all day will be unlikely to have the same jargon, patterns of behaviour, values and beliefs as HR staff or marketing teams.

Consequences of culture clashes

Many businesses have turned themselves around, converting potential bankruptcy into commercial success. Very often this transformation has been achieved by changing the culture of the business. The existing culture of a business can become inappropriate and clash with new objectives needed to achieve growth, development and success. For example:

- A traditional family firm which has favoured members of the family for promotion into senior posts converts to a public limited company. New investors demand more transparency and recognition of natural talent from recruited employees. A different leadership style may lead to a clash with the existing culture of the business – hence the need to change existing values and beliefs.
- A product-led business needs to respond to changing market conditions by encouraging more staff involvement. A team or task culture may need to be adopted.
- A recently privatised business, formerly run on bureaucratic principles, needs to become more profit orientated and customer focused. An entrepreneurial culture may need to be introduced for the first time.
- A merger or takeover may result in one of the businesses having to adapt its culture to ensure consist-

ACTIVITY 15.3

Read the case study below and then answer the questions that follow.

Porsche culture contributes to success

Perhaps one of the reasons for the astonishing success of the Porsche motor manufacturing business is the culture embodied by the views of its former boss, Wendelin Wiedeking. 'The Porsche philosophy is that first comes the client, then come the workers, then the suppliers and finally the shareholders. When the first three are happy, then so are the shareholders.' Compare this with the typical view in US- and UK-based businesses that often promote 'shareholder culture' as being most important. These differences in outlook and culture help to explain why high-profile integrations between BMW and Rover Cars and then Chrysler and Mercedes-Benz were such disasters.

The collapse of the merger between car giants Chrylser and Mercedes-Benz was largely due to differences in corporate culture

20 marks, 35 minutes

1 Explain the term 'corporate culture'. [2]

2 Outline **two** factors that may have affected Porsche's corporate culture. [4]

3 Analyse why Porsche's philosophy of focusing on the needs of clients, workers and suppliers will ultimately satisfy shareholders. [6]

4 Discuss the problems of adapting the corporate culture of a car manufacturer when it is taken over by or merges with a foreign car manufacturer. [8]

ency within the newly created larger business unit. The danger of culture clashes as a result of mergers and takeovers is very real, particularly when the integration involves companies from different countries. The culture clash between the management team at Mercedes (German) and Chrysler (US) is often used as an example of how cross-border integration sometimes fails.

- Declining profits and market share may be the consequences of poorly motivated staff and a lack of interest in quality and customer service. A person culture may help to transform the prospects of this business.

Changing organisational culture

Changing the value system of a business and attitudes of all staff who work for it is never going to be an easy task. The process could take several years before all staff and processes have been fully 'converted'. It means changing the way people think and react to problem situations. It can mean directly challenging the way things have been done for years. It can also involve substantial changes of personnel, job descriptions, communication methods and working practices.

The key common elements in effective cultural change are:

- Concentrate on the positive aspects of the business and how it currently operates and enlarge on these. This will be much easier and more popular with staff than focusing on, and trying to change, negative aspects.
- Obtain the full commitment of people at the top of the business and all key personnel. If they cannot or will not change, it might be easier to replace them altogether. Unless the key personnel model the behaviour they expect to see in others, change will be very difficult to achieve.
- Establish new objectives and a mission statement that accurately reflect the new values and attitudes that are to be adopted – these also need to be communicated to all staff.
- Encourage 'bottom-up' participation of workers when defining existing problems or when devising new solutions. The biggest mistake could be to try to impose a new culture on workers without explaining the need for change or without giving them the opportunity to propose alternative ways of working.
- Train staff in new procedures and new ways of working to reflect the changed value system of the business. If people believe in the change and understand the benefits of it, then it will become more acceptable to them.
- Change the staff reward system to avoid rewarding success in the 'old ways' and ensure that appropriate behaviour that should be encouraged receives recognition. People need to be reassured that if they adjust to the new approach, then they will gain from it.

ACTIVITY 15.4

A housing development for disabled workers has been owned and operated by a profit-making private company for many years. A charity has just been successful in buying the development from the company.

6 marks, 10 minutes

Explain the steps the new management might have to take to change the culture of the organisation. [6]

Evaluating organisational culture

The significance and power of an organisation's culture to drive people's behaviour and attitudes should not be underestimated. The impact of culture goes beyond the desire of most people to conform with accepted values. The following examples reinforce the importance of organisational culture:

- The values of a business establish the norms of behaviour of staff – what is and what is not acceptable in certain situations. For example, is it acceptable in this organisation to offer bribes to attract large contracts 'as long as we are not found out'?
- Culture determines the way in which company managers and workers treat each other. For example, if the chief executive is open and receptive to new ideas and proposals from senior managers, then this approach is likely to filter through the whole organisation – to its potential long-term benefit.
- A distinctive organisational culture can support a business's brand image and relationships with customers. For example, The Body Shop almost invented the 'ethical trading' culture. Will this approach to business now change after its takeover by L'Oréal?
- Culture determines not just how decisions are made – with the participation of staff or by top managers alone – but also the type of strategic decisions that are taken. For example, the culture of the UK National Health Service in target setting and giving rewards for meeting short waiting times within Accident and Emergency departments is, it is claimed, encouraging hospital managers to decide to leave patients in ambulances for up to two hours. How different would it be if doctors were actually taking these decisions?
- Organisational culture has been clearly linked to the economic performance and long-term success of organisations. Businesses dedicated to continuous improvement with staff involvement have been shown to be more profitable in the long term. Toyota is the prime example of success based on this principle.

THEORY OF KNOWLEDGE

'Much has been written about the importance of having a single, unified corporate culture. Companies spend enormous amounts of energy and money on it, on the assumption that it's a guiding force for good and a necessity for corporate success.'

Source: Forbes.com (18 May 2010)

What evidence would you use to establish whether a strong corporate culture is good for business?

OVER TO YOU

REVISION CHECKLIST

1 If you were appointed to a management position in a well-known business, what evidence would you need to identify the culture of the organisation?

2 Explain the possible problems of changing the culture of a business with a small but loyal staff and customer base.

3 How might a business attempt to establish a people culture?

4 Explain **two** reasons why the culture of a fast-food restaurant might need to be changed.

5 Explain **two** reasons why workers may resist attempts to change the culture of the organisation they work for.

6 Examine the differences between role culture and entrepreneurial culture. Include examples of different circumstances of when each culture might be appropriate.

REVISION ACTIVITY

Read the case study below and then answer the questions that follow.

Changing culture – from state ownership to private-sector ownership

British Airways (BA) used to be a nationalised, state-owned business. It was overstaffed and customers' satisfaction ratings were low. Privatisation brought a profit focus to all strategic decisions. Staff numbers were reduced, but productivity and profits increased. Managers were encouraged to be enterprising in taking decisions to increase customer numbers and profits. The new culture brought risks too. In 2008, BA agreed to pay compensation to thousands of passengers who, for two years, had been overcharged a fuel surcharge that BA had illegally fixed with Virgin Atlantic. Possibly additional staff training may have helped to demonstrate those circumstances where 'how we do things around here' might conflict with legal obligations.

12 marks, 21 minutes

1 Why might culture clashes have resulted from the switch from state control to a public limited company? [6]

2 Explain why a culture clash might develop if BA were to be taken over by an Indian-owned, low-cost airline. [6]

EXAM PRACTICE QUESTION

Read the case study below and then answer the questions that follow.

REGAL SUPERMARKETS – A CASE STUDY IN CULTURAL CHANGE

As one of the UK's largest family-owned chain of supermarket stores, Regal Supermarkets had established a culture among its staff that had contributed to its success and growth. Loyalty to the family managers was very high. Staff often commented on the whole business being like a 'big family'. Promotion was based on long service and loyalty. Relationships with suppliers had been built up over many years and long-term supply contracts were in place. Customer service was a priority and was especially important as Regal never intended to be the cheapest shop in the towns it operated in. However, profits were not high and the younger members of the owning family lacked the skills to take over.

It was clear to some industry experts that some of these values and attitudes had to change once it was sold by the family and converted into a public limited company. The new chief executive, Sally Harte, had experience in the USA as Walmart's chief food buyer. She announced on the first day of her appointment: 'This business is like a sleeping giant. There is so much shareholder value that I can unlock to allow for higher dividends and to underpin a higher share price.' Within five weeks, 50% of the directors and key managers had been replaced. Suppliers' terms were changed, on Sally's insistence, to '5% below the cheapest or we drop you' and the staff salary and pension scheme was replaced for new recruits with flexible pay and conditions contracts. Staff turnover increased sharply.

Sally had not predicted the adverse media coverage of these changes. She said, 'I am only trying to adapt the organisational culture of this business to one which allows us to be successful in a highly competitive national marketplace where consumers want low prices and fresh goods.'

25 marks, 45 minutes

1 Explain **one** possible reason why Sally thought it necessary to change the organisational culture of Regal Supermarkets. [4]

2 Outline the type of culture that Sally seems to be introducing at Regal Supermarkets. [4]

3 Analyse the key steps that Sally should have taken to manage cultural change more effectively. [8]

4 To what extent will the change in culture guarantee future success for this business? [9]

16 Employer and employee relations

This chapter covers syllabus section 2.7 (Higher level only)

On completing this chapter you should be able to:

- (H) analyse the dynamic relationships between employees, employers and their representatives
- (H) examine the methods used by employees and their representatives in pursuit of their objectives
- (H) examine the methods used by employers to put pressure on employees and evaluate their impact
- (H) identify the sources of conflict in the workplace and evaluate alternative approaches to conflict resolution.

SETTING THE SCENE

Cathay Pacific avoids damaging strike just before busy holiday season

Cathay Pacific has avoided a threatened strike by cabin crew after it agreed a compromise deal with the flight attendants' union. The union welcomed the deal, which gave it most of what it was asking for, and called off the strike. The industrial dispute was over a new money-saving health insurance scheme that Cathay wanted to introduce for its 10 000 workers that would have forced them to pay for visits to the doctor. Cathay has now agreed to drop these charges until May and then to allow ten free visits to the doctor each year. The company refused to say how much the compromise would cost. 'I hope that the management will now improve labour–management relations and continue to work with us,' said Becky Kwan, the chairwoman of the flight attendants' union.

Source: www.iht.com

Points to think about:

- What was the cause of the conflict between employees and the employer?
- Suggest **three** other possible causes of conflict between an employer and its employees.
- Examine the likely reasons for Cathay Pacific agreeing to the costly compromise to solve this dispute.

16 Employer and employee relations

Introduction

Conflict resulting from differing objectives may be inevitable between labour and management within business. How can these conflicts be resolved or at least reduced so that the disagreement is not so great that it prevents all forms of co-ordination and working together? How can positive co-operation be achieved between these two groups for the benefit of the business and all stakeholders?

The methods used by employees and employers to achieve their objectives will depend on the relative 'strength' of each side. Much also depends on the culture and legal structure of the country in which the organisation operates, as well as the culture of the business itself. In some countries, trade unions are still illegal or their operations are strictly controlled. At the other extreme, in the European Union, workers' rights over minimum pay levels, security of employment and working conditions are protected by laws that restrict quite substantially the independence of management in deciding on such issues.

Collective bargaining

KEY TERM

collective bargaining the negotiations between employees' representatives (trade unions) and employers and their representatives on issues of common interest such as pay and conditions of work

The opposite of collective bargaining is individual bargaining, where each worker discusses separately with his/her employer issues such as pay and conditions. This process becomes unwieldy in large organisations. Instead, many employees belong to trade unions or professional associations and these bodies bargain or negotiate on their behalf. In some countries, employers also belong to employers' associations that negotiate with unions and any agreements made will cover all firms that belong to the association.

The growing power and membership of trade unions in the twentieth century in the USA and Europe led to the widespread development of national collective bargaining. These collective negotiations can make trade union leaders very powerful as they may be able to threaten and actually call for strike action from all of their members, which could bring the entire industry to a halt.

This form of collective bargaining was never used in some countries where unions were weak or illegal. Even in Europe and the USA, national collective bargaining is now much less common as national agreements are not always suitable or affordable for smaller or less profitable businesses. Agreements are now often made by individual businesses or business units negotiating with employees' representatives regionally or locally.

Trade unions and their role

KEY TERMS

trade union an organisation of working people with the objective of improving the pay and working conditions of its members and providing them with support and legal services

industrial action measures taken by the workforce or trade union to put pressure on management to settle an industrial dispute in favour of employees

WHY WORKERS JOIN TRADE UNIONS

1 'Power through solidarity' has been the basis of union influence and this is best illustrated by their ability to engage in 'collective bargaining'. This is when trade unions negotiate on behalf of all of their members in a business. This puts workers in a stronger position than if they negotiated individually to gain higher pay deals and better working conditions.
2 Individual industrial action – one worker going on strike, for example, is not likely to be very effective. Collective industrial action could result in much more influence over employers during industrial disputes.
3 Unions provide legal support to employees who claim unfair dismissal or poor conditions of work.
4 Unions pressurise employers to ensure that all legal requirements are met, e.g. health and safety rules regarding the use of machinery.

UNION RECOGNITION

KEY TERM

trade union recognition when an employer formally agrees to conduct negotiations on pay and working conditions with a trade union rather than bargaining individually with each worker

In many countries it is not a legal requirement to recognise trade unions. In the UK, employers did not have to 'recognise' a union in the workplace until the law was changed in 2000. This meant that the employer could choose not to bargain collectively with a union official representing the workforce. Instead, all workers would be treated individually and negotiations over pay and conditions and matters of discipline would only be dealt with between the employer and each individual worker. Since 2000, workers have been able to vote on whether they should demand employer recognition of their union. If a majority support this idea, then it will be illegal for an employer not to deal with union officials. Such a law is likely to boost union membership and influence.

ACTIVITY 16.1

Read the case study below and then answer the questions that follow.

Trade union? India's BPO workers say 'no'

From Europe to North America, India's offshore workers (Business Process Outsourcing) – call-centre operators, data-entry clerks and telemarketers – may seem like the sweatshop labourers of the information age, toiling for long hours with modest pay, but an international alliance of unions that wants them to become union members is finding it very hard to recruit them. These workers think of themselves as members of a relatively well-paid, respected professional elite in no need of union protection. The back office outsourcing industry in India employs around 400 000 workers, yet the Union Network International (UNI) organisation has only recruited 500 of them so far. 'A union would make sense if we had no job security,' said K. V. Sudhakar, a technical support worker for IMB, 'but there are so many jobs and so few qualified staff that firms are trying all possible means to keep employees happy so they will not leave.'

A similar situation has arisen in the USA where unions have lost many members as traditional manufacturing industries decline. They find it very difficult to recruit white-collar workers and professional workers in the finance and other service industries.

An Indian worker who did join UNI is Raghavan Iyengar, a call centre supervisor. He said companies give incentives to those who work beyond contracted time and young workers often ignore health problems, such as insomnia and bad backs, to earn extra money. 'The industry's motto is 'shut your mouth and take your money', he said, 'and we want to change that.'

Source: www.rediff.com

Most workers in call centres in India see little point in joining a trade union

15 marks, 25 minutes

1 Explain why employers might not want employees to join trade unions. **[5]**

2 If you were a call-centre worker in India, would you join the UNI? Give both advantages and disadvantages before explaining your decision. **[10]**

It could also have benefits for the employers:

- Employers would be able to negotiate with one officer from the union rather than with individual workers.
- The union system could provide an additional, useful channel of communication with the workers – two-way communication in the sense that workers' problems could be raised with management by the union and the plans of the employers could be discussed via the union organisation.
- Unions can impose discipline on members who plan to take hasty industrial action that could disrupt a business – this makes such action less likely.
- The growth of responsible, partnership unionism has given employers an invaluable forum for discussing issues of common interest and making new workplace agreements. Very often, these will lead to increased productivity, which should help to secure jobs and raise profits.

EXAM TIP

You will need to know about trade unions in your own country. Are they legal? If so, do the majority of workers belong to them? What actions do unions take in your country?

ACTIVITY 16.2

Investigate a recent industrial dispute in your country. Analyse the causes of the dispute, what actions were taken by employees and employers to settle the dispute and how it ended.

Industrial action by Italian metal workers – businesses may have to shut down while workers are on strike

Action taken by employees and employers

UNIONS

Trade union objectives include higher pay, improved conditions and security of employment. Union leaders can use a number of measures to 'encourage' employers to accept their demands for improvements in pay and conditions:

- Negotiations – and, possibly, agreeing to arbitration (see page 168).
- Go slow – a form of industrial action in which workers keep working but at the minimum pace as demanded by their contract of employment. Bonus payments may be lost by workers, but at busy times of the year this action can be very disruptive and costly for employers.
- Work to rule – a form of industrial action in which employees refuse to do any work outside the precise terms of the employment contract. Overtime will not be worked and all non-contractual co-operation will be withdrawn.
- Overtime bans – industrial action in which workers refuse to work more than the contracted number of hours each week. During busy times of the year, this could lead to much lost output for the employer.
- Strike action – the most extreme form of industrial action in which employees totally withdraw their labour for a period of time. This may lead to production stopping completely. Strike action leads to the business shutting down during the industrial action.

EMPLOYERS

Settling disputes with unions can increase the long-term profits of the business. Settlement may be reached in a variety of ways:

- Negotiations – these aim to reach a compromise solution. If face-to-face negotiations with union leaders fail to reach an agreement, then the dispute may require arbitration – (see page 168).
- Public relations – using the media to try to gain public support for the employer's position in the dispute. This may put pressure on the union to settle for a compromise solution.
- Threats of redundancies – these threats would, again, put pressure on unions to agree to a settlement of the dispute, but they might inflame opinions on the employees side and could be looked upon as 'bullying' and lead to poor publicity for the employer.
- Changes of contract – if employees are taking advantage of their employment contracts to work to rule or ban overtime, then new contracts could, when the old ones are due for renewal, be issued that insist on higher work rates or overtime working.
- Closure – closure of the business or the factory/office where the industrial dispute takes place would certainly solve the dispute! It would lead to redundancy for all of the workers and no output and profit for the business owners. This is a very extreme measure and would only be threatened or used if the demands of the union would, if agreed to, lead to a serious loss being made by the business or factory anyway.
- Lock-outs – short-term closure of the business or factory to prevent employees from working and being paid. Some workers who are not keen on losing pay for long periods may put pressure on their union leaders to agree to a reasonable settlement of the dispute.

WHICH SIDE IS STRONGER?

The power and influence of employers and unions in an industrial dispute will depend on a number of factors as outlined in Table 16.1.

Sources of conflict at work

Employers aim to achieve satisfactory profit levels by keeping costs, including labour costs, as low as possible. However, workers – remember that wage costs are often a major part of total business costs – will seek to obtain

Union/employee power will be strong when:	Employer power will be strong when:
• most workers belong to one union • all workers agree to take the industrial action decided on • the business is very busy, operating close to full capacity, does not want to disappoint customers and profits are high • industrial action rapidly costs the employer large amounts of lost output/revenue/profits • there is public support for the union case, e.g. for very low-paid workers • inflation is high so a high wage increase would seem 'reasonable' to maintain living standards • labour costs are a low proportion of total costs.	• unemployment is high – there are few alternative jobs for workers to take • the employer takes action, e.g. lock-out has a very quick impact on workers' wages • there is public support for the employer, e.g. when unions are asking for rises much higher than other workers receive • profits are low and threats of closure are taken seriously • threats of relocation to low-cost countries are taken seriously, e.g. the business has already closed other plants and relocated them.

Table 16.1 *The relative strength of unions and employers*

high pay and shorter working hours. There is clear scope for conflict here, but it is not the only source of possible clashes of interest between labour and management. Some other common areas of dispute or conflict are shown in Table 16.2.

Strategies to reduce conflict

KEY TERMS

single-union agreement an employer recognises just one union for purposes of collective bargaining

no-strike agreement unions agree to sign an agreement with employers not to strike in exchange for greater involvement in decisions that affect the workforce

SINGLE-UNION AGREEMENT

Single-union deals are one strategy to reduce conflict at work. Just 50 years ago, the UK still had over 100 separate trade unions. This number is now much reduced, but it is still possible for the workforce of one business to have members in several different unions. This makes collective bargaining much more difficult and time consuming. In addition, it can lead to inter-union disputes over which skills or grades of workers should get the highest pay rise. It can also reduce the flexibility of a workforce if members of one union are prevented from doing the work of other workers belonging to another union. This is called a demarcation dispute and reduces total productivity.

Many employers now insist on signing recognition deals with just one union. There has been a great deal of competition among unions for these deals, as total membership depends on them. Two potential consequences of such deals are that the newly united workforce and its union representatives may be able to exert greater influence during collective bargaining, and that just one union may not effectively represent the range of skilled staff, and their needs at work, that exist in most businesses. The growth of single-union agreements has led to further mergers between unions to prevent smaller unions being gradually excluded from all such industrial deals.

NO-STRIKE AGREEMENTS

At first glance, these seem rather unusual agreements for a union to sign with an employer. Why give up the most effective form of industrial action? There are two main reasons:

Cause of conflict	Common management view	Common employee view
Business change, e.g. relocation or new technology	Change is necessary to remain competitive and profitable.	Change can lead to job losses, may result in retraining in new skills that causes uncertainty over ability to cope. Demands for increased 'flexibility' from staff may reduce job security.
Rationalisation and organisational change	Business needs to cut overheads and be flexible and adaptable to deal with 'globalised' low-cost competition.	Cost cuts and rationalisation always seem to fall on employees – not the senior managers or owners of the business. Reduced job security will damage employee motivation.

Table 16.2 *Common causes of labour–management conflict*

1 It improves the image of the union as being a responsible representative body and this could encourage employees to become members.
2 These deals are often agreed to in exchange for greater union involvement in both decision-making and in representing employees in important negotiations. This has led to union–employer agreements to change working methods and increase labour flexibility that lead to higher productivity, higher profits *and* higher pay and worker participation. This is sometimes referred to as a win–win settlement as both employer and employee will gain from this new partnership approach to industrial relations.

CONCILIATION AND ARBITRATION

KEY TERMS

conciliation the use of a third party in industrial disputes to encourage both employer and union to discuss an acceptable compromise solution

arbitration resolving an industrial dispute by using an independent third party to judge and recommend an appropriate solution

In the UK, ACAS (Advisory, Conciliation and Arbitration Service) was set up in 1975. Its primary function is to reduce conflict in UK industry by improving employment relations between employers and employees. It gives advice to employers and employees and their representatives on issues likely to cause disputes between them. Most countries have a similar organisation. As a conciliator in industrial disputes, ACAS would listen to both sides of the argument – perhaps over pay or working conditions – and attempt to find common ground. This might then be used as a basis for an eventual compromise agreement.

Arbitration is different. An ACAS official will again listen to both sides of a dispute, but will now make a decision for resolving the disagreement. This might be a compromise between the opposing views of employer's and union's officials. If both parties agreed to accept this, then this becomes binding arbitration. The risk of the arbitrator setting the compromise closer to 'one side' than the other can lead to both groups establishing extreme negotiating positions. For example, in wage negotiations, a union might ask for a rise of 10% rather than a more realistic figure of, say, 5%. This is in the hope that the final decision of the arbitrator may be influenced by the high pay claim and will set a 'compromise' of 7.5% – which is what the union was hoping to achieve anyway!

An alternative form of arbitration, designed to prevent this union strategy (and also to discourage employers from offering a very low increase) is called 'pendulum arbitration'. In this case, both sides must accept the decision of the arbitrator and the arbitrator is forced to accept either the union's pay claim or the employer's pay offer because no compromise is allowed. Thus, if a union submitted a very high claim or if employers offered a very low rise, then the arbitrator would be tempted to 'swing' the decision towards the other side completely.

EMPLOYEE PARTICIPATION AND INDUSTRIAL DEMOCRACY

These are attempts to reduce industrial conflict by achieving a closer working relationship between employees and employers. This then might lead to commonly agreed objectives. Participation at work by employees can take different forms:

- Industrial democracy, in its purest form, implies workers' control over industry, perhaps linked to workers' ownership of the business, e.g. producer co-operatives.
- Employee or trade union directors on the company's board of directors represent the workers' approach to major company issues at the highest decision-making level.
- Works councils, e.g. European Works Councils, discuss issues such as the employment situation, major investment projects planned by the business, major organisational changes and health and safety.
- Autonomous work groups and quality circles lead to employee participation in decision-making and help to avoid the 'them and us' environment. By involving workers in everyday decisions that impact on their working lives, such as work schedules, improvements in work practices and how to plan team working, the threat of industrial disputes is reduced.

THEORY OF KNOWLEDGE

IBERIA SET FOR MORE STRIKE ACTION

Unions representing Spanish airline Iberia's cabin crews have announced a further eight days of strikes unless a pay agreement can be reached.

The airline has been forced to ground hundreds of flights due to strike action. Cabin staff are in dispute with the airline's management over plans for a hiring and wage freeze. Analysts believe that unless Iberia's management can force through cost-cutting measures, the airline will have to make large-scale redundancies.

Source: www.bbc.co.uk/news (adapted)

Trade unions are often thought to act in a way that promotes the best interests of their members. To what extent is there a conflict between reason and a union acting in the interests of its members?

OVER TO YOU

REVISION CHECKLIST

1 Explain **two** reasons why good labour–management relations are important to a business.
2 Define collective bargaining.
3 State **two** benefits to a business of collective bargaining with representatives of the workforce.
4 State **three** possible benefits to a worker from joining a trade union.
5 Would you advise a firm to sign a single-union deal with one particular union? Explain your answer.
6 Would you advise an employer to agree to pendulum arbitration when attempting to settle a pay dispute with a trade union? Explain your answer.
7 Why would a union sign a no-strike deal with employers? What would it expect in return?
8 There is an industrial dispute between the managers and the employees' trade union of a large hotel in your town/city. Discuss the factors that will influence whether the final agreement to settle the dispute is a better deal for the employer or employees.

REVISION ACTIVITY

Read the case study below and then answer the questions that follow.

Safeguard Investments Ltd

Joe Hussain, the union representative responsible for pay negotiations at Safeguard Investments, had important decisions to make regarding this year's pay negotiations. First, the human resources manager had offered binding arbitration to resolve any dispute between them and to avoid the lengthy and bitter negotiations that had taken place last year. The manager had told Joe, 'We need to be responsible about these negotiations as the business wants a motivated workforce, but we cannot offer a rise above the level of inflation – just 2% a year.' Joe was convinced that an independent arbitrator would consider this to be unacceptable given the very low levels of unemployment in the finance industry and the high profitability of Safeguard. Joe had to put forward a pay claim – should he ask for 5%, which is the average increase for the industry this year, or 10%, assuming that the arbitrator would find a compromise between his position and that of the HR manager? His views were also being influenced by the last statement from the HR manager, 'Perhaps we ought to go for pendulum arbitration to avoid both of us going for ridiculous figures.'

16 marks, 28 minutes

1 Consider the arguments for and against Joe accepting the principle of binding arbitration for this year's pay settlement. **[6]**

2 Assume that he agrees to binding arbitration. Prepare a short report for Joe stating the case for and against a 5% or 10% pay claim:
   a if pendulum arbitration is to be adopted
   b if non-pendulum arbitration is to be adopted. **[10]**

EXAM PRACTICE QUESTION

Read the case study below and then answer the questions that follow.

'SINGLE GLOBAL SUPER UNION WITHIN A DECADE'

An international trade union could be created within a decade, the leader of one of Europe's biggest trade unions has declared. The UK union Amicus has signed solidarity agreements with IG Metall in Germany and two unions in the USA. It is looking for agreements with other unions in other countries.

Derek Simpson, general secretary of Amicus said, 'Our aim is to create a powerful single union that will cross international boundaries to challenge the global forces of capital. It will increase the collective bargaining power of unions.'

Trade union leaders are worried by the growth of globalisation that has weakened their power and reduced their membership. Because employers can now easily transfer production to low-cost countries, the unions' power to bargain and negotiate higher pay deals has been much weakened. The answer, according to Amicus, is to 'globalise trade unions' too. A single global union would be able to negotiate with multinationals on behalf of members throughout the world and this might prevent worker exploitation in very low-wage economies.

'Our aim is to match up to globalised industry. We will force multinational companies to sign deals with one single international union. This will stop them making changes to workers' pay and rights in one country without consulting unions elsewhere.'

20 marks, 35 minutes

1 Explain what is meant by:
   a a 'single-union deal (or agreement)'
   b 'collective bargaining'. [4]

2 Analyse **two** potential benefits to both workers and employees of a 'globalised union'. [7]

3 To what extent would any one multinational company be likely to be affected by the development of one large global trade union? [9]

17 Crisis management and contingency planning

This chapter covers syllabus section 2.8 (Higher level only)

On completing this chapter you should be able to:

- H explain the difference between crisis management and contingency planning
- H evaluate the costs and benefits of contingency planning
- H discuss how far it is possible to plan for a crisis.

SETTING THE SCENE

Planning for the worst pays off

When arsonists destroyed the head office of marketing agency, FDS Group, chairwoman Allison Williams ensured her 75 employees were relocated and the business fully operational within three working days. 'Having a disaster recovery plan as part of our corporate plan helped to re-house the entire business in days and sent out a strong positive signal to our customers,' said Allison. 'Our contingency planning routines meant that our data were backed up off site. We made use of our contacts in the local business community and had two temporary offices to view within 24 hours. The company secretary made sure the insurance company's loss adjustor was on site by noon of the day after the fire. I've never been so proud of my staff, and suppliers fell over themselves to help us too. There was no time to dwell on the situation – most of our customers are blue-chip businesses and they wanted the reassurance that we could be operational again as soon as possible.'

Managers from FDS held several informal meetings with customers within days of the fire to reassure them that it was 'business as usual'. This was also part of the firm's contingency plan. This demonstration of the firm's commitment to its customers paid off as it showed that customers' needs were valued above everything else.

Source: www.businesslink.gov.uk (adapted)

Points to think about:

- Explain whether you think the time spent by this business in planning for disasters was worthwhile or not.
- What problems might this business have experienced if it had not 'prepared for the worst'?
- Do you think that even very small businesses should engage in some form of contingency planning? Justify your answer.

17 Crisis management and contingency planning

Introduction

KEY TERMS

contingency planning preparing the immediate steps to be taken by an organisation in the event of a crisis or emergency

crisis management steps taken by an organisation to limit the damage from a crisis by handling, retaining and resolving it

Contingency planning is also known as 'business continuity planning' or 'disaster-recovery planning', which perhaps gives a better idea of what it is for. Unplanned events can have a devastating effect on businesses of any size. Crises such as fire, floods, damage to stock, illness of key staff, IT system failure or accidents on the business's premises or involving its vehicles could all make it difficult or impossible to carry out normal everyday activities. At worst, important customers could be lost or the firm could go out of business altogether. Contingency planning helps with crisis management – by being prepared with a series of procedures to be put into effect if an emergency occurs, the organisation will be better able to manage most crisis situations.

Effective contingency planning allows a business to take steps to minimise the potential impact of a disaster – and ideally prevent it from happening in the first place.

Key steps in contingency planning

1. Identify the potential disasters that could affect the business. Some of these are common to all businesses, but others will be specific to certain industries. For example, the oil industry must plan for oil tankers sinking, explosions at refineries and leakages in oil and gas pipelines.
2. Assess the likelihood of these occurring. Some incidents are more likely to occur than others and the degree of impact on business operations varies too. It seems obvious to plan for the most 'common' disasters, but the most unlikely occurrences can have the greatest total risk to a business's future. These issues need to be balanced carefully by managers when choosing which disaster events to prepare for most thoroughly.
3. Minimise the potential impact of crises. Effective planning can sometimes remove a potential risk altogether. When this is not possible, the key is to minimise the damage a disaster can do. This does not just mean protecting fixed assets and people, but also the company's reputation and public goodwill, as far as possible. This is often best done by the publicity department telling the truth, indicating the causes when known and giving full details of how to contact the business and the actions being taken to minimise the impact on the public. Staff training and practice drills with mock incidents are often the most effective ways of preparing to minimise negative impact.
4. Plan for continued operations of the business. As in the 'Setting the scene' case study above, prior planning can help with alternative accommodation and IT data – the sooner the business can begin trading again, the less the impact is likely to be on customer relationships.

Table 17.1 lists the benefits and limitations of contingency planning.

Benefits	Limitations
• Reassures staff, customers and local residents that concerns for safety are a priority. • Minimises negative impact on customers and suppliers in the event of a major disaster. • Public relations response is much more likely to be speedy and appropriate with senior managers being used to promote what the company intends to do, by when and how.	• Costly and time consuming – not just the planning process but the need to train staff and have practice drills of what to do in the event of fire, IT failure, terrorist attack, accident involving company vehicles and so on. • Needs to be constantly updated as the number and range of potential disasters can change over time. • Staff training needs to be increased if labour turnover is high. • Avoiding disasters is still better than planning for what to do if they occur.

Table 17.1 Contingency planning – benefits and limitations

THEORY OF KNOWLEDGE

CRISIS AS NATIONAL FOOTBALL TEAM REFUSES TO TRAIN

France's football players refused to train on Sunday following Nicolas Anelka's expulsion from the squad for verbally abusing coach Raymond Domenech. Domenech read out a statement from his squad which said: 'To show our opposition to the decision taken [on Anelka], all the players decided not to take part in training.' The French Football Federation's managing director subsequently quit. Moments before a public training session was about to begin, Domenech had to separate captain Patrice Evra and fitness coach Robert Duverne. Duverne is understood to have stormed away from an argument with the Manchester United defender, throwing his accreditation badge to the ground.

Source: www.bbc.co.uk/news 21/6/2010 (adapted)

To what extent is a manager's response to a crisis instinctive?

OVER TO YOU

REVISION CHECKLIST

1 Explain, with business examples, the difference between crisis management and contingency planning.
2 Explain the steps your school or college should take in planning for the effects of a serious fire.
3 How can contingency planning reduce the chances of some crises from occurring?
4 Explain why contingency planning cannot remove all risks of emergencies occurring.
5 Explain the consequences for an oil company of not having planned for how to deal with a major oil-tanker disaster.

REVISION ACTIVITY

Read the case study opposite and then answer the questions that follow.

Stop and think: Cadbury had a plan ready

The risk of salmonella contaminating millions of chocolate bars put Cadbury's corporate plan in doubt. The problem was caused by a leaking pipe in Cadbury's UK factory but the company's contingency plan swung into action. Over a million chocolate bars were recalled by the company, they were disposed of in a completely safe way and the Food Standards Agency was informed. Retailers were fully compensated for stock that was destroyed. Cadbury apologised to all customers. Business consultants doubted whether the incident would cause any long-term damage to the company's image or brand names because of the detailed contingency plan that was put into operation.

20 marks, 30 minutes

1 Outline **two** other incidents or 'disasters' that could have a major impact on Cadbury's sales and reputation. [8]

2 Evaluate the importance of contingency planning in this case. [12]

THE BP GULF OF MEXICO DISASTER

On 20 April 2010, the Deepwater Horizon drilling rig exploded in the Gulf of Mexico, killing 11 workers and causing an oil spill that soon became the worst environmental disaster in US history. The rig was drilling in about 1525m of water, pushing the boundaries of deep-water drilling technology. Following the explosion the Deepwater Horizon sank to the bottom of the Gulf after burning for 36 hours.

The US Coast Guard quickly became involved with the incident putting a **crisis management** plan into place. Environmental experts raised concerns that the Macondo well Deepwater Horizon was drilling could be releasing up to 40 000 barrels of oil per day into the sea. A few days after the disaster, oil from the leaking well began washing ashore in Louisiana; fragile coastal wetlands were inundated with thick, brown mud, beaches were covered in black tar and a black shadow appeared over hundreds of square miles of the Gulf of Mexico. The US Administration reacted furiously to the incident accusing BP of 'criminal negligence'.

BP made a number of vain attempts to cap the leaking well until it finally stopped the leak in July. BP, under considerable political pressure, announced in June that it would place $20 billion in a fund to compensate victims of the oil spill and said it would not pay a shareholder dividend in 2010. By early July BP's share price had fallen by 50 per cent since the start of the crisis. The BP CEO, Tony Hayward, came under pressure because of his perceived mishandling of the crisis and received a 'tongue-lashing' at a hearing in the US Congress because BP seemed to have no **contingency plan** to deal with the crisis. Tony Hayward was eventually forced to resign.

EXAM PRACTICE QUESTION

Read the case study and then answer the questions that follow.

25 marks, 45 minutes

1 Define the following terms:
   a crisis management
   b contingency plan [4]

2 Outline the key steps BP would have gone through to produce a contingency plan for a crisis such as the Deepwater Horizon. [5]

3 Analyse the reasons why the BP share price fell by 50 per cent following the Deepwater Horizon crisis. [7]

4 Discuss the likely benefits and limitations of BP's contingency planning when preparing for any future disasters like Deepwater Horizon. [9]

18 Sources of finance

This chapter covers syllabus section 3.1

On completing this chapter you should be able to:

- understand internal and external finance
- analyse the different sources of long-, medium- and short-term finance
- understand the role played by the main financial institutions
- evaluate the advantages and disadvantages of each form of finance for a given situation.

SETTING THE SCENE

Two US companies – different sources of finance

The financial differences between two of the USA's biggest companies could not be greater. The globally recognised brands of General Motors (GM) and Coca-Cola face very different futures too. The soft drinks company announced record sales and profits for the three months to October 2008 – net profits exceeded $1.8 billion! It has over $5 billion in cash with high profit margins and its share price has not slumped in the same way as that of most companies during the global recession. It can afford to launch more new products and enter new markets without the need to borrow or sell further shares. In contrast, General Motors is in deep trouble. Its share price fell to a 60-year low in November 2008 – just $3.36. Some analysts believe the price could fall to below $1 a share, so to try to raise finance from selling new shares would be pointless – who would want to buy them? The company already has $300 billion of debt and it made a huge loss of $4.2 billion in just three months. It is selling assets – closed factory sites, for example – to raise funds, and has also appealed to the US government for emergency finance. GM already has access to $25 billion of cheap US government loans and grants to help it over the current crisis.

Source: http://newsvote.bbc.co.uk and http://articles.moneycentral.msn.com (adapted)

Points to think about:

- List all of the possible sources of business finance contained in this case study.
- Why is Coca-Cola able to finance expansion without loans or selling shares? What are the advantages of this?
- Do you think that the US government should provide more financial aid to General Motors?
- What impact does it have on a public limited company if its share price falls rapidly?

Introduction

Finance is required for many business activities. Below are some examples:

- Setting up a business will require start-up capital of cash injections from the owner(s) to purchase essential capital equipment and, possibly, premises.
- Businesses need to finance their working capital – the day-to-day finance needed to pay bills and expenses and to build up stocks.
- Business expansion needs finance to increase the capital assets held by the firm – and, often, expansion will involve higher working capital needs.
- Expansion can be achieved by taking over other businesses. Finance is then needed to buy out the owners of the other firm.
- Special situations will often lead to a need for greater finance. A decline in sales, possibly as a result of economic recession, could lead to cash needs to keep the business stable; or a large customer could fail to pay for goods, and finance is quickly needed to pay for essential expenses.
- Apart from purchasing fixed assets, finance is often used to pay for research and development into new products or to invest in new marketing strategies, such as opening up overseas markets.

Some of these situations will need investment in the business for many years. Others will need only short-term funding – for around one year or less. Some finance requirements of the business are for between one and five years – medium-term finance. The important point to note about the list above is that all of these situations will need different types of finance. In practice, this means that no one source or type of finance is likely to be suitable in all cases.

KEY TERMS

start-up capital capital needed by an entrepreneur to set up a business

working capital the capital needed to pay for raw materials, day-to-day running costs and credit offered to customers. In accounting terms: working capital = current assets – current liabilities

Capital and revenue expenditure

Capital expenditure is the purchase of assets that are expected to last for more than one year, such as buildings and machinery. Revenue expenditure is spending on all costs and assets other than fixed assets and includes wages and salaries and materials bought for stock. These two types of spending will be financed in different ways as the length of time that the money is 'tied up' will be very different.

Sources of finance

This section deals initially with sources of finance for limited companies – and then considers sole traders and partnerships. Companies are able to raise finance from a wide range of sources. It is useful to classify these into:

- internal money raised from the business's own assets or from profits left in the business (ploughed-back or retained profits)
- external money raised from sources outside the business.

Another classification is also often made, that of short-, medium- and long-term finance; this distinction is made clearer by considering Figure 18.1.

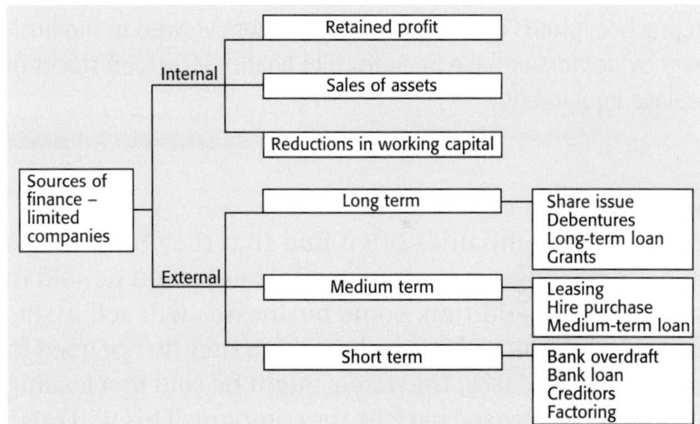

Figure 18.1 Sources of finance for limited companies

INTERNAL SOURCES OF FINANCE

Profits retained in the business

If a company is trading profitably, some of these profits will be taken in tax by the government (corporation tax) and some is nearly always paid out to the owners or shareholders (dividends). If any profit remains, it is kept in the business and this retained profit becomes a source of finance for future activities. Clearly, a newly formed company or one trading at a loss will not have access to this source of finance. For other companies, retained profits are a very significant source of funds for expansion – see again the Coca-Cola situation in 'Setting the scene' case study above. Once invested back into the business, these retained profits will not be paid out to shareholders, so they represent a permanent source of finance.

Coca-Cola finances most of its global expansion from retained profits

EXAM TIP

Do not assume that a profitable business is cash rich – and that it can use all of its profits as a source of finance for future projects. In practice, profits are often 'tied up' in money owed to the business by debtors or have been used to finance increased stocks or replace equipment.

Sale of assets

Established companies often find that they have assets that are no longer fully employed. These could be sold to raise cash. In addition, some businesses will sell assets that they still intend to use, but which they do not need to own. In these cases, the assets might be sold to a leasing specialist and leased back by the company. This will raise capital – but there will be an additional fixed cost in the leasing and rental payment.

In 2008, AIG insurance company planned to sell off some of its subsidiaries to raise cash to help the company through difficult times. For example, the sale of one of the world's largest aircraft leasing companies, International Lease Finance, could raise several billion dollars. In the previous year, HSBC sold its huge London headquarters for \$2 billion, but will stay in the building and lease it back from the new owners – at an annual rent of \$80 million.

Managing working capital more efficiently

When businesses increase stock levels or sell goods on credit to customers (debtors), they use a source of finance. When companies reduce these assets – by reducing their working capital – capital is released, which acts as a source of finance for other uses. There are risks in cutting down on working capital, however. As will be seen in Chapter 20, managing working capital by cutting back on current assets by selling stocks or reducing debts owed to the business may reduce the firm's liquidity – its ability to pay short-term debts – to risky levels (see page 196).

Internal sources of finance – an evaluation

This type of capital has no direct cost to the business, although there may be an opportunity cost and if assets are leased back after being sold, there will be leasing charges. Internal finance does not increase the liabilities or debts of the business. There is no risk of loss of control by the original owners as no shares are sold. However, it is not available for all companies, for example newly formed ones or unprofitable ones with few 'spare' assets. Solely depending on internal sources of finance for expansion can slow down business growth, as the pace of development will be limited by the annual profits or the value of assets to be sold. Thus, rapidly expanding companies are often dependent on external sources for much of their finance.

EXAM TIP

Do not make the mistake of suggesting that selling shares is a form of internal finance for companies. Although the shareholders own the business, the company is a separate legal unit and, therefore, the shareholders are 'outside' it.

EXTERNAL SOURCES OF FINANCE

Short-term finance

There are three main sources of short-term external finance:

- bank overdrafts
- trade credit
- debt factoring.

Bank overdrafts

A bank overdraft is the most 'flexible' of all sources of finance. The amount of finance can vary from day to day, depending on the needs of the business. The bank allows the business to 'overdraw' on its account at the bank by writing cheques to a greater value than the balance in the account. This overdrawn amount should always be agreed in advance and always has a limit beyond which the firm should not go. Businesses may need to increase the overdraft for short periods of time if customers do not pay as quickly as expected or if a large delivery of stocks has to be paid for. This form of finance often carries high interest charges. In addition, if a bank becomes concerned about the stability of one of its customers, it can 'call in' the overdraft and force the firm to pay it back. In extreme cases, this may lead to business failure.

Trade credit
By delaying the payment of bills for goods or services received, a business is, in effect, obtaining finance. Its suppliers, or creditors, are providing goods and services without receiving immediate payment. The downside to these periods of credit is that they are not 'free' – discounts for quick payment and supplier confidence are often lost if the business takes too long to pay its suppliers.

Debt factoring
When a business sells goods on credit, it creates a debtor. The longer the time allowed to this debtor to pay, the more finance the business has to find to carry on trading. One option is to sell these claims on debtors to a debt factor. In this way immediate cash is obtained but not for the full amount of the debt. This is because the debt-factoring company's profits are made by discounting the debts and not paying their full value. When full payment is received from the original customer, the debt factor makes a profit. Smaller firms who sell goods on hire purchase often sell the debt to credit-loan firms, so that the credit agreement is never with the firm but with the specialist provider.

KEY TERMS

overdraft bank agrees to a business borrowing up to an agreed limit as and when required

factoring selling of claims over debtors to a debt factor in exchange for immediate liquidity – only a proportion of the value of the debts will be received as cash

Medium-term finance
There are two main sources of medium-term external finance:

- hire purchase and leasing
- medium-term bank loan.

Hire purchase and leasing
These methods are often used to obtain fixed assets with a medium life span – one to five years. Hire purchase is a form of credit for purchasing an asset over a period of time. This avoids making a large initial cash payment to buy the asset.

Leasing involves a contract with a leasing or finance company to acquire, but not necessarily to purchase, assets over the medium term. A periodic payment is made over the life of the agreement, but the business does not have to purchase the asset at the end. This agreement allows the firms to avoid cash purchase of the asset. The risk of using unreliable or outdated equipment is reduced as the leasing company will repair and update the asset as part of the agreement. Neither hire purchase nor leasing is a cheap option, but they do improve the short-term cash-flow position of a company compared to outright purchase of an asset for cash.

KEY TERMS

leasing obtaining the use of equipment or vehicles and paying a rental or leasing charge over a fixed period. This avoids the need for the business to raise long-term capital to buy the asset. Ownership remains with the leasing company

hire purchase an asset is sold to a company which agrees to pay fixed repayments over an agreed time period – the asset belongs to the company

ACTIVITY 18.1

6 marks, 12 minutes

In each of the following cases, explain briefly why internal sources of finance might be unavailable or inadequate:

a a business needs to pay creditors after a period when it has made losses and the value of its assets have fallen
b the rapid expansion of a business, which requires expenditure several times greater than current profits
c the purchase of additional stocks by a retailer just before Christmas. [6]

Long-term finance
The two main choices here are debt or equity finance. Debt finance increases the liabilities of a company. Debt finance can be raised in two main ways:

- long-term loans from banks
- debentures (also known as loan stock or corporate bonds).

KEY TERMS

long-term loans loans that do not have to be repaid for at least one year

equity finance permanent finance raised by companies through the sale of shares

Long-term loans from banks
These may be offered at either a variable or a fixed interest rate. Fixed rates provide more certainty, but they can turn out to be expensive if the loan is agreed at a time of high interest rates. Companies borrowing from banks will often have to provide security or collateral for the loan; this means the right to sell an asset is given to the bank, if the company cannot repay the debt. Businesses with few assets to act as security may find it difficult to obtain loans – or may be asked to pay higher rates of interest.

ACTIVITY 18.2

Read the case study below and then answer the questions that follow.

EIB loans €30 million for research and development in aeronautics

A French company specialising in high-precision screws and other fasteners for the aeronautical industry has applied for – and been granted – a massive €30 million loan by the European Investment Bank. The capital will be used to finance a long-term research and development project at the group's headquarters near Paris to design new fasteners using lighter and stronger materials. It was thought that, with interest rates falling due to the global downturn and share prices also very volatile and uncertain, this form of finance was the best one to use at this time. Investors in shares are understandably nervous at the present time with uncertain share prices but also with research and development projects in particular, which can take years before they see any profit returned to the business.

Source: http://bulletin.sciencebusiness.net

12 marks, 21 minutes

Do you agree that loan capital was the best source of finance for this company for this project? Justify your answer. **[12]**

THEORY OF KNOWLEDGE

Many great businesses never really get started or are doomed to failure because banks do not like lending to people or organisations that have a significant risk of failing. How many products and services never reach the market to benefit consumers? How many people are never employed and how much wealth is never created because banks are reluctant to lend?

In groups, discuss the following statement: 'Banks have a moral responsibility to lend as much money as possible to new businesses.'

Debentures

KEY TERM

debentures or long-term bonds bonds issued by companies to raise debt finance, often with a fixed rate of interest

A company wishing to raise funds will issue or sell these to interested investors. The company agrees to pay a fixed rate of interest each year for the life of the debenture, which can be up to 25 years. The buyers may resell to other investors if they do not wish to wait until maturity before getting their original investment back. Debentures are usually not 'secured' on a particular asset. When they are secured the debentures are known as mortgage debentures. Debentures can be a very important source of long-term finance – in BT's 2007 accounts, for example, the total value of issued loan stock amounted to £3000 million. Convertible debentures can be, if the borrower wants to, switched into shares after a certain period of time and this means that the company issuing them will never have to pay the debenture back.

Sale of shares – equity finance

All limited companies issue shares when they are first formed. The capital raised will be used to purchase essential assets. Both private and public limited companies are able to sell further shares – up to the limit of their authorised share capital – in order to raise additional permanent finance. This capital never has to be repaid unless the company is completely wound up as a result of ceasing to trade. Private limited companies can sell further shares to existing shareholders. This has the advantage of not changing the control or ownership of the company – as long as all shareholders buy shares in the same proportion to those already owned. Owners of a private limited company can also decide to 'go public' and obtain the necessary authority to sell shares to the wider public. This would obviously have the potential to raise much more capital than from just the existing shareholders – but with the risk of some loss of control to the new shareholders.

In the UK, this can be done in two ways and these are quite typical for many countries:

- Obtain a listing on the Alternative Investment Market (AIM), which is that part of the London Stock Exchange concerned with smaller companies that want to raise only limited amounts of additional capital. The strict requirements for a full Stock Exchange listing are relaxed.
- Apply for a full listing on the London Stock Exchange by satisfying the criteria of (a) selling at least £50 000 worth of shares and (b) having a satisfactory trading record to give investors some confidence in the security of their investment. This sale of shares can be undertaken in two main ways:
  - Public issue by prospectus – this advertises the company and its share sale to the public and invites them to apply for the new shares. This is expensive, as the prospectus has to be prepared and issued.

The share issue is often underwritten or guaranteed by a merchant bank, which charges for its services.
- Arranging a placing of shares with institutional investors without the expense of a full public issue – once a company has gained plc status, it is still possible for it to raise further capital by selling additional shares. This is often done by means of a rights issue of shares.

KEY TERM

rights issue existing shareholders are given the right to buy additional shares at a discounted price

By not introducing new shareholders, the ownership of the business does not change and the company raises capital relatively cheaply as no public promotion or advertising of the share offer is necessary. However, as the rights issue increases the supply of shares to the stock exchange, the short-term effect is often to reduce the existing share price, which is unlikely to give existing shareholders too much confidence in the business if the share price falls too sharply.

Debt or equity capital – an evaluation

Which method of long-term finance should a company choose? There is no easy answer to this question, and, as seen above, some businesses will use both debt and equity finance for very large projects.

Debt finance has the following advantages:

- As no shares are sold, the ownership of the company does not change and is not 'diluted' by the issue of additional shares.
- Loans will be repaid eventually (apart from convertible debentures), so there is no permanent increase in the liabilities of the business.
- Lenders have no voting rights at annual general meetings.

ACTIVITY 18.3

Read the case studies below and then answer the questions that follow.

Indian companies take AIM

Four Indian companies floated on the London AIM market in the last 12 months. Between them these companies have raised a total of $387 million – without the costs or controls of a full public listing on the Stock Exchange. The companies are: KEF, Indus Gas, Mortice and OPG Power Ventures. The head of equity markets at the London Stock Exchange (LSE), Tracey Pierce, said: 'These companies have chosen to go global through AIM as they benefit from a pool of international capital, a professional investor base and a commitment from LSE to serve emerging economies.'

Source: http://www.londonstockexchange.com

Peacocks to go public

Peacocks, the discount clothing and houseware retailer, has issued its prospectus to the public. The company is going public to raise £42 million (after expenses) to fund further expansion and to repay outstanding debt. The managing director believes that there are great benefits in replacing debt finance with equity or share finance.

Source: www.timesonline.co.uk

Rights issue from Australian company

Australian fertiliser maker Incitec Pivot Ltd plans to raise A$1.17 billion through a rights issue of shares. Some of the capital will be used to repay loans and the rest will be used for long-term investment and research. The rights issue is being offered at A$2.50 per share, a 40% discount to the company's latest traded share price. The share issue is likely to reduce the market share price, at least in the short term. The company has also announced a tripling of annual profits, reflecting gains from a recent takeover and high fertiliser prices.

Source: http://malaysia.news.yahoo.com

26 marks, 45 minutes

1 Why do you think the Indian companies decided to join AIM rather than the full Stock Exchange? [4]

2 Peacocks decided to issue shares by prospectus to the general public. Why do you think this method of selling shares was selected? [4]

3 What did the managing director of Peacocks mean when he said that there were advantages in selling shares to repay debt? What are the advantages of repaying debts? [6]

4 Why do you think Incitec Pivot decided to use a rights issue of shares to raise capital? [4]

5 Evaluate whether a shareholder in Incitec Pivot would be advised to buy the rights issue of shares being offered. [8]

- Interest charges are an expense of the business and are paid out before corporation tax is deducted, while dividends on shares have to be paid from profits after tax.
- The gearing of the company increases and this gives shareholders the chance of higher returns in the future. This point is dealt with more fully in Chapter 23 (see page 235).

Equity capital has the following advantages:

- It never has to be repaid – it is permanent capital.
- Dividends do not have to be paid every year. In contrast, interest on loans must be paid when demanded by the lender.

Other sources of long-term finance

Grants

There are many agencies that are prepared, under certain circumstances, to grant funds to businesses. The two major sources in most European countries are the central government and the European Union. Usually, grants from these two bodies are given to small businesses or those expanding in developing regions of the country. Grants often come with 'strings attached', such as location and the number of jobs to be created, but if these conditions are met, grants do not have to be repaid.

Venture capital

Small companies that are not listed on the Stock Exchange can gain long-term investment funds from venture capitalists. These specialist organisations, or sometimes wealthy individuals, are prepared to lend risk capital to, or purchase shares in, business start-ups or small to medium-sized businesses that might find it difficult to raise capital from other sources. This could be because of risks of the business. These risks could come from the new technology that the company is dealing in or the complex research it is planning, in which other providers of finance are not prepared to get involved. Venture capitalists take great risks and could lose all of their money – but the rewards can be great. The value of certain 'high-tech' businesses has grown rapidly and many were financed, at least in part, by venture capitalists. Venture capitalists generally expect a share of the future profits or a sizeable stake in the business in return for their investment.

KEY TERM

venture capital risk capital invested in business start-ups or expanding small businesses, that have good profit potential, but do not find it easy to gain finance from other sources

FINANCE FOR SOLE TRADERS AND PARTNERSHIPS

Unincorporated businesses – sole traders and partnerships – cannot raise finance from the sale of shares and are most unlikely to be successful in selling debentures as they are likely to be relatively unknown firms. Owners of these businesses will have access to bank overdrafts, loans and credit from suppliers. They may borrow from family and friends, use the savings and profits made by the owners and, if a sole trader wishes to do this, take on partners to inject further capital.

An owner or partner in an unincorporated business runs the risk of losing all property owned if the firm fails. Lenders are often reluctant to lend to smaller businesses, which is what sole traders and partnerships tend to be, unless the owners give personal guarantees, supported by their own assets, should the business fail.

Grants are available to small and newly formed businesses as part of most governments' assistance to small businesses.

EXAM TIP

When answering case study examination questions, you should analyse what type of legal structure the business has and what sources of finance are available to it.

Micro-finance

This approach to providing small capital sums to entrepreneurs has grown in importance in recent years. In 1974, an economics lecturer at the University of Chittagong, Bangladesh, lent $27 to a group of very poor villagers. Not only did they repay this loan in full after their business ideas had been successful, but it led to the lecturer, Muhammad Yunus, eventually winning the

Muhammad Yunus, founder of the Grameen Bank, which makes small loans to people with no bank accounts

Nobel Peace Prize. He founded the Grameen Bank in 1983 to make very small loans – perhaps $20 a time – to poor people with no bank accounts and no chance of obtaining finance through traditional means. Since its foundation, the Grameen Bank has lent $6 billion to over 6 million Asian people, many of whom have set up their own very small enterprises with the capital.

Many business entrepreneurs in Bangladesh and other Asian countries have received micro-finance to help start their business.

ACTIVITY 18.4

SOURCES OF FINANCE

Copy out the following table and complete it by ticking the appropriate boxes alongside each source of finance.

Sources of finance	**Long-term finance**	**Medium-term finance**	**Short-term finance**	**Available to unincorporated businesses**	**Available to private limited companies**	**Available to public limited companies**
Sale of shares to the public						
Sale of debentures						
Leasing						
Debt factoring						
Loans from family						
Take on partners						
Rights issue of shares						
Ten-year bank loan						
Bank overdraft						

EXAM TIP

You should be able to recommend appropriate sources of finance for businesses needing capital for different reasons.

Making the financing decision

The size and the profitability of the business are clearly key considerations when managers make a financing choice. Small businesses are unlikely to be able to justify the costs of converting to plc status. They might also have limited internal funds available if the existing profit levels are low. These and other factors that are considered before making the financing choice are analysed in Table 18.1.

Factor influencing finance choice	Significance
Use to which finance is to be put – which affects the time period for which finance is required	• It is very risky to borrow long-term finance to pay for short-term needs. Businesses should match the sources of finance to the requirement. • Permanent capital may be needed for long-term business expansion. • Short-term finance would be advisable to finance a short-term need to increase stocks or pay creditors.
Cost	• Obtaining finance is never 'free' – even internal finance may have an opportunity cost. • Loans may become very expensive during a period of rising interest rates. • A stock exchange flotation can cost millions of dollars in fees and promotion of the share sale.
Amount required	• Share issues and sales of debentures, because of the administration and other costs, would generally only be used for large capital sums. • Small bank loans or reducing debtors' payment period could be used to raise small sums.
Legal structure and desire to retain control	• Share issues can only be used by limited companies – and only public limited companies can sell shares directly to the public. Doing this runs the risk of the current owners losing some control – except if a rights issue was used. • If the owners want to retain control of the business at all costs, then a sale of shares might be unwise.
Size of existing borrowing	• This is a key issue – the higher the existing debts of a business (compared to its size), the greater the risk of lending more. Banks and other lenders will become anxious about lending more finance. • This concept is referred to as gearing and is fully covered in Chapter 23 (see page 235).
Flexibility	• When a firm has a variable need for finance – for example, it has a seasonal pattern of sales and cash receipts – a flexible form of finance is better than a long-term and inflexible source.

Table 18.1 *Factors to be considered in making the 'source of finance' decision*

ACTIVITY 18.5

Read the case studies below and then answer the questions that follow.

Telkonet raises $3.5 million by sale of debentures

Telkonet Inc., the provider of energy management systems, has arranged to sell $3.5 million of 13% three-year debentures. The company plans to use the finance to cover working capital needs and to invest in expansion of its range of products. The announcement was made as world share prices recorded another bad day with further falls in most of the major indices.

Source: http://findarticles.com (adapted)

CuraGen raises $125 million from the sale of convertible debentures

This drug research and development company has issued $125 million of convertible debentures. The capital raised will be used to finance further long-term research into genomics-based drugs for medical purposes. The debentures offer a fixed 6% per year and are convertible into CuraGen's shares in seven years' time at a conversion price of $127 per share.

Source: http://bulletin.sciencebusiness.net

14 marks, 18 minutes

1 Explain the terms:
   a convertible debentures
   b working capital. [4]

2 Explain the benefits to both companies of raising finance through the sale of debentures rather than either selling shares or a long-term bank loan with variable interest rates. [10]

OVER TO YOU

REVISION CHECKLIST

1 State **three** examples of business situations that require additional finance.
2 Outline **two** ways in which businesses can raise finance from internal sources.
3 Explain the difference between long- and short-term finance.
4 Why might a new business find it difficult to raise external finance?
5 What is trade credit and why is it a source of finance?
6 Discuss whether a business would find debt factoring a suitable form of finance.
7 State **two** drawbacks to long-term loan finance.
8 Why might the managers of a private limited company be reluctant to apply for public limited company status for the business, despite the prospect of additional finance?
9 Why might a firm decide to lease new equipment rather than to purchase it outright?
10 Why is the management of working capital important to a firm's survival?
11 Examine the case for a company using a rights issue of shares rather than a full public offer of shares.
12 Why is increasing the long-term loans of a business beyond a certain level often described as being 'risky'?
13 State **two** factors that a manager should consider before deciding between loan and share capital to raise additional long-term finance.
14 Discuss the importance of the **two** factors you identified in question 13 in detail.
15 What information is a bank manager likely to request before granting additional loan capital to a business?

REVISION ACTIVITY

Read the case study below and then answer the questions that follow.

Tata rights issue leads to fall in share price

Shares in India's Tata Motors fell as much as 6.6% as volatile markets raised concerns that investors may reject its huge $885 million rights issue. Shares in India's top vehicle maker have taken a hit on the company's fund-raising plans and the grim outlook for the car and commercial vehicles market where demand has slowed right down due to high fuel prices and the global economic slowdown. Some shareholders seem keen to take up the rights issue, but others are wary. They are worried about future share prices if the company's expansion plans are not successful.

Tata Motors has also said that it was looking at selling assets in some subsidiaries to raise capital, and independent investment analysts say that this is preferable to diluting ownership equity by the rights issue method. The company is offering one new ordinary share for 340 rupees for every six currently held by shareholders. The capital raised will be used to pay off the loans taken out by Tata when it purchased Jaguar and Land Rover for $2.3 billion from Ford in 2008.

Source: http://uk.reuters.com

20 marks, 35 minutes

1 What was the strategic decision that required the capital Tata raised from the rights issue? [2]

2 Using evidence from the text and your own knowledge, explain why you think that Tata used a rights issue of shares rather than continuing to use long-term loans. [6]

3 Evaluate the likely reaction of shareholders to this financing decision in:
   a the short term [6]
   b the longer term. [6]

EXAM PRACTICE QUESTION

Read the case study below and then answer the questions that follow.

EASYJET TAKES OFF TO 342P SHARE PRICE

easyJet, Europe's second largest low-cost airline, saw its share price rise strongly on its first day of trading as a public limited company, rising 10% to 342p. The offering was priced at 310p a share with the issue of 63 million shares raising £195 million. The issue, solely to institutional investors, represented about 25% of the enlarged share capital. The stake held by Stelios Haji-Ioannou, founder and chairman of the company, was valued at about £328 million. Mr Haji-Ioannou and his brother and sister still control a stake of about 75% in easyJet.

Investment bankers said the issue attracted strong interest. The performance of the shares had been helped by the strong rise of Ryanair, the leading European low-cost airline, which has been used by investors as a yardstick for the easyJet offering. easyJet shares have also proved attractive because the company has seen its passenger numbers rise markedly over previous years. Capital raised from the share issue is earmarked to support the purchase of new aircraft as part of the group's plans for a rapid expansion during the next few years, which includes the addition of 32 new Boeing 737-700s, more than doubling the size of the fleet.

25 marks, 45 minutes

1 Define the terms:
   a public limited company
   b share price. [4]

2 Outline two possible sources of long-term finance available to easyJet. [6]

3 Explain why an expansion in easyJet's passenger numbers has increased the need for short- and long-term finance. [6]

4 Evaluate the view that easyJet's decision to raise long-term finance by selling shares is preferable to raising it through borrowing. [9]

19 Investment appraisal

This chapter covers syllabus section 3.2

On completing this chapter you should be able to:

- understand what investment means, why appraising investment projects is essential and the information needed for investment appraisal
- assess why forecasting future cash flows adds uncertainty to investment appraisal
- apply and analyse the payback method of investment appraisal
- apply and analyse the average rate of return method of investment appraisal
- analyse the importance of qualitative or non-numerical factors in many investment decisions
- (H) understand discounted cash flows and apply and analyse the net present value method of investment appraisal.

SETTING THE SCENE

Glasgow NHS invests in RFID to reduce costs

Greater Glasgow and Clyde NHS has invested in a wireless networking project in one of its hospitals. It tracks medical equipment with RFID (radio frequency identification) tags. The scheme will cost £70 000 and 1500 items of medical equipment will eventually be tagged. According to NHS clinical scientist, Jason Britton, the hospital loses between £20 000 and £40 000 a year in wasted time looking for misplaced equipment such as defibrillators, infusion pumps and blood pressure monitors. 'Devices can get lost in the system for years before they are discovered,' he said. With RFID, a central office will know exactly where each of the tagged items is in the hospital. Doctors will be able to locate the equipment quickly, so improving the level of patient care. The investment should pay back within two to three years.

Source: www.silicon.com

Nigerian Water privatisation appears to be a good investment

The privatisation scheme selected by the Nigerian government for water supply involved private firms buying 20-year contracts to build and operate water-supply services to regions of the country. These were risky investments for private sector businesses as it was unclear how much consumers would be prepared to pay for clean water supplies. An analysis of the likely profitability of these projects concluded that:

- profit in today's values might be around $67 million
- the average rate of return should be close to 28%
- the payback period would be approximately 3.8 years.

Source: http://wedc.lboro.ac.uk

19 Investment appraisal

Points to think about:

- Both of these investment projects were expected to earn returns greater than the original cost. Why might it be difficult to forecast future returns from an investment?
- Both articles refer to the time to 'pay back' the investment cost. Why do you think this might be important?

Introduction

Investment means purchasing capital goods – such as equipment, vehicles and new buildings – and improving existing fixed assets. Many investment decisions involve significant strategic issues – such as relocation of premises or the adoption of computer-assisted engineering methods. Other investment plans are less important to the overall performance of the business – such as replacing worn-out photocopiers. Relatively minor investment decisions will not be analysed to the same degree of detail as more substantial decisions on capital expenditure.

What is investment appraisal?

KEY TERM

investment appraisal evaluating the profitability or desirability of an investment project

Investment appraisal is undertaken by using quantitative techniques that assess the financial feasibility of the project. Non-financial issues can also be significant and therefore qualitative appraisal of a project might also be very important. In some businesses, especially those dominated by the founding entrepreneur, formal investment appraisal may not be applied. Instead, the owner may develop a 'feel' for what is likely to be most successful and go ahead with that project even though no formal analysis has been undertaken. The use of such 'intuitive' or 'hunch' methods of taking investment decisions cannot be easily explained or justified – unless they turn out to be very successful.

QUANTITATIVE INVESTMENT APPRAISAL

Quantitative investment appraisal requires the following information:

- the initial capital cost of the investment, including any installation costs
- the estimated life expectancy – how many years can returns be expected from the investment?
- the residual value of the investment – at the end of their useful lives will the assets be sold, earning additional net returns?
- the forecasted net returns or net cash flows from the project – these are the expected returns from the investment less the annual running cost.

Methods of quantitative investment appraisal include:

- payback period
- average rate of return
- net present value using discounted cash flows. 

Forecasting cash flows in an uncertain environment

All of the techniques used to appraise investment projects require forecasts to be made of future cash flows. These figures are referred to as 'net cash flows'.

KEY TERM

annual forecasted net cash flow forecasted cash inflow – forecasted cash outflows

We assume for the IB examinations, rather simplistically, that the cash inflows are the same as the annual revenues earned from the project and the cash outflows are the annual operating costs.

These net cash-flow figures can then be compared with those of other projects and with the initial cost of the investment. Forecasting cash flows is not easy and is rarely likely to be 100% accurate. With long-term investments, forecasts several years ahead have to be made and there will be increased chances of external factors reducing the accuracy of the figures. For instance, when appraising the construction of a new airport, forecasts of cash flows many years ahead are likely to be required. Revenue forecasts may be affected by external factors such as:

- an economic recession could reduce both business and tourist traffic through the airport
- increases in oil prices could make air travel more expensive than expected, again reducing revenue totals
- the construction of a new high-speed rail link within the country might encourage some travellers to switch to this form of transport.

These future uncertainties cannot be removed from investment appraisal calculations. The possibility of uncertain and unpredicted events making cash-flow forecasts inaccurate must, however, be constantly borne in mind by managers. All investment decisions involve some risk due to this uncertainty.

ACTIVITY 19.1

Cash-flow uncertainties

15 marks, 18 minutes

For each of the following investment projects explain **one** reason why there is likely to be some uncertainty about the future net cash-flow forecasts earned by them:

a a project to construct a factory to make large and expensive luxury cars [3]

b an investment in a new computerised banking system offering customers new services using state-of-the-art equipment that has not yet been thoroughly tested [3]

c cash-flow forecasts for a new sports centre that are based on a small market research sample of the local population [3]

d the building of a new toll motorway between two cities [3]

e the construction of an oil-fired power station. [3]

QUANTITATIVE TECHNIQUES OF INVESTMENT APPRAISAL

Payback method

KEY TERM

payback period length of time it takes for the net cash inflows to pay back the original capital cost of the investment

If a project costs $2 million and is expected to pay back $500 000 per year, the payback period will be four years. This can then be compared with the payback on alternative investments. It is normal to refer to 'year 0' as the time period in which the investment is made. The cash flow at this time is therefore negative – shown by a bracketed amount – see Table 19.1. This shows the forecasted annual net cash flows and cumulative cash flows. This latter figure shows the 'running total' of cash flows and becomes less and less negative as further cash inflows are received. Notice that in year 3 it becomes positive – so the initial capital cost has been paid back during this year. But when during this year? If we assume that the cash flows are received evenly throughout the year (this may not be the case, of course), then payback will be at the end of the fourth month of the third year. How do we know this? At the end of year 2, $50 000 is needed to pay back the remainder of the initial investment. A total of $150 000 is expected during year 3; $50 000 is a third of $150 000 and one-third of a year is the end of month 4. To find out this exact month use this formula:

$$\frac{\text{additional cash inflow needed}}{\text{annual cash flow in year 3}} \times 12 \text{ months}$$

$$= \frac{\$50000}{\$150000} \times 12 \text{ months} = 4 \text{ months}$$

Year	Annual net cash flows ($)	Cumulative cash flows ($)
0	(500 000)	(500 000)
1	300 000	(200 000)
2	150 000	(50 000)
3	150 000	100 000
4	100 000 (including residual value)	200 000

Table 19.1 *Cash flows of an investment*

Importance of payback of a project

Managers can compare the payback period of a particular project with other alternative projects so as to put them in rank order. Alternatively, the payback period can be compared with a 'cut-off' time period that the business may have decided on – for example, it may not accept any project proposal that pays back after five years.

- A business may have borrowed the finance for the investment and a long payback period will increase interest payments.
- Even if the finance was obtained internally, the capital has an opportunity cost of other purposes for which

it could be used. The speedier the payback, the more quickly the capital is made available for other projects.
- The longer into the future before a project pays back the capital invested in it, the more uncertain the whole investment becomes. The changes in the external environment that could occur to make a project unprofitable are likely to be much greater over ten years than over two.
- Some managers are 'risk averse' – they want to reduce risk to a minimum so a quick payback reduces uncertainties for these managers.
- Cash flows received in the future have less real value than cash flows today, owing to inflation. The more quickly money is returned to an investing company, the higher will be its real value.

Virgin Atlantic invested £200 000 in a new technology communication system which provides direct contact with potential customers, giving details about special fare offers. The system earned extra cash flow of £200 000 in three months – a very rapid payback.

Evaluation of payback method

The payback method is often used as a quick check on the viability of a project or as a means of comparing projects. However, it is rarely used in isolation from the other investment appraisal methods (see Table 19.2).

Average rate of return (ARR)

KEY TERM

average rate of return (ARR) measures the annual profitability of an investment as a percentage of the initial investment

$$\text{ARR (\%)} = \frac{\text{annual profit (net cash flow)}}{\text{initial capital cost}} \times 100$$

This may also be referred to as the accounting rate of return. If it can be shown that Project A returns, on average, 8% per year while Project B returns 12% per year, then the decision between the alternative investments will be an easier one to make. For simplicity, we will assume that the net cash flows equal the annual profitability.

Table 19.3 shows the expected cash flows from a business investment into a fleet of new fuel-efficient vehicles. The inflows for years 1 to 3 are the annual cost savings made. In year 4, the expected proceeds from selling the vehicles are included.

Year	Net cash flow
0	($5 million)
1	$2 million
2	$2 million
3	$2 million
4	$3 million (including residual value)

Table 19.3 *Net cash flows for fleet investment*

Advantages	Disadvantages
• It is quick and easy to calculate. • The results are easily understood by managers. • The emphasis on speed of return of cash flows gives the benefit of concentrating on the more accurate short-term forecasts of the project's profitability. • The result can be used to eliminate or 'screen out' projects that give returns too far into the future. • It is particularly useful for businesses where liquidity is of greater significance than overall profitability.	• It does not measure the overall profitability of a project – indeed, it ignores all of the cash flows after the payback period. It may be possible for an investment to give a really rapid return of capital but then to offer no other cash inflows. • This concentration on the short term may lead businesses to reject very profitable investments just because they take some time to repay the capital. • It does not consider the timing of the cash flows during the payback period – this will become clearer when the principle of discounting is examined in the other two appraisal methods (average rate of return and net present value).

Table 19.2 *Payback method – advantages and disadvantages*

The four stages in calculating ARR:

1 Add up all positive cash flows = \$9 million
2 Subtract cost of investment = \$9 million – \$5 million = \$4 million (this is total profit)
3 Divide by life span = \$4 million/4 = \$1 million (this is annual profit)
4 Calculate the % return to find the ARR = \$1 million/\$5 million × 100 = 20%

What does this result mean? It indicates to the business that, on average over the life span of the investment, it can expect an annual return of 20% on its investment. This could be compared with:

- the ARR on other projects
- the minimum expected return set by the business – known as the criterion rate. In the example above, if the business refused to accept any project with a return of less than 15%, the new vehicle fleet would satisfy this criterion
- the annual interest rate on loans – if the ARR is less than the interest rate, it will not be worthwhile taking a loan to invest in the project.

KEY TERM

criterion rate or level the minimum level (maximum for payback period) set by management for investment appraisal results for a project to be accepted

Evaluation of average rate of return

ARR is a widely used measure for appraising projects, but it is best considered together with payback results. The two results then allow consideration of both profits and cash-flow timings (see Table 19.4).

ACTIVITY 19.2

Read the case study below and then answer the questions that follow.

Textile company plans investment

A textile business is planning an investment programme to overcome a problem of demand exceeding capacity. It is considering two alternative projects involving new machinery. The initial outlays and future cash outflows are given below. Project Y machinery is forecast to have a life expectancy of just four years.

Year	Project X	Project Y
1	(\$50 000)	(\$80 000)
2	\$25 000	\$45 000
3	\$20 000	\$35 000
4	\$20 000	\$17 000
5	\$15 000	\$15 000
6	\$10 000	–

33 marks, 65 minutes

1 Calculate the payback for both projects. [6]

2 Explain which project should be selected if payback is the only criterion used – and why. [6]

3 Calculate ARR for both projects. [6]

4 The business has a cut-off or criterion rate of 11% for all new projects. Would either project be acceptable with this restriction? [3]

5 Taking both the results of payback and ARR together, which project would you advise the business to invest in and why? [7]

6 What additional information would help you advise the business on the more suitable project? [5]

Advantages	Disadvantages
• It uses all of the cash flows – unlike the payback method. • It focuses on profitability, which is the central objective of many business decisions. • The result is easily understood and easy to compare with other projects that may be competing for the limited investment funds available. • The result can be quickly assessed against the predetermined criterion rate of the business.	• It ignores the timing of the cash flows. This could result in two projects having similar ARR results, but one could pay back much more quickly than the other. • As all cash inflows are included, the later cash flows, which are less likely to be accurate, are incorporated into the calculation. • The time value of money is ignored as the cash flows have not been discounted – this concept is considered in the section on net present value.

Table 19.4 *Average rate of return – advantages and disadvantages*

Gezhouba Dam, China – most major projects are evaluated using investment appraisal

HIGHER LEVEL

Discounting future cash flows

If you have worked through Activity 19.2 you will realise that managers may be uncertain which project to invest in if the two methods of investment appraisal used give conflicting results: if project A is estimated to pay back at the end of year 3 at an ARR of 15%, should this be preferred to project B with a payback of four years but an ARR of 17%?

Managers need another investment appraisal method, which solves this problem of trying to compare projects with different returns and payback periods. This additional method considers both the size of cash flows and the timing of them. It does this by discounting cash flows. If the effects of inflation are ignored, most people would rather accept a payment of $1000 today instead of a payment of $1000 in one year's time. Which would you choose? The payment today is preferred for three reasons:

- It can be spent immediately and the benefits of this expenditure can be obtained immediately. There is no waiting involved.
- The $1000 could be saved at the current rate of interest. The total of cash plus interest will be greater than the offer of $1000 in one year's time.
- The cash today is certain, but the future cash offer is always open to uncertainty.

This is called taking the 'time value of money' into consideration. Discounting is the process of reducing the value of future cash flows to give them their value in today's terms. How much less is future cash worth compared to today's money? The answer depends on the rate of interest. If $1000 received today can be saved at 10%, then it will grow to $1100 in one year's time. Therefore, $1100 in one year's time has the same value as $1000 today at 10% interest. This value of $1000 is called the present value of $1100 received in one year's time. Discounting calculates the present values of future cash flows so that investment projects can be compared with each other by considering today's value of their returns.

Discounting – how is it done?

The present value of a future sum of money depends on two factors:

- the higher the interest rate, the less value future cash has in today's money
- the longer into the future cash is received, the less value it has today.

These two variables – interest rates and time – are used to calculate discount factors. You do not have to calculate these – they are available in discount tables and an extract of one is given in Table 19.5. To use the discount factors to obtain present values of future cash flows, multiply the appropriate discount factor by the cash flow. For example, $3000 is expected in three years' time. The current rate of interest is 10%. The discount factor to be used is 0.75 – this means that $1 received in three years' time is worth the same as 75p today. This discount factor is multiplied by $3000 and the present value is $2250.

Year	6%	8%	10%	12%	16%	20%
1	0.94	0.93	0.91	0.89	0.86	0.83
2	0.89	0.86	0.83	0.79	0.74	0.69
3	0.84	0.79	0.75	0.71	0.64	0.58
4	0.79	0.74	0.68	0.64	0.55	0.48
5	0.75	0.68	0.62	0.57	0.48	0.40
6	0.71	0.63	0.56	0.51	0.41	0.33

Table 19.5 *Extract from discounted cash flow table*

Net present value (NPV)

KEY TERM

net present value (NPV) today's value of the estimated cash flows resulting from an investment

This method once again uses discounted cash flows. It is calculated by subtracting the capital cost of the investment from the total discounted cash flows. The three stages in calculating NPV:

1 Multiply discount factors by the cash flows. Cash flows in year 0 are never discounted as they are today's values already.
2 Add the discounted cash flows.
3 Subtract the capital cost to give the NPV.

The working is clearly displayed in Table 19.6. The initial cost of the investment is a current cost paid out in year 0. Current cash flows are not discounted.

Year	Cash flow	Discount factors @ 8%	Discounted cash flows (DCF)
0	($10 000)	1	($10 000)
1	$5 000	0.93	$4 650
2	$4 000	0.86	$3 440
3	$3 000	0.79	$2 370
4	$2 000	0.74	$1 480

Table 19.6 *Discounted cash flows*

Net present value is now calculated.

total discounted cash flows = $11 940
original investment = ($10 000)
NPV = $1 940

This result means that the project earns $1940 in today's money values. So, if the finance needed can be borrowed at an interest rate of less than 8%, the investment will be profitable. What would happen to NPV if the discount rate was raised, perhaps because interest rates have increased? This will reduce NPV as future cash flows are worth even less when they are discounted at a higher rate. The choice of discount rate is, therefore, crucial to the assessment of projects using this method of appraisal.

Usually, businesses will choose a rate of discount that reflects the interest cost of borrowing the capital to finance the investment. Even if the finance is raised internally, the rate of interest should still be used to discount future returns. This is because of the opportunity cost of internal finance – it could be left on deposit in a bank to earn interest. An alternative approach to selecting the discount rate to be used is for a business to adopt a cut-off or criterion rate. The business would use this to discount the returns on a project and, if the net present value is positive, the investment could go ahead.

Evaluation of net present value

Net present value is a widely used technique of investment appraisal in industry, but, as it does not give an actual percentage rate of return, it is often considered together with the internal rate of return percentage, which is not an IB specification topic (see Table 19.7).

Advantages	Disadvantages
• It considers both the timing of cash flows and the size of them in arriving at an appraisal. • The rate of discount can be varied to allow for different economic circumstances. For instance, it could be increased if there was a general expectation that interest rates were about to rise. • It considers the time value of money and takes the opportunity cost of money into account.	• It is reasonably complex to calculate and to explain – especially to non-numerate managers! • The final result depends greatly on the rate of discount used, and expectations about interest rates may be inaccurate. • Net present values can be compared with other projects, but only if the initial capital cost is the same. This is because the method does not provide a percentage rate of return on the investment (internal rate of return).

Table 19.7 *Net present value – advantages and disadvantages*

EXAM TIP

When calculating investment appraisal methods, set out your working carefully, using the same type of tables used in this chapter.

ACTIVITY 19.3

Discounting cash flows

19 marks, 28 minutes

1 Calculate the present-day values of the following cash flows:
   a $10 000 expected in four years' time at prevailing rate of interest of 10%
   b $2000 expected in six years' time at prevailing rate of interest of 16%
   c $6000 expected in one year's time at prevailing rate of interest of 20%. [6]
2 The following net cash flows have been forecasted by a manufacturer for a major purchase:

Year	Net cash flows ($)
0	(15 000)
1	8 000
2	10 000
3	5 000
4	5 000

a Calculate the payback period. [3]
b Calculate the average rate of return (ARR). [4]
c Discount all cash flows at a rate of discount of 10%. [3]
d Calculate the net present value. [3]

The discounted cash flows of an investment project at varying rates of interest are shown in Table 19.8. As the discount rate increases, so the net present value declines until a negative value is eventually reached.

Year	Net cash flows	DCF @ 8%	DCF @ 12%	DCF @ 20%
0	($35 000)	($35 000)	($35 000)	($35 000)
1	$15 000	$13 950	$13 350	$12 450
2	$15 000	$12 900	$12 000	$10 350
3	$10 000	$7 900	$7 100	$5 800
4	$10 000	$7 400	$6 400	$4 800
NPV		$7 150	$3 850	($1 600)

Table 19.8 *Discounted cash flows at varying rates of interest*

ACTIVITY 19.4

Net present value

12 marks, 21 minutes

Using the data in Table 19.8:

- recalculate the net present value at a discount rate of 20% [4]
- explain why the net present value is negative [2]
- explain why the project would not be viable if the business had to borrow finance at 20%. [2]

If the criterion rate used by the business for new investments is 10%, would this project have a positive net present value, and would it therefore be acceptable? [4]

QUALITATIVE INVESTMENT APPRAISAL

Investment appraisal techniques provide numerical data, which are important in taking decisions. However, no manager can afford to ignore other factors which cannot be expressed in a numerical form but may have a crucial bearing on a decision. These are referred to as qualitative factors and include the following:

- The impact on the environment and the local community. Bad publicity stemming from the announcement of some proposed investment plans may dissuade managers from going ahead with a project because of the long-run impact on image and sales. An example is the dispute over the building of a third runway at London's Heathrow airport.
- Planning permission. Certain projects may not receive planning permission if they are against the interests of local communities. Local planners weigh up the social costs and benefits of a planned project. Community members will often have a direct role through a public enquiry or may set up a pressure group to make their views known and try to achieve a particular outcome.
- Aims and objectives of the business. The decision to close bank branches and replace them with internet and telephone banking services involves considerable capital expenditure – as well as the potential for long-term savings. Managers may, however, be reluctant to pursue these investment policies if there is concern that the aim of giving excellent and personal customer service is being threatened. Similarly, the decision to replace large numbers of workers with labour-saving machinery may be reversed if the negative impact on human relations within the business appears to be too great.
- Risk. Different managers are prepared to accept different degrees of risk. No amount of positive quantitative data will convince some managers, perhaps as a result of previous experience, to accept a project that involves a considerable chance of failure.

EXAM TIP

Unless the question asks **only** for an analysis of numerical or quantitative factors, your answers to investment appraisal questions should include an assessment of qualitative factors too.

THEORY OF KNOWLEDGE

Business forecasting has always been a key part of managing an organisation. Forecasting, however, was traditionally based less on comprehensive data and more on management intuition and common sense. Now business forecasting has become much more scientific, with a variety of theories, methods and techniques designed for forecasting certain types of data. The growth of IT and the internet has led to a major expansion in the use of forecasting. Projecting the right levels of goods to buy or products to produce now means using sophisticated software and electronic networks using complex data and advanced mathematical algorithms tailored to an organisation's particular market conditions and line of business.

a Using techniques you have learned in the course analyse how business people go about knowing the possible future consequences of their decisions.
b Discuss the usefulness of the forecasting techniques for business people.
c To what extent is business decision-making more about intuition as opposed to scientific forecasting?

OVER TO YOU

REVISION CHECKLIST

1 Give **three** examples of new projects that a supermarket could invest in.
2 List **four** types of information usually required to undertake quantitative investment appraisal.
3 What is meant by the 'annual net cash flow' from an investment project?
4 Examine **two** reasons why the forecast annual net cash flows for an investment in a new clothes shop could prove to be inaccurate.
5 Explain what a 'payback of two years and six months' means for an investment project.
6 State **three** reasons why a manager might select an investment project with a short payback period.
7 Explain any **one** of the reasons you identified in question 6.
8 Write down the formula for calculating the 'average rate of return' for an investment project.
9 Explain why a manager would prefer, other things being equal, to select an investment project with an ARR of 12% rather than one with an ARR of 8%.
10 What does a 'criterion rate of return' mean?
11 Explain why qualitative factors might be significant to an investment decision to replace bank branches with an internet banking service.
12 Explain how environmental considerations could affect an investment decision.
13 Explain why a business's objectives could influence an investment decision to open a factory in a low-income developing country.
(H) 14 Why is discounting of future net cash flows often used in investment appraisal?
(H) 15 Explain what a 'net present value of $4500' means.
(H) 16 Explain what happens to the net present value of a project when the discount rate is increased – and why.

REVISION ACTIVITY

Read the case study below and then answer the questions that follow.

Location investment decision

A shoe shop owner is planning to open another branch and has to decide between two new locations that involve large capital investment – the business cannot afford both of them. He has forecasted the following annual net cash flows for these two locations. These forecasts are based on market research and cost estimates. The cash flows are as follows:

Year	Location A	Location B
0	($12 000)	($12 000)
1	$3 000	$6 000
2	$4 000	$5 000
3	$5 000	$3 000
4	$6 000	$2 000
5	$5 000	$5 000

36 marks, 65 minutes

1 Calculate the simple payback period for both projects and comment on your results. [4]
2 Calculate the ARR for both projects. [4]
3 Explain why the manager might find it difficult, in the light of your results, to make a choice between these two projects. [4]
(H) 4 Using the discount factors on page 190, calculate the net present value of both locations at:
a 10% discount and
b 20% discount. [6]

[continues]

5 Comment on your results to question 4. [4]

6 Using all of your results, recommend to the manager which location you consider should be selected, on the basis of quantitative data. [8]

7 How reliable are these cash-flow forecasts likely to be? [6]

INVESTING TO STAY COMPETITIVE

Asia Print plc is a large printing firm offering a range of services to industry, such as printed catalogues, leaflets and brochures. It operates in a very competitive market as it is relatively easy for new firms to join using the latest computer software 'page-making' packages. In an effort to maintain market share, the directors of Asia Print plc are considering several new investment projects. The two most promising schemes are:

Project Y – a newly designed highly automated printing press with fast changeover facilities and full colour ability. Direct internet links with customers would allow for rapid input of new material to be printed. Two highly trained operatives will be required and this would mean six redundancies from existing staff.

Project Z – a semi-automated machine with a more limited range of facilities but with proven reliability. Existing staff could operate this machine but there would be three redundancies. It is very noisy and local residents might complain.

The finance director was asked to undertake an investment appraisal of these two machines. He had gathered the following data. Each additional unit produced would be sold for an average of $1.25, but there would be additional variable costs of $0.5 per unit. In addition, the annual operational cost of the two machines is expected to be $1 million for Y and $0.5 million for Z. The introduction of either machine would involve considerable disruption to existing production. Staff would have to be selected and trained for project Y and the trade union is very worried about potential job cuts. The residual value of Y is expected to be $1 million and of Z, $0.5 million.

	Project Y	Project Z
Purchase price ($m)	20	12
Expected life expectancy	5 years	4 years
Forecast annual sales (million units)	8	6

EXAM PRACTICE QUESTION

Read the case study and then answer the questions that follow.

25 marks, 45 minutes

1 Define the following terms:
 a residual value
 b expected life expectancy. [4]

2 Explain how Asia Print might have forecast future annual sales. [6]

3 Calculate for each project:
 a the payback period
 b the average annual rate of return (ARR). [8]

4 On the basis of your results and any other relevant factors, discuss which project Asia Print should choose. [7]

20 Working capital

This chapter covers syllabus section 3.3

On completing this chapter you should be able to:

- define working capital and explain the working capital cycle
- prepare a cash-flow forecast from given information
- evaluate strategies for dealing with liquidity problems.

SETTING THE SCENE

Asian Glasses runs out of cash

Asian Glasses had been making spectacles for years but had reached a critical point with no sales growth and low profits. A new managing director, Jerry Xue, did not take long to make changes. He aimed to raise the annual sales revenue from $1 million to $4 million in two years by specialising in fashion sunglasses. New designs were developed. Jerry's contacts within the industry helped him gain big orders from some of the leading retailers. The sunglasses sold for high prices. These large orders were profitable, but there was a major problem. The biggest retailers were the slowest payers as they expected several months of credit. They also demanded such high standards that some production had to be scrapped.

Jerry started to worry about the firm's cash position. Suppliers were demanding payment. The bank overdraft had reached record levels. Overtime working by staff to complete orders on time took cash out of the business. Then Jerry discovered that his bookkeeper had not included transport costs in the monthly cash-flow forecast – the business had even less money than they thought.

The situation went from bad to worse. On the day that Jerry had appointments with a department store buyer in the morning and the bank manager in the afternoon, the glass lens machine broke down and a major supplier refused to supply materials. Within weeks, the assets of the business had been sold off and the creditors owed money by Asian Glasses received a fraction of what they were owed.

Points to think about:

- As the business is profitable, how could Asian Glasses run out of cash?
- How useful would an accurate forecast of cash flows have been to Jerry?
- What could Jerry have done to improve the cash position of Asian Glasses?
- Why did this business need day-to-day finance?

20 Working capital

Introduction

Working capital is often described as the 'lifeblood' of a business. All businesses need finance to pay for everyday expenses such as wages and the purchase of stock.

Without sufficient working capital a business will be illiquid – unable to pay its immediate or short-term debts. Either the business raises finance quickly – such as a bank loan – or it may be forced into 'liquidation' by its creditors, the firms it owes money to.

KEY TERMS

working capital the capital needed to pay for raw materials, day-to-day running costs and credit offered to customers. In accounting terms: making capital = current assets – current liabilities

liquidity the ability of a firm to be able to pay its short-term debts

liquidation when a firm ceases trading and its assets are sold for cash

Where does working capital come from?

The simple calculation for working capital is: current assets less current liabilities. Current assets are stocks, debtors and cash. Virtually no business could survive without these three assets, although some business owners refuse to sell any products on credit so there will be no debtors. This is very rare for businesses beyond a certain size.

Where does the capital come from to purchase and hold these current assets? Most businesses will obtain some of this finance in the form of current liabilities – overdrafts and creditors are the main forms. However, it would be unwise to obtain all of the funds needed from these sources. First, they may have to be repaid at very short notice, meaning the firm is again left with a liquidity problem. Secondly, it will leave no working capital for buying additional stocks or extending further credit to customers when required.

HOW MUCH IS NEEDED?

Sufficient working capital is essential to prevent a business from becoming illiquid and unable to pay its debts. Too high a level of working capital is a disadvantage; the opportunity cost of too much capital tied up in stocks, debtors and idle cash is the return that money could earn elsewhere in the business – invested in fixed assets perhaps.

The working capital requirement for any business will depend upon the 'length' of this 'working capital cycle'.

KEY TERM

working capital cycle the period of time between spending cash on the production process and receiving cash payments from customers

The longer this time period from buying materials to receiving payment from customers, the greater will be the working capital needs of the business. Figure 20.1 shows the simple cycle of a business that produces goods but neither asks for nor offers credit. Credit given to customers by the business will lengthen the time before a sale is turned into cash – extending the working capital cycle. Credit received by the business from suppliers will reduce the length of this cycle. To give more credit than is received is to increase the need for working capital. To receive more credit than is given is to reduce the need for working capital.

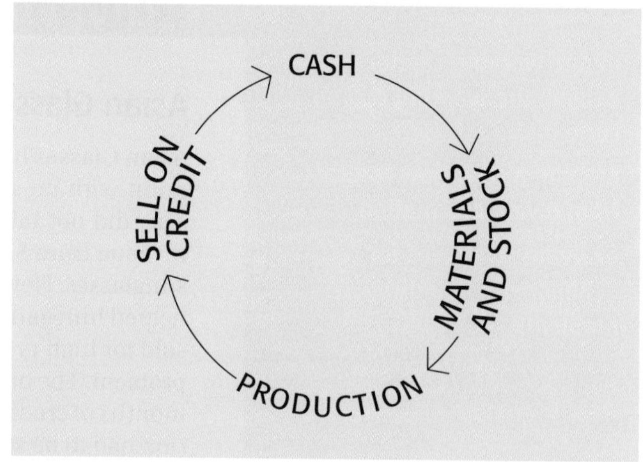

Figure 20.1 The simple working capital cycle – the longer this cycle takes to complete, the more working capital a business will need

ACTIVITY 20.1

Sheila and her friend Alison have decided to run their own mobile hairdressing business using the training they have received at college and the experience they both gained working for three years for a local hairdresser. Investigate, locally, the equipment and working stock they will need. From this, estimate the capital they will need to set up the business and survive the first year. Write a brief report on your findings.

The importance of cash flow

The Asian Glasses case study in 'Setting the scene' above allows us to see the importance of cash flow to all businesses – even those that claim to be making a profit! Profit does not pay the bills and expenses of running a business – but cash does. Of course, profit is important – especially in the long term when investors expect rewards and the business needs additional finance for investment. Cash is always important – short and long term. Cash flow relates to the timing of payments to workers

ACTIVITY 20.2

Read the case study below and then answer the questions that follow.

Directphone Ltd

Directphone Ltd operates a direct insurance service to motorists. As part of a recent expansion programme, the finance director calculated that stocks of stationery, such as insurance certificates, would have to rise by 10% from $10 000. More motorists would be encouraged to use the company by being offered extended credit terms. This would increase debtors to an estimated $50 000 from the existing $40 000. Cash reserves to pay out for accidents would rise to $35 000 from $30 000. The only current liability was creditors (garages that had not yet been paid for accident work). This amounted to $40 000 and the director hoped to be allowed to increase this to $50 000.

10 marks, 18 minutes

1 Calculate the proposed increase in the working capital requirements of the business resulting from the expansion. [6]

2 Outline two ways in which this increase in working capital might be financed. [4]

and suppliers and receipts from customers. If a business does not plan the timing of these payments and receipts carefully, it may run out of cash even though it is operating profitably. If suppliers and creditors are not paid in time, they can force the business into liquidation of its assets if it appears to be insolvent.

KEY TERMS

cash flow the sum of cash payments to a business (inflows) less the sum of cash payments made by it (outflows)

liquidation turning assets into cash may be insisted on by courts if suppliers have not been paid

insolvent when a business cannot meet its short-term debts

So, cash flow is certainly important, especially to small business start-ups. Cash-flow planning is vital for entrepreneurs for several reasons:

- Business start-ups are often offered much less time to pay suppliers than larger, well-established firms – they are given shorter credit periods.
- Banks and other lenders may not believe the promises of new business owners as they have no trading record. They will expect payment at the agreed time.
- Finance is often very tight at start-up, so not planning accurately is of even more significance for new businesses.

Cash and profit

Cash and profit – what's the difference? To many failed business owners there was none – which is why their business collapsed. It is very common for profitable businesses to run short of cash. On the other hand, loss-making businesses can have high cash inflows in the short term. The essential difference between cash and profit can be explained with a simple example.

Example

Shula owns Fine Foods, a specialist delicatessen. Last month she bought $500 of fresh goods from a supplier who offers her one month's credit. The goods sold very slowly during the month and she was forced to cut her prices several times. Eventually, she sold them all for only $300, paid in cash by her customers.

- What was her profit or loss (ignoring all other costs)? A loss of $200 – because even though she has not yet paid for the goods they are still recorded as a cost.
- What was the difference between her cash outflow and inflow? A positive inflow $300 – because she has not paid the supplier yet. So Shula has a positive cash flow from these goods this month even though she made a loss on them.
- Cash was not the same as profit for this business.

KEY TERMS

cash inflows payments in cash received by a business, such as those from customers (debtors) or from the bank, e.g. receiving a loan

outflows payments in cash made by a business, such as those to suppliers and workers

EXAM TIP

When given the opportunity, emphasise the importance of having enough cash in the short term. Profit can wait to be earned in the long term – but cash payments are always being made.

Forecasting cash flow

Forecasting cash flow is estimating future cash inflows and cash outflows, usually on a month-by-month basis. Let's take the case of Mohammed, an entrepreneur planning to open a car-valeting service offering car cleaning to individual customers and owners of car fleets, such as taxi firms.

FORECASTING CASH INFLOWS

Where to start? The business owner will probably attempt to forecast cash inflow first. Some of these will be easier to forecast than others. Here are some examples of cash inflows and how they might be forecast:

- Owners' own capital injection – easy to forecast as this is under Mohammed's direct control.
- Bank loan payments – easy to forecast if they have been agreed with the bank in advance, both in terms of amount and timing.
- Customers' cash purchases – difficult to forecast as they depend on sales, so a sales forecast will be necessary – but how accurate might this be?
- Debtors' payments – difficult to forecast as these depend on two unknowns. First, what is the likely level of sales on credit and, secondly, when will debtors actually pay? One month's credit may have been agreed with them, but payment after this period can never be guaranteed.

KEY TERM

debtors customers who have bought products on credit and will pay cash at an agreed date in the future

FORECASTING CASH OUTFLOWS

Again, some of these will be much easier to forecast than others. Here are some examples:

- Lease payment for premises – easy to forecast as this will be in the estate agent's details of the property.
- Annual rent payment – easy to forecast as this will be fixed and agreed for a certain time period. The landlord may increase the rent after this period, however.
- Electricity, gas, water and telephone bills – difficult to forecast as these will vary with so many factors, such as the number of customers, seasonal weather conditions and energy prices.
- Labour cost payments – these forecasts will be based largely on demand forecasts and the hourly wage rate that is to be paid. These payments could vary from week to week if demand fluctuates and if staff are on flexible contracts.
- Variable cost payments such as cleaning materials – the cost of these should vary consistently with demand, so revenue forecasts could be used to assess variable costs too. How much credit will be offered by suppliers? The longer the period of credit offered, the lower will be the start-up cash needs of the business.

EXAM TIP

Never fall into the trap of referring to forecasts as **actual** accounts – they are financial estimates that are dealing with the future.

Structure of cash-flow forecasts

Due to the crucial importance of cash as the lifeblood of any successful business, all firms should engage in cash-flow forecasting to help identify cash-flow problems before it is too late.

A simplified cash-flow forecast is shown in Table 20.1. It is based on Mohammed's car-valeting service. Although there are different styles of presenting this information, all cash-flow forecasts have three basic sections:

Section 1 Cash inflows This section records the cash payments to the business, including cash sales, payments for credit sales and capital inflows.

Section 2 Cash outflows This section records the cash payments made by the business, including wages, materials, rent and other costs.

Section 3 Net monthly cash flow and opening and closing balance This shows the net cash flow for the period and the cash balances at the start and end of the period – the opening cash balance and the closing cash balance. If the closing balance is negative (shown by a figure in brackets), then a bank overdraft will almost certainly be necessary to finance this.

KEY TERMS

cash-flow forecast estimate of a firm's future cash inflows and outflows

net monthly cash flow estimated difference between monthly cash inflows and outflows

opening cash balance cash held by the business at the start of the month

closing cash balance cash held at the end of the month becomes next month's opening balance

What does the forecast in Table 20.1 tell Mohammed about the prospects for his business? In cash terms, the business appears to be in a good position at the end of four months. This is because:

	All figures in £000	Jan	Feb	Mar	Apr
Cash inflows					
	Owner's capital injection	6	0	0	0
	Cash sales	3	4	6	6
	Payments by debtors	0	2	2	3
	Total cash in	9	6	8	9
Cash outflows					
	Lease	8	0	0	0
	Rent	1	1	1	1
	Materials	0.5	1	3	2
	Labour	1	2	3	3
	Other costs	0.5	1	0.5	1.5
	Total cash out	11	5	7.5	7.5
Net cash flow	Net monthly cash flow	(2)	1	0.5	1.5
	Opening balance	0	(2)	(1)	(0.5)
	Closing balance	(2)	(1)	(0.5)	1

***Table 20.1** Mohammed's cash-flow forecast for the first four months (figures in brackets are negative)*

- in April the closing cash balance is positive, so the bank overdraft has been fully repaid
- there was only one month – the first month of operation – in which the monthly net cash flow was negative
- the monthly net cash flow is increasing each month.

Remember, these are only forecasts – the accuracy of the cash-flow forecast will depend greatly on how accurate Mohammed was in his demand, revenue and material cost forecasts.

ACTIVITY 20.3

4 marks, 7 minutes

Think of **one** more likely cash payment that could be received by a business and **one** more cash payment made by a business.

ACTIVITY 20.4

April cash flow

8 marks, 14 minutes

Using Table 20.1, draw up a revised cash-flow forecast for April assuming:

- cash sales are forecast to be $1000 higher
- materials are forecast to be $500 higher
- other costs are forecast to be $1000 higher. [8]

Benefits of cash-flow forecasts

Cash-flow forecasting has a number of benefits, especially for start-up businesses:

- By showing periods of negative cash flow, plans can be put in place to provide additional finance, e.g. arranging a bank overdraft or preparing to inject more owner's capital.
- If negative cash flows appear to be too great, then plans can be made for reducing these, e.g. by cutting down on purchase of materials or machinery or by not making sales on credit, only for cash.
- A new business proposal will never progress beyond the initial planning stage unless investors and bankers have access to a cash-flow forecast – and the assumptions that lie behind it.

Limitations of cash-flow forecasts

Although an entrepreneur should take every reasonable step to improve the accuracy of cash-flow forecasts, it would be unwise to assume that they will always be accurate. So many factors, either internal to the business or in the external environment, can change to blow a cash-flow forecast off course. This does not make them useless – but they must be used with caution. Here are the most common limitations of them:

- Mistakes can be made in preparing the revenue and cost forecasts or they may be drawn up by inexperienced entrepreneurs or staff.
- Unexpected cost increases can lead to major inaccuracies in forecasts. For example, fluctuations in oil prices can cause the cash-flow forecasts of even major airlines to be misleading.
- Wrong assumptions can be made in estimating the sales of the business, perhaps based on poor market research, and this will make the cash-inflow forecasts inaccurate.

ACTIVITY 20.5

Read the case study below and then answer the questions that follow.

Fashion-shop forecasts look good

'I have stood outside some of these fashion shops for hours counting the number of people coming out with their carrier bags and I am convinced my sales forecasts are OK,' announced Sayuri to her business partner, Korede. They were both putting the finishing touches to their business plan for an exclusive 'top brands only' fashion store in the city. Sayuri's primary research was not the only evidence they had used in arriving at the sales forecasts and the cash-inflow forecasts. Some desk research on the internet had also revealed the rapid growth of high-income consumer numbers spending increasing amounts on expensive clothing.

Cash-outflow forecasts had been based on estimates of electricity and telephone usage. Korede had found what he thought was a suitable shop, so they knew how much the rent would be. They would pay themselves a salary of £2000 a month each initially. Other labour costs were less certain. Should they employ full-time salaried staff or part-time hourly wage employees? The cost of buying the clothes was also uncertain. There would be no problem if they sold all the suits and dresses that they bought in – but how likely was that? And what would happen to cash-flow forecasts if stock was left unsold and huge price reductions had to be advertised? Both Sayuri and Korede realised why they had to construct a cash-flow forecast for their business plan. The almost completed forecast is shown below.

	All figures in $000	April	May	June	July
Cash inflows					
	Owner's capital injection	28	0	0	0
	Cash sales	6	8	12	9
	Payments by debtors (e.g. credit card companies)	0	2	2	3
	Total cash in	34	10	14	12
Cash outflows					
	Lease	18	0	0	0
	Rent	2	2	2	2
	Clothes purchases	6	4	3	4
	Labour	3	3	4	3
	Other costs	6.5	2	2.5	1.5
	Total cash out	35.5	11	11.5	*y*
Net cash flow	Net monthly cash flow	*x*	(1)	2.5	*z*
	Opening balance	0	(1.5)	(2.5)	0
	Closing balance	(1.5)	(2.5)	0	1.5

26 marks, 45 minutes

1 Complete the cash-flow forecast by inserting values for *x*, *y* and *z*. [3]

2 Analyse **two** problems that Sayuri and Korede might have experienced when drawing up their cash-flow forecast. [6]

3 The first three months' actual trading was poor and cash sales were 20% below forecast. Draw up a new cash-flow forecast for July assuming 20% lower cash sales, 20% lower clothes purchases, an opening cash balance of (£2000); all other factors remain unchanged. [7]

4 To what extent would drawing up a cash-flow forecast increase the chances of this business being successful? [10]

Causes of cash-flow problems

LACK OF PLANNING

Cash-flow forecasts help greatly in predicting future cash problems for a business. This form of financial planning can be used to predict potential cash-flow problems so that business managers can take action to overcome them in plenty of time.

EXAM TIP

Remember, cash-flow forecasts do not solve cash-flow problems by themselves – but they are an essential part of financial planning and can help prevent cash-flow problems from developing.

POOR CREDIT CONTROL

The credit control department of a business keeps a check on all customers' accounts – who has paid, who is keeping to agreed credit terms and which customers are not paying on time. If this credit control is inefficient and badly managed, then debtors will not be 'chased up' for payment and potential bad debts will not be identified.

KEY TERMS

credit control monitoring of debts to ensure that credit periods are not exceeded

bad debt unpaid customers' bills that are now very unlikely to ever be paid

ALLOWING CUSTOMERS TOO MUCH CREDIT

In many trading situations, businesses will have to offer trade credit to customers in order to be competitive. Assume a customer has a choice between two suppliers selling very similar products. If one insists on cash payment 'on delivery' and the other allows two months' trade credit, then customers will go for credit terms because it improves their cash flow. Allowing customers **too** long to pay means reducing short-term cash inflows, which could lead to cash-flow problems.

EXPANDING TOO RAPIDLY

When a business expands rapidly, it has to pay for the expansion and for increased wages and materials months before it receives cash from additional sales. This over-trading can lead to serious cash-flow shortages – even though the business is successful and growing.

KEY TERM

overtrading expanding a business rapidly without obtaining all of the necessary finance so that a cash-flow shortage develops

UNEXPECTED EVENTS

Unforeseen increases in costs – a breakdown of a delivery van that needs to be replaced, or a dip in predicted sales income, or a competitor lowers prices unexpectedly – could lead to negative net monthly cash flows.

ACTIVITY 20.6

Taxi firm's cash flow

8 marks, 14 minutes

How would the following events be likely to affect the cash flow of a taxi operating company?

- An increase in oil prices.
- An increase in unemployment.
- Lower train fares. [8]

Ways to improve cash flow

There are two main ways to improve net cash flow:

- increase cash inflows
- reduce cash outflows (see Figure 20.2).

Care needs to be taken here – the aim is to improve the cash position of the business, **not** sales revenue or profits. These are different concepts. For example, a decision to advertise more in order to increase sales, which will eventually lead to increased cash flows, will make the short-term cash position worse as the advertising has to be paid for.

Tables 20.2 and 20.3 outline the methods used to increase cash inflows and reduce cash outflows.

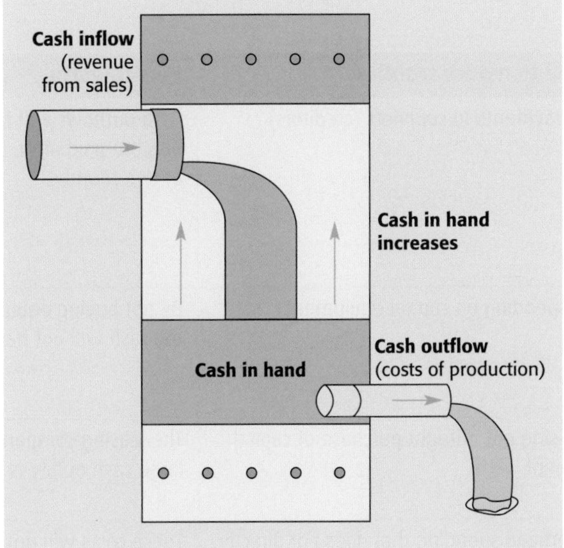

Figure 20.2 Symbolic drawing of cash-flow 'tank' with leakages and injections of cash

Method to increase cash flow	How it works	Evaluation
Overdraft	Flexible loans can be arranged on which the business can draw as necessary up to an agreed limit.	• Interest rates can be high – there may be an overdraft arrangement fee. • Overdrafts can be withdrawn by the bank and this often causes insolvency.
Short-term loan	A fixed amount can be borrowed for an agreed length of time.	• The interest costs have to be paid. • The loan must be repaid by the due date.
Sale of assets	Cash receipts can be obtained from selling off redundant assets, which will boost cash inflow.	• Selling assets quickly can result in low price. • The assets might be required at a later date for expansion. • The assets could have been used as collateral for future loans.
Sale and leaseback	Assets can be sold, e.g. to a finance company, but the asset can be leased back from the new owner.	• The leasing costs add to annual overheads. • There could be loss of potential profit if the asset rises in price. • The assets could have been used as collateral for future loans.
Reduce credit terms to customers	Cash flow can be brought forward by reducing credit terms from, say, two months to one month.	• Customers may purchase products from firms that offer extended credit terms.
Debt factoring	Debt-factoring companies can buy the customers' bills from a business and offer immediate cash – this reduces the risk of bad debts too.	• Only about 90–95% of the debt will now be paid by the debt-factoring company – this reduces profit. • The customer has the debt collected by the finance company – this could suggest that the business is in trouble.

Table 20.2 *Ways to increase cash inflows and their possible drawbacks*

EXAM TIP

When answering an examination question about improving cash flow, just writing 'the firm should increase sales' will not demonstrate a true understanding of the difference between sales revenue and cash flow.

EXAM TIP

If you suggest 'cutting staff and cheaper materials', this may reduce cash outflows, but what will be the negative impact on output, sales and future cash inflows? This suggestion will nearly always be inappropriate for an examination question on improving cash flow.

Method to reduce cashflow	How it works	Evaluation
Delay payments to suppliers (creditors)	Cash outflows will fall in the short term if bills are paid after, say, three months instead of two months.	• Suppliers may reduce any discount offered with the purchase. • Suppliers can either demand cash on delivery or refuse to supply at all if they believe the risk of not being paid is too great.
Delay spending on capital equipment	By not buying equipment, vehicles and so on, cash will not have to be paid to suppliers.	• The business may become less efficient if outdated and inefficient equipment is not replaced. • Expansion becomes very difficult.
Use leasing not outright purchase of capital equipment	The leasing company owns the asset and no large cash outlay is required.	• The asset is not owned by the business. • Leasing charges include an interest cost and add to annual overheads.
Cut overhead spending that does not directly affect output, e.g. promotion costs	These costs will not reduce production capacity and cash payments will be reduced.	• Future demand may be reduced by failing to promote the products effectively.

Table 20.3 *Ways to reduce cash outflows and their possible drawbacks*

THEORY OF KNOWLEDGE

Thousands of firms have gone out of business in California since the recession hit the state in 2008. Panicky bank managers have been quick to call in overdrafts and loans if businesses look vulnerable and are slow to make repayments. This has brought misery to many owners and employees in California's ailing economy.

In groups, discuss the following question: 'Is it ethical for banks to call in their loans and force a business into bankruptcy if it falls behind with its repayments?'

OVER TO YOU

REVISION CHECKLIST

1 Explain the working capital cycle for (a) a shipbuilding business, (b) a sweet shop.
2 Outline **two** reasons why businesses should prepare cash-flow forecasts.
3 Explain why a bank manager would be particularly keen to see a cash-flow forecast in the business plan of a new business when applying for a loan.
4 What is meant by 'monthly net cash flow'?
5 What is meant by 'closing cash balance'?
6 How can sale and leaseback of fixed assets improve business cash flow?
7 Is there any purpose in cash-flow forecasts if they can be made inaccurate by external events?
8 How could a business vary its debtor/creditor policy to improve its cash-flow position?
9 How does a cash-flow forecast assist a business in planning its finance requirements?
10 What particular problems would a new business have in establishing a cash-flow forecast?

REVISION ACTIVITY

Read the case study below and then answer the questions that follow.

Cash flow drying up for Indian small firms

Madhu Gupta has a problem. His company, Mojj Engineering Systems, makes large-scale equipment for food and chemical plants. His customers keep ringing up and saying: 'We don't need the equipment yet – hold it in stock,' 'Can we have an extra discount?' or even 'We will only buy it if you give us credit.'

'Three months ago we had no idea things could happen as quickly as this,' said Mr Gupta. 'It was too sudden to prepare for it.' He was, of course, complaining about the global recession and the speed with which it hit many businesses.

Mr Gupta has already paid cash for all of his raw materials. Completed machines are filling up the yard in his factory. He will not get the money back for materials bought, or for labour costs, until he delivers these machines and is paid for them. The finance the business was planning to use for expansion to a new factory is now being used to pay for the increase in working capital.

24 marks, 40 minutes

1 Explain the term 'working capital'. [3]

2 Explain why Mr Gupta is finding it so difficult to control his working capital. [9]

3 Evaluate **three** ways in which Mr Gupta could try to reduce the finance tied up in working capital. [12]

EXAM PRACTICE QUESTION

Read the case study below and then answer the questions that follow.

'COFFEE CALL' SEEKS FUNDS FOR EXPANSION

Coffee Call is a small, independent coffee shop. It is run by two brothers, Erin and Carl Shutter. They are keen to increase sales by using the shop space more effectively and installing three new tables. This will, however, require a significant investment and the brothers have approached the bank with a business plan for the expansion with the aim of securing loan finance. The brothers have also been approached by a venture capitalist who is willing to fund the expansion in return for a 20% stake in Coffee Call. The brothers are concerned to keep the liquidity of the business secure during the expansion.

The following cash-flow data have been produced by Coffee Call's accountant for the period January to June:

- Sales for the first three months of the year will be $20 000, rising to $40 000 in the following three months once Coffee Call has installed the extra seating.
- Material costs are 50% of sales and are paid each month.
- Electricity and gas cost $4000, with half paid in February and the remainder in September.
- Staff wages of $2000 are paid each month, but this will rise to $3000 after three months once Coffee Call has expanded.
- Erin and Carl draw $10 000 each out of the business in March and December.
- Marketing costs of $500 are paid each month.
- A loan of $20 000 is taken out in February to fund the expansion.
- The $20 000 cost of fitting the new tables is paid in March.
- The brothers believe the tables can be fitted in three days without any disruption to sales.
- The opening cash balance is $7000.

25 marks, 45 minutes

1 Define the following terms:
  a loan finance
  b liquidity. [4]

2 Explain why material costs have been forecast to be 50% of sales. [4]

3 Draw up a cash-flow forecast for Coffee Call for the first six months of the year. [8]

4 Discuss the advantages and disadvantages of Coffee Call using the venture capitalist as a source of finance. [9]

21 Budgeting

This chapter covers syllabus section 3.4 (Higher level only)

On completing this chapter you should be able to:

- understand the importance of budgeting for organisations
- calculate and interpret variances

- analyse the role of budgets and variances in strategic planning.

SETTING THE SCENE

Ford's budgets set back by recession

The Ford Motor Company starts its budgeting process in May each year. Objectives for each market it sells cars in are set based on forecasted total market sales and expected market share. Targets are set for each model and body style. Financial budgets or targets are established for costs of production. The marketing promotion budget needed to reach the sales targets is determined.

Costs are budgeted in considerable detail – there are over 2000 cost centres in its UK operations alone. Each manager with delegated authority for a cost centre prepares a detailed budget for the coming year. The main costs included in the cost-centre budget of Ford manufacturing plant are:

- direct labour costs
- overheads including indirect labour, power, depreciation and maintenance.

Once this process is complete for all cost/profit centres, the overall budgets are submitted to Ford's board of directors for approval. The actual performance of each operational section is measured against its cost budget – this gives financial control. Similarly, sales budgets are compared with actual performance to assess how effectively targets have been reached.

The global recession of 2008–9 resulted in Ford's sales in the USA falling by 20% in 12 months. This was a much worse performance than forecast and made the company's cost and sales budgets for this financial year very unrealistic. Despite this, Ford estimated that its market share in the USA increased in December 2008 compared to a year earlier due to demand for its newer fuel-efficient models.

Source: www.competition-commission.org.uk and http://uk.biz.yahoo.com (adapted)

21 Budgeting

Points to think about:

- What are the likely benefits to any business of making financial plans?
- Do you think managers of each department or cost centre should have some responsibility for setting these budgets or plans? Explain your answer.
- Does the impact of an economic recession mean that financial budgeting/planning is a waste of time? Explain your answer.

Introduction

The financial planning process is known as budgeting. A budget is a detailed, financial plan for a future time period. If no financial plans are made, an organisation drifts without real direction and purpose. Managers will not be able to allocate the scarce resources of the business effectively without a plan to work towards. Employees working in an organisation without plans for future action are likely to feel demotivated, as they have no targets to work towards – and no objective to be praised for achieving. If no targets are set, then an organisation cannot review its progress because it has no set objective against which actual performance can be compared.

Benefits of setting budgets

Strategic planning for the future must consider the financial needs and likely consequences of these plans. This is the budgeting process. Setting and agreeing financial targets for each section of a business will have many benefits.

KEY TERMS

budget a detailed financial plan for the future

budget holder individual responsible for the initial setting and achievement of a budget

Budgets are set for both sales revenue and costs and it is usual for each cost and profit centre to have budgets set for the next 12 months, broken down on a month-by-month basis. Setting budgets and establishing financial plans for the future have seven main purposes:

- Planning – the budgetary process makes managers consider future plans carefully so that realistic targets can be set.
- Effective allocation of resources – budgets can be an effective way of making sure that the business does not spend more resources than it has access to. There will be priorities to discuss and to agree on since what can be done is always likely to be greater than resources will permit.
- Setting targets to be achieved – most people work better if they have a realisable target at which to aim. This motivation will be greater if the budget holder or the cost- and profit-centre manager has been given some delegated accountability for setting and reaching budget levels. These then become delegated budgets.
- Co-ordination – discussion about the allocation of resources to different departments and divisions requires co-ordination between these departments. Once budgets have been agreed, people will have to work effectively together if targets set are to be achieved.
- Monitoring and controlling – plans cannot be ignored once in place. There is a need to check regularly that the objective is still within reach. All kinds of conditions may change and businesses cannot afford to assume that everything is fine.
- Modifying – if there is evidence to suggest that the objective cannot be reached and that the budget is unrealistic, then either the plan or the way of working towards it must be changed.
- Assessing performance – once the budgeted period has ended, variance analysis will be used to compare actual performance with the original budgets.

Key features of budgeting

A budget is not a forecast, although much of the data on which it is based will come from forecasts, since we are looking into the future. Budgets are plans that organisations aim to fulfil. A forecast is a prediction of what could occur in the future.

Budgets may be established for any part of an organisation as long as the outcome of its operation is quantifiable. There may be sales budgets, capital expenditure budgets, labour cost budgets and so on.

Co-ordination between departments when establishing budgets is essential. This should avoid departments making conflicting plans. For example, the marketing department may be planning to increase sales by lowering prices, yet the production department may be planning to reduce output and the direct-labour cost budget. These targets will conflict and need to be reconciled.

Decisions regarding budgets should be made with the subordinate managers who will be involved in putting them into effect. Those who are to be held responsible for fulfilling a budget should be involved in setting it. This sense of 'ownership' not only helps to motivate the department concerned to achieve the targets but also leads to the establishment of more realistic targets. This approach to budgeting is called delegated budgets.

KEY TERM

delegated budgets control over budgets is given to less senior management

The budget will be used to review the performance of a department and the managers of that department will be appraised on their effectiveness in reaching targets. Successful and unsuccessful managers can therefore be identified.

These stages of involvement in constructing the budget, taking responsibility for its operation and being appraised in terms of success are the human aspects of the process. They have a very important role to play in the motivation of staff.

EXAM TIP

When discussing delegated budgeting try to link this in your answer with the motivational approach of Herzberg – making work more challenging and rewarding.

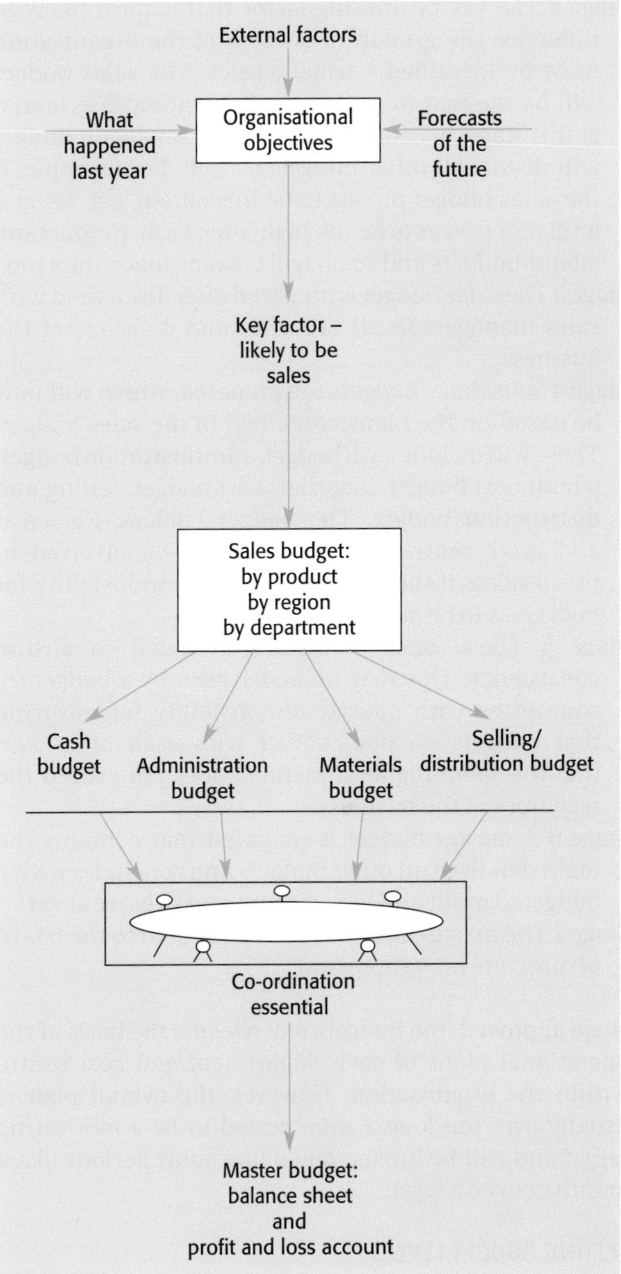

Figure 21.1 How budgets are commonly prepared

Preparation of budgets

STAGES IN SETTING BUDGETS

Figure 21.1 shows how budgets are commonly prepared. This involves seven stages:

Stage 1 The most important organisational objectives for the coming year are established – these will be based on:

- the previous performance of the business
- external changes likely to affect the organisation
- sales forecasts based on research and past sales data.

Stage 2 The key or limiting factor that is most likely to influence the growth or success of the organisation must be identified – usually sales. The sales budget will be the first to be prepared. Accuracy is essential at this stage, because an error in the key-factor budget will distort all other budgets as well. For example, if the sales budget proves to be inaccurate, e.g. set at a level that proves to be too high, then cash, production, labour budgets and so on will become inaccurate too.

Stage 3 The sales budget is prepared after discussion with sales managers in all branches and divisions of the business.

Stage 4 Subsidiary budgets are prepared, which will now be based on the plans contained in the sales budget. These will include cash budget, administration budget, labour cost budget, materials cost budget, selling and distribution budget. The budget holders, e.g. cost- and profit-centre managers, should be involved in this process if the aim of delegated responsibility for budgets is to be achieved.

Stage 5 These budgets are co-ordinated to ensure consistency. This may be undertaken by a budgetary committee with special responsibility for ensuring that budgets do not conflict with each other and that the spending level planned does not exceed the resources of the business.

Stage 6 A master budget is prepared that contains the main details of all other budgets and concludes with a budgeted profit and loss account and balance sheet.

Stage 7 The master budget is then presented to the board of directors for its approval.

Once approved, the budgets will become the basis of the operational plans of each department and cost centre within the organisation. However, the overall plan is usually over too long a time period to be a motivating target and will be broken down into short periods like a month or even a week.

SETTING BUDGET LEVELS

Incremental budgeting and zero budgeting are the two methods most widely used to set budget levels.

Incremental budgeting

In many businesses that operate in highly competitive markets there may be plans to lower the cost budget for departments each year, but to raise the sales budgets. This puts increased pressure on many staff to achieve higher productivity. Incremental budgeting does not allow for unforeseen events. Using last year's figure as a basis means that each department does not have to justify its whole budget for the coming year – only the change or 'increment'.

Zero budgeting

This approach to setting budgets requires all departments and budget holders to justify their whole budget each year. This is time consuming, as a fundamental review of the work and importance of each budget-holding section is needed each year. However, it does provide added incentive for managers to defend the work of their own section. Also, changing situations can be reflected in very different budget levels each year.

KEY TERMS

incremental budgeting uses last year's budget as a basis and an adjustment is made for the coming year

zero budgeting setting budgets to zero each year and budget holders have to argue their case to receive any finance

Potential limitations of budgets

- Lack of flexibility. If budgets are set with no flexibility built into them, then sudden and unexpected changes in the external environment can make them very unrealistic – see the 'Setting the scene' case study on page 205. These external changes include unplanned increases in materials and energy-cost inflation.
- Focused on the short term. Budgets tend to be set for the relatively short term, e.g. the next 12 months. Managers may take a short-term decision to stay within budget that may not be in the best long-term interests of the business. For example, a decision to reduce the size of the workforce to stay within the labour budget may limit the firm's ability to increase output if sales were to rise unexpectedly quickly in the future.
- Result in unnecessary spending. When the end of the budgeting period approaches and managers realise that they have underspent their budgets, unnecessary spending decisions might be made so that the same level of budget can be justified next year. If a large surplus exists at the end of the budget period, how could managers justify the same level of resources next year?
- Training needs must be met. Setting and keeping to budgets is not easy and all managers with delegated responsibility for budgets will need extensive training in this role.
- Setting budgets for new projects. When a major new project is being undertaken, perhaps a one-off building scheme such as a large bridge or tunnel, setting realistic budgets may be difficult and frequent revisions in the budgets might be necessary.

Budgetary control – variance analysis

During the period covered by the budget and at the end of it the actual performance of the organisation needs to be compared with the original targets and reasons for differences must be investigated. This process is known as variance analysis. A variance is the difference between budgeted and actual figures. Variance analysis is an essential part of budgeting for a number of reasons:

- It measures differences from the planned performance of each department both month by month and at the end of the year.
- It assists in analysing the causes of deviations from budget. For example, if actual profit is below budget, was this due to lower sales revenue or higher costs?
- An understanding of the reasons for the deviations from the original planned levels can be used to change future budgets in order to make them more accurate. For example, if sales revenue is lower than planned as a result of market resistance to higher prices, then this knowledge could be used to help prepare future budgets.
- The performance of each individual budget-holding section may be appraised in an accurate and objective way.

KEY TERM

variance analysis the process of investigating any differences between budgeted figures and actual figures

If the variance has had the effect of increasing profit, for example sales revenue higher than budgeted for, then it is termed a favourable variance. If the variance has had the effect of reducing profit, for example direct material costs are higher than budget, then it is termed an unfavourable or adverse variance. See the West Indian Carpets worked example on page 210.

KEY TERMS

adverse variance exists when the difference between the budgeted and actual figure leads to a lower than expected profit

favourable variance exists when the difference between the budgeted and actual figure leads to a higher than expected profit

RESPONDING TO VARIANCE ANALYSIS RESULTS

Managers may need to respond quickly to both adverse and favourable variances. Clearly, adverse variances will need to be looked at in some detail to see if cheaper supplies or working methods could be adopted. However, an adverse variance caused by an increase in output leading to higher raw material costs is of much less concern.

Favourable variances cannot be ignored either. They may reflect a poor and inaccurate budgeting process where cost budgets were set too high. A favourable direct cost variance caused by output being much less than planned for is not very promising – why were sales and output lower than planned for?

Budgetary control and strategic planning

Setting, agreeing and controlling budgets is time consuming. Budgets can fail to reflect changing circumstances and become inflexible. Budget holders can look upon a budget as a limit up to which they can spend, whether their department needs all of the resources or not. Therefore, is the budgetary process worthwhile?

Try to think of the alternative:

- Without a detailed and co-ordinated set of plans for allocating money and resources of the business, who would decide 'who gets what'?
- Without a clear sales budget as the cornerstone of the budgetary process, how would departments know how much to produce or to spend on sales promotion or how many people to employ?
- Would it be possible to assess how the business had done or how well individual departments had performed without a clear series of targets with which to compare performance?
- Without figures to monitor progress during the budgetary period, how would it be possible to know where the business is or to suggest changes that might be made?
- Budgets have to be agreed and controlled. This gives responsibility and a sense of direction to those delegated to work with them. These human advantages are difficult to ensure without planned money values to work with.

Based on these arguments in favour of budget setting and budgetary control, all businesses are likely to undertake some form of financial planning.

THEORY OF KNOWLEDGE

Sereena Mushtaq is a meticulous planner. As a finance specialist, she believes in detail and accuracy and never leaves things to chance. As a maths graduate, she likes the idea of certainty and control. As the finance director of Aztec Ltd, one of Pakistan's leading software businesses, she prides herself on the accuracy of her forecasts and budgets.

Examine the ways Sereena, as a finance specialist, can make the future financial outcomes more certain. To what extent is certainty attainable when Sereena is setting her budgets?

VARIANCE ANALYSIS – WORKED EXAMPLE FOR WEST INDIAN CARPETS LTD

Financial variable	Budget ($)	Actual result ($)	Variance ($)	Favourable or adverse
Sales revenue	15 000	12 000	3 000	Adverse – this reduces profit
Direct costs	5 000	4 000	1 000	Favourable – this increases profit
Overhead costs	3 000	3 500	500	Adverse – this reduces profit
Net profit	7 000	4 500	2 500	Adverse – profit is below forecast

Table 21.1 *West Indian Carpets Ltd*

The variance calculations for West Indian Carpets Ltd, shown in Table 21.1, can be verified by checking the net profit variance ($2500 adverse) against the net sum of the other variances ($3500 adverse–$1,000 favourable = $2500 adverse). The benefits to be gained from regular variance analysis include:

1 Identifying potential problems early so that remedial action can be taken. Perhaps, in this case, a new competing carpet retailer has opened up and West Indian Carpets will have to quickly introduce strategies to combat this competition.

2 Allowing managers to concentrate their time and efforts on the major, or exceptional, problem areas – this is known as management by exception. In this case, it seems that managers should urgently investigate the likely causes of the lower than expected sales figures.

Table 21.2 identifies the possible causes of adverse and favourable variances.

Adverse variances	Favourable variances
1 Sales revenue is below budget *either* because units sold were fewer than planned for *or* the selling price had to be lowered due to competition. 2 Actual raw material costs are higher than planned for *either* because output was higher than budgeted *or* the cost per unit of materials increased. 3 Labour costs are above budget *either* because wage rates had to be raised due to shortages of workers *or* the labour time taken to complete the work was longer than expected. 4 Overhead costs are higher than budgeted, perhaps because the annual rent rise was above forecast.	1 Sales revenue is above budget *either* due to higher than expected economic growth *or* problems with one of the competitor's products. 2 Raw material costs are lower *either* because output was less than planned *or* the cost per unit of materials was lower than budget. 3 Labour costs are lower than planned for *either* because of lower wage rates *or* quicker completion of the work. 4 Overhead costs are lower than budgeted, perhaps because advertising rates from TV companies were reduced.

Table 21.2 *Possible causes of adverse and favourable variances*

OVER TO YOU

REVISION CHECKLIST

1 What is the difference between a forecast and a budget?
2 Explain **three** advantages to a new business of operating an extensive budgeting system.
3 What is meant by 'master budget'?
4 Outline why a fashion clothing business might face problems when setting its sales revenue budget.
5 A food retailing business with many branches is planning to introduce delegated budgeting for the first time.
   a Explain **two** possible benefits of this to the business.
   b Outline **two** possible limitations of doing this.
6 Explain why a firm might decide to use zero budgeting.
7 Examine **two** advantages for a business of using variance analysis.
8 Distinguish, with the aid of numerical examples, between 'favourable variances' and 'adverse variances'.
9 Discuss **two** ways that a sports shoe retailing business might use to correct an adverse sales revenue variance.

REVISION ACTIVITY

Look at the case study below and then answer the questions that follow.

Kinibali Timber Ltd

$000	Budgeted figures	Actual figures
Sales revenue	66	70
Direct labour	15	18
Direct materials	12	17
Fixed costs	6	5
Profit	–	–

Budgeted and actual figures for the year ending 31 December 2010

16 marks, 28 minutes

1 Calculate the budgeted profit and actual profit figures. [2]
2 Using variance analysis, discuss whether the management of Kinibali Timber Ltd should be satisfied with the performance of the business over the last 12 months. [10]
3 Outline **two** other pieces of information that would have helped you in your answer to question 2. [4]

VARIANCE ANALYSIS AT OASIS COOKERS LTD

Oasis Cookers Ltd makes gas and electric ovens. The business has a good reputation for quality products. These are sold through a number of selected retailers who have agreed to display and market the ovens in ways that differentiate them from cheaper models. The national economy is experiencing a downturn with no economic growth. The government has been forced to increase interest rates to control cost-push inflation and this has contributed to an appreciation of the currency's exchange rate. Foreign oven imports are falling in price because of this. The management of Oasis Cookers Ltd are studying the latest variance analysis results:

$000	Budgeted figures	Actual figures	Variance
Sales revenue	165	150	
Cost of materials	80	70	
Labour costs	22	23	
Gross profit	63	57	
Overheads	40	43	
Net profit	23	14	

EXAM PRACTICE QUESTION

Read the case study and then answer the questions that follow.

25 marks, 45 minutes

1 Define the following terms:
   a budgeted figures
   b variance. [4]
2 Explain how a manufacturing business sets budgets for sales and costs. [4]
3 Complete the table by calculating the variances, indicating whether they are adverse or favourable. [6]
4 Using the variance results, comment on the performance of Oasis Cookers during the year. [4]
5 Evaluate the usefulness of budgets to a business such as Oasis Cookers. [7]

22 Financial accounts

This chapter covers syllabus section 3.5

On completing this chapter you should be able to:

- explain the purpose of accounts
- construct and amend accounts from information given
- evaluate the importance of final accounts to each stakeholder group
- identify and understand the main components of a profit and loss account
- identify and understand the main components of a balance sheet
- (H) calculate depreciation and stock valuations
- (H) understand what intangible assets are and understand the difficulties of valuing them.

SETTING THE SCENE

Sky's the limit for satellite dishes

Rashid sold and fitted ten TV satellite dishes in his first month of trading. He had bought 50 satellite dishes from a website specialising in stock sell-offs from failed businesses. He paid $100 each. This used up most of his start-up capital. He rented a small truck for $120 a month. A large advertising sign had cost him $120. Other advertising costs in his first month had been more than expected. The local newspaper had increased its classified rates – $150 was $30 more than planned. He sold the satellite dishes for $275 fully fitted. Rashid could have just sold the dishes themselves but he wanted to 'add value' to them by doing the fitting too. Each fitting kit cost Rashid $10. Other costs – such as road tax and insurance on the truck – totalled $200 per month, just as predicted.

He started to work out his profit for the first month. His only real worry was that two of his customers had asked if they could delay paying him. He had agreed as he wanted to make the sale. But when would they pay? Should he include these two satellite dishes when working out his first monthly profits?

Points to think about:

- Why do you think it is important for Rashid to keep accurate financial records (accounts)?
- Do you think he made a profit in his first month of trading? How would you try to work this out?
- Why will profit be important to Rashid?
- If you were Rashid, would you have offered the two customers credit?

Introduction

All businesses have to keep detailed records of purchases, sales and other financial transactions. Table 22.1 lists some problems that would immediately arise if accounts were not kept. We can therefore say that accounts are financial records of business transactions, which are needed to provide essential information to groups both within and outside the organisation.

Problem	Groups affected
How much did we buy from our suppliers and have they been paid yet?	Managers and suppliers (creditors)
How much profit did the business make last year?	Managers, shareholders and the tax authorities
Is the business able to repay the loan to the bank?	Managers and the bank
Did we pay wages to the workers last week?	Managers and workers
What is the value of the fixed assets and by how much did they depreciate last year?	Managers and shareholders

Table 22.1 *Accounts and the interests of stakeholders*

Stakeholders and accounting information

There are internal and external stakeholder users of accounts. The managers, as internal users, will have access to much more detailed and up-to-date data than other groups. External users include banks, government, employees and shareholders and other stakeholders of the business. The list below identifies the main stakeholders and how they use business accounts.

Business managers

- Measure the performance of the business to compare against targets, previous time periods and competitors.
- Help them take decisions, such as new investments, closing branches and launching new products.
- Control and monitor the operation of each department and division of the business.
- Set targets or budgets for the future and review these against actual performance.

Banks

- Decide whether to lend money to the business.
- Assess whether to allow an increase in overdraft facilities.
- Decide whether to continue an overdraft facility or a loan.

Creditors, such as suppliers

- Assess whether the business is secure and liquid enough to pay off its debts.
- Assess whether the business is a good credit risk.
- Decide whether to press for early repayment of outstanding debts.

Customers

- Assess whether the business is secure.
- Determine whether they will be assured of future supplies of the goods they are purchasing.
- Establish whether there will be security of spare parts and service facilities.

Government and tax authorities

- Calculate how much tax is due from the business.
- Determine whether the business is likely to expand and create more jobs.
- Assess whether the business is in danger of closing down, creating economic problems.
- Confirm that the business is staying within the law in terms of accounting regulations.

Investors, such as shareholders in the company

- Assess the value of the business and their investment in it.
- Establish whether the business is becoming more or less profitable.
- Determine what share of the profits investors are receiving.
- Decide whether the business has potential for growth.
- As potential investors, compare these details with those from other businesses before making a decision to buy shares in a company.
- As actual investors, to decide whether to consider selling all or part of their holding.

Workforce

- Assess whether the business is secure enough to pay wages and salaries.
- Determine whether the business is likely to expand or be reduced in size.
- Determine whether jobs are secure.
- Find out whether, if profits are rising, a wage increase can be afforded.
- Find out how the average wage in the business compares with the salaries of directors.

Local community

- See if the business is profitable and likely to expand, which could be good for the local economy.
- Determine whether the business is making losses and whether this could lead to closure.

The main business accounts

At the end of each accounting period, usually one year, accountants will draw up the financial statements of the business. For companies, these will be included in the annual report and accounts, which are sent to every shareholder. Table 22.2 gives details of the financial statements of limited companies, as these are the accounts you are most likely to come across in IB Business and Management.

RECENT LAYOUT CHANGES

There have been many recent changes to the layout of published accounts to comply with the International Financial Reporting Standards (IFRS). These changes include different titles to important items on published accounts. This book employs the traditional layouts and titles, as used by the IB examinations, but you should be aware that accounts may be presented in slightly different ways and using slightly different terminology.

The account	What it shows
Income statement	The gross and net profit of the company. Details of how the net profit is split up (or appropriated) between dividends to shareholders and retained profits.
Balance sheet	The net worth of the company. This is the difference between the value of what a company owns (assets) and what it owes (liabilities).
Cash-flow statement	Where cash was received from and what it was spent on.

Table 22.2 *Final accounts of limited companies – what they contain*

THE INCOME STATEMENT

This account used to be known as the profit and loss account. In old examination papers or company accounts drawn up some years ago, this term may be used.

KEY TERM

income statement records the revenue, costs and profit (or loss) of a business over a given period of time

- A detailed income statement is produced for internal use because managers will need as much information as possible. It may be produced as frequently as managers need the information – perhaps once a month.
- A less detailed summary will appear in the published accounts of companies for external users. It will be produced at least once a year. The content of this is laid down by the Company Acts and provides a minimum of information to prevent competitors having insight into their rivals' strengths and weaknesses.

The version used in this chapter is one based on the published accounts, but with additional information where this aids understanding. An example is given in Table 22.3.

	Sales turnover	3060	Trading account
(minus)	Cost of sales	(1840)	
(equals)	Gross profit	1220	
(minus)	Overheads	(580)	Profit and loss account
(equals)	Net profit or profit before tax and interest	640	
(minus)	Interest	(80)	
(equals)	Pre-tax profits	560	
(minus)	Tax @ 20%	(112)	
(equals)	Profit after tax	448	
(minus)	Dividends to shareholders	200	Appropriation account
(equals)	Retained profit	248	

Table 22.3 *Income statement for Energen plc for the year ended 29 March 2010 (£000s)*

The three sections of an income statement

1 The trading account

This shows how gross profit (or loss) has been made from the trading activities of the business.

It is most important to understand that, as not all sales are for cash in most businesses, the sales turnover figure is not the same as cash received by the business. The formula for calculating sales turnover is: selling price × quantity sold. Therefore, if 120 items are sold at $2 each, the sales turnover is $240.

KEY TERMS

gross profit equal to sales revenue less cost of sales

sales revenue (or sales turnover) the total value of sales made during the trading period = selling price × quantity sold

cost of sales (or cost of goods sold) this is the direct cost of purchasing the goods that were sold during the financial year

2 Profit and loss account

This section of the income statement calculates both the net profit (or profit before interest and tax) and the profit after tax of the business.

ACTIVITY 22.1

Calculating gross profit

12 marks, 20 minutes

1 Calculate gross profit for Cosy Corner Retailers Ltd for the financial year ending 31 March 2010. Show all workings.
   a 1500 items sold for $5 each; cost of goods sold = 1500 @ $2. [3]
   b Explain two reasons why you think it is important for any business to make a profit. [6]

2 Cambridge Boxes Ltd sold 3500 units in the last financial year ending 31 December 2009. The selling price was $4. All boxes cost the company $2 each. Calculate the company's gross profit in 2009. [3]

ACTIVITY 22.2

Read the case study below and then answer the questions that follow.

Calculating profits

Rodrigues buys second-hand computers, updates them and then sells them in his small shop. He has many customers who are keen to buy computers at prices below those charged for new machines. Rodrigues took out a bank loan to buy his shop – he has since repaid half of this loan. He employs three electricians to help him with the computer work. He is the main shareholder in the business – three of his friends also invested in the company when it was first set up.

	$
Sales revenue (4000 items @ $3 each)	12 000
Cost of goods sold (@ $1 per item)	4 000
Gross profit	*V*
Overhead expenses	3 000
Operating profit (net profit)	*W*
Interest	1 000
Profit before tax	*X*
Corporation tax @ 20%	800
Profit after tax	*Y*
Dividends paid	1 200
Retained profit	*Z*

Profit and loss account for Rodrigues Traders Ltd for the year ending 31 October 2009

17 marks, 35 minutes

1 Calculate the missing values *V–Z* for the different types of profit for Rodrigues Traders. [5]

2 State **three** stakeholders in this business who would be interested in these profit figures. [3]

3 For each stakeholder group identified, explain why the profits of this business are important. [9]

Overheads are costs or expenses of the business that are not directly related to the number of items made or sold. These can include rent and business rates, management salaries, lighting costs and depreciation. Operating profit (sometimes called net profit or profit before interest and taxation) is the profit made before tax and interest have been subtracted, but after all costs of sales and overheads have been deducted from sales turnover. Limited companies pay corporation tax on their profits before paying dividends.

KEY TERMS

operating profit (net profit) gross profit minus overhead expenses

profit after tax operating profit minus interest costs and corporation tax

3 Appropriation account

This final section of the income statement (which is not always shown in published accounts) shows how the profits after tax of the business are distributed between the owners – in the form of dividends to company shareholders – and as retained profits.

KEY TERMS

dividends the share of the profits paid to shareholders as a return for investing in the company

retained profit the profit left after all deductions, including dividends, have been made. This is 'ploughed back' into the company as a source of finance

Using income statements

- They can be used to measure and compare the performance of a business over time or with other firms – and ratios can be used to help with this form of analysis.

- The actual profit data can be compared with the expected profit levels of the business.
- Bankers and creditors of the business will need the information to help decide whether to lend money to the business.
- Potential investors may assess the value of investing in a business from the level of profits being made.

All of these users of profit data need to be aware of the limitations of accounting data; for example, they might have been 'window dressed' by managers to flatter the performance of the business. In addition, they should also consider the 'quality' of the profit being recorded. For example, a high profit figure resulting from the sale of a valuable asset for more than its expected value might not be repeatable and is, therefore, said to be low-quality profit. Profits made from developing, producing and selling exclusive product designs, however, are high-quality profits because this is likely to be a continuous source of profit for some time to come.

KEY TERMS

low-quality profit one-off profit that cannot easily be repeated or sustained

high-quality profit profit that can be repeated and sustained

THE BALANCE SHEET

KEY TERMS

balance sheet an accounting statement that records the values of a business's assets, liabilities and shareholders' equity at one point in time

assets items of monetary value that are owned by a business

liabilities a financial obligation of a business that it is required to pay in the future

shareholders' equity total value of assets *less* total value of liabilities

share capital the total value of capital raised from shareholders by the issue of shares

The balance sheet records the net wealth or shareholders' equity of a business at one moment in time. In a company this net wealth 'belongs' to the shareholders. The aim of most businesses is to increase the shareholders' equity by raising the value of the business's assets more than any increase in the value of liabilities. Shareholders' equity comes from two main sources:

- The first and original source was the capital originally invested in the company through the purchase of shares. This is called share capital.
- The second source is the retained earnings of the company accumulated over time through its operations. These are sometimes referred to as reserves – which is rather misleading as they are not reserves of cash.

Table 22.4 shows an example of a balance sheet with key terms and explanatory notes. The figures have been presented in two columns to help understanding of how sub-totals are arrived at. In published accounts, all figures will be presented in one column. The IB format of the balance sheet is given, but the latest IFRS terminology is given in brackets.

Further points to note:

- Companies have to publish the income statement and the balance sheet for the previous financial year as well in order to allow easy comparison.
- The titles of both accounts are very important as they identify both the account and the company.
- Whereas the income statement covers the whole financial year, the balance sheet is a statement of the estimated value of the company at one moment in time – the end of the financial year.

Fixed assets

The most common examples of fixed assets are land, buildings, vehicles and machinery. These are all tangible assets as they have a physical existence and are expected to be retained and used by the business for more than 12 months. Businesses can also own intangible assets – these cannot be seen but still have value in the business. See page 219 for problems of their valuation.

Current assets

These are very important to a business, as will be seen when liquidity is assessed later in this chapter. The most common examples are inventories, accounts payable (debtors who have bought goods on credit) and cash/bank balance.

Current liabilities

Typical current liabilities include accounts payable (suppliers who have allowed the business credit), bank overdraft and unpaid dividends and unpaid tax.

	$m	$m	Key term	Notes
ASSETS				
Fixed (non-current) assets:			*assets to be kept and used by the business for more than one year*	*Previously referred to as fixed assets.*
Property	300			
Vehicles	45			
Equipment	67			
Intangible assets	30		*items of value that do not have a physical presence, such as patents and trademarks*	
		442		
Current assets:			*assets that are likely to be turned into cash before the next balance sheet date*	
Stocks (inventories)	34		*stocks held by the business in the form of materials, work in progress and finished goods*	
Debtors (accounts receivable)	28		*the value of payments to be received from customers who have bought goods on credit*	*Also known as 'trade receivables'.*
Cash	4			*Also known as 'cash and cash equivalents'.*
	66			
CURRENT LIABILITIES			*debts of the business that will usually have to be paid within one year*	
Creditors (accounts payable)	42		*value of debts for goods bought on credit payable to suppliers*	*Also known as 'trade payables'.*
Short-term loans	31			*These loans will include the company's overdraft with the bank.* *Other current liabilities might include provisions to pay for tax and dividends.*
	73			
Net current assets		(7)	*current assets – current liabilities*	*Also known as 'working capital'.*
NET ASSETS		**435**		
Long-term (non-current) liabilities:			*value of debts of the business that will be payable after more than one year*	
Long-term loans		125		*Other long-term liabilities might include debentures issued by the company.*
SHAREHOLDERS' EQUITY:				*Definitions for all of the following terms have already been given.*
Share capital	200			
Retained earnings	110			*Also referred to as 'retained profit'.*
		310		
CAPITAL EMPLOYED		**435**		*This balances with net assets!*

Table 22.4 *Example of a balance sheet with key terms and explanatory notes*

ACTIVITY 22.3

Understanding balance sheets
Copy out this table and indicate in which category the following items would appear on a company balance sheet.

	Fixed tangible assets	Fixed intangible assets	Current assets	Current liabilities	Long-term liabilities	Shareholders' equity
Company car						
Work in progress						
Four-year bank loan						
Money owed to suppliers						
Issued share capital						
Dividends owed to shareholders						
Value of patents						
Payments due from customers						
Retained earnings						
Cash in bank						

Working capital

You will recall this concept from Chapter 20 and it can be calculated from the balance sheet by the formula: current assets – current liabilities. It can also be referred to as net current assets.

Shareholders' equity

This is sometimes referred to as shareholders' funds. It represents the capital originally paid into the business when the shareholders bought shares (share capital) or the retained earnings/profits of the business that the shareholders have accepted should be kept in the business. These are also known as reserves. Other reserves can also appear on the balance sheet if a company believes that its fixed assets have increased in value (revaluation reserve) or if it sells additional shares for more than their 'nominal' value (share premium reserve). Shareholders' equity is the permanent capital of the business – it will not be repaid to shareholders (unless the company ceases trading altogether), unlike loans that are repaid to creditors.

The most common misunderstanding regarding reserves is to believe that they are 'cash reserves' that can be called upon as a source of finance. They are not. Retained earnings arise due to profits being made which are not paid out in tax or dividends, but they have nearly always been invested back into the business by being used to purchase additional assets. They are, therefore, no longer available as a source of liquid funds. The only cash funds available in the business are those indicated under 'cash' in the current assets section.

Long-term liabilities
These are the long-term loans owed by the business. They are due to be paid over a period of time greater than one year and include loans, commercial mortgages and debentures. The value of non-current assets compared to the total capital employed by the business is a very important measure of the degree of risk being taken by the company's management.

ACTIVITY 22.4

Mauritius Telecom
Study the simplified version of the 2008 balance sheet for Mauritius Telecom as at 31 December 2008 (000 Mauritian rupees).

	2007	2008
Fixed assets	7520978	7841517
Current assets:		
Stocks (inventories)	92726	153521
Debtors (accounts receivable)	2230290	2059528
Cash and cash equivalents	2484847	3651527
Total current assets	4807863	5864576
TOTAL ASSETS	12328841	13706083
Total long-term liabilities	1763981	1744768
Total current liabilities	3553079	4243430
Shareholders' capital and reserves (shareholders' equity)	7011781	7717885
TOTAL EQUITY AND LIABILITIES	12328841	13706083

30 marks, 40 minutes (plus research time)

1 Define the following terms:
   a debtors/accounts receivable
   b stocks/inventories
   c current assets
   d long-term liabilities. [12]

2 Explain why it is important to stakeholders of Mauritius Telecoms to be provided with two years of balance sheet values in the published accounts. Try to make references to some of the data in your answer. [6]

3 Use the internet to research the latest year's accounts from Mauritius Telecoms http://www.mauritiustelecom.com (or another plc of your choice). Read the Chairman's statement, the Report of Directors and the Auditors' report. How useful do you think these reports would be to:
   a shareholders
   b workers in the company
   c any other stakeholder group?

   Explain your answers. [12]

Valuing intangible assets

The reputation and prestige of a business that has been operating for some time also give value to the business over and above the worth of its physical assets. This is called the 'goodwill' of a business. This should normally only feature on a balance sheet just after it has been purchased for more than its assets are worth, or when the business is being prepared for sale. At other times, goodwill will not appear on company accounts – it is 'written off' as soon as possible if it has been included in the purchase of another company. This is because business reputation and good name can disappear very rapidly – for example, with a scare over products that risk consumers' health.

Let's look at an example of goodwill. If business A buys out business B for $2 million, yet the net asset value of B is only $1.5 million, then A has paid $0.5 million for the 'goodwill' of business B. Why might business A have been prepared to pay this extra $0.5 million?

Goodwill has value when the business being sold is well known, well established and has good trading links with both customers and suppliers. A newly formed business does not yet have goodwill, but an existing business is said to be a 'going concern' with the intangible advantages listed above. Hence, other firms are prepared to pay a price exceeding net asset value in order to purchase this goodwill.

There are two accounting conventions regarding goodwill:

- It should not appear as an asset of an existing business because it is so difficult to value and can disappear rapidly, e.g. following an accident that damages the environment and destroys a firm's reputation.

- It will appear on the balance sheet of a business that has bought another firm and has paid for goodwill. It will appear as a non-current intangible asset. However, this should be taken off the balance sheet (written off) as soon as possible for the same reason as above – it is not necessarily permanent and just because it was worth $0.5 million last year does not mean that the reputation and customer contacts are still worth that amount this year.

Goodwill is an example of an intangible asset, but it is not the only one. Patents, copyrights, well-established brand names and capital spent on research and development into new products – these are all assets that do not exist in a physical sense, yet they add value to a company.

- Intangible assets are difficult to put a value on as they are rarely bought and sold on the open market. In addition, unlike buildings or equipment which can be valued by specialist surveyors who can be fairly confident in their assessment, the value of intangible assets can fluctuate wildly. The damage to Toyota's brand image (and hence brand valuation) by the 2010 recall for safety reasons of millions of cars worldwide is a good example. Disputes can arise between accountants about the valuation of intangible assets and there is a current debate regarding the asset value of well-known brand names. There is scope for varying the value of these and other intangibles on the balance sheet in order to give a better picture of the company's position. This is one aspect of 'window dressing' of accounts that can reduce the objectivity of published accounts.
- Balance sheets prepared under normally accepted accounting rules do not usually record these assets – often known as intellectual property – unless acquired through takeover or merger.
- For many companies, they are their main source of future earnings, especially in a world increasingly dominated by the 'knowledge-based economy', e.g. scientific research companies, publishing and music companies, companies with famous brand names and so on.
- The market value of companies with many intangible assets will be much greater than the balance sheet or book value.

KEY TERMS

goodwill arises when a business is valued at or sold for more than the balance sheet values of its assets

intellectual property an intangible asset that has been developed from human ideas and knowledge

market value the estimated total value of a company if it were taken over

Depreciation of assets

Nearly all fixed/non-current assets will depreciate or decline in value over time. It seems reasonable, therefore, to record only the value of each year's depreciation as a cost on each year's profit and loss account. This will overcome both of the problems referred to above:

- The assets will retain some value on the balance sheet each year until fully depreciated or sold off.
- The profits will be reduced by the amount of that year's depreciation and will not be under- or over-recorded.

KEY TERM

depreciation the decline in the estimated value of a non-current asset over time

Assets decline in value for two main reasons:

- normal wear and tear through usage
- technological change, making either the asset, or the product it is used to make, obsolete.

Technological change makes office equipment obsolete, even if it was purchased quite recently

CALCULATING DEPRECIATION

There are a number of different methods accountants can use to calculate depreciation – but only two will be tested by the IB examination papers: straight line and reducing balance.

KEY TERMS

straight-line depreciation a constant amount of depreciation is subtracted from the value of the asset each year

net book value the current balance sheet value of a non-current asset = original cost–accumulated depreciation
reducing balance method calculates depreciation by subtracting a fixed percentage from the previous year's net book value

Straight-line method of depreciation

The title of this method indicates the way in which depreciation is calculated.

To calculate the annual amount of depreciation the following information will be needed:

- the original or historical cost of the asset
- the expected useful life of the asset
- an estimation of the value of the asset at the end of its useful life – this is known as the residual value of the asset.

The following formula is then used to calculate the annual depreciation charge:

$$\text{annual depreciation charge} = \frac{\text{original or historical cost of asset} - \text{expected residual value}}{\text{expected useful life of asset (years)}}$$

Straight-line depreciation has both advantages and limitations:

- It is easy to calculate and understand. It is widely used by limited companies. You can check this for yourself. Look in the annual accounts of any plc and you will find a statement about the depreciation methods it has used – more often than not, it will have used this method.
- It requires estimates to be made regarding both life expectancy and residual value. Mistakes at this stage will lead to inaccurate depreciation charges being calculated.
- In addition, cars, trucks and computers are examples of assets that tend to depreciate much more quickly in the first and second years than in subsequent years. This is not reflected in the straight-line method of calculation – all annual depreciation charges are the same. The diminishing balance method of depreciation (see below) depreciates assets by a greater amount in the first few years of life than in later years.
- There is no recognition of the very rapid pace at which advances in modern technology tend to make existing assets redundant.

CALCULATING DEPRECIATION USING THE STRAIGHT-LINE METHOD – WORKED EXAMPLE

A firm of lawyers purchases three new computers costing \$3000 each. Experience with previous computers suggests that they will need to be updated after four years. At the end of this period, the second-hand value of each machine is estimated to be just \$200. Using straight-line depreciation, the annual depreciation charge will be:

$$\$9000 - \$600 = \frac{\$8400}{4} = \$2100$$

So an annual depreciation charge of \$2100 will be made. This will be included in the firm's overhead expenses on the profit and loss account. On the balance sheet, the annual depreciation charge will be subtracted from the value of the computers. At the end of four years, each computer will be valued at \$200 on the balance sheet. Table 22.5 shows how the value of the computers falls over the four-year period.

Year	Annual depreciation charge	Net book value of the three computers
Present	0	\$9000
1	\$2100	\$6900
2	\$2100	\$4800
3	\$2100	\$2700
4	\$2100	\$600

Table 22.5 *Net book value declines with each annual depreciation*

Suppose that at the end of the fourth year, the computers are sold for more than their expected residual value. If they are sold for a total of \$900, then the firm has made a surplus of \$300. If, however, the computers were scrapped, because they had become so out of date compared with more recent models, the firm would have to record a loss, in the fourth year, on the disposal of these assets.

- The repairs and the maintenance costs of an asset usually increase with age and this will reduce the profitability of the asset. This is not adjusted for by the fixed depreciation charge of the straight-line method.

Reducing (diminishing) balance method

This method of calculating depreciation solves some of the problems identified by the straight-line method. It leads to higher levels of depreciation in the early years of an asset's life but lower depreciation as the asset ages. The rate of depreciation is calculated using the formula:

$$1 - \sqrt[n]{\frac{\text{residual value}}{\text{cost}}} \times 100$$

CALCULATING DEPRECIATION USING THE REDUCING BALANCE METHOD – WORKED EXAMPLE

A delivery company purchases a vehicle for $16 000. It estimates the residual value as $4000, with an expected life span of four years. Table 22.6 shows the depreciation and net book value.

Year	Depreciation	Net book value
0	0	$16 000
1	$4 800 ($16 000×30%)	$11 200
2	$3 360 ($11 200×30%)	$7 840
3	$2 352 ($7 840×30%)	$5 488
4	$1 646 ($5 488×30%)	$3 842

Table 22.6 *Net book value declines with each annual depreciation*

Note that:

- the *amount* of depreciation falls each year but the *rate* remains constant
- the residual value at the end of year 4 is just below the forecasted figure because the rate of depreciation used was rounded up from the 'true' rate of 29.29%.

The reducing balance method also has advantages and limitations:

- It is more accurate than the straight-line method, especially where assets lose more value in their early years.
- Another rationale for using this method is that many assets are more efficient and profitable when new, so it is more logical to 'match' a higher amount of the cost of the asset against this higher profit.
- It is slightly more difficult to calculate than the straight-line method.
- By calculating a 'precise' rate of depreciation it suggests a level of accuracy for the process of depreciation which is unjustified – the residual value and expected life span are always estimates and this detracts from the achievement of complete accuracy.

Stock valuation

The value of closing stock on a balance sheet is a major factor influencing:

- the value of a company's balance sheet
- the profit recorded – the higher the value given to closing stock, the lower will be the cost of goods sold, thereby raising the profit figure.

The valuation of stocks can vary greatly depending on the method used and the rate of inflation.

LAST IN FIRST OUT (LIFO)

KEY TERM

last in first out (LIFO) valuing closing stocks by assuming that the last one purchased was sold first

During a period of rising prices, valuing stocks using the LIFO method will tend to reduce the declared profits of the business – giving a potential saving in corporation tax.

LIFO – WORKED EXAMPLE

A company selling TVs to retailers received three deliveries of stock in February 2011:

Date	Stock purchased
2 Feb 2011	10 TVs @ $200
7 Feb 2011	50 TVs @ $220
16 Feb 2011	100 TVs @ $250

There were 10 TVs in stock on 1 February bought at $190 each. During February 2011 the company sold 130 TVs at a price of $400 each.

Question 1: What was the value of the goods sold?

Answer: Assuming LIFO, the earliest (lowest price) TVs are still assumed to be in stock. The value of the goods sold or 'issued' and the value of closing stocks is shown in Table 22.7.

value of goods sold = 10 @ $200 + 40 @ $220 + 80 @ $250 = $30 800

Date	Stock purchased	Stock issued	Closing stock
1 Feb 2011			10 @ $190
2 Feb 2011	10 @ $200		10 @ $190 10 @ $200
5 Feb 2011		10 @ $200	10 @ $190
7 Feb 2011	50 @ $220		10 @ $190 50 @ $220
		40 @ $220	10 @ $190 10 @ $220
16 Feb 2011	100 @ $250		
		80 @ $250	10 @ $190 10 @ $220 20 @ $250

Table 22.7 *Using LIFO: value of TVs sold and value of closing stocks*

Question 2: What is the value of closing stocks at the end of February?

Answer: 10 TVs @ $190 + 10 TVs @ $220 + 20 TVs @ $250 = $9100

Question 3: What is the gross profit made by the business during February?

Answer: gross profit = sales revenue – cost of goods sold = $52 000 – $30 800 = $21 200

FIRST IN FIRST OUT (FIFO)

KEY TERM

first in first out (FIFO) valuing stocks by assuming that the first ones bought in were sold first

During a period of rising prices, valuing stocks using the FIFO method will record a higher closing stock value than LIFO and a higher profit figure.

Points to note about LIFO and FIFO:

- These are stock valuation methods *not* rules for the physical movement or sale of stock.
- During inflationary periods LIFO will lower profits, reduce corporation tax charges and improve a firm's liquidity.
- During inflationary periods LIFO results in a lower valuation of closing stocks and net assets.
- The method used will have an impact on important ratios such as stock turnover.

FIFO – WORKED EXAMPLE

Using the data from the worked example above:

1. value of goods sold = 10 @ $190 + 10 @ $200 + 50 @ $220 + 60 @ $250 = $29 900
2. value of closing stocks = 40 @ $250 = $10 000
3. gross profit = $52 000 – $29 900 = $22 100

Date	Stock purchased	Stock issued	Closing stock
1 Feb 2011			10 @ $190
2 Feb 2011	10 @ $200		10 @ $190 10 @ $200
5 Feb 2011		10 @ $190	10 @ $200
7 Feb 2011	50 @ $220		10 @ $200 50 @ $220
		40 = 10 @ $200 30 @ $220	20 @ $220
16 Feb 2011	100 @ $250		
		80 = 20 @ $220 60 @ $250	40 @ $250

Table 22.8 *Using FIFO: value of TVs sold and value of closing stocks*

- Many governments do not allow the use of LIFO for the calculation of published profits on which corporation tax is based.
- An alternative method of stock valuation exists – AVCO – which takes the average value of stocks used over a period for the calculation of profits.

THEORY OF KNOWLEDGE

1. The balance sheet measures the financial value of a business and the profit and loss account (income statement) measures the financial trading success of a business. Discuss other ways you might use to measure the value and success of a business.
2. Many companies think being ethical is only about producing a corporate social responsibility report. However, acting ethically in business involves more than spending money on marketing and PR. The world's leading ethical business are the ones that act to improve society's welfare.

a Each member of your class or group should prepare an ethical profit and loss account for a business of their choice. Instead of revenues, identify the things the business does to improve society's welfare; instead of costs, identify the things the business does that damage society's welfare.

b As a class, prepare an ethical league table for the businesses you have studied.

c Discuss the problems of producing such a league table.

OVER TO YOU

REVISION CHECKLIST

1 List **four** likely external users of the accounts of a large plc such as Microsoft and explain what they would use these accounts for.

2 Outline why managers need more detailed accounts than external users.

3 What is meant by 'window dressing' the accounts?

4 What are the **three** sections of an income statement and what do they show?

5 What is the difference between gross and net/operating profit?

6 What are the **two** ways in which profit after tax may be appropriated?

7 What does a balance sheet show about a business?

8 Explain the difference between fixed assets and current assets.

9 What is meant by the term 'capital employed' on a balance sheet?

(H) 10 What is meant by goodwill and why should it be written off the accounts of a business buying another firm as quickly as possible?

(H) 11 Explain why it might be difficult for a music publishing business such as EMI to include intangible assets on its accounts.

(H) 12 Explain, using numerical examples, why the reducing balance method of depreciation is often considered to be more accurate than the straight-line method.

(H) 13 Explain, using numerical examples, how LIFO can lead to a lower recorded gross profit figure than FIFO during a period of rising prices.

REVISION ACTIVITY

Read the case study below and then answer the questions that follow.

Shivani's first balance sheet

Shivani has been in business for just one year. She is a qualified beauty therapist. Despite lacking experience in accounting, she is determined to save money by trying to draw up her end-of-year accounts herself. The initial attempt to construct a balance sheet is shown below.

Assets	
Fixed assets:	
Stock of materials	15
Equipment	25
Current assets:	
Cash	1
Creditors	5
Overdraft	3
Net assets	49
Current liabilities:	
Debtors	3
Long-term liabilities:	
Loan	20
Share capital	10
Shareholders' equity:	
Retained earnings	6
Capital employed	39

Shivani Beauty Salon Ltd: year ending 31 March 2011 ($000)

As you can see, she has not made a very good first attempt. Some assets and liabilities are incorrectly placed and net assets do not equal capital employed!

10 marks, 15 minutes

Draw up a correct version of Shivani's balance sheet, using headings and making sure that it finally balances. **[10]**

EXAM PRACTICE QUESTION

Read the case study below and then answer the questions that follow.

CARLOS CHAVES'S ACCOUNTS

Carlos Chaves is a sole trader who has recently opened a small, specialist food shop. His main competitors are the large supermarket chains. Carlos prides himself on the quality of his products and the personal service he offers. For each month in 2010:

- the shop's sales averaged $80 000
- the cost of goods sold was 75% of sales revenue
- the indirect costs were constant at $20 000.

Carlos has just bought a new van for $40 000 to provide customers with a delivery service. The van has a useful life of four years and he expects to sell the van for $8000 at the end of its life.

20 marks, 35 minutes

1 List **two** advantages that the large supermarket chains will have over Carlos's shop. [2]

2 a Prepare a trading and profit and loss account for the year ending 31 December 2010. Show all workings. [6]

(H) b Calculate the annual depreciation expense of the van. [4]

c Discuss the usefulness of Carlos's profit and loss account to different stakeholders. [8]

23 Ratio analysis

This chapter covers syllabus section 3.6

On completing this chapter you should be able to:

- calculate ratios
- use ratios to interpret and analyse financial statements from the perspective of various stakeholders

- evaluate possible financial and other strategies to improve the values of ratios.

SETTING THE SCENE

Comparing the accounts of the cola giants

How can stakeholders in PepsiCo and Coca-Cola, the world's two best-known soft drink businesses, compare their performance? One way is to analyse their accounting results. Using ratio analysis – taking a result and comparing it with other data – is widely used by shareholders, banks and managers to assess and compare company performance.

Here are extracts from both companies' 2009 (end of December, in $ million) published accounts:

	Sales revenue	Cost of goods sold	Current assets	Current liabilities	Stocks	Accounts receivable	Net profit	Capital employed
PepsiCo	43 232	20 099	12 571	8 756	2 618	4 624	5 946	31 092
Coca-Cola	30 990	11 088	9 151	13 721	2 354	3 758	6 824	34 950

The liquidity of both companies can be assessed by using the current ratio, and the gross and net profit margin ratios can be calculated from using the data above. This would be a good starting point in comparing the performance of these two businesses. But these ratios do not give us the complete picture. Which company is making more profitable use of the capital invested in it? Which one seems to handle inventories more effectively? Does Coca-Cola or PepsiCo manage its payments from debtors better? If a potential shareholder was planning to buy shares in just one of these companies, which one might be the better investment?

These and other questions can be answered by further analysis of published accounts.

Points to think about:

- Would it be sensible to compare these two companies' accounts with those from a construction company? Explain your answer.
- Do you think a high level of stocks compared to the total cost of sales is a sign of good management or not? Explain your answer.
- Why would it be useful for stakeholders to make a comparison between profits and capital invested into a business?

Introduction

When studying a company's accounts it is easy to compare one year's profit figure with the previous year. Changes in sales revenue can also be identified – as can differences from one year to the next in current assets, current liabilities and shareholders' equity. Similar comparisons can be made between different companies too. However, in making these comparisons, one essential problem arises. Look at the company results of two printing firms:

	Operating profit 2010 ($000)
Nairobi Press Ltd	50
Port Louis Press Ltd	500

Is Port Louis Press more successful than Nairobi Press? Are the managers of Nairobi Press less effective? Are the companies becoming more profitable? Would they make good investments for future shareholders? Are the strategies adopted by Port Louis Press much more successful than those of Nairobi Press?

The answer to all of these questions is the same – we cannot tell from the information given. The only correct statement that can be made is that one company (Port Louis Press) made a net profit ten times greater than that of the other company.

Now look at other information about these two businesses:

	Sales revenue 2010 ($000)
Nairobi Press Ltd	250
Port Louis Press Ltd	3200

The additional data give us a more detailed picture of the performance of these two businesses in 2010, especially if we compare the data above with the earlier profit results. Which management team has been more effective at converting sales revenue into profit? Accountants make this assessment by relating two accounting results to each other in the form of a ratio.

Accounting ratios

There are five main groups of ratios:

- profitability ratios
- liquidity ratios
- financial efficiency ratios
- shareholder or investment ratios
- gearing ratios.

PROFITABILITY RATIOS

Profit margin ratios

Gross profit margin and net profit margin ratios are used to assess how successful the management of a business has been at converting sales revenue into both gross profit and net profit. They are used to measure the performance of a company and its management team.

KEY TERMS

gross profit margin (%) $= \frac{\text{gross profit}}{\text{sales revenue}} \times 100$

net profit margin (%) $= \frac{\text{net profit}}{\text{sales revenue}} \times 100$

Using the two businesses referred to above (all figures for 2010), the gross profit margin may be calculated as follows:

	Gross profit ($000)	Sales revenue ($000)	Gross profit margin
Nairobi Press Ltd	125	250	$\frac{125}{250} \times 100 = 50\%$
Port Louis Press Ltd	800	3200	$\frac{800}{3200} \times 100 = 25\%$

Points to note:

- Port Louis Press's gross profit margin could be lower because it is adopting a low-price strategy to increase sales or because it has higher cost of sales. The company might have higher material costs or higher direct labour costs compared to Nairobi Press.
- Port Louis Press's gross profit margin could increase its ratio by reducing the cost of sale, while maintaining revenue – say, by using a cheaper supplier – or by increasing revenue without increasing cost of sales – say, by raising prices but offering a better service.
- The gross profit margin is a good indicator of how effectively managers have 'added value' to the cost of sales.
- It is misleading to compare the ratios of firms in different industries because the level of risk and gross profit margin will differ greatly.

The net profit margin of the two companies may be calculated as follows:

	Gross profit ($000)	Sales revenue ($000)	Net profit margin
Nairobi Press Ltd	50	250	$\frac{50}{250} \times 100 = 20\%$
Port Louis Press Ltd	500	3200	$\frac{500}{3200} \times 100 = 15.6\%$

Points to note:

- The profitability gap between these two businesses has narrowed. Whereas the difference in gross profit margins was substantial, the net profit margins are much more alike. This suggests that Nairobi has relatively high overheads compared to sales, when contrasted with Port Louis.
- Port Louis could narrow the gap further by reducing overhead expenses while maintaining sales or by increasing sales without increasing overhead expenses.
- As with all ratios, a comparison of results with those of previous years would indicate whether the performance and profitability of a company were improving or worsening. The net profit margin – and the trend in this ratio over time – is a good indicator of management effectiveness at converting sales revenue into net profits.

HIGHER LEVEL

See Table 23.1 for an evaluation of ways to increase profit margins.

EXAM TIPS

- Many candidates state that to 'increase profit margins the business should increase sales'. This is a poor answer *unless* sales revenue can be increased at a greater rate than the costs of the business.
- Many examination questions will ask for methods of increasing profitability of a business. If the question needs an evaluative answer, it is very important that you consider at least one reason why your suggestion might not be effective.

Return on capital employed (RoCE)

This is the most commonly used means of assessing the profitability of a business – it is often referred to as the primary efficiency ratio.

KEY TERMS

return on capital employed $(\%) = \frac{\text{net profit}}{\text{capital employed}} \times 100$

capital employed = (non-current assets + current assets) − current liabilities OR non-current liabilities + shareholders equity

From the results below it is clear that the management of Nairobi Press is more effective at making the capital invested in the business earn profit.

	Net profit ($m)	Capital employed ($m)	RoCE
Nairobi Press Ltd	50	400	$\frac{50}{400} \times 100 = 12.5\%$
Port Louis Press Ltd	500	5,000	$\frac{500}{5000} \times 100 = 10\%$

Points to note:

- The higher the value of this ratio, the greater the return on the capital invested in the business.
- The return can be compared both with other companies and the RoCE of the previous year's performance. Comparisons over time enable the trend of profitability in the company to be identified.

HIGHER LEVEL

Method to increase profit margins	Examples	Evaluation
Increase gross and operating profit margin by reducing direct costs.	1 Use cheaper materials, e.g. rubber not leather soles on shoes. 2 Cut labour costs by relocating production to low labour-cost countries, e.g. Dyson relocating the manufacture of vacuum cleaners to Malaysia. 3 Cut labour costs by increasing productivity through automation in production, e.g. the Hyundai production line uses some of the most advanced labour-saving robots in the world. 4 Cut wage costs by reducing workers' pay.	1 Consumers' perception of quality may be damaged and this could hit the product's reputation. Consumers may also expect lower prices, which may cut the gross profit margin. 2 Quality may be at risk – communication problems with distant factories. 3 Purchasing machinery will increase overhead costs (gross profit could rise but net profit fall); remaining staff will need retraining – short-term profits may be cut due to these costs. 4 Motivation levels might fall, which could reduce productivity and quality.
Increase gross and operating profit margin by increasing price.	1 Raise the price of the product with no significant increase in variable costs, e.g. BT raising the price of its broadband connections. 2 Petrol companies increase prices by more than the price of oil has risen.	1 Total profit could fall if too many consumers switch to competitors – this links to Chapter 27 and price elasticity. 2 Consumers may consider this to be a 'profiteering' decision and the long-term image of the business may be damaged.
Increase net profit margin by reducing overhead costs.	Cut overhead costs, such as rent, promotion costs or management costs, but maintain sales levels, for example by: 1 moving to a cheaper head office location 2 reducing promotion costs 3 delayering the organisation.	1 Lower rental costs could mean moving to a cheaper area, which could damage image, e.g. of a restaurant. 2 Cutting promotion costs could lead to sales falling by more than fixed costs. 3 Fewer managers – or lower salaries – could reduce the efficient operation of the business.

Table 23.1 *Evaluation of ways to increase profit margins*

- The result can also be compared with the return from interest accounts – could the capital be invested in a bank at a higher rate of interest with no risk?
- RoCE should be compared with the interest cost of borrowing finance – if it is less than this interest rate, then any increase in borrowings will reduce returns to shareholders.
- The RoCE can only be raised by increasing the profitable, efficient use of the assets owned by the business, which were purchased by the capital employed.
- The method used for the calculation of capital employed is not universally agreed and this causes problems for comparisons between companies.

LIQUIDITY RATIOS

These ratios assess the ability of the firm to pay its short-term debts. They are not concerned with profits but with the working capital of the business. If there is too little working capital, then the business could become illiquid and be unable to settle short-term debts. If it has too much money tied up in working capital, then this could be used more effectively and profitably by investing in other assets.

Current ratio

KEY TERM

$$\text{current ratio} = \frac{\text{current assets}}{\text{current liabilities}}$$

The result can either be expressed as a ratio (2:1, for example) or just as a number (for example, 2). There is no particular result that can be considered a universal and reliable guide to a firm's liquidity. Many accountants recommend a result of around 1.5–2, but much depends on the industry the firm operates in and the recent trend in the current ratio. For instance, a result of around 1.5 could be a cause of concern if, last year, the current ratio had been much higher than this.

The current ratios for the printing companies may be calculated as follows (all figures as at 31 December 2010):

	Current assets ($000)	Current liabilities ($000)	Current ratio
Nairobi Press Ltd	60	30	$\frac{60}{30} = 2$
Port Louis Press Ltd	240	240	$\frac{240}{240} = 1$

Points to note:

- Nairobi Press is in a more liquid position than Port Louis Press. Nairobi Press has twice as many current assets as current liabilities. For every $1 of short-term debts it has $2 of current assets to pay for them. This is a relatively 'safe' position – indeed, many accountants advise firms to aim for current ratios between 1.5 and 2.0.
- The current ratio of Port Louis Press is more worrying. It only has $1 of current assets to pay for each $1 of short-term debt. It could be in trouble in the (unlikely) event that all of its short-term creditors demanded repayment at the same time, especially if some of its current assets could not be converted into cash quickly. For this reason, the next ratio, the acid test, is often more widely used.
- Very low current ratios might not be unusual for businesses, such as food retailers, that have regular inflows of cash, such as cash sales, that they can rely on to pay short-term debts.
- Current ratio results over 2 might suggest that too many funds are tied up in unprofitable inventories, debtors and cash and would be better placed in more profitable assets, such as equipment to increase efficiency.
- A low current ratio might lead to corrective management action to increase cash held by the business. Such measures might include: sale of redundant assets, cancelling capital spending plans, share issue, or taking out long-term loans.

Acid test ratio

Also known as the quick ratio, this is a stricter test of a firm's liquidity. It ignores the least liquid of the firm's current assets – stocks, which have not yet been sold and there is no certainty that they will be sold in the short term. By eliminating the value of stocks from the acid test ratio, the users of accounts are given a clearer picture of the firm's ability to pay short-term debts.

KEY TERMS

acid test ratio = $\frac{\text{liquid assets}}{\text{current liabilities}}$

liquid assets = current assets – stocks

The acid test ratios for the printing companies may be calculated as follows (all figures as at 31 December 2010):

	Liquid assets ($000)	Current liabilities ($000)	Acid test ratio
Nairobi Press Ltd	30	30	1
Port Louis Press Ltd	180	240	0.75

HIGHER LEVEL

See Table 23.2 for an evaluation of ways to improve liquidity.

Method to increase liquidity	Examples	Evaluation
Sell off fixed assets for cash – could lease these back if still needed by the business.	• Land and property could be sold to a leasing company.	• If assets are sold quickly, they might not raise their true value. • If assets are still needed by the business, then leasing charges will add to overheads and reduce net profit margin.
Sell off inventories for cash – *note:* this will improve the acid test ratio, but not the current ratio.	• Stocks of finished goods could be sold off at a discount to raise cash. • Just-in-time (JIT) stock management will achieve this objective.	• This will reduce the gross profit margin if inventories are sold at a discount. • Consumers may doubt the image of the brand if inventories are sold off cheaply. • Inventories might be needed to meet changing customer demand levels – JIT might be difficult to adopt in some industries.
Increase loans to inject cash into the business and increase working capital.	• Long-term loans could be taken out if the bank is confident of the company's prospects.	• These will increase the gearing ratio. • These will increase interest costs.

***Table 23.2** Evaluation of ways to improve liquidity*

Points to note:

- Results below 1 are often viewed with caution by accountants as they mean that the business has less than $1 of liquid assets to pay each $1 of short-term debt. Therefore, Port Louis Press may well have a liquidity problem.
- The full picture needs to be gained by looking at previous years' results. For example, if last year Port Louis Press had an acid test of 0.5, this means that over the last 12 months its liquidity has actually improved and this is more favourable than if its results last year had been 1, showing a decline in liquidity in the current year.
- Firms with very high inventory levels will record very different current and acid test ratios. This is not a problem if inventories are always high for this type of business, such as furniture retailers. It would be a problem for other types of businesses, such as computer manufacturers, where stocks lose value rapidly due to technical changes.
- Whereas selling inventories for cash will not improve the current ratio – both items are included in current assets – this policy will improve the acid test ratio as cash is a liquid asset but inventories are not.

ACTIVITY 23.1

Use the information in the case study below to answer the questions that follow.

Has BP plc got enough liquidity to pay its short-term debts?

The following information is taken from BP plc's accounts for the year ending 31 December 2007 (all figures in $ million). The data have been simplified for ease of understanding.

Current assets: inventories 26 554; trade receivables (debtors) 38 020; cash 3 562.
Current liabilities: trade payables (creditors) 43 152; short-term loans 15 394.

20 marks, 35 minutes

1 Calculate BP's current ratio. [3]

2 Calculate BP's acid test ratio. [3]

3 Comment on BP's liquidity. [6]

4 Why would it be useful to BP's stakeholders to have liquidity ratio results for the previous year and for other oil companies? [8]

EXAM TIP

When commenting on ratio results, it is often advisable to question the accuracy of the data used and the limitations of just using a limited number of ratio results in your analysis.

ACTIVITY 23.2

Read the case study below and then answer the questions that follow.

How is my business doing?

Mohammed Ahmed is the chief executive of Ahmed Builders plc. The company specialises in the quality fitting out of shops for internationally famous retailers. These customers demand that work is finished to very tight time limits, so it is important for Ahmed Builders to keep stocks of important materials. Mohammed is keen to compare the performance and liquidity of his company with those of another building company which does similar work. He obtained a set of published accounts for Flash Builders plc and used ratios to help him in the comparison. These were the figures he used from both companies.

	Ahmed ($000)	Flash ($000)
Gross profit (2010)	100	150
Net profit (2010)	20	60
Sales revenue (2010)	350	600
Current assets (as at 31/12/10)	100	150
Inventories (as at 31/12/10)	50	60
Current liabilities (as at 31/12/10)	45	120

46 marks, 75 minutes

1 Calculate **two** profit margin ratios for both companies. Show all workings. [6]

2 Comment on the profitability of both businesses. Should Ahmed be pleased about the performance of his business compared to Flash Builders? Explain your answer. [10]

3 Explain and evaluate **two** ways in which Ahmed might attempt to increase the net profit margin ratio for his business. [10]

4 Calculate **two** liquidity ratios for both businesses. Show all workings. [6]

5 Comment on your results to question 4. [6]

6 Explain and evaluate **two** ways in which Flash Builders plc might be able to improve its liquidity position. [8]

FINANCIAL EFFICIENCY RATIOS

There are many efficiency or activity ratios that can be used to assess how efficiently the assets or resources of a business are being used by management. The two most frequently used are stock turnover ratio and debtor days ratio.

Stock (inventory) turnover ratio

In principle, the lower the amount of capital used in holding stocks, the better. Modern stock control theory focuses on minimising investment in inventories. This ratio records the number of times the stock of a business is bought in and resold in a period of time. In general terms, the higher this ratio is, the lower the investment in stocks will be. If a business bought stock just once each year, enough to see it through the whole year, its stock turnover would be 1 and investment in stocks high.

KEY TERM

stock (inventory) turnover ratio $= \dfrac{\text{cost of goods sold}}{\text{value of stock (average)}}$

This ratio uses average stock holding, that is the average value of inventories at the start of the year and at the end.

An alternative formula that measures the average number of days that money is tied up in stocks is:

$$\text{stock turnover ratio (days)} = \frac{\text{value of stocks}}{\text{cost of sales / 365}}$$

According to the 2010 stock turnover ratio (see below), Nairobi Press has more effective control over inventory management – it has a lower level of inventories compared to costs of goods sold than Port Louis Press. If Port Louis Press introduced a system of 'just-in-time' stock management, then inventory deliveries would be more frequent but smaller in size and this would increase its stock turnover ratio.

	Cost of goods sold 2010 ($m)	Stocks 31/12/10 ($m)	Stock turnover ratio
Nairobi Press Ltd	125	25	$\frac{125}{25} = 5$
Port Louis Press Ltd	2400	600	$\frac{2400}{600} = 4$

Points to note:

- The result is not a percentage but the number of times stock turns over in the time period – usually one year.
- The higher the number, the more efficient the managers are in selling stock rapidly. Very efficient stock management – such as the use of the just-in-time system – will give a high inventory turnover ratio.
- The 'normal' result for a business depends very much on the industry it operates in – for instance, a fresh-fish retailer would (hopefully) have a much higher inventory turnover ratio than a car dealer.
- For service sector firms, such as insurance companies, this ratio has little relevance as they are not selling 'products' held in stock.

Debtor days ratio

This ratio measures how long, on average, it takes the business to recover payment from customers who have bought goods on credit – the debtors. The shorter this time period is, the better the management is at controlling its working capital.

KEY TERM

debtor days (days' sales in receivables)

$$= \frac{\text{trade debtors (accounts receivable)}}{\text{sales turnover}} \times 365 \text{ (days)}$$

It can also be calculated by using total credit sales, thus excluding sales for cash from the calculation – which could be explained as being more accurate, as cash sales will never lead to debtors.

The printing companies' debtor days have been calculated as follows:

	Debtors 31/12/10 ($m)	Sales turnover year ending 31/12/10 ($m)	Debtor days
Nairobi Press Ltd	75	250	$\frac{75 \times 365}{250} = 109.5$ days
Port Louis Press Ltd	600	3200	$\frac{600 \times 365}{3200} = 87.5$ days

This result shows that both companies give their customers a very long time to pay debts. Perhaps the printing market is very competitive in these cities and to gain business, long credit periods have to be offered. Debtor days ratios as high as these put a great strain on companies' working capital requirements.

Points to note:

- There is no 'right' or 'wrong' result – it will vary from business to business and industry to industry. A business selling mainly for cash will have a very low ratio result.
- A high trade debtor days ratio may be a deliberate management strategy – customers will be attracted to businesses that give extended credit. However, the results shown above are higher than average for most businesses and could result from poor control of debtors and repayment periods.
- The value of this ratio could be reduced by giving shorter credit terms – say, 30 days instead of 60 days – or by improving credit control. This could involve refusing to offer credit terms to frequent late payers. The impact on sales revenue of such policies must always be borne in mind – perhaps the marketing department wants to increase credit terms for customers to sell more, but the finance department wants all customers to pay for products as soon as possible.

ACTIVITY 23.3

Read the case study below and then answer the questions that follow.

Pakistan State Oil Company Ltd (PSO)

A sharp fall in the world price of crude oil at the end of 2008 caused PSO to record a large loss in the last three months of the year. The following table gives some accounting ratio results for PSO as at 10 February 2008:

Return on capital employed	Gross profit margin	Inventory turnover	Current ratio	Acid test ratio	Debtors turnover*
14.78%	2.93%	13.1	1.1	0.6	15.6

* to convert this to the number of days debtors are given to pay, divide this figure into 365.

Source: http://www.PSOPK.com

Pakistan State Oil facilities

20 marks, 35 minutes (plus research time)

1 Use the internet link above to compare the latest ratio results for PSO with those in the table above.

2 Evaluate the performance of the business over the time period between the two sets of ratios. [10]

3 Use the internet to research the accounting ratios of another oil company – perhaps one that operates in your country. Compare these ratio results with those for PSO in the table above. [10]

Creditor days ratio

This measures how quickly a business pays its suppliers during the year.

KEY TERM

creditor days ratio $= \frac{\text{trade creditors}}{\text{credit purchases}} \times 365$

The printing companies' creditor days ratios are as follows:

	Trade creditors 31/12/10 (\$m)	Credit purchases (\$m)	Creditor days
Nairobi Press Ltd	20	100	$\frac{20}{100} \times 365 = 91$ days
Port Louis Press Ltd	250	1125	$\frac{250}{1125} \times 365 = 81$ days

Points to note:

- A high number of days reduces the firm's cash outflow to pay suppliers in the short term.
- Suppliers may object to not being paid promptly and may offer less discount and support the business less when it needs rapid deliveries.

SHAREHOLDER OR INVESTMENT RATIOS

These are of interest to prospective investors in a business. Buying shares in a company has the potential for capital gains by the share price rising. In addition, companies pay annual dividends to shareholders unless profits are too low or losses are being made. The shareholder ratios give an indication of the prospects for financial gain from both of these sources.

Dividend yield ratio

This measures the rate of return a shareholder gets at the current share price.

KEY TERMS

dividends the share of the profits paid to shareholders as a return for investing in the company

share price the quoted price of one share on the stock exchange

dividend yield ratio (%) $= \frac{\text{dividend per share}}{\text{current share price}} \times 100$

dividend per share $= \frac{\text{total annual dividends}}{\text{total number of issued shares}}$

Shareholders in Nairobi Press are earning a higher return on their investment than if they had bought shares in Port Louis Press:

	Dividends 2010 (\$m)	Number of shares (m)	Dividend per share (\$)	Market share price 31/12/10 (\$)	Dividend yield (%)
Nairobi Press Ltd	21	140	0.15	\$1.50	$\frac{\$0.15}{\$1.50} = 10\%$
Port Louis Press Ltd	140	200	0.70	\$10.00	$\frac{0.70}{\$10.00} = 7\%$

Points to note:

- If the share price rises, perhaps due to improved prospects for the business, then with an unchanged dividend the dividend yield will fall.
- If the directors propose an increased dividend, but the share price does not change, then the dividend yield will increase.
- This rate of return can be compared with other investments, such as bank interest rates and dividend yields from other companies.
- The result needs to be compared with previous years and with other companies in a similar industry to allow effective analysis.
- Potential shareholders might be attracted to buy shares in a company with a high dividend yield as long as the share price is not expected to fall in coming months.
- Directors may decide to pay a dividend from reserves even when profits are low or a loss has been made in order to keep shareholder loyalty.
- Directors may decide to reduce the annual dividend even if profits have not fallen in an attempt to increase retained profits – this could allow further investment into expanding the business.
- A high dividend yield may not indicate a wise investment – the yield could be high because the share price has recently fallen, possibly because the stock market is concerned about the long-term prospects of the company.

Earnings per share ratio
This ratio measures the amount that each share is earning for the shareholder. This can then be compared with the price of the share – and compared also with other companies' data.

KEY TERM

earnings per share profit earned per share in the company

$$= \frac{\text{profit after tax}}{\text{total number of ordinary shares}}$$

GEARING RATIO
This measures the degree to which the capital of the business is financed from long-term loans. The greater the reliance of a business on loan capital, the more 'highly geared' it is said to be. There are several different ways of measuring gearing, but this is one of the most widely used ratios.

KEY TERM

$$\textbf{gearing ratio (\%)} = \frac{\text{long-term loans}}{\text{capital employed}} \times 100$$

Nairobi Press is less dependent on long-term loans to finance its assets than is Port Louis Press – see below. This is a safer business strategy – but could the directors of Nairobi Press be missing some potentially profitable investment opportunities by their reluctance to increase debts? On the other hand, if interest rates and company profits fell as a result of a recession, then the directors of Port Louis Press might start to regret their decision to raise finance from debts.

	Long-term loans 31/12/10 ($m) (non-current liabilities)	Capital employed 31/12/10 (shareholders equity + non-current liabilities) ($m)	Gearing ratio
Nairobi Press Ltd	40	400	$\frac{40}{400} = 10\%$
Port Louis Press Ltd	2000	5000	$\frac{2000}{5000} = 40\%$

Points to note:

- The gearing ratio shows the extent to which the company's assets are financed from external long-term borrowing. A result of over 50%, using the ratio above, would indicate a highly geared business.
- The higher this ratio, the greater the risk taken by shareholders when investing in the business. This risk arises for two main reasons:
  - The larger the borrowings of the business, the more interest must be paid and this will affect the ability of the company to pay dividends and earn retained profits. This is particularly the case when interest rates are high and company profits are low – such as during an economic downturn.
  - Interest will still have to be paid – but from declining profits.
- Debts have to be repaid eventually and the strain of paying back high debts compared to capital could leave a business with low liquidity.
- A low gearing ratio is an indication of a 'safe' business strategy. It also suggests that management are not borrowing to expand the business. This could be a problem for shareholders if they want rapidly increasing returns on their investment. The returns to shareholders may not increase as they might for a highly geared business with a vigorous growth strategy. Shareholders in a company following a successful growth strategy financed by high debt will find their returns increasing much faster than in a slower growth company with low gearing.
- The gearing ratio of a business could be reduced by using non-loan sources of finance to increase capital employed, such as issuing more shares or retaining profits. These increase shareholders' funds and capital employed and lower the gearing ratio.

Ratio analysis – an evaluation
All of the external and internal users of accounts could find ratio analysis of great help when studying the degree of success of a company's strategy. The ratios we have considered are widely used by company analysts and prospective investors before making assessments and taking important decisions on:

- whether to invest in the business
- whether to lend it more money
- whether the profitability is rising or falling
- whether the management are using resources efficiently.

ACTIVITY 23.4

Look at the table below, which compares data from two furniture manufacturers, and then answer the questions that follow.

Financial efficiency and gearing ratios

	Value of stocks 31/12/10 ($m)	Cost of sales 2010 ($m)	Sales revenue ($m)	Capital employed ($m)	Long-term loans ($m)
Company X	73	580	1120	1575	500
Company Y	150	750	1460	2050	1025

28 marks, 50 minutes

1 Calculate for both companies:
 a debtors days ratios
 b stock turnover ratio
 c gearing ratio.
 Show all workings. [12]

2 Company Y is planning to invest in a new expansion project costing $75 million.
 a Would you advise the business to raise all of this finance by selling off stock and reducing its inventory levels? Explain your answer. [4]
 b Would you recommend Company Y to finance this expansion with a bank loan? Explain your answer. [8]

3 Recalculate the new gearing ratio. (*Hint:* you must increase both long-term loans and capital employed by the amount of the increased loan.) [4]

However, as with any analytical tool, ratio analysis needs to be applied with some caution as there are quite significant limitations to its effectiveness. These will now be considered to allow a full evaluation of this approach to be made.

LIMITATIONS OF RATIO ANALYSIS

1 One ratio result is not very helpful – to allow meaningful analysis to be made, a comparison needs to be made between this one result and either:
- other businesses, called inter-firm comparisons or
- other time periods, called trend analysis (see Figure 23.1).

2 Inter-firm comparisons need to be used with caution and are most effective when companies in the same industry are being compared. Financial years end at different times for businesses and a rapid change in the economic environment could have an adverse impact on a company publishing its accounts in June compared to a January publication for another company.

3 Trend analysis needs to take into account changing circumstances over time which could have affected the ratio results. These factors may be outside the companies' control, such as an economic recession.

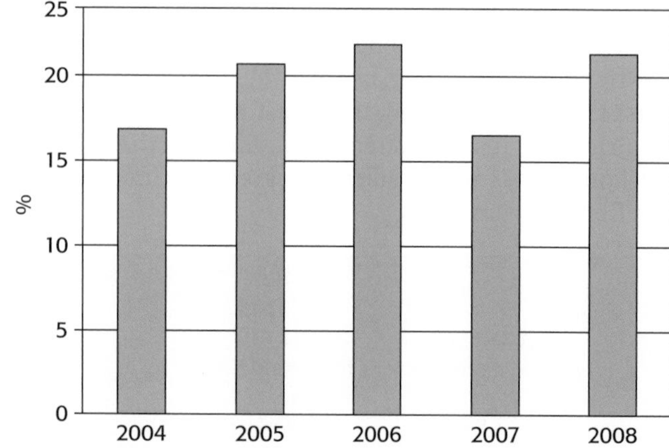

Figure 23.1 An example of trend analysis: BP's return on capital employed
Source: http://www.investis.com/bp

4 As noted above, some ratios can be calculated using slightly different formulae, and care must be taken only to make comparisons with results calculated using the same ratio formula.

5 Companies can value their assets in different ways, and different depreciation methods can lead to different capital employed totals, which will affect certain ratio results. Deliberate window dressing of accounts would obviously make a company's key ratios look more favourable – at least in the short term.

6 Ratios are only concerned with accounting items to which a numerical value can be given. Increasingly, observers of company performance and strategy are becoming more concerned with non-numerical aspects of business performance, such as environmental audits and human rights abuses in developing countries that the firms may operate in. Indicators other than ratios must be used for these assessments.

7 Ratios are useful analytical tools, but they do not solve business problems. Ratio analysis can highlight issues that need to be tackled – such as falling profitability or liquidity – and these problems can be tracked back over time and compared with other businesses. On their own, ratios do not necessarily indicate the true cause of business problems and it is up to good managers to locate these and form effective strategies to overcome them.

ACTIVITY 23.5

Ratio analysis

42 marks, 75 minutes

1 Make a list of the ratios which would be of most use to:
   a managers of a company
   b the workforce of a company
   c prospective shareholders of a company
   d bankers of a company.
   Justify your selection in each case. [12]

2 Look as the table below. Using the data taken from the published accounts of two construction companies, calculate as many of the profitability ratios, financial efficiency ratios and liquidity ratios for 2010 as you have information for. All figures are in $ million. [14]

3 Using your results, compare the performance, efficiency and liquidity of these two businesses. [8]

4 Assess the limitations of the ratio analysis you have just undertaken. [4]

5 Explain what additional information would be useful when making this comparison. [4]

Company	Capital employed	Non-current liabilities	Current assets	Current liabilities	Gross profit	Operating profit	Sales revenue	Inventories
A	3000	1500	1200	1400	1100	750	4000	400
B	200	50	70	70	75	25	300	35

THEORY OF KNOWLEDGE

'You just needed to look at the figures: sales were rising, profit margin was good and return on capital was the best in the industry. So it was a bit of a shock when ARL Leisure went into administration. Accounting irregularities, directors making figures look good to drive up the share price and good old-fashioned fraud were at the heart of ARL's problems.'

a Examine the role of evidence in making judgements about an organisation's performance.

b To what extent does financial gain lead to unethical practices in organisations?

OVER TO YOU

REVISION CHECKLIST

1 How is the return on capital employed ratio calculated and what does the result indicate about a business?
2 Explain **two** ways in which directors of a carpet manufacturing business could attempt to increase its RoCE ratio.
3 Explain to a manager what the financial efficiency ratios could tell her about the business.
4 Analyse why, with examples, it is difficult to make a realistic comparison between the stock turnover ratios of companies in different industries.
5 Why would introducing just-in-time inventory control be likely to reduce the stock turnover ratio for a car manufacturer?
6 Would you advise a prospective investor to analyse the shareholder ratios before purchasing shares in a company? Explain your answer by referring to **three** ratios.
7 Explain how a high gearing ratio might lead to high shareholder returns in the future.
8 Would you advise a business to attempt to raise or lower its gearing ratio during a period of economic uncertainty with rising interest rates? Explain your answer.
9 What is meant by:
- trend analysis of accounts and
- inter-firm comparisons?

10 Explain **two** drawbacks to using accounting ratios to assess the performance of one business compared to another.
(H) 11 A soft drink manufacturer operates in a very competitive market. The business currently has low liquidity levels. Would you advise the business to offer longer credit periods to retail store owners who buy large quantities of its drinks? Explain your answer.

REVISION ACTIVITY 1

Read the case study below and then answer the questions that follow.

Habib Manufacturing Ltd

Habib Manufacturing Ltd produces a range of saucepans and cooking pots. The saucepans and pots are mainly sold through mail-order catalogues. Since becoming managing director of the family business four years ago, Asif Habib has taken the following decisions:

- New machinery has been purchased leading to higher than expected staff retraining costs. Half of the necessary finance was borrowed. The government recently announced higher interest rates to deal with inflation.
- Cheaper raw materials and components were bought in, with orders only taking place twice a year, to maximise scale economies.
- Advertising and promotional expenses were doubled in efforts to increase sales.
- Payments to suppliers have been delayed.

Despite these changes, the overall performance of the business is not encouraging. Habib has asked the company accountant to prepare the following ratios:

	2008	2009	2010
Return on capital employed (%)	15	9	7
Gross profit margin (%)	38	42	43
Operating profit margin (%)	20	15	12
Stock (inventory) turnover	5	4	3
Current ratio	2	1.5	1.4
Acid test ratio	1.5	0.9	0.4

Habib Manufacturing Ltd: ratio analysis of accounts 2008–10

Asif has two more plans. His first idea is to increase the prices of the most popular range of saucepans and pots. This will aim these products at higher-income segments of the market.

His second plan is to relocate the factory away from its expensive site near the city centre. This site could be sold and a new factory on the edge of the city would be built.

30 marks, 52 minutes

1 Analyse the possible reasons for the changing performance of the business over the last three years. [10]
2 Explain the problems this business might experience from:
- declining liquidity
- declining stock turnover ratio. [8]

(H) 3 Evaluate two ways in which Habib might attempt to increase profitability. [12]

REVISION ACTIVITY 2

Read the case studies below and then answer the questions that follow.

IBM bucks gloom with rosy outlook

IBM's latest quarterly profits rose 12% – a rare ray of light for the pessimistic technology sector of industry.

IBM sales are increasing during the recession as other firms are keen to cut costs by improving their IT network. The American computer giant has been able to cut costs sharply. The company's operating profit in the fourth quarter of 2008 rose 12% from a year earlier to $4.4 billion. Directors are expecting the company to earn $9.20 per share in 2009. IBM's operating profit margin increased to 47.9%. The news boosted IBM's share price. It climbed 4.5% to $85.64.

Source: www.bbc.co.uk/news

Intel profits fall by 90% in last 3 months of 2008

Intel, the world's largest maker of microchips, recorded net profits down by 90% in the last quarter of 2008. For the three months to the end of 2008, it reported profits of $234 million, down from $2.27 billion in the same period in 2008. Intel partly blames the drop in profits on the big reduction in demand for PCs as the world economy hit the financial crisis at the end of 2008. Directors were optimistic about the future though: 'Our new technologies and new products will help us achieve sales growth when the economy recovers.' The company also announced cost cuts of $800 million in 2008. Intel has just announced price cuts of up to 48% on some of its chips and the company expects its gross profit margin to fall to around 43% in 2009.

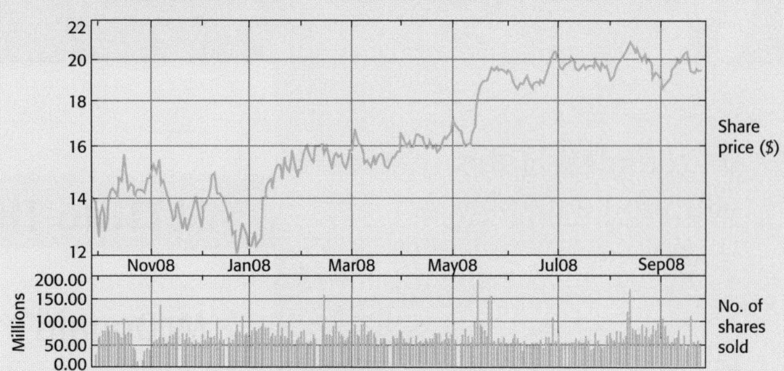

Intel's share prices, November 2007–September 2008
Source: http://seekingalpha.com

18 marks, 30 minutes

1 Explain why IBM's share price increased after the profits announcement. [4]

2 Explain the sentence: 'IBM's operating profit margin rose to 47.9%.' [4]

3 Discuss the most important factors a potential investor should consider before taking a decision to purchase shares in Intel. [10]

EXAM PRACTICE QUESTION

KARACHI PAPER PRODUCTS PLC

Look at the extracts from the published accounts for Karachi Paper Products plc and then answer the questions that follow.

	Year ending 31/10/10 ($m)	Year ending 31/10/09 ($m)
Sales turnover	400	330
Cost of goods sold	120	100
Net profit	35	33
Profit after tax and interest	30	29
Inventories (Stock)	58	36
Accounts receivable (Debtors)	80	70
Current assets	140	120
Current liabilities	140	120
Dividends paid	20	15
Long-term (non-current) liabilities	150	120
Capital employed	300	260

25 marks, 45 minutes

1 Define the following terms:
  a current assets
  b capital employed. [4]

2 Explain one ratio you would use to measure Karachi's liquidity. [4]

3 Calculate the following ratios for 2009 and 2010:
  a return on capital employed
  b gross profit margin
  c net profit margin
  d gearing
  e debtors days. [10]

4 On the basis of the ratios you have calculated, evaluate the change in performance of Karachi Paper Products over the two years. [7]

24 The role of marketing

This chapter covers syllabus section 4.1

On completing this chapter you should be able to:

- understand what marketing is and the role of marketing
- recognise the difference between market orientation and product orientation
- assess the main features of markets, such as size, growth and share
- understand the distinction between consumer goods and service markets and industrial markets
- analyse the marketing of non-profit-making organisations
- describe the elements of a marketing plan
- (H) analyse asset-led marketing and social marketing.

SETTING THE SCENE

McDonald's – marketing does not stand still

What food do you think of when you hear 'McDonald's'? Most people would still say 'burger and chips'! But the multinational fast-food business is working hard to change its brand image. There are several reasons for this but two stand out:

- The global economic downturn between 2008 and 2010 has created market opportunities for 'premium products' aimed at consumers who are short of cash and cannot afford a meal in a three-star restaurant.
- Increasing concern about the bad health effects of fast food – especially the youth obesity problem of today – means that healthier menu options are becoming much more popular.

McDonald's claims: 'We are constantly researching consumer wants, and as many people cannot now afford full restaurant meals, we are revising our menu to appeal to them with luxury beef and chicken products in specialist ciabatta bread. The company is also committed to increasing its range of salads and other healthy options.' At the same time, McDonald's is also aware of the cash limits on its traditional customers and is targeting them with a new 'dollar-saver' menu.

No business can afford to stand still – there are always competitors to worry about. Burger King is also trying new ingredients, such as Spanish sausages and tiger prawns. It promoted its new upmarket menu with a world record-breaking $95 burger with the most expensive beef in the world! It captured the newspaper headlines, but it will not become a regular product.

Points to think about:

- What do you think marketing managers do? Make a list of as many marketing tasks as you can from this case study.
- Explain why McDonald's is changing its food menu.
- Do you think it will be easy to change the company's 'brand image'? Explain your answer.
- Why are 'researching consumer wants' and promotion important to firms such as McDonald's and Burger King?

Introduction

Most people think of marketing as just being about advertising and selling of products. However, this is a very limited view – marketing embraces much more than just telling people about a product and selling it to them. There are thousands of definitions of marketing. One of the shortest and clearest is from the Chartered Institute of Marketing:

> Marketing is the management process responsible for identifying, anticipating and satisfying consumers' requirements profitably.

Another definition comes from *Contemporary Marketing Wired*, by Boone and Kurtz (9th edition, 1998):

> Marketing is the process of planning and undertaking the conception, pricing, promotion and distribution of goods and services to create and maintain relationships that will satisfy individual and organisational objectives.

It seems from this definition that marketing involves a number of related management functions. These include:

- market research
- product design
- pricing
- advertising
- distribution
- customer service
- packaging.

So, marketing is a very important business activity! Marketing activities are all those associated with identifying the particular wants and needs of target-market customers and then trying to satisfy those customer needs better than your competitors do. This means that market research is needed to identify and analyse customer needs. With this knowledge, strategic decisions must then be taken about product design, pricing, promotion and distribution.

Market: size, growth and share

KEY TERMS

marketing the management task that links the business to the customer by identifying and meeting the needs of customers profitably – it does this by getting the right product at the right price to the right place at the right time

market size the total level of sales of all producers within a market

market growth the percentage change in the total size of a market (volume or value) over a period of time

market share the percentage of sales in the total market sold by one business

MARKET SIZE

This can be measured in two ways: volume of sales (units sold) or value of goods sold (revenue).

The size of a market is important for three reasons:

- A marketing manager can assess whether a market is worth entering or not.
- Firms can calculate their own market share.
- Growth or decline of the market can be identified.

MARKET GROWTH

Some markets are obviously growing faster than others; some, such as non-HD TVs, are declining rapidly. Is it always better to be operating in a rapidly growing market? In many cases, yes, but not always – there might be many competitors entering the market at the same time so profits might not be high. The pace of growth will depend on several factors including economic growth, changes in consumer incomes, development of new markets, changes in consumer tastes and technological change, which can boost market sales through innovative products. The rate of growth will also depend on whether the market is 'saturated' or not. In most western countries, the sales of washing machines are not rising each year as most households already have one – most purchases are, therefore, replacement models. Sales of laptop computers are still rising in India and China as most potential consumers have yet to purchase one.

EXAM TIP

You may be asked to do some simple calculations about market growth and market share – remember to take your calculator into the examination with you!

MARKET SHARE

This is calculated by the following formula:

$$\text{market share \%} = \frac{\text{firm's sales in time period}}{\text{total market sales in time period}} \times 100$$

'Firm's sales' and 'total market sales' can be measured in either units (volume) or sales value in this market. Market share, and increases in it, is often the most effective way to measure the relative success of one business's marketing strategy against that of its competitors. If a firm's market share is increasing, then the marketing of its products has been relatively more successful than most of its competitors. The product with the highest market share is called the 'brand leader'. Why might it be important for a brand or a manufacturer to have market leadership in this way?

ACTIVITY 24.1

Read the case study below and then answer the questions that follow.

China's auto market growing rapidly

At 23, Shi Lingxi bought his first car. He considered a Ford Focus, but last week he negotiated a huge discount of 35 000 yuan off a brand-new Nissan Bluebird. Like millions of other new motorists in China, he does not plan to use it much – it's too hard to find a parking space – but he looks forward to the freedom the car brings. China's auto industry is now growing by around 1 million extra vehicles a year – a rate of 23% last year. Although not the biggest market in the world – that is still in the USA – the growth rate is the fastest. Whereas car sales did not increase at all in the USA in 2008, in China they are forecast to grow by 10% a year for at least a decade. No wonder 100 global and Chinese vehicle manufacturers are now competing in this market.

Source: www.chinadaily.com

10 marks, 18 minutes

1 Explain the difference between 'market size' and 'market growth'. [4]
2 Explain why it is important to a car manufacturer selling to China that the car market is growing rapidly. [6]

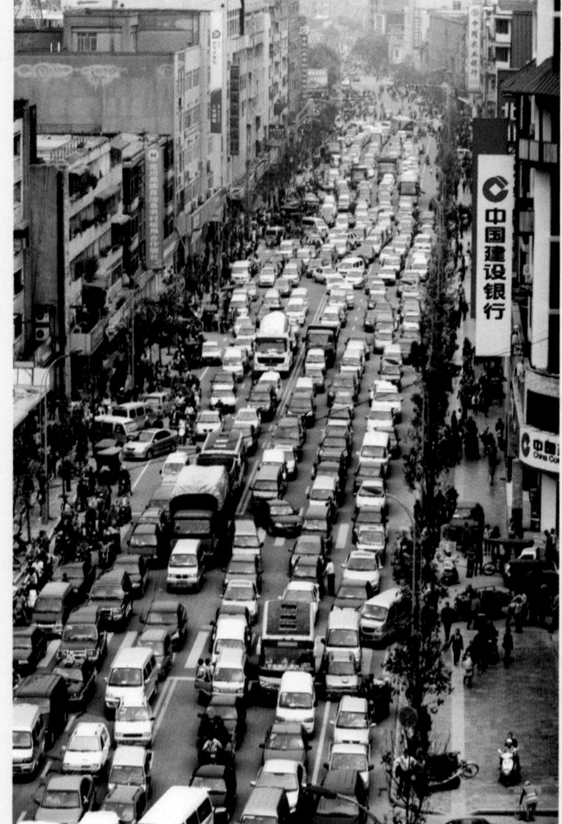

The demand for cars is growing faster in China than any other country

ACTIVITY 24.2

Read the case study below and then answer the questions that follow.

A tale of two markets

Total sales in market A in 2009 were 54 000 units. The average selling price was $3.
Total sales in market B in 2009 were 10 000 units. The average selling price was $15.
In 2010, sales volume of market A increased by 5% and the selling price increased by 10%.
In 2010, total sales value of market B was $180 000, despite the average price falling to $12.

12 marks, 21 minutes

1 Calculate the percentage increase in the total value of sales for market A between 2009 and 2010. [6]

2 Calculate the percentage increase in total sales volume in market B between 2009 and 2010. [6]

The benefits of being the brand leader with highest market share include the following:

- Sales are higher than those of any competing business in the same market and this could lead to higher profits too.
- Retailers will be keen to stock and promote the best-selling brands. They may be given the most prominent position in shops.
- As shops are keen to stock the product, it might be sold to them with a lower discount rate – say 10% instead of 15%, which has to be offered by the smaller, competing brands. The combination of this factor and the higher sales level should lead to higher profitability for the producer of the leading brand.
- The fact that an item or brand is the market leader can be used in advertising and other promotional material. Consumers are often keen to buy the most popular brands.

It is not always easy to measure market growth or market share in an unambiguous way. Different results may be obtained depending on whether the growth and share rates are measured in volume or value terms. For example, if total sales in the market for jeans rose from 24 million pairs at an average price of $32 to 26 million pairs at an average price of $36, then market growth can be measured in two ways:

- by volume – the market has risen from 24 to 26 million units, an increase of 8.33%
- by value – the revenue has risen from $768 million to $936 million, an increase of 21.87%.

Which of these two figures – value or volume – should be used for measuring the changing market share for any one jeans manufacturer? The manufacturer could use the measure that reflects best on its own position. It may, therefore, be difficult to compare firms' changing market shares. A cosmetic company that specialises in selling low volumes of expensive products is likely to have a higher market share in value terms than when measured by volume.

EXAM TIP

It is very important to understand that a firm's market share can fall even though its sales are rising. This is because, if the total market sales are increasing at a faster rate than one firm's sales, the market share will fall.

Consumer markets and industrial markets

Different marketing strategies will often be used between these two markets, for example a business selling computers to both consumers – perhaps through retail shops – and industrial customers.

KEY TERMS

consumer markets markets for goods and services bought by the final user of them

industrial markets markets for goods and services bought by businesses to be used in the production process of other products

MARKETING BUSINESS TO BUSINESS

When selling to other businesses a computer manufacturer, for example, will:

- not focus on retail stores, but use more resources on industrial exhibitions and direct or personal selling to companies
- customise each computer system to the exact requirements of each business customer

ACTIVITY 24.3

Tesco is market leader in Thailand

Tesco Lotus – the brand name used by the European supermarket in Thailand – had 31% of total Thai supermarket sales of $35 billion in 2008. Two French-owned companies operating in Thailand were second and third on the list of firms' market shares – Big C had 24% and Carrefour 14%.

Being market leader gives Tesco Lotus a huge advantage – and it is not standing still. It has plans both to open new stores and enter new markets. In 2008 for example, Tesco Lotus entered the fast-growing school uniform market, with £140 million a year, with prices 20–30% lower than traditional shops.

This expansion is not without its critics and the new Thai government has taken action to protect locally owned shops and to ensure good consumer choice is maintained. A new law is proposed that would severely restrict the opening of all new foreign-owned stores. Consumer groups are split on the new law – they want to keep the variety offered by local stores, but they enjoy the big stores and low prices too.

Source: www.ethicalcorp.com

A Tesco Lotus superstore in Bangkok

23 marks, 39 minutes

1 Calculate Tesco Lotus's sales in the Thai supermarket industry in 2008. [3]

2 If Tesco Lotus's sales increased by $2 billion in 2009, but the total size of the Thai market increased by $10 billion, calculate Tesco Lotus's 2009 market share. [6]

3 Explain **two** advantages Tesco Lotus might gain from being 'market leader' in Thailand. [6]

4 Do you think the Thai government should put restrictions on Tesco Lotus's future growth? Explain your answer. [8]

- promote the product as being a cost-saving and profitable choice – not something that will satisfy a consumer desire or need
- produce technical promotions and literature that will recognise that business customers will very likely be knowledgeable and will be making an informed choice.

MARKETING CONSUMER GOODS AND SERVICES

Tangible goods are often marketed in different ways to intangible consumer services. Managers responsible for selling services – such as banking services or hotel services – have to consider a number of factors:

- Services are consumed immediately – they cannot be stored – so empty hotel bedrooms during the off-peak season may have to be filled by charging much lower prices.
- Services cannot be taken back to be repaired or replaced – so the service quality must be right first time or the consumer will not return.
- Consumers find it much more difficult to compare service quality than manufactured goods – so promotion of services must be informative and detailed about the precise nature of the range and quality of services offered.
- People (trained, approachable and helpful staff) are very important to the successful marketing of services. By contrast, products such as Nintendo's Wii, often 'sell themselves' due to their innovative features.

Marketing approaches

MARKET ORIENTATION AND PRODUCT ORIENTATION

KEY TERMS

market orientation an outward-looking approach basing product decisions on consumer demand, as established by market research

product orientation an inward-looking approach that focuses on making products that can be made – or have been made for a long time – and then trying to sell them

This is an important distinction. Most businesses would today describe themselves as being 'market oriented' or 'market led'. This approach requires market research and market analysis to indicate present and future consumer demand. The consumer is put first – the business attempts to produce what consumers want rather than try to sell them a product they may not really want to buy. It has advantages, especially in fast-changing, volatile consumer markets. In these cases, increasing consumer awareness of competitors' products, prices and image can result in significant fluctuations in popularity of goods and services. The benefits of market orientation are threefold:

- The chances of newly developed products failing in the market are much reduced – but not eliminated – if effective market research has been undertaken first. With the huge cost of developing new products, such as cars or computers, this is a convincing argument for most businesses to use the market-oriented approach.
- If consumer needs are being met with appropriate products, then they are likely to survive longer and make higher profits than those that are being sold following a product-led approach.
- Constant feedback from consumers – market research never actually ends – will allow the product and how it is marketed to be adapted to changing tastes before it is too late and before competitors 'get there first'.

The days of traditional product-oriented businesses, which assume there will always be a market for the products they make, are fast disappearing. However, product-led marketing still exists to an extent and the following instances help to explain why:

1 Product-oriented businesses invent and develop products in the belief that they will find consumers to purchase them. The development of the WAP mobile phone was driven more by technical innovation than by consumer needs – consumers were not aware that such versatile products were likely to be made available until the basic concept had been invented and developed into an innovative new product. Pure research in this form is rare but still exists, for example in pharmaceutical and electronic industries. Here there is still the belief that if they produce an innovative product of a good enough quality, then it will be purchased.
2 Product-oriented businesses concentrate their efforts on efficiently producing high-quality goods. They believe quality will be valued above market fashion. Such quality-driven firms do still exist, especially in product areas where quality or safety is of great importance, such as bottled-water plants or the manufacture of crash helmets.

Evaluation of these two approaches

The trend then is towards market orientation, but there are limitations. If a business attempts to respond to every passing consumer trend or market fashion, then it may well overstretch its resources and end up not doing anything particularly well. Trying to offer choice and range so that every consumer need is met can be expensive. In contrast, researching and developing an innovative product can be successful, even if there has been no formal market research – consider Dyson's hugely profitable cyclone vacuum cleaner, for example.

HIGHER LEVEL

ASSET-LED MARKETING

A third approach – between market and product orientation – is asset-led marketing.

KEY TERM

asset-led marketing an approach to marketing that bases strategy on the firm's existing strengths and assets instead of purely on what the customer wants

This is based on market research too, but does not attempt to satisfy all consumers in all markets. Instead, the firm will consider its own strengths (or 'competencies') in terms of people, assets and brand image and will only make those products that use and take advantage of those strengths. Using this approach, Levi Strauss restricts its product to clothing – but it does offer a wider range of clothing than ever before. Similarly, BMW does not enter the commercial-vehicle or motor-caravan markets – but it does use its brand strength to market sports and luxurious 4 × 4 SUVs (sports utility vehicles). These, and many other firms, focus on their existing strengths, assets and products rather than entering entirely new markets trying to meet every new consumer taste and fashion.

It is very important to realise that not all market-oriented businesses will succeed. Market research and identifying consumer needs are not a guarantee of business success – the new products developed in this way may come to market too late or fail to impress consumers compared to rivals' products. Success and survival in the competitive and globalised markets of the twenty-first century depend upon the whole marketing process – not just the use of market research.

SOCIAL MARKETING

This approach to marketing adopts a wider perspective than the previous forms of orientation. It focuses on other stakeholders as well as the business and its consumers. Social responsibility is becoming increasingly popular among organisations and can be regarded as an important strategic marketing tool. This raises the question of what the central purpose of marketing should be. Is it 'a management tool to help maximise profits' or should it be 'a means of satisfying consumer needs profitably, but with minimum damage and costs to society'? Managers who believe in 'social marketing' claim the latter concept of marketing is the correct one to adopt. The term 'social (or societal) marketing' was first coined by Kotler in 1972.

KEY TERM

social (societal) marketing this approach considers not only the demands of consumers but also the effects on all members of the public ('society') involved in some way when firms meet these demands

These other members of the public or stakeholders include employees, shareholders, suppliers, competitors, government, the community and the natural environment. Examples of societal marketing include The Body Shop, which promises not to support animal testing of its products and purchases its supplies from sustainable sources produced in non-environmentally damaging ways. These products are not the cheapest – but they do meet society's long-term interests. Another example is the sale of dolphin-safe tuna fish, which has been caught by rod and line rather than nets that can entrap dolphins. This tuna is more expensive – but it is more appealing to society's concerns.

The social marketing concept has the following implications:

- It is an attempt to balance three concerns: company profits, consumer wants, society's interests.
- There may be a difference between short-term consumer wants (low prices) and long-term consumer and society welfare (protecting the environment and paying workers reasonable wages). Social marketing considers long-term welfare.
- Businesses should still aim to identify consumer needs and wants and to satisfy these more efficiently than competitors do – but in a way that enhances consumers' and society's welfare.
- Using this concept could give a business a significant competitive advantage. Many consumers prefer to purchase products from businesses that are seen to be socially responsible.
- A social marketing strategy, if successful, could lead to the firm being able to charge higher prices for its products as benefiting society becomes a unique selling point.

Tins of dolphin-safe tuna – an example of social marketing

Marketing in non-profit-making organisations

In a recent survey of UK charities, the consultants Robson Rhodes reported that:

76% of charities admitted to failing to monitor the results of their marketing activities

58% of charities revealed that they did not set any performance indicators for their promotional campaigns – such as their reach and impact

31% of respondents had attempted to re-brand their charities in the previous two years to appeal to different market segments.

In some ways, marketing and non-profit making might appear to be opposing concepts. Yet charities have very clear fund-raising objectives – to support their cause – and this money needs to be raised in the most cost-effective way, so there are in fact many similarities between marketing consumer goods and charities. For example:

- Market research – how does the public view our charity and which groups are most likely to donate?
- The best ways to communicate effectively with donors – many charities have moved away from expensive and ineffective direct-mail shots to internet and viral marketing campaigns. A recent blog-driven campaign helped to raise funds for waterforpeople (see website: www.waterforpeople.org).
- The need to assess the effectiveness of different promotions and campaigns to increase value for money in the future.

What are the differences in marketing non-profit-marketing organisations?

- The importance of maintaining high ethical standards to avoid alienating the public.
- Constant feedback on the success of charity campaigns – and future issues to be addressed – to maintain public interest and awareness.
- Free publicity, with the aim of capturing the public's imagination, for example for fund-raising events and stunts, is much more important for charitable causes than for most consumer products.

Marketing plans

KEY TERM

marketing plan a detailed report on an organisation's marketing strategy

A marketing plan is an essential component of any successful marketing campaign. Successful marketing does not just 'happen', it has to be planned and prepared for. The key components of a marketing plan include:

- SMART marketing objectives, e.g. to increase sales by 10% in each of the next three years
- strategic plans – an overview of the steps to be taken to achieve these objectives, e.g. selling existing products in new markets and how this will be attempted
- specific marketing actions, e.g. Which new markets? By when? Which methods of promotion to be used?
- a marketing budget – the finance that will be needed to pay for the overall cost of the marketing strategy and actions.

See Table 24.1 for the benefits and limitations of marketing plans.

Benefits	Limitations
• Plans provide focus to the work of the marketing department. • Marketing strategies linked to SMART objectives will increase the likelihood of the marketing campaign's success. • The budget should be adequate to achieve the campaign's objectives.	• Plans that are not revised to meet changing internal or external conditions will become outdated. • Plans are insufficient on their own – they need to be reviewed constantly and the final outcome must be judged against the original objectives to aid future decision-making.

Table 24.1 *Marketing plans – benefits and limitations*

THEORY OF KNOWLEDGE

1 'You can pay over $60 for a Ralph Lauren Cotton Oxford shirt although you could purchase a similar type of product for $25 from a major supermarket chain; a packet of 16 Nurofen costs over $3 when the same unbranded drug ibuprofen sells for 70% less; Moët et Chandon champagne sells for around $50 a bottle and yet good-quality sparkling white wine can be bought for around $10.'
   a Find out **three** more examples where there is a significant difference between the price of branded and unbranded products.
   b In the light of your research and the information in the text, discuss the extent to which consumers apply logic when buying branded products.

2 'Have you seen the latest Heineken beer advert? Coca-Cola has increased its funding of grass-roots football. McDonald's is giving away free plastic figures from the latest blockbuster children's film and cable television is full of adverts for law firms seeking out clients for personal injury claims.' The marketing objective of many businesses is to create a desire for their products.

   To what extent is it ethical for businesses to pursue this aim?

OVER TO YOU

REVISION CHECKLIST

1 Why is 'marketing' not just 'selling and advertising'?
2 Using examples, differentiate between market orientation and product orientation.
3 Why is it usually better for a firm to be market oriented?
4 Explain **three** examples of problems that might result from failing to link marketing decisions with other departments in the business.
5 State **four** possible examples of marketing objectives that a business might set.
6 Which **one** of these objectives do you think would be most appropriate for Coca-Cola in your country? Explain your answer.
7 Using numerical examples, explain the difference between market share and market size.
8 Why would a business that had the second largest market share be keen to become market leader?
9 List **three** factors that could lead to an overall decline in the size of a market.
10 Outline **three** factors that could lead to a business experiencing declining market share in a growing market.
11 Outline **three** ways in which a manufacturer of jeans might increase market share.
12 How might a retailer of sports clothing attempt to 'add value' to the products?
13 Measure company A's market share and the growth rate of the market it operates in from the following data. Comment on your results.

	2010	2011
Total market sales (units)	36 000	48 000
Total market value ($m)	5.0 million	6.5 million
Company A's sales (units)	3600	5000
Company A's sales value ($m)	0.5	0.6

(H) 14 Explain the difference between market orientation, asset-led marketing and social marketing.

REVISION ACTIVITY

Read the case study below and then answer the questions that follow.

The Classic Watch Company

The Classic Watch company was in trouble. Sales had fallen for each of the last three years. The founder of the company, Harry Brainch, could not understand the reasons for this. His business had been making the Classic Ladies' wrist watch for the last 20 years. The current model had been updated but was still essentially the same design as the original watch. Consumers had been attracted to its simple, robust design and good value. These were very important qualities during the economic crisis that the country had suffered from for much of the last few years.

More recently, consumer incomes had started to rise. Old manufacturing industry had been replaced by service sector businesses that offered many supervisory and managerial jobs. Youth unemployment, in particular, had fallen and young consumers had much more money to spend than previously. Both men and women were becoming much more fashion conscious as their consumer tastes changed with higher incomes. Harry knew his business had to change, but he did not know which new styles of watches to introduce. He almost wished a return to the good old days when shoppers were happy to buy a recognised design at a reasonable price.

24 marks, 45 minutes

1 Is the Classic Watch Company product or market oriented? Explain your answer. [4]
2 Analyse why Harry's original marketing strategy no longer increases sales. [6]
3 Outline **three** ways in which Harry might separate or segment consumers into different groups, producing watches for these groups, in order to increase overall sales. [6]
(H) 4 Evaluate whether this business should adopt an asset-led marketing approach. [8]

EXAM PRACTICE QUESTION

Read the case study below and then answer the questions that follow.

MICROSOFT LAUNCHES ITS NEW SMART-PHONE

The Kin, Microsoft's new smart-phone, is the US giant's latest attempt to take on Apple and Google in the mobile phone market. The Kin's distinctive design feature is a slide-out keyboard, which makes the product smaller than its rivals. It will be on sale in the US in the next few weeks and it arrives in Europe later in the year.

Microsoft sees the smart-phone as increasingly important, as analysts suggest that the next generation of web users will mainly access the internet on mobile devices rather than a PC. The company has developed its new devices through a project called Pink. Windows Phone Series 7 was announced back in February and a number of mobile phone producers are working on devices that use the new software.

Microsoft has tried in vain to gain market share in the mobile phone sector, in contrast to its dominance of the personal computer market. Its share of the US smart-phone market dropped to 15.1% in February from 19.1% in November, while Google's Android increased its share from 3.8% to almost 9%. Apple has maintained its 25% share and is still the leading player in the sector. It is thought that the reason for the success of Apple's iPhone is the company's market-orientated approach to promoting its products. Microsoft has a long way to go if it wants to get anywhere near the market share Apple's iPhone enjoys.

25 marks, 45 minutes

1 Explain how Microsoft's 15.1% share of the mobile phone market would have been calculated. [2]

2 Analyse two ways Microsoft could increase its market share of the mobile phone market. [8]

3 Explain the characteristics of Apple's market-orientated approach to promoting the iPhone. [6]

(H) 4 Discuss the benefits mobile phone producers could gain by adopting a more social approach to marketing their products. [9]

25 Marketing planning

This chapter covers syllabus section 4.2

On completing this chapter you should be able to:

- apply the elements of the marketing mix to given situations
- discuss the effectiveness of a marketing mix in achieving marketing objectives and evaluate marketing strategies
- discuss the ethics of marketing
- explain the value of a marketing audit
-  apply Porter's Five Forces to analyse competitive pressures in the marketplace
- examine the appropriateness of marketing objectives
- analyse the role of market research
- evaluate the different methods of market research
- understand segmentation and targeting
- discuss how organisations can differentiate themselves and their products
-  analyse sales-forecasting methods and evaluate their significance for marketing and resource planning.

SETTING THE SCENE

Nivea Pearl & Beauty launch based on market research results

The successful launch of a new deodorant product aimed at young women was aided by extensive market research. The market researchers used both existing data and newly gathered data. The existing data on consumer usage of deodorant products and competitors' sales were out of date, so new research was very important if the company wanted to find out what today's women want in a deodorant product and what its key features should be.

Using these data, the company produced test products and tried these on small discussion groups of women. Women seemed to prefer the most beautifying and caring product and this was the one that went into production. One of the most important questions to answer was about price – what price would encourage the groups of women to switch brands? How many would buy it at different prices? A mid to high price was acceptable to the majority. But what was the image of the packaging and the advertisements – did they give the correct brand image? These were shown to the groups and their reactions and opinions were used to adapt both packaging and the advertisements. The product is now one of the best-selling deodorants to the target market – 18–30-year-old fashion-oriented women.

Source: www.thetimes100.co.uk (adapted)

Points to think about:

- Why did Nivea use both existing and new market research data?
- Explain **four** uses of the data collected to Nivea.
- Was the use of market research the only factor that led to this product's success?

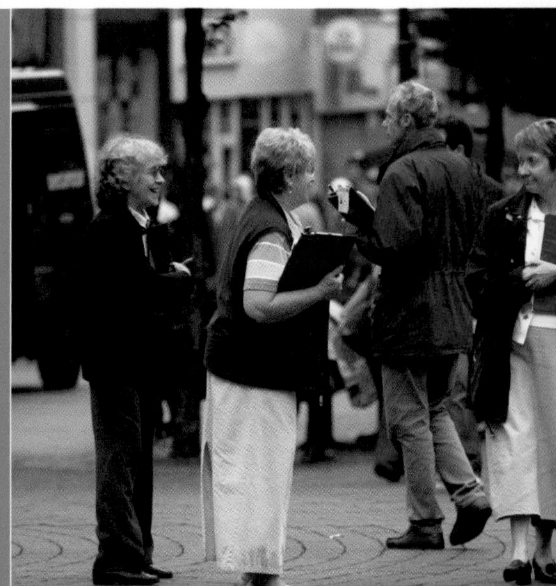

Introduction

KEY TERM

marketing planning the process of formulating appropriate strategies and preparing marketing activities to meet marketing objectives

A market plan is often a formal written document which outlines in detail how the business unit intends to achieve the marketing objectives derived from the corporate objectives. Effective market planning is nearly always based on clear awareness of market trends, competitors' actions and consumer wants so market research is vital. The plan will then contain detailed action programmes, budgets, sales forecasts and strategies – and these strategies will be based on adaptations of the firm's marketing mix.

Marketing mix

The marketing mix for a product is a major factor in influencing whether a business can sell it profitably.

KEY TERM

marketing mix the key decisions that must be taken in the effective marketing of a product

The marketing mix is made up of seven interrelated decisions – the 7Ps. The four key ones are **product**, **price**, **promotion** (including advertising and packaging) and **place** (where and how a product will be sold to consumers). The other 3Ps largely relate to marketing services – **people**, **process** and **physical evidence**.

- Consumers require the right product. This might be an existing product, an adaptation of an existing product or a newly developed one.
- The right price is important too. If set too low, then consumers may lose confidence in the product's quality; if too high, then many will be unable to afford it.
- Promotion must be effective – telling consumers about the product's availability and convincing them that 'your brand' is the one to choose. Packaging is often used to reinforce this image.
- Place refers to how the product is distributed to the consumer. If it is not available at the right time in the right place, then even the best product in the world will not be bought in the quantities expected.
- Selling services successfully requires people who can interact positively with customers and create the correct impression to encourage them to return. This is particularly relevant in the hotel and restaurant industry.
- The processes that a business has in place to satisfy customers' wants reliably and consistently form an important part of marketing services. For example, banks replacing an out-of-date debit card without the customer having to ask for one.
- Physical evidence means allowing customers to see for themselves the quality of the service being provided. This will reduce the element of risk in buying a service as opposed to a tangible product. For example, a clean and well-presented reception area in a hotel would raise appropriate expectations in the mind of the customer.

Not all of the 7Ps have the same degree of significance in every case. It is vital that these elements fit together into a coherent and integrated plan. An appropriate marketing mix will ensure that these marketing decisions are interrelated. They must be carefully co-ordinated to make sure that customers are not confused by conflicting messages being given about the good or service being sold.

KEY TERM

co-ordinated marketing mix key marketing decisions complement each other and work together to give customers a consistent message about the product

AN APPROPRIATE MARKETING MIX

- If an expensive, well-known brand of perfume was for sale on a **market stall**, would you be suspicious?
- If the most exclusive shop in your town sold expensive gifts and wrapped them in **newspaper**, would you be surprised?
- If a cheap range of children's clothing was advertised in a **glossy colour magazine** aimed at professional women, would this advert lead to many sales?

These are all examples of poorly integrated marketing decisions. The marketing strategies – shown in bold – lack integration with the rest of the marketing mix and are therefore inappropriate. If the messages consumers receive about a product are confused or lacking in focus, they may fail to recognise the true identity or 'personality' of the product. Consumers are likely to reject products where the marketing mix has not communicated a clear and unambiguous message, resulting in fewer long-term sales.

If just one part of the marketing is inconsistent or does not integrate with the rest, it may lead to the failure of even the best marketing plan. The most appropriate marketing mix decisions will therefore be:

- based on marketing objectives that are affordable within the marketing budget
- co-ordinated and consistent with each other
- targeted at the appropriate consumers.

EXAM TIP

IB questions may ask you to recommend and evaluate a marketing strategy for a product. As with an actual business, the key point here is to suggest a fully co-ordinated marketing mix which is appropriate for achieving a set marketing objective.

ACTIVITY 25.1

Look at the examples of four marketing mix decisions and then answer the questions that follow.

What went wrong?

	Product	Price	Place	Promotion
Mix A	Fast sports car	High – based on top-range competitors' prices	Exclusive dealers in impressive city showrooms	Advertised on radio only
Mix B	Range of furniture for families with low incomes	Low – low costs allow prices to be set below competitors'	Sold only over the internet	Advertised on posters and in free local newspapers
Mix C	Ladies' fashion hairdressing salon with cutting by well-known stylists	Low-price offers to large family groups	Salon located in wealthy area of city	Advertised in fashion and beauty magazines
Mix D	Fast-food restaurant	Skimming or high-price strategy	Expensive business district location with many top-class restaurants	Advertised in business magazines, loyalty card scheme operated together with quality retail department stores

16 marks, 30 minutes

1 In each case, identify which marketing mix decision seems to be 'out of place' and not integrated with the other decisions. [4]

2 In each case, recommend and justify a change to one of the marketing decisions to create an integrated mix. [12]

The ethics of marketing

Chapter 3 looked at the importance of ethical standards in business decision-making. These are of particular significance to the work of marketing departments as the examples of ethical issues given in Table 25.1 show.

Ethical marketing issues are becoming increasingly significant in a period of rapid globalisation. What may be acceptable and normal marketing practice in one country may be viewed as offensive and unethical in others. Many of these issues were discussed in Chapter 3 (see pages 31–33).

The value of a marketing audit

KEY TERM

marketing audit a regular review of the cost and effectiveness of a marketing plan including an analysis of internal and external influences

A marketing audit is conducted not just at the conclusion of a marketing plan but also during its implementation. Its purpose is to alert management to the progress being made, for example, with the launch of a new product, so

Marketing mix decision	Is it ethical to:
Pricing	• sell a computer printer cheaply and then tie in customers to buy expensive refill cartridges? • offer low airfares on the internet and then add taxes on after a purchase has been made?
Promotion	• advertise toys on TV to young children who may not be able to distinguish between programme and advert? • use sexual images to sell products in countries with deeply held religious views?
Place	• close all retail branches and sell only over the internet when many elderly consumers may not have access to a computer?
Product	• buy cheap and potentially dangerous supplies in order to cut prices? • design clothes for young children that are sexually provocative?

Table 25.1 *Marketing and ethics*

that changes may be made to the marketing mix if necessary. A marketing audit should provide an answer to the question: What is the current marketing situation?

A marketing audit consists of three key features:

1. An analysis of the business's internal strengths and weaknesses and how they have changed since the last audit – for example, a successful marketing manager might have left the company, which would be considered a weakness.
2. An analysis of the external opportunities and threats and how these have changed since the last audit – for example, the entry of a new rival into the market would add to the threats faced by the business. SWOT and PEST analyses are central to the first two stages of the marketing audit. Review their importance by re-reading the relevant sections in Chapters 5 (see pages 46–47) and 6 (see pages 64–65).
3. Review the progress of the marketing plan. This will analyse:
   - market share – compare with objectives set at the start of the plan
   - actual sales performance compared with the original sales budgets
   - whether the company is achieving its SMART objectives.

Once the audit has been completed, then changes to the marketing mix might be needed to respond to any of the changes identified by it.

HIGHER LEVEL

Porter's Five Forces analysis

Michael Porter provided a framework that analyses an industry as being influenced by five forces. It has been suggested that management, attempting to establish a competitive marketing advantage over rivals, can use this model to understand the industry context in which the business operates and take appropriate strategic decisions. Figure 25.1 shows these five forces with the key one – competitive rivalry – at the centre.

1 Threat of entry

This means the ease with which other firms can join the industry and compete with existing businesses. The threat of entry is greatest when:

- economies of scale are low in the industry
- technology needed to enter the industry is relatively cheap
- distribution channels are easy to access, e.g. retail shops are not owned by existing manufacturers in the industry
- there are no legal or patent restrictions on entry
- the importance of product differentiation is low, so extensive advertising may not be required to get established.

2 The power of buyers

This refers to the power that customers have on the producing industry. For example, if there are four major supermarket groups that dominate this sector of retailing, their buyer power over food and other producers will be great. Buyer power will also be increased when:

- there are many undifferentiated small supplying firms, e.g. many small farmers supplying milk or chicken to large supermarket businesses
- the cost of switching suppliers is low
- buyers can realistically and easily buy from other suppliers.

3 The power of suppliers

Suppliers will be relatively powerful compared with buyers when:

- the cost of switching is high, e.g. from PC computers to AppleMacs
- when the brand being sold is very powerful and well known, e.g. Cadbury's chocolate or Nike shoes
- suppliers could realistically threaten to open their own forward-integration operations, e.g. coffee suppliers open their own cafés

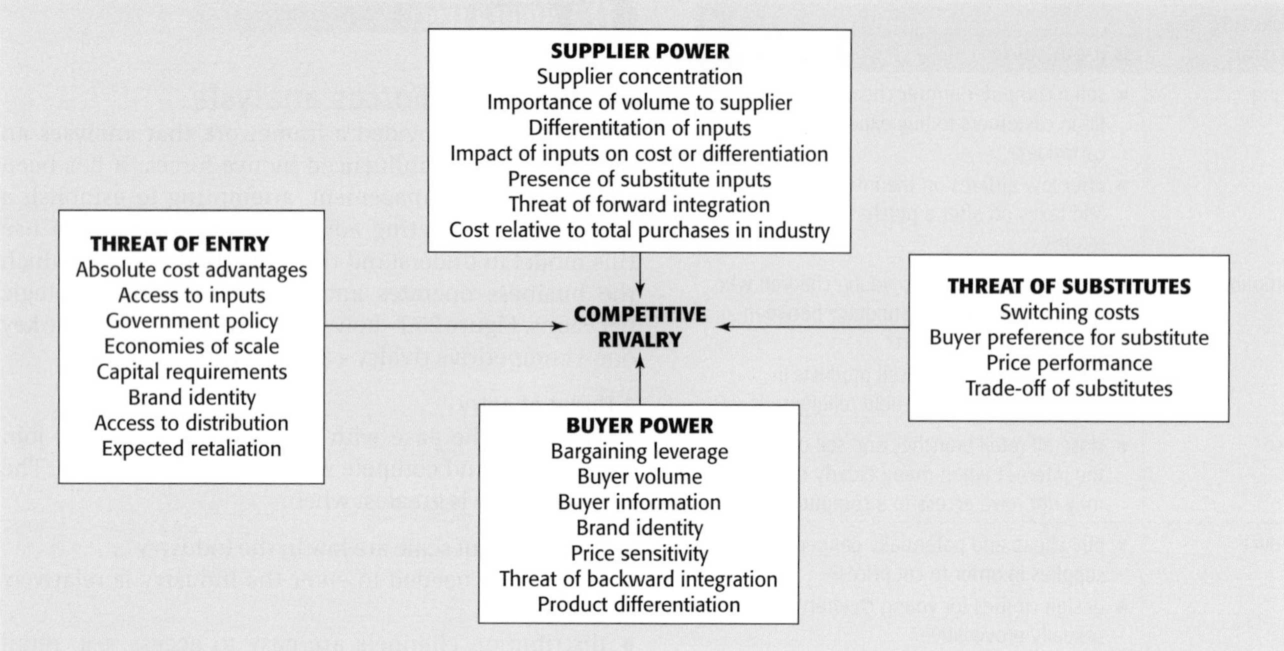

Figure 25.1 *Porter's Five Forces model*

- customers have little bargaining power as they are small firms and fragmented, e.g. dispersed around the country as with independent petrol stations.

4 The threat of substitutes

In Porter's model, 'substitute products' does not mean alternatives in the same industry such as Toyota for Honda cars. It refers to substitute products in other industries. For instance, the demand for aluminium for cans is partly affected by the price of glass for bottling and plastic for containers. These are substitutes for aluminium, but they are not rivals in the same industry. Threats of substitution will exist when:

- new technology makes other options available such as satellite TV instead of traditional antenna reception
- price competition forces customers to consider alternatives, e.g. lower bus fares might make some travellers switch from rail transport
- any significant new product leads to consumer spending that results in less being spent on other goods, e.g. increasing spending on mobile phones by young people reduces the cash they have available to spend on clothes.

5 Competitive rivalry

This is the key part of this analysis – it sums up the most important factors that determine the level of competition or rivalry in an industry. It is based on the other four forces which is why it is often illustrated in the centre of the Five Forces diagram. Competitive rivalry is most likely to be high where:

- it is cheap and easy for new firms to enter an industry
- there is a threat from substitute products
- suppliers have much power
- buyers have much power.

There will also be great rivalry between competing firms in an industry when:

- there are a large number of firms with similar market share
- high fixed costs force firms to try to obtain economies of scale
- there is slow market growth that forces firms to take share from rivals if they wish to increase sales.

ACTIVITY 25.2

Porter's Five Forces model

20 marks, 35 minutes

Choose an industry/market such as supermarkets, newspapers or hotels in your own country. Based on your own research, analyse the industry/market using Porter's Five Forces model. Write a report of your findings, assessing the overall degree of competitive rivalry. [20]

PORTER'S FIVE FORCES AND STRATEGIC DECISIONS

How does this analysis of the competitive situation in an industry help businesses take important strategic marketing decisions?

1 By analysing new markets in this way, it helps firms decide whether to enter them or not. It provides an insight into the potential profitability of markets. Is it better to enter a highly competitive market or not?
2 By analysing the existing markets a business operates in, decisions may be taken about: 'Do we stay in these markets in the future if they are becoming more competitive?' and 'How could we reduce the level of competitive rivalry in these markets – and thus increase potential profitability?'
3 With the knowledge gained and the power of competitive forces, businesses can develop strategies that might improve their own competitive position. Examples include:

- product differentiation, e.g. Honda hybrid cars with a distinctive appearance
- using patents and other forms of protection to prevent simple copying of products
- focusing on different market segments that might be less competitive, e.g. Nestlé entering niche confectionery markets such as vegetarian chocolates
- merging with or taking over suppliers or customers in order to reduce supplier and buyer influence over the business – this is a major strategic decision that would have a considerable marketing impact
- signing exclusivity agreements with buyers and tying in customers with long-term service agreements that would make it more expensive for them to switch to another supplier.

Marketing objectives and corporate objectives

The long-term objectives of the company will have a significant impact on both the marketing objectives and marketing strategy adopted. A business with clear short-term profit targets will focus on maximising sales at the highest prices possible. In contrast, a business with longer-term objectives, which may include both profitability as well as the achievement of goals of social responsibility, may adopt a social marketing approach.

KEY TERMS

marketing objectives the goals set for the marketing department to help the business achieve its overall objectives

marketing strategy long-term plan established for achieving marketing objectives

Examples of marketing objectives include:

- increasing market share – perhaps to gain market leadership
- increasing brand awareness
- increasing total sales levels – either in terms of volume or sales value
- development of new markets for existing products to spread risks.

To be effective, marketing objectives should:

- fit in with the overall aims and mission of the business – they should reflect the aims of the whole organisation and should attempt to aid the achievement of these.
- be determined by senior management – they will determine the markets and products a business trades in for years to come and these issues must be dealt with by managers at a very senior level in the company.

- be realistic, motivating, achievable, measurable and clearly communicated to all departments in the organisation.

Why are marketing objectives important?

- They provide a sense of direction for the marketing department.
- Progress can be monitored against these targets.
- They can be broken down into regional and product sales targets to allow for management by objectives.
- They form the basis of marketing strategy. These marketing objectives will have a crucial impact on the marketing strategies adopted, as without a clear vision of *what* the business hopes to achieve for its products, it will be pointless discussing *how* it should market them.

The role of market research

KEY TERM

market research process of collecting, recording and analysing data about customers, competitors and the market

Market research is a broad and far-reaching process. It is concerned not just with finding out, as accurately as possible, whether consumers will buy a particular product or not, but also with trying to analyse their reaction to:

- different price levels
- alternative forms of promotion
- new types of packaging
- different methods of distribution.

The results of market research can have a great impact on decisions made in all areas of the marketing process:

1 To reduce the risks associated with new product launches

By investigating potential demand for a new product or service the business should be able to assess the likely chances of a new product achieving satisfactory sales. Although market research cannot guarantee success, market research is still a key part of new product development (NPD). Table 25.2 summarises how NPD is supported by market research.

2 To predict future demand changes

A travel firm may wish to investigate social and other changes to see how these might affect the demand for holidays in the future. For instance, the growth in the number of single-person households may suggest that there could be a rising demand for 'singles' holidays.

The NPD process		The market research process
identify consumer needs and tastes	→	primary and secondary research into consumer needs and competitors
product idea and packaging design	→	testing or product and packaging with consumer groups
brand positioning and advertising testing	→	pre-testing of the product image and advertisements
product launch and after launch period	→	monitoring of sales and consumer response

Table 25.2 *Summary of how NPD is supported by market research*

3 To explain patterns in sales of existing products and market trends

Market research is not just undertaken for new or planned products, it needs to be conducted for existing products too. Sales at the fashion retailer Gap had, by the end of 2008, fallen in 28 of the last 31 months. Unless Gap managers were prepared to find out why this happened, they would not be able to take remedial action.

4 To assess the most favoured designs, flavours, styles, promotions and packages for a product

Consumer tests of different versions of a product or of the proposed adverts to promote it will enable a business to focus on the aspects of design and performance that consumers rate most highly. These can then be incorporated into the final product.

Market research can, therefore, be used to discover information about:

- market size and consumer tastes and trends
- the product and its perceived strengths and weaknesses
- the promotion used and its effectiveness
- competitors and their claimed unique selling propositions
- distribution methods most preferred by consumers
- consumers' preferences for packaging the product.

Sources of market research data

Primary research collects 'first-hand' data as they are being collected by the organisation for the first time for its own needs. In contrast, secondary research is the use and analysis of data that already exist. These data were originally collected by another organisation, often for a different purpose, and are often referred to as 'second-hand' data.

Secondary research should be undertaken first – but only if the data exist, which they may not if the planned

ACTIVITY 25.3

Read the case study below and then answer the questions that follow.

We know who our customers are

IKEA is one of the world's best-known furniture retailers. In 2009, it had 267 stores in 25 countries serving 590 million customers.

Peter Hogstead, one of its senior managers, has researched its consumer base very carefully:

- It is largely middle class and the middle class in most countries of the world is increasing.
- Its core customers are between 25 and 50 years old.
- They are fashion conscious but want good-value products.
- Eighty per cent are female.
- The majority have children.

12 marks, 21 minutes

Explain **four** benefits to IKEA's managers of having detailed research information about their customers. [12]

product is so different that no second-hand data exist. Why undertake secondary research first? It is because of the benefits that secondary research offers over primary methods. Assume that a US-owned supermarket business is thinking about expanding into Trinidad and Tobago. The following data could be obtained from secondary sources, without the manager leaving his or her desk – which is why it is sometimes called desk research.

- The two-island republic has one of the highest per capita GDPs in the Caribbean.
- The retail market is made up of over 500 chain stores (supermarkets, grocery stores and petrol stations), with sales estimated at $817 million in 2009.
- Aiming for a 'one-stop' shopping experience, many supermarket chains have begun to renovate and remodel their stores.
- In-house bakeries and delis are becoming more common.
- Retail food sales rose by nearly 45% between 2000 and 2009.
- Supermarkets are increasing the amount of low-fat and health-food products on offer.

Much more detailed information about the supermarket sector in Trinidad and Tobago could then be obtained by the US business purchasing a second-hand market research report from an agency specialised in this market in the republic.

KEY TERMS

primary research the collection of first-hand data that are directly related to a firm's needs

secondary research collection of data from second-hand sources

SOURCES OF SECONDARY DATA

Secondary data can be obtained from the following well-known sources.

1 Government publications

In most countries, sources, such as the following from the UK, could be referred to:

- *population census*
- *Social Trends*
- *Annual Abstract of Statistics*
- *Family Expenditure Survey.*

Therefore, if a furniture manufacturer was undecided whether to produce new designs for teenagers' bedrooms or electric reclining armchairs for the elderly, reference to government publications for the forecasted age distribution of the population over the next ten years would be a useful starting point.

2 Local libraries and local government offices

If the research data needed were only for a small area – investigating the viability of a new café, for example – then local not national data would be necessary:

- local population census – total population size, age and occupation distributions
- number of households in the area
- proportions of the local population from different ethnic and cultural groups.

3 Trade organisations

Trade organisations produce regular reports on the state of the markets their members operate in. For example:

- Society of Motor Manufacturers and Traders
- Furniture Retailers Association
- Engineering Employers Federation.

If a garage owner wanted to start stocking new cars for sale, then details of the type and size of car that is most popular with consumers could be obtained from the first source listed above. Clearly, further research might then be needed to see if, locally, these national data were reflected in consumer demand in the garage's own area.

4 Market intelligence reports
These are extremely detailed reports on individual markets and industries produced by specialist market research agencies. They are very expensive, but they are usually available at local business libraries. Examples are:

- Mintel reports
- Key Note reports
- Euromonitor.

If the owner of a small hotel planned to expand the business by opening a hotel in the capital city, one of these reports on the hotel and catering market would provide huge amounts of detail on market and consumer trends, eating and holiday habits of consumers, number of tourists and so on.

5 Newspaper reports and specialist publications

- *Marketing* – this journal provides weekly advertising spend data and consumer 'recall of adverts' results
- The *Grocer*
- *Motor Trader*
- The *Financial Times* – regular articles on key industries such as IT and detailed country reports – essential for potential exporters.

6 Internal company records
If the business has been trading for some time, a large quantity of secondary data will already be available for further analysis from:

- customer sales records
- guarantee claims from customers
- daily, weekly and monthly sales trends
- feedback from customers on product, service, delivery and quality.

7 The internet
The internet has transformed secondary data collection. Whenever secondary research is conducted just from the internet, the accuracy and relevance of the source should always be checked upon.

Initial secondary research will nearly always indicate the focus that subsequent primary research should have. However, on its own, it is rarely sufficient, which is why primary research is also usually undertaken. Table 25.3 summarises the advantages and disadvantages of secondary research. Secondary research gathers background data, but only primary research can provide detailed, up-to-date information from consumers within the firm's target market.

ACTIVITY 25.4 RESEARCH ACTIVITY

Read the case study below and then answer the questions that follow.

What do you want to know about Malaysia?
If you are prepared to pay for it, the range of secondary market research data available for businesses operating in Malaysia is incredible. Four examples, from many thousands of reports available are:

- Clothing and footwear in Malaysia (Euromonitor)
- Pet food in Malaysia (Euromonitor)
- Gardening in Malaysia (Euromonitor)
- Malaysian desktop and notebook demand 2009–13 (IDC).

Research into a market for a product or service in your own country. Find out as much as you can about the size of the market, any segments that exist within it and the features of 'typical' consumers for this product.

Advantages	Disadvantages
• Often obtainable very cheaply – apart from the purchase of market intelligence reports. • Identifies the nature of the market and assists with the planning of primary research. • Obtainable quickly without the need to devise complicated data-gathering methods. • Allows comparison of data from different sources.	• May not be updated frequently and may therefore be out of date. • As it was originally collected for another purpose, it may not be entirely suitable or presented in the most effective way for the business using it. • Data-collection methods and accuracy of these may be unknown. • Might not be available for completely new product developments.

Table 25.3 *Secondary research – advantages and disadvantages*

Primary research

Table 25.4 summarises the advantages and disadvantages of primary research.

METHODS OF PRIMARY RESEARCH

Primary – or field – research can itself be divided into quantitative and qualitative research.

Advantages	Disadvantages
• Up to date and therefore more useful than much secondary data. • Relevant – collected for a specific purpose – directly addresses the questions the business wants answers to. • Confidential – no other business has access to this data.	• Costly – market research agencies can charge thousands of dollars for detailed customer surveys and other market research reports. • Time consuming – secondary data could be obtained from the internet much more quickly. • Doubts over accuracy and validity – largely because of the need to use sampling and the risk of sampling error.

Table 25.4 *Primary research – advantages and disadvantages*

KEY TERMS

quantitative research research that leads to numerical results that can be presented and analysed

qualitative research research into the in-depth motivations behind consumer buying behaviour or opinions

Qualitative research

Finding out about the quantities that consumers might purchase is clearly important information, but what is often even more revealing is why consumers will or will not buy a particular product. Qualitative research should discover the motivational factors behind consumer buying habits. For example, quantitative research might establish the size of the potential market for a new luxury ice cream. But will consumers buy it for its taste and the quality of its ingredients or because it will be promoted as a lifestyle product that will reflect on the consumers' image of themselves? Only qualitative research, perhaps by the use of focus groups, can establish the answer to the last question – and it is important because it will help the business in its pricing and promotional decisions for the new product.

KEY TERM

focus groups a group of people who are asked about their attitude towards a product, service, advertisement or new style of packaging

In these discussion groups, questions are asked and the group are encouraged to actively discuss their responses about a product, advertising, packaging and so on. All members of the group are free to talk with other group members. These discussions are often filmed and this is then used by the market research department as a source of data. Information is often believed to be more accurate and realistic than the responses to individual interviews or questionnaires, where respondents do not have this discussion opportunity presented. There might, however, be the risk of researchers leading or influencing the discussion too much, leading to biased conclusions.

Focus groups are an important method for gathering consumers' opinions and responses – qualitative research

Quantitative research techniques

1 Test marketing

This takes place after a decision has been made to produce a limited quantity of a new product but before a full-scale, national launch is made. It involves promoting and selling the product in a limited geographical area and then recording consumer reactions and sales figures. It reduces the risks of a new product launch failing completely, but the evidence is not always completely accurate if the total population does not share the same characteristics and preferences as the region selected.

KEY TERM

test marketing marketing a new product in a geographical region before a full-scale launch

2 Consumer surveys

These involve directly asking consumers or potential consumers for their opinions and preferences. They can be used to obtain both qualitative and quantitative

ACTIVITY 25.5

Read the case study below and then answer the questions that follow.

Carlos plans a new restaurant

Carlos Sanchez is a chef specialising in Spanish cuisine. He has always wanted to work for himself and has decided to open his own small restaurant. Property prices are too high in the capital, so he has moved to a small coastal resort about 100 kilometres from the capital. He has many important decisions to make. He is not sure whether Spanish cooking will be popular with the locals and the tourists. He is able to prepare many other types of dishes too. He could open just a restaurant or a takeaway too. If Carlos offers takeaway meals, he could either serve these in plastic containers for microwave heating, which are expensive, or in paper trays, which are cheaper. Carlos has noticed that there are few other restaurants in the area and no takeaways, although one well-known fast-food chain has recently closed down. There are no other Spanish-based restaurants. After finding a suitable shop site, Carlos then has to decide whether to decorate it for younger people's tastes with loud pop music or in a more sober style with traditional-style Spanish music.

24 marks, 44 minutes

1 Explain the benefits to Carlos of undertaking market research before he opens his new business. [6]

2 List **four** questions Carlos needs answers to from marketing research. [4]

3 Assuming Carlos lives in your country, list four sources of secondary research that he could refer to. [4]

4 Assess the likely usefulness of secondary research to Carlos. [10]

research. For example, here are two questions asked in a recent survey of shoppers:

'How many foreign holidays did you take last year?'
'What do you look for in an ideal foreign holiday?'

The first question will provide quantitative data, which can be presented graphically and analysed statistically. The second question is designed to find out the key qualitative features of a holiday that would influence consumer choice. There are four important issues for market researchers to consider when conducting consumer surveys:

- Who to ask? In most cases it is impossible or too expensive to survey all potential members of a target market (the survey population). A 'sample' from this population is therefore necessary. The more closely this sample reflects the characteristics of the survey population, the less chance of sampling error.
- What to ask? The construction of an unbiased and unambiguous questionnaire is essential if the survey is to obtain useful results.
- How to ask? Should the questionnaire be self-completed and returned by post or filled in by an interviewer in a face-to-face session with the respondent? Could a telephone or internet survey be conducted instead?
- How accurate is it? Assessing the likely accuracy and validity of the results is a crucial element of market research surveys.

KEY TERMS

sample group of people taking part in a market research survey selected to be representative of the target market overall

sampling error errors in research caused by using a sample for data collection rather than the whole target population

Who to ask? – sample size and sampling methods

Generally speaking, the larger the sample, the more confidence can be given to the final results. In surveying consumer reaction to a new advertising campaign for a major brand of chocolate, a sample of ten people is unlikely to be sufficient. The first ten people chosen might show a positive reaction to the new advertisement. Yet another ten might show a majority with negative reactions. A sample of ten is too small to be confident about the result, as chance variations from the views of the whole target population occur because of the limited number of respondents. A sample of 100 or even 1000 will produce results that will reflect much more accurately the total preferences of the whole survey population. There will be much less risk of pure chance distorting the results causing sampling error.

What prevents all primary research being based on a sample size of 1000? Cost and time are the two major constraints here – the bigger the samples, the greater the cost and the longer the time needed to collect and interpret results.

There are several different ways of selecting an appropriate sample. The ones below are the most commonly used.

1 Random sampling

Each member of the target population has an equal chance of being included in the sample. To select a random sample the following are needed:

- a list of all of the people in the target population
- sequential numbers given to each member of this population
- a list of random numbers generated by computer.

If a sample of 100 is required, then the first 100 numbers on the random number list are taken and the people who had these numbers allocated to them will form the sample – but it may take time to contact these specific people. Just asking the first 100 pedestrians who pass by during a survey on a main shopping street is *not* random sampling – it is called convenience sampling and will be biased because different groups of people tend to frequent the main shopping streets at different times.

2 Stratified sampling

This method recognises that the target population may be made up of many different groups with many different opinions. These groups are called strata or layers of the population and for a sample to be accurate it should contain members of all of these strata – hence the term, stratified sampling.

If you were asked to sample 100 students in a school about soft drink preferences for the school shop, it would be more accurate if, instead of asking 100 friends, you split the school up into certain strata, such as class groups, ages or gender. So, if the whole school or college contains 1000 students of whom 50 are girls in year group 8, an accurate sample of 100 would contain five girls from year group 8 ($50/1000 \times 100$). This process would be repeated with all year groups until the total required sample of 100 was reached. The people to be surveyed in each stratum should be selected randomly. Stratified sampling may also be used when a product is designed to appeal to just one segment of the market, for example if a computer game is aimed at 16–24-year-olds, only people from this stratum of the population will be included in the sample.

3 Cluster sampling

When a full sampling frame list is not available or the target population is too geographically dispersed, then cluster sampling will take a sample from just one or a few groups – not the whole population. This might be just one town or region and this will help to reduce costs – but it may not be fully representative of the whole population. Random methods can then be used to select the sample from this group. A multinational wanting to research global attitudes towards its product would save time and money by concentrating on just a few areas for its research.

4 Quota sampling

The population is first segmented into mutually exclusive sub-groups – such as male and female. Then the interviewer or researcher uses his or her judgement to select people from each segment based on a specified proportion; for example, an interviewer may be told to sample 200 females and 300 males between the ages of 45 and 60 years. In quota sampling the selection of the sample is non-scientific and may therefore be biased – interviewers might be tempted to interview those who look most helpful or most attractive. The main weakness of quota sampling is that not everyone gets a chance of selection.

5 Snowball sampling

The first respondent refers a friend who then refers another friend...and so the process continues. This is a cheap method of sampling and can be operated through social networking sites. However, it is likely to lead to a biased sample, as each respondent's friends are likely to have the same kind of lifestyle and opinions.

EXAM TIP

Each method of sampling has its own advantages and limitations – so which is best? This depends on the size and financial resources of the business and how 'different' consumers are in their tastes between different age groups and so on. Remember, cost-effectiveness is important in all market research decisions.

KEY TERMS

random sampling every member of the target population has an equal chance of being selected

stratified sampling this draws a sample from a specified sub-group or segment of the population and uses random sampling to select an appropriate number from each stratum

cluster sampling using one or a number of specific groups to draw samples from and not selecting from the whole population, e.g. using one town or region

quota sampling gathering data from a group chosen out of a specific sub-group, e.g. a researcher might ask 100 individuals between the ages of 20 and 30 years

snowball sampling using existing members of a sample study group to recruit further participants through their acquaintances

ACTIVITY 25.6

Read the case study below and then answer the questions that follow.

Low market share at Cosmos

The Cosmos Soft Drink Co. Ltd is concerned about its low market share despite extensive press advertising and colourful displays in large retailers. The image the company was trying to create was a 'sport energy drink' for youthful consumers. This was because the directors had used census data to discover that the proportion of the population under 18 was forecast to rise in the next ten years and the sports participation rates of most age groups were increasing. The directors believed that this image was the correct one to have and that other factors were to blame for the poor sales performance. Market research was undertaken using a telephone survey as they believed that quick results were essential to allow them to take the right measures to boost sales. A questionnaire was drawn up asking for details of soft drinks bought and the reasons for purchase decisions, names and addresses of the respondents so that free vouchers could be sent, income levels to identify consumer profiles and many other details that the directors thought might be useful. One hundred people were to be contacted by picking names at random from the telephone directory.

The results of the survey were disappointing. Many calls were not answered, some people refused to answer some of the questions and some elderly respondents said that all soft drinks were too sweet and fizzy for them anyway. The directors were no clearer after the survey about what could be done to increase sales of Cosmos soft drinks.

21 marks, 39 minutes

1 What evidence is there in the case study that this business has used secondary research methods? [3]

2 Analyse **two** possible reasons why the results of the telephone survey were so disappointing. [8]

3 Suggest and justify **two** alternative sampling methods that Cosmos could have used to achieve more useful results. [10]

Market segmentation and consumer profile

KEY TERMS

market segment a sub-group of a whole market in which consumers have similar characteristics

market segmentation identifying different segments within a market and targeting different products or services to them

consumer profile a quantified picture of consumers of a firm's products, showing proportions of age groups, income levels, location, gender and social class

Segmentation is sometimes referred to as differentiated marketing. Instead of trying to sell just one product to the whole market as in mass marketing, different products are targeted at different segments. This is a form of niche marketing. To be effective, firms must research and analyse the total market carefully to identify the specific consumer groups or segments that exist within it.

Below are some examples of market segmentation:

- Computer manufacturers, such as Hewlett Packard, produce PCs for office and home use, including games, but also make laptop models for business people who travel.
- Coca-Cola not only makes the standard cola drink but also Diet Coke for slimmers and flavoured drinks for consumers with particular tastes.
- Renault, the car maker, produces several versions of its Mégane model, such as a coupe, saloon, convertible and 'people carrier' – all appealing to different groups of consumers.

Sometimes firms only market their goods or services to one segment and deliberately do not aim to satisfy other segments. Gap is a clothing retailer that aims only at the youth market, Nike shoes are only for sports use and Coutts Bank only offers banking services to the seriously rich. These businesses make a virtue out of concentrating on one segment and developing an image and brand that suits that segment.

IDENTIFYING DIFFERENT CONSUMER GROUPS

Successful segmentation requires a business to have a very clear picture of the consumers in the target market it is aiming to sell in. This is called the consumer profile. The main characteristics of consumers contained in a consumer profile are income levels, age, gender, social class and region. Marketing mix decisions need to be appropriate for the consumer profile of the target market.

A well-targeted product will need less advertising and promotional support than one which does not really meet the needs of the consumers that it is aimed at.

KEY TERM

target market the market segment that a particular product is aimed at

Markets may be segmented in a number of different ways. The three commonly used bases for segmentation are shown below.

1 Geographic differences

Consumer tastes may vary between different geographic areas and so it may be appropriate to offer different products and market them in 'location-specific' ways.

2 Demographic differences

These are the most commonly used basis for segmentation as age, sex, family size and ethnic background can all be used to separate markets. A house construction firm will use demographic data to help determine which segment of the market a new block of apartments should be aimed at. Should they be retirement flats with a resident caretaker? Should they be small studio flats for young, single people? Should they offer large reception rooms to encourage certain ethnic groups that live in extended families to be attracted to the apartments? The construction firm may not attempt to attract all market segments – but having decided on the most appropriate one, it will be essential to gear the price and promotion strategies towards this segment.

An individual's social class may have a great impact on their expenditure patterns. This will be largely due to income differences between different classes of employment. The wealthy will have very different consumption patterns from the 'working class'. The jobs people do are one of the main factors influencing people's income levels. Other forces apart from income levels could operate, however. For instance, top professional groups would be expected to spend more money on, say, power boating and golfing, as these tend to be class-related activities.

Many marketing acronyms exist as abbreviations for different demographic groups of consumers. Here are just three:

DINKY – double income no kids yet
NILK – no income lots of kids
WOOF – well-off older folk

3 Psychographic factors

These are to do with differences between people's lifestyles, personalities, values and attitudes. Lifestyle is a very broad term which often relates to activities undertaken, interests and opinions rather than personality. The huge increase in TV channels and TV viewing in many countries has contributed to the growth of 'TV dinners', which are pre-prepared meals ready to eat without missing any of your favourite programmes.

Table 25.5 summarises the advantages and limitations of market segmentation.

Advantages	Limitations
• Businesses can define their target market precisely and design and produce goods that are specifically aimed at these groups leading to increased sales. • It helps to identify gaps in the market – groups of consumers that are not currently being targeted – and these might then be successfully exploited. • Differentiated marketing strategies can be focused on target market groups. This avoids wasting money on trying to sell products to the whole market – some consumer groups will have no intention of buying the product. • Small firms unable to compete in the whole market are able to specialise in one or two market segments. • Price discrimination can be used to increase revenue and profits.	• Research and development and production costs might be high as a result of marketing several different product variations. • Promotional costs might be high as different advertisements and promotions might be needed for different segments – marketing economies of scale may not be fully exploited. • Production and stock holding costs might be higher than for the option of just producing and stocking one undifferentiated product. • By focusing on one or two limited market segments there is a danger that excessive specialisation could lead to problems if consumers in those segments change their purchasing habits significantly.

Table 25.5 *Market segmentation – advantages and limitations*

POSITIONING

Before targeting a niche market, businesses often analyse consumers' perceptions of existing brands. This is called positioning the product by using a technique such as market mapping. The first stage is to identify the features of this type of product considered to be important to consumers – as established by market research. These key features might be price, quality of materials used, perceived image, level of comfort offered (hotels) and so on. They will be different for each product category. The example in Figure 25.2 uses the criteria of price and healthy image to 'map' the market for soft drinks. This analysis could be used in a number of ways:

The tourist market can be segmented in many ways to allow for differentiated marketing

- It identifies a potential gap in the market for a cheaper drink with a healthy image. This could be the segment that the business should aim for. Alternatively, the firm could play safe and position the new product in with others – less risky but likely to be less profitable too.
- Having identified the sector with the greatest 'niche' potential the marketing manager is then made aware of the key feature(s) of the product that should be promoted most heavily.
- Lastly, when this analysis is used to monitor the position of existing brands a firm can easily see if a repositioning of one of them is required. This could involve a new advertising campaign or restyled packaging rather than a newly launched product.

CORPORATE IMAGE

KEY TERM

corporate image consumer perception of the company behind a brand

In a competitive business climate many businesses actively work to create and communicate a positive image

ACTIVITY 25.7

'Understanding market segmentation key to repeat visits by tourists'

According to a study by Cathy Hsu of the School of Tourism at Hong Kong University, the key to boosting the number of tourists re-visiting the region is for companies to understand market segmentation. In a survey of 1300 tourists passing through Hong Kong international airport, Professor Hsu identified six distinct groups of tourists who, she claimed, needed to be treated differently by marketing activities.

The six groups were:

- leisure travellers 55 years or younger
- first-time mature travellers 55 years +
- repeat mature travellers
- business travellers with incomes over $50 000 per year
- business travellers with incomes under $50 000 per year
- travellers visiting friends or family in Hong Kong.

These groups needed a different marketing focus to encourage repeat visits. Young, single leisure travellers might be attracted by 'bring a friend' promotions. High-income business travellers could be more influenced by promotions about the wide range of leisure and shopping facilities in the region. Mature repeat travellers made up just 4.5% of the total sample, suggesting that this was a market segment that needed to be more fully developed. The segment that needed little additional marketing focus was made up of those visiting family and friends – they would be likely to visit Hong Kong again anyway.

Source: www.eturbonews.com

24 marks, 44 minutes

1 Why does successful market segmentation need to be supported by market research? Use this case study as an example in your answer. [6]

2 Explain **two** of the ways that this research has segmented the total tourist market to Hong Kong. [6]

3 Discuss the possible benefits and limitations to a Hong Kong travel company of targeting different segments of the tourist market with different marketing activities. [12]

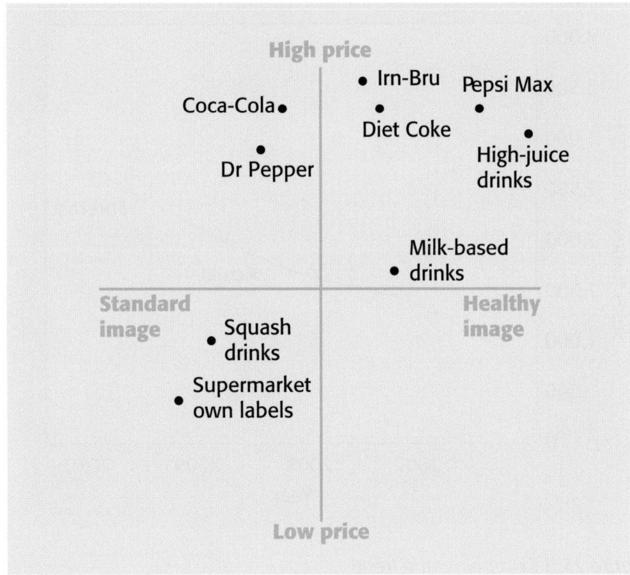

Figure 25.2 A market map for soft drinks

to their customers and other stakeholders. This helps to build a good reputation, has a positive impact on sales and makes the successful launch of new products easier to achieve. In *Building Your Company's Good Name* (1996), Davis Young recommends the following steps to achieving a positive corporate image:

- Focus on long-term reputation, not short-term profits.
- Insist on honesty in all business dealings.
- Uphold the stakeholders' right to information about the company and its activities.
- Develop good company policies, e.g. towards staff, rather than trying to control damage caused by bad company policies.

Young notes, 'A good corporate image can take years to build and only moments to destroy.' This saying was certainly true in the case of Toyota in 2010. The carefully crafted image of 'quality products' and 'customer comes first' was shattered by revelations about faulty, potentially dangerous cars being produced and sold in the USA and Europe even though, it has been alleged, the company knew about potential problems. Toyota initially responded slowly to these concerns and was then forced to take very expensive remedial action to millions of cars worldwide. Would this action be enough to save the company's image and reputation? Only time – and sales figures – will tell.

UNIQUE SELLING POINT/PROPOSITION (USP)

KEY TERM

unique selling point/proposition (USP) differentiating factor that makes a company's product unique, designed to motivate customers to buy

Unless a business can pinpoint what makes its product unique in a world of homogeneous competitors, its sales efforts will not be targeted effectively. Customers are often attracted towards goods or services that offer a distinctive image, service, feature or performance. Establishing a USP is about differentiating a company from its competitors. USPs can be based on any aspect of the marketing mix. For example:

- **Product.** Dyson's vacuum cleaners offer 'dual cyclone technology' that is unique (and patented) and the company has become the world number two manufacturer of vacuum cleaners in just 20 years.
- **Price.** 'Never knowingly undersold' is the classic advertising slogan for the John Lewis Partnership's department stores in the UK. The retailer checks and matches its high street competitors' prices regularly, both at national and local level. The company achieved 10% sales growth in the UK in 2009 despite the most severe economic recession for 60 years.
- **Place.** Dell became the first computer manufacturer to focus almost exclusively on internet sales. Keeping its costs down allowed it to offer competitive prices.
- **Promotion.** 'When it absolutely, positively has to be there overnight' (FedEx courier service) is one of the most famous promotional slogans of recent years. It helped to establish in customers' minds the unique quality of service that this company claimed to offer.

H HIGHER LEVEL

Sales forecasting

KEY TERM

sales forecasting predicting future sales levels and sales trends

POTENTIAL BENEFITS

If marketing managers were able to predict the future accurately, the risks of business operations would be much reduced. If a precise forecast of monthly sales over the next two years could be made, the benefits to the whole organisation would be immense:

- The production department would know how many units to produce and what quantity of materials to order and would hold the correct level of stocks.

- The marketing department would be aware of how many products to distribute and whether changes to the existing marketing mix were needed to increase sales.
- Human resources workforce plan would be more accurate, leading to the appropriate level of staffing.
- Finance could plan cash flows with much greater accuracy.

In reality, such precision in forecasting is impossible to achieve, because of the external factors that can influence sales performance. Consider the difficulties in forecasting, even for a short-term period, the sales of films on DVDs. Apart from changes in film tastes, new developments in recording, playback and downloading technology will impact on DVD sales; the growth of internet shopping, rather than buying from stores, and the general economic climate will also have a great effect on future sales levels. Despite these problems, most firms make sales forecasts in order to reduce to an acceptable minimum the unforeseen nature of future changes.

Market forecasts form an essential part of the market planning process and of the screening process before new products are launched on to the market. These forecasts will be based on market research data, gained from both primary and secondary sources. For existing products sales forecasts are commonly based on past sales data.

QUANTITATIVE SALES FORECASTING METHODS – TIME-SERIES ANALYSIS

This method of sales forecasting is based entirely on past sales data. Sales records are kept over time and, when they are presented in date order, they are referred to as a 'time series'.

Extrapolation

Extrapolation involves basing future predictions on past results. When actual results are plotted on a time-series graph, the line can be extended, or extrapolated, into the future along the trend of the past data – see Figure 25.3. This simple method assumes that sales patterns are stable and will remain so in the future. It is ineffective when this condition does not hold true.

Moving averages

This method is more complex than simple graphical extrapolation. It allows the identification of underlying factors that are expected to influence future sales. These are the trend, seasonal variations, cyclical variations and random variations. The moving-average method is used to analyse these in Table 25.7 on ice-cream sales. Once they have been identified, then short-term sales forecasts can be made.

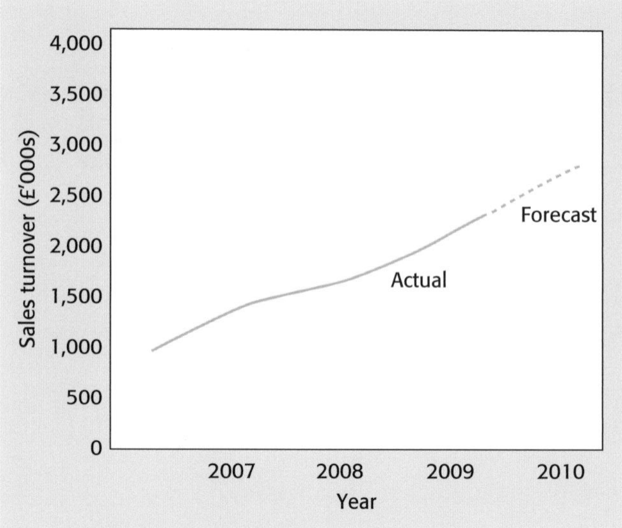

Figure 25.3 Extrapolating a trend

KEY TERMS

trend underlying movement of the data in a time series

seasonal variations regular and repeated variations that occur in sales data within a period of 12 months or less

cyclical variations variations in sales occurring over periods of time of much more than a year – they are related to the business cycle

random variations may occur at any time and will cause unusual and unpredictable sales figures, e.g. exceptionally poor weather, or negative public image following a high-profile product failure

Key stages of the moving-average method:

- The method involves calculating moving totals from a number of sales figures. Each total in column 4 of Table 25.7 is made up of four results. This is why the total is called a four-period moving total. A four-period moving total was used because the data clearly vary consistently over this period of time. For example, sales are always highest in quarter 3. If other data were used,

Quarter	Sales	Four-quarter total	Four-quarter average
1	20		
2	30		
3	50		27.5
4	10	110/4	

Table 25.6 Four-period moving total – but the four-quarter average is not yet centred

perhaps daily sales figures, then a seven-period total would have been used, because the regular variation in sales would have been over seven days. Monthly sales data may require the use of a 12-period moving total.

- If this four-quarter moving total was divided by 4 in order to calculate the average, the result would not lie alongside any one quarter. This would not make sense – to have a result which does not 'belong' to any one time period (see Table 25.6). The problem is overcome by 'centring' the average so that it lies alongside one actual quarter. This is done by adding two four-quarter moving totals together. This gives an eight-period moving total. This is divided by 8 to give the moving average.

The moving average is known as the trend of the data. The underlying movement of the data has been identified by averaging out the regular seasonal fluctuations.

- The difference between the actual sales and this trend must have been largely due to seasonal fluctuations. These can then be calculated as shown in Table 25.7.

seasonal variation (col. 7) = actual result (col. 3) – moving average (trend) (col. 6)

Make sure you obtain the correct plus or minus sign for your results. If the result is negative, it means that in that quarter sales are usually below the trend or average for seasonal reasons.

- The average seasonal variation smoothes out the actual seasonal variations. This is obtained by adding up all of the seasonal variations for each separate quarter and then dividing by the number of results. For example, quarter 3 seasonal variations are:

$$43.75 + 52.5 + 58.75 = \frac{155}{3} = 51.67$$

Any further variation in sales, not accounted for by the seasonal fluctuations in demand for ice cream, is caused either by cyclical factors or random factors. In the table shown, only random factors are assumed to exist. In quarter 4 2008, sales were lower than average due to seasonal variation but not by as much as the average seasonal variation for that period indicated. The difference of $6650 was caused by random factors – perhaps there had been production problems at a competitor's factory and this meant that sales did not fall as much as normal in quarter 4 in this year.

Forecasting using the moving-average method

The results from Table 25.7 can now be used for short-term forecasting. You will need to:

1. plot the trend (moving average) results on a time-series graph (see Figure 25.4)
2. extrapolate this into the future – short-term extrapolations are likely to be the most accurate
3. read off the forecast trend result from the graph for the period under review, e.g. quarter 2 in year 2011
4. adjust this by the average seasonal variation for quarter 2.

1 Year	2 Quarter	3 Sales revenue	4 Four-quarter moving total	5 Eight-quarter moving total	6 Quarterly moving average (trend)	7 Seasonal variation	8 Average seasonal variation	9 Random variation
2007	1	120						
	2	140						
	3	190			146.25	43.75	51.67	–7.92
	4	130	580		150.00	–20	–15.4	–4.6
2008	1	130	590	1170 ÷ 8	156.25	–26.25	–33.3	6.8
	2	160	610	1200	163.75	–3.75	–4.6	1.1
	3	220	640	1250	167.5	52.5	51.67	0.83
	4	160	670	1310	168.75	–8.75	–15.4	6.65
2009	1	130	670	1340	172.5	–42.5	–33.3	–9.2
	2	170	680	1350	176.25	–6.25	–4.6	–1.65
	3	240	700	1380	181.25	58.75	51.67	–7.08
	4	170	710	1410	187.5	–17.5	–15.4	–2.1
2010	1	160	740	1450	191.25	–31.25	–33.3	2.05
	2	190	760	1500	193.75	–3.75	–4.6	0.85
	3	250	770	1530				
	4	180	780	1550				

Table 25.7 *Moving averages for ice-cream sales ($000s)*

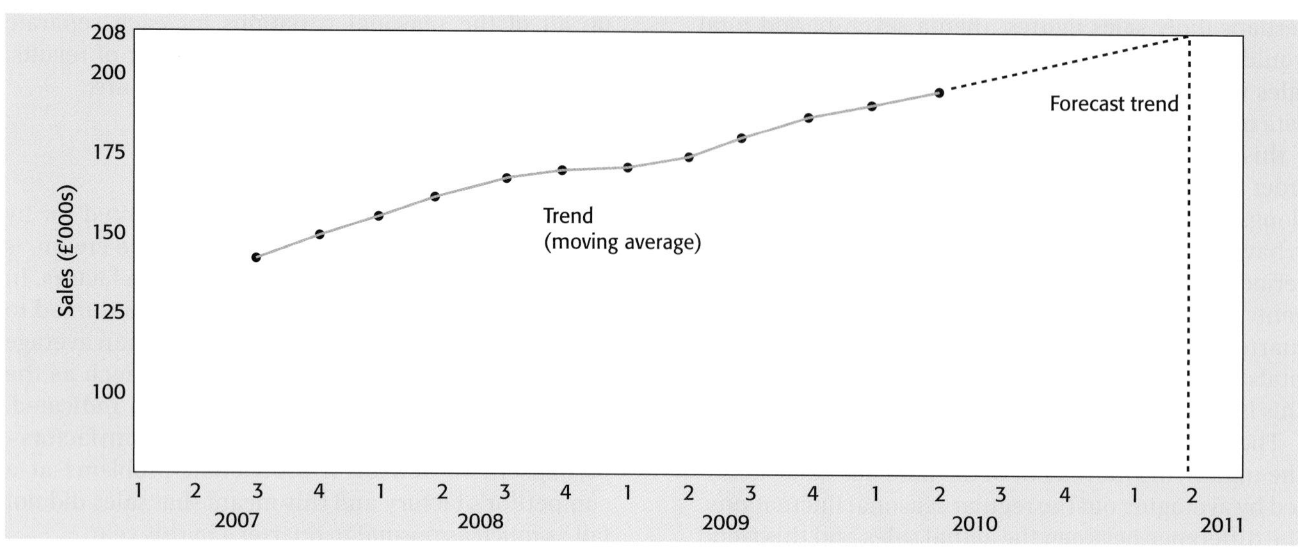

Figure 25.4 Forecasting future trend sales figures

Thus, for quarter 2 in the year 2011: the actual forecast will be the extrapolated trend forecast for this quarter, \$208 000, plus the average seasonal variation of –£4600 = £203 400.

See Table 25.8 for the advantages and disadvantages of the moving-average method.

Advantages	Disadvantages
• Useful for identifying and applying the seasonal variation to predictions. • Reasonably accurate for short-term forecasts in reasonably stable economic conditions. • Identifies the average seasonal variations for each time period and this can assist in planning for each quarter in future.	• Fairly complex calculation. • Forecasts further into the future become less accurate as the projections made are entirely based on past data. • Forecasting for the longer term may require the use of more qualitative methods that are less dependent on past results.

Table 25.8 Moving-average method – advantages and disadvantages

EXAM TIP

You should be prepared to discuss the limitations of sales forecasting techniques as well as the potential benefits of predicting future sales.

THEORY OF KNOWLEDGE

The table below lists some of the richest entrepreneurs in the world. To what extent is the successful marketing of products about the intuition of entrepreneurs?

Name	Business	Worth in \$billions	Industry
Bill Gates	Microsoft	40	Computer software
Carlos Slim	Telmex	35	Telecommunications
Larry Ellison	Oracle	23	Computer software
Ingvar Kamprad	IKEA	22	Retail
Karl Albrecht	Aldi	22	Retail
Mukesh Ambani	Reliance	20	Steel, petroleum
Amancio Ortega	Zara	18	Retail

H

OVER TO YOU

REVISION CHECKLIST

1. Outline the key features of a marketing mix of a product that you have recently purchased.
2. Why is 'people' one of the important marketing mix factors for consumer services?
3. Explain why some people consider direct advertising of toys to young children is unethical.
4. Explain **two** benefits of a marketing audit.
5. State **two** possible marketing objectives for the Starbucks Coffee Company in your country.
6. Differentiate between primary and secondary market research.
7. Differentiate between quota and random sampling.
8. Explain **two** ways in which a producer of TV programmes might use market segmentation.
9. What would the benefits be of using a targeted marketing strategy for a clothing retailer?
10. Explain the USP of any company of your choice.
11. (H) Use Porter's Five Forces model to assess competitive pressures in either food retailing or car retailing in your country
12. (H) Differentiate between the 'trend' and the 'seasonal variation' of time-series sales data.

REVISION ACTIVITY

Read the case study below and then answer the questions that follow.

Sodhi's sales forecast

The sales of Sodhi's convenience store were recorded over a four-year period. The owner of the store has started to undertake a short-term forecasting exercise to help plan future purchases and stocks of goods.

	Quarter	Sales ($000)
Year 1	1	18
	2	24
	3	35
	4	27
Year 2	1	19
	2	26
	3	38
	4	29
Year 3	1	23
	2	27
	3	40
	4	32
Year 4	1	25
	2	30
	3	42
	4	35

25 marks, 45 minutes

1. What is meant by:
   a. sales forecasting? [2]
   b. the moving-average method? [3]
2. Copy out the table above and add columns for: four-quarter moving total, eight-quarter moving total, quarterly moving average (trend), seasonal variation, average seasonal variation, random variation (assume no cyclical variation). Calculate values in these columns. [6]
3. Graph the actual sales data and quarterly moving average data and draw a line of extrapolation. [6]
4. Estimate sales for year 5 quarter 4. [2]
5. Discuss briefly how useful this forecast is likely to be for Sodhi. [6]

EXAM PRACTICE QUESTION

Read the case study below and then answer the questions that follow.

LE SPORTIF HEALTH AND SPORTS CLUB

Le Sportif is a health and sports club located in Paris. The club has performed well over the last two years but now faces competition from two clubs, Wellness and Glides, which have just opened. Wellness has been particularly successful and has attracted a number of customers from Le Sportif.

The management of Le Sportif conducted some extensive market research to find out more information about their customers. They used a series of focus groups to find out about customers' views on Le Sportif and a questionnaire to provide them with more precise data about the way customers used the club.

Le Sportif has responded positively to its market research by adopting the following strategies:

- introducing a family membership scheme
- introducing a range of family-based classes to encourage health and fitness
- opening a coffee shop.

The management of Le Sportif believe that this new customer-oriented approach, which targets health and fitness for the whole family, will give the club a unique selling point and will enable it to stand out from the competition.

25 marks, 45 minutes

1 Define the following terms:
   a market research
   b unique selling point. [4]

2 Explain the way focus groups could have been used to provide Le Sportif with market research information. [6]

(H) 3 Using Porter's Five Forces model, analyse **two** forces that might have affected Le Sportif. [6]

4 Evaluate the advantages and disadvantages of Le Sportif using market research to guide its new strategy of targeting the family market. [9]

26 Product

This chapter covers syllabus section 4.3

On completing this chapter you should be able to:

- classify products by line, range and mix
- describe the importance of new product design and development
- analyse the stages of a typical product life cycle and the relationship between this and the marketing mix, profit and cash flow
- understand product portfolio analysis and the application of the Boston Consulting Group matrix
- discuss the importance and role of branding
- (H) use the Boston matrix to develop future strategic direction
- (H) distinguish between different types of branding and analyse the role of branding in a global market.

SETTING THE SCENE

Global brands

According to the magazine *Business Week*, the best builders of brand image are the companies that have focused on developing simple, integrated messages consistent with the products they sell, in every market around the world and with every contact with consumers. The best brand builders are also very creative in getting their products' message across to consumers. Thirty years ago, several 45-second advertisements on the main TV channels was enough to get a brand recognised by most consumers. With the explosion in the number of TV channels and other forms of electronic media, this approach no longer works. Establishing and selling a brand these days has to be done through a variety of media: the web, live events, cellphones and handheld computers.

The link between brand messages and entertainment is proving increasingly popular. Apple launched a special iPod player in partnership with the band U2. The iPod had U2 on the front, the band's signatures on the back, the band starred in a TV ad and buyers got $50 off the download of 400 U2 songs. 'It's hard to tell where the brand message ends and where the entertainment begins,' says Ryan Barker, a brand consultant.

Source: www.businessweek.com

Points to think about:

- What do you understand by the idea of a product's brand?
- Why is establishing a distinctive global brand important for multinational companies?
- What methods would you use to try to build a brand image for a new computer games console?

Introduction

It is sometimes said that 'you can sell any product to consumers once, but to establish loyalty and good customer relationships, the product must be right'. If the product does not meet customer expectations, as discovered by market research, regarding:

- quality
- durability
- performance
- appearance…

then no matter how low the price or how expensive the advert for it costs, it will not sell successfully in the long term.

The term 'product' includes consumer and industrial goods and services. Goods have a physical existence, such as washing machines and chocolate bars. Services have no physical existence but satisfy consumer needs in other ways – hairdressing, car repairs, childminding and banking are examples of services. Industrial products such as mining equipment are purchased by businesses not final consumers.

KEY TERMS

product the end result of the production process sold on the market to satisfy a customer need

consumer durables manufactured products that can be re-used and are expected to have a reasonably long life, such as cars and washing machines

product line a set of related products sold by a business

product mix the variety of product lines that a business produces or a retailer stocks

product range all of the types of products made by a business

New product design and development

New product development (NPD) is crucial to the success of some businesses operating in markets with constant technological changes, such as computer games consoles. It is also important in the pharmaceuticals industry, where the opportunities to make huge profits from newly patented drugs are great, and in industrial markets, such as machine tools, where robots have revolutionised production methods. In contrast, in other markets, it is possible to sell the same product for many years or to adjust and adapt it slightly to meet changing tastes and to enter new segments, such as Pepsi Cola.

Financing NPD can be a major problem as the research and development costs often have to be paid years before any returns are earned from the sale of the innovative products.

THE NEW PRODUCT DEVELOPMENT PROCESS

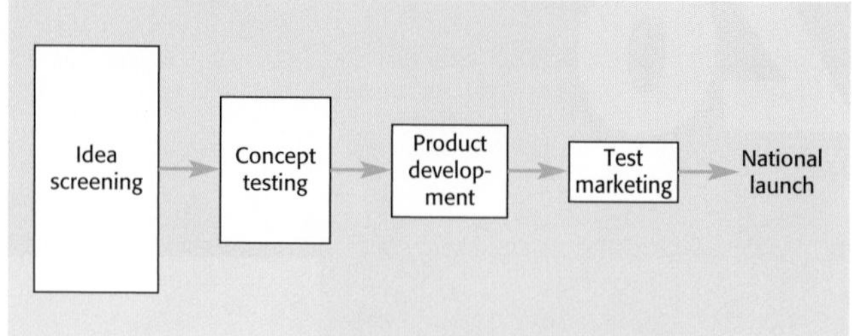

Figure 26.1 Not all new ideas are turned into successful products

There are seven stages in the NPD process:

1. Generating new ideas, e.g. market research, brainstorming, adapting existing products.
2. Idea screening – eliminate those ideas that have the least chance of being commercially successful.
3. Concept testing – establishing most likely consumers, possible cost of production, specific features that the product will have.
4. Business analysis – analysing likely impact of the new product on revenue, costs and profits.
5. Product testing – developing prototypes to assess performance and to obtain feedback.
6. Test marketing – launching the developed product in a small but representative section of the market to assess likely sales following a national launch.
7. Commercialisation – full-scale launch of the product with appropriate promotion and distribution.

A very small proportion of new ideas ever reach the commercialisation stage – the NPD process should reduce the risk of failure by eliminating unsuitable and unprofitable products before they reach the final stage.

Product life cycle

KEY TERM

product life cycle the pattern of sales recorded by a product from launch to withdrawal from the market

Knowing when to launch a new product or update an existing one can give a business a crucial advantage. Allowing existing models of cars or computers to 'soldier on' in the market when other firms are introducing attractive new or revamped ones is a classic business error that has led to many failures. An awareness of the product life cycle principle can assist greatly in dealing with this problem. The life cycle of a product records the sales of that product over time. There are several stages in this life cycle and these are shown in Figure 26.2.

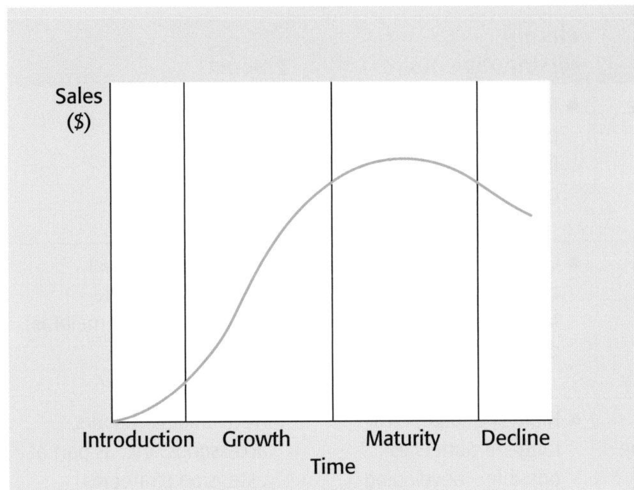

Figure 26.2 *Product life cycle – the length of each stage will vary from product to product*

Points to note on the first three stages:

- Introduction. This is when the product has just been launched after development and testing. Sales are often quite low to begin with and may increase only quite slowly – but there are exceptions, such as a newly launched DVD by a major rock star.
- Growth. If the product is effectively promoted and well received by the market, then sales should grow significantly. This stage cannot last for ever, although all firms wish that it would. Eventually, and this may take days, weeks or even years, sales growth will begin to slow and might stop altogether, which leads the product into the next stage. The reasons for declining growth include increasing competition, technological changes making the product less appealing, changes in consumer tastes and saturation of the market.
- Maturity or saturation. At this stage, sales fail to grow, but they do not decline significantly either. This stage can last for years, for example Coca-Cola. The saturation of consumer durables markets is caused by most consumers who want a certain product having already bought one. The best recent example is mobile phones. Although the world market has grown phenomenally in recent years, in 2009 sales growth ended altogether. This was put down to the vast number of consumers who already possessed a mobile. It is only when their own phone breaks down or is replaced by newer technology that a further spurt to sales growth will be received. This is why all phone companies are working so hard on the next generation of mobile phone – to make existing models obsolete.

EXTENSION STRATEGIES

KEY TERM

extension strategies marketing plans that extend the maturity stage of the product before a brand new one is needed

Such strategies include developing new markets for existing products, for example export markets, new uses for existing products and product relaunches involving new packaging and advertising (see Figure 26.3).

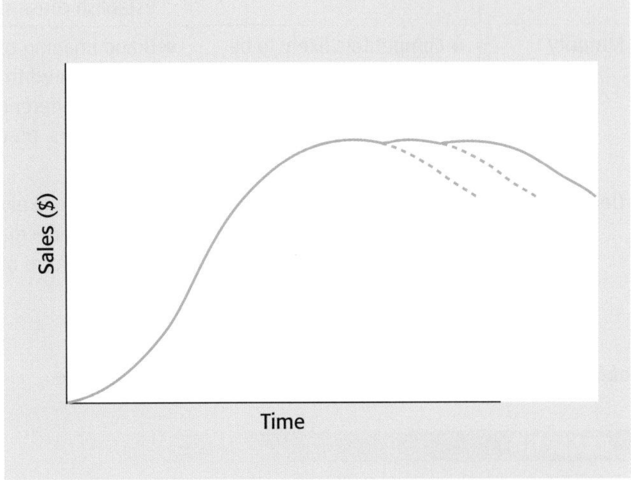

Figure 26.3 *Product life cycle – showing the effect of extension strategies*

During the 'decline' phase, sales will fall steadily. Either no extension strategy has been tried, or it has not worked or the product is so obsolescent that the only option is replacement. Newer competitors' products are the most likely cause of declining sales and profits – and when the product becomes unprofitable or when its replacement is ready for the market, it will be withdrawn.

USES OF THE PRODUCT LIFE CYCLE

The life-cycle concept has two main uses.

Assisting with the planning of marketing mix decisions

- When would you advise a firm to lower the price of its product – at the growth or at the decline stage?
- In which phase is advertising likely to be most important – during introduction or at maturity?
- When should variations be made to the product – during introduction or at maturity?

Table 26.1 explains how marketing mix decisions can be influenced by knowledge of the product life cycle.

Product life-cycle phase	Price	Promotion	Place (distribution outlets)	Product
Introduction	• May be high compared to competitors (skimming) or low (penetration).	• High levels of informative advertising to make consumers aware of the product's arrival on the market.	• Restricted outlets – possibly high-class outlets if a skimming strategy is adopted.	• Basic model.
Growth	• If successful, an initial penetration pricing strategy could now lead to rising prices.	• Consumers need to be convinced to make repeat purchases – brand identification will help to establish consumer loyalty.	• Growing numbers of outlets in areas indicated by strength of consumer demand.	• Planning of product improvements and developments to maintain consumer appeal.
Maturity	• Competitors likely to be entering market – there will be a need to keep prices at competitive levels	• Brand imaging continues – growing need to stress the positive differences with competitors' products.	• Highest geographical range of outlets as possible – developing new types of outlets where possible.	• New models, colours, accessories, etc. as part of extension strategies.
Decline	• Lower prices to sell off stock – or if the product has a small 'cult' following, prices could even rise.	• Advertising likely to be very limited – may just be used to inform of lower prices.	• Eliminate unprofitable outlets for the product.	• Prepare to replace with other products – slowly withdraw from certain markets.

Table 26.1 *The marketing mix and phases of the product life cycle*

EXAM TIP

When discussing the product life cycle it is important to remember that no two products are likely to have exactly the same pattern of sales growth/maturity and decline.

Identifying how cash flow might depend on the product life cycle

- Cash flow is vital to business survival and ignoring the link between cash flow and product life cycles could be very serious. Figure 26.4 shows this typical relationship.

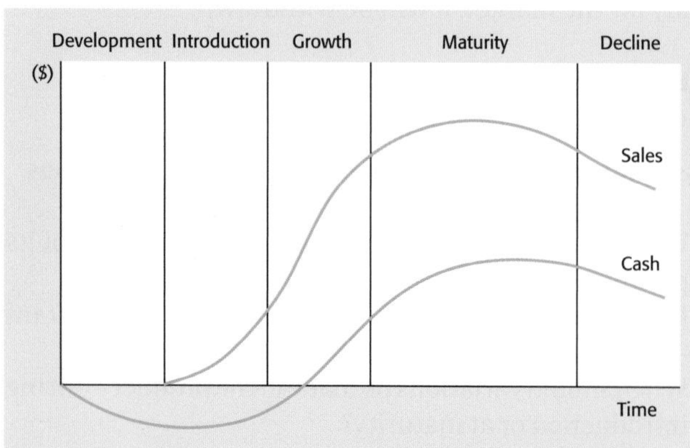

Figure 26.4 *The link between cash flow and product life cycle*

- Cash flow is negative during the development of the product as costs are high, but nothing has yet been produced or sold.
- At introduction, the development costs might have ended but heavy promotional expenses are likely to be incurred – and these could continue into the growth phase. In addition, there is likely to be much unused factory capacity at this stage which will place a further strain on costs. As sales increase, then cash flow should improve – precisely when will depend on the length of consumer credit being offered.
- The maturity phase is likely to see the most positive cash flows, because sales are high, promotional costs might be limited and spare factory capacity should be low.
- As the product passes into decline, so price reductions and falling sales are likely to combine to reduce cash flows. Clearly, if a business had too many of its products either at the decline or the introduction phase then the consequences for cash flow could be serious. Firms will benefit from a balanced portfolio of products, at different stages of their life cycles, so that cash from those entering maturity can be used to provide investment funds for developing eventual replacement products.

When do you think this photo was taken?

Boston Matrix – product portfolio analysis

This method of analysing the market standing of a firm's products and the firm's overall product portfolio was developed by the Boston Consulting Group (see Figure 26.5)

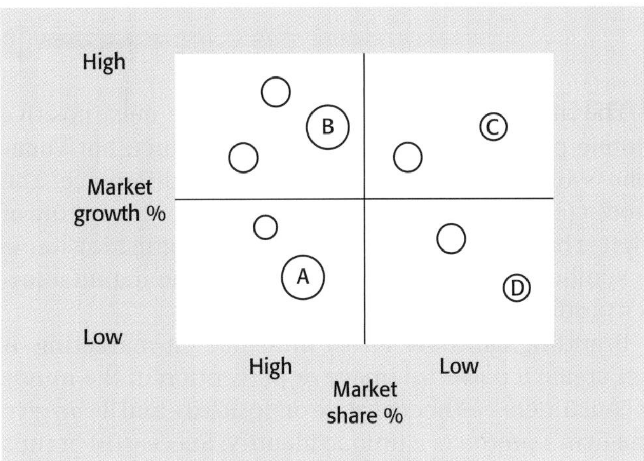

Figure 26.5 *The Boston Matrix*

KEY TERM

Boston Matrix a method of analysing the product portfolio of a business in terms of market share and market growth

It highlights the position of each of a firm's products when measured by market share and market growth. This allows not only an analysis of the existing product portfolio but also what future strategies the firm could take next. The size of each circle represents the total revenue earned by each product. The four sectors created by the matrix can be analysed in the following way.

Low market growth – high market share: product A 'Cash cow'

This is a well-established product in a mature market. Typically, this type of product creates a high positive cash flow and is profitable. Sales are high relative to the market and promotional costs are likely to be low, as a result of high consumer awareness. The cash from this product can be 'milked' and injected into some of the other products in the portfolio – hence, this product is often referred to as a 'Cash cow'. The business will want to maintain cash cows for as long as possible, especially if the high market share can be maintained with little additional promotional spending.

High market growth – high market share: product B 'Star'

This is clearly a successful product as it is performing well in an expanding market – because of this it is often called a 'Star'. The firm will be keen to maintain the market position of this product in what may be a fast-changing market – therefore, promotional costs will be high to help differentiate the product and reinforce its brand image. Despite these costs a star is likely to generate high amounts of income. If their status and market share can be maintained, they should become the cash cows of the future as the market matures and market growth slows.

High market growth – low market share: product C 'Problem child'

The 'Problem child' consumes resources but it generates little return – at least in the short term. If it is a newly launched product, it is going to need heavy promotional costs to help become established – this finance could come from the cash cow. The future of the product may be uncertain, so quick decisions may need to be taken if sales do not improve, such as revised design, relaunch or even withdrawal from the market. It should, however, have potential as it is selling in a market sector that is growing fast and businesses need to analyse carefully which problem children are worth developing and investing in and which are the best ones to drop and stop selling.

Low market growth – low market share: product D 'Dog'

'Dogs' seem to offer little to the business either in terms of existing sales and cash flow or future prospects, because the market is not growing. They may need to be replaced shortly, or the firm could decide to withdraw from this market sector altogether and position itself into faster-growing sectors.

BOSTON MATRIX AND STRATEGIC ANALYSIS

By identifying the position of all of the firm's products a full analysis of the portfolio is possible. This should help focus on which products need support or which need corrective action. This action could include the following strategies:

- Building – supporting problem child products with additional advertising or further distribution outlets. The finance for this could be obtained from the established cash cow products.
- Holding – continuing support for star products so that they can maintain their good market position. Work may be needed to 'freshen' the product in the eyes of the consumers so that high sales growth can be sustained.
- Milking – taking the positive cash flow from established products and investing in other products in the portfolio.
- Divesting – identifying the worst performing dogs and stopping the production and supply of these. This strategic decision should not be taken lightly as it will involve other issues, such as the impact on the workforce and whether the spare capacity freed up by stopping production can be used profitably for another product.

These strategies can only be undertaken if the business has a balanced portfolio of products. If there are too many dogs or problem children, then the overall shortage of cash may not allow the firm to take appropriate action.

EVALUATION OF THE BOSTON MATRIX

This analytical tool has relevance when:

- analysing the performance and current position of existing products
- planning action to be taken with existing products
- planning the introduction of new products.

No technique can guarantee business success – this will depend on the accuracy of the analysis by the marketing managers and the skills they possess in employing appropriate marketing strategies.

The Boston Matrix helps to establish the current situation in which the firm's products find themselves – but it is of little use in 'predicting' future success or failure.

- On its own it cannot tell a manager what will happen next with any product. Detailed and continuous market research will help – but at all times, decision-makers must be conscious of the potentially dramatic effects of competitors' decisions, technological changes and the fluctuating economic environment.
- It is only a planning tool and it has been criticised as simplifying a complex set of factors determining product success.
- The assumption is made that higher rates of profit are directly related to high market shares – this is not necessarily the case if sales are being gained by reducing prices and profit margins.

ACTIVITY 26.1

Applying the Boston Matrix

Undertake detailed research into the product portfolio of one well-known business in your country that sells a range of different products. For example, this might be a chocolate manufacturer, soft drinks producer, car manufacturer and so on. Try to discover the market share of the different products sold and the rate of growth of the market segment the products are sold in.

24 marks, 35 minutes

1 Analyse the firm's product portfolio using the Boston Matrix. **[12]**

2 Evaluate **two** strategies that the business could adopt for any **one** of its products. **[12]**

H

Branding

Mobile phones are an example of a product, but Vodafone is an example of a brand. What is the difference? The product is the general term used to describe the nature of what is being sold. The brand is the distinguishing name or symbol that is used to differentiate one manufacturer's products from another.

Branding can have a real influence on marketing. It can create a powerful image or perception in the minds of consumers – either negative or positive – and it can give one firm's products a unique identity. Successful brands can often charge premium prices as consumers are loyal to the product and the image that it generates. This helps to make the price elasticity of demand for the brand low (see Chapter 27).

However, attempting to establish a new brand is often expensive. Increasing brand awareness and brand loyalty are primary goals of promotional activity in the early months or years of a product's launch. It can cost millions of dollars to attempt to create an effective brand image – and success cannot be guaranteed. If a brand image receives bad publicity – such as Nestlé's marketing of powdered baby milk in developing countries – then the image of all products in the 'corporate brand' will be damaged.

KEY TERMS

brand an identifying symbol, name, image or trademark that distinguishes a product from its competitors

brand awareness extent to which a brand is recognised by potential customers and is correctly associated with a particular product – can be expressed as a percentage of the target market

brand development measures the infiltration of a product's sales, usually per thousand population. If 100 people in 1000 buy a product, it has a brand development of 10

brand loyalty the faithfulness of consumers to a particular brand as shown by their repeat purchases irrespective of the marketing pressure from competing brands

TYPES OF BRANDING

Table 26.2 looks at the different types of branding, their benefits and limitations.

KEY TERMS

family branding a marketing strategy that involves selling several related products under one brand name (also known as umbrella branding)

product branding each individual product in a portfolio is given its own unique identity and brand image (also known as individual branding)

company or corporate branding the company name is applied to products and this becomes the brand name

own-label branding retailers create their own brand name and identity for a range of products

manufacturers' brands producers establish the brand image of a product or a family of products, often under the company's name

Type of branding	Examples	Benefits	Limitations
Family branding	• Mars Bar was the original product – now joined by Mars ice cream, Mars energy drink and Mars muffins.	• Marketing economies of scale when promoting the brand. • Makes new product launches easier.	• Poor quality of one product under the brand may damage them all.
Individual branding	• Toyota created the Lexus brand of luxury cars. • Procter & Gamble sells Head and Shoulders, Pampers, Duracell and Braun with separate brand identities.	• Each product is perceived as its own unique and separate brand – unconnected in consumers' minds with the parent company.	• Loses the positive image of a strong company brand.
Company or corporate branding	• Virgin – airlines, rail services, mobile phone provider – all marketed under single brand name. • Disney products.	• Similar points to family branding – but now applies to all products produced under the company's brand name.	• As for individual branding.
Own-label branding	• Walmart has numerous own brands, e.g. Sam's Choice (premium food products), Faded Glory (Americana clothing), Life (menswear), Metro 7 (womenswear).	• Often cheaper than name-brand products. • Each own-brand label appeals to different consumer groups and tastes. • Often little spent on advertising – in-store promotions used instead.	• Consumers often perceive products to have a lower quality image.
Manufacturers' brands	• Levi's • Coca-Cola • Mercedes-Benz	• Successful branding by manufacturers establishes a unique 'personality' for the product which many consumers want to be associated with – and will often pay premium prices to purchase.	• The brand has to be constantly promoted and defended.

Table 26.2 Different types of branding – limitations and benefits

THE ROLE OF BRANDING IN A GLOBAL MARKET

Branding is now an international process, not confined to one country or region. Establishing a successful brand image across national borders opens up the potential for increased sales and economies of scale – especially in terms of globally marketing products with the same range of promotions under the same name. It is increasingly important that businesses which have a multinational presence build up a consistent and recognisable brand image that is transferable between countries. UBS Bank has achieved this. Created by a series of mergers and takeovers that gave it many separate brand names and products, the bank lacked recognition in markets outside Switzerland. It merged many products under the UBS name and re-launched itself as a global bank serving local needs but with the prestige and image that come from being the sixth largest bank in the world.

Globalised branding and marketing can have substantial benefits (see Chapter 29 'International marketing and e-commerce'), but there are limitations too if the international brand and image fail to link in with localised culture and customer tastes.

THEORY OF KNOWLEDGE

Microsoft 'is king of UK brands'

Microsoft takes back the number one position in a survey of UK brands

US computer giant Microsoft has won back its crown as the number one consumer brand in the UK. A list of about 1400 brands was considered by a panel of experts, with more than 2000 UK consumers taking part in a vote. At number two was Rolex, while Google slipped two places to third. Lego and Coca-Cola were new to the top ten.

Prepare a presentation to give to the rest of the class. What role do emotion, logic and experience play in making leading brands so attractive to consumers?

OVER TO YOU

REVISION CHECKLIST

1 Use an example to explain the difference between product line and product range.
2 Outline the stages of new product development.
3 Identify different products which could be classified into the stages of a typical product life cycle (PLC).
4 Explain **one** use of the PLC to a car manufacturer.
(H) 5 Explain **one** use of the Boston Matrix to a multi-product firm of your choice.
(H) 6 Differentiate, with examples, between brands and products.

REVISION ACTIVITY 1

Read the case study below and then answer the questions that follow.

Body Shop held back by product errors

Mistakes with new products and a failure to control stock properly caused underlying profits to drop by a fifth last year at Body Shop International. 'I take responsibility for the performance of the company,' said Patrick Gournay, chief executive of the retailer best known for its green and ethical stance. 'We have been going through a huge change process, and some of the things we did have not gone so well. We tried to do too many things, too fast. For instance, we changed the packaging on a new haircare range and discontinued some existing lines. The customers didn't like it very much,' he admitted.

Improvements are under way, Mr Gournay said, including launching fewer products and making sure they were closer to the brand's ethical traditions that customers identified with. He also wants to keep better control of costs, so that new products do not sell at lower margins than the goods they were replacing. He expected profit this year to be higher than last time, but warned that more intense seasonal sales fluctuations would depress first-half results below last year's £6.8 million.

12 marks, 23 minutes

1 What evidence is there that Body Shop did not undertake sufficient market research before making 'product' changes? [4]

2 Why might it be important for the future sales success and profitability of Body Shop for it to keep 'closer to the brand's traditions' and a 'better control on costs'? [8]

REVISION ACTIVITY 2

Read the case study below and then answer the questions that follow.

Chocolate wars lead to melt down

Jupiter Confectionery Ltd manufactures four brands of chocolate bar. It is an old-established business and relies heavily on the traditional qualities of rich-tasting chocolate and prestige packaging to sell its products. It rarely introduces new brands – its last launch was three years ago, but the other three brands are each over ten years old. The products are:

Orion – the newest brand, designed to appeal to teenagers with 'star wars' wrappers and a competitive price. Sales are increasing at a steady rate.

Venus – the original product of the company, a rich, dark chocolate bar with a black and gold wrapper. The same size as most bars, but slightly more expensive – to suit its image. Sales and cash flow from this product have helped to finance the launch of the other three.

Sun – the firm's only attempt at boxes of chocolates. There was intense competition in this high-value and high-profit margin market sector. Sales figures are given below.

Year	Sales of Sun boxes of chocolates (units)
2007	120 000
2008	125 000
2009	115 000
2010	123 000
2011	124 000

Mercury – this was a very sweet soft-centred bar that has been very popular with older consumers. Sales have declined in recent years because of imports of healthier 'low-fat' chocolates. Old stocks are being returned by retailers.

The marketing manager is concerned both about sales of Mercury bars and the sales record of Sun boxes. Should they both be dropped or could sales be revived? The manager decided to analyse the current sales of the range of products by using product life cycles.

39 marks, 70 minutes

1 What is meant by the term 'product life cycle'? [3]

2 What stage of its product life cycle does the Sun box of chocolates appear to be in? Explain your answer. [4]

3 Outline the options available to the marketing manager for the Sun box of chocolates product. [4]

4 A decision has been made to try to extend the life of this product. Evaluate **three** extension strategies that the business could use in your country for this product. [12]

5 Outline **two** problems this business could face as a consequence of launching very few new products. [6]

6 Evaluate the factors that the business should consider before deciding to withdraw the Mercury bar from the market. [10]

EXAM PRACTICE QUESTION

Read the case study below and then answer the questions that follow.

TOSHIBA DROPS HD DVD AFTER PROMISING START

The battle for the high-definition (HD) DVD formats between Sony Blu-Ray and Toshiba HD DVD has finally been won by Sony. Despite a promising early sales performance, Toshiba has admitted defeat and withdrawn its rival product from the market many years before it was expected to experience sales decline. This defeat is costly. Toshiba has spent millions of dollars developing the product and promoting it, so cash flows from it have been negative. Marketing analysts see this as a classic situation where a 'problem child product fails to grow up'. The unexpected acceptance by all of the major international film-producing companies, such as Disney and MGM, of the Sony Blu-Ray format and their refusal to release films on Toshiba's rival system was the final factor behind the company's decision to withdraw it from the market. Toshiba's management felt the strength of the Blu-Ray brand had made it very difficult for competing technologies in this highly competitive market.

25 marks, 45 minutes

1 Define the following terms:
   (H) a problem child product
   b brand. [4]

2 Explain the new product development stages a product like Toshiba DVD would go through before it is launched. [6]

3 Analyse **two** possible reasons, other than the acceptance of Blu-Ray by major film-producing companies, why Blu-Ray succeeded and HD DVD did not. [6]

(H) 4 Evaluate the usefulness of models like the Boston Matrix to firms like Toshiba. [9]

27 Price

This chapter covers syllabus section 4.4

On completing this chapter you should be able to:

- analyse different pricing strategies: cost-based, competition-based, market-based (includes H)
- analyse the appropriateness of different pricing strategies (includes H)
- H evaluate the impact of changes in the conditions of supply and demand
- H calculate and interpret price, income, cross and advertising elasticity of demand
- H explain the relationship between elasticity and the product life cycle
- H analyse the relationship between price elasticity and sales revenue.

SETTING THE SCENE

Xbox price cut brings console war to the USA

Microsoft has effectively declared war on Sony in the US, cutting the price of its top-of-the-range Xbox 360 Elite console by $100 to $299 – exactly the same price as Sony's PlayStation 3 Slim, launched in September. In the same month, Microsoft will start to offer two versions of the Xbox 360, the Elite and the Pro retailing at $249. The new PlayStation 3 has the same memory – 130GB – as the Elite and can play games in high definition.

The USA is the world's largest market for video games and consoles with annual software sales alone amounting to $6 billion. In recent weeks, the Xbox has been outselling the PS3 by almost two to one, and Microsoft is determined not to give up market share to Sony when the PS3 Slim is launched.

Source: http://technology.timesonline.co.uk

Points to think about:

- Explain why Microsoft reduced the price of its Xbox console at this time.
- Why do you think all of the prices quoted above are just below a 'round figure', e.g. $299 and not $300?
- Since the first games console was launched, retail prices have fallen steadily. Why is the price trend for this product falling?

27 Price

Introduction

Price is the amount paid by consumers for a product. Price is a vital component of the marketing mix as it impacts on the consumer demand for the product.

The pricing level will also:

- determine the degree of value added by the business to bought-in components
- influence the revenue and profit made by a business due to the impact on demand
- reflect the marketing objectives of the business and help establish the psychological image and identity of a product.

Get the pricing decision wrong and much hard work in market research and product development can be put at risk.

Factors determining the price decision

There are a number of factors that will determine the pricing decision for a product:

1. costs of production
2. competitive conditions in the market
3. competitors' prices
4. marketing objectives
5. price elasticity of demand
6. whether it is a new or an existing product.

The significance of these is discussed in this chapter.

Pricing strategies

COST-BASED PRICING

The central idea is that firms will assess their costs of producing or supplying each unit, and then add an amount on top of the calculated cost. There are a number of different methods of cost-based pricing that may be adopted.

Cost-plus pricing

KEY TERM

cost-plus pricing adding a fixed mark-up for profit to the unit price of a product

This method is often used by retailers, who take the price that they pay the producer or wholesaler for a product, and then just add a percentage mark-up. The size of the mark-up usually depends upon a combination of the strength of demand for the product, the number of competitors and the age and stage of life of the product. Sometimes it also depends on traditional practice in the industry.

Example 1:
Cost of bought-in materials: $40
50% mark-up on cost = $20
Selling price: $60

 **HIGHER LEVEL**

Marginal-cost pricing

KEY TERM

marginal-cost price basing the price on the extra cost of making one additional unit of output

If an airline has an empty seat on a particular flight, to gain additional (marginal) customers it could offer a price lower than the average cost as long as it at least covered the marginal cost of carrying an extra passenger. As long as this 'special promotional price' did not become universally known – in which case all customers would demand it – this pricing method could increase sales and market share. Not all customers can be offered special deals that just cover the marginal cost – total revenue must at least cover total costs for a profit to be made.

Contribution-cost pricing

KEY TERM

contribution-cost pricing setting prices based on the variable costs of making a product in order to make a contribution towards fixed costs and profit

A product makes a contribution to fixed costs and profit if selling price is greater than variable costs. The business calculates a unit variable cost for the product and then adds an extra amount – this becomes the contribution to fixed costs. If enough units are sold, the total contribution will be enough to cover the fixed costs and to return a profit. This is widely used by:

- multi-product businesses that would find it almost impossible to allocate or divide fixed costs accurately between different products
- firms that want to attract new orders from potentially important customers
- businesses that want to sell off stock to make way for new inventories.

Example 2: A product has a variable cost of $2 per unit. The business sets a price of $3, perhaps to remain competitive, which includes a contribution to fixed costs of $1. If the firm sells 40 000 units in the year, then a total contribution of $40 000 is made. If the business allocates fixed costs of $40 000 to this product, then it will start to make a profit after 40 000 units have been sold. If the firm sells 60 000 units, then the fixed costs will be covered and there will be $20 000 profit made.

A product that makes a positive contribution to fixed costs should, generally, continue to be produced so long as there is spare capacity in the firm. There are many firms that have excess capacity and use contribution pricing to attract extra business which will absorb the excess capacity. Examples are train companies, for which there is substantial excess capacity except in the morning and evening rush hours. It is also widely used in making one-off decisions – such as a price for a special order and the assumption is that no additional fixed costs will be incurred.

Example 3: A business makes a single product design with a variable cost per unit of $4. The annual fixed costs or overheads are $80 000. The firm decides on a contribution of $2 per unit sold. Therefore, the selling price is $6. If the business sells 50 000 units in one year, the total contribution to fixed costs becomes 50 000 × $2 = $100 000. A profit of $20 000 has been made. This firm would have to sell at least 40 000 units per year in order to break even.

H

Full-cost (or absorption-cost) pricing

KEY TERM

full-cost/absorption-cost pricing setting a price by calculating a unit cost for the product (allocated fixed and variable costs) and then adding a fixed profit mark-up

This is similar in principle to cost-plus pricing. It is often used by firms making a single type of product. For multi-product firms, full-cost pricing involves the allocation of fixed costs to different products and the calculation of the 'full cost' for each one.

Example 4: A business produces DVDs. One of its products is a range of industrial training DVDs. The annual overheads or fixed costs allocated to this product are $10 000. The variable cost of producing each training DVD is $5. The business is currently producing 5000 units per year. The total costs of this product each year are:

$$\$10\,000 + (5000 \times \$5) = \$35\,000$$

The average or unit cost of

$$\text{making each DVD} = \frac{\$35\,000}{5000} = \$7$$

The business will have to charge at least $7 each in order to break even on each unit. If the firm now adds a 300% profit mark-up, then the total selling price becomes $28.

Competition-based pricing

An example of competition-based pricing is price leadership.

KEY TERMS

competition-based pricing a firm will base its price upon the price set by its competitors

price leadership one dominant firm in a market sets a price and other firms simply charge a price based upon that set by the market leader

This often occurs in oligopolistic markets – dominated by a few firms. In petrol retailing, for example, all prices charged tend to move in line with each other – following the market leader. Is this a result of illegal collusion between the companies? This is very difficult to prove in practice. It might just be because one major player in the market, often with lowest average cost, leads a price change and the others feel obliged to follow.

H HIGHER LEVEL

Predatory or destroyer pricing

KEY TERM

predatory pricing deliberately undercutting competitors' prices in order to try to force them out of the market

This is an illegal pricing strategy in the European Union as it favours the strong, established companies unfairly compared to new entrants. In practice, it is very difficult to prove – businesses often claim that they are just adopting a loss-leader strategy – see below.

H

Going-rate pricing

KEY TERM

going-rate pricing the price charged is based upon a study of the conditions that prevail in a certain market and the prices charged by major competitors

The internet has made going-rate pricing more common because of the greater transparency that now exists as result of this global information base. Consumers can quickly compare prices of, for example, DVDs or computers, and purchase from the cheapest supplier. More firms are therefore being forced to lower their prices to the 'going rate', especially if they cannot add value to it in the form of special customer service which might have justified higher prices.

See Table 27.1 for a summary of pricing strategies.

Methods	Advantages	Disadvantages
Full-cost pricing (also applies to cost-plus)	• Price set will cover all costs of production. • Easy to calculate for single-product firms where there is no doubt about fixed cost allocation. • Suitable for firms that are 'price makers' due to market dominance.	• Not necessarily accurate for firms with several products where there is doubt over the allocation of fixed costs. • Does not take market/competitive conditions into account. • Tends to be inflexible, e.g. there might be opportunities to increase price even higher. • If sales fall, average fixed and average total costs rise – this could lead to the price being raised using this method.
Contribution-cost pricing	• All variable costs will be covered by the price – and a contribution made to fixed costs. • Suitable for firms producing several products – fixed costs do not have to be allocated. • Flexible – price can be adapted to suit market conditions or to accept special orders.	• Fixed costs may not be covered. • If prices vary too much – due to the flexibility advantage – then regular customers might be annoyed.
Competition-based and going-rate pricing	• Almost essential for firms with little market power – price takers. • Flexible to market and competitive conditions.	• Price set may not cover all of the costs of production. • May have to vary price frequently due to changing market and competitive conditions.
(H) Price discrimination (one method of market-based pricing)	• Uses price elasticity knowledge to charge different prices in order to increase total revenue.	• Administrative costs of having different pricing levels. • Customers may switch to lower priced market. • Consumers paying higher prices may object and look for alternatives.

Table 27.1 *Summary of main pricing methods*

MARKET-BASED PRICING STRATEGIES

These are normally split into two different approaches depending on the marketing objectives of the business.

Penetration pricing

KEY TERM

penetration pricing setting a relatively low price often supported by strong promotion in order to achieve a high volume of sales

Firms tend to adopt penetration pricing because they are attempting to use mass marketing and gain a large market share. If the product gains a large market share, then the price could slowly be increased.

Market skimming

KEY TERM

market skimming setting a high price for a new product when a firm has a unique or highly differentiated product with low price elasticity of demand

This aims to maximise short-run profits, before competitors enter the market with a similar product, and to project an exclusive image for the product. If rivals do launch similar products, it may be necessary for the price to be reduced over a period of time. An example of this is pharmaceutical firms, who are often given a legal monopoly for a certain number of years for new drugs. They are able to charge high prices in order to recoup their considerable investments in research and to make high profits. It is not uncommon for them to lower their prices in the last year of their legal monopoly in order to hold their market share when other companies enter. This is a typical example of market-skimming price strategy – see Figure 27.1.

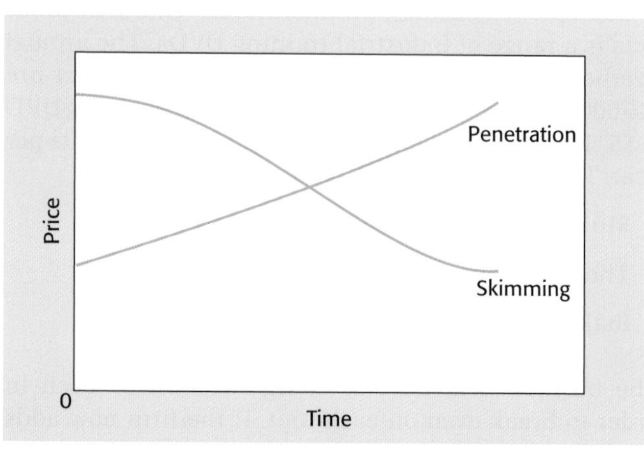

Figure 27.1 *Market-skimming and penetration pricing strategies*

Price discrimination

This takes place in markets where sub-groups of consumer exist and it is possible to charge different consumer groups different prices for the same product. An example of this would be airline operators who charge many different rates for the same journey. Firms can price discriminate if there are different groups of consumers with different elasticities of demand (see page 288). Also the firm must avoid resale between the groups and it must not cost too much to keep the groups of consumers separate. Other examples of price discrimination include selling train and bus tickets more cheaply to children or the elderly and setting different prices for products in different export markets.

Loss leaders

KEY TERM

loss leader product sold at a very low price to encourage consumers to buy other products

Loss leaders are widely used by supermarkets. Selling milk or bread at very low prices – perhaps below cost price – will encourage consumers into the stores to buy other goods on which the supermarket makes a higher profit margin. Is this fair on smaller retailers of milk and bread who cannot buy in supplies as cheaply as the large supermarkets? Other examples include computer printers sold for $40 – but the replacement ink cartridges can cost $30 each.

Psychological pricing

KEY TERM

psychological pricing setting prices that take account of customers' perception of value of the product

This has two aspects. First, it is very common for manufacturers and retailers to set prices just below key price levels in order to make the price appear much lower than it is. Therefore, $999 is used instead of $1001, and $1.99 not $2.01. In addition, psychological pricing also refers to the use of market research to avoid setting prices that consumers consider to be inappropriate for the style and quality of the product. A very low price for cosmetics or perfume, even though the costs of production may not be high, will not create the status and exclusive image that the firm is trying to portray. Potential consumers may be put off by the fact that too many people can now afford the product and the quality may not be as high as they originally believed. Similarly, prices can be so high that they exceed consumer perceptions of the quality and image of the product, and sales will be damaged as a result.

Promotional pricing

KEY TERM

promotional pricing special low prices to gain market share or sell off excess stock – includes 'buy one get one free' (see Chapter 28, pages 296 and 298)

A very widely used pricing strategy, it tends to operate for limited periods only to boost sales at times of low demand or to support the opening of a new store.

ACTIVITY 27.1

Read the case study below and then answer the questions that follow.

Car prices to rise in China?

Although Volkswagen has denied the rumour of 'general price hikes in April' for its cars in China, business analysts are predicting substantial car price rises. Due to rising costs of production – steel and other raw materials and higher labour costs – the cost of making each car in China increased on average by $400 in 2009. Can manufacturers resist these cost pressures? By how much are they prepared to cut their profit margins to stay competitive?

However, the fierce competition in China's car market has deterred many manufacturers from putting up prices. In recent years, due to increased numbers of cars being made in China and more manufacturers exporting to China, competitive pressures have put car prices on a downward trend, but that could change now that costs are rising so fast.

To avoid consumer resistance to price increases, manufacturers are increasing their profit margins in other ways. Dealers are promising quick delivery of cars to customers if they order expensive accessories and luxury items – such as leather seats. The profit margin on these decorative accessories can be as high as 30–40%, which helps to make up for very low margins on the cars themselves. So, indirect price increases could be the solution to the very small profit margins on selling basic car models.

Source: ChinaBizIntel.com (adapted)

16 marks, 28 minutes

1 Explain why increasing costs usually lead manufacturers to raise prices to consumers. [4]

2 Why, in this case, are car manufacturers reluctant to raise prices? [4]

3 Analyse how car manufacturers such as BMW or Mercedes might still sell cars profitably in a competitive market. [8]

H

ACTIVITY 27.2

Read the case study below and then answer the questions that follow.

Does the price fit?

Hartwood Hats manufactures caps for sportswear companies. The caps cost $3 each for materials and labour – the only variable costs. Last year, a total of 400 000 caps were produced and sold to two big sports firms. The fixed costs of the business amount to $200 000 per year. The marketing manager has to decide on pricing levels for the coming year and is uncertain whether to use full-cost or contribution pricing. Last year a price of $6 was set. The firm was left with spare capacity of around 100 000 caps.

15 marks, 25 minutes

1 What does contribution mean and what was the contribution per cap last year? [4]

2 What price would be charged if full-cost pricing was used and 100% mark-up added to the unit cost? [3]

3 Refer to your answer to question 3. Advise the firm on what factors it should consider before fixing the price at this level. [4]

4 If there were a 50% increase in variable costs and the contribution was lowered to $2, what profit would be made if sales remained unchanged? [4]

ACTIVITY 27.3

Read the case studies below and then answer the questions that follow.

Prices rise – but for different reasons

Case 1 Florida's theme parks increase prices

Universal Orlando is raising its one-day, one-park adult ticket prices from $63 to $67 just days after Disney World also raised its prices. A Universal spokesman refused to comment on whether the price rise was in response to Disney's announcement. Disney has raised its ticket prices twice this year. The latest increase takes an adult ticket to $67 – Universal has set exactly the same price.

Case 2 Carib Cement price adjustment

Caribbean Cement Company Limited has announced that from July the price of cement products would be adjusted by an average of 15%. The company blamed significant increases in input costs, such as electricity and oil prices. A spokesperson said, 'The price rises were inevitable as when costs rise, our profits will decline unless prices are increased too.' The company claims that its prices are still among the lowest in the region.

Case 3 Growing demand allows ethanol producers to increase prices

Growing demand in the USA for the corn-based fuel, ethanol, has boosted prices for this environmentally friendly alternative to petrol. The supply of ethanol is limited due to no spare capacity in the industry, but 33 new plants are being planned for the USA. Currently, ethanol fuel is now no cheaper than ordinary petrol.

18 marks, 23 minutes

1 Identify the different pricing methods used in case 1 and case 2. [2]

2 In case 1, explain **two** potential benefits to Universal of the company *not* increasing its prices following the decision by Disney World to increase its entry fee. [6]

3 Under what circumstances might you recommend to the managing director of Carib Cement that the company should *not* increase its prices, despite higher costs. Explain your answer. [6]

4 Explain what might happen to the price of ethanol in the USA when the 33 new plants start producing it. [4]

H HIGHER LEVEL

Supply and demand

In a free market, the market or equilibrium price is determined by supply and demand. The prices of most of the world's commodities, such as agricultural goods, oil, copper, lead and so on, are determined by the forces of supply and demand. This applies to foreign currency exchange rates – have you ever noticed how frequently these change? Supply means the quantity that producers are willing to sell at the existing market price. If supply *increases* for a product, such as cocoa, then the world price is likely to *fall*. Factors that determine supply and could cause an increase in the supply of cocoa include:

- good harvest conditions
- more growers entering the market
- government subsidies to growers
- release of unsold stocks on to the market.

Demand means the quantity that customers are willing and able to buy at the existing market price. An *increase* in demand for cocoa is likely to *increase* the world price for it. Factors that could increase demand for cocoa include:

- increasing consumer incomes
- more advertising for chocolate
- increased prices of non-chocolate-based confectionery
- rising population.

PRICE ELASTICITY OF DEMAND (PED)

The quantity demanded for most products increases as the price of them falls. This can be shown on a demand curve – look at Figures 27.2 and 27.3. Notice that D_2 has a steeper gradient than D_1. What impact does the slope or gradient of the curves have on the demand levels for these two products when prices are changed? You will notice that, when the price of both products is increased by the same amount, the reduction in demand is greater for product B than it is for product A. This could be very important information for the marketing manager because the total revenue (total revenue = price × quantity) for product A has actually increased, but for B it has fallen, as can be seen by the size of the shaded areas.

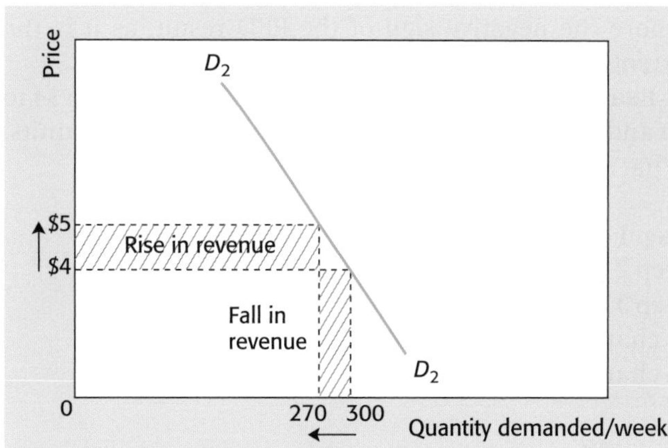

Figure 27.2 Demand curve for product A

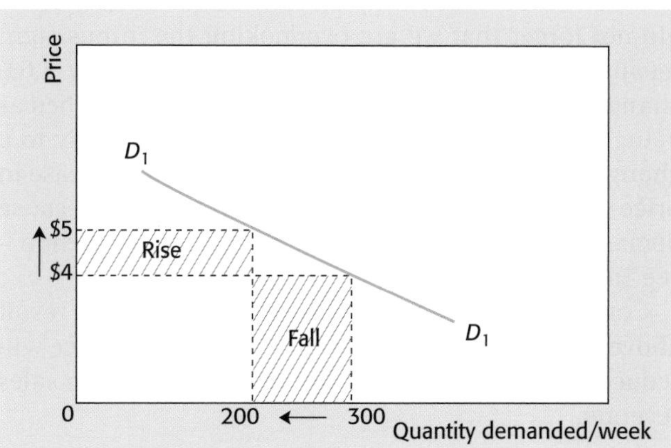

Figure 27.3 Demand curve for product B

This relationship between price changes and the size of the resulting change in demand is known as price elasticity of demand.

KEY TERM

price elasticity of demand measures the responsiveness of demand following a change in price

This concept can be demonstrated on demand curves as shown above – product A's demand is less elastic or less responsive to a price change than product B. This idea can also be measured mathematically. The formula for price elasticity of demand (PED) is:

$$\frac{\text{percentage change in quantity demanded}}{\text{percentage change in price}}$$

The value of PED is normally negative because a fall in price (–ve) usually results in a rise in demand (+ve). This is called an inverse relationship. It is quite common to ignore the negative sign of the PED result, as it is the extent of the change that is important.

Example: In Figure 27.2, the price increased from $4 to $5 and demand fell from 300 units per week to 270 units. What is the PED?

Step 1 Calculate the percentage change in price.
Step 2 Calculate the percentage change in demand.
Step 3 Use the PED formula:
% change in demand = 10
% change in price = 25

$$\text{PED} = \frac{10}{25} = 0.4$$

It is now important to explain this result. A PED of 0.4 (do not forget that we are overlooking the minus sign) means that demand changes by 0.4% for every 1.0% change in price. As this is less than one, it is described as being inelastic. Consumers do not respond greatly to a change in the price in this product so that an increase in price will raise sales revenue and a fall in price, because demand will change little, will reduce sales revenue – see Table 27.2.

Conversely, when demand is price elastic (PED result above 1, ignoring the minus sign) then a rise in price will reduce sales revenue and a fall in price will raise sales revenue.

ACTIVITY 27.4

6 marks, 10 minutes

1 Using the information in Figure 27.3, calculate the PED following the rise in price of product B. [2]

2 Comment on the likely impact on sales revenue as a result of this price increase. [4]

Value of PED	Classification	Explanation and impact on sales revenue
Between 0 and 1	Inelastic demand	The percentage change in demand is less than the percentage change in price. If a firm faces this elasticity of demand, it can raise the price, not lose much demand and increase sales revenue. However, this cannot keep happening. As the price continues to rise, demand will become more elastic.
Unitary	Unit elasticity	The percentage change in demand is equal and opposite to the percentage change in price, so any price change will lead to an equal change in demand. Total sales revenue will remain constant.
Between 1 and infinity (∞)	Elastic demand	The percentage change in demand is greater than the percentage change in price. If a firm faces this elasticity of demand, then it can lower the price, pick up a lot more demand and increase sales revenue.

Table 27.2 *Price elasticity of demand and its effects on sales revenue (minus sign not shown)*

Factors that determine price elasticity of demand

- How necessary the product is.
- The number of similar competing products or brands.
- The level of consumer loyalty to the brand.
- The price of the product as a proportion of consumers' incomes.

ACTIVITY 27.5

Read the case study below and then answer the questions that follow.

The *Daily Times*

The *Daily Times* newspaper editor is concerned about falling circulation (sales). He believes that newspaper readers are mainly influenced by price when making their decisions over which papers to buy. He decided to cut the price of the paper from $1.50 to $1.20. In the following week, circulation increased by 150 000 copies to 1 650 000. After four weeks, however, sales had fallen back to their original level. The owner was confused about the possible reasons for this and wondered whether he should cut the price again to $1.

25 marks, 45 minutes

1 From the information above, calculate the PED in the first week after the price reduction. [4]

2 Comment on your result in terms of the apparent price elasticity of this product. [2]

3 Calculate the newspaper's daily sales revenue before and after the price cut. Comment on your results. [5]

4 Explain **two** possible reasons why demand fell back to the original level some weeks after the price reduction. [6]

5 Discuss the action the newspaper's owner should now take to increase sales. [8]

ACTIVITY 27.6

A firm sells three products. The price elasticity of demand is estimated to be:

A −3, B −0.5, C −1

12 marks, 21 minutes

1 Explain what these results mean. [6]
2 Explain what the effect on (a) sales and (b) sales revenue will be for each product if all prices rise by 10%. [6]

INCOME ELASTICITY OF DEMAND (YED)

KEY TERM

income elasticity measures the responsiveness of demand for a product following a change in consumers' incomes

Income elasticity of demand is calculated by the following formula:

$$\text{Income elasticity} = \frac{\%\text{ change in demand}}{\%\text{ change in income}}$$

- Normal products such as DVDs and airline travel will have positive income elasticity of demand. It is positive because if incomes rise, the demand for the product is likely to increase.
- Necessity goods are likely to have low income elasticity of demand – a 10% increase in consumers' incomes is unlikely to have much impact on the demand for salt.
- Luxury goods are likely to have a high income elasticity – the demand for Ferraris tends to increase at a faster rate than consumers' incomes during an economic boom.
- Inferior goods have negative income elasticity. As they have a preferred competing product, the demand for inferior goods falls as income rises. The demand for bus and rail travel has fallen greatly in the USA as consumers, with higher incomes to spend, have preferred private car use or travel by air.

CROSS ELASTICITY OF DEMAND (XED)

KEY TERM

cross elasticity measures the responsiveness of demand for a product following the change in the price of another product

$$\text{Cross-elasticity} = \frac{\%\text{ change in demand for product X}}{\%\text{ change in price of product Y}}$$

If two goods are close substitutes, such as Xbox and PlayStation, then a fall in the price of Xbox is likely to lead to a reduction in the price of PlayStations. The cross elasticity is positive.

If two goods are often bought together, as they are complements such as Apple iPhones and iPhone applications, then an increase in the price of the phone is likely to lead to a reduction in the demand for applications. The cross elasticity will be negative.

ADVERTISING ELASTICITY OF DEMAND (AED)

KEY TERM

advertising elasticity measures the responsiveness of demand for a product following a change in the advertising spending on it

$$\text{Advertising elasticity} = \frac{\%\text{ change in demand for product}}{\%\text{ change in advertising spend on product}}$$

For many products, especially consumer goods, advertising elasticity will be high – demand is responsive to more advertising. However, this is not always the case if:

- rival firms are spending even more on advertising
- the campaign is expensive but poorly received by consumers
- other elements of the marketing mix are not working well – perhaps they are not integrated with the promotional campaign and consumers are getting mixed messages about the product
- industrial product sales are less responsive to advertising – product quality, after-sales service and delivery dates may be more significant.

Elasticity and the product life cycle

Table 27.3 explains the relationships between elasticity and the product life cycle.

EXAM TIP

When discussing the importance of these measures of elasticity it is important to make clear that nearly all elasticity results are estimates and depend very much on all other factors affecting demand remaining unchanged.

Stage of the product life cycle	Application of elasticity
Launch and growth	• PED likely to be low – consumers may be prepared to pay high prices. • AED likely to be high – informative advertising could lead to considerable consumer interest. • XED depends on number and closeness of substitutes – a unique new design will have very low XED as price changes of other goods will have little impact on demand for this unique product. • YED depends on whether the product is launched at a prestige niche market (high YED) or low-image mass market (low YED).
Saturation/ maturity	• PED might be increasing as new rivals come into the market and appear more attractive – business may have to lower prices. • AED likely to be low – most consumers will now be aware of the product. • XED – more competition and if prices of rival products are lowered, XED likely to be high and positive. • YED depends on nature of product.
Decline	• PED – prices may be lowered at this stage but PED might be low if consumers would really prefer a newer product. Time for an extension strategy? • AED – low unless advertising is used as part of a product re-launch extension strategy. • XED – high and positive as rivals' substitute products increase in number. • YED – the product may now become an 'inferior' good and YED could be negative.

***Table 27.3** Applying elasticity to a product life cycle*

ACTIVITY 27.7

'Levi claims Tesco cut-price jeans bad for brand image'

The maker of Levi's jeans has asked the European Court of Justice to prevent Tesco and Costco selling their jeans at knock-down prices. The manufacturer fears that its brand image and reputation will be damaged if its jeans are sold in supermarkets. Judges are being asked to decide if Tesco has infringed Levi's trademark rights by importing and selling branded jeans from outside Europe without consent.

The jeans come from the United States, Canada and Mexico. Levi stopped supplying Mexican wholesalers when it discovered that its jeans were being sold for export. Several years ago, Levi started legal action against Tesco. The retailer argued that it was entitled to buy jeans from abroad and sell them freely. Alan Christie, Levi's vice-president of public affairs, said that Tesco had undermined Levi's ability to control its own brand. He said: 'Tesco is trying to use our investment in our brand to build its own reputation, and it is doing so illegitimately. For a company that makes as much money as Tesco does, that is simply unacceptable.' Christie denied that Tesco was providing a service to consumers by making branded products available at a cheaper price. 'We have retail criteria that describe the conditions under which we want our products to be sold. Tesco does not meet those criteria because it does not specialise in retailing clothing,' he said. 'People want to experience a premium brand like Levi's in the right environment.'

Source: Daily Telegraph, *17 January 2001 (adapted)*

12 marks, 21 minutes

Do you think Levi's is right to try to limit the sale of its clothing products at 'knock-down' prices? Justify your answer. **[12]**

THEORY OF KNOWLEDGE

Major supermarkets like Tesco and Asda say that low prices are good for consumers and therefore good for society. Others argue that low prices are bad for producers who supply businesses, lead to over-consumption and have a negative effect on the environment.

In groups, discuss to what extent supermarkets selling goods at very low prices is good for society.

OVER TO YOU

REVISION CHECKLIST

1 State **two** reasons why the pricing decision is such an important one.
2 Why should pricing decisions not be taken in isolation to other marketing mix decisions?
3 Define full-cost/absorption pricing.
4 Differentiate between skimming pricing strategies and penetration pricing strategies.
(H) 5 State the formula for price elasticity of demand.
(H) 6 A manager is reviewing the pricing levels of two products and, from past data, the PED for product X is –0.5 and for product Y –1.6. In which case would you advise the manager to consider increasing price and in which case would a price reduction seem to be more appropriate? Explain your answer with diagrams or calculations.
(H) 7 Explain one situation in which contribution-cost pricing would seem to be more appropriate than full-cost pricing.
(H) 8 What do you understand by 'psychological pricing'?
(H) 9 Under what circumstances would it seem to be relevant to use a loss leader strategy?
(H) 10 How could variations in the price of a product be used to extend its life cycle?
(H) 11 Using your knowledge of price elasticity of demand, explain why many businesses use a policy of price discrimination.
(H) 12 Would consumers benefit from a policy of predatory pricing? Explain your answer.

REVISION ACTIVITY

Read the case study below and then answer the questions that follow.

Pricing decision for new computer game

The 'Time Traveller' computer game has just been developed by Access Games Inc. The life cycle of new computer games tends to be very short due to the pace of change in the industry. Should the company adopt a skimming price strategy for the launch of this new game? Alternatively, is it more important to carve out a substantial market share to begin with, by using penetration pricing, and then develop improved versions to maintain consumer interest? The decision has to be taken quickly – the promotional material is being developed – and there would only be the one chance to get the price right. The following data are available:

- annual fixed costs $400 000
- variable costs per unit $4
- expected annual output level 50 000
- competitors' prices varied from $10 to $30 per game (although most were at least 12 months old).

25 marks, 45 minutes

1 If the company uses full-cost pricing using a mark-up of 50% on total unit costs, calculate the price to be charged for 'Time Traveller'. [4]

2 Recommend whether an even higher price than this should be charged in order to adopt a skimming strategy for this new product. Justify your recommendation. [6]

(H) 3 The latest market research suggests that 40 000 units might be sold each year at a price of $26 but that 50 000 units could be sold at a price of $20. Calculate the price elasticity of demand if this research is assumed to be accurate. Comment on your result. [7]

(H) 4 Evaluate the impact that knowledge of the game's life cycle might have on the price charged for it after launch. [8]

EXAM PRACTICE QUESTION

Read the case study below and then answer the questions that follow.

DELL TO CONTINUE PRICE CUTS AS PC SALES SLOW DOWN

'It's only a price war if you are losing money and losing market share.' Dell Computers, one of the world's largest computer makers, promised to continue its price-cutting offensive (some industry insiders described this as a destroyer or predatory pricing). This is bad news for other, smaller, computer manufacturers. The company pledged further cuts in the price of laptop and desktop PCs, storage units and computer servers to increase its share of the slowing US PC market. It said its low stock levels enabled it to pass on price falls in microchips faster than rivals in the industry; recently, there have been profits warnings from Gateway, Apple and Hewlett-Packard. Dell has dismayed some analysts by reducing profit margins through discounting its prices. But Michael Dell, chairman and chief executive, said the move was intended to undercut high-margin rivals, such as EMC and Sun Microsystems. 'You have not seen the last of our price-cutting,' Mr Dell said yesterday. 'It's only a price war if you are losing money and losing market share. We are gaining market share and increasing sales revenue.'

Source: Carlos Grande, Financial Times, *31.1.2001*

25 marks, 45 minutes

1 Define the terms:

(H) a destroyer or predatory pricing

b sales revenue. [4]

2 Explain the impact a reduction in the price of computers might have on the demand for computer software. [4]

(H) 3 The demand for Dell computers is thought to be price elastic.

a Explain what this statement means. [2]

b Analyse **one** reason why the demand for Dell computers might be price elastic. [6]

c Discuss the advantages and disadvantages to Dell of reducing the price of its computers to increase market share. [9]

28 Promotion and place (distribution)

This chapter covers syllabus sections 4.5 and 4.6

On completing this chapter you should be able to:

- identify differences between sales promotion and advertising, above-the-line and below-the-line promotion
- analyse different promotional tools and discuss their effectiveness
- prepare an appropriate promotional mix
- discuss different distribution channels and assess their appropriateness in different circumstances
- (H) evaluate the effectiveness of different distribution channels
- (H) examine how organisations can increase the efficiency of the supply chain.

SETTING THE SCENE

Nikon Coolpix promotion exceeds targets

The global digital camera market is saturated with many well-recognised brands. Nikon's Coolpix camera had to be promoted in exciting new ways to become the number one choice for retailers to stock and for consumers to buy. Three objectives of Nikon's promotional campaign were:

- encourage consumers to visit camera retailers to try out Coolpix
- give incentives to shop staff to demonstrate and recommend this camera
- meet or exceed sales targets based on a 10% increase from last year.

Promotions focused on a target group of consumers: digital-camera users, of which 58% were men concentrated in the 35–44 age group, 81% married with children and with household incomes greater than $70000 a year. The three key features of the promotional campaign were:

- 500000 leaflets enclosing a photo memory card were posted to target group consumers.
- People receiving the card were invited to a camera retailer to test it in a Nikon Coolpix camera – if the LCD screen showed a 'prize image', the consumer could claim the prize, such as a holiday to Australia.
- Retail shop staff were motivated to sell the cameras by winning the same prize as consumers.

Sales increased by 30% and consumer recognition of the Coolpix brand increased even after the campaign ended. The budget of $2 million for the prizes was not exceeded and the campaign increased sales by much more than this figure anyway.

Source: Institute of Sales Promotion

Points to think about:

- Explain the importance of aiming a promotional campaign at a clearly defined target audience.
- Why was it important to have both clear objectives and a budget limit for this campaign?
- Nikon sells most of its cameras through traditional retailers. Would there be any benefits for Nikon opening its own chain of shops?

28 Promotion and place (distribution)

Introduction

Promotion is about communicating with actual or potential customers. Effective promotion not only increases awareness of products, but can create images and product 'personalities' that consumers can identify with. Advertising is only one form of promotion and other techniques include direct selling and sales promotion offers. The combination of all forms of promotion used by a business for any product is known as the 'promotion mix'. The amount firms spend on promotion – the promotion budget – is often a key decision, but successful communication is not just about the total amount spent. It is also about how the budget is allocated between the competing forms of promotion available.

KEY TERM

promotion the use of advertising, sales promotion, personal selling, direct mail, trade fairs, sponsorship and public relations to inform consumers and persuade consumers to buy

Promotional objectives

Promotional objectives should aim to:

- increase sales by raising consumer awareness of a new product
- remind consumers of an existing product and its distinctive qualities
- encourage increased purchases by existing consumers or attract new consumers
- demonstrate the superior specification or qualities of a product compared to those of competitors – often used when the product has been updated or adapted in some way
- create or reinforce the brand image or 'personality' of the product
- correct misleading reports about the product or the business and reassure consumers after a 'scare' or an accident involving the product
- develop or adapt the public image of the business – rather than the product
- encourage retailers to stock and actively promote products to the final consumer.

EXAM TIP

When writing about promotion of a product try to consider the marketing objectives of the business. Is the promotion being used likely to help achieve these objectives?

Above-the-line promotion

KEY TERM

above-the-line promotion a form of promotion that is undertaken by a business by paying for communication with consumers, e.g. advertising

Advertising

Advertising is communicating information about a product or business through the media, such as radio, TV and newspapers. These advertisements are usually directed towards the appropriate target market by selecting the right media – but it is possible that many people who are unlikely to purchase the product may see the advertisements too. Successful advertising campaigns have led to substantial increases in consumer awareness and sales, and this effect can last for a considerable length of time if brand loyalty can be established. Advertisements are often classified into two types, but in practice this distinction is often quite blurred.

1. Informative advertising – these are adverts that give information to potential purchasers of a product, rather than just trying to create a brand image. This information could include price, technical specifications or main features and places where the product can be purchased. This style of advertising could be particularly effective when promoting a new product that consumers are unlikely to be aware of or when communicating a substantial change in price, design or specification.
2. Persuasive advertising – this involves trying to create a distinct image or brand identity for the product. It may not contain any details at all about materials or ingredients used, prices or places to buy it. This form of advertising is very common, especially in those markets where there might be little actual difference between products and where advertisers are trying to create a perceived difference in the minds of consumers.

In reality, there is little difference between these two styles of advertising: 'The more informative your advertising, the more persuasive it will be' (David Ogilvy, *Confessions of an Advertising Man*, New York: Ballantine Books, 1971).

Advertising decisions – which media to use?

The bigger the firm and the greater the advertising budget, the more 'media' choice there is. Limited resources will restrict options to the cheaper media. However, the most expensive forms of communication are not always the most effective. Choosing the right media means considering a number of factors:

1. Cost – TV and radio advertising can be very expensive per minute of advert, but the actual cost will depend on the time of day that the advertisements are to be transmitted and the size of the potential audience. National newspapers will be more expensive than local ones. Other media include posters, magazines of general and specific interest and cinema advertising. Marketing managers compare the cost of these media and assess whether they fall within the marketing budget. Buying media time or space is not the only cost. The advert still has to be written and produced and the use of celebrities in TV, radio or cinema adverts can soon increase the total cost greatly.
2. The profile of the target audience in terms of age, income levels, interests and so on – this should reflect as closely as possible the target consumer profile of the market being aimed for. For instance, there is likely to be little point in advertising a new children's toy after 10 p.m. at night. Using a mass-market, low-priced daily newspaper to advertise a new range of exclusive clothing would be aiming at the wrong target.
3. The type of product and the message to be communicated – written forms of communication are likely to be most effective for giving detailed information about a product that needs to be referred to more than once by the potential consumer. However, if an image-creating advert is planned, perhaps for a new range of clothes or sports equipment, then a dynamic and colourful TV advert is possibly more effective.

An example of informative advertising

An example of persuasive advertising

ACTIVITY 28.1

Read the case study below and then answer the questions that follow.

The Cadbury gorilla advertisement

This is one of the most famous and effective advertisement campaigns of recent years. The aims of the campaign were to:

- improve the public's perception of Cadbury and the Dairy Milk chocolate brand after a number of public relations disasters such as the 2006 food poisoning scare at one of the company's factories
- increase annual sales of Dairy Milk, which seemed to have reached market saturation point.

The TV advert featured an actor in a gorilla costume playing a well-known drum solo from the Phil Collins' hit record 'In the air tonight'. The 'gorilla' has a look of concentration and passion on its face – at times closing its eyes and looking skywards. The performance lasts for 90 seconds until fading to a computer-generated shot of a Dairy Milk bar over the slogan 'A glass and a half full of joy' (Cadbury have always claimed that each bar contains a glass and a half of fresh milk).

The production of the advertisement and the TV time slots were budgeted to cost \$12 million. One TV advert was timed during the commercial break of the 2007 Rugby World Cup and this cost \$1.4 million alone. The campaign was very successful. The advert was uploaded on to the video-sharing website YouTube and was viewed over 500 000 times in the first week alone. Market research reports suggested that the public's view of Cadbury and Dairy Milk had improved and sales rose by 9% in 2007 – higher than the original target.

23 marks, 40 minutes

1 Was this an example of an informative or a persuasive advertisement? Explain your answer? [5]

2 Can the expenditure of \$12 million on advertising a chocolate bar ever be justified? Explain your answer. [12]

3 Explain why it is important for advertisers to check and monitor the effectiveness of a promotional campaign. [6]

4 The other aspects of the marketing mix – the link between the other parts of the mix and the media chosen for adverts could be crucial to success. The use of exclusive and glossy women's magazines to advertise a new 'budget' range of ready-cooked meals could be counterproductive.

5 The law and other constraints – a widespread ban on tobacco advertising in Formula One grand prix racing has forced many sponsors to use other media for presenting their cigarette advertising. In some countries, there are restrictions on the use of TV advertising aimed at children, claiming that it exercises too much influence over young minds.

Advertising expenditure and the trade cycle

The evidence from the advertising industry is that in most countries firms tend to spend more when the economy is booming than when it is in recession.

Below-the-line promotion

KEY TERMS

below-the-line promotion promotion that is not a directly paid-for means of communication but based on short-term incentives to purchase, e.g. sales promotion techniques

sales promotion incentives such as special offers or special deals directed at consumers or retailers to achieve short-term sales increases and repeat purchases by consumers

Sales promotion

Sales promotion generally aims to achieve short-term increases in sales. There is a huge range of incentives and activities that come under the umbrella term 'sales promotion' (see Table 28.1 on page 298). They include:

- price deals – a temporary reduction in price, such as 10% reduction for one week only
- loyalty reward programmes – consumers collect points, airmiles or credits for purchases and redeem them for rewards
- money-off coupons – redeemed when the consumer buys the product
- point-of-sale displays in shops, e.g. 'aisle interrupter' – a sign that juts into the supermarket aisle from a shelf; and 'dump bin' – a free-standing bin centrally placed full of products 'dumped' inside to attract attention
- 'buy one get one free' (BOGOF)
- games and competitions, e.g. on cereal packets
- public relations
- sponsorship.

ACTIVITY 28.2

Read the case study below and then answer the questions that follow.

Ad spending in the USA to rise by 4.8% in 2008 – but could fall in 2009

The weaker US economy will see slow growth in advertising spending in 2008. If it weren't for the Olympics boosting TV adverts, the total amount spent by industry on advertising could fall. Internet display ad spending is forecast to rise by 15% and, for the first time in US history, will exceed radio advertising in importance. Advertising spending in newspapers and trade magazines is expected to fall by 1%.

In 2009, the picture is altogether gloomier. A further decline in the US economy and no Olympic Games could mean that business saves on costs by cutting advertising spending. Is this how firms should react to an economic downturn?

Source: www.forbes.com/advertising (adapted)

18 marks, 23 minutes

1 Why do you think internet advertising is now more important in the USA than radio advertising? [4]

2 Explain why the Olympic Games led to a boost in advertising spending by companies, especially on TV. [4]

3 Is it a good idea for a business to cut costs during a recession by reducing advertising expenditure? Give reasons for your answer. [10]

Sales promotion can either be directed at:

- the final consumer to encourage purchase (pull strategy) or
- the distribution channel, e.g. the retailer, to encourage stocking and display of the product (push strategy).

The possible impact of sales promotions are shown in Table 28.1 on page 298.

The promotion mix

KEY TERM

promotion mix the combination of promotional techniques that a firm uses to communicate the benefits of its products to customers

The promotional mix is part of the wider marketing mix. A successful promotional mix uses a balance of advertising, public relations, sales promotion, direct marketing and personal selling in a planned and structured way. A single 'tool' rarely works well in isolation. There are eight stages in deciding on a promotional mix:

1 Decide on the image of the product.
2 Develop a profile of the target market.
3 Decide on the messages to communicate.
4 Set an appropriate budget.
5 Decide how the messages should be communicated.
6 Establish how the success of the promotional mix is to be assessed.
7 Undertake the promotional plan and the mix elements of it.
8 Measure its success.

EXAM TIP

Don't confuse advertising and sales promotion – they are both forms of promotion, but they are not the same.

PROMOTION AND THE PRODUCT LIFE CYCLE

Table 28.2 (on page 300) summarises some promotion mix options at different stages of a product's life cycle.

'Place' decisions in the marketing mix

'Place' decisions are concerned with how products should pass from manufacturer to the final customer. Several different channels of distribution are available for firms to use.

KEY TERM

channel of distribution this refers to the chain of intermediaries a product passes through from producer to final consumer

Method explained	Possible limitations
Price promotions – these are temporary reductions in price, also known as price discounting. They are aimed at encouraging existing customers to buy more and attracting new customers to buy the product.	• Increased sales gained from price reductions will affect gross profit on each item sold. • There might be a negative impact on the brand's reputation from the discounted price.
Money-off coupons – these are a more versatile and better-focused way of offering a price discount. Coupons can appear on the back of receipts, in newspaper adverts or on an existing product pack.	• They may simply encourage consumers to buy what they would have bought anyway. • Retailers may be surprised by the increase in demand and not hold enough stocks, leading to consumer disappointment. • Proportion of consumers using the coupon might be low if the reduction it offers is small.
Customer loyalty schemes, such as airmiles or customer loyalty cards – focused on encouraging repeat purchases and discouraging consumers from shopping with competitors. Information stored through loyalty cards provides a great deal of information about consumers' buying preferences.	• The discount offered by such schemes cuts the gross profit on each purchase. • There are administration costs to inform consumers of loyalty points earned and these may outweigh the benefits from increased consumer loyalty. • Most consumers now have many loyalty cards from different retailers, so their 'loyalty' impact is reduced.
Money refunds – these are offered when the receipt is returned to the manufacturer.	• These involve the consumer filling in and posting off a form and this might be a disincentive. • Delay before a refund is received may act as a disincentive.
BOGOF – 'buy one get one free' – this encourages multiple purchases, which reduces demand for competitors' products too.	• There could be substantial reduction in gross profit margin. • Consumers may consider that if this scheme is able to operate, are they paying a 'normal' price that is too high? • Is the scheme being used to sell off stock that cannot be sold at normal prices – impact on reputation? • Current sales might increase, but future sales could fall as consumers have stocked up on the product.
Point-of-sale displays – maximum impact on consumer behaviour is achieved by attractive, informative and well-positioned displays in stores.	• The best display points are usually offered to the market leaders – products with high market share. • New products may struggle for best positions in stores – unless big discounts are offered to retailers.
Public relations – the use of free publicity provided by newspapers, TV and other media to communicate with and achieve understanding of the public.	• This is not easily controllable as some 'free publicity' might not be positive towards the company or its products, e.g. newspaper reviews.
Sponsorship – payment by a company to team owners or event organisers so that the company name becomes associated with the event.	• The success of the sponsorship is largely out of the company's control. If the team loses every match or the event is a failure, this might reflect badly on the sponsor.

Table 28.1 *Common methods of sales promotion*

ACTIVITY 28.3

Does promotion work?

A survey of over 200 supermarket shoppers in Hong Kong found that some sales promotions worked better than others. Price discounts and buy-one-get-one free offers were felt by consumers to be the most effective promotional tool for encouraging consumers to bring purchases forward (buying this week rather than next week), stockpiling and spending more. In-store displays and demonstrations were felt to be effective in encouraging consumers to try a product for the first time. Loyalty cards and rewards for spending more were effective in encouraging consumers to buy just from one store. Competitions and games, in contrast, were felt to be ineffective in terms of generating all types of consumer response. A supermarket manager said, 'We have to be careful with the cost of sales promotions – if they reduce our profits through the cost of them, but they fail to lead to longer-term increases in sales or brand switching, are they really worthwhile?'

20 marks, 30 minutes

1 Explain why it is important for shop managers to compare the cost and effectiveness of sales promotions. [8]

2 Assume you are a supermarket manager. You have been asked by head office to promote one very profitable brand of breakfast cereal. What promotional mix would you use for this product? Explain and justify your answer. [12]

Solo long distance yachtswoman Ellen MacArthur and her Kingfisher-sponsored boat – sponsorship of this boat in a well-publicised race secured 'free' publicity worth $200 million

ACTIVITY 28.4

Read the case study below and then answer the questions that follow.

Can Gap win back lost customers?

Only a few years ago Gap was one of the most rapidly growing retail fashion retailers. Gap Inc sells clothes under the Gap, Banana Republic and Old Navy brand names. Consumers and investors were very excited about the bright and lively store designs, the simple, classic fashion look and the unusual style of advertising. Recently things have gone badly wrong. Its core customer base has aged – and the brand has failed to attract younger shoppers. Some analysts believe that Gap's shops look dated and their fashions are less appealing than those of main rivals Zara and Uniqlo. In fact, in 2008, Zara overtook Gap to become the world's biggest clothing retailer. The table shows how Gap's sales have fallen in recent years.

It is therefore quite surprising that Gap has decided to reduce spending on both design teams and marketing promotions. Surely, the business should be aiming to introduce more cutting-edge fashions and spend more on marketing when sales have stooped expanding? But is Gap in need of a fundamental change in branding rather than just new fashions and more advertising?

	% change in sales in July 2009 compared to July 2008
Total Gap Inc sales	-9
Gap branded stores	-10
Gap stores North America	-10
Banana Republic North America	-20
Old Navy North America	-7
International sales	-5

Source: GAP website.

22 marks, 40 minutes

1 Explain why Gap's managers should be worried about the sales trends shown in the table and the loss of market leadership to Zara. [8]

2 Recommend a new promotional strategy for Gap in your own country that could reverse this decline in sales. Consider advertising campaigns, displays in shops, special offers and the image that you think the business should try to create for its products in your country. [14]

ACTIVITY 28.5

Read the case study below and then answer the questions that follow.

Olympus targets youth with i-snap

Olympus, the camera maker, made its first venture into the youth market with the launch of a colourful kids' camera, the i-snap. Olympus did not actively advertise the camera, which is white with green or pink trim, until several months after it was launched. Marketing director Sara Cubitt hoped that the camera's unusual design, high-profile packaging and point-of-sale displays would set it apart from its rivals. As well as window and in-store displays, point-of-sale promotions included floor stickers directing customers to the cameras, which were priced at around $40.

22 marks, 40 minutes

1 Explain the term 'point-of-sale displays'. [2]

2 Do you think it was a good idea not to use 'above-the-line' promotion in the first few months after the launch of this product? Explain your answer. [10]

3 Assume that a similar camera is launched in your own country. Prepare a fully justified recommendation to Olympus for the promotional mix it should use. [10]

Stage of the cycle	Promotional options
Introduction	• Informative advertising and PR to make consumers aware of the product. • Sales promotion offering free samples or trial periods to encourage consumers to test the product.
Growth	• Focus shifts to 'brand' building and persuasive advertising. • Sales promotion to encourage repeat purchases. • Attempt to develop brand loyalty.
Maturity	• Advertising to emphasise the differences between this product and competitors. • Sales promotion incentives to encourage brand development and loyalty.
Decline – assuming no extension strategy	• Minimal advertising. • Sales promotion – there may be little additional support for the product if the intention is to withdraw it.

Table 28.2 *How promotional mix may vary over the life cycle of a product*

Below are some reasons why the choice of distribution channel is important:

- Consumers may need easy access to a firm's products to allow them to see and try them before they buy, to make purchasing easy and to allow, if necessary, for the return of goods.
- Manufacturers need outlets for their products that give as wide a market coverage as possible, but with the desired image of the product appropriately promoted.
- Retailers – firms that sell goods to the final consumer – will sell producers' goods but will demand a mark-up to cover their costs and make a profit, so, if price is very important, using few or no intermediaries would be an advantage.

CHANNEL STRATEGY

In deciding on an appropriate channel strategy, a business must answer these questions:

- Should the product be sold directly to consumers?
- Should the product be sold through retailers?
- How long should the channel be (how many intermediaries)?
- Where should the product be made available?
- Should electronic methods of distribution be used?
- How much will it cost to keep the stock of products on store shelves and in channel warehouses?
- How much control does the business want to have over the marketing mix?
- How will the distribution channel selected support the other components of the marketing mix?

Factors influencing choice of distribution channel include the following:

- Industrial products tend to be sold more directly with fewer intermediaries than consumer goods.
- Geographical dispersion of the target market – if the target market is large but widely dispersed throughout the country, then the use of intermediaries is more likely.

- The level of service expected by consumers, e.g. after-sales servicing of a car means that internet selling is not appropriate for most manufacturers.
- Technical complexity of the product, e.g. business computers are sold directly as they require a great deal of technical sales staff know-how and a supporting service team.
- Unit value of the product – it may be worth employing sales staff to sell directly to customers if the unit cost of, for example, a luxury yacht is $5 million, but not worthwhile if items of jewellery are being sold for $5.
- Number of potential customers – if the number of potential customers is few, as with commercial aircraft, direct selling might be used, but Nike, Inc. or Reebok with their millions of customers for sports shoes worldwide would use intermediate channels to distribute their products.

The channel strategy must be integrated with the marketing objectives of the business. For example, if the aim is to secure a niche market with a high-quality image product (e.g. branded cosmetics), then selling it through street vendors will not achieve this objective. If, however, the marketing aim is to achieve maximum sales and distribution coverage (e.g. sweets), then selling through a few carefully selected and exclusive food retailers will not be successful. As with all components of the marketing mix, distribution channel strategy must be clearly linked to marketing objectives and to the other components of the mix for an effective and convincing overall marketing strategy to be developed.

EXAM TIP

Do not confuse 'place' or 'distribution' decisions with transportation methods. Place is about how and where the product is to be sold to a customer – transportation is about how the product is to be physically delivered.

Distribution channels

The most commonly used distribution channels are shown in Figures 28.1–28.3. Figure 28.1 shows the direct route which gives the producer full control over marketing of products. This is sometimes known as direct selling or direct marketing. The growth of the internet has led to a rapid rise in the popularity of this channel of distribution.

With the increasing size of many modern retailers, the 'single-intermediary channel' depicted in Figure 28.2 is becoming more common. These huge retailers have great purchasing power. They are able to arrange their own storage and distribution systems to individual stores.

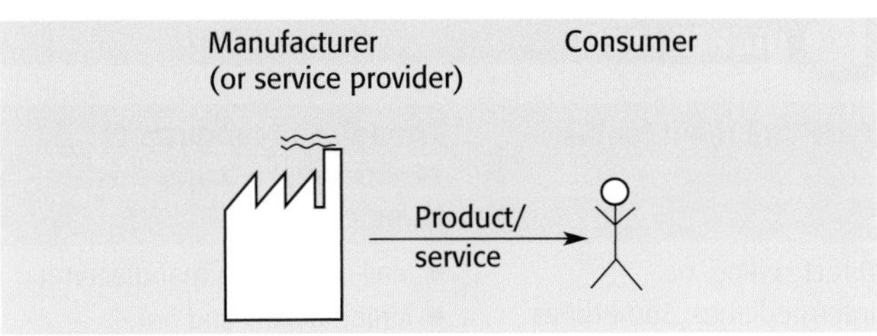

Figure 28.1 Direct selling to consumer

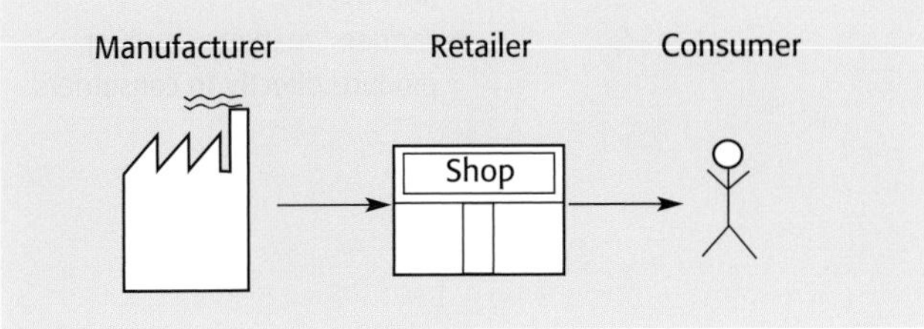

Figure 28.2 Single-intermediary channel

In Figure 28.3 we see what is often known as the traditional two-intermediaries channel as, until recent developments in retailing and the internet, it was the most common of all channels of distribution.

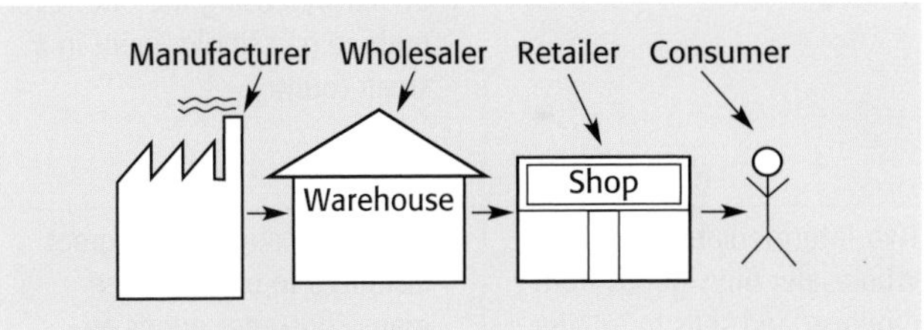

Figure 28.3 Two-intermediaries channel

Effectiveness of distribution channels

See Table 28.3 on page 302 for the benefits and limitations of distribution channels.

KEY TERM

agent business with the authority to act on behalf of another firm, e.g. to market its products

Appropriate distribution channels

Recent trends in distribution channels in recent years include:

- The increased use of the internet for direct selling of goods and services. In the service sector this can be seen with internet banking and direct selling of insurance policies online.

HIGHER LEVEL

Type and main features	Examples of products or services often using this channel	Possible benefits	Possible drawbacks
Direct selling: no intermediaries. Sometimes referred to as 'zero intermediary' channel.	• Mail order from manufacturer. • Airline tickets and hotel accommodation sold over the internet by the service providers. • Farmers' markets – selling produce directly to consumers.	• No intermediaries, so no mark-up or profit margin taken by other businesses. • Producer has complete control over the marketing mix – how the product is sold, promoted and priced to consumers. • Quicker than other channels. • May lead to fresher food products. • Direct contact with consumers offers useful market research.	• All storage and stock costs have to be paid for by producer. • No retail outlets limits the chances for consumers to 'see and try' before they buy. • May not be convenient for consumer. • No advertising or promotion paid for by intermediaries and no after-sales service offered by shops. • Can be expensive to deliver each item sold to consumers.
One-intermediary channel. Usually used for consumer goods but could also be an agent for selling industrial products to businesses.	• Holiday companies selling holidays via travel agents. • Large supermarkets that hold their own stocks rather than using wholesalers. • Where the whole country can be reached using the one-level route, e.g. a single agent in a small country.	• Retailer holds stocks and pays for cost of this. • Retailer has product displays and offers after-sales service. • Retailers often in locations that are convenient to consumers. • Producers can focus on production – not on selling the products to consumers.	• Intermediary takes a profit mark-up and this could make the product more expensive to final consumers. • Producers lose some control over marketing mix. • Retailers may sell products from competitors too, so there is no exclusive outlet. • Producer has delivery costs to retailer.
Two-intermediaries channel. Wholesaler buys goods from producer and sells to retailer.	• In a large country with great distances to each retailer, many consumer goods are distributed this way, e.g. soft drinks, electrical goods and books.	• Wholesaler holds goods and buys in bulk from producer. • Reduces stock-holding costs of producer. • Wholesaler pays for transport costs to retailer. • Wholesaler 'breaks bulk' by buying in large quantities and selling to retailers in small quantities. • Maybe the best way to enter foreign markets where producer has no direct contact with retailers.	• Another intermediary takes a profit mark-up – may make final goods more expensive to consumer. • Producer loses further control over marketing mix. • Slows down the distribution chain.

Table 28.3 *Distribution channels – main benefits and potential limitations*

- Large supermarket chains perform the function of wholesalers as well as retailers, as they hold large stocks in their own central warehouses. By owning another link in the distribution chain, the business is engaging in vertical marketing.
- Businesses are increasingly using a variety of different channels, e.g. an ice-cream manufacturer may have its own ice-cream vans to sell directly to consumers as well as supplying retailers. Hotels may sell room accommodation directly as well as through travel agents and holiday companies.
- There is increasing integration of services where a complete package is sold to consumers, e.g. air flights, car hire, hotel accommodation all sold or distributed to consumers at same time.

ACTIVITY 28.6

Read the case study below and then answer the questions that follow.

Coke chief's latest Daft idea – a cola tap in every house

It may be just a pipe dream, but Douglas Daft, the chief executive of Coca-Cola, is planning to compete with water by channelling Coke through taps in customers' homes. The business has created a system to mix carbonated water with Coke's secret syrup and pipe it around houses. It would be mixed inside homes rather than pumped in from an external source. Daft does not see Pepsi as his main competitor and will be happy only when people are turning on taps in their homes to drink Coke rather than water. This idea is not yet ready to be launched, Mr Daft said. The syrup would be sold as a concentrate in sealed containers directly by Coca-Cola, over the internet.

'You would have water mixing automatically with the concentrate and then connect it all up so that when you turn on your tap you have Coke at home. There's a lot more to it than that to ensure quality and it has to be a sealed unit so people can't alter the formula to destroy the value of the brand,' he said. Businesses already have closed systems. Cafés and branches of McDonald's, the burger chain, have stored the raw materials in basements and produced Coke on the spot for years.

22 marks, 40 minutes

1 Explain the importance of the Coca-Cola brand name to the company. [6]

2 This is an example of direct selling from the manufacturer to the consumer. Discuss the advantages and disadvantages of this channel of distributing Coca-Cola from the point of view of both the company and consumers. [10]

3 Outline **three** other methods Coca-Cola could use to 'place' or distribute its product to more consumers more often. [6]

HIGHER LEVEL

Supply chain management (SCM)

KEY TERM

supply chain management (SCM) managing the network of businesses that are involved in the provision of products to the final consumers

Managing and co-ordinating all of the separate businesses involved in supplying a car or computer to the end consumer is a complex process that is now aided by specialised software. The purpose of SCM is to ensure that products are consistently made available on time to consumers by integrating supply and demand management across all of the companies involved.

This logistical process involves many activities. SCM can increase the efficiency of a firm's supply chain by:

- ensuring all supply companies are kept well informed of the changing material needs of the business
- making appropriate transport arrangements for materials and for finished goods
- reducing the total number of suppliers
- planning production to meet consumer demand
- ensuring adequate supplies are delivered, on time, to retailers or other intermediaries.

THEORY OF KNOWLEDGE

Luciano Benetton's clothing retail business, Benetton, has always chosen to shock and even outrage people with its advertising. The picture above is typical of the images used to promote their brand. Other images used include a new-born baby, an anorexic girl and a black woman breast feeding a white baby.

a Find **five** examples of the images Benetton has used to advertise its brand.

b Do businesses such as Benetton have a moral obligation to promote their products in a responsible way?

ACTIVITY 28.7

Why the marketing mix must be integrated

Here are four examples of marketing mix decisions:

	Product	Price	Place	Promotion
Mix A	Six-year-old design of family car made in low-wage-cost country – few additional extras or features	Skimming strategy to try to develop exclusive image	Car showrooms in town centre with personal selling by experienced sales staff	Advertised in high-income segment magazines only
Mix B	Range of furniture for mid-income families with unique, modern designs	Low – low prices to be set below competitors to establish high market share	Sold over the internet and in some well-known department stores	Advertised on TV at times of most popular programmes
Mix C	Ladies' fashion hairdressing salon with cutting by well-known stylists	High prices to create top market image	Salon located in out-of-town shopping centre	Advertised in fashion and beauty magazines
Mix D	High-technology computer games with advanced interactivity functions	Skimming price strategy	Sold exclusively through the internet	Advertised on commercial radio stations at times most likely to be heard by young listeners

20 marks, 35 minutes

1 In each case, identify which marketing mix decision is not integrated with the other decisions. [4]

2 In each case, recommend a change to one of the marketing decisions to create an integrated mix. Explain and justify your recommendations. [16]

OVER TO YOU

REVISION CHECKLIST

1 Explain the differences between advertising and sales promotion.
2 State **three** reasons why a business might advertise an existing product.
3 Explain **one** example of how a sports show manufacturer might use both above- and below-the-line promotion to support the launch of a new product.
4 Outline **three** reasons why spending more money on advertising might fail to increase sales to the expected level.
5 Explain why it is important to assess whether a promotional campaign has achieved its objectives or not.
6 State **three** ways, other than an increase in sales, that a business might use to assess the effectiveness of a promotional campaign.
7 How can promotion be used to extend a product's life cycle?
8 For which products might point-of-sale displays be a useful form of promotion?
9 What is meant by 'public relations' and why is this important to a business?
10 Outline **two** functions performed by wholesalers in a traditional channel of communication.
11 Compare the promotional mix of two large stores in your area. Consider advertising, sales promotion, own-branded goods and public relations. Analyse the differences between the two promotional mixes and suggest how effective they might be in attracting customers to the stores.
(H) 12 State **two** channels of distribution that could be used by a manufacturer of mountain bikes. Compare the advantages to the business and consumers of these two channels.

REVISION ACTIVITY

Read the case study below and then answer the questions that follow.

Promoting golf equipment

Penang Golf Kit Ltd produces golfing equipment. The product range includes clubs, bags, golfing shoes and clothing. Sales have grown steadily in recent years, but no more rapidly than the expansion of the overall market for golf and golfing equipment. The firm's products are well known for their quality and relatively high prices. Promotion is based around sponsorship of one major championship each year and three famous golfers. This helps provide some public relations exposure when golf is being televised. A limited amount of advertising is paid for in the country's best-known golfing magazine. The firm has recently started designing a new range of golfing equipment and clothing aimed at the youth market (under 21 years). The number of young people playing golf has increased by 50% over the last ten years compared to an overall growth of 20% in the total number of players. The business has yet to decide how this new range of goods should be promoted. A total marketing budget of $1 million has been allocated for this purpose. The aim is not to lower the image of the brand name with these new products. The following data have been gathered – use them to advise the firm on an appropriate promotional strategy.

TV advertising – $0.5 million is the minimum promotion budget required for buying TV time. This purchases five minutes of TV time in 10–30 second slots. Two times are suggested:

- During the interval of the Saturday evening football match on TV. The audience is forecast to be 5 million – 25% of whom are likely to be under 21. The average income of viewers is around $10 000 per year.
- Friday evenings after a popular sports quiz show. Audience figures suggest an average number of 6 million viewers, 25% under 21. The average income of viewers is around $8000 The cost of producing the advertisement for TV will be a further $400 000.

National newspaper advertising – one popular paper will offer ten full-page adverts for $0.5 million. This paper has a circulation of 2 million and, on average, three people read each edition. Another paper, a quality daily usually bought by high-income groups, offers six pages for the same price. The readership is 1 million but four people on average read this paper. The cost of producing a newspaper advert will be $20 000, but a colour magazine advert will cost $50 000.

A monthly golfing magazine – aimed at all ages it will offer one full page in the next ten editions for $300 000. Circulation is only 30 000 but an estimated ten people read each edition.

Other options include radio advertising and street posters.

22 marks, 30 minutes

1 Explain **two** ways in which the company could have decided on the size of the total marketing budget of $1 million. **[6]**

2 Using all of the data and any other information you have, prepare a fully supported recommendation to the marketing manager concerning the promotional mix that could be adopted for this range of products. **[12]**

3 Explain **two** other pieces of information that would help you in coming to your recommendation. **[4]**

EXAM PRACTICE QUESTION

Read the case study below and then answer the questions that follow.

APPLE OPENS MORE OF ITS OWN STORES

Apple computers has announced plans to open more of its own branded stores in the USA and China as it continues to develop this distribution channel. Just a few years ago, the Silicon Valley company, famous for the first popular personal computer in the 1970s and more recently the iPod, always relied on other retailers and its website to sell its ever-growing range of products. The new retail stores are likely to be well received by consumers if recent reports from London and New York are any guide.

Some business analysts believe that Apple runs a real risk of coming into conflict with its existing retail partners – including the US chain CompUSA. 'Why should other retail stores bother to sell and promote Apple products if the company is going to compete directly with them on the high street?' said one investment specialist. There are also fears that Apple could fall into the same trap as Gateway, another PC maker focused on the consumer market. Gateway had to close about 40% of its North American stores, saying it had over-extended itself at a time of slowing sales of PCs. Apple is investing heavily in property and there is always the risk of stock build-up at a time of slower world economic growth.

Apple plans to open its two new stores in high-profile shopping centres near Las Vegas in the USA and in the Chaoyang district of China. Apart from selling the usual Apple products – computers, iPods, Apple TV and the like – the main draw in the shops will be the Genius Bar – a counter where shoppers will find several highly trained Mac Geniuses ready to advise on any technical questions. There will be a hands-on Apple Retail Store Experience giving consumers the chance to test drive Apple's entire product mix. The stores will also run a series of daily creative workshops to teach customers how to make the most of the programs available.

Sources: www.timeout.com and http://uk.reuters.com (adapted)

25 marks, 45 minutes

1 Define the following terms:
 a distribution channel
 b product mix. [4]

2 Outline the different distribution channels Apple could use to distribute its products. [6]

3 Analyse the effects on existing retailers of Apple products of the opening of new Apple stores. [6]

4 Evaluate Apple's decision to open new Apple stores as a way of distributing its products. [9]

29 International marketing and e-commerce

This chapter cover syllabus sections 4.7 and 4.8

On completing this chapter you should be able to:

- evaluate the opportunities and threats posed by entry into international markets
- analyse the cultural, legal, political, social and economic issues of entering international markets
- analyse the effect of e-commerce on the marketing mix
- discuss the costs and benefits of e-commerce to firms and consumers.

SETTING THE SCENE

IKEA expands in China

Since being set up in Sweden in 1943, IKEA has grown to become the world's largest furniture retailer. The company's latest plans include the opening of two huge shopping centres in China – one in Beijing and one in Wuxi City. These will take the total number of IKEA stores worldwide to over 310. The products sold in each of these stores are remarkably similar. IKEA has largely ignored the retailing 'rule' that international success involves tailoring product lines to match national tastes and consumer preferences. The founder of the company – Ingvar Kamprad – had the vision that stores should sell a product range that is 'typically Swedish'. This has led to substantial cost benefits (huge production runs of identical products lead to economies of scale), which have helped to cancel out the high transport costs that international furniture retailers experience. The largely product-oriented company sells largely 'flat-pack' furniture that has to be assembled at home, further reducing the cost of supplying stores around the globe.

Some consumers do object to the standardised product formula. IKEA did have to make some product design changes in the highly competitive US market where furniture such as beds and wardrobes tend to be larger than average. The company recognises that, particularly in China, it does only seem to appeal to middle class consumers and that there are other market segment opportunities. Apart from its out-of-town shops, IKEA also has a highly developed internet selling division with an advanced website. This accounts for a small – but increasing – proportion of total sales.

Points to think about:

- Outline likely reasons why IKEA is planning expansion in China.
- What advantages and disadvantages might IKEA have from using the same marketing strategy (e.g. product ranges and low prices) in all the countries it which it operates?
- Examine whether IKEA stores could one day be entirely replaced by internet sales (e-commerce).

29 International marketing and e-commerce

Introduction

Selling in foreign markets was once too risky and expensive for most firms, so only large businesses – growing too large for their national markets – used this form of marketing. Improved communications, better transport links and freer international trade – all key features of globalisation – have changed all this. For many firms, international marketing is now an opportunity to profitably expand their sales, and indeed for some firms it is no longer an option but a necessity.

KEY TERM

international marketing selling products in markets other than the original domestic market

Why sell products in other countries?

Here are some of the reasons why companies may decide to sell in foreign markets:

- Saturated home markets – sales of personal computers in developed economies fell by 7.9% in 2010 yet rose by 11% in emerging markets.
- Potential to increase profits through rapid sales growth and low costs in emerging markets.
- Spreading risks between different markets – selling cars in China with a GDP growth rate of 11% in 2009 was easier than in the UK where GDP fell by over 4%.
- Poor trading conditions in the home market – perhaps due to the entry of new rivals.

Why international marketing is different

POLITICAL DIFFERENCES

Changes of governments can cause instability in some countries and this can increase the risk of doing business there. Acts of terrorism or threats of civil violence, which might lead to destruction of a company's assets, will all add to the problems of marketing abroad.

ECONOMIC AND SOCIAL DIFFERENCES

Average living standards vary greatly across the globe. The country with the highest GDP per head of the population is Luxembourg (US$78 559), and the lowest is Burundi (US$160) (source: World Bank 2009). Location decisions about a firm's marketing activities will need to take this into account as well as differences in tax rates, interest rates and the age structure of the population. The role of women and the importance of marriage in society vary substantially too and these and other social factors may have a considerable impact on the products to be sold and the marketing strategies used to sell them.

LEGAL DIFFERENCES

There are many of these and they will impact on international marketing in key ways. For example:

- Some goods, such as guns, can be sold in the USA, but are illegal in other countries.
- It is illegal to advertise directly to children below the age of 12 on Swedish TV – and there are other restrictions in other countries.
- Product safety and product labelling controls are much stricter in the European Union (EU) than in some African states.

CULTURAL DIFFERENCES

This is a key factor in international marketing, yet it is often difficult to define and measure. Cultural differences are not written down as laws are, yet they can exercise as powerful an impact on people's behaviour. Failure to recognise cultural and language differences can have a disastrous effect on a firm's marketing strategy. Some words have unfortunate meanings when translated into a foreign language. The use of male and female models in advertisements would not be acceptable in some countries with strong religious traditions. Colours can have different significance too – in the Far East, white rather than black is associated with mourning.

DIFFERENCES IN BUSINESS PRACTICES

Accounting standards and rules can vary in different parts of the world. The ease of setting up a limited company varies widely – it can take a few days in the UK, yet the formalities and form filling can exceed one year in Sierra Leone.

EXAM TIP

Keep up to date with business practices and legal changes in your own country – you may be asked to evaluate a business strategy used by a business operating in your country. Specific references to differences between your country and others could be useful.

Entry into international markets

EXPORTING

Exporting can be undertaken either by selling the product directly to a foreign customer – perhaps the order has been placed via the company website – or indirectly through an export intermediary, such as an agent or trading company based in the country.

INTERNATIONAL FRANCHISING

International franchising means that foreign franchisees are used to operate a firm's activities abroad. This can either take the form of one foreign company being used as a franchisee for *all* the branches in their own country or individual franchisees are appointed to operate each outlet. McDonald's uses just one franchisee business to operate its branches in Argentina, for example.

JOINT VENTURES

These are agreements between at least two companies to own and operate a new business venture. An example of this method to enter an international market is the 50–50 joint venture between McDonald's and two Indian restaurant chains, Hardcastle Restaurants and Connaught Plaza restaurants.

LICENSING

Licensing involves the business allowing another firm in the country being entered to produce its branded goods or patented products under licence, which will involve strictly controlled terms over quality. This means that goods do not have to be physically exported, saving on time and transport cost – and making food products fresher too. The parent firm avoids the capital cost of setting up its own operating bases abroad. The limitations of this approach include quality issues and unethical production methods may be used by the licensee to cut costs, reflecting badly on the business offering the licence.

DIRECT INVESTMENT IN SUBSIDIARIES

Studies have shown that setting up company-owned subsidiaries in foreign countries can achieve higher success rates than taking over or merging with locally based companies.

The business cultures, organisational structures and technology differences between the company and the locally acquired business can often present obstacles too great to be overcome. Subsidiaries can be factories set up in foreign countries, as with Toyota in the EU and South America, or retailing operations, as with Tesco in Thailand and China. They may be almost completely decentralised – where local managers take most key decisions – or organised with centralised control from head office in the home country.

International marketing – alternative strategies

One feature of globalisation is that national and regional differences in tastes, culture, fashion and wants are becoming less obvious. According to some analysts (e.g. Levitt) the world is becoming more standardised in the goods and services that it is demanding. If this is true, then the opportunities for companies to use technology to gain massive economies of scale by selling the same product across the globe are huge.

Other writers (e.g. Douglas and Wind) suggest that substantial differences still exist in consumer needs in different countries markets. Standardisation is only one option for entering these markets, and this will sometimes fail. The alternative is for businesses to adapt a global marketing mix to local needs and conditions – this is called localisation.

The two broad approaches to selling goods and services internationally are known as 'pan-global marketing' and 'global localisation'. See Table 29.1 on page 311 for the advantages and disadvantages of a pan-global or pan-regional marketing strategy.

KEY TERMS

pan-global marketing adopting a standardised product across the globe as if the whole world were a single market – selling the same goods in the same way everywhere

global localisation adapting the marketing mix, including differentiated products, to meet national and regional tastes and cultures

Pan-global marketing may continue to be important for two groups of products in particular: upmarket brands with international appeal for their exclusivity such as Rolex watches, Rolls-Royce cars and Versace dresses. The opportunity to buy the same product as international celebrities is the key promise made by these brands. Consumers do not want them adapted to their markets. Secondly, mass-appeal brands, such as Levi's, Apple and Nike, have substantial opportunities for global campaigns and standardised products – and the economies of scale that result from these.

However, with growing concern about 'cultural imperialism' from US and European businesses and an expanding anti-globalisation movement, there will be increasing scope for other businesses to benefit from adapting and selling products that are geared directly towards the particular cultural, religious and consumer requirements of each country using localisation strategies.

Global localisation

'Thinking global – acting local' is sometimes how this approach to international marketing is summed up. YUM, the world's largest fast-food organisation with top brands such as KFC and Pizza Hut, has adopted this approach with great success. It offers all of its franchisees and branches around the globe the benefits and security offered by a giant multinational corporation. However, it

ACTIVITY 29.1

Read the case study below and then answer the questions that follow.

The franchising path to international marketing

Dunkin' Donuts, a US-based coffee and baked goods franchise, has opened its 50th United Arab Emirates (UAE) store. Continental Foods is the UAE-based business that owns the master franchise for Dunkin' Donuts in this country. Michale Cortelletti, Dunkin' Donuts International Director for the Middle East, said, 'UAE is an important growth market for the brand and has seen ground-breaking innovation, such as the opening of the first drive-through.'

Cartridge World, the ink-cartridge filling business, founded in South Australia in 1988, is set to continue its Asian expansion. It already has franchised outlets in India and is aiming to launch stores in Nepal, Sri Lanka, Bangladesh and Bhutan through international franchising. Without the quick growth offered by franchising and the local market expertise offered by local franchisees, the business would not have been able to grow to over 1300 branches in 36 countries so rapidly.

Yogen Fruz, a Canada-based frozen yoghurt chain, has signed franchise deals for Argentina and Peru with Fruzco Chile SA. This company already owns and operates Yogen Fruz franchises in Chile. Argentina has one of the fastest-growing economies of Southern America and has a high GDP per head. The President of Yogen Fruz said, 'We needed a locally based company with experience of the region to introduce our brands in these other countries.' Yogen Fruz does not have to pay the high capital costs of setting up its own subsidiaries in these other countries.

Source: Franchise International (adapted)

28 marks, 50 minutes

1 Explain **two** likely reasons why these companies are all operating in international markets. [8]

2 Analyse **three** differences one of these franchisor companies might experience from selling goods in international markets compared to their home market. [10]

3 Assess reasons why all three companies have decided to enter international markets through franchising. [10]

A Dunkin' Donuts franchise in China

Advantages	Disadvantages
• A common identity for the product can be established. This aids consumer recognition, especially in a world of increasing international travel by consumers and the widespread use of satellite TV channels with 'international' advertising. • Cost reduction can be substantial. The same product can be produced for all markets allowing substantial economies of scale. This is particularly important for firms that have to spend huge sums on developing new products that may have only a short product life cycle. The same marketing mix can be used. This allows just one marketing agency and advertising strategy to be used for the whole world or region rather than different ones for each country. • It recognises that differences between consumers in different countries are reducing – it is often said that teenagers in different countries have more in common with each other than they have with their parents! Therefore, a pan-global strategy for a product aimed at teenagers could be developed.	• Despite growing similarity between consumer tastes in different countries, it might still be necessary to develop different products to suit cultural or religious variations – see the revision activity on McDonald's at the end of this chapter. Market opportunities could be lost by trying to sell essentially the same product everywhere. • Legal restrictions can vary substantially between countries. This does not just apply to product restrictions, e.g. it is illegal to use promotions involving games or gambling in certain countries. There may also be restrictions on what can be shown in advertisements too. • Brand names do not always translate effectively into other languages. They might even cause offence or unplanned embarrassment for the company if the selection of the brand name to be used in all markets is not made with care. • Setting the same price in all countries will fail to take into account different average income levels that exist.

Table 29.1 *Pan-global or pan-regional marketing strategy – advantages and disadvantages*

differentiates most aspects of its marketing mix between different countries and markets. For example:

- In China, it sells products that are not available in other countries to suit local consumers' tastes. So, although it was the first company to introduce the Chinese to pizzas, in 1990, its best-selling lines today include 'KFC Dragon Twister'.
- Price levels are varied between different countries to reflect different average incomes.
- Advertisements always contain local 'ethnic' people.
- Its distribution and place decisions are tested for local markets too. In China, it tried out 14 new Chinese quick-service restaurants offering authentic Chinese food in surroundings designed in a local style.

See Table 29.2 for the benefits and limitations of global localisation.

Benefits	Limitations
• Local needs, tastes and cultures are reflected in the marketing mix of the business and this could lead to higher sales and profits. • There is no attempt to impose foreign brands/products/advertisements on regional markets. • The products are more likely to meet local national legal requirements than if they are standardised products. • There will be less local opposition to multinational business activity.	• The scope for economies of scale is reduced. • The international brand could lose its power and identity if locally adapted products become more popular than the 'international' product. • There will be additional costs of adapting products, adverts, store layouts, etc. to specific local needs – these costs might lead to higher prices than a 'global marketing' strategy would result in.

Table 29.2 *Global localisation – benefits and limitations*

E-commerce

KEY TERM

e-commerce the buying and selling of goods and services on the internet

E-commerce or internet marketing can involve several different marketing functions. Some businesses employ all of these but others just one or two:

- Selling of goods and services directly to final customers (consumers) as orders are placed online through the company website. This is called 'business to consumer' or b2c.
- Selling/buying of goods and services to/from other businesses. This is called 'business to business' or b2b. The volume of these transactions is much greater than b2c because the production of most products requires parts and components from a large number of suppliers, yet the final product is only sold once.
- Advertising by using the company's own website or by placing a banner advert or pop-up on other firms' websites, e.g. a motor insurance company might pay to have a banner advert on a car manufacturer's website. This allows adverts to be well targeted at potential consumers.

ACTIVITY 29.2

Zumo the energy drink

Launched in the mid-1980s, this energy product is aimed at fitness-conscious men and women between 20 and 45. Zumo is offered in four flavours and is distributed through supermarkets and sports clubs. Advertising is based on TV and radio media with endorsements from well-known European sports stars. It is currently sold only in Europe, where average incomes are high. It is priced above an equivalent non-energy soft drink, such as Coca-Cola, but is not as expensive as some energy drinks.

Zumposa is the food and drinks company based in Valencia, Spain that produces Zumo. The managers want to make Zumo a global brand. They know that Zumo is seen as a Spanish drink – this might not be suitable when developing a global image. The board of directors has decided to focus first on South America and Asia to launch a global campaign – the aim is for a 10% market share in the first year. Decisions are needed on:

- price – should this vary to reflect different average income levels in different countries?
- flavours – does it keep the same flavours across the globe or adapt products to different markets?
- packaging – should the design and colours on the can be the same everywhere?
- advertising – should different adverts be used in each country or could a global advert be made with different languages added?
- name and brand image – should these be changed or should a global image and name be established?

20 marks, 35 minutes

As a business analyst, write a report to Zumposa's board of directors recommending an appropriate marketing strategy for this product in your country. It should contain: explanations of global marketing and localisation; advantages and disadvantages of both strategies for this product in your country; details of the changes you would recommend for the integrated marketing strategy in your country. **[20]**

- Sales leads are established by visitors to a site leaving their details and then the company emails or phones them to attempt to make a sale.
- Collecting market research data by encouraging visitors to the website to answer questions that can provide important consumer data.

IMPACT ON BUSINESS AND CONSUMERS

Internet marketing has had a huge impact on several industries that used to be entirely focused on retail stores to sell their products. These include music, film, banking,

THEORY OF KNOWLEDGE

Since the late 1980s ICT has revolutionised business and retailing – email communication, online buying and selling, internet advertising, websites and so on.

a Prepare a presentation on the impact of ICT on your school or college in the last 15 years.

b 'The growth in the use of ICT can only be good for schools and colleges.' Discuss the validity of this statement.

insurance, travel and tourism. The relative decline in the importance of traditional retail stores has been rapid. In 2010, Apple's iTunes online store was the largest seller of music in the USA. Of individuals who have a bank account in the UK, over 40% only use the internet for their transactions. Internet auctions have grown in popularity. Specialised e-stores sell items ranging from antiques to old movie posters. Increasingly, potential consumers are using eBay and other sites to make price comparisons before making a purchase. See Table 29.3 for the benefits and limitations of internet marketing.

IMPACT OF E-COMMERCE ON THE MARKETING MIX

Product

Each consumer can be communicated with individually and individual product requirements can be built into the product or service to suit different needs. Examples include airline tickets (time/class of seat/luggage/car hire and so on) and computers assembled to match the individual specification of each customer. Businesses selling over the internet – because of the greater market potential – can afford to stock a much wider range of goods than nearly all shops could justify, for example ASOS clothing.

Price

Markets are now much more competitive as prices can be compared so rapidly – in both b2b and b2c. Price-comparison websites will even do the search for you! Competitive pricing is much more likely to be used than cost plus which means customers are now more in control.

Promotion

Banners, pop-ups, text messages, web pages, viral marketing – all these terms were unheard of 15 years ago. Promotional opportunities have been greatly expanded by the internet and other ICT developments, and at the same time the costs of reaching huge numbers of potential customers have been cut. Will we still be reading newspaper adverts and watching TV adverts in years to come?

Place

The internet is transforming the buying/shopping experience. Is the day of the high-street store passed? Eventually, will all products be bought online?

Benefits	Limitations
• It is relatively inexpensive when compared to the ratio of cost and the number of potential consumers reached. • Companies can reach a worldwide audience for a small proportion of traditional promotion budgets. • Consumers interact with the websites and make purchases and leave important data about themselves. • The internet is convenient for consumers to use – if they have access to a computer. They can quickly compare prices from many suppliers worldwide. • Accurate records can be kept on the number of 'clicks' or visitors, and the success rate of different web promotions can be quickly measured. • Computer ownership and usage are increasing in all countries of the world. • Selling products on the internet involves lower fixed costs than traditional retail stores – these could be passed on in lower prices.	• Some countries have low-speed internet connections and in poorer countries, computer ownership is not widespread. • Consumers cannot touch, smell, feel or try on tangible goods before buying – this may limit their willingness to buy certain products online. • Product returns may increase as consumers are dissatisfied with their purchase once it has been received. • The cost and reliability of postal services in some countries may reduce the cost advantage of internet selling. • The website must be kept up to date and user friendly – good websites can be expensive to develop. • Worries about internet security – e.g. consumers may wonder who will use information about them or their credit card details – may reduce future growth potential.

Table 29.3 *Internet marketing – benefits and limitations*

KEY TERM

viral marketing the use of social networking sites or SMS text messages to increase brand awareness or sell products

OVER TO YOU

REVISION CHECKLIST

1 Analyse **two** differences between selling clothing products in a home market and selling them internationally.
2 Explain **two** reasons why Apple sells its products internationally.
3 If a soft drinks manufacturer based in your country wanted to sell its products in foreign markets, explain **three** factors it should consider before deciding on the entry method for these markets.
4 Differentiate, with examples, between global marketing and global localisation strategies.
5 Why are many businesses now using localisation rather than standardisation (global marketing) to compete in foreign markets?

REVISION ACTIVITY

Read the case study below and then answer the questions that follow.

McDonald's – pan-global strategy or global localisation?
The world's best-known fast-food restaurant sets high standards for hygiene and levels of service in all countries it operates in. The principle of a common world approach is also extended to the marketing mix used by the business – same products, same décor, same promotions, same pricing levels. When the company first expanded internationally in the 1970s, it was selling the 'American dream', but that is no longer acceptable in many countries of the world. The emphasis has now changed to 'global brand but local marketing'.

The need to be aware of cultural and religious factors when designing a global marketing strategy was made clear when McDonald's was sued by Indian Hindus. The company had to apologise to all religious and secular vegetarians for not making clear that beef flavouring is added to its chips in the USA. It is claimed that there are at least 16 million vegetarians in the USA, who may have eaten these chips, and who could be suffering from emotional distress as a result. In India, restaurant windows were smashed and dirt was smeared on statues of 'Ronald McDonald'. Hindu leaders called for the food chain to be expelled from the country.

There are benefits to standardisation, however – the McDonald's double-arch logo is now the best recognised in the world, for example, and internationally standardised adverts as used by Coca-Cola offer economies of scale as well as reinforcing the global nature of the brand.

However, McDonald's is not alone in increasingly adopting the 'think globally, act locally' concept. Products that are heavily focused on US culture, tastes and consumer needs are much less well received in some countries than they used to be. Adapting well-known brands to meet the cultural and social demands of other countries is now a priority for companies like McDonald's. In India McDonald's had to move away from reliance on beef and has an Indian menu with local flavours, such as McCurry Pan and Chicken Maharaja Mac. In France, red and yellow colour schemes are replaced with more 'adult' colour schemes. External restaurant signs are discreet and blend in with the neighbourhood. There are real leather seats, gas fireplaces and hardwood floors. Organic ingredients are used and healthy eating messages are displayed on every wall. French desserts are offered instead of the standard options and a big seller is 'le p'tit moutarde' – a small hamburger with a French mustard sauce. McDonald's sales in France rose by 8% in 2008 after some years of much slower growth – perhaps meeting local needs and responding to national consumer tastes is the way forward.

McDonald's annual % sales growth:

	2007	2008
USA	6.7	4.3
Europe	7.6	7.7
Asia, Middle East, Africa	7.2	9.9

Source: www.moneymorning.com and www.mcdonalds.com

28 marks, 50 minutes

1 Explain the likely reasons why McDonald's decided to enter international markets. [8]

2 Discuss the advantages and disadvantages to McDonald's of initially using a pan-global marketing strategy for its restaurants. [10]

3 Evaluate how and why you might adapt McDonald's marketing strategy to a new restaurant in your town to suit local market conditions. [10]

EXAM PRACTICE QUESTION

Read the case study below and then answer the questions that follow.

E-TAILING ON THE INCREASE

Online retailing is becoming an increasingly important part of e-commerce. Online sales have increased by 32% in 2008 compared to high-street sales growth of 1.2%, according to industry analyst Verdict Research. E-tailing now accounts for almost 7% of total retail spending and this share could double to 14% by 2015. 74% of consumers surveyed by Verdict said the internet was better for cheaper goods and 67% agreed that it is better for comparing prices. Typical of the move to e-tailing was the decision by Dixons, the electrical goods retailer, to:

- close many of its high-street stores
- rebrand those remaining into Currys.digital
- move the Dixons brand completely online.

The strategy cost £7 milliion, but was expected to increase sales as well as deliver administration cost savings of £3 million annually.

'I am very excited about the prospects for the Dixons brand as a pure e-tailer,' said the chief executive of Dixons. 'Consumer buying behaviours are developing with the market growth in broadband and we constantly innovate to support how our customers shop.'

E-tailing is now an indispensable part of the fashion industry too. Yoox.com is a virtual boutique that saw over 3 million visitors per month in 2008. When another site, Net-a-Porter, partnered fashion label Halston, one dress sold out in 45 minutes after the launch of the site. There is also potential for young new designers keen to enter the industry to show off their styles to a huge online audience. However, when consumer spending fell in 2009, online traders reported lower 'conversion rates' (online shoppers actually buying) and there were signs of consumer resistance. Tesco withdrew its clothing ranges from Tesco Direct after its initial claim of 'selling online will enable us to reach a greater number of customers eager to buy items from our collections' was not supported by sales figures.

There are familiar customer complaints about 'difficult to use sites', 'delays in postal deliveries' and 'it was not as it seemed on screen', so perhaps high-street shops are not doomed after all. 'The high street will not die,' said Neil Saunders, director of Verdict Research. 'Internet retailing is set to become more significant, but shopping is a tactile process and for many people it is a leisure activity – e-tailing does not really deliver these two things.'

Source: www.talkingretail.com and www.silicon.com/webwatch (adapted)

25 marks, 45 minutes

1 Define the following terms:
   a e-commerce
   b market growth. [4]

2 Explain **two** factors that might have led to the rise in the number of consumers shopping online. [6]

3 Analyse **two** ways in which a high-street retailer might be able to compete effectively with online retailers. [6]

4 Discuss the advantages and disadvantages to retailers of selling their products online. [9]

30 Production methods

This chapter covers syllabus section 5.1

On completing this chapter you should be able to:

- describe and compare the features and applications of job, batch, line, flow and mass production
- (H) analyse the implications for functional departments that arise from changing the production method
- (H) analyse the most appropriate method of production for a given situation
- (H) understand the need for some organisations to use more than one production method.

SETTING THE SCENE

Cell production at Dr. Martens

World-famous Dr. Martens footwear is made using cell production methods. Production workers are divided into individual cells or teams made up of up to 17 people. Each team is responsible for its own production. Staff work 39 hours a week, but each cell (or pod) can divide that time how they wish. For example, if a cell prefers to work four long days and have a day off, it can do so. For every extra 100 pairs of shoes each cell makes over its target, its members receive extra money. Each cell does everything apart from the cutting and stitching, which still use mass production methods. Each cell is responsible for:

- organising work schedules
- planning output
- meeting order deadlines
- quality.

Everyone in each cell is multi-skilled – they can carry out all the tasks needed to produce the boots. This has two advantages: absence of any staff member means production can continue and doing a variety of tasks – with the increased responsibility that cell production brings – reduces boredom and increases motivation. Since introducing the cell production system, productivity has improved – yet so has quality.

Points to think about:

- Do you think all products could be made using cell production? Explain your answer.
- What additional costs might there be from introducing cell production?
- Analyse the potential advantages of cell production – making reference to motivation theorists.

Introduction

There are several different ways in which goods and services can be produced. They are usually classified into:

- job production
- batch production
- flow production and mass production
- mass customisation
- (H) cell production.

EXAM TIP

Although mass customisation is not examined specifically in IB examinations, this important recent production development may be used for comparison purposes.

KEY TERMS

job production producing a one-off item specially designed for the customer

batch production producing a limited number of identical products – each item in the batch passes through one stage of production before passing on to the next stage

flow production producing items in a continually moving process – also known as line production

mass production producing large quantities of a standardised product

mass customisation the use of flexible computer-aided production systems to produce items to meet individual customers' requirements at mass production cost levels

Production methods

JOB PRODUCTION

This is normally used for the production of single, one-off products. These products may be small or large and are often unique. Good examples of job production would be a specially designed wedding ring or made-to-measure suits or the Yangtze dam in China. In order to be called job production, each individual product has to be completed before the next product is started. At any one time, there is only one product being made. New, small firms often use labour-intensive job production, before they get the chance to expand and purchase advanced equipment. Job production enables specialised products to be produced and tends to be motivating for workers, because they produce the whole product and can take pride in it.

However, this production method tends to result in high unit costs, often takes a long time to complete, and is usually labour intensive. The labour force also needs to be highly skilled and this is not always easy to achieve. Aston Martin is an example of a very expensive car that is individually produced for the needs of each customer. Each engine is hand built and carries a plate with the engineer's name on it.

Job production – every Aston Martin engine is built by hand

BATCH PRODUCTION

Batch production makes products in separate groups and the products in each batch go through the whole production process together. The production process involves a number of distinct stages and the defining feature of batch production is that every unit in the batch must go through an individual production stage before the batch as a whole moves on to the next stage.

A good example of this form of production is a baker making batches of rolls. First, the dough is mixed and kneaded. Then, after being left for a time, the dough is separated into individual amounts, the right size for rolls. After this, the rolls are baked together and then they are left to cool. When they have cooled, they are put on display in the shop and another batch can be prepared. Each roll has gone through the process with the other rolls in the batch and all the rolls have undergone each stage of the batch before going on to the next stage.

Batch production allows firms to use division of labour in their production process and it enables economies of scale if the batch is large enough. It is usually employed in industries where demand is for batches of identical products – such as 500 school uniforms for the students at one school. It also allows each individual batch to be specifically matched to the demand, and the design and composition of batches can be easily altered.

The drawbacks are that batch production tends to have high levels of work-in-progress stocks at each stage

Batch production of identical bread rolls

of the production process. The work may well be boring and demotivating for the workers. If batches are small, then unit costs are likely to remain high. There is often a need to clean and adjust machinery after each batch has passed through.

Batch production should not be confused with flow production. Some firms produce 'batches' of products using a flow production system. For example, a soft drinks firm may bottle a batch of 20000 cans of orange drink before resetting the line and producing a 'batch' of another drink. This is not, however, batch production. The individual items are free to move through the process without having to wait for others, so it must be flow production.

FLOW PRODUCTION

This method is used when individual products move from stage to stage of the production process as soon as they are ready, without having to wait for any other products. Flow production systems are capable of producing large quantities of output in a relatively short time and so it suits industries where the demand for the product in question is high and consistent. It also suits the production of large numbers of a standardised item that only requires minimal alterations. This is why it is often referred to as mass production. Flow production usually takes place on a production line – hence the use of the term line production.

An example would be a Coca-Cola production plant like the one in Ho Chi Minh City, Vietnam. Here, the product is standardised in that it is a can of soft drink of a standard size. The system is flow production because the cans move through the various stages independently. However, the firm can make changes to the contents of the cans and the labelling on them without having to alter the flow production system. They are capable of producing Coke, Sprite and Schweppes Soda Water on the same production line. It is essential that the flow production process be very carefully planned, so that there are no disruptions in the system. In a perfect system, the production process would be broken down so that all of the stages were of equal duration and producing equal output levels.

Flow production has a number of advantages over other types of production. Labour costs tend to be relatively low, because much of the process is mechanised and there is little physical handling of the products. The constant output rate should make the planning of inputs relatively simple and this can lead to the minimisation of input stocks through the use of just-in-time (JIT) stock control. Quality tends to be consistent and high and it is easy to check the quality of products at various points throughout the process. The main disadvantage is the high initial set-up cost. By definition, capital intensive, high-technology production lines are going to cost a great deal of money. In addition, the work involved tends to be boring, demotivating and repetitive.

Flow production at the Coca-Cola plant in Ho Chi Minh City, Vietnam

EXAM TIP

It is important to weigh up the advantages and disadvantages of each production method if a question asks you to compare production methods.

MASS CUSTOMISATION

The search for production methods that combine the advantages of job production – flexibility and worker satisfaction – with the gains from flow/mass production – low unit costs – has led to the development of mass customisation. This method is only possible because of tremendous advances in technology such as computer-aided design (CAD) and computer-aided manufacturing (CAM). These have allowed much quicker developments of new products, designs that feature many common components and robotic machinery that can be switched to making different parts. Developments in the organisation of the production flow lines have also reduced the alienating effects of typical mass production. The emphasis on repetitive, boring tasks has been a major factor in poor worker motivation.

The mass customisation process combines the latest technology with multi-skilled labour forces to use production lines to make a range of varied products. This allows the business to move away from the mass marketing approach with high output of identical products. Instead, focused or differentiated marketing can be used which allows for higher added value – an essential objective of all operations managers. So, Dell Computers can make a customised computer to suit the customer's specific needs in a matter of hours. By changing just a few of the key components, but keeping the rest the same, low unit costs are maintained with greater product choice.

Table 30.1 summarises the main features, advantages and disadvantages of the four methods of production.

CELL PRODUCTION

KEY TERM

cell production splitting flow production into self-contained groups that are responsible for whole work units

Cell production is a form of flow production, but instead of each individual worker performing a single task, the production line is split into several self-contained, mini-production units – known as cells. Each individual cell produces a complete unit of work, such as a complete washing machine motor and not just a small part of it. Each cell has a team leader and below that a single level of hierarchy made up of multi-skilled workers. The performance of each cell is measured against pre-set targets. These targets will include output levels, quality and lead times. Cells are responsible for the quality of their own complete units of work – this links in with total quality management (TQM) (see Chapter 33, page 346), job enrichment and team working (see Chapter 14, page 152).

The cell production system has led to:

- significant improvements in worker commitment and motivation because there is team work and a sense of 'ownership' of the complete unit of work
- job rotation within the cell
- increased productivity.

Success of cell production depends on a well-trained and multi-skilled workforce prepared and able to be flexible and accept a more responsible style of working (see Figure 30.1).

ACTIVITY 30.1

Read the case study below and then answer the questions that follow.

Sunburst Bakeries

Sunburst Bakeries is a supplier of all kinds of bread and cakes to leading supermarkets. It has a huge factory that makes the entire range of products – no finished items are bought in from other bakers. Production facilities are split into three main areas. Different production methods are used in these three areas. The demand patterns for three of the best-known Sunburst products are very different. Standard loaves are bought by supermarkets every day, all year round. There is some variation in demand through the seasons – but very little. Large, family-sized cakes are mainly bought at weekends – whereas doughnuts are most often bought midweek for children's lunch boxes. Finally, the business is famous for its hand-made wedding cakes, each one to a different design. There have been rumours among the workers that one section of the factory that uses batch production might be converted into flow-line production.

22 marks, 40 minutes

1 Explain the key differences between job and batch production. [6]

2 For each of the products referred to above, suggest and justify an appropriate production method. [8]

3 Explain the possible effects on Sunburst's stock levels and profitability if it replaced batch production with flow line production. [8]

30 Production methods

	Job	Batch	Flow/mass	Mass customisation
Main feature	• Single one-off items	• Group of identical products pass through each stage together	• Mass production of standardised products	• Flow production with many standardised components but customised differences too
Essential requirements	• Highly skilled workforce	• Labour and machines must be flexible to switch to making batches of other designs	• Specialised, often expensive, capital equipment – but can be very efficient • High steady demand for standardised products	• Many common components • Flexible and multi-skilled workers • Flexible equipment – often CAM to allow for variations in the product
Main advantages	• Able to undertake specialist projects or jobs, often with high value added • High levels of worker motivation	• Some economies of scale • Faster production with lower unit costs than job production • Some flexibility in design of product in each batch	• Low unit costs due to constant working of machines, high labour productivity and economies of scale • JIT stock management easier to apply than with other methods	• Combines low unit costs with flexibility to meet customers' individual requirements
Main limitations	• High unit production costs • Time consuming • Wide range of tools and equipment needed	• High levels of stocks at each production stage • Unit costs likely to be higher than with flow production	• Inflexible – often very difficult and time consuming to switch from one type of product to another • Expensive to set up flow-line machinery and each section needs to be carefully synchronised	• Expensive product redesign may be needed to allow key components to be switched to allow variety • Expensive flexible capital equipment needed

Table 30.1 *Summary of main production methods*

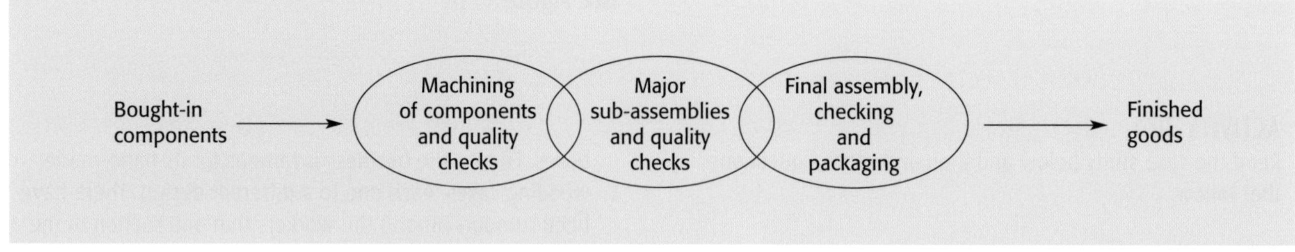

Figure 30.1 *How cell production might be organised in an assembly plant*

Impact of changing production methods

A change in production methods will impact on the different functional departments of a business.

FROM JOB TO BATCH

- Finance:
  - cost of equipment needed to handle large numbers in each batch
  - additional working capital needed to finance high levels of stocks and work in progress.

- Human resources: staff demotivation – less emphasis placed on an individual's craft skills.

- Marketing:
  - can no longer promote the product as being 'customised to each consumer'
  - may have to promote the benefits of lower prices and consistent quality.

FROM JOB OR BATCH TO FLOW

- Finance:
  - cost of capital equipment needed for flow production
  - any production delays during the change-over period may impact on cash flow.
- Human resources: risk of low motivation and boredom if traditional line production techniques are used.
- Marketing:
  - mass production requires mass marketing so market research will be vital to identify largest market segments
  - accurate estimates of future demand to ensure that output matches demand
  - promotion and pricing decisions will have to be geared towards a mass marketing approach – not niche marketing, so the orientation of the business might have to change.

FROM BATCH OR FLOW TO CELL PRODUCTION

- Finance: expensive CAM methods may be needed to allow cells to switch from one product to another.
- Human resources:
  - recruitment of flexible, adaptable staff keen to work in teams
  - staff training will be needed to achieve multi-skilling.
- Marketing: productivity and quality improvements should allow competitive pricing and promotion of the improved quality products.

Choosing appropriate production methods

The following factors will influence whether a business adopts one of the four methods of production considered above – that is job, batch, flow or flow production with the development to mass customisation.

SIZE OF THE MARKET

If the market is very small, such as for designer clothes, then job production is likely to be used. Flow production is most efficiently adopted when the market for similar or identical products is very large and consistent throughout the year. If mass production is used in this way, then mass marketing methods will also have to be adopted to sell the high output levels that can be manufactured. Even in a market for mass produced items, such as cars, there may be market niches that will allow smaller manufacturers to survive by making one-off products or batches of identical goods before changing the design or style for another model. If the market demands a large number of units, but at different times of the year, for example textbooks at the start of the academic year, then batch production might be most appropriate.

THE AMOUNT OF CAPITAL AVAILABLE

A purpose-built flow production line is difficult and expensive to construct. Small firms are unlikely to be able to afford this type of investment and are more likely to use job or batch production.

AVAILABILITY OF OTHER RESOURCES

Large-scale flow production often requires a supply of relatively unskilled workers and a large, flat land area. Job production needs skilled crafts people. If any of these resources are unavailable, or very limited in supply, then the production method may have to be adapted to suit available resources, given the market constraint referred to above.

MARKET DEMAND FOR PRODUCTS ADAPTED TO CUSTOMER REQUIREMENTS

If firms want the cost advantages of high volumes combined with the ability to make slightly different products for different markets, then mass customisation would be most appropriate. As was seen above, technology is giving firms the flexibility to produce a variety of models from the one basic design and production process.

Using more than one method

Most firms do not just use *one* production method. It is quite common for many businesses to use all three production methods to gain the benefits that they offer. A French restaurant might have a continuous supply of staple items on the menu – such as frites – but make batches of a dish that can be kept hot for a long time (or even frozen and reheated easily) such as boeuf bourguignon. Specialist dishes that have to be cooked at the table, such as flambés, will use job production. Standard Land Rover models are made on a line production system of mass production. Orders for military versions with special features in common will be made together in one batch. One-off orders, such as a bullet-proof, gold-plated model for an oil prince would be hand assembled and finished.

Final evaluation

The traditional differences between the three basic production methods are becoming much less obvious. Many complex products, such as computers and industrial engines, can be adapted to meet different consumers' different requirements. The flexibility offered by technology to large businesses could put at risk the survival of small firms that used to exploit small market niches with hand-built or batch-produced products. However, there is always likely to be a demand from increasingly wealthy consumers for original and specialist products, such as architect-designed, one-off houses, and small firms with non-mass production methods will still thrive in these market segments.

THEORY OF KNOWLEDGE

The production line in one of Indonesia's most productive garment manufacturers is a difficult place to work: always hot, very noisy, with a high risk of injury and frighteningly long hours. It is, however, very profitable, employs hundreds of people and it delivers top-brand clothing to the US and Europe at low prices.

In groups, discuss the following statement. 'There is no place for sweat-shop working conditions in a socially responsible society'.

OVER TO YOU

REVISION CHECKLIST

1 Why do many small firms use job production?
2 Explain **one** advantage and **one** disadvantage that batch production has compared to job production.
3 What is meant by a 'flow-line production system'?
4 Why is there a trend towards more customisation in flow production?
(H) 5 Under what circumstances would you advise a manufacturer of jeans and T-shirts to switch from batch to flow production?
(H) 6 Give an example of a business – other than a restaurant – that might use all three of the main methods of production.

REVISION ACTIVITY

Read the case study below and then answer the questions that follow.

In search of quality in quantity

The spread of mass customisation techniques across industries is starting to spell an end to the old production line. Mass production using flow production, based on standardised parts and processes, was introduced by Henry Ford early in the twentieth century. It greatly cut the costs of making each unit, but the main drawback was that all goods coming off a single production line were identical. In mass customisation the line can be varied to make different products, either individually or in small batches.

Caterpillar, the US supplier of construction and power equipment, says that virtually all of the 11 000 engines it makes each year are different. The variation comes from changes to 10–20% of the 1000 parts that go into each product. Software for the engine controls can also be varied. Cessna makes a wide range of general aviation aircraft from the single-engine piston to business jets on several different production lines. Of the 17 different models produced last year, Cessna produced and delivered over 1200 planes to customers. By producing a variety of models, Cessna is able to market its products to a much wider range of customers, meeting their individual requirements and adding higher value to the components used. Mass customisation needs:

- advanced and flexible capital equipment, e.g. car paint robots can now paint vehicles in 'one-off' colours in between lines of cars in standard colours
- skilled and well-trained workers able to operate this machinery and adapt it to make different products
- product designs that contain as many standardised parts as possible in different versions
- reliable suppliers able to supply slight variations in standard parts or components.

The consultancy Strategic Horizons says mass customisation has increased greatly in the last few years. 'Some time this century mass customisation will be the main form of manufacturing.'

12 marks, 23 minutes

1 Explain the difference between traditional flow or mass production and mass customisation. [6]
2 Examine the benefits of mass customisation to either a computer manufacturer or a dress-making business. [6]

EXAM PRACTICE QUESTION

Read the case study below and then answer the questions that follow.

PRODUCTION AT BMW

The Mini was one of the few parts of the former Rover group to be retained by BMW following its takeover in 1994. The Mini was seen as a valuable brand by BMW and it continued to develop it with the introduction of a new model in 2001. Production of the car was transferred to the Cowley plant in Oxford and the company spent £230 million on improvements to production facilities. The plant currently produces over 210 000 vehicles a year, but BMW is keen to increase this further.

BMW changed the culture of the organisation by introducing a new system of working at Cowley. It moved away from traditional flow production to a team-based approach. The workforce was reorganised into self-managing teams or cells of between eight and 15 people. The teams can make production decisions and have job rotation schemes. Responsibility for achieving plant-wide targets are now in the hands of those teams. Each team has more of a stake in the way the business develops rather than a hierarchical system where workers feel alienated from decision-making, stifling initiative and leading to a dependency culture. The organisation also introduced fortnightly team talks where plans, decisions, suggestions and points of view could be aired.

http://www.bized.co.uk (adapted)

25 marks, 45 minutes

1 Define the following terms:
   a flow production
   b job rotation. [4]

2 Analyse **two** disadvantages BMW may have encountered using flow production. [6]

H 3 Explain the characteristics of cell production. [6]

H 4 Discuss the advantages and disadvantages to BMW of switching from flow production to cell production. [9]

31 Costs and revenues

This chapter covers syllabus section 5.2

On completing this chapter you should be able to:

- explain and give examples of the different types of production costs
- explain the meaning of revenue and comment on sources of revenue for different firms
- understand the uses to which cost data can be put
- explain and calculate the contribution to fixed costs
- (H) explain the nature of cost and profit centres and analyse their value
- (H) analyse product viability using contribution analysis.

SETTING THE SCENE

Cutting costs to increase profits

Three important international businesses have recently announced cost reductions that will increase the chances of them making profits. Despite disappointing sales trends at its stores due to less consumer spending, Gap has reported an increase in quarterly net profit. This is the result of cost cuts – it is holding less stock, so variable costs are lower and fixed operational expenses such as management salaries have also been cut back.

Vodafone aims to save nearly $2 billion in costs after reporting a poor six-monthly performance. The mobile phone operator said UK profits over this period had halved to about $260 million. Jobs will be cut in the company. It will also spend less on promotion chasing new customers – it will instead focus on trying to get existing customers to use their phones more. This is a cheaper method of promotion.

Ryanair, Europe's leading low-cost operator, announced that it would just break even this year – no loss but no profit either – if the oil price stays below $100 a barrel. The recent fall in the price of oil – a huge variable cost for all airlines – means that Ryanair will not be forced to increase fares again.

Source: http://www.guardian.co.uk and http://newsvote.bbc.uk (adapted)

Points to think about:

- Using these cases, why is it important for a business to be able to identify and calculate its costs?
- Why do you think it is important for a company to cut costs during periods of low sales?
- Using Gap as starting point, explain which are likely to be the easiest types of costs for a business to cut back on.
- If oil prices increased again, would you advise Ryanair to increase passenger fares to try to raise revenue? Explain your answer.

Introduction

Management decisions can cover a wide range of issues and they require much information before effective strategies can be adopted. These business decisions include location of the operations, which method of production to use, which products to continue to make and whether to buy in components or make them within the business. Such decisions would not be possible without cost data. Here are some of the major uses of cost data:

- Business costs are a key factor in the 'profit equation'. Profits or losses cannot be calculated without accurate cost data. If businesses do not keep a record of their costs, then they will be unable to take profitable decisions, such as where to locate.
- Cost data are important to departments, such as marketing. Marketing managers will use cost data to help inform their pricing decisions.
- Keeping cost records also allows comparisons to be made with past periods of time. In this way, the efficiency of a department or a product's profitability may be measured and assessed over time.
- Past cost data can help to set budgets for the future. These will act as targets to work towards for the departments concerned.
- Cost variances can be calculated by comparing cost budgets with actual data.
- Comparing cost data can help a manager make decisions about resource use. For example, if wage rates are very low, then labour-intensive methods of production may be preferred over capital-intensive ones.
- Calculating the costs of different options can assist managers in their decision-making and help improve business performance.

Production costs

TYPES OF FINANCIAL COSTS

The financial costs incurred in making a product or providing a service can be classified in several ways. Cost classification is not always as clear cut as it seems and allocating costs to each product is not usually very straightforward in a business with more than one product. Some costing methods require this allocation to be made, some do not.

Before we can begin to use cost data to assist in making important decisions, it is important to understand the different cost classifications. The most important categories are:

- direct costs
- indirect costs
- fixed costs
- variable costs
- semi-variable costs
- marginal costs.

Direct costs

KEY TERM

direct costs these costs can be clearly identified with each unit of production and can be allocated to a cost centre

- One of the direct costs of a hamburger in a fast-food restaurant is the cost of the meat.
- One of the direct costs for a garage in servicing a car is the labour cost of the mechanic.
- One of the direct costs of the business studies department is the salary of the business studies teacher.

The two most common direct costs in a manufacturing business are labour and materials. The most important direct cost in a service business, such as retailing, is the cost of the goods being sold.

Indirect costs

KEY TERM

indirect costs costs which cannot be identified with a unit of production or allocated accurately to a cost centre – also known as overhead costs

Indirect costs are often referred to as overheads. Examples are:

- One indirect cost to a farm is the purchase of a tractor.
- One indirect cost to a supermarket is its promotional expenditure.
- One indirect cost to a garage is the rent.
- One indirect cost of running a school is the cost of cleaning it.

They are usually classified into four main groups:

- Production overheads – these include factory rent and rates, depreciation of equipment and power.
- Selling and distribution overheads – these include warehouse, packing and distribution costs and salaries of sales staff.
- Administration overheads – these include office rent and rates, clerical and executive salaries.
- Finance overheads – these include the interest on loans.

HOW ARE COSTS AFFECTED BY THE LEVEL OF OUTPUT?

It is important for management to understand that not all costs will vary directly in line with production increases or decreases. In the short run – the period in which no changes to capacity can be made – costs may be classified as follows:

- Fixed costs – these remain fixed no matter what the level of output, such as rent of premises.
- Variable costs – these vary as output changes, such as the direct cost of materials used in making a washing machine or the electricity used to cook a fast-food meal.
- Semi-variable costs – these include both a fixed and a variable element, e.g. the electricity standing charge plus cost per unit used, sales person's fixed basic wage plus a commission that varies with sales.
- Marginal costs – these are the additional variable costs of producing one more unit of output.

KEY TERMS

fixed costs costs that do not vary with output in the short run
variable costs costs that vary with output
semi-variable costs costs that have both a fixed cost and a variable cost element
marginal costs the extra cost of producing one more unit of output

Revenue

KEY TERMS

revenue the income received from the sale of a product
total revenue total income from the sale of all units of the product = quantity × price

Revenue is *not* the same as cash in a cash-flow forecast *unless* all goods have been sold for cash. Revenue is recorded on a firm's accounts whether the cash has been received from the customer/debtor or not. Revenue is *not* the same as profit either. All costs of operating the business during a time period have to be subtracted from total revenue to obtain the profit figure.

A business may receive income from sources other than its normal operating activities, for example from:

- the sale of non-current or fixed assets no longer required
- rent from factory or office space to another business
- dividends on shares held in another business
- interest on deposits held in a bank.

ACTIVITY 31.1

Types of costs

18 marks, 23 minutes

1 Identify **one** indirect/overhead cost for each of these businesses:
   a a building firm
   b a high-street bank
   c a TV repairer
   d an oil-fired power station. [4]

2 Explain why the cost is indirect in each case. [4]

3 Identify **one** direct cost for each of these business activities:
   a a carpenter making a wardrobe
   b an insurance company issuing a new motor insurance policy
   c a brewery delivering beer to a hotel
   d a bank agreeing an overdraft
   e an oil-fired power station. [5]

4 Why do you think it is important to identify the direct costs of producing a product? [5]

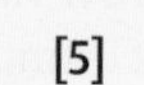

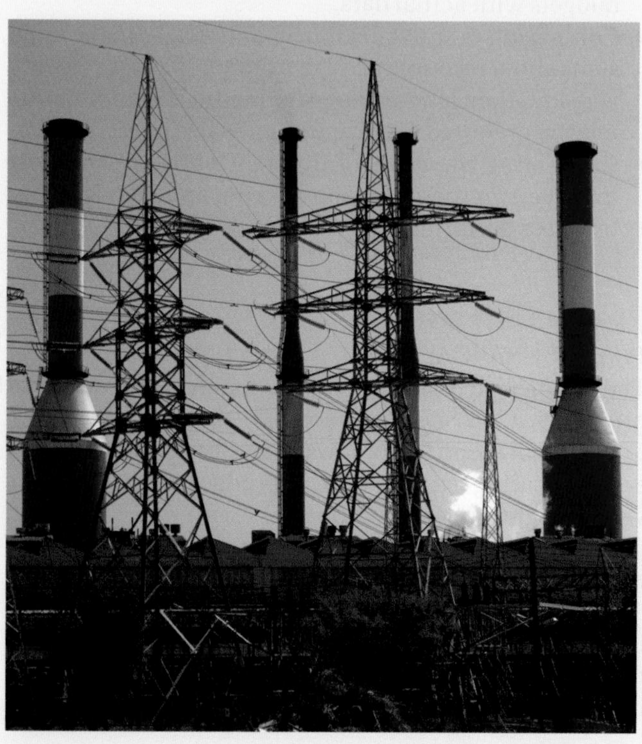

Oil-fired power station in Cyprus – indirect costs are a very high proportion of total costs in electricity generation

ACTIVITY 31.2

16 marks, 20 minutes

Classifying costs

The management of a furniture manufacturing firm is trying to classify the costs of the business to help in future decision-making. It makes a range of wooden tables and chairs. You have been asked to assist in this exercise.

1 Classify these costs by ticking in the appropriate boxes in the following table. [8]

2 Explain why you have classified these costs in the way you have. [8]

Cost	Direct	Indirect	Fixed	Variable
Rent of factory				
Management salaries				
Electricity				
Piece-rate labour wages of production staff				
Depreciation of equipment				
Lease of company cars				
Wood and other materials used in production				
Maintenance cost of special machine used to make one type of wooden chair				

Contribution to fixed costs

This is an important business concept – and must never be confused with profit. The contribution of a product refers to how much it contributes to the fixed costs and profit of the business once variable costs have been covered. It can be calculated either *per unit* of output or in terms of *total contribution* of all units produced.

KEY TERMS

contribution per unit selling price of a product less variable costs per unit

total contribution total revenue from sale of a product less total variable costs of producing it

Why is contribution not the same as profit? You can see that an important cost has not been considered – fixed cost. Profit is calculated by subtracting *all costs* (fixed and variable) from revenue. Contribution ignores fixed costs and only considers any surplus left once variable costs have been subtracted from revenue. Hence, contribution is what a product contributes towards the fixed costs of the business and, once these are paid, the profits of the business.

Costing products

Managers need to know, as accurately as possible, the cost of each product or service produced by the firm. One reason for this is the need to make a pricing decision. In fact, buyers of many products will want an estimated price or a quotation before they agree to purchase. Managers may also need to decide whether production should be stopped, stepped up or switched to new methods or new materials. Managers also need to compare actual product costs with original budgets and to compare the current period with past time periods.

In calculating the cost of a product, both direct labour and direct materials are often easy to identify and allocate to each product. For instance, the materials used in making product X are allocated directly to the cost of that product. These are not the only costs involved. Overheads, or indirect costs, cannot be allocated directly to each product but must be 'shared' between all of the items produced by a business. There is more than one costing method that can be used to apportion these costs and, therefore, there may be more than one answer to the question: 'How much does a product cost to produce?'

EXAM TIP

The only costing method required in the IB examination is contribution costing.

31 Costs and revenues

HIGHER LEVEL

COST AND PROFIT CENTRES

Before studying an important costing method, two important concepts need to be understood.

1 Cost centres

KEY TERM

cost centre a section of a business, such as a department, to which costs can be allocated or charged

Examples of cost centres are:

- in a manufacturing business – products, departments, factories, particular processes or stages in the production, such as assembly
- in a hotel – the restaurant, reception, bar, room letting and conference section.

Different businesses will use different cost centres that are appropriate to their own needs.

2 Profit centres

KEY TERM

profit centre a section of a business to which both costs and revenues can be allocated

Examples of profit centres are:

- each branch of a chain of shops
- each department of a department store
- in a multi-product firm, each product in the overall portfolio of the business.

Why do businesses divide operations into cost and profit centres?

If an organisation is divided into these centres, certain benefits are likely to be gained:

- Managers and staff will have targets to work towards – if these are reasonable and achievable, this should have a positive impact on motivation.
- These targets can be used to compare with actual performance and help identify those areas performing well and those not so well.
- The individual performances of divisions and their managers can be assessed and compared.
- Work can be monitored and decisions made about the future. For example, should a profit centre be kept open or should the price of a product be increased?

However, the following problems might arise when using these centres:

- Managers and workers may consider that their part of the business to be more important than the whole organisation itself. There could be damaging competition between profit centres to gain new orders.
- Some costs – indirect costs – can be impossible to allocate to cost and profit centres accurately and this can result in arbitrary and inaccurate overhead cost allocations.
- Reasons for good or bad performance of one particular profit centre may be due to external factors not under its control.

EXAM TIP

You may be asked to evaluate the usefulness of dividing a business into cost or profit centres.

Contribution costing approach

KEY TERM

contribution costing costing method that only allocates direct costs to cost/profit centres not overhead costs

This approach to costing solves the problem of how to apportion or divide overhead costs between products – it does not apportion them at all. Instead, the method concentrates on two very important accounting concepts:

- Marginal cost is the cost of producing an extra unit. This extra cost will clearly be a variable direct cost. For example, if the total cost of producing 100 units is $400 000 and the total cost of producing 101 units is $400 050, the marginal cost is $50.
- The contribution to fixed costs and profit. This is the revenue gained from selling a product less its variable direct costs. This is not the same as profit, which can only be calculated after overheads have also been deducted. For example, if that 101st unit with a variable (marginal) cost of $50 is sold for $70, it has made a contribution towards fixed costs of $20. The unit contribution is found as the difference between the sale price ($70) and the extra variable cost ($50), that is $20.

ACTIVITY 31.3

Cost centres at school

12 marks, 18 minutes

1 Identify and list **four** possible cost centres within your own school or college. Discuss with the managers or heads of these cost centres the benefits and drawbacks of using this form of organisation. Check with your bursar/college accountant the accuracy of your answer. [4]

2 Explain the difference between a cost centre and a profit centre. [4]

3 Explain whether any of the cost centres identified in question 1 above are, in fact, profit centres. Explain your answer. [4]

CONTRIBUTION COSTING AND DECISION-MAKING

Contribution costing has very important advantages over full costing when management plans to take important decisions based on cost data. An example contribution costing statement is shown in Table 31.1.

	Novel	Textbook
$000		
Sales revenue	50	100
Direct materials	15	35
Direct labour	20	50
Other direct costs	10	5
Total marginal cost	45	90
Contribution	5	10

Table 31.1 *Marginal costing/contribution statement for Cambridge Printers Ltd*

As can be seen in Table 31.1, this statement avoids allocating overhead costs between these two products. Overheads cannot be ignored altogether, however. They are needed to calculate the profit or loss of the business:

Total contribution for Cambridge Printers Ltd = $15 000
If total overheads amounted to $12 000, then:

profit = contribution − overheads

Therefore, the business has made a profit of $3000.

This link between contribution to overheads and profit is a crucial one and you can see the role of contribution costing in pricing decisions if you read the pricing section in Chapter 27 'Price' (see page 282).

MULTI-PRODUCT FIRMS – ASSESSING VIABILITY OF EACH PRODUCT

If a business makes more than one product or provides more than one service, contribution costing shows managers which product or service is making the greatest or least contribution to overheads and profit. If all costs, including overheads, were divided between the products instead, a manager could decide to stop producing a product that seemed to be making a loss, even though it might still be making a positive contribution. Activity 31.4 – some of which has been worked out for you – illustrates this point.

Should a business accept a contract or a purchase offer at below full cost?

If a firm has spare capacity or if it is trying to enter a new market segment, marginal costing assists managers in deciding whether to accept an order at below the full cost of the product or service. Hotels often offer very low rates to customers in off-peak seasons, arguing that it is better to earn a contribution from additional guests than to leave rooms empty.

If contracts are accepted or customers gained by using prices below full unit cost, this can, in certain circumstances, lead to an increase in the total profits of the

This hotel in Scotland may offer reduced rates in the off-season months

ACTIVITY 31.4

Should product Z be dropped?
An electrical assembly firm produces three products. The following data (in $) are available:

Products	X	Y	Z
Unit direct costs:			
Labour	5	7	9
Materials	4	12	10
Selling price	20	30	21
Current annual output (units)	500	1000	400

Total overhead costs are $10 000. The company currently uses full costing and each product is apportioned a proportion of overheads on the basis of floor space taken up: X 30%, Y 50%, Z 20%.

20 marks, 35 minutes

1 Calculate the unit contribution of each product:
Answer: X = $20 – $9 = $11
Calculate the unit contribution of Y and Z. [4]

2 If annual output is all sold, calculate the total contribution of each product.
Answer: X = 500 × $11 = $5500
Calculate the total contribution of Y and Z. [4]

3 Calculate the profit or loss made by each product using full costing at the current output level.
Answer: X: total contribution = $5500.
Allocated overheads = 30% of $10 000 = $3000
Total profit on product X = $2500
Calculate the profit or loss made by Y and Z. [6]

4 Calculate the impact on the total profit of the business if production of product *Z* is stopped. (Do not forget that the overhead costs allocated to product Z will still have to be paid.) [6]

business. This is because the fixed overhead costs are being paid anyway and if an extra contribution can be earned, profits will increase. There are dangers in this policy, however:

- Existing customers may learn of the lower prices being offered and demand similar treatment. If all goods or services being sold by a business are sold at just above marginal cost, then this could make earning a profit very unlikely.
- When high prices are a key feature in establishing the exclusivity of a brand, then to offer some customers lower prices could destroy a hard-won image.
- Where there is no excess capacity, sales at contribution cost may be losing sales based on the full cost.
- In some circumstances, lower priced goods or services may be resold into the higher priced market.

The following example illustrates this principle of using contribution in accepting new business:

Yelena is a dressmaker who pays $45 a day to use a workshop. This covers all the fixed costs of her small business. She makes three dresses a day and sells them for $30 each. Materials cost her $8 a dress. So, unit costs per dress using full costing are:

Fixed costs per dress	$15
Material cost	$8
Unit cost	$23

One day she has orders for only two dresses. Today, a new customer telephoned and wants to buy a dress but will only pay $20. Should she accept this order? Surely she will make a loss on this dress?

If she does *not* accept the order, she will make a loss of $1 today: {2×$30 – (2× $8+$45)}

If she *does* accept the order, she will make a profit of $11: {2×$30+$20} – {3×$8+$45}

EXAM TIP

Remember, fixed costs have to be paid whether the factory or workshop is busy or not.

ACTIVITY 31.5

Read the case study below and then answer the questions that follow.

Bureau Office Supplies Ltd

The marketing director was determined to gain a large order for computer desks from a major local authority. There was spare capacity on the production line as a recent contract had just been cancelled. The buyer wanted to purchase 1000 desks at a price of $70 each. Bureau's marketing director knew this was a price lower than that offered to most of its customers. The order was being discussed at a board meeting and the production manager presented the following cost data:

Computer desks full unit cost statement	
Direct labour	$25
Direct materials	$30
Apportioned overheads	$30
Full unit cost	$85

The production manager was amazed at the willingness of the marketing department to sell the desks for $70 each. 'How can you possibly justify selling these desks at a total loss of $15 000?' he asked.

Who has the better case? Is the marketing director justified in his attempt to capture this order? Is the production manager right to be concerned at the apparent loss the order will make? The appropriate answer depends on the following factors:

- Does the order make a contribution to overheads by the price exceeding direct costs?
- Is there spare capacity?
- Can the order be accepted without further overhead expenditure – e.g. a special machine needed just to make goods for this order?
- Are other orders likely?
- Is there another customer who is prepared to pay a higher price for these goods?
- Will the price of the order become known to other customers?

25 marks, 45 minutes

1 Use the contribution principle to calculate whether the new order will add to the profits of the business or not. **[10]**

2 Prepare a brief report, containing a contribution costing statement, to the board, together with a recommendation on whether to accept the order or not. Consider both quantitative and qualitative factors in coming to your recommendation. **[15]**

ACTIVITY 31.6

Read the case study below and then answer the questions that follow.

Onyx Garages

The managing director of Onyx Garages Ltd is concerned about the profitability of the business. She asked for cost details of the three divisions of the business – repairs, petrol sales and spare parts – together with a breakdown of sales revenue. Unaware of the differences between costing approaches, she asked for overheads to be apportioned on full-cost principles according to labour cost. The following data were provided.

2010 ($000s)	Repairs	Petrol	Parts
Sales revenue (A)	27	300	68
Direct labour cost	15	25	10
Direct materials	5	180	35
Other direct costs	4	10	5
Apportioned overheads (total $60 000)	18	30	12
Total cost (B)	42	245	62
Profit/(Loss) (A – B)	(15)	55	6

When the managing director saw these details, she said, 'If we close down our repair division, then total annual profits will rise – they would have been $15 000 higher last year if we had shut down repairs in 2010.'

overall profit made by the business in 2009
= (55 000 + 6000) – 15 000 = $46 000

As a trainee accountant working with this company, you have been asked for your opinion on the figures above.

20 marks, 35 minutes

1 Use the contribution costing method and produce a new costing statement. **[10]**

2 Do you agree with the managing director that the repairs division should be closed in order to increase overall garage profits? Justify your answer with both quantitative and qualitative reasons. **[10]**

EXAM TIP

Remember, even though a positive contribution can be made by accepting an order, there are real dangers that other customers will find out that a lower price is being offered on a particular contract. Qualitative factors are important too.

Using contribution costing – a summary

- Overhead costs are not allocated to cost centres, so contribution costing avoids inaccuracies and arbitrary allocations of these costs.
- Decisions about a product or department are made on the basis of contribution to overheads – not 'profit or loss' based on what may be an inaccurate full-cost calculation.
- Excess capacity is more likely to be effectively used, as orders or contracts that make a positive contribution will be accepted.

But:

- By ignoring overhead costs until the final calculation of the business's profit or loss, contribution costing does not consider that some products and departments may actually incur much higher fixed costs than others. In addition, single-product firms have to cover the fixed costs with revenue from this single product, so using contribution costing is unlikely to be so appropriate.
- It emphasises contribution in decision-making. It may lead managers to choose to maintain the production of goods just because of a positive contribution – perhaps a brand new product should be launched instead which could, in time, make an even greater contribution.
- As in all areas of decision-making, qualitative factors may be important too, such as the image a product gives the business. In addition, products with a low contribution may be part of a range of goods produced by the firm and to cease producing one would reduce the appeal of the whole range.

THEORY OF KNOWLEDGE

Calculating costs and revenues is critical for a business to know where it is in terms of trading performance. It is another part of business that relies on the skill of the mathematician.

Discuss the importance of mathematics in facilitating business people knowing about their organisations.

OVER TO YOU

REVISION CHECKLIST

1 Explain **two** reasons why cost data would be useful for operations managers.
2 Distinguish between direct and indirect costs.
3 Distinguish between fixed and variable costs.
4 Explain the differences between: revenue, contribution and profit.
5 Using the following data, calculate the contribution to overheads/profits made by a product:

Sales revenue	$14 000
Variable/direct material costs	$6 000
Variable/direct labour	$4 000
Overheads	$3 000

Explain your result.

6 Explain the term 'overheads' and give **three** examples.
(H) 7 Distinguish between a profit centre and a cost centre.
(H) 8 Analyse why the use of profit centres might have significant advantages for a multi-product business with several departments.
(H) 9 Explain the usefulness of contribution costing.
(H) 10 Assume that firm A is offered a supply of essential components by an outside supplier for a price less than the full cost of firm A making them. Explain why firm A might reject this offer.

REVISION ACTIVITY

Read the case study below and then answer the questions that follow.

Cosmic Cases

Cosmic Cases manufacture a range of suitcases. There are four sizes of case, ranging from a small vanity case to a large luggage case with wheels for mobility. The cases are sold mainly through department stores, either as a complete set or, more frequently, as individual items. The latest six-monthly costing statement (see below) had just been prepared, together with the sales figures for the same period. Jill Grealey, the managing director, was concerned about the performance of the medium-sized case and wanted to discuss the data with the finance director.

Costing statement for six months ending 31/3/2010

	Vanity case	Small suitcase	Medium suitcase	Large suitcase
Total direct costs	$30 000	$35 000	$12 000	$20 000
Allocated overheads	$15 000	$12 500	$10 000	$10 000
Total costs	$45 000	$47 500	$22 000	30 000
Total output	5 000	4 000	1 000	1 500

The selling prices to the department stores were: Vanity case $15, Small case $18, Medium case $20, Large case $25

20 marks, 35 minutes

1 Calculate the total revenue (price × quantity sold) for each size of case. [4]

2 Calculate the total profit/loss made by each size of case. [2]

3 Calculate the total contribution made by each size of case. [4]

(H) 4 Jill Grealey wanted to stop production of the medium-sized case. She said to the finance director, 'If we stop making this case, then our total profits will rise.' The finance director was convinced that this would be the wrong decision to make. As a management consultant, write a report to the managing director giving your recommendation for the action to be taken with the medium-sized case. You should justify your recommendation with both numerical and non-numerical factors. [10]

EXAM PRACTICE QUESTION

Read the case study below and then answer the questions that follow.

MIDTOWN IMPERIAL HOTEL

'We would be mad to accept this special request at $1850 below our normal price and $500 below the cost of providing the conference facilities and equipment hire.'

The hotel manager, Rajesh, was annoyed that Sheila Burns, the conference manager of the Imperial Hotel, had even bothered to consult him about the enquiry from the Friends of General Hospital for the use of the conference suite for their annual general meeting involving 100 people. Sheila had been asked for a price to organise the Friends' AGM and had used the normal hotel practice of adding a 50% mark-up to the total cost of the facility. This had been too much for the charity, so they had requested a reduction and had suggested a lower figure of $2200. As the AGM was planned for the end of February, a very slack time for all hotels, Sheila had been tempted to take up the offer and had put it to Rajesh for his approval. She knew that many of the Friends were quite influential people with business interests and she believed that this could be to the hotel's long-term advantage.

The costing statement for the conference suite was as follows:

Variable cost per delegate including food, three drinks each and waiting staff $15

Hotel overhead allocation per conference $1000

In addition, the Friends had requested some special audiovisual equipment, which the hotel would have to hire in for the day at a cost of $200

25 marks, 45 minutes

1 Define the following terms:
   a mark-up
   b variable cost. [4]

2 Using the cost information from the text, calculate:
   a the full cost of the conference for the Friends of the General Hospital (including the equipment hire) [4]
   b the price that the hotel would normally charge for a conference of this size with the equipment requested [3]
   c the profit the hotel would make at the normal price [2]
   d the contribution to the hotel's overheads and profit if the conference suite were let out for $2200. [3]

(H) 3 Using monetary and non-monetary information evaluate Sheila Burns's decision to offer the hospital the conference facilities at the reduced price. [9]

32 Break-even analysis

This chapter covers syllabus section 5.3

On completing this chapter you should be able to:

- use graphical and quantitative methods to calculate the break-even quantity, profit and margin of safety
- (H) use these methods to analyse the effects of changes in price or cost on break even, profit and margin of safety
- (H) calculate the required output level for a given target revenue or profit
- (H) analyse the assumptions and limitations of break-even analysis.

SETTING THE SCENE

Burj Dubai tower sets records and makes profits

'As of today we have sold 90% of the building,' said Mohamed Ali Alabbar, chairman of the property company that constructed the world's tallest building. 'Originally we thought that we would be lucky to break even.'

Completing such a huge building during one of the world's biggest economic downturns was not ideal, but the revenue from the sold apartments and office space is on target. Selling only around 80% of the space available would have meant that the construction company, Emaar, would have just broken even. But by attracting and retaining the interest of enough corporations so that only 10% of space was vacant meant that the Burj Dubai is already profitable – in the week it was completed.

Source: http://newsvote.bbc.co.uk (adapted)

Points to think about:

- What is the difference between 'revenue' and 'profit'?
- What do you think 'breaking even' means?
- If only 80% of the Burj Dubai office space and apartments had been sold, would you have advised the developers to reduce prices of the remaining space?

32 Break-even analysis

Introduction

KEY TERM

break-even point of production the level of output at which total costs equal total revenue

If a business is able to calculate the break-even quantity that must be sold to cover all costs, it will be easier to make important production and marketing decisions. At the break-even level of output and sales, profit is zero. This must mean that at break even:

total costs = total revenue

No profit or loss is made.

Calculating break even – methods

Break-even analysis can be undertaken in three ways:

- table of costs and revenues method
- graphical method
- formula method.

THE TABLE METHOD

Table 32.1 shows the cost and revenue data for a hamburger stall at a Premier League football match. The stall has to pay the club $500 for each match day – these are the fixed costs. Each hamburger costs $1 in ingredients and labour (variable costs) and they are sold for $2 each.

The break-even level of sales for the operator of the hamburger stall is 500. At this level of sales, total costs equal total revenue.

THE GRAPHICAL METHOD – THE BREAK-EVEN CHART

The break-even chart requires a graph with the axes shown in Figure 32.1. The chart itself is usually drawn showing three pieces of information:

- fixed costs, which, in the short term, will not vary with the level of output and which must be paid whether the firm produces anything or not
- total costs, which are the addition of fixed and variable costs; we will assume, initially at least, that variable costs vary in direct proportion to output
- sales revenue, obtained by multiplying selling price by output level.

Figure 32.2 shows a typical break-even chart. Note the following points:

- The fixed cost line is horizontal showing that fixed costs are constant at all output levels.
- The variable cost line starts from the origin (0). If no goods are produced, there will be no variable costs. It increases at a constant rate and, at each level of output shows that total variable costs = quantity × variable cost per unit. The line is not necessary to interpret the chart and is often omitted.
- The total cost line begins at the level of fixed costs, but then follows the same slope/gradient as variable costs.
- Sales revenue starts at the origin (0) as if no sales are made, there can be no revenue. It increases at a constant rate and, at each level of output shows that total revenue = quantity × price.
- The point at which the total cost and sales revenue lines cross (*BE*) is the break-even point. At production levels below the break-even point, the business is making a loss; at production levels above the break-even point, the business is making a profit.
- Profit is shown by the positive difference between sales revenue and total costs – to the right of the *BE* point.
- Maximum profit is made at maximum output and is shown on the graph.

Quantity sold	Fixed cost ($)	Variable costs ($)	Total costs ($)	Revenue (Price × quantity) ($)	Profit / (Loss) ($)
0	500	0	500	0	(500)
100	500	100	600	200	(400)
200	500	200	700	400	(300)
300	500	300	800	600	(200)
400	500	400	900	800	(100)
500	500	500	1000	1000	0
600	500	600	1100	1200	100
700	500	700	1200	1400	200

Table 32.1 *Cost and revenue data for sale of hamburgers*

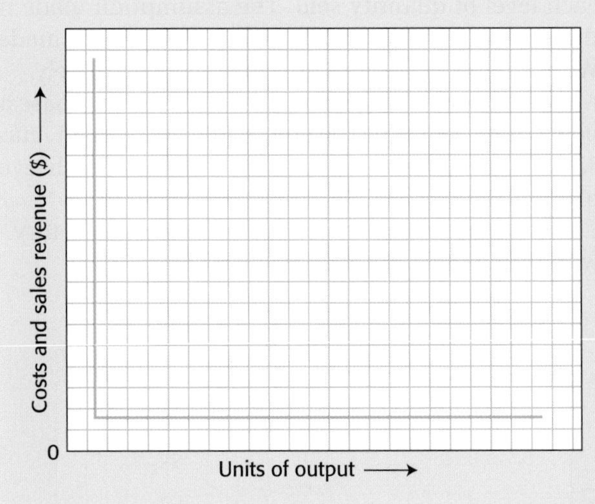

Figure 32.1 *The axes for a break-even chart*

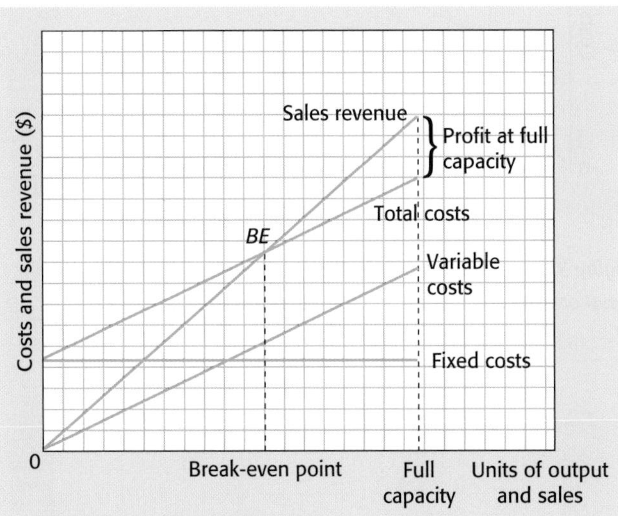

Figure 32.2 *A typical break-even chart*

ACTIVITY 32.1

14 marks, 23 minutes

1 Draw a break-even graph for the data given in Table 32.1 and confirm the break-even level of output. [10]

2 Indicate on the graph the margin of safety and the profit at maximum output – 700 hamburgers. [4]

Margin of safety

KEY TERM

margin of safety the amount by which the sales level exceeds the break-even level of output

This is a useful indication of how much sales could fall without the firm falling into loss. For example, if break-even output is 400 units and current production is 600 units, the margin of safety is 200 units. This can be expressed as a percentage of the breakeven point. For example:

production over break-even point = 200 = 50.0%

If a firm is producing below break-even point, it is in danger. This is sometimes expressed as a negative margin of safety. Hence, if break-even output is 400 and the firm is producing at 350 units, it has a margin of safety of –50 (see Figure 32.3). The minus sign simply tells us that the production level is below break even.

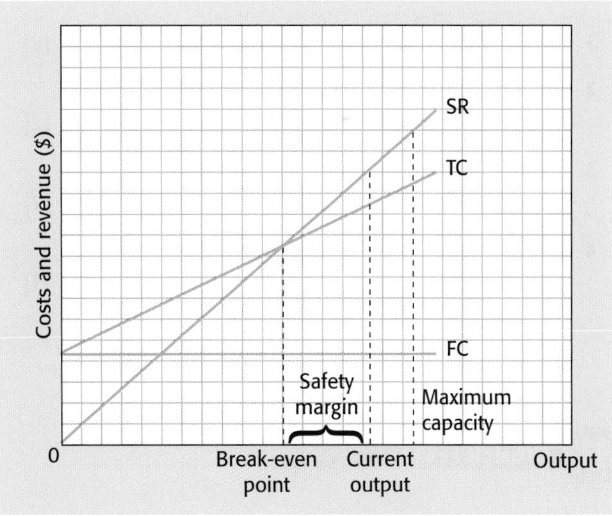

Figure 32.3 *A break-even chart showing the safety margin*

THE BREAK-EVEN FORMULA

A formula can be used to calculate break even:

$$\text{break-even level of output} = \frac{\text{fixed cost}}{\text{contribution per unit}}$$

KEY TERM

contribution per unit selling price of a product less variable costs per unit

If fixed costs are \$200 000 and the contribution per unit of output is \$50, then the break-even level of production is:

$$\frac{200000}{50} = 4000 \text{ units}$$

This is an exact answer and, therefore, likely to be more accurate than many break-even graphs.

ACTIVITY 32.2

Break-even charts

The following data relate to a single-product business:

- direct labour per unit \$12
- direct materials per unit \$18
- variable overheads per unit \$5
- fixed costs \$200 000
- selling price \$45
- maximum capacity of the factory is 30 000 units.

13 marks, 18 minutes

1 Draw a break-even chart using these data. [8]

2 Show the break-even point and identify the break-even level of output. [2]

3 Identify from the graph the profit expected at maximum capacity. [2]

4 What is the margin of safety at an output level of 25 000 units? [1]

HIGHER LEVEL

Break-even analysis – further uses

In addition to obtaining break-even levels of production and margins of safety, break-even techniques can also be used to assist managers in making key decisions.

The charts can be redrawn showing a potential new situation and this can then be compared with the existing position of the business. Care must be taken in making these comparisons, as forecasts and predictions are usually necessary. Here are three examples of further uses of the break-even technique:

1 A marketing decision – the impact of a price increase (see Figure 32.4). This raises the sales revenue line at each level of quantity sold. The assumption made in this example is that maximum sales will still be made. With a higher price level, this may well be unlikely.

2 An operations management decision – the purchase of new equipment with lower variable costs (see Figure 32.5). This will lower the variable cost line at each level of quantity.

3 Choosing between two locations for a new factory – with different fixed and variable costs.

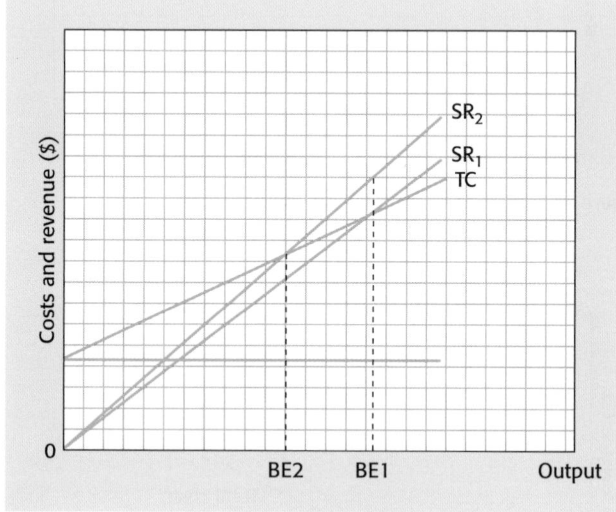

Figure 32.4 *A break-even chart showing the effect on the break-even point and maximum total profit of a price rise (BE2)*

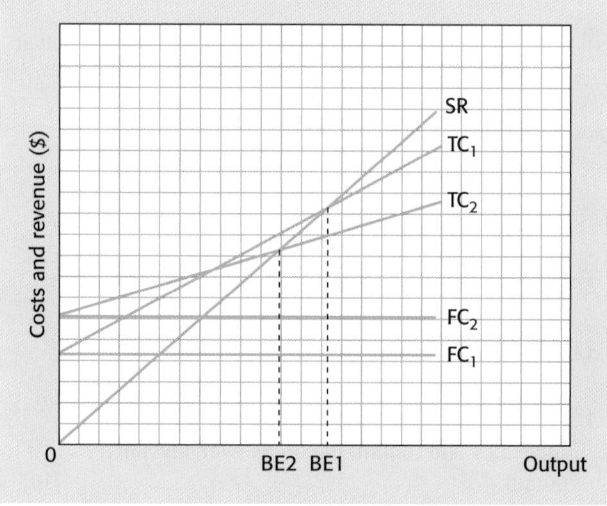

Figure 32.5 *A break-even chart showing the possible impact of new equipment (raising fixed costs), but offering lower variable costs (BE2)*

Target revenue and profit

An adapted version of the break-even formula can be used if the business wants to determine a target profit level and establish the level of output required to achieve it. The formula now becomes:

$$\text{target profit level of output} = \frac{\text{fixed costs} + \text{target profit}}{\text{contribution per unit}}$$

Suppose the target profit is \$25 000, fixed costs are \$200 000 and contribution per unit \$50. The level of output needed to earn the target profit is:

$$\frac{200000 + \$25000}{50}$$

$$= \frac{225000}{50} = 4500 \text{ units}$$

Break-even revenue

KEY TERM

break-even revenue the amount of revenue needed to cover both fixed and variable costs so that the business breaks even

Break-even revenue can be calculated using the following formula:

$$\text{break-even revenue} = \frac{\text{Fixed costs}}{1-(\text{variable cost/price})}$$

Here is an example: in service businesses, in particular, such as lawyers or surveyors, it is useful to be able to know how much income the business needs to cover all of its costs. If the monthly fixed costs of a law practice are \$60 000, lawyers are paid \$15 per hour (variable costs) and clients are charged a price of \$30 per hour, the break-even revenue will be:

$$\frac{\$60000}{1-(\$15/\$30)} = \$120000$$

Break-even analysis – an evaluation

USEFULNESS OF BREAK-EVEN ANALYSIS

- Charts are relatively easy to construct and interpret.
- It provides useful guidelines to management on break-even points, safety margins and profit/loss levels at different rates of output.
- Comparisons can be made between different options by constructing new charts to show changed circumstances. In the example above, the charts could be amended to show the possible impact on profit and break-even point of a change in the product's selling price.
- The equation produces a precise break-even result.
- Break-even analysis can be used to assist managers when taking important decisions, such as location decisions, whether to buy new equipment and which project to invest in.

LIMITATIONS OF BREAK-EVEN ANALYSIS

- The assumption that costs and revenues are always represented by straight lines is unrealistic. Not all variable costs change directly or 'smoothly' with output. For example, labour costs may increase as output reaches maximum due to higher shift payments or overtime rates. The revenue line could be influenced by price reductions made necessary to sell all units produced at high output levels. The combined effects of these assumptions could be to create two break-even points in practice (see Figure 32.6).
- Not all costs can be conveniently classified into fixed and variable costs. The introduction of semi-variable costs will make the technique much more complicated.
- There is no allowance made for stock levels on the break-even chart. It is assumed that all units produced are sold. This is unlikely to always be the case in practice.
- It is also unlikely that fixed costs will remain unchanged at different output levels up to maximum capacity.

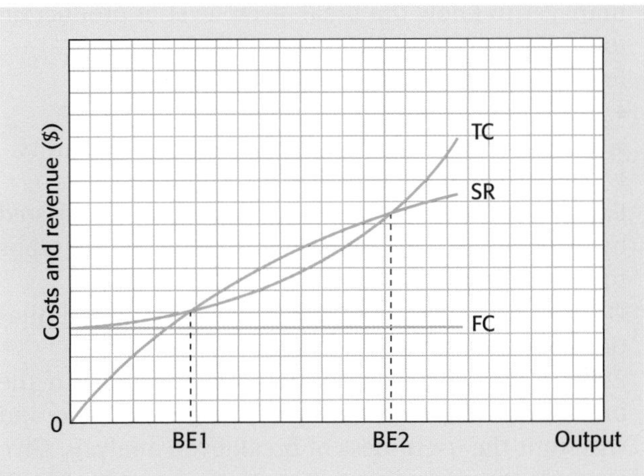

Figure 32.6 A break-even chart showing how non-linear assumptions can lead to two break-even points

EXAM TIP

It is very important to remember that a break-even graph or calculation is only accurate for a limited period of time, for example because of cost changes or changes in market conditions that mean the price has to be changed.

THEORY OF KNOWLEDGE

FOOD FOR THOUGHT

Marketing director George Berkoff began his presentation to Vinz Foods' directors: 'This product will make 30 million euros in its first three years and it will cover its initial set-up costs and break even within eight months. It will add significantly to the value of our business and I must have the green light to go ahead with the product launch.'

Examine the way numbers, data, statistics, graphs and quantitative techniques affect the way knowledge claims in business and management are valued.

ACTIVITY 32.3

Location decisions and break even

The following data have been collected about two possible locations:

	Fixed costs ($)	Variable costs per unit ($)	Forecast selling price per unit ($)	Maximum capacity due to space limits (units)
Site A	60 000	3	6	40 000
Site B	80 000	2.50	6	50 000

24 marks, 42 minutes

1 Use the data above to calculate, for each site:
  a break-even level of output
  b safety margin
  c total maximum profit assuming all units sold. [9]
2 Advise the business on which location to choose. You should explain your *BE* results in your answer. [10]
3 List **five** other factors that you consider the business should consider before making this location decision. [5]

OVER TO YOU

REVISION CHECKLIST

1 Explain why it would be useful to an operations manager to know the break-even level of production for his factory.
2 From the graph identify:
  - the break-even point
  - the margin of safety at output level of 15 000 units
  - the level of fixed costs.
3 Explain **two** business decisions that would be assisted by using break-even analysis – use sketches of graphs to aid your explanation.
H 4 Discuss, using graph sketches if necessary, **two** limitations of the break-even technique.
H 5 Explain why the assumptions that the lines in the break-even chart are straight are not realistic and will limit the usefulness of break-even analysis. Give examples to support your argument.

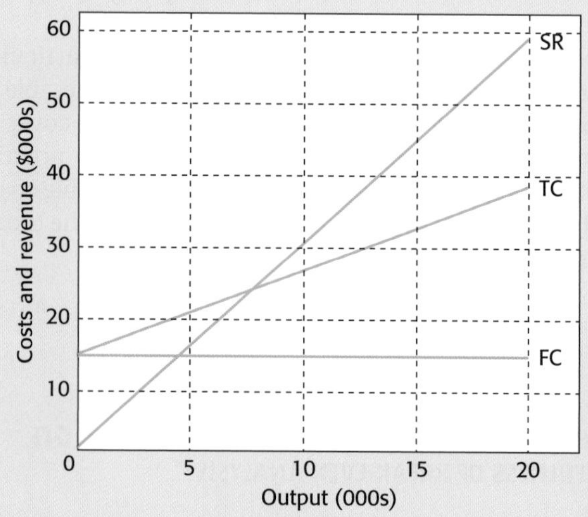

REVISION ACTIVITY

Read the case study below and then answer the questions that follow.

Decision time at the pottery

A pottery business sells clay pots for $3 each. It expects to produce and sell 5000 pots this year, although there is a total production capacity of 7500. Fixed costs are $4000 per year. The variable costs of production are $1.50 per pot.

16 marks, 23 minutes

1 Draw a break-even graph to represent these data, identifying the break-even level of production and the safety margin. [6]

 2 The manager is considering two options in an effort to increase profits:

- Purchase a new energy-efficient kiln. This would raise fixed costs by $1000 per year but reduce variable costs to $1.20 per pot. Output would remain unchanged.
- Reduce price by 10%. Market research indicates that this could raise sales by 20%. By drawing two new graphs, compare the break-even points of all three situations (including the original), the total levels of profit and the safety margins.

Advise the firm, on the basis of your results, whether to remain as it is or to adopt one of the two options above. Justify your answer. [10]

EXAM PRACTICE QUESTION

Read the case study below and then answer the questions that follow.

WINDCHEATER CAR ROOFRACKS

The sole owner of Windcheater Car Roofracks needs to expand output as a result of increasing demand from motor accessory shops. The business uses batch production to produce its roofracks. Current output capacity has been reached at 5000 units per year. Each rack is sold to the retailers for $40. Production costs are:

- direct labour $10
- direct materials $12
- fixed costs $54 000.

The owner is considering two options for expansion:

Option 1 Extend the existing premises, but keep the same method of production. This would increase fixed costs by $27 000 per year, but direct costs would remain unchanged. Capacity would be doubled.

Option 2 Purchase new machinery, which will speed up the production process and cut down on wasted materials. Fixed costs would rise by $6000 per year, but direct costs would be reduced by $2 per unit. Output capacity would increase by 50%.

25 marks, 45 minutes

1 Define the following terms:
a batch production
b fixed cost. [4]

2 Draw a break-even chart for options 1 and 2 and show the break-even points for each option. [8]

(H) 3 On the basis of your break-even charts, explain which option Windcheater should choose. [4]

(H) 4 Evaluate the usefulness of break-even analysis to businesses like Windcheater. [9]

33 Quality assurance

This chapter covers syllabus section 5.3

On completing this chapter you should be able to:

- explain the concept of quality
- understand the difference between quality control and quality assurance – total quality management
- (H) explain the role of Kaizen in quality improvement
- (H) evaluate different approaches to quality improvement
- (H) explain the role of local and national standards in assuring quality for consumers.

SETTING THE SCENE

Toyota's approach to quality

A new approach to achieving quality products was developed in the USA by many specialists, most famously by W. Edwards Deming. They advocated many changes to traditional quality-control systems. In the mid-1940s, many Japanese manufacturers listened to their ideas and then started to re-think and re-develop their approach to quality.

Toyota has achieved a reputation for the production of very high-quality vehicles in many countries around the world. The company considers quality assurance as a key part of the activities to produce goods and services economically and to be of a standard which exceeds customers' needs. Customer satisfaction is at the heart of everything that Toyota does. In order to satisfy customer needs the company includes all 'members' (Toyota's name for its workers) in quality assurance activities. Everybody – from research and development to manufacturing, retailing and servicing – contributes to the quality process. All members have two roles – their own job and quality assurance. At Toyota this is referred to as 'company-wide quality control'.

Some people understand quality assurance to mean the inspection of parts after they are made. This is not Toyota's belief – total quality is carried out using two basic principles: quality is built in at every stage and quality is continually improved.

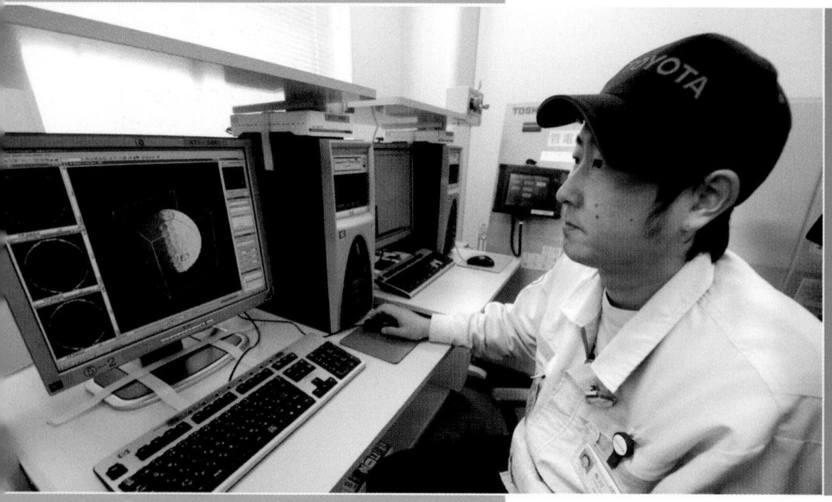

Points to think about:

- Why does Toyota take quality so seriously? How can it gain a competitive advantage from this approach?
- Why do you think it is important to involve all staff members in striving for higher quality?
- What do you understand by the term 'quality product'?

Introduction

A quality product does not necessarily have to be the 'best possible'. Read Activity 33.1 to find out why.

KEY TERM

quality product a good or service that meets customers' expectations and is therefore 'fit for purpose'

ACTIVITY 33.1

Read the case study below and then answer the questions that follow.

Are expensive products always the best quality?

The operations manager at Athletic Shoes was proud of the quality standards his business achieved. 'Our sports shoes sell for a retail price of $25, so they are not the best or most stylish on the market. However, only four customers returned shoes because of serious problems over the last year when we sold 50 000 pairs. All workers are accountable for the products reaching minimum standards of quality at each stage of production. Of course, there are better shoes available, but our customers know what they are getting.'

The customer service manager at the Exclusive Footwear shoe shop was about to return a pair of hand-made leather fashion shoes to Ital Fashion Shoe producers. 'We retail these for $400 a pair and customers paying such high prices expect, reasonably in my view, a near-perfect product. Even the smallest scratch or imperfection means the customers reject them. Although Ital checks every shoe made at each stage of production a few very minor blemishes are sometimes missed.'

14 marks, 23 minutes

1 The consumers of these different types of shoes seem to have different product expectations. Explain why this is. [4]

2 Using just this case study, how would you attempt to explain what 'quality' means? [4]

3 Briefly explain how the two different methods used for achieving quality seem to operate. [6]

The concept of quality

As Activity 33.1 showed, consumer expectations will be very different for goods and services sold at different prices. A quality product does not *have* to be made with the highest-quality materials to the most exacting standards – but it must meet consumer requirements for it.

In certain cases, a product must meet the highest quality standards and the high cost of it becomes almost insignificant. Internal parts for a jet engine used on a passenger plane will be expected to have a failure rate of less than 1 in 1 million. However, if fashion clothing was made to the same exacting standards with regards to stitching, buttons, zips and so on – how much would a pair of jeans cost then? Designing too much quality into a product that consumers do not expect to last for many years can make the product very expensive and uncompetitive.

A Rolls-Royce aircraft engine – customer expectations of quality mean that it has been constructed to the highest possible standard

A quality product does not have to be expensive. If low-cost light bulbs and clothes pegs last for several years in normal use, then they have still met consumer expectations and have been of the required quality. So, a highly priced good may still be of low quality if it fails to come up to consumer requirements. A cheap good can be considered of good quality if it performs as expected. It should now be clear that quality is a relative concept and not an absolute one – it depends on the product's price and the expectations of consumers.

KEY TERM

quality standards the expectations of customers expressed in terms of the minimum acceptable production or service standards

33 Quality assurance

It is easy to think of quality standards in terms of manufactured goods – the reliability of cars or the wear rate of clothes, for example. However, quality is a crucial issue for service providers too. For example, the quality of service offered by UK banks is claimed to be inferior to those in other countries in terms of:

- time taken to answer the telephone
- no indication of waiting time on the telephone
- queuing time in branches
- contact with the same person on each occasion
- number of accounts errors made
- quality of financial advice given.

The advantages of producing quality products and services are:

- easier to create customer loyalty
- saves on the costs associated with customer complaints, e.g. compensation, replacing
- defective products and loss of consumer goodwill
- longer life cycles
- less advertising may be necessary as the brand will establish a quality image through the performance of the products
- a higher price – a price premium – could be charged for such goods and services. Quality can, therefore, be profitable.

EXAM TIP

Quality is often viewed by candidates as an absolute concept and not a relative one. Quality must be explained in reference to the expectations of the target market consumers. The level of quality selected by any business must be based on the resources available to it, the needs of the target market and the quality standards of competitors.

Quality control and quality assurance

KEY TERMS

quality control this is based on inspection of the product or a sample of products

quality assurance this is a system of agreeing and meeting quality standards at each stage of production to ensure consumer satisfaction

These two terms are used to classify two very different approaches to managing and achieving quality in any business.

Quality control is the traditional approach to achieving quality based on inspection or checking, usually of the completed product or of the service as it is being provided to a consumer. For example:

- an MP3 player being tested at the end of the production line for battery-charging capability
- a telephone-banking adviser having a call to a customer listened to and recorded.

QUALITY-CONTROL TECHNIQUES

There are three stages to effective quality control:

1. Prevention – this is the most effective way of improving quality. If the design of the product follows the requirements of the customer and allows for accurate production, then the other two stages will be less significant. Quality should be 'designed into' a product.
2. Inspection – traditionally this has been the most important stage – but it has high costs and these could be reduced by 'zero-defect' manufacturing that is the aim of total quality management (TQM).
3. Correction and improvement – this is not just about correcting faulty products but is also concerned with correcting the process that caused the fault in the first place. This will improve quality in the future.

Inspecting for quality

Traditionally, quality has been checked by inspecting products at the end of the production process. Some checking might take place at different stages of the process, but the emphasis was on the quality of the finished article. Quality inspection is expensive – qualified engineers have to be used – and such checks can involve damaging the product, for example dropping computers to see if they still work. As a result, a sampling process must be used and this cannot guarantee that every product is of the appropriate quality. When quality checks are used during the production process statistical techniques are used to record and respond to results.

Weaknesses of inspecting for quality

The key point about inspected quality is that it involves a group of quality-control inspectors who check the work of workers. There are several problems related to this approach to quality:

- It is looking for problems and is, therefore, negative in its culture. It can cause resentment among workers, as the inspectors believe that they have been 'successful' when they find faults. Workers are likely to view the inspectors as management employees who are there just to check on output and to find problems with the work. Workers may consider it satisfying to get a faulty product passed by this team of inspectors.

- The job of inspection can be tedious, so inspectors become demotivated and may not carry out their tasks efficiently.
- If checking takes place only at specific points in the production process, then faulty products may pass through several production stages before being identified. This could lead to a lot of time being spent finding the source of the fault between the quality checkpoints.
- The main drawback is that it takes away from the workers the responsibility for quality. As the inspectors have full authority for checking products, the workers will not see quality as their responsibility and will not feel that it is part of their task to ensure that it is maintained. Ultimately, this lack of responsibility is demotivating and will result in lower-quality output.

Inspecting for quality, therefore, has many weaknesses. It is hardly surprising that there has been a move away from this approach in recent years.

QUALITY ASSURANCE

Quality assurance is based on setting agreed quality standards at all stages in the production of a good or service in order to ensure that customers' satisfaction is achieved. It does not just focus on the finished product. This approach often involves self-checking by workers of their own output against these agreed quality standards. The key differences between the two methods are that quality assurance:

- puts much more emphasis on prevention of poor quality by designing products for easy fault-free manufacture, rather than inspecting for poor-quality products – 'getting it right first time'
- stresses the need for workers to get it right the first time and reduces the chances of faulty products occurring or expensive reworking of faulty goods
- establishes quality standards and targets for each stage of the production process – for both goods and services
- checks components, materials and services bought into the business at the point of arrival or delivery – not at the end of the production process by which stage much time and many resources may have been wasted.

The quality-assurance department will need to consider all areas of the firm. Agreed standards must be established at all stages of the process from initial product idea to it finally reaching the consumer:

- Product design – will the product meet the expectations of consumers?
- Quality of inputs – quality must not be let down by bought-in components. Suppliers will have to accept and keep to strict quality standards.
- Production quality – this can be assured by total quality management (TQM) and emphasising with workers that quality levels must not drop below pre-set standards.
- Delivery systems – customers need goods and services delivered at times convenient to them. The punctuality and reliability of delivery systems must be monitored.
- Customer service including after-sales service – continued customer satisfaction will depend on the quality of contact with consumers after purchase.

For example:

- Nissan car factories have predetermined quality standards set and checked at each stage of the assembly of vehicles – by the workers accountable for them.
- First Direct, a European telephone banking organisation, sets limits on waiting times for calls to be answered, average times to be taken for meeting each customer's requests and assurance standards to monitor that customer requests have been acted on correctly.

Quality assurance has the following advantages:

- It makes everyone responsible for quality – this can be a form of job enrichment.
- Self-checking and making efforts to improve quality increases motivation.
- The system can be used to 'trace back' quality problems to the stage of the production process where a problem might have been occurring.
- It reduces the need for expensive final inspection and correction or reworking of faulty products.

EXAM TIP

Remember, quality is not just an issue for large businesses. Small and medium-sized firms must ensure that the quality level selected and the quality-assurance methods used are within their resources. In fact, by using quality assurance that helps to reduce wasted faulty products and on staff self-checking quality levels, these businesses can save money in the long term.

Importance of quality-assurance systems

There are several reasons why it is important for businesses to establish quality-assurance systems:

- to involve all staff and this can promote team work and a sense of belonging which aids motivation
- to set quality standards for all stages of production so that all materials and all production phases are

checked before it is 'too late' and the whole product has been completed
- to reduce costs of final inspection as this should become less necessary as all stages and sub-sections of the process have been judged against quality standards
- to reduce total quality costs – by instilling in the whole organisation a culture of quality, it is possible for quality assurance to lead to reduced costs of wastage and faulty products
- to gain accreditation for quality awards – these can give a business real status or kudos. The most widely recognised quality award within the European Union is ISO 9000.

ISO 9000

KEY TERM

ISO 9000 internationally recognised certificate that acknowledges the existence of a quality procedure that meets certain conditions

This award is given to firms that can demonstrate that they have a quality-assurance system in place which allows for quality to be regularly measured and for corrective action to be taken if quality falls below these levels. This award does not prove that every good produced or service provided by the business is of good quality. It is an indication that a business has a system of quality in place that has relevant targets set and activities ready to deal with a quality problem.

To obtain ISO 9000 accreditation the firm has to demonstrate that it has:

- staff training and appraisal methods
- methods for checking on suppliers
- quality standards in all areas of the business
- procedures for dealing with defective products and quality failures
- after-sales service.

The benefits for a firm of being forced to establish a quality-assurance framework and to have this externally monitored are clear. There are, however, drawbacks such as costs of preparing for inspection and bureaucratic form filling to gain the certificate.

EXAM TIP

Remember, ISO 9000 is not a guarantee of good quality.

Total quality management (TQM)

This approach to quality assurance requires the involvement of all employees in an organisation. It is based on the principle that everyone within a business has a contribution to make to the overall quality of the finished product or service. By reducing waste and cost of rejected low-quality products TQM is a key component of the approach to operations management known as lean production.

KEY TERMS

total quality management an approach to quality that aims to involve all employees in the quality improvement process

lean production producing goods and services with the minimum of wasted resources while maintaining high quality

TQM often involves a significant change in the culture of an organisation. Employees can no longer think that quality is someone else's responsibility. Every worker should think about the quality of the work they are performing because another employee is, in effect, their internal customer. All departments are expected to meet the standards expected by its customer. These departmental relationships are sometimes known as quality chains. All businesses can, therefore, be described as a series of supplier and customer relationships.

For example:

- A truck driver who drops off supplies to retailers is the internal customer of the team loading the vehicle – goods must be handled carefully and loaded in the right order. The truck driver has to face the retailer if goods are damaged or the wrong ones delivered.
- A computer assembly team is the internal customer of the teams producing the individual components – a fault with any of these means the assembled computer will not meet quality standards.

To be effective the TQM concept must be fully explained and training given to all staff. TQM is not a technique, it is a philosophy of quality being everyone's responsibility. The aim is to make all workers at all levels accept that the quality of the work they perform is important. They should be empowered with the responsibility of checking this quality level before passing their work on to the next production stage. This approach fits in well with the Herzberg principles of job enrichment (see Chapter 14 'Motivation', page 145). TQM should almost eliminate the need for a separate quality-control department with inspectors divorced from the production line itself.

ACTIVITY 33.2

Read the case study below and then answer the questions that follow.

Trinidad Tractor Factory Ltd (TTF) – quality becomes an issue

The last meeting between the marketing director and the operations manager of TTF was very heated. They each blamed the other for the disappointing data below. The marketing director had complained that 'The number of faulty tractors leaving our factory has increased and this has directly led to both rising customer complaints and lower sales. Our reputation is being damaged by these faults and many former customers are now buying imported tractors. We have just lost a government order for 15 tractors as our competitor was able to boast about their ISO 9000 certificate.' The operations manager had replied by saying that customers were becoming much more demanding and it was up to the marketing department to provide good after-sales service. 'I have increased the number of quality control engineers from five to eight and we are correcting more faults in completed products than ever before.'

	TTF customer complaints	TTF sales (units)
2009	53	2345
2010	78	2124

26 marks, 45 minutes

1. Outline the problems that TTF has because of low-quality products. [6]
2. Discuss whether the increase in the number of quality-control inspectors was the best way to try to improve quality. [8]
3. Explain the difference between quality control and quality assurance. [4]
4. Do you think that TTF should establish a quality-assurance system and apply for an ISO award? Justify your answer. [8]

TQM aims to cut the costs of faulty or defective products by encouraging all staff to 'get it right first time' and to achieve 'zero defects'. This is in contrast to traditional inspected quality methods that considered quality control as being a cost centre of the business. Under TQM, if quality is improved and guaranteed, then reject costs should fall and the demand for the products rises over time. However, TQM will only work effectively if everyone in the firm is committed to the idea. It cannot just be introduced into one section of a business if defective products coming from other sections are not reduced. The philosophy requires a commitment from senior management to allow the workforce authority and empowerment, as TQM will not operate well in a rigid and authoritarian structure.

KEY TERMS

internal customers people within the organisation who depend upon the quality of work being done by others

zero defects the aim of achieving perfect products every time

Jaguar uses quality-assurance systems and it now has one of the highest US customer satisfaction ratings of any car maker

Kaizen – continuous improvement

ROLE OF KAIZEN IN QUALITY IMPROVEMENT

KEY TERM

Kaizen Japanese term meaning continuous improvement

The philosophy behind this idea is that all workers have something to contribute to improving the way their business operates and the way the product is made. Traditional styles of management – possibly based on a Theory X approach (see Chapter 14, page 144) – never give workers the opportunity to suggest improvements to the way things are done because the assumption is that trained managers 'know best'. The objective of managers adopting this approach is to keep production up to the mark and then look for one-off improvements in the form of inventions or to make investments in machines to increase productivity.

The Kaizen philosophy suggests that, in many cases, workers actually know more than managers about how a job should be done or how productivity might be improved. Someone who works at a task every day is actually much more likely to know how to change it to improve either quality or productivity than a manager with, perhaps, no hands-on experience of production at all.

Another key feature of this idea is that improvements in productivity do not just result from massive one-off investments in new technology. A series of small improvements, suggested by staff teams, can, over time, amount to as big an improvement in efficiency as a major new investment. This idea is illustrated in Figure 33.1.

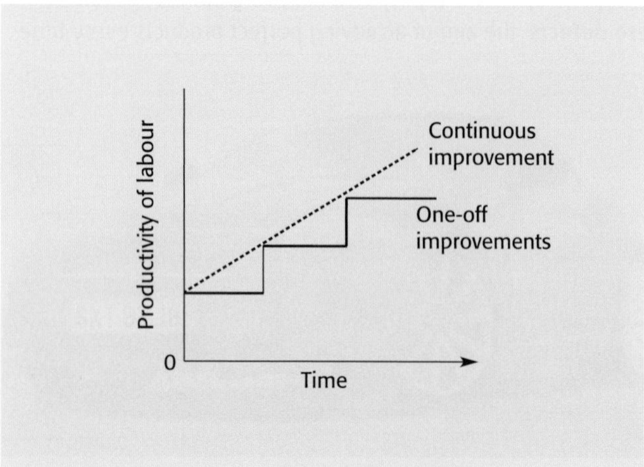

Figure 33.1 Kaizen compared to 'one-off' changes

Conditions necessary for Kaizen to operate:

1. Management culture must be directed towards involving staff and giving their views and ideas importance – managers must accept that in many areas of the business work experience will count for as much as theoretical knowledge.
2. Team working – suggesting and discussing new ideas to improve quality or productivity is best done in groups. Kaizen groups are likely to be drawn from the work team – or cell – operating in the place of work. Each Kaizen group should meet regularly – management must provide the time and necessary training – to discuss problems that they have identified. Recommendations for change could then be put forward to managers, or each group may be empowered to put their own ideas into practice.
3. Empowerment – by giving each Kaizen group the power to take decisions regarding workplace improvements, this will allow speedier introduction of new ideas and motivate staff to come up with further ideas. You should now be able to link this suggestion with the work of Herzberg and the concept of job enrichment. If every idea and suggestion made by a Kaizen group had to be put to managers – who could then either ignore it or accept it after consideration – staff would become quickly fed up with the process.
4. All staff should be involved.

EXAM TIP

In examination answers, it would be good analysis to link the Kaizen principle to the work of Herzberg on job enrichment.

KAIZEN – AN EVALUATION

There are some limitations to the Kaizen approach:

- Some changes cannot be introduced gradually and may need a radical and expensive solution: for example, the need for Kodak to invest heavily in the manufacture of digital cameras rather than film-based cameras when the new technology was introduced.
- There may be very real resistance from senior managers to such a programme due to their existing culture. Kaizen will only work effectively if there is genuine empowerment of the groups involved – authoritarian managers would find this impossible to accept.
- At least in the short term there may be tangible costs to the business of such a scheme, such as staff training to organise meetings and lost output as a result of meeting time.
- The most important advances tend to be made early on during the Kaizen programme – later changes can be less significant and this has led some observers to believe that there could be 'diminishing returns' from such an approach.

Benchmarking

KEY TERM

benchmarking comparing the performance – including quality – of a business with performance standards throughout the industry

The full title for benchmarking is 'best practice benchmarking'. This comparison with 'the best' will identify areas of the business that need to be improved to meet the highest standards of quality and productivity.

ACTIVITY 33.3

Read the case study below and then answer the questions that follow.

Kaizen thinking fires productivity

Mike Brookes, co-owner of Ambi-Rad, when asked why he failed for many years to introduce new ideas aimed at increasing competitiveness, gives a simple answer: he was too busy expanding. His Midlands engineering company is a European leader in gas-fired, 'radiant tube' heating systems. But Mr Brookes found little time to think about how to increase quality and productivity. 'We were a top-down company with all the new ideas coming from the directors,' explains Mr Brookes. The government minister for industry is particularly keen that smaller manufacturers should take on board 'Kaizen', or continuous improvement programmes of the kind initially introduced by Japanese firms in the past 20 years. The competitiveness problems were highlighted in a recent EU report, which put Britain in 11th position out of 15 in the EU productivity league table.

At Ambi-Rad, Mr Brookes decided to take action and implement 'Kaizen' thinking under which workers in the company hierarchy are given more control over decisions and encouraged to come up with suggestions for quality and efficiency improvements. Most of the 150 workers at Ambi-Rad's main plant in the UK are divided into eight groups, each one responsible for specific aspects of production. Team leaders encourage new ideas and link the shop floor and senior managers. One recent idea came from Jean Cox, an assembly worker at Ambi-Rad for 13 years. She suggested punching holes in a piece of metal in a different place to shorten the overall production process. The proposal was implemented, leading to a small but worthwhile productivity improvement. 'I feel I am much more involved,' says Ms Cox. 'As a problem occurs, rather than carry on regardless, we are now encouraged to think of a way round it.'

Some of the ideas are very simple, but suggestions from people like Ms Cox have taken $600 000 a year off the company's costs. The Kaizen scheme has enabled Ambi-Rad to maintain profits at a time of severe difficulties in the engineering business. In the past two years, many comparable UK companies have seen orders and earnings hit by the economic recession and weak demand in important markets.

'Partly because of the new manufacturing ideas we have kept pre-tax profits at 10 per cent of sales, which is really excellent by the standards of other engineering companies,' Mr Brookes says. This year Ambi-Rad expects to have sales of £18 million, more than twice the figure five years ago, and exports roughly a quarter of its turnover. Mr Brookes wants savings from Kaizen-based ideas to reach £1 million annually over the next few years.

36 marks, 60 minutes

1. Explain how Kaizen groups can help reduce costs for businesses such as Ambi-Rad. [6]
2. Identify and evaluate the benefits for three stakeholder groups in Ambi-Rad from the firm adopting Kaizen. [12]
3. Examine the conditions that are necessary for the Kaizen philosophy to be successful at businesses such as Ambi-Rad. [8]
4. Using the case study as a starting point, assess the possible relationship between the use of Kaizen groups and the leadership style of an organisation. [10]

Stages in the benchmarking process:

1. Identify the aspects of the business to be benchmarked – perhaps by interviewing customers and finding out what they consider to be most important. For example, research may reveal that the most important factors are reliability of the product, speed of delivery and after-sales service. These are the areas that the firm would first benchmark.
2. Measure performance in these areas – for example, reliability records, delivery records and the number of customer complaints.
3. Identify the firms in the industry that are considered to be the best – this process might be assessed by management consultants or by benchmarking schemes operated by government or industry organisations.
4. Use comparative data from the best firms to establish the main weaknesses in the business – these data might be obtained from firms by mutual agreement, from published accounts, specialist industry publications and contact with customers/suppliers.
5. Set standards for improvement – these might be the standards set by the best firms or they could be set even higher to create a competitive advantage.
6. Change processes to achieve the standards set – this may require nothing more than a different way of performing one task, but more substantial changes may be necessary.
7. Re-measurement – the changes to the process need to be checked to see if the new, higher standards are

being reached. Benchmarking is not a 'one-off ' exercise and to be effective it should become a continuous process to achieve long-term improvements in productivity and quality.

See Table 33.1 for an evaluation of benchmarking.

Benefits	Limitations
• Offers a faster and cheaper way of solving problems than firms attempting to solve production or quality problems without external comparisons. • Areas of greatest significance for customers are identified and action can be directed to improving these. • A process that can assist the firm to increase international competitiveness. • Comparisons between firms in different industries, such as customer service departments in a retailer compared to a bank, can encourage a useful crossover of ideas. • If the workforce is involved in the comparison exercise, then their participation can lead to better ideas for improvement and increased motivation.	• The process depends on obtaining relevant and up-to-date information from other firms in the industry. If this is difficult to obtain, then the benchmarking exercise will be limited. • Merely copying the ideas and practices of other firms may discourage initiative and original ideas. • The costs of the comparison exercise may not be recovered by the improvements obtained from benchmarking.

Table 33.1 Benchmarking – benefits and limitations

Quality issues – an evaluation

- Quality is not an 'option'. It is a fundamental aspect of all successful businesses.
- Quality is an issue for all firms, in all sectors of industry. It is essential for businesses to put quality of products and customer service at the top of their priorities to survive in competitive markets. Improving quality has obvious cost advantages if the rate of defective products is reduced.
- Satisfying customers will give clear marketing advantages when seeking further sales.
- Involving staff in quality improvement programmes can lead to a more motivated workforce.

ACTIVITY 33.4

Read the case study below and then answer the questions that follow.

Benchmarking is key to efficiency

Lord Simon is former chief executive of BP, and was responsible for introducing benchmarking to the oil company. 'Knowing the opposition and where it is making better profits is one of the most crucial bits of information you can get in business,' says Simon. 'In BP we faced the fact that American companies always achieved a higher return on capital than UK equivalents. Why should this be? We set ourselves a target to equal or exceed Exxon, at that time the best performer, within five years. It was a great way of focusing the mind.' Simon now promotes the benefits of benchmarking to all firms, especially to small and medium enterprises. 'They need clear data on where competitors are extracting greater profit margins, whether in production, marketing or distribution. Such data can change, enabling better decisions about how to allocate resources.'

Benchmarking also improves the focus and motivation of everybody in the company. 'When managers talk to staff about the need for change it can seem like just another demand,' says Simon. 'But if staff look at a benchmark and see the competition is doing better, they say, if they can do that, so can we.'

Closing the Gap, a DTI (Department of Trade and Industry) report, has indicated startling variations in performance. The top 25% of companies achieve profit margins five times greater than those in the bottom quartile. They achieve 98% supplier accuracy and delivery reliability against 60% accuracy and 85% reliability for bottom quartile companies. Spending on training is ten times greater and staff absenteeism rates up to 75% lower than in the bottom quartile.

12 marks, 21 minutes

1 Explain 'benchmarking'. [3]

2 Analyse **three** benefits to small and medium-sized enterprises of adopting benchmarking. [9]

H

THEORY OF KNOWLEDGE

'8 out of 10 owners said their cats prefer Whiskas' [catfood]
'Carlsberg is probably the best lager in the world'
BMW – 'The ultimate driving machine'
'Nothing acts faster than Anadin' [painkillers]

Businesses often make claims about the superior quality of their products.

a Find **four** more advertising slogans where businesses make claims about the superiority of their products.
b To what extent do organisations have a moral responsibility to meet these claims?

OVER TO YOU

REVISION CHECKLIST

1 Why does 'quality' not always mean 'making the best product possible'?
2 Explain **three** benefits to a business from producing quality products.
3 Why might 'designed-in' quality be better than 'inspected quality'?
4 Explain **two** drawbacks to inspected quality.
5 Outline the key features of total quality management.
6 Are the following statements true or false? Briefly explain your decision in each case.
 a An expensive product is always of higher quality than a cheaper one.
 b Insisting on higher quality standards always costs a business more.
 c ISO 9000 ensures products are of a high quality.
 d Quality-assurance systems can result in lower total costs for a business.
7 Explain why improving quality is important in an increasingly competitive market.
8 Use the example of a small manufacturer of fashion clothing to explain how quality assurance could be adopted.
(H) 9 Distinguish between quality control and quality assurance.
(H) 10 What are the problems often associated with effective benchmarking?
(H) 11 Examine **two** conditions that are necessary for a Kaizen programme to operate successfully.
(H) 12 Explain how a service-based business could benefit from adopting benchmarking.

REVISION ACTIVITY

Read the case study below and then answer the questions that follow.

Wiping out defects at Wheeler's

Wheeler's manufactures pumps, cables, controls and drums used by washing-machine producers. The company is a major supplier to most of the leading firms in the industry. The firm buys in a huge range of materials and components to make up the products it sells to the washing-machine makers. Wheeler's makes over 2000 different items. Today's consumers have high expectations for their new washing machines. They look for value for money and reliability. Manufacturers expect suppliers like Wheeler's to turn out parts to a high quality at the lowest possible cost. To satisfy these demands and to maintain an edge over cheaper foreign imports, Wheeler's follows a strict quality-assurance system. It has been awarded ISO 9000 – a certificate now demanded by many of its customers. There is a world of difference between setting targets for zero defects and low costs and actually achieving them. The growing demand for Wheeler's products is due in no small part to its reputation for quality, which is based on workers checking their own work using statistical control charts and recording the results of quality checks at regular intervals. Wheeler's operations manager believes that the company's success depends on three key operations management features:

- The lean production system has made 'just in time' a priority. They now produce what is wanted when it is wanted. This requires Wheeler's own suppliers to be reliable and to be involved in the design and quality of each component so that it is perfect for the task it has to perform.
- A well-trained, multi-skilled and flexible workforce. Workers have to be prepared to operate different machines and produce different items. They work in cells

or teams of between six and ten. Each cell is empowered to implement its own quality improvements established through regular Kaizen-type meetings. The workers have been successful in achieving very high productivity levels. Staff turnover is low.

- A quality-assurance system that puts the emphasis on 'prevention not detection'. Employees share responsibility for making defect-free products. For example, the team making electrical switches checks the quality of output at each stage. They will not pass any item on to the final assembly and packing stage – their 'internal customers' – unless it is defect free. This approach helped the company gain the ISO 9000 award.

24 marks, 42 minutes

1 What is meant by the terms:
   a ISO 9000
    b Kaizen groups
   c quality assurance
   d internal customers
   e total quality management
   f zero defects? [12]

2 An objective of the company is to achieve 'quality output at low costs'. Evaluate the importance of the **three** factors listed in the case study in helping to achieve this objective. [12]

EXAM PRACTICE QUESTION

Read the case study below and then answer the questions that follow.

QUALITY ASSURANCE AT THE HAIRDRESSERS

The Kuala Lumpur branch of FatBoyTrims had come bottom of all of the company's branches for customer satisfaction. The number of complaints received at head office about this branch and the quality of its haircutting and styling services had been much greater than for any other location. Revenue had fallen in recent months and the number of repeat customers had fallen to 15% of total custom. A competing business nearby, that charged at least 30% more, was always full. As a consequence, this branch of FatBoyTrims had spent more on advertising for new business than any other. The revenue per customer was also low as high-value services – such as colouring and tinting – were avoided by customers. A new manager had just been appointed to the branch and she immediately set about establishing a quality-assurance approach to improve customer satisfaction. She set quality targets for each stage of the customer experience. These included:

- maximum time for phone to ring
- maximum waiting time for appointment time
- maximum time between hair wash and cutting
- all customers to be offered refreshments
- minimum time spent by stylists with each customer
- feedback forms to be filled in by 20% of clients and stylists responsible for each client to discuss answers with client.

Each member of staff was given responsibility for at least one of these targets in an attempt to achieve continuous improvement in the hairdressers. A record had to be kept of the branch's success at meeting these targets. At first, branch costs increased as an additional staff member had to be recruited to help meet the quality standards. After two months, the number of repeat clients had reached 36% and the branch reduced its advertising expenditure. After four months, revenue had climbed by 38% and the branch had reached third place in the company league table for customer satisfaction. The competing branch had reduced many prices by 15%.

25 marks, 45 minutes

1 Define the following terms:
   a quality assurance
   b continuous improvement. [4]

2 Outline **two** drawbacks to this business of not meeting customer expectations. [5]

3 Analyse the benefits to this hairdressers of improving the quality of their service. [7]

4 Discuss the problems the new manager of FatBoyTrims might have when trying to implement the quality targets she has set. [9]

34 Location

This chapter cover syllabus sections 5.5

On completing this chapter you should be able to:

- explain the causes and consequences of location and relocation – domestically and internationally
- (H) consider the effects of globalisation on location
- (H) assess the importance of location decisions to the success of a business and on functional departments.

SETTING THE SCENE

Locating in Trinidad and Tobago

Two multinational food companies have located in Trinidad for similar reasons. P. R. Trinidad Ltd is a subsidiary of French drinks group Pernod Ricard. The 100-employee company extracts anise oil, which is used as flavouring, from the leaves of anise bushes planted on land leased at a reasonable rent from the government. Before deciding on Trinidad as the best location, the company 'looked first at the economic and political stability of the country,' reported the operations manager. 'Trinidad also enjoys the right climate for anise production and we found a large area of flat land suitable for its production,' he added. Other reasons given by the company for its location decision were the well-trained workforce with a good supply of qualified technicians from the local university. The company is planning some joint ventures with other local businesses – so the existence of other businesses in the drinks industry was an important factor in moving to Trinidad too.

Coca-Cola recently opened a bottling plant in Trinidad and employs 350 staff there. The flow production method is used with much automated machinery. The demand for soft drinks in the Caribbean is high all year round. The general manager Bob Ramchand believes that 'the government is in favour of private sector industry and supports it. Many of the qualified young professionals in the Caribbean come from the University of West Indies and this was important to us.' Trinidad is viewed as the key island for manufacturing within the regional free trade area known as CARICOM. Being a member of this organisation allows free trade between members for goods manufactured on the island. Many of the other countries in the region are too small to have the resources needed for a large operation such as Coca-Cola. 'I believe that in the long term the decision will prove to be an even better one as the CARICOM area opens up more and more and Trinidad is well located to supply all of its members,' added Mr Ramchand.

34 Location

Points to think about:

- List and explain **six** reasons for these companies locating in Trinidad.
- Do you think that the location decision is a very important one for all businesses? Explain your answer by referring to soft drink manufacturers, hotels and hairdressing businesses.

Photo © TriniGourmet.com

Introduction

Deciding on the best location for a new business – or relocating an existing one – is often crucial to its success. Location decisions – choosing new sites for expansion or relocation of the business – are some of the most important decisions made by management teams. Selecting the best site will have a significant effect on many departments of the business and, ultimately, on the profitability and chances of success of the whole firm. Location decisions have three key characteristics:

- They are strategic in nature – as they are long term and have an impact on the whole business.
- They are difficult to reverse if an error of judgement is made – due to the costs of relocation.
- They are taken at the highest management levels and are not delegated to subordinates.

An 'optimal' location decision is one that selects the best site for expansion of the business or for its relocation, given current information. This best site should maximise the long-term profits of the business. The optimal site is nearly always a compromise between conflicting benefits and drawbacks. For example:

1. A well-positioned high-street shop will have the potential for high sales but will have higher rental charges than a similar sized shop out of town.
2. A factory location which is cheap to purchase due to its distance from major towns might have problems recruiting staff due to lack of a large and trained working population.

So an optimal location is likely to be a compromise one that balances:

- high fixed costs of the site and buildings with convenience for customers and potential sales revenue
- the low costs of a remote site with limited supply of suitably qualified labour
- quantitative factors with qualitative ones (see below)
- the opportunities of receiving government grants in areas of high unemployment with the risks of low sales as average incomes in the area may be low.

KEY TERM

optimal location a business location that gives the best combination of quantitative and qualitative factors

Some of the potential problems of non-optimal location decisions are shown in Table 34.1.

EXAM TIP

Do not assume that the 'best' location for a business will always be competitive – cost and other factors can change over a period of time and this accounts for many firms 'relocating' to new sites – but this can be expensive.

Factors influencing location decisions

QUANTITATIVE FACTORS

KEY TERM

quantitative factors these are measurable in financial terms and will have a direct impact on either the costs of a site or the revenues from it and its profitability

Problem	Disadvantages to business
High fixed site costs	• High break-even level of production. • Low profits – or even losses. • If operating at low-capacity utilisation, unit fixed costs will be high.
High variable costs, e.g. labour	• Low contribution per unit produced or sold. • Low profits – or even losses. • High unit variable costs reduce competitiveness.
Low unemployment rate	• Problems with recruiting suitable staff. • Staff turnover likely to be a problem. • Pay levels may have to be raised to attract and retain staff.
High unemployment rate	• Average consumer disposable incomes may be low – leading to relatively low demand for income elastic products.
Poor transport infrastructure	• Raises transport costs for both materials and finished products. • Relatively inaccessible to customers. • Difficult to operate a just-in-time (JIT) stock management system due to unreliable deliveries.

Table 34.1 *Disadvantages to a business of non-optimal location decisions*

Site and other capital costs such as building or shop-fitting costs

These vary greatly from region to region within a country and between countries. The best office and retail sites may be so expensive that the cost of them is beyond the resources of all but the largest companies. The cost of building on a greenfield site – one that has never previously been developed – must be compared with the costs of adapting existing buildings on a developed site.

Labour costs

The relative importance of these as a locational factor depends on whether the business is capital or labour intensive. An insurance company call centre will need many staff, but the labour costs of a nuclear power station will be a very small proportion of its total costs. The attraction of much lower wage rates overseas has encouraged many European businesses to set up operations in other countries – for example, bank and insurance company call centres.

Transport costs

Businesses that use heavy and bulky raw materials – such as steel making – will incur high transport costs if suppliers are at a great distance from the steel plant. Goods that increase in bulk during production will, traditionally, reduce transport costs by locating close to the market. Service industries, such as hotels and retailing, need to be conveniently located for customers and transport costs will be of less significance.

Sales revenue potential

The level of sales made by a business can depend directly on location. Confectionery shops and convenience stores have to be just that – convenient to potential customers. In addition to this, certain locations can add status and image to a business and this may allow value to be added to the product in the eyes of the consumers. This is true for high-class retailers situated in London's Bond Street or Ngee Ann City in Singapore, but also for financial specialists operating from an address in New York's Wall Street.

Government grants

Governments across the world are very keen to attract new businesses to locate in their country. Grants may be offered to act as an incentive. Existing businesses operating in a country can also be provided with financial assistance to retain existing jobs or attract new employment to deprived areas of high unemployment.

ACTIVITY 34.1

Read the case study below and then answer the questions that follow.

Government support

Senior management at Nissan were initially reluctant to build the new Micra at their Sunderland factory. However, a UK government grant of £3.26 million helped to clinch the decision to invest a total of £95 million into the new production facilities at this factory in the north of the UK. It secured 250 jobs in this area of high unemployment.

16 marks, 28 minutes

1 Explain the benefits the regional economy would gain as a result of this new investment. [6]

2 Discuss whether the location that offered the highest government grant would always be the best site for a new car factory. [10]

Once these quantitative factors have been identified and costs and revenues estimated, the following techniques can be used to assist in the location decision:

1 Profit estimates

By comparing the estimated revenues and costs of each location the site with the highest annual potential profit may be identified.

ACTIVITY 34.2

Profits in different locations

12 marks, 21 minutes

1 Calculate the estimated annual profit from these two possible locations for a mobile-phone shop: [6]

	Site A – city centre location	Site B – shopping arcade out of the city
Estimated annual costs (including rent and labour costs)	£975 000	£498 000
Expected annual sales (units)	25 000	17 000
Forecast selling price per unit	£50	£45

2 In future years, why might the annual profits made from each location change? [6]

ACTIVITY 34.3

Which site is the best investment?

8 marks, 14 minutes

TLC Cosmetics is planning to open a new branch of its shops selling upmarket cosmetics. The company has expanded rapidly and it has substantial loans. Some economists are predicting an increase in interest rates by the Bank of England. Using the investment appraisal results in the table and any other information, which of these two sites would you recommend the company should choose for the new shop? [8]

	Site X – capital cost £2 million	Site Y – capital cost £3 million
Length of time to repay initial capital cost (payback period)	2.5 years	3.8 years
Annual profit made as % of initial cost	12%	14%

2 Investment appraisal

Location decisions often involve a substantial capital investment. Investment appraisal methods can be used to identify locations with the highest potential returns over a number of years. The simplest of these, the payback method, can be used to estimate the location most likely to return the original investment most quickly. This could be of particular benefit to a business with a capital shortage or in times of economic uncertainty. Calculating the annual profit as a percentage of the original cost of each location is another useful measure.

3 Break-even analysis

This is a straightforward method of comparing two or more possible locations. The lower the break-even level of output the better the site is, other things being equal. This information might be particularly important for businesses that face high levels of fixed costs and which may benefit from a location with lower overheads. (See Chapter 32 'Break-even analysis'.)

QUALITATIVE FACTORS

There are other important factors that cannot be measured in financial terms. These are called qualitative factors.

ACTIVITY 34.4

Which site covers its costs at a lower output level?

ICT Chemicals Ltd plans to open a new paint factory with a maximum capacity of 10 million litres per year. It has narrowed the choice of sites down to Site C in the UK, located five miles away from a large city and Site D in a less economically developed country with very low labour wage rates and few health and safety controls. The figures exclude transport costs.

	Site C	Site D
Level of output needed to cover all costs (break-even output)	4 million litres	2 million litres

10 marks, 18 minutes

1 Suggest to the business which location should be selected by using the data shown in the table. The expected annual production level is 6 million litres. Briefly explain your answer. [6]

2 What other factors do you think the business should consider before taking the final location decision? [4]

KEY TERM

qualitative factors non-measurable factors that may influence business decisions

Safety

To avoid potential risk to the public and damage to the company's reputation as a consequence of an accident that risked public safety, some industrial plants will be located in remote areas, even though these may increase transport and other costs.

Room for further expansion

It is expensive to relocate if a site proves to be too small to accommodate an expanding business. If a location has room for further expansion of the business, then this might be an important long-term consideration.

Managers' preferences

In small businesses, managers' personal preferences regarding desirable work and home environments could influence location decisions of the business. In larger organisations, such as a plc, this is unlikely to be a factor, as earning profits and increasing returns to shareholders will be key objectives that will take priority in location decisions.

Labour supply

Apart from the cost of labour, the availability or non-availability of workers with appropriate skills will be an important factor for most business location decisions.

Ethical considerations

A business deciding to relocate from the UK is likely to make workers redundant. This will cause bad publicity and could also be contrary to the ethical code of the business and may be viewed by stakeholders as being immoral. In addition, if the relocation is to a country with much weaker controls over worker welfare and the environment, there could be further claims that the business is acting unethically.

Environmental concerns

A business might be reluctant to set up in an area that is particularly sensitive from an environmental viewpoint, as this could lead to poor public relations and action from pressure groups.

Infrastructure

The quality of the local infrastructure, especially transport and communication links, will influence the choice of location. Singapore's huge port facilities have encouraged many of the world's largest shipping firms to set up a base there. The quality of IT infrastructure varies considerably around the world and this is an important consideration for companies that need quick communication with their different sites or customers, for example call centres or selling via the internet. The growing popularity of online shopping in developed countries may lead to some retailers opening fewer high-street stores and more 'warehouse' operations to supply consumers.

ACTIVITY 34.5

Read the case study below and then answer the questions that follow.

Rolls-Royce goes for a quality location

Choosing the lowest cost location for the Rolls-Royce factory was not a priority. When BMW moved production from the industrial northern town of Crewe, it chose one of the most crowded and expensive parts of the country – the south-east of England. The Goodwood factory has many advantages but low cost is not one of them. One of its main benefits is its proximity to a small airport where the helicopters and executive jets of intending purchasers of Rolls-Royce cars can arrive in style. Potential buyers are identified by the company and invited to visit the factory and attend events held at the nearby exclusive marina and horse-race and motor-race courses. The area has been termed a 'playground for the wealthy' and future customers often spend a day or two at the races or a morning at the marina before browsing the cars – and more often than not, signing an order form.

Source: http://business.timesonline (adapted)

8 marks, 14 minutes

Explain why qualitative factors were considered to be so important in this case when Rolls-Royce could find much cheaper locations to produce its cars. [8]

Low cost was not a priority when locating the Rolls-Royce factory

OTHER LOCATIONAL ISSUES

The pull of the market

This is less important with the development of transport and communication industries and with the world becoming a single market for so many goods. The internet can achieve a massive amount in terms of rendering location of a retailing business less important, but the market is still very important for the service industries and the power of the car has taken many of these out of the convenient centres of towns and on to the ring roads. The cinema is a good example. Once the centrepiece of a town, it is found regenerated on the ring roads. Superstores and other retail stores have relocated in a similar fashion.

Planning restrictions

Local authorities have a duty to serve the interests of their populations. On the one hand, they want business and industry because they provide employment. On the other hand, they want to protect the environment of the towns and villages. In some areas, large development corporations have been set up to develop a town or city into a much more successful combination of dwellings and industrial activity. In most countries, local or central government has set up industrial estates and business parks that both businesses and consumers find very attractive.

External economies of scale

These are cost reductions that can benefit a business as the industry 'clusters' and grows in one region. It is common for firms in the same industry to be clustered in the same region – Silicon Valley in the USA and Bangalore in India have a very high concentration of IT-focused businesses. All IT firms in these regions will benefit from the attraction of a pool of qualified labour to the area, local college courses focused on IT and a network of suppliers whose own scale economies should offer lower component costs. In addition, it will be easier to arrange co-operation and joint ventures when the businesses are located close to each other.

Multi-site locations

See Table 34.2 for the advantages and disadvantages of multi-site locations.

Advantages	Disadvantages
• Greater convenience for consumers, e.g. McDonald's restaurants in every town. • Lower transport costs, e.g. breweries can supply large cities from regional breweries rather than transport from one national brewery. • Production-based companies reduce the risk of supply disruption if there are technical or industrial relations problems in one factory. • Opportunities for delegation of authority to regional managers from head office – help to develop staff skills and improve motivation. • Cost advantages of multi-sites in different countries.	• Co-ordination problems between the locations – excellent two-way communication systems will be essential. • Potential lack of control and direction from senior management based at head office. • Different cultural standards and legal systems in different countries – the business must adapt to these differences. • If sites are too close to each other, there may be a danger of 'cannibalism' where one restaurant or store takes sales away from another owned by the same business.

Table 34.2 *Multi-site locations – advantages and disadvantages*

ACTIVITY 34.6

Read the case study below and then answer the questions that follow.

One company, many factories

Toyota is one of the best examples of a multi-site business with 52 manufacturing facilities in 26 different countries. In a typical recent 12-month period, it opened its first factory in Mexico and opened its 13th manufacturing facility in the USA – in Mississippi. In 2007, concerns were expressed by the company that its production capacity in the USA was starting to outstrip demand for vehicles, so this could be the last new factory the company builds there for some time.

Source: http://reuters.com (adapted)

12 marks, 21 minutes

Discuss the advantages and disadvantages to Toyota of operating factories in so many different countries. **[12]**

H HIGHER LEVEL

Globalisation and international location decisions

The issues considered so far could apply to any location decision – a new business start-up, the relocation or expansion of existing business. These issues are all relevant whether the location decision is a regional, national or international one. However, there are some additional factors that need to be weighed up when a firm is considering locating in another country.

One of the main features of globalisation is the growing trend for businesses to relocate completely to another country or to set up new operating bases abroad. This process is often referred to as 'offshoring'. The world's largest corporations are now virtually all multinationals.

KEY TERMS

offshoring the relocation of a business process done in one country to the same or another company in another country

multinational a business with operations or production bases in more than one country

EXAM TIP

Do not confuse offshoring with outsourcing, although they may be linked. Outsourcing is transferring a business function, such as human resources, to another company. It is only offshoring if this company is based in another country.

REASONS FOR LOCATION DECISIONS AND IMPACT ON FUNCTIONAL DEPARTMENTS

1 To reduce costs

This is undoubtedly the major reason explaining most company moves abroad. The potential for higher profits will benefit the finance department despite the initial set-up costs in overseas locations. With labour wage rates in India, Malaysia, China and eastern Europe being a fraction of those in western Europe and the USA, it is not surprising that businesses that wish to remain competitive have to seriously consider relocation to low-wage economies. Examples include:

Norwich Union Insurance call centres → India
Panasonic TV production → Czech Republic
Hornby Toy Trains → China
Dyson vacuum cleaners → Malaysia.

In developing countries, because of the shortage of jobs, the human resource department will find it easy to recruit unskilled or semi-skilled workers.

Look at the data in Table 34.3 for labour costs in different countries compared with German labour costs, which are some of the highest in the world. It is now easy to see what cost advantages multinational companies have when they operate in countries such as Bulgaria, Hungary, India and China.

Country	Weekly pay in euros	Compared with Germany (= 100)
India	26	3
China	43	6
Bulgaria	45	6
Brazil	62	8
Hungary	165	22

Table 34.3 *Labour costs in different countries compared with German labour costs*
Source: Federation of European Employers, January 2010

2 To access global markets

Rapid economic growth in developing countries has created huge potential for the marketing department to exploit. Access to these markets is often best achieved by direct operation in the countries concerned. Markets for some products in western Europe have reached saturation point and further sales growth can only be achieved by expanding abroad. Some businesses have reached the limit of their internal domestic expansion as the market may have reached saturation. There may be threats from government regulatory bodies about increasing monopoly power. All of these reasons help explain Tesco's recent international expansion. Tesco shops are now common sights in Thailand and eastern Europe and it has also become the only major UK-based retail business to expand successfully into the USA. The Fresh&Easy convenience stores opened by Tesco in California have quickly become established and profitable, helping to make up for slow growth in the UK grocery market.

Many businesses' international location decisions are in response to competitors' location decisions. These are often called defensive actions. So the expansion of the French supermarket chain Carrefour into China – gaining first mover advantage in the process – has encouraged Tesco to make similar strategic location decisions in the burgeoning market.

3 To avoid protectionist trade barriers

KEY TERM

trade barriers taxes (tariffs) or other limitations on the free international movement of goods and services

Barriers to free international trade are rapidly being reduced, but some still exist – notably between the large trading blocs, such as the EU, North American Free Trade Association (NAFTA) and Association of South East Asian Nations (ASEAN). To avoid tariff barriers on imported goods into most countries or trading blocs, it is necessary to set up operations within the country or trading bloc concerned. Examples include Honda's factory in Swindon that produces cars for the EU market and Toyota's new factory in Mexico that gives tariff-free access to this country's car market.

4 Other reasons

These include substantial government financial support to relocating businesses, good educational standards (as in India and China) and highly qualified staff and avoidance of problems resulting from exchange rate fluctuations. This last point makes pricing decisions difficult for the marketing department, especially for products that are not made within the country, but are imported, when its currency fluctuates considerably. One way around this problem is to locate production in this country.

EXAM TIP

Do your own research during the Business and Management course on major location decisions, both at home and abroad, of businesses based in your country.

THEORY OF KNOWLEDGE

'Globalisation, as defined by rich people like us, is a very nice thing ... you are talking about the internet, you are talking about cell [mobile] phones, you are talking about computers. This doesn't affect two-thirds of the people of the world.' *Jimmy Carter, former US president*

In groups, in the light of this statement, discuss the claim that 'globalisation only benefits people in the richest countries in the world'.

ACTIVITY 34.7

Read the case study below and then answer the questions that follow.

TRG's excellent experience in Pakistan

TRG is a company listed on the Karachi Stock Exchange. The business takes controlling stakes in firms offering services to other businesses – such as web- and phone-based customer service centres – and prepares them for rapid expansion. It has operations in Lahore, Karachi, the Philippines and Morocco. The company's decision to base its head office in Lahore, Pakistan was based on a number of factors:

- large pool of English-proficient graduates
- well-organised capital market giving opportunities to raise the finance needed
- land costs 30% less than India or the Philippines
- wages 60% less than the USA
- government willing to offer incentives, a 15-year tax 'holiday' and willing to invest in IT infrastructure.

There were some initial problems:

- cultural differences – workers did not expect to work US business hours
- lack of general management experience among the graduates – they had to be trained in this
- lack of support organisations, such as specialist personnel recruitment firms or training institutes, as TRG were one of the first businesses in this industry in the country.

Source: www.sourcingmag.com

22 marks, 40 minutes

1 Using knowledge of your own country, do you think TRG would be advised to move its head office to your country or remain in Pakistan? Give reasons for your answer. [10]

Students in Pakistan: Evaluate the main reasons for TRG's decision to base the company in Pakistan.

2 Explain why another business services firm setting up in Lahore might benefit from TRG's presence there. [6]

3 Outline **two** of TRG's functional departments that would be affected by a relocation to your country. [6]

Students in Pakistan: Outline **two** of TRG's functional departments that would be most affected by location of operations in Pakistan.

POTENTIAL LIMITATIONS OF INTERNATIONAL LOCATION AND IMPACT ON FUNCTIONAL DEPARTMENTS

International locations can also add to the number of drawbacks that might result from an inappropriate location decision. Here are some of the major additional issues that need to be weighed up carefully before going offshore.

1 Language and other communication barriers

Distance is often a problem for effective communication. This human resources problem is made worse when company employees, suppliers or customers use another language altogether. This is one of the reasons for India's success in attracting offshoring companies – English is one of the official languages.

2 Cultural differences

These are important for the marketing department if products are being sold in the country concerned – consumer tastes and religious factors will play a significant role in determining what goods should be stocked. Cultural differences also exist in the workplace and impact on human resource management. Toyota found that the typical Mexican worker is self-reliant and independent, yet the Toyota manufacturing system depends greatly on team work and co-operation. Effective staff training may be necessary to ensure that cultural differences do not prevent successful overseas expansion. For example, Oscar Rodriguez was only 20 when he was employed by Toyota's new Tijuana factory. 'I was self reliant and I would conceal production problems and try and fix them myself,' he said. 'But I was taught how to communicate and I have learned that there is never a stupid question. The company supervisors teach us well and they are patient' (www.detnews.com).

3 Level of service concerns

This operations management issue applies particularly to the offshoring of call centres, technical support centres and functions such as accounting. Some consumer groups argue that off-shoring of these services has led to inferior customer service due to time difference problems, time delays in phone messages, language barriers and different practices and conventions, for example with accounting systems.

4 Supply-chain concerns

The operations management department will also be concerned about the loss of control over quality and reliability of delivery with overseas manufacturing plants. This reason is always cited by Zara, the clothing company, for its decision to not offshore clothing production to cheaper countries as 'fast fashion' requires very close contact with suppliers. Using just-in-time manufacturing may become much riskier if important supplies have to be shipped thousands of miles to an assembly plant.

5 Ethical considerations

There may be a loss of jobs when a company locates all or some of its operations abroad and this may, as in the case of Burberry clothing, led to a consumer boycott as there were claims that the company's decision to close its Welsh factory was not 'the right thing to do'. In addition, there are several reports of high-street clothing retailers sourcing supplies from Asian factories using child labour and very low-wage labour. Could this negative publicity cancel out the competitive advantage of low-cost supplies? Will the marketing department experience lost sales from negative publicity and will human resources find it more difficult to recruit well-qualified staff if the business is viewed as being unethical?

EXAM TIP

Remember, the lowest cost location may not always be the optimal location – if quality suffers or if there is negative public reaction to products being made by low-wage workers, then low costs may be outweighed by even lower revenue!

Is it right to sell clothing in European shops that has been made by low-wage labour in Asian countries?

H

OVER TO YOU

REVISION CHECKLIST

1 What would be meant by the term 'optimal location' for a new Walmart supermarket?
2 Outline possible reasons why Tesco chose the USA as a country in which to expand.
3 Analyse **two** ways in which the location of a retail shop could affect its competitiveness.
4 Examine the quantitative factors that a hairdressing business might take into account when deciding whether to relocate.
5 What is meant by 'clustering' of similar firms in an industry and why might this be of significance in the location decision for a new car factory?
6 Why do governments often award grants to firms setting up in certain areas of the country?
7 Explain why the location of a new clothes retailer is of strategic importance to the business.
8 Outline **two** examples of qualitative factors that might be considered by an insurance company planning to relocate its offices to a cheaper region, far away from its existing operations.
9 How might the increasing use of internet shopping have an impact on the location decisions of businesses that sell to final consumers?
(H) 10 Why might a high-technology business decide to locate in Germany, despite the huge labour cost advantages that some developing countries have?

REVISION ACTIVITY

Read the case studies below and then answer the questions that follow.

Indo European Foods to manufacture ethnic foods in the UK

'There is a huge potential market for our authentic Indian spices, sauces, pastes and chutneys in the UK and the rest of Europe,' said Dave Roberts the operations director of Indo European Foods. By locating a factory in eastern England the company will be able to supply this market more quickly, efficiently and profitably than importing directly from India. Felixstowe offers the business a suitable site of over 9000 square metres, close proximity to ports, excellent rail links and east–west road connections via the A14. 'This area also gives us a good base for finding a suitably skilled multi-cultural workforce,' added Mr. Roberts.

Electrolux factory to close in Durham with loss of 500 jobs

An Electrolux cooker factory in Durham is to close with the loss of 500 jobs. It has been making increased losses. Only three years ago, the company believed this was still the best location for manufacturing cookers and invested £7 million in the plant with the aid of a government grant of £1.6 million. Now, the company believes that the sterling exchange rate and wage and other cost pressures make it uncompetitive and have decided to switch production to a factory in Poland. It has been estimated that the break-even level of production at this new plant will be less than half that of the UK factory.

Source: www.bbc.co.uk (adapted)

33 marks, 60 minutes

1 Explain why a good location is important to both of these businesses. [6]
2 Analyse **five** factors referred to in the cases that influenced these two location decisions. [10]
3 Explain why the 'best' location for a business might change over time. [5]
4 Discuss the problems and benefits that Electrolux might experience following the decision to relocate to Poland. [12]

EXAM PRACTICE QUESTION

Read the case study below and then answer the questions that follow.

GERMAN EFFICIENCY IN AN EGYPTIAN LOCATION

Two large banners hanging from the ceiling – 'Zero defect is perfection' and '0.01 of a millimetre makes a difference' – remind the staff of their employer's quality standards. Welcome to the Egyptian German Automotive company, an oasis of German efficiency 30 kilometres south-west of the busy streets of Cairo. Almost every one of the 1600 Mercedes sold in Egypt comes from this plant, a joint venture set up in 1996 by Mercedes and a group of Egyptian entrepreneurs.

The company had no choice other than to set up its own operations in order to serve this market, where some 65 000 cars are sold a year. Very high import duties, imposed by the government to safeguard local industries and jobs, force manufacturers to charge exorbitant prices for imported cars. 'Egypt is a local assembly market because the average import duty on a car is 230%. If you want to sell in this market, you have to be here,' says Roland Sabais, managing director of Mercedes Egypt.

Once set up, foreign companies have to deal with many rules and regulations designed to help local producers. A recent example was the government's decision to increase the percentage of local parts in the car from 40% to 45% virtually overnight. Despite these hurdles the operations are profitable and have met the targets set by head office. One of the reasons why the company is profitable, despite the 'non-tariff trade barriers', is that labour is cheap and productivity is high. The 400 workers in the Cairo Mercedes plant are paid on average 80% less than their counterparts in Germany, even though they are trained and perform to similar standards. Infrastructure costs are also low. The factory cost Daimler-Benz E£150 million ($38.5 million), but its revenues are tax-free for ten years because it is located in one of the government-sponsored industrial zones.

25 marks, 45 minutes

1 Define the following terms:
 a joint venture
 b import duties. [4]

2 Explain **two** qualitative factors Mercedes might take into account when choosing to locate in Cairo. [4]

3 Analyse the **two** reasons why Mercedes chose to use a joint venture when entering the Egyptian economy. [8]

4 Discuss the advantages and disadvantages to Mercedes of expanding into the developing economies like Egypt. [9]

35 Innovation

This chapter covers syllabus section 5.6 (Higher level only)

On completing this chapter you should be able to:

- (H) explain the importance of research and development for a business
- (H) explain the role and importance of intellectual property for a business
- (H) analyse the factors affecting innovation.

SETTING THE SCENE

Future iPads will include a camera

Apple's non-stop programme of innovative products seems set to continue. Not content with gaining worldwide publicity from the launch of the iPad, Apple seems to have allowed themselves the option of fitting this class-leading product with a webcam. This would further enhance the capabilities of this product, keep it fresh in consumers' minds as well as giving an excuse for more well-publicised product launches.

Apple is one of the world's great innovators – and it has the consumer loyalty and profitability to prove it. Such is the interest in its new products that interest in the iPad steadily built in the months before its unveiling. This is the first product that combines a 9.7-inch LED display, Wi-Fi, 3G and an e-book reader. The potential is huge. Roughly 140 000 apps are available to iPad users from the App Store.

Source: www.eweekeurope.co.uk (adapted)

Points to consider

- How do innovative products benefit consumers?
- What benefits does Apple appear to gain from launching innovative products?
- Are all innovative products necessarily a marketing success?

Introduction

Few markets avoid change, which involves new products or new ways of making existing products. Some industries are more likely to undergo substantial changes brought about by new technologies and new adaptations of existing technologies. The IT, computer and mobile-phone markets are experiencing more innovation than most. How do businesses benefit from introducing radical new products and what factors influence the range and pace of innovation? These are the main issues explained in this chapter.

The importance of research and development

KEY TERMS

research and development the scientific research and technical development of new products and processes

invention the formulation or discovery of new ideas for products or processes

innovation the practical application of new inventions into marketable products

product innovation new, marketable products such as the Apple iPad

process innovation new methods of manufacturing or service provision that offers important benefits, e.g. Pilkington's float-glass process

Spending on research and development (R&D) is growing globally and in most industrial sectors. The benefits to a country of encouraging R&D spending include:

- creation of high-tech jobs
- creation of high-added-value products that may then be manufactured in that country
- prestige – a country being linked to scientific and technological breakthroughs
- attraction of investment by multinational corporations.

In 2009–10, R&D spending increased at a faster rate in emerging economies than in developed economies – reflecting the benefits that some governments see in R&D being the engine for further development. Table 35.1 looks at the share of total global R&D spending in selected countries.

The benefits gained from successful R&D spending can be considerable. Why else would Toyota claim to be spending $1.1 million an hour on developing new products and processes? The companies with the largest R&D budgets in 2008–9 are shown in Table 35.2 (source: Booz and Company). Despite the global downturn between 2008 and 2010, 90% of the respondents to Booz and Company's survey said that innovation was critical in preparing for the upturn. Barry Januzelski, a partner at Booz and Company, said, 'Reducing efforts on innovation would be similar to unilateral disarmament in wartime. Now is the opportune time to build advantage over competitors with R&D spending, especially weaker ones that may have to skimp on R&D for financial reasons.' One exception to this was General Motors which had been so badly hit by the economic downturn that in 2010 it slipped to being the 50th largest spender on R&D.

	2008	2009	2010
USA	35.4	35.0	34.8
Asia	32.0	33.5	34.6
China	9.1	11.1	12.2
India	2.4	2.5	2.9
Europe	24.9	24.0	23.2

Table 35.1 *Percentage share of total global R&D spending (selected countries/regions)*
Source: Battelle-R&D Magazine

Company	R&D spending, 2008–09 (US$ billion)	As percentage of sales
Toyota (cars – Japan)	8944	4.4
Nokia (mobile phones – Finland)	8733	11.8
Roche (health – Switzerland)	8168	19.4
Microsoft (IT – USA)	8164	13.5
General Motors (cars – USA)	8000	5.4
Pfizer (health – USA)	7945	16.5
Johnson & Johnson (health – USA)	7577	11.9

Table 35.2 *The largest corporate R&D budgets, 2008–9*
Source: Booz and Company

THE IMPORTANCE OF R&D TO BUSINESS

The benefits of successful R&D spending – that is, spending that leads to innovative products – include:

- competitive advantage over competitors – Dyson has become one of the world's leading vacuum-cleaner manufacturers in 20 years as a result of its 'dual cyclone' technology
- customer loyalty – Microsoft's continuous development and improvement programme for its computer

operating systems help to keep customers loyal to the brand even though competitors are becoming more numerous

- high, premium prices – being first into a market with an innovative product can allow high prices to be charged, e.g. the tiny but expensive Smart Car was marketed not as a low-cost form of transport but an eco-friendly vehicle, worth paying 'extra' for
- publicity – Apple receives free worldwide publicity for each new innovative product it launches
- lower costs – Pilkington, the glass maker, revolutionised float-glass making and slashed the cost of making glass to give it substantial cost advantages.

RESEARCH AND DEVELOPMENT – LIMITATIONS

- R&D does not always lead to innovation. Billions of dollars have been spent by pharmaceutical companies to develop a cure for the common cold – so far they have all failed.
- R&D is expensive and has an opportunity cost. Would the money spent on R&D be more wisely invested in marketing existing products more intensively?
- Inventions do not always lead to successful innovative products. Examples of product failures after extensive R&D spending include the Sinclair C5 battery-powered vehicle, smokeless cigarettes, New Coca-Cola and disposable paper clothing.
- Competing R&D spending may result in even more successful products. Toshiba lost millions of dollars that it had invested in HD-DVD technology when it was knocked out of the market by Sony's Blu-ray system.
- Ethical issues can sometimes outweigh the potential commercial benefits. Consumers still reject genetically modified (GM) food crops and there is no certainty that big GM R&D spenders such as Monsanto will receive a return on their investments.

Intellectual property rights

KEY TERMS

intellectual property refers to creations of the mind such as inventions, literary and artistic works and symbols, names, images and designs used in business

intellectual property rights legal property rights over the possession and use of intellectual property

patent legal right to be the sole producer and seller of an invention for a certain period of time

copyright legal right to protect and be the sole beneficiary from artistic and literary works

trademark a distinctive name, symbol, motto or design that identifies a business or its products – can be legally registered and cannot be copied

As a type of property, intellectual property is intangible, a creation of the mind, with no physical existence. With a tangible object – such as a computer – property rights cease when the object is destroyed. With intellectual property, since there is nothing physical, property rights only exist for as long as the law says they do.

This does not mean that property rights – the rights to possess, use, license, sell and financially benefit from property – are not worth anything. Far from it, as they can:

- set a business apart from its competitors and encourage increased sales as a result of this distinctiveness
- be sold or licensed to provide an important revenue stream
- form a key part of the branding process and assist in the marketing of the firm's products
- be given a financial value on a business balance sheet which increases its net assets.

There may be problems protecting intellectual property. Copying without permission of the copyright holder has always been a problem, but the ability to download digital versions of music, film and other material, which has led to illegal downloading, has made the task of protecting revenue earned by the intellectual property even more difficult. In addition, brand names and trademarks can be damaged by bad publicity and this can 'write-off' a great deal of value from a balance sheet or the value of the business.

Factors affecting innovation

Several factors may influence the level of R&D and innovation by a business:

- The nature of the industry. Rapidly changing technologies – and consumer expectations – in pharmaceutical products, defence, computer and software products and motor vehicles lead to the need for substantial investment in R&D by leading firms. Other businesses, such as hotels and hairdressing, would need to spend much less as the scope for innovation is more limited.

- The R&D and innovation spending plans of competitors. In most markets, it is essential to innovate as much as or more than competitors if market share and technical leadership are to be maintained. However, a monopoly may limit R&D spending if it believes that the risk of a more technically advanced competitor entering the market is limited. On the other hand, profits from a monopoly could be used to finance research into innovative products if the risk of competitor entry into the industry is high.
- Business expectations. If business managers are optimistic about the future state of the economy and the rate of economic growth and consumer demand, then they are more likely to agree to substantial budgets for R&D and aim to introduce more innovative products.
- The risk profile or culture of the business. The attitude of the management to risk and whether shareholders are prepared to invest for the long term will have a significant effect on the sums that businesses can inject into R&D programmes. 'Short termism' is an accusation made towards many major UK financial institutions and the need to satisfy these investors could discourage managers from investing in R&D.
- Government policy towards grants to businesses and universities for R&D programmes and the range and scope of tax allowances for such expenditure will influence decisions by businesses.
- Finance is needed for effective R&D. In many firms this may be limited and will restrict the number of new innovations that could be made.

THEORY OF KNOWLEDGE

Agriculture and food: the genetically modified crop marches on

In agricultural biotechnology, the big theme is still the march of genetically modified crops across the world's farmland. The most authoritative annual survey of GM planting, carried out by the International Service for the Acquisition of Agri-biotech Applications, showed a 7% annual increase last year in the area covered to 134 million hectares (330 million acres) in 25 countries.

Source: Clive Cookson, FT.com, 4 May 2010

In the light of growth of the market for GM crops, how do you know whether society benefits from research and development into different types of products? Prepare a presentation on this topic to give to your class.

OVER TO YOU

REVISION CHECKLIST

1 Explain, with examples, the difference between invention and innovation.
2 Explain the distinction between market research and research and development.
3 Outline **two** potential benefits to a pharmaceutical company such as Pfizer of being able to patent a new drug following extensive research and development.
4 Why might an innovative product allow a business to successfully charge high prices for it?
5 Explain why high R&D spending might not lead to increased sales and profits for the business.
6 Explain why R&Dspending accounts for a higher proportion of spending for some businesses than others. Use business examples in your answer.

REVISION ACTIVITY

Read the case studies below and then answer the questions that follow.

Toyota is top-value car brand (2008)

Brand value is impossible to measure accurately and it can be affected by numerous volatile factors. If, however, a consumer is willing to pay more for one brand over another, then brand value becomes a vital indicator of a company's overall value. This then translates into the market value of the business being greater than the sum of its tangible assets – so brand value adds to the take-over price that a predator business would have to pay.

One of the best indicators of how valuable each brand is compared to its rivals is the annual Best Global Brands survey conducted by consultancy firm Interbrand. Once again, Coca-Cola has taken top spot followed by IBM, Microsoft and

General Motors. When it comes to car manufacturers, Toyota as usual dominates its competitors with 6th rank overall. In 2008, the brand value of Toyota was estimated at $34 billion.

Source: www.motorauthority.com

Toyota's image in freefall (2010)

Toyota's reputation and brand value is in 'near freefall' after well-publicised faults plaguing eight of its models, said brand experts in February 2010. The world's leading car maker launched a recall of more than 400 000 Prius cars over brake problems – in addition to the 8 million other cars being recalled for repairs to accelerator pedals. BrandIndex, which tracks consumers' brand perceptions, has predicted that Toyota's reputation has suffered from its failure to react quickly to consumer worries over the faults. It has predicted that Toyota's reputation and brand image would suffer long-term damage following the recalls.

Source: http://news.scotman.com

18 marks, 35 minutes

1 What do you understand by 'brand value'? [2]

2 Explain why the problems referred to in the second case study have damaged Toyota's brand value. [6]

3 Discuss **two** measures that the company could take to attempt to restore its reputation and brand value. [10]

EXAM PRACTICE QUESTION

Read the case study below and then answer the questions that follow.

GILLETTE: MANAGING PRODUCT INNOVATION

Gillette has always believed that continuous new product development resulting from extensive R&D is necessary to differentiate itself from competitors. True to its corporate mantra of 'innovation is Gillette', the company has introduced some of the most successful and widely acclaimed innovative products in the consumer products industry. Its product range, protected by trademarks, is legendary with such brands as Sensor, SensorExcel, Mach 3 and Gillette for Women Venus.

The company's policy is to generate 40% of its sales from products launched within the last five years. One reason for Gillette's strong focus on new product development is that the competition has successfully learned to copy its products very quickly. For example, Schick (part of Warner Lambert, later taken over by Pfizer but known as Wilkinson Sword in many parts of the world) had imitated Gillette's Trac II twin-blade razor within five months of the product's launch.

Further product launches have added to the brand value of Gillette. It has succeeded, in some markets, in making razors less of a commodity product – which consumers just buy on price and convenience considerations – but a branded consumer product that customers will pay a premium price for.

Source: www.icmrindia.org (adapted)

25 marks, 45 minutes

1 Define the following terms:
   a innovative products
   b trademarks. [4]

2 Explain how the use of innovative products and trademarks can add to the value of a company such as Gillette. [4]

3 Analyse the importance of companies such as Gillette continuing to spend large sums on R&D even in a global downturn. [8]

4 Evaluate the factors that determine the level of innovation in an industry. [9]

36 Production planning

This chapter covers syllabus section 5.7

On completing this chapter you should be able to:

- understand why businesses hold stocks and the costs of stock holding
- analyse the advantages and disadvantages of traditional stock-control systems
- discuss and compare the just-in-case approach and the just-in-time (JIT) stock management system
- (H) explain outsourcing and subcontracting
- (H) discuss the arguments for and against outsourcing and subcontracting
- (H) make appropriate calculations to support a decision to make or buy.

SETTING THE SCENE

The shocking cost of holding stocks

It is commonly accepted that the cost to a business of holding stock is between 4% and 10% of the stock's value. So, if an average stock level is $1 million, the annual cost of actually keeping and looking after the stocks could be up to $100 000. Recent research has shown that the figure could be as high as 40%. These costs include:

- storage costs
- stock-handling costs
- loss and damage of stocks
- obsolescence
- opportunity cost of capital.

But how to cut down on these costs? Could businesses manage their operations with lower stocks – or even no stocks at all? The experience of a Scottish supermarket group suggests that it is possible to move away from holding large stocks 'just in case' there is a demand for the products. The managers of Scotmid decided on an IT-driven stock-ordering system that re-ordered goods from suppliers automatically as remaining goods on the shelves were purchased by customers. 'We now have much tighter control of stock, wastage and improved cash flow. Stockholding has reduced dramatically with huge benefits throughout the supermarket group,' said Robin Kilpatrick, IT manager, Scotmid.

Source: http://www.logisticsit.com and www.vmeretail.com (adapted)

Points to think about:

- Give examples of stocks held by: (a) a supermarket, (b) a housebuilder and (c) an insurance company.
- Explain as many reasons as you can why businesses hold stocks.
- Could a business manage with 'zero' stocks? Explain your answer.

Introduction

KEY TERM

stock (inventory) materials and goods required to allow for the production of and supply of products to the customer

All businesses hold stocks of some kind. Banks and insurance companies will hold stocks of stationery, and retailers have stocks of goods on display and in their warehouses. Manufacturing businesses will hold stocks in three distinct forms:

1 Raw materials and components. These will have been purchased from outside suppliers. They will be held in stock until they are used in the production process.
2 Work in progress. At any one time the production process will be converting raw materials and components into finished goods and these are 'work in progress'. For some firms, such as construction businesses, this will be the main form of stocks held. Batch production tends to have high work-in-progress levels.
3 Finished goods. Having been through the complete production process goods may then be held in stock until sold and despatched to the customer.

EXAM TIP

Remember to apply your answer to the business in the question of the case study when writing about stocks and stock-handling systems – for example, if the business sells toys, it is likely to hold high stocks of toys at festival times.

Stock-holding costs

There are three costs associated with stock holding:

1 Opportunity cost. Working capital tied up in stocks could be put to another best alternative use. The capital might be used to pay off loans, buy new equipment or pay off suppliers, or could be left in the bank to earn interest.
2 Storage costs. Stocks have to be held in secure warehouses. They often require special conditions, such as refrigeration. Staff will be needed to guard and transport the stocks which should be insured against fire or theft.
3 Risk of wastage and obsolescence. If stocks are not used or sold as rapidly as expected, then there is an increasing danger of goods deteriorating or becoming outdated. This will lower the value of such stocks. Goods often become damaged while held in storage – they can then only be sold for a much lower price.

COSTS OF NOT HOLDING ENOUGH STOCKS

There are risks to holding very low stock levels – and these risks may have financial costs for the firm. These costs are often called 'stock-out' costs:

1 Lost sales. If a firm is unable to supply customers 'from stock', then sales could be lost to firms that hold higher stock levels. This might lead to future lost orders too. In purchasing contracts between businesses, it is common for there to be a penalty payment clause requiring the supplier to pay compensation if delivery dates cannot be met on time.
2 Idle production resources. If stocks of raw materials and components run out, then production will have to stop. This will leave expensive equipment idle and labour with nothing to do. The costs of lost output and wasted resources could be considerable.
3 Special orders could be expensive. If an urgent order is given to a supplier to deliver additional stock due to shortages, then extra costs might be incurred in administration of the order and in special delivery charges.
4 Small order quantities. Keeping low stock levels may mean only ordering goods and supplies in small quantities. The larger the size of each delivery, the higher will be the average stock level held. By ordering in small quantities, the firm may lose out on an important economy of scale such as discounts for large orders.

The optimum stock level will be at the lowest point of the total stock cost graph (see Figure 36.1).

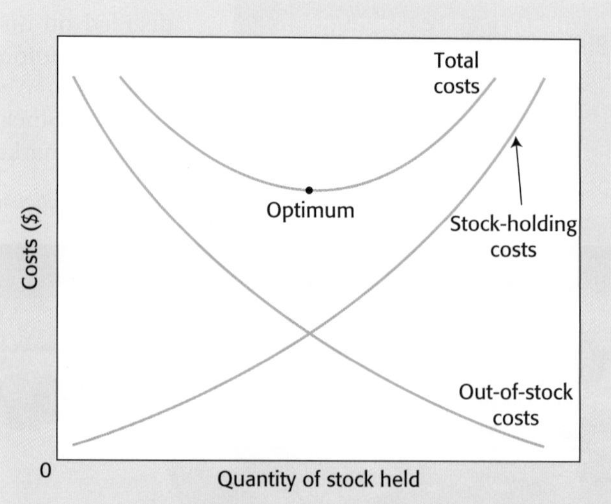

Figure 36.1 Total stock-holding costs

Optimum order size

Purchasing managers might be tempted to order huge quantities of stocks in order to gain economies of scale and to ensure that the firm never runs out. Ordering and administration costs will be low as few orders will need to be placed. Continuous production should be ensured and special order costs for out-of-stock materials should be unnecessary.

However, stock-holding costs will be higher as the large orders will have to be stored until they are needed. Opportunity costs will be higher due to more capital being tied up. The danger of stock becoming obsolete and out of date is increased. What, then, is the optimum order size? It will differ for every firm and every kind of stock. The economic order quantity (EOQ) can be calculated for each product, but for the IB examinations it is sufficient just to know the forces that influence the size of this optimum order size. These can be summarised in Figure 36.2.

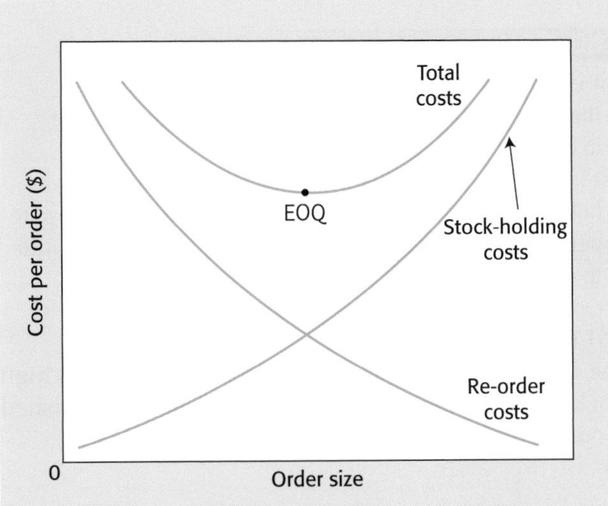

Figure 36.2 Factors influencing the economic order quantity

KEY TERM

economic order quantity (EOQ) the optimum or least-cost quantity of stock to re-order taking into account delivery costs and stock-holding costs

EXAM TIP

You will not be asked to calculate the optimum order size, but it is advised that you remember the costs of stock holding and the costs of being out of stocks – and apply these to the business in the question.

Controlling stock levels – a graphical approach

Stock-control charts or graphs are widely used to monitor a firm's stock position. These charts record stock levels, stock deliveries, buffer stocks and maximum stock levels over time. They aid a stock manager in determining the appropriate order time and order quantity (see Figure 36.3).

Figure 36.3 has certain key features:

1. Buffer stocks. The more uncertainty there is about delivery times or production levels, the higher the buffer stock level will have to be. Also, the greater the cost involved in shutting production down and restarting, the greater the potential cost savings from holding high buffer stocks.

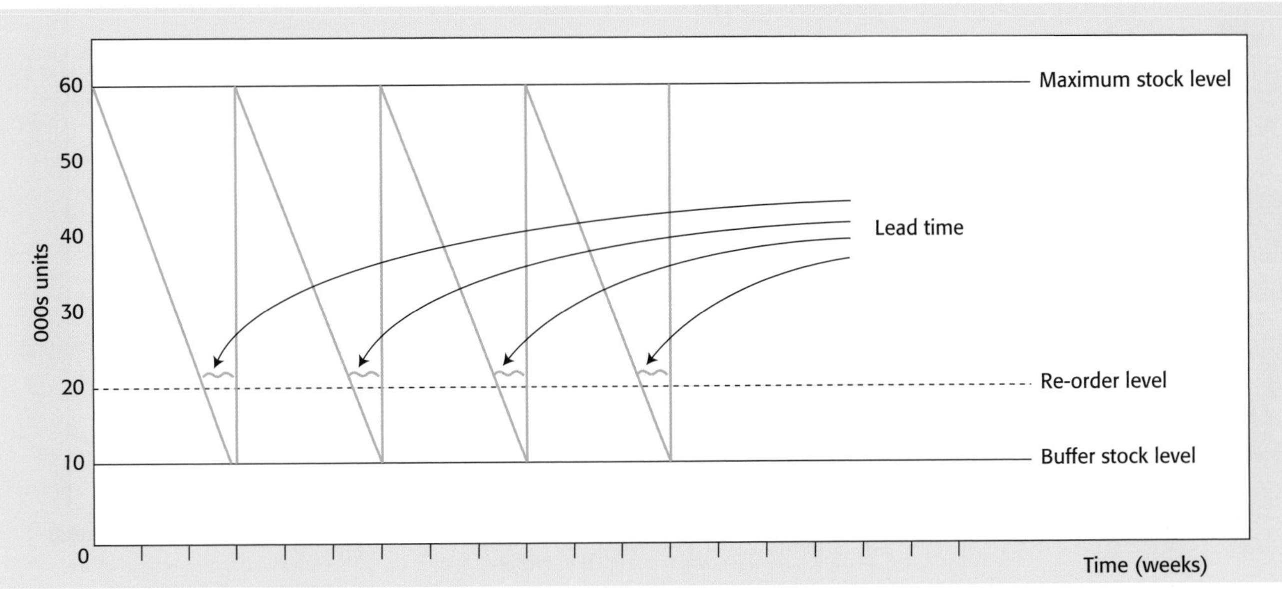

Figure 36.3 A typical stock-control chart

2 Maximum stock level. This may be limited by space or by the financial costs of holding even higher stock levels. One way to calculate this maximum level is to add the EOQ of each component to the buffer stock level for that item.
3 Re-order quantity. This will be influenced by the economic order quantity concept referred to above.
4 Lead time. The longer this period of time, then the higher will have to be the re-order stock level. The less reliable suppliers are, the greater the buffer stock level might have to be.
5 Re-order stock level. It is now very common for computers to be used to keep a record of every sale and every delivery of stock. The re-order quantity and re-order stock level can be programmed into the computer and it can then reorder automatically from the supplier when stocks fall to the re-order stock level. The stock control chart can also be prepared by the computer and Figure 36.4 shows the sale of Popsquash soft drinks from one retailer over a ten-week period.

As can be seen from Figure 36.4, the stock level does not follow the regular and consistent pattern of the previous chart. The sales have been affected by two important factors, shown by the more steeply sloping lines, and deliveries were delayed one week. This is a more realistic situation and helps to illustrate the usefulness of this type of chart for future decision-making regarding stocks.

KEY TERMS

buffer stocks the minimum stocks that should be held to ensure that production could still take place should a delay in delivery occur or production rates increase

re-order quantity the number of units ordered each time

lead time the normal time taken between ordering new stocks and their delivery

re-order stock level the level of stocks that will trigger a new order to be sent to the supplier

Just in case and just in time stock systems

KEY TERMS

just in case (JIC) holding high stock levels 'just in case' there is a production problem or an unexpected upsurge in demand

just in time (JIT) a stock control method that aims to avoid holding stocks by requiring supplies to arrive just as they are needed in production and completed products are produced to order

JUST IN CASE

The traditional view of stock holding was to hold high stock levels, especially of raw materials and finished goods, to meet unexpected situations such as:

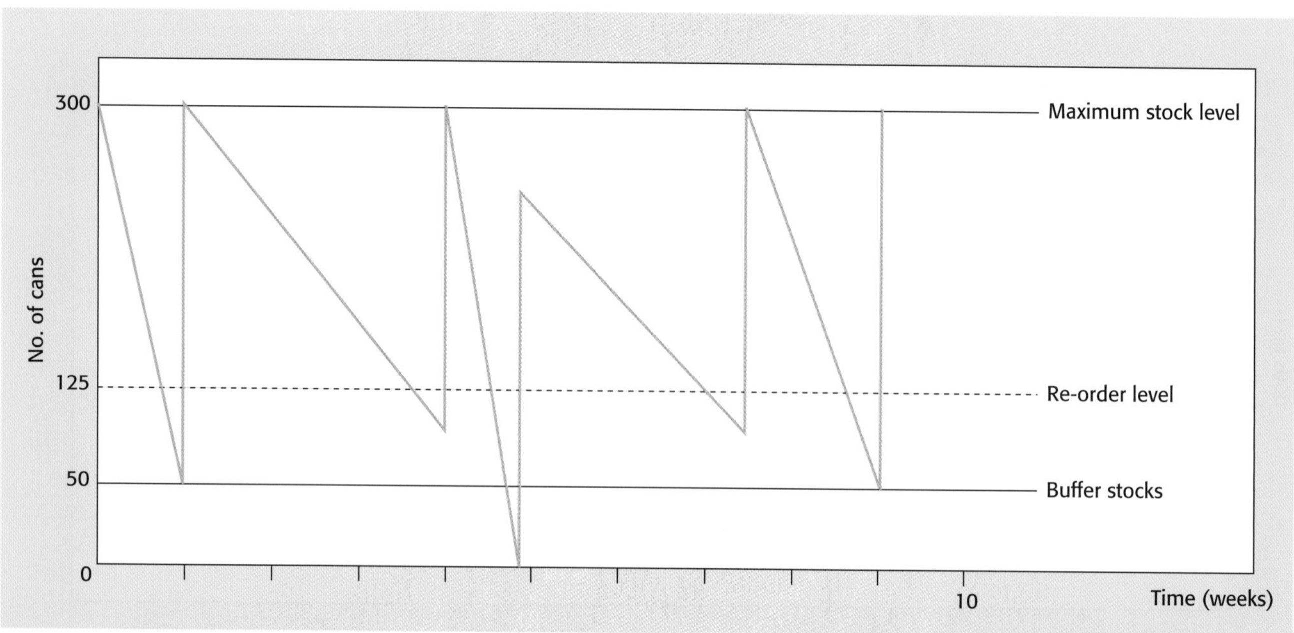

Figure 36.4 Stock-control chart for 'Popsquash' soft drinks

ACTIVITY 36.1

Stock control at Saiko

Refer to the stock-control chart below.

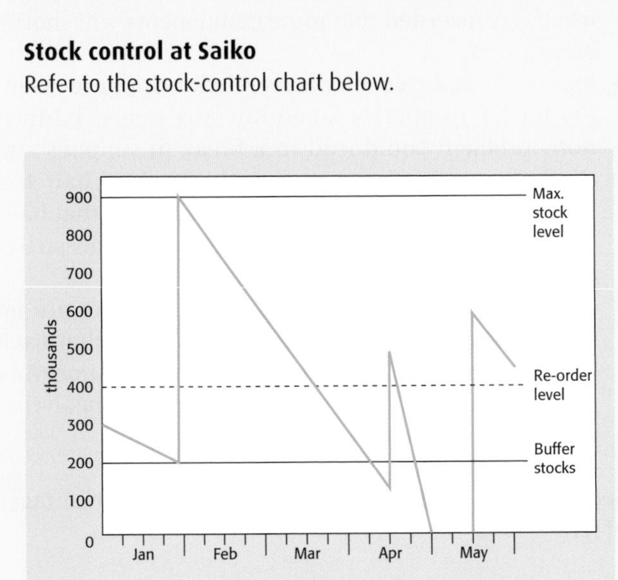

Stock-control chart for Saiko Trading Ltd

20 marks, 35 minutes

1 What factors may have determined the size of the maximum stock level? [4]

2 What size of order was received at the end of January? [2]

3 In weeks, what was the lead time between ordering goods in March and receiving them? [2]

4 Suggest why stocks fell to zero in April. [4]

5 Discuss the problems Saiko Trading Ltd might experience from the pattern of stock usage shown by the chart. [8]

- failure of a supplying firm to deliver on time
- production problems halting output
- increased consumer demand.

Table 36.1 summarises the advantages and disadvantages of the just-in-case management approach.

Advantages	Disadvantages
• Stocks of raw materials can be used to allow the firm to meet increases in demand by increasing the rate of production quickly. • Raw-material supply hold-ups will not lead to production stopping. • Economies of scale from bulk discounts will reduce average costs. • Stocks of finished goods can be displayed to customers and increase the chances of sales. • Stocks of finished goods used to meet sudden, unpredicted increases in demand – customers can be satisfied without delay. • Firms can stockpile completed goods to meet anticipated increases in demand as with seasonal goods or products, such as toys at festival times.	• High opportunity costs of working capital tied up in stock. • High storage costs. • Risk of goods being damaged or becoming outdated. • 'Getting it right first time' – a key component of lean production – matters less than with JIT as other supplies are kept in stock to replace defective items. • Space used to store stock cannot be used for productive purposes.

Table 36.1 *Just-in-case stock management approach – advantages and disadvantages*

JUST IN TIME

Originating in Japan, the JIT approach to stock control is now influencing stock-holding decisions in businesses all over the world. JIT requires that no buffer stocks are held, components arrive just as they are needed on the production line and finished goods are delivered to customers as soon as they are completed.

Important conditions for JIT to be successful

1 Relationships with suppliers have to be excellent. Suppliers must be prepared and able to supply fresh supplies at very short notice – short lead time. This often means that a firm will only have one, or at most two, suppliers for each component, so that a relationship of mutual benefit can be built up.

2 Production staff must be multi-skilled and prepared to change jobs at short notice. Each worker must be able to switch to making different items at very short notice so that no excess supplies of any one product are made. For example, if a worker in a clothing factory usually makes men's denim jeans, but demand is falling, then the worker should be able to switch to making other garments that are still in demand.
3 Equipment and machinery must be flexible. Old-fashioned manufacturing equipment tended to be designed to produce one range of very similar products. This equipment would be most unsuitable for JIT-based systems. The machinery would have to produce large batches of one type of component before being converted to making another item. Stocks of each item produced would be needed to cope with demand while it was producing other goods. Modern, computer-controlled equipment is much more flexible and adaptable – often able to be changed with no more than a different software program. In this way, very small batches of each item can be produced which keeps stock levels to an absolute minimum. Such equipment is expensive and, therefore, JIT may not be so appropriate for small or underfinanced firms.
4 Accurate demand forecasts will make JIT a much more successful policy. If it is very difficult for a firm to predict likely future sales levels, then keeping zero stocks of materials, parts and finished goods could be a very risky strategy. Demand forecasts can be converted into production schedules that allow calculation of the precise number of components of each type needed over a certain time period.
5 The latest IT equipment will allow JIT to be more successful. Accurate data-based records of sales, sales trends, re-order levels and so on will allow very low or zero stocks to be held. Similarly, if contact with suppliers can be set up with the latest electronic data exchanges, then automatic and immediate ordering can take place, when it is recorded that more components will shortly be required.
6 Excellent employee–employer relationships are essential for JIT to operate smoothly. Any industrial-relations problem could lead to a break in supplies and the entire production system could grind to a halt. It is no coincidence that many of the businesses that have adopted JIT in Japan and in Europe have a 'no-strike' deal with the major trade unions.
7 Quality must be everyone's priority. As there are no spare stocks to fall back on, it is essential that each component and product must be right first time. Any poor-quality goods that cannot be used will mean that a customer will not receive goods on time.

See Table 36.2 for the advantages and disadvantages of JIT.

EXAM TIP

Any question about JIT that involves discussing how appropriate it is in different business cases should lead to an answer that considers the potential drawbacks of the approach as well as the more obvious benefits of it.

JIT – an evaluation

JIT requires a very different organisational culture to that of JIC stock-control systems. This change in culture requires staff to be held much more accountable for their performance and suppliers to be very reliable as any failure to meet targets will lead to production stopping.

Advantages	Disadvantages
• Capital invested in inventory is reduced and the opportunity cost of stock holding is reduced. • Costs of storage and stock holding are reduced. • Space released from holding of stocks can be used for a more productive purpose. • Much less chance of stock becoming outdated or obsolescent. Less stock held also reduces the risk of damage or wastage. • The greater flexibility that the system demands leads to quicker response times to changes in consumer demand or tastes. • The multi-skilled and adaptable staff required for JIT to work may gain from improved motivation.	• Any failure to receive supplies of materials or components in time caused by, for example, a strike at the supplier's factory, transport problems or IT failure, will lead to expensive production delays. • Delivery costs will increase as frequent small deliveries are an essential feature of JIT. • Order administration costs may rise because so many small orders need to be processed. • There could be a reduction in the bulk discounts offered by suppliers because each order is likely to be very small. • The reputation of the business depends significantly on outside factors such as the reliability of supplying firms.

Table 36.2 *JIT stock control – advantages and disadvantages*

ACTIVITY 36.2

Read the case studies below and then answer the questions that follow.

Nissan cuts stock to almost zero

Nissan's car factories now operate on an average of just 1.6 days' worth of component and raw-material stocks. This is one of the lowest in the entire motor industry. Computer links with suppliers, which are often located in the same area as the Nissan factories, allow special coded messages to be sent from the Nissan production line. These contain details of the models and colours of cars being assembled. The supplier, for example of car carpets, then knows that it must supply particular colours of carpets directly to the factory. In fact, some suppliers will make up to 120 deliveries in a day. The parts are taken straight to the assembly line – they do not pass through a traditional warehouse first. Nissan production control directors claim that this method brings huge savings in stock holding and internal stock handling as well as great space-saving advantages.

Toyota production is halted

A fire at a major supplier of parts to Toyota's Japanese factories has brought all car production to a stop. Toyota's JIT production system relies on suppliers delivering only the necessary volume of vehicle parts to the assembly line at precisely the point in the manufacturing process at which they are required. The problem is that when things go wrong at just one supplier – Aisin Seiki's fire, for example – the lack of stock of parts can lead to serious problems. Toyota always relies on one supplier for all major parts, because it believes that this brings huge economies of scale. These suppliers not only have to agree to be 100% reliable – excluding events such as fires or earthquakes – but also accept that they must design parts for Toyota's cars themselves. This special relationship with suppliers has helped Toyota reduce its costs by $820 million in each of the past three years.

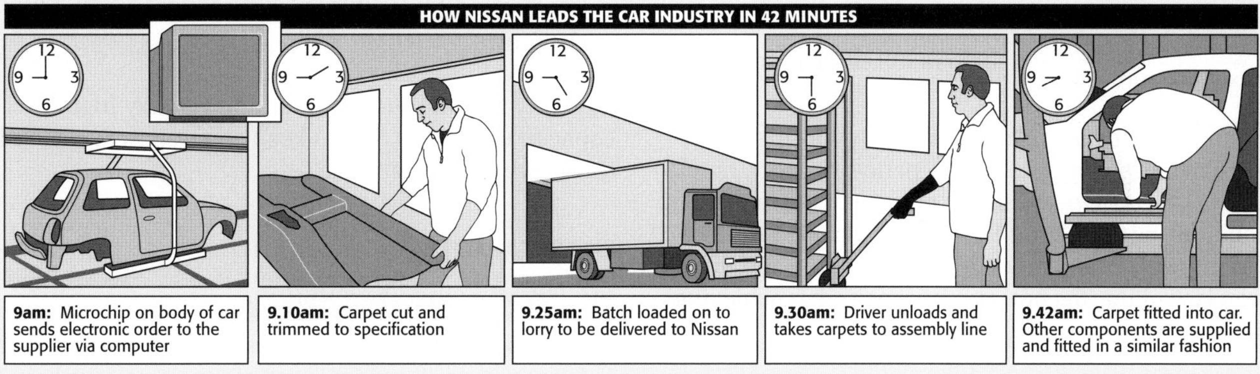

HOW NISSAN LEADS THE CAR INDUSTRY IN 42 MINUTES
9am: Microchip on body of car sends electronic order to the supplier via computer
9.10am: Carpet cut and trimmed to specification
9.25am: Batch loaded on to lorry to be delivered to Nissan
9.30am: Driver unloads and takes carpets to assembly line
9.42am: Carpet fitted into car. Other components are supplied and fitted in a similar fashion

24 marks, 42 minutes

1 Examine the benefits to both Nissan and Toyota of:
   a the JIT system of stock control that both use
   b their reliance on just one supplier for each major component. [12]

2 Using evidence drawn from the case studies and from your own knowledge, examine the potential drawbacks to the adoption of the JIT concept for manufacturing businesses. [12]

JIT may not be suitable for all firms at all times:

- There may be limits to the application of JIT if the costs resulting from production being halted when supplies do not arrive far exceed the costs of holding buffer stocks of key components.
- Small firms could argue that the expensive IT systems needed to operate JIT effectively cannot be justified by the potential cost savings.
- In addition, rising global inflation makes holding stocks of raw materials more beneficial as it may be cheaper to buy a large quantity now than smaller quantities in the future when prices have risen. Similarly, higher oil prices will make frequent and small deliveries of materials and components more expensive.

THEORY OF KNOWLEDGE

JIT is more than just a business system; it is a Japanese management philosophy. First developed by Taiichi Ohno for use in Toyota's manufacturing plants, it was seen as a way of quickly meeting consumer demand and maximising production efficiency.

To what extent do a nation's culture and philosophy shape its business decision-making?

HIGHER LEVEL

Capacity utilisation

KEY TERM

capacity utilisation the proportion of maximum output capacity currently being achieved

Capacity utilisation is calculated by the formula:

$$\frac{\text{current output level}}{\text{maximum output level}} \times 100 = \text{rate of capacity utilisation}$$

Maximum capacity is the total level of output that a business can achieve in a certain time period. So, for a hotel, monthly total capacity will be the number of 'room nights' available during this period. For a factory, it will be the total level of output that all of the existing resources can produce. If a firm is working 'flat out' at full capacity, it is achieving 100% capacity utilisation with no spare capacity.

IMPACT ON AVERAGE FIXED COSTS

When capacity utilisation is at a high rate, average fixed costs will be spread out over a large number of units – unit fixed costs will be relatively low. When utilisation is low, fixed costs will have to be borne by fewer units and unit fixed costs will rise (see Table 36.3).

Do all firms aim to produce at 100% capacity at all times? In theory, the cost advantages of this would appear to be great. Unit fixed costs will be at their lowest possible level and this should help to lift profits. The business will be able to claim how successful it is as it has no spare capacity. For example, hotels will put up 'No vacancy' signs and airlines will not have any unsold seats. Employees will have a sense of job security too.

There are also potential drawbacks to operating at full capacity for a long period of time:

- Staff may feel under pressure due to the workload and this could raise stress levels. Operations managers cannot afford to make any production scheduling mistakes, as there is no slack time to make up for lost output.
- Regular customers who wish to increase their orders will have to be turned away or kept waiting for long periods. This could encourage them to use other suppliers with the danger that they might be lost as long-term clients.
- Machinery will be working flat out and there may be insufficient time for maintenance and preventative repairs and this could lead to increased unreliability in the future.

100-bed hotel	All bedrooms occupied (100% of capacity)	50 bedrooms occupied (50% of capacity)
Hotel fixed costs per day, e.g. rent and salaries	$2500	$2500
Average fixed costs per room per day	$25	$50

Table 36.3 *How unit fixed costs vary with capacity utilisation*

So many firms attempt to maintain a very high level of capacity utilisation, but to keep some spare capacity for unforeseen eventualities.

EXCESS CAPACITY

KEY TERM

excess capacity exists when the current levels of demand are less than the full capacity output of a business – also known as spare capacity

EXAM TIP

When making decisions about how to deal with excess capacity it is important to consider both the length of time that the spare capacity might exist for and the causes of the problem.

FULL-CAPACITY WORKING

The potential problems connected with operating at full capacity have been referred to. When business is operating close to or at full capacity, then other decisions have to be taken:

- Should the firm increase its scale of operation by acquiring more production resources?
- Should it keep existing capacity but outsource or subcontract more work to other firms?

ACTIVITY 36.3

Read the case studies below and then answer the questions that follow.

NEC to raise capacity in China

NEC, a major manufacturer of semi-conductors, has just announced that it will invest $300 million on expanding capacity in its Chinese factories. These are already working at full capacity and most analysts predict that the Chinese market will continue to expand – but possibly at a slower rate. NEC hopes that this new investment in its Chinese plants will raise monthly production from 20 000 to 30 000 semi-conductor chips. Also announced recently is a move by Sony to integrate its operations in southern Japan into just one factory – currently it produces at three different plants.

Dell to increase capacity at Malaysian plant (2001)

Dell Computer Corporation, the world's leading direct marketer of computers, plans to double manufacturing capacity for the Asia-Pacific region. It is confident that global sales growth will justify this increase in capacity. Last year, its sales rose by 39% in Asia and 70% in China. Simon Wong, the managing director for Dell's Asian-Pacific division, said that the new factory would produce 2 million units within three years. 'We are stretched right to the limit. The growth of the whole region is creating tremendous demand.'

Dell plans further job cuts (2009)

Dell has announced it is seeking to cut costs by more than $3 billion over the next four years. This will result in 8800 job cuts. Michael Dell, founder of the firm, said that cost-cutting measures would also include reform of the supply network and outsourcing more of its manufacturing operations. Production capacity will be cut back – a manufacturing plant in Texas, USA, is being shut down with the loss of 900 jobs. A company spokesperson would not say what proportion of further job cuts will be made in the USA but insisted that the job reduction programme would be global.

The company is responding to two pressures:

- extreme competition in the computer industry
- global economic downturn which is reducing demand for business and home computers.

Source: https://business.timesonline.co.uk

30 marks, 52 minutes

1 Explain, with reference to the first two case studies, what is meant by the term 'to raise capacity'. [5]

2 Examine why both companies have taken this decision at this time. [5]

3 If the monthly overheads of NEC's expanded Chinese plant rise from $1 million to $1.2 million each month, calculate the change in unit overhead costs as a result of the expanded capacity. [4]

4 Explain why Dell, in 2009, decided to cut jobs and production capacity eight years after increasing capacity. [6]

5 Evaluate how a business such as Dell can respond to changing demand levels for its products. [10]

- Could the quality of products obtained from subcontractors be assured?
- Should it keep working at full capacity and not expand, perhaps because of the danger that demand might fall in the near future?

KEY TERM

full capacity when a business produces at maximum output

CAPACITY SHORTAGE

What options is a firm faced with if the demand for its products exceeds current output capacity? It is essential to analyse the cause of the excess demand and how long it is likely to last. If it results from a reduction in output caused by a faulty machine that will be repaired next month, then drastic action to raise capacity is unlikely. If, however, the firm has been producing at 100% capacity for some time and there seems to be no sign of demand falling, then two options need to be weighed up (see Table 36.4).

Long-term capacity shortage		
	Advantages	**Disadvantages**
Option 1. Use subcontractors or outsourcing of supplies, components or even finished goods	• No major capital investment is required. • Should be quite quick to arrange. • Offers much greater flexibility than expansion of facilities – if demand falls back, then the contracts with other firms can be ended.	• Less control over quality of output. • May add to administration and transport costs. • May be uncertainty over delivery times and reliability of delivery. • Unit cost may be higher than in-house production due to the supplier's profit margin.
Option 2. Capital investment into expansion of production facilities	• Long-term increase in capacity. • Firm is in control of quality and final delivery times. • New facilities should be able to use latest equipment and methods. • Other economies of scale should be possible too.	• Capital cost may be high. • Problems with raising capital. • Increases total capacity, but problems could occur if demand should fall for a long period. • Takes time to build and equip a new facility – customers may not wait.

Table 36.4 *How to overcome long-term capacity shortage problems*

Outsourcing

KEY TERMS

capacity shortage when the demand for a business's products exceeds production capacity

outsourcing (or subcontracting) using another business (a 'third party') to undertake a part of the production process rather than doing it within the business using the firm's own employees. When this is done by firms in another country it is called 'offshoring'

business process outsourcing (BPO) a form of outsourcing which uses a third party to take responsibility for certain business functions, such as human resources and finance

The growth of outsourcing in recent years by many businesses is not just driven by shortage of capacity. These are several major reasons for outsourcing:

- Reduction and control of operating costs. Instead of employing expensive specialists that might not be kept busy at all times it could be cheaper to 'buy in' specialist services or products as and when needed. Outsourcing firms may be cheaper because they benefit from economies of scale, as they may provide similar services to a large number of other businesses. Much outsourcing involves offshoring – buying in services, components or completed products from low-wage economies.
- Increased flexibility. By removing departments from the staff payroll and buying in services when needed, fixed costs are converted into variable costs. Additional capacity can be obtained from outsourcing only when needed and contracts can be cancelled if demand falls much more quickly than closing down whole factories owned by the business.
- Improved company focus. By outsourcing 'peripheral' activities the management of a business can concentrate on the main aims and tasks of the business. These are called the 'core' parts of the business. So, a small hotel might use management time to improve customer service and outsource the accounting function completely.
- Access to quality service or resources that are not available internally. Many outsourcing firms employ quality specialists that small to medium-sized businesses could not afford to employ directly.
- Free up internal resources for use in other areas. If the human resources department of an insurance company is closed and the functions bought in, then the resulting office space and computer facilities could be made available to improve customer service.

There are potential drawbacks to outsourcing too:

- Loss of jobs within the business. Workers who remain directly employed by the organisation may experience a loss of job security, reducing motivation. Bad publicity may result from redundancies, especially if the business is accused of employing very low-wage employees in other countries to replace the jobs lost. The firm's ethical standards could be questioned.
- Quality issues. Internal processes will be monitored by the firm's own quality assurance system. This will not be so easy when outside contractors are performing important functions. A clear contract with minimum service-level agreements will be needed. The company contracting out the functions may have to send quality assurance staff out to the business undertaking the tasks to ensure that product quality and customer service standards are being met.

- Customer resistance. This could take several forms. Overseas telephone call centres have led to criticism about inability to understand foreign operators. Customers may object to dealing with overseas outsourced operations. Bought-in components and functions may raise doubts in customers' minds over quality and reliability.
- Ethical concerns. If outsourcing is undertaken by firms in countries with poor human rights or employment rights records, it may be cheaper for the business that has outsourced – but how will the media and consumers view this potentially unethical decision?
- Security. Using outside businesses to perform important IT functions may be a security risk – if important data were lost by the business, who would take responsibility for this?

EXAM TIP

You may be asked for your advice on outsourcing an activity. Generally, the more important an activity is to the overall aims and reputation of the business, the less likely it is that outsourcing should be adopted.

MAKE-OR-BUY DECISIONS

The potential cost advantages of outsourcing are an important part of the make-or-buy decision. The cost to buy a component or service can be obtained from estimates given by potential suppliers. The cost to make should use contribution costing, that is only the additional costs of making a product or component or providing a service should be considered. Overheads that would still have to be paid if the outsourcing option was used should *not* be included in the calculation. An example can be used to demonstrate this. An operations manager of a computer assembly firm has obtained an estimate from a specialist supplier of keyboards: 'To supply 1000 keyboards each month at $3 each = total cost of $3000'.

The manager has estimated the internal variable and direct costs of making keyboards in-house at $3.50 each. Obtaining 1000 keyboards from an outsourcing company would save the computer business $500 per month. The cost to buy is less than the cost to make.

EXAM TIP

For make-or-buy decisions remember to consider: Will the supplier increase prices once the firm has closed down its own production capability? Will the quality be as good? Is the supplier reliable?

OUTSOURCING – AN EVALUATION

The global trend towards outsourcing seems likely to continue as firms seek ways of improving competitiveness and more opportunities arise due to globalisation. This process is not without its risks. Before any substantial business process outsourcing of complete functions is undertaken or before any stage of the production process is outsourced, the company must undertake a substantial cost–benefit analysis of the decision. Having closed or run down a whole department to outsource its functions, it would be expensive to re-open and re-establish it if it was found that the outsourcing had failed.

One of the key factors in any business decision on outsourcing is to decide what is a truly core activity that must be kept within the direct control of the business. These core activities will vary from business to business.

H

OVER TO YOU

REVISION CHECKLIST

1 Explain the following terms:
 a buffer stock level
 b stock re-order size
 c lead time.

2 From the diagram below, identify:
 a buffer stock level
 b order size
 c lead time.

3 State **three** types of stock that are likely to be held by a chocolate manufacturer.

4 Explain why most manufacturers will hold stocks in the form of 'work in progress'.

5 Explain **two** factors that would determine the maximum stock level held by a food-processing business.

6 Explain **two** conditions that must exist for JIT stock control to work effectively.

7 Explain two risks to a business from operating a JIT system.

8 If a business currently has an annual production capacity of 50 000 units, what will be its rate of capacity utilisation if its annual production is:
 a 20 000 units
 b 30 000 units
 c 45 000 units
 d 50 000 units?
 Show your working.

(H) 9 What is meant by 'full capacity working'?

(H) 10 Explain **two** reasons why firms may not wish to operate at 100% capacity.

(H) 11 Explain **two** advantages and **two** disadvantages to a computer manufacturing business of using subcontractors/outsourcing to solve a problem of capacity shortage.

(H) 12 Apart from production, list **four** business functions or processes that can be outsourced.

(H) 13 Would you advise an airline to outsource recruitment and training of airline cabin crew? Explain your answer.

(H) 14 Explain **two** benefits to an insurance company of outsourcing its customer service telephone answering system to an overseas call centre.

(H) 15 Are there some functions that you believe a large international hotel business should *not* consider outsourcing? Explain your answer.

(H) 16 Refer to the table opposite:
 a Calculate the capacity utilisation rates in each of the three years.
 b Calculate the average fixed costs in each of the three years. Comment on your results.

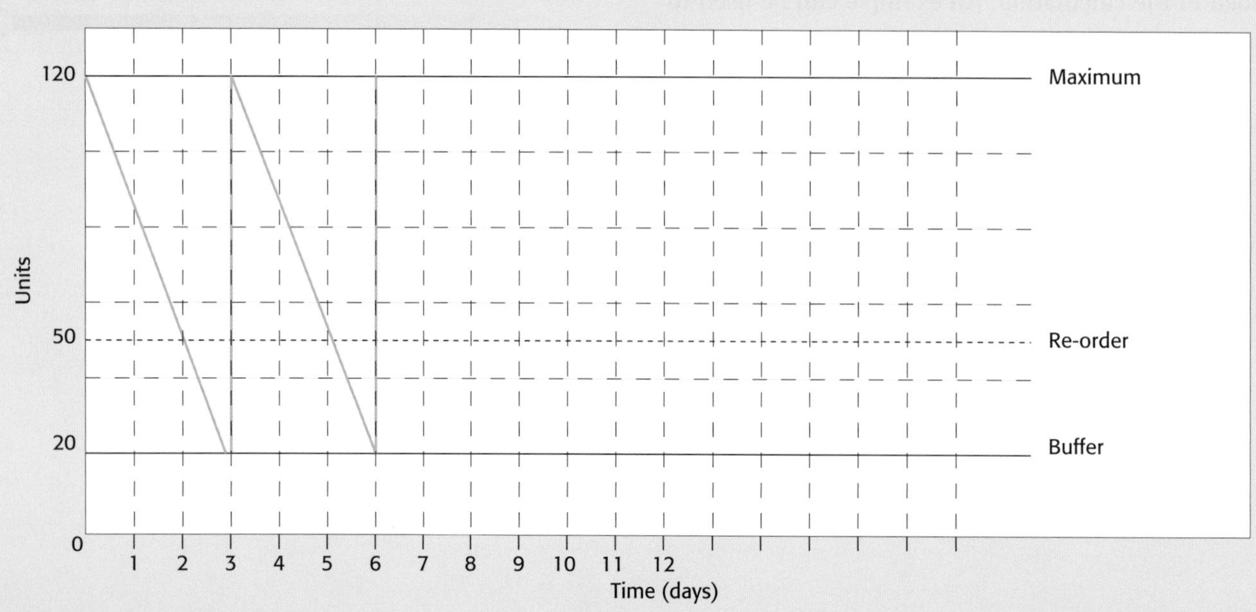

	2008	2009	2010
Maximum capacity (metres)	5 million	5 million	5 million
Actual annual output (metres)	4 million	3.7 million	3 million
Annual fixed costs	$3 million	$3 million	$3 million

HIGHER LEVEL

REVISION ACTIVITY 1

Read the case study below and then answer the questions that follow.

World's airlines increase outsourcing

Major national airlines and their cut-price competitors agree on one thing – aircraft maintenance is a lot cheaper when it's performed by low-paid mechanics working for outsourcing companies. JetBlue, Southwest, Qantas, America West and United are among the big airlines which outsource all major maintenance of their aircraft to contractors in other countries. JetBlue's A320 Airbus planes are sent to El Salvador for maintenance, for example. US Airways recently cut 2000 skilled mechanics' jobs as it outsourced most of its maintenance and repair work.

It wasn't long ago that all global airlines employed their own teams of highly qualified and highly paid aircraft engineers. They were all licensed by their own country's civil aviation authority and could earn at least $60 an hour. Mechanics working for outsourcers do not have to be licensed – only their supervisors must be fully qualified. In El Salvador the mechanics earn between $10 and $20 an hour.

Most airlines have also outsourced customer enquiry call centres, baggage handling, in-flight catering and merchandising. Malaysia Airlines recently denied rumours that it was about to outsource its in-flight retail operation called Golden Boutique. The airline has made clear its desire to 'mutually separate' non-core operations. The company described its in-flight business as 'non-core but good value', so it may want to remain in complete control of this with its own employees.

Aircraft mechanics in El Salvador – should aircraft maintenance be outsourced?

Source: http://www.dfnionline.com and http://www.consumeraffairs.com

33 marks, 60 minutes

1 Explain the term 'outsourcing'. [3]

2 Analyse **two** potential benefits to a major airline from outsourcing the maintenance of its aircraft. [8]

3 Explain **two** reasons why Malaysia Airlines may not want to outsource in-flight retailing. [8]

4 As a business consultant, write a report to the chief executive of your own national airline discussing the process of outsourcing and recommending whether all non-core activities should be outsourced. [14]

36 Production planning

HIGHER LEVEL

REVISION ACTIVITY 2

Read the case studies below and then answer the questions that follow.

Capacity utilisation

Lothian Buses in Scotland has recently undertaken research into the passenger occupancy levels of their main bus routes. The company wanted to know if some buses were operating at full capacity – in which case perhaps they needed to buy more vehicles – and if some were operating way below full capacity – in which case, could they cancel some bus routes altogether? The research was aiming to see if the company was managing its operations and capacity effectively.

On some routes at peak times (8–9 a.m.) buses were completely full but with an average seat utilisation of 86%. Passengers on some routes were being turned away or had to wait a long time. At off-peak times, some buses only had an average of 39% of seats filled, which meant that large expensive buses with well-paid drivers were less than half full.

Source: http://www.scotland.gov.uk

Outsourcing

Deutsche Bank has outsourced the design and operation of its IT system that deals with customer relations to a Russian company, Luxoft. The bank does not employ its own IT software developers, preferring to use other specialist companies. Luxoft has 100 developers working on the Deutsche Bank customer system, which covers details such as dates of meetings with customers, amount lent and copies of all documents. Getting the details right is essential, so quality checks on the Luxoft system are essential.

Source: http://management.silicon.com

18 marks, 30 minutes

1 Why might it *not* be most effective to have all buses and all factories operating at 100% of capacity? [6]

2 Suggest **two** ways in which Lothian Buses might overcome the capacity problem during peak periods other than buying more buses. [4]

3 What might be the benefits and risks to Deutsche Bank of outsourcing some important operations to another business? [8]

EXAM PRACTICE QUESTION

Read the case study below and then answer the questions that follow.

MFLEX TO EXPAND OPERATIONS IN MALAYSIA

MFLEX, the leading global maker of high-quality advanced circuit boards to the electronics industry, has leased a 35 000 square metre factory in Johor Darul Takzim, Malaysia. It has purchased new manufacturing equipment for the plant and employed 125 workers, which will mean a considerable increase in capacity and scale of operation for the company.

The factory will allow the business to respond more rapidly and flexibly to just-in-time demands from its customers. The company will also expect its suppliers to be able to deliver materials and components on a JIT basis and it has signed exclusive deals with certain suppliers and is connected to them by computer link to speed up ordering.

Rapid inflation in Malaysia, as in other countries, is forcing some businesses to re-think their use of JIT manufacturing systems. With rising costs of industrial materials and components and much higher charges for transport, some operations managers are looking again at whether the 'no buffer stock' policy of the JIT method with frequent small orders being delivered is actually costing more than a large stock-order policy.

Source: http://biz.yahoo.com/prnews (adapted)

25 marks, 45 minutes

1 Define the following terms:
   a increase in capacity
   b increase in scale of operation
   c no buffer stock. [4]

2 Explain the difference between stock-holding costs and the costs of not holding enough stock. [6]

3 Analyse **two** criteria MFLEX needs to meet in order to use JIT stock management successfully. [6]

4 Evaluate MFLEX's decision to use JIT stock management. [9]

37 Project management

This chapter covers syllabus section 5.8 (Higher level only)

On completing this chapter you should be able to:

- (H) construct and interpret a network diagram
- (H) analyse how critical path analysis (CPA) and network diagrams can be used to help with project management
- (H) apply CPA to different projects
- (H) evaluate the usefulness of a network in the management of projects.

SETTING THE SCENE

Building a new bridge

The Eastern Construction Company has just received its first major bridge-building contract from a foreign government. The company managers have been keen to sign this contract as it means that they will be able to add to the range of building projects that they have worked on. Jimmy Chen has been appointed project manager for this key contract. He has seen government officials on several occasions to obtain agreement on:

- the exact size and specifications of the bridge
- the expected completion date
- the value of the contract – the price the government has agreed to pay for the completed bridge.

Jimmy has a team of managers to help him calculate the exact materials and equipment needs of this building project – they will take responsibility for seeing the project through to completion. IT specialists have been asked to draw up a diagram showing all of the different tasks of the project, the estimated time for each task and the resources needed for each. This diagram has shown that some tasks can be done together – such as laying the tarmac on the road and painting the steel structure, and other tasks must be completed before any other work can start – such as building an access road and laying foundations for the bridge.

After six months, building work has started and the project is on time – so far. Some costs have exceeded estimates – but others are lower than expected. Both Jimmy and his senior managers hope that if the project is seen as a success, other bridge contracts will be awarded to the company.

37 Project management

Points to think about:

- Why is careful management of this project particularly important to this company?
- Why would a diagram of activities be useful to Jimmy and his team?
- What problems might there be in making sure this diagram was as accurate as possible?

Introduction

KEY TERMS

project a specific and temporary activity with a start and end date, clear goals, defined responsibilities and a budget

project management using modern management techniques to carry out and complete a project from start to finish in order to achieve pre-set targets of quality, time and cost

Examples of business projects include:

- setting up a new IT system
- relocating the company operations
- installing machinery
- developing and launching a new product
- building a factory.

To be completed successfully, a project needs to be planned and managed, costs determined and times allocated, problems dealt with and, eventually, concluded. Formal methods of managing a project offer clear guidelines and deadlines. The key elements of project management include:

- defining the project carefully, including the setting of clear objectives
- dividing the project up into manageable tasks and activities
- controlling the project at every stage to check that time limits are being kept to
- giving each team member a clear role
- providing controls over quality issues and risks.

Failure to manage projects successfully can have serious consequences for any organisation. In the 'Setting the scene' case study above, any failure to complete the building of the bridge on time and within budget could result in:

- penalty payments having to be paid to the customers
- bad publicity in the construction industry
- loss of future contracts.

A Standish Report on project management suggested that major projects failed because:

- customers were not involved in the planning and development process
- the project had inadequate or no resources that were vital for its completion
- senior management did not seem interested in seeing the project through
- the project specification kept changing during the life of the project
- planning was poor
- the project's scope had become outdated due to change in the business environment
- the project team was technically incompetent.

Critical path analysis (CPA)

Operational resources are expensive and the most expensive resource is that which is unused or underused – unused stocks take up space and working capital; machinery left idle wastes capital and can require protective maintenance; labour waiting for supplies to arrive will add unnecessarily to the wages bill. Efficient firms will always aim to use their resources as intensively as possible and avoid wasted time and idle assets. Keeping assets busy is not always as easy as it sounds, especially when the project is a complex one.

Consider the construction of a house:

- The builder only wants to employ specialist staff on a subcontract basis when the job is ready for their particular skills.

- He also wants to order bricks and other materials to arrive just as they are needed, not weeks before, blocking up the site, wasting working capital and inviting theft.
- He certainly does not want them three days after the bricklayers require them.
- Specialist equipment is often hired and to keep this a day more than necessary will raise costs and affect cash flow.

How can all of the different tasks involved in building a house be put into order so that the right goods and labour can be employed just at the right time? The answer for many businesses is to use a technique known as critical path analysis (CPA) – also known as network analysis.

KEY TERM

critical path analysis planning technique that identifies all tasks in a project, puts them in the correct sequence and allows for the identification of the critical path

THE CRITICAL PATH ANALYSIS PROCESS

CPA involves drawing a network diagram that indicates the shortest possible time in which a project can be completed. The activities – that must be completed to achieve this shortest time – make up what is known as the critical path. The process of using CPA involves the following steps:

1. Identify the objective of the project, e.g. building a factory in six weeks.
2. Put the tasks that make up the project into the right sequence and draw a network diagram.
3. Add the durations of each of the activities.
4. Identify the critical path – those activities that must be finished on time for the project to be finished in the shortest time.
5. Use the network as a control tool when problems occur during the project.

KEY TERMS

network diagram the diagram used in critical path analysis that shows the logical sequence of activities and the logical dependencies between them – and the critical path can be identified

critical path the sequence of activities that must be completed on time for the whole project to be completed by the agreed date

USING CRITICAL PATH ANALYSIS

Constructing a simple network diagram to identify the critical path

The objective is to see if a new machine can be installed and the staff trained to operate it within three weeks (assume a five-day working week) (see Figure 37.1). A network diagram uses the following notation:

- An arrow indicates each activity.
- An activity takes up time and resources.
- A node (circle) indicates the end of each activity.

The activities involved in this project and the estimated time for each activity (duration) are as follows:

- Strip out old machine (A) – three days.
- Order new machine and await arrival (B) – one day.
- Prepare site for new machine (C) – two days.
- Assemble new machine (D) – two days.
- Install new machine (E) – one week.
- Demonstrate to workers (F) – two days.
- Obtain necessary raw materials (G) – one day.
- Trial test run (H) – three days.

You will notice from the diagram that from the first node, two activities can start. This is because stripping out the old machine and ordering the new one are independent activities. They can be done simultaneously and do not have to be done in sequence.

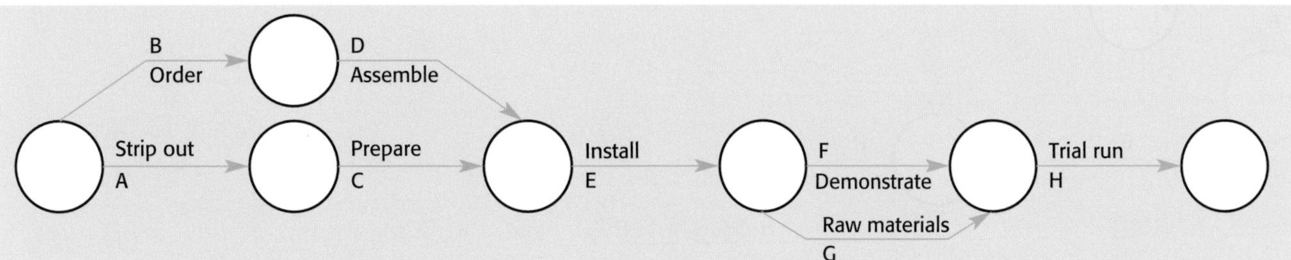

Figure 37.1 Installing a new machine – the network diagram

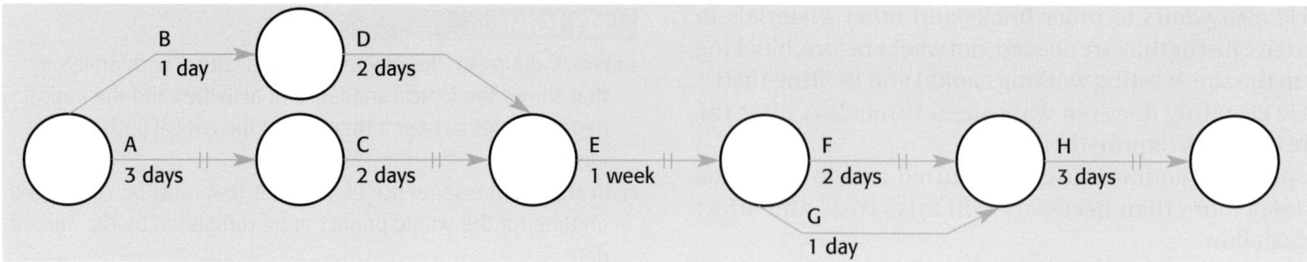

Figure 37.2 Adding durations to find the critical path

Clearly, this is a relatively simple project and, if these durations are added to the network diagram, it is possible to determine visually:

- which is the critical path of activities – these activities are indicated with pairs of short parallel lines
- that the project can be completed within three weeks – see Figure 37.2.

It is clear that the 'critical' activities are A, C, E, F and H. If these should be delayed in any way, for example if the preparation of the site takes more than two days, then the whole task will take longer than three weeks. It can be seen that the other activities are not critical – these, in fact, may have some spare time. This is termed float time. In more complex projects, this can be useful for achieving an even more efficient use of resources.

How the critical path is determined: a more complex example

The objective is to construct a house in 42 days. To create the network diagram, the tasks to be performed in order to build the house have been broken down into ten main activities, such as digging foundations and tiling the roof. These activities must be done in a certain order – the roof cannot be tiled before the walls are built, for instance – and this order of tasks is as shown in Table 37.1. The network diagram for these activities is shown in Figure 37.3.

Activity	Preceding activities
A	–
B	–
C	A
D	B and C
E	A
F	E
G	F and D
H	B and C
I	G and H
J	I

***Table 37.1** The order of tasks in building a house – the objective is to build a house in 42 days*

You will notice from the diagram that each of the nodes has been numbered for ease of reference. The duration times for each activity, shown in Table 37.2, can now be added to the network diagram (see Figure 37.4).

These durations are very important. They allow us to calculate both the critical path and the spare time – or float time – for the non-critical activities. The critical path is indicated by calculating, at each node, the earliest start time (EST) and the latest finish time (LFT). These have already been added to the nodes in Figure 37.4. Figure 37.5 opposite illustrates how the node numbering should be shown.

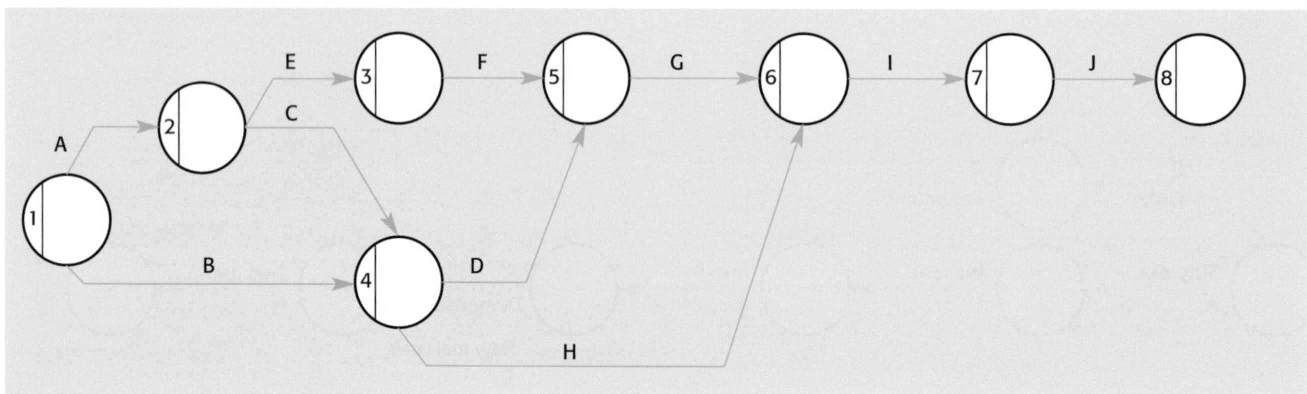

Figure 37.3 The main stages of building a house

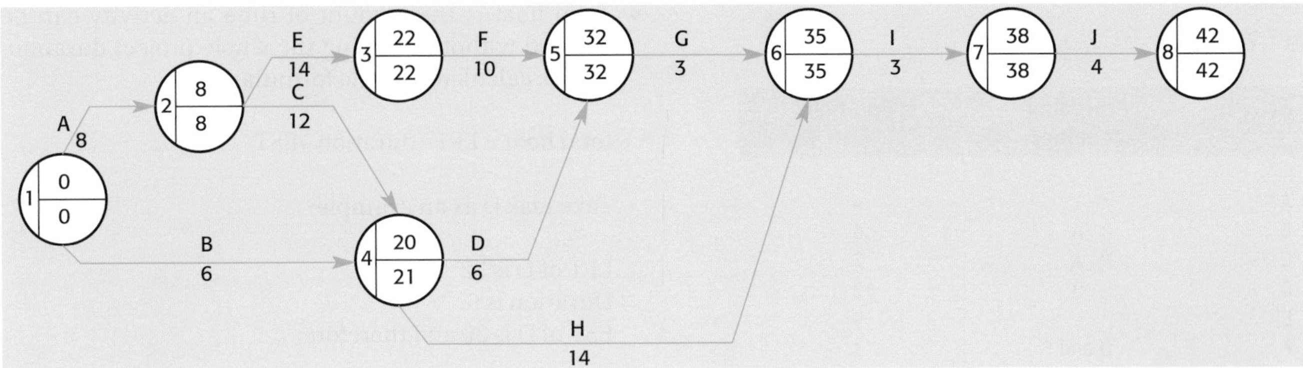

Figure 37.4 Adding in the activities and durations

Activity	Duration (days)
A	8
B	6
C	12
D	6
E	14
F	10
G	3
H	14
I	3
J	4

Table 37.2 *Duration times of the tasks in building a house*

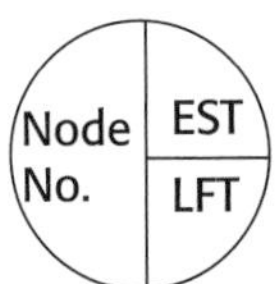

Figure 37.5 Node numbering

Critical path analysis helps avoid delays on construction projects

ACTIVITY 37.1

Verify the ESTs in Figure 37.4 by working through the diagram from left to right, taking the longest route, in days, to each node.

What is the earliest start time and how is it calculated?

It is the earliest time each activity can begin, taking into account all of the preceding activities. So, activity E cannot start before day 8 because A will not be finished before then. And D cannot start before day 20 because both A and C have to be completed first.

What is the latest finish time and how is it calculated?

It is the latest time an activity can finish without delaying the whole project. So, I (and all preceding activities) must be finished by day 38 or the entire project will take longer than 42 days (because 4 days must be allowed to finish J itself). Task F (and all preceding activities) must finish by day 32 or the time taken to complete G, I and J will take the total project time over 42 days.

The easiest way to calculate the LFTs is to work from right to left. The LFT at node 8 must be 42 – the total project time. The duration of activity J is now subtracted from this to give 38. This is the LFT at node 7.Where there is a choice of routes back to a node, the aim is to achieve the lowest number for LFT. The LFT for node 4 is therefore 21, achieved by working back through J, I and H, even though a higher number could be reached by working through J, I, G and D. Remember, the lowest number at each node is what is required for the LFT.

ACTIVITY 37.2

Verify all of the LFTs by your own calculation.

ACTIVITY 37.3

Activity	Preceding activities	Duration
A	–	4
B	A	6
C	A	7
D	B	12
E	C	9
F	D and E	3
G	A	16
H	G and F	3

Activities and durations for Project X

20 marks, 35 minutes

1 Draw the network for Project X. [6]

2 Use the duration times to calculate the EST and LFT of each activity. [6]

3 Identify the critical path. [2]

4 Explain the importance of this critical path to the operations manager. [6]

What is the critical path for this project?

Those activities that have no spare time are the critical ones. These activities are shown by those nodes where EST and LFT are equal. Take node 3 as an example. The EST of F is 22. This is the same as the LFT of E. Therefore no delay is possible – F must start on time or the whole project will over-run. Therefore, the critical path is made up of activities A, E, F, G, I and J. These will take 42 days to complete, so this becomes the project duration. Float times have very significant applications in managing resources – see advantages of network analysis.

Calculating float times for non-critical activities

Look at the network diagram for building a home (Figure 37.4). Non-critical activities B, C, D and H will have 'float' time. All of the non-critical activities, those not on the critical path, will have a certain amount of spare time. This spare time is called float. There are two types of float:

- Total float is the amount of time an activity can be delayed without delaying the whole project duration. This is calculated by the formula:

  total float = LFT – duration – EST

  Take task D as an example:

  LFT of D is 32
  Duration is 6
  EST of D is 20 and therefore:

  total float for D = 32 – 6 – 20 = 6 days

  D could be delayed by up to 6 days without extending the total project duration or changing the critical path.

- Free float is the length of time an activity can be delayed without delaying the start of the following activities. This is calculated by the formula:

  free float = EST (next activity) – duration – EST (this activity)

  Take task B as an example:

  EST of next activity after B is 20
  Duration of B is 6
  EST at the start of B is 0 and, therefore:

  free float for B = 20 – 6 – 0 = 14

B could be delayed by 14 days without delaying the start of either H or D, the following activities. See Table 37.3.

Activity	Total float	Free float
B	15	14
C	1	0
D	6	6
H	1	1

***Table 37.3** Float time for all non-critical activities*

Dummy activities

A dummy activity is not strictly an activity at all. It is shown by a dotted line on a network diagram. It does not consume either time or resources. What it shows is a 'logical dependency' between other activities that must be included in certain networks to prevent an illogical path from being created. Consider these activities and the relationships between them:

- The activities A and B are the start of the project. They have no preceding activities.
- C follows A.
- D follows A and B.

How can the network be drawn? Figure 37.6 shows one attempt – but it is wrong. Can you see why? The network shows that both C and D require A and B to be finished, whereas C only requires A to finish before it can start.

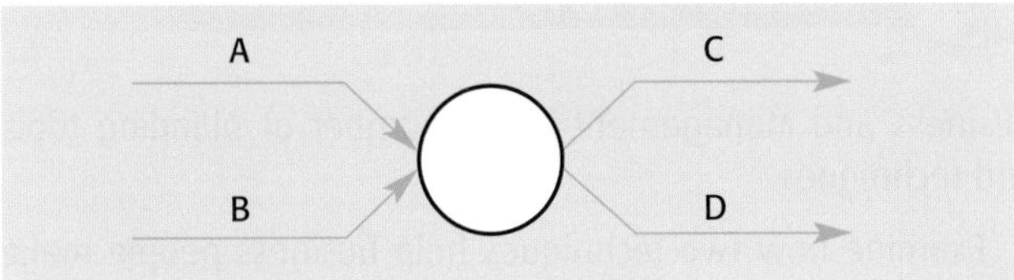

Figure 37.6 *First attempt at drawing a network*

The correct network is shown in Figure 37.7, which shows the correct logical dependencies – C starts when A is finished, but D has to wait before both A and B are finished. The dummy activity shows the relationship between B and D – with the arrow indicating the direction of the dependency.

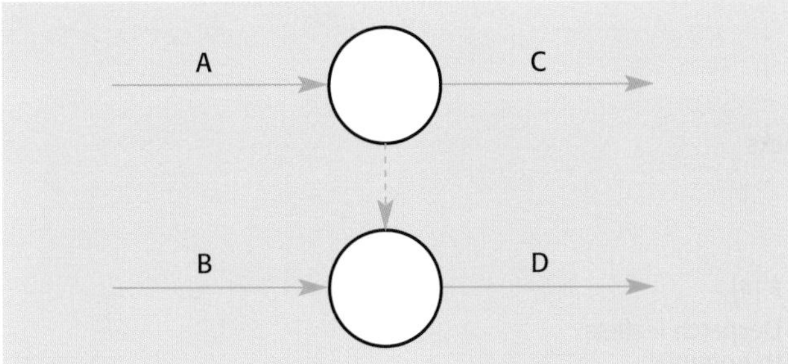

Figure 37.7 *The correct network*

THE ADVANTAGES OF NETWORK ANALYSIS

It has already been stated that network analysis can be used to assist the planning and management of complex projects. The following are some of the advantages that result from using the technique:

- Using the diagram to calculate the total project duration allows businesses to give accurate delivery dates. Customers may insist on a particular completion date and the critical time shows whether the firm can make this date or not.
- Calculating an EST for each activity allows the operations manager to order special equipment or materials needed for that task at the correct time. This ties the use of network analysis in with JIT strategies and assists in the control of cash flow and working capital.
- Calculating the LFT of each activity provides a useful control tool for the operations manager. The manager will be able to see whether the project is up to schedule by checking the actual completion times of activities against the network LFT.
- Knowing the critical path can be very useful. If there is a delay on a critical activity, there is no float because it is critical and the delay will, unless quick action is taken, put back the whole project. This could lead to expensive damage claims from the customer. By knowing the critical path, the operations manager can see which other activities need to be speeded up if one has been delayed. For instance, in the house-building example above, if E was delayed by two days due to bad weather or non-arrival of equipment, the operations manager would know that one of the following critical activities needs to be accelerated to catch up on time lost.
- The additional resources for speeding up a critical activity could come from the non-critical ones. To use the house-building example, if F is to be reduced to eight days to counter the delay on E, the resources of labour, materials and machinery could be taken from D or H, as they both have spare time. This will allow a better and more efficient use of the firm's resources. This shows how the existence of float times on D and H allows resources to be allocated more efficiently.
- The sequential and logical structure of the diagram lends itself well to computer applications and nearly all business applications of network analysis will now be run on computer.
- The need to put all activities into sequence in order to structure the diagram forces managers to plan each project carefully by putting activities in the correct order.
- The need for rapid development of new products has never been greater in the fast-changing consumer markets of today. Network analysis gives design and engineering departments a positive advantage by showing them the tasks that can be undertaken simultaneously in developing a new product. This will help to reduce the total time taken by the new project and supports the principle of 'simultaneous engineering'.

EXAM TIP

No planning technique, however good, can ensure that a project will reach a successful conclusion – refer to all of the reasons mentioned at the start of this chapter that can cause a project to fail.

NETWORK ANALYSIS – AN EVALUATION

Network analysis is a planning and control technique to assist with project management. It cannot guarantee a successful project by itself and, as with any plan, requires skilled and motivated staff to put it into effect. In addition, a plan is only as good as the management putting it into effect – if management of the project is poor, then even a good critical path network diagram will not ensure success. This is particularly true when attempting to make up for lost time on a critical activity – experienced managers will need to identify the cheapest option for using and switching resources from non-critical activities.

Staff will feel more committed to the plan of operation if they have been consulted during its construction, for example over likely duration times for each activity.

When using CPA for a completely new project, there may be considerable guesswork involved in estimating the durations for each activity – as there will be no previous experience to go on. Although the manipulation of the network and of duration and float times is likely to be aided by computer, it can take skilled labour hours to put a complex project on to a computer. This time and the related expense must be justified by the subsequent cost and efficiency savings of applying the technique.

THEORY OF KNOWLEDGE

Business and Management has a number of planning tools and techniques.

a Examine how **two** techniques help business people make better decisions.

b 'Embarking on a project without a logically thought out plan risks a high probability of failure.' To what extent is logic an important part of business decision-making?

ACTIVITY 37.4

The launch of a new product

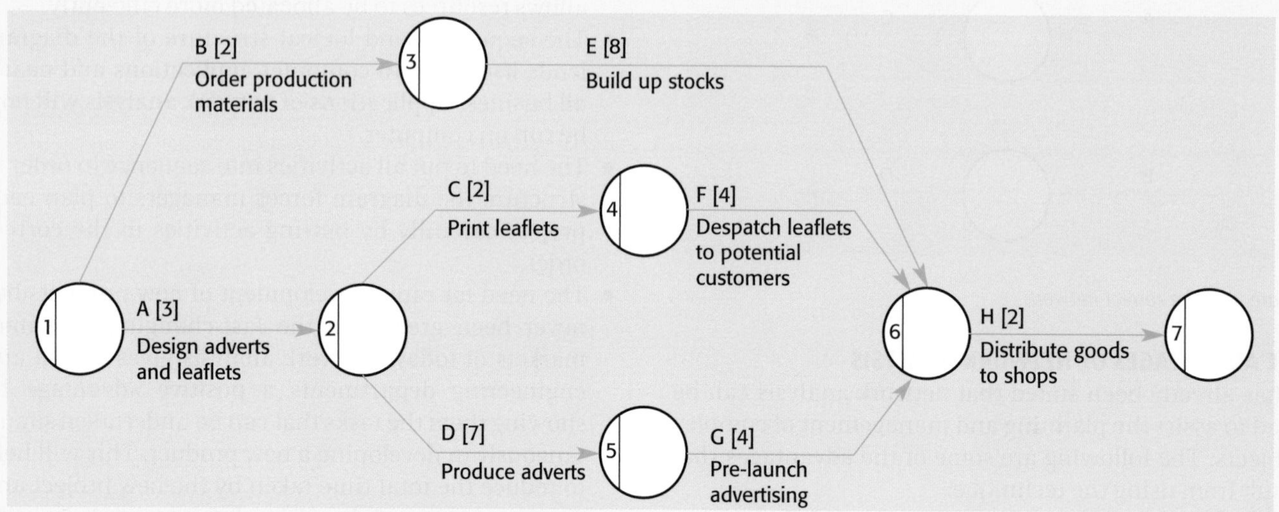

Network diagram showing the launch of a product

25 marks, 45 minutes

1 Calculate the EST and LFT at each node (all durations in weeks). [6]

2 Identify the critical path. [1]

3 Calculate the total floats and free floats for each non-critical activity. [6]

4 If D is delayed by an over-run in the production of the advertisements, suggest how the marketing manager might still be able to complete the launch in the original project time. [4]

5 Explain how the use of network analysis might have assisted the marketing manager during this project. [8]

OVER TO YOU

REVISION CHECKLIST

1 What is meant by 'project management'?
2 Why is it important to manage projects effectively?
3 What are the **four** key factors in project management?
4 What is meant by the 'critical path' in network analysis?
5 Explain why it important for an operations manager to monitor carefully the critical activities on a network diagram.
6 Explain the difference between the earliest start time of an activity and its latest finish time.
7 Distinguish between a non-critical activity's total float and free float in network analysis.
8 Outline **two** advantages for a road-building firm of using critical path analysis.
9 Suggest **one** other business that might benefit greatly from using critical path analysis.
10 Outline **two** limitations of critical path analysis.
11 Why might a project not be completed successfully, even though a detailed critical path analysis has been undertaken?

REVISION ACTIVITY

18 marks, 28 minutes

1 Calculate all ESTs and LSTs for the network shown in the diagram below. [6]

2 Calculate the duration of the critical path. [2]

3 Calculate total floats on all of the non-critical activities. [6]

4 Explain the disadvantages to the operations manager of ordering goods needed for task D to arrive on:
- day 25
- day 15. [4]

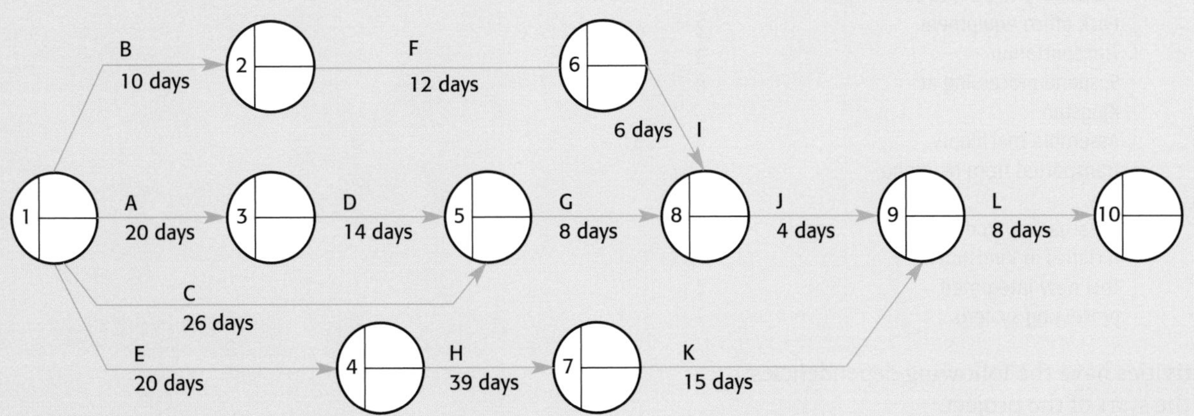

Critical path

EXAM PRACTICE QUESTION

Read the case study below and then answer the questions that follow.

SHUT DOWN AT JAMAICA PHOTOS

Jamaica Photos is a medium-sized private limited company. The firm specialises in photographic processing. It currently operates from two sites in Jamaica. After considerable consultation with employees, it is planning to close one of these sites, at Montego Bay, and to concentrate film processing at its Kingston branch. The managers of the company want to make sure that the closure should be carefully planned to reduce to a minimum the adverse effects on production and customer delivery times. A project management team has been drawn from all levels within the company to carry through this plan. The team has been offered a bonus if it can complete the task within 15 working days.

Closing the factory involves a number of activities as shown below:

Activity	Description	Duration (days)
A	End processing in Montego Bay; run down stocks of materials	2
B	Dismantle machinery	4
C	Knock out doorway to allow machinery to be moved	2
D	Pack office equipment	2
E	Transportation	3
F	Suspend processing at Kingston	8
G	Assemble machinery transported from Montego Bay	3
H	Re-organise production facilities in Kingston	2
I	Test new integrated processing system	2

The activities have the following dependencies:

- A is the start of the project.
- B, C and D cannot start until A is complete.
- E follows B, C and D.
- F has no preceding activity.
- F must be completed before I can commence.
- G and H follow E.
- I follows G and H.

25 marks, 45 minutes

1 Define the following terms:
   a private limited company
   b project management. [4]

2 Based on the information on the factory closure:
   a construct a network diagram for closing the factory [6]
   b calculate the ESTs and LFTs for each activity [4]
   c identify the critical path. [2]

3 Evaluate the usefulness of critical path analysis to the management of Jamaica Photos. [9]

38 Business strategy

This chapter covers syllabus section 6 (Higher level only)

On completing this chapter you should be able to:

- (H) understand the meaning of business strategy and strategic management
- (H) discuss the three key elements of the strategic framework – strategic analysis, strategic choice and strategic implementation
- (H) recommend and evaluate business strategies in a variety of business contexts.

SETTING THE SCENE

New corporate strategy for Hitachi

Hitachi's new corporate strategy aims to achieve 'profits through creativity'. The basic policy is to focus on a market-oriented approach and profit creation. Several strategic decisions have been taken, after an analysis of where the company stands in its current markets, to guide the large Japanese electronics firm towards these goals. They are:

- creating a portfolio of products with higher profitability – the research and development departments will work more closely with the marketing side of operations
- increasing collaboration with business partners to create more innovative products – an example of this is the strengthened partnership between Hitachi and Clarion to develop new car entertainment systems
- each business group within Hitachi to be given increased autonomy and profit responsibilities
- allocate more resources to business areas where Hitachi is strong, such as storage systems and in-car information systems.

Points to think about:

- What do you understand by the term 'strategy' from this case study?
- What are likely to be the benefits to Hitachi of introducing the plans outlined above? Explain your answer.
- In setting a new future strategy why do you think it is important to assess 'where the business is now'?

38 Business strategy

Introduction

Topic 6 of the IB Business and Management course is very different from topics 1–5. These covered important subject content and nearly all of the questions on the standard level (SL) and higher level (HL) papers will be focused on this extensive content and your ability to understand, apply and analyse it. Topic 6 is different because it adds no new business or management content to learn and understand. Instead it brings together – or synthesises – the business ideas, concepts and techniques that form part of the HL course to allow you to make strategic choices or decisions. These decisions have an impact on all functional departments – cross-functional decisions – not just one of them, and they are called strategic decisions. These strategic approaches will be examined in section C on HL Paper 1 and they will also be expected in the preparation and presentation of the research project for the HL internal assessment.

Business strategy – what does it mean?

In simple terms a strategy is a plan for 'getting from where we are now to where we want to be in the future'. A successful business will have a vision or ultimate goal. Its corporate strategy will be a clear plan and set of policies that should push it towards achieving this vision.

KEY TERMS

business strategy a long-term plan of action for the whole organisation, designed to meet the needs of markets and to fulfil stakeholder expectations.

strategic management the role of management when setting long-term goals and implementing cross-functional decisions that should enable a business to reach these goals

tactic short-term policy or decision aimed at resolving a particular problem or meeting a specific part of the overall strategy

A longer explanation of business strategy is that it is a plan, based on an assessment of the company's current position and the external environment, containing key business objectives and the decisions needed to achieve these. So business strategy asks the big questions – such as 'Which markets and products do we want to be in?' – and makes the big decisions – such as 'expanding manufacturing operations into retailing too'. Businesses organisations need a corporate strategy to provide integration, direction and focus.

Elements of the strategic framework

The process of strategic management has three key stages (see Figure 38.1):

1 strategic analysis
2 strategic choice
3 strategic implementation (see Table 38.1).

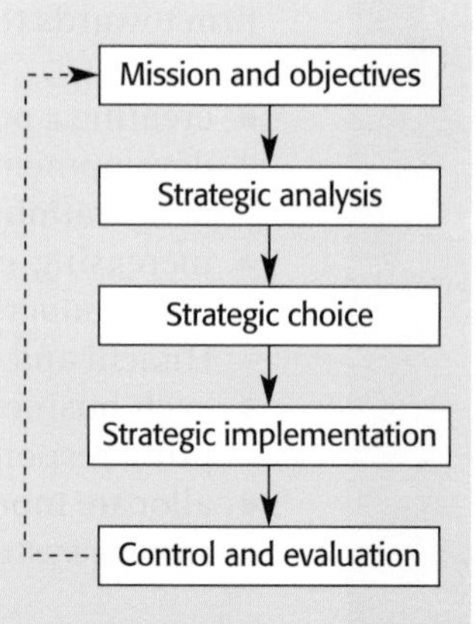

Figure 38.1 *Strategic management*

Key stages of strategic management	Reasons why important
1 STRATEGIC ANALYSIS • Assessing the current position of the company in relation to its market, competitors and the external environment.	• Decisions that do not start from knowledge of 'where the business is now' may be inappropriate and ineffective.
2 STRATEGIC CHOICE • Setting the company's mission, vision and objectives – these may be new if the business is undergoing a significant change of direction. • Taking important long-term decisions that will push the business towards the objectives set.	• Chapter 3 examined the importance of having clear and well-defined aims and objectives to provide a clear sense of overall direction to the work of the whole organisation. • A new direction for a business will require key decisions to be taken about products and markets.
3 STRATEGIC IMPLEMENTATION • Integrating and co-ordinating the activities of the different functional areas. • Allocating sufficient resources to put decisions into effect. • Evaluating success – evaluating the overall performance of the business and its progress towards objectives.	• As strategic decisions are cross-functional, departments must work together to implement them successfully. So, a decision to enter a new geographical market will need input from finance, marketing, HR and operations management. • Changing strategy is rarely 'cheap' and resources must be provided at the right time and in sufficient quantities to allow the new policies to work. • The outcome of the strategy should be measured against the original objectives set for it. Lessons can be learnt from both 'failed' and 'successful' strategies.

Table 38.1 *What strategic management involves – the strategic framework*

Strategy hierarchy

Strategic management is the highest level of managerial activity. It is undertaken by, or at least closely supervised by, the chief executive officer and approved by the board of directors. In most large organisations there are several layers of management. Under the broad corporate strategy role of the senior directors there are, typically, business unit competitive strategies and functional department strategies. These must be co-ordinated with the overall corporate strategy to increase the chances of achieving the organisation's long-term aims (see Table 38.2).

Corporate strategy	The overall strategy development for the whole corporation
Business strategy	Separate business divisions of a large corporation – product or geographical market business units – form strategies to achieve and sustain competitive advantage. If successful, the corporate strategy is also likely to succeed.
Functional strategies	These plans are limited to the department's own functional responsibilities such as product development strategies, marketing strategies and human resource strategies.

Table 38.2 *The strategy hierarchy*

Tactics, on the other hand, are concerned with making smaller-scale decisions aimed at reaching more limited and measurable goals, which themselves are part of the longer-term strategic aim. It is important to be clear about the distinction between tactics and strategies – this is shown in Table 38.3.

Strategic decisions, e.g. to develop new markets abroad	**Tactical decisions, e.g. to sell product in different-sized packaging**
Long term	Short to medium term
Difficult to reverse once made – departments will have committed resources to it	Reversible, but there may still be costs involved
Taken by directors and/or senior managers	Taken by less senior managers and subordinates with delegated authority
Cross-functional – will involve all major departments of the business	Impact of tactical decisions is often only on one department

Table 38.3 *Key differences between tactical decisions and strategic decisions*

ACTIVITY 38.1

BUSINESS STRATEGY OR BUSINESS TACTICS?

15 marks, 30 minutes

Copy and complete the table below. Are the decisions strategic or tactical? Explain your answer in each case. **[15]**

Business context	**Decision**	**Strategic or tactical – and explanation**
Multinational drinks company	Switch from cans to plastic bottles.	
Supermarket business	Start selling non-food items, such as clothes, for the first time.	
Steel-making company	Recruit production supervisors internally not externally.	
Holiday tour operator	Increase prices of holidays to a popular destination.	
Major computer manufacturer	Develop a range of advanced mobile phones with internet capability.	

Strategic analysis

KEY TERMS

strategic analysis the process of conducting research on the business environment within which a business operates and on the organisation itself in order to develop strategy

Strategic analysis is concerned with analysing the strengths and weaknesses of a business's position and understanding the important external factors that may influence that position. Before a business can plan a future strategy it is essential to assess 'where it is now'. Strategic analysis tries to find answers to three key questions:

- Where is the business now?
- How might the business be affected by what is happening, or likely to happen?
- How could the business respond to these likely changes?

Effective strategic analysis will lead to clearer and more relevant business goals, better quality strategic decisions and a less risky future for a business as it should be better prepared.

The process of strategic analysis is aided by a number of tools which have already been discussed in earlier sections of this book:

1 The starting point for this analysis is likely to be SWOT and PEST analysis (see Chapters 5 and 6). Internal analysis of the business and external environmental analysis will investigate issues such as:
   - What are the present aims, objectives and core principles of the business?
   - Is it a new or established business?
   - To what extent has the business planned for its future direction?
   - What are the objectives of the business's stakeholders?
   - Does the existing vision or mission statement reflect what the business is doing now?
   - What new market opportunities are available?
   - What resources are available to the business?
   - What are the attitudes of the business to risk?
   - Is entrepreneurship encouraged?
2 Porter's Five Forces analysis. (See Chapter 25.)
3 Assessing how expansion could be financed. (See ratio analysis, Chapter 23, and sources of finance, Chapter 18.)
4 Is the business in the private or public sector? Does it operate in the profit or not-for-profit sector? (See Chapter 2.)
5 Is the business a multinational or does it operate only in domestic markets? (See Chapter 9.)
6 Analysing the organisation's present financial position and assessing whether it is conducive to change. (See Chapter 23.)
7 Is the present product portfolio adequate and appropriate? (See Boston Matrix, Chapter 26.)

Source: IB Diploma Programme Business and Management guide (adapted)

These techniques and tools will provide the essential content knowledge that you will need to demonstrate when answering an IB question which requires a discussion of strategic analysis. The remainder of this section focuses on developing one key theme in strategic decision-making – competitive advantage – and on case study examples of business strategy.

BUSINESS STRATEGY AND COMPETITIVE ADVANTAGE

World trade is growing faster than world GDP – this is a key consequence of globalisation. Trade barriers are being reduced and protectionist policies are no longer acceptable to the many countries that believe in the free-trade concept. This means that companies must compete not only with domestic rivals but with competitors from across the globe. Many of these competitors will have either:

- lower costs

  or
- differentiated products.

According to Michael Porter, these are the two main factors that can lead to a significant competitive advantage. Business managers must decide whether they want business strategy to focus on competitiveness gained through low costs (and prices) or differentiated products that would allow higher prices to be charged.

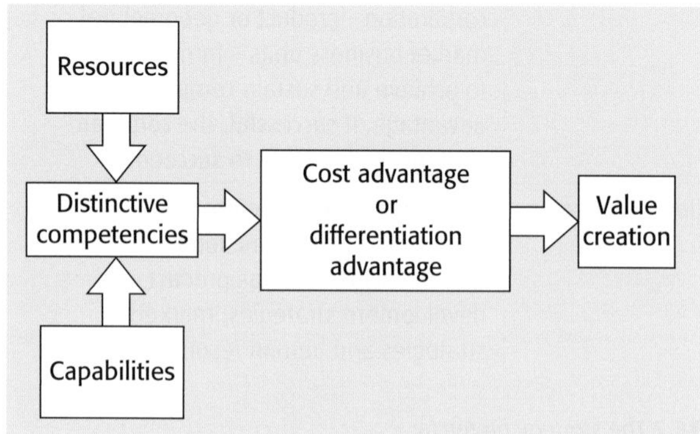

Figure 38.2 *A model of competitive advantage*

What strategies can be adopted to increase a business's competitive advantage when faced with a globalised marketplace? Here are three examples:

1 Automation. BMW's takeover of the iconic Mini brand led to an investment of over $400 million in 230 new robots at the UK factory. These offer some of the most advanced and productive manufacturing production facilities in the world. This helps to reduce the costs of manufacture, but it also allows a flexible production system that can make all three types of Mini body shell on the same production line. So, in effect, both lower costs and differentiated products were achieved by this automation strategy.
2 Rationalisation. The merger of two of Europe's main travel companies, Thomas Cook and MyTravel, aimed to cut costs to increase competitiveness. It seemed to achieve its aims because, within two years, cost savings of over $300 million had been achieved by a combination of redundancies – especially when job titles were unnecessarily duplicated after the merger – and bulk purchasing of holiday accommodation.

3 Research and development (R&D). Shell, the oil giant, increased its R&D spending by 36% in 2008. The company has a strategy of technological developments to allow diversification away from its original oil and gas business. This strategy is partly driven by the fact that it has relatively low reserves of oil and gas compared to other big firms in the industry. Product differentiation by means of R&D at Shell is focusing on biotechnology, carbon emission storage and alternative fuels.

All three of the above strategies will, if successful, allow these business to gain or sustain their competitive advantages in an increasingly tough competitive world. These examples also illustrate the fundamental importance of businesses having a clear corporate strategy that focuses on plans that should allow the achievement of long-term goals.

CORE COMPETENCIES

Another approach to competitive advantage was developed by Hamel and Prahalad (1990). They studied the importance of developing a business's 'core competencies' and argued that if a business develops core competencies, then they may gain competitive advantage over other firms in the same industry.

KEY TERMS

core competence an important business capability that gives it a competitive advantage

core product product made from a business's core competencies, but not for final consumer or 'end' user

To be of commercial and profitable benefit to a business, a core competence should:

- provide recognisable benefits to consumers
- not be easy for other firms to copy, e.g. a patented design
- be applicable to a range of different products and markets.

According to Hamel and Prahalad, core competencies lead to the development of core products. Core products are not necessarily sold to final consumers. Instead they are used to produce a large number of end-user products. For example, Black & Decker, it is claimed, has a core competence in the design and manufacture of small electric motors. These core products are used in a huge variety of different applications from power tools, such as drills, to lawnmowers and food processors.

Developing core competencies

It is important to realise that a business might be particularly good at a certain activity – it might have competence in this activity – but this does not necessarily make it a core competence *if* it is not exceptional or is easy to copy. So, a computer-assembly business might be very efficient and produce computers at low cost, but if it depends on easily available and cheap bought-in components from suppliers, this is not a core competence. It does not make the business very different from many other computer-assembly firms.

Developing a core competence, according to Prahalad and Hamel, depends on integrating multiple technologies and different product skills that probably already exist in the business. It does not necessarily mean spending huge amounts on R&D – although patented production processes, such as Pilkington's float-glass process, may give a core competence. If a management team can effectively bring together and co-ordinate designers, production specialists, IT experts and so on, into a team to develop new and different competencies, then these may become differentiated and core competencies. Two excellent business examples are the development of Philip's expertise in optical media and Sony's ability to miniaturise electronic components that has led to many core products.

Core competencies and business strategy

Once a core competence has been established, it opens up strategic opportunities for developing core products and then new 'end' products and new markets, as shown in Figure 38.3. The business units in the diagram are the divisions of a business that will use the core products. So, they might be 'consumer products business' and 'industrial products business' but they would both use the core competencies of the business, for example a new very fast microchip or a new design of electric motor. By building up new products for new markets in this way there will now be a greater opportunity to gain economies of scale in the manufacture of the core products.

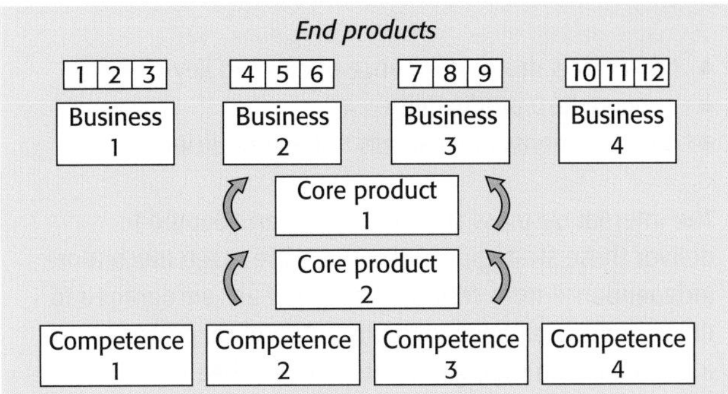

Figure 38.3 Core competences to end products
Source: www.quickmba.com/strategy/core-competencies

ACTIVITY 38.2

Core competencies in practice

Honda is often claimed to have a core competence in building powerful and efficient petrol engines. Black & Decker is recognised as having a core competence in making small electric motors.

Research into the range of products offered either by Honda or Black & Decker. Discuss the benefits to either of these businesses of having the core competence outlined above.

ACTIVITY 38.3

Read the case study below and then answer the questions that follow.

GlaxoSmithKline (GSK) – strategy influenced by competition

GSK is a large multinational pharmaceutical business. It spends billions of dollars each year researching new medicines – at any one time it has over 150 projects in clinical development. The company's mission statement is to: 'improve the quality of human life by enabling people to do more, feel better and live longer'. It aims to launch several new drugs for medical purposes each year – in 2008, five important new medicines were marketed, including cancer drugs and one for reducing risk of heart failure. However, sales of existing products are being increasingly affected by the rise of 'generic drugs' made by companies that copy the successful GSK formula when the patent period has ended.

The company strategy for the next few years is to:

- maximise sales performance of existing key products
- improve R&D productivity
- ensure patients have access to new medicines.

The internal business structure has been adapted to deliver these strategies. R&D groups are given much more independence from central control and are encouraged to deliver novel solutions to important medical problems. In addition, an 'emerging markets' unit has been created to increase sales from the growing markets of China, India, Brazil and Russia. Its chief executive said in a statement:

'Making the changes required to develop our business for the next decade needs a rigorous and disciplined focus on corporate strategy. A key element of the organisational changes is to proactively seek new business opportunities to expand our global reach and drive sales growth.'

Source: www.canadianbusiness.com and www.icis.co.v2companies9145279 (adapted)

24 marks, 42 minutes

1 Do you think GSK's strategies reflect the company's mission statement? Explain your answer. [8]

2 Explain how competition is affecting GSK's strategies. [6]

3 Discuss the importance of the link between business strategy and business organisational structure by references to GSK and other business examples. [10]

ACTIVITY 38.4

Read the case study below and then answer the questions that follow.

Which industry is more competitive?

It is interesting to compare two completely different industries in terms of competitive rivalry. The world fashion industry has many famous names that compete for our attention and for our 'consumer dollar'. The images of these businesses, such as Versace, Armani and Chanel, have been carefully built up with celebrity endorsements and expensive advertising. It would be difficult for new firms trying to break into the industry to compete with these. Certainly, using low prices to attract consumers to buy an 'exclusive' new brand of clothing is unlikely to be successful. Exclusive shops often have agreements with fashion companies to be their exclusive outlets – again making it difficult for new firms to get established. However, the rapid growth of technology could make traditional retailers old fashioned and consumers may be happy in future to buy even top fashion names through e-commerce.

The world car industry has huge excess capacity. An industry specialist has forecast that total car sales in 2009 were 40 million, yet the production capacity of the world's car factories is around 60 million. The only new mass-market producers in recent years have come from Korea, such as Hyundai, and China, and the cost advantages they enjoy have reduced output in the USA and Europe, which has reduced the economies of scale of producers in these countries. The technological expertise and capital needed to build a new mass-market car factory make it very unlikely that new firms will now join the world car industry. There is likely to be a number of mergers and takeovers. However, small niche market producers – such as makers of electric cars or super-fast sports cars – are still launching new products in a desperate attempt to create product differentiation.

20 marks, 35 minutes

Using Porter's Five Forces model, the information above and any other information you have researched, compare the likely competitive rivalry of these two markets. [20]

Strategic choice

Strategic choice is the next logical element in the strategic decision-making process. Choice is at the centre of strategy formulation. If there are no important choices to be made, there is no point in giving much consideration to the decision-making process at all. Strategic choice is concerned with the identification of different strategic options and deciding between them. Good strategic choices have to be challenging enough to gain competitive advantage, but also achievable and within the resource capabilities of the organisation. There are logical techniques available to assist managers in making strategic choices, but judgement and skill are also very important.

KEY TERMS

strategic choice identifying strategic options, evaluating them and then choosing between them

The process of strategic choice is aided by a number of techniques that have been discussed already in this book:

- The processes of decision-making:
  - scientific and formal decision-making (see Chapter 6)
  - decision trees (see Chapter 6)
  - fishbone diagram – cause-and-effect diagram (see Chapter 6)
  - force-field analysis (see Chapter 8).
- Forecasting future market changes:
  - sales forecasting (see Chapter 25).
- The future options available to a business:
  - core competencies (see Chapter 38)
  - growth strategies as analysed by Ansoff's matrix (see Chapter 7)
  - investment appraisal (see Chapter 19).
- Target setting and benchmarking to measure success – especially against competitors:
  - return on investment (see Chapter 23)
  - benchmarking (see Chapter 33).

Source: IB Diploma Programme Business and Management guide (adapted)

CORPORATE PLANS
What do they contain?

KEY TERMS

corporate plan a methodical plan containing details of the organisation's central objectives and the strategies to be followed to achieve them

A typical corporate plan will include:

1. The overall objectives of the organisation within a given time frame – perhaps three to four years. These could be:
   - profit target
   - sales growth
   - market share target.
2. The strategy or strategies to be used to attempt to meet these objectives. For instance, to achieve sales growth the business could consider the choices as analysed by Ansoff's matrix:
   - increase sales of existing products – market penetration
   - develop new markets for existing products – market development
   - research and develop new products for existing markets – product development
   - diversify – new products for new markets.
3. The main objectives for the key departments of the business derived from the overall objective (see Figure 38.4).

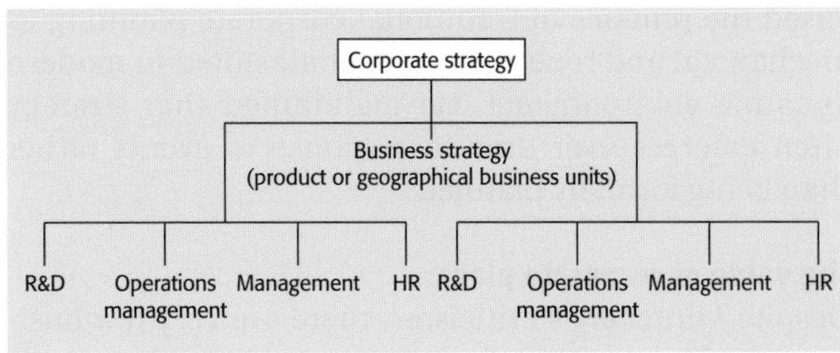

Figure 38.4 *Setting objectives and strategy for key functional departments which must be based on corporate objectives and strategy*

What are corporate plans for?

Potential benefits

The value of corporate planning for several years ahead is that senior managers have a clear focus and sense of purpose for what they are trying to achieve and the strategies they should use to reach these aims. Hopefully, they will communicate this sense of purpose and focus to all managers and staff below them in the organisation – and this is an important requirement for corporate plans to be effective. This advantage is important to any business organisation – a start-up firm or an established one, small firms or large corporations.

An important benefit of any corporate plan is the 'control and review' process. The original objectives can be compared with actual outcomes to see how well the businesses performance matched its aims.

The actual planning process is a very useful exercise as well. When effectively done, actually preparing for and producing the corporate plan can have the benefits of forcing senior managers to consider the organisation's strengths and weaknesses in relation to its environment and to think about how all of the different functional departments of the firms interrelate.

Potential limitations

Plans are great if nothing else changes. The best-laid plans of any business can be made obsolete by rapid and unexpected internal or external changes. This does not mean that planning is useless – far from it, as part of the planning process may well be looking ahead to consider how to respond to unforeseen events (see contingency planning, Chapter 17). What change does mean, however, is that if a business puts, say, a five-year plan into effect and then refuses to make any variations or adaptations to it no matter how much external environmental factors might change, then this inflexibility will be punished. The planning process and the plans that result from it should be as adaptable and flexible as possible to allow them to continue to be relevant and useful during periods of change. Henry Mintzberg, in his book *The Rise and Fall of Corporate Planning* (1994), criticised the practice of traditional corporate planning as mechanical and repetitive – not at all suited to modern dynamic environments. He maintained that strategy often emerges over time in response to events rather than being formally planned.

The value of corporate plans

Despite Mintzberg's criticisms, there are very few businesses without a formal planning process. The plan is not just for senior management, it will be essential to share the contents of such a document with:

- potential investors when a share sale is considered
- major lenders to the organisation
- other stakeholder groups, e.g. the government if requesting development grants for expanding into an area of high unemployment
- all staff – in the form of specific and tangible objectives for all departments, sections and individuals that will be based on the original objectives and strategies contained in the corporate plan.

The main influences on a corporate plan

Internal

- Financial resources – can the new proposed strategies be afforded?
- Operating capacity – will this be sufficient if expansion plans are approved by directors?
- Managerial skills and experience – this may be a major constraint on the plan's success, especially if the diversification strategy is chosen.
- Staff numbers and skills – workforce planning is a key factor in the success of any corporate plan.
- Culture of the organisation – discussed in detail below.

External

- Macro-economic conditions – expansion may have to be put 'on hold' during a recession.
- Central bank and government economic policy changes.
- Likely technological changes – these could make even the best-laid plans appear very outdated quite rapidly.
- Competitors' actions – the competitive nature of the market was explained in Chapter 35 (page 364).

EXAM TIP

Remember, the relative importance of these factors will vary from business to business. A company producing income-elastic luxury products may find its corporate plan is most influenced by macro-economic forecasts. The directors of a small company may consider that the plan for their business is most constrained by internal financial limits.

Strategic implementation

This is the final section of the strategic management process. Implementation literally means 'putting into effect or carrying out an idea'. So this stage of strategic management involves putting the strategic plans that have been analysed and chosen 'into effect'.

KEY TERMS

strategic implementation the process of allocating and controlling resources to support the chosen strategies

ACTIVITY 38.5

Read the case study below and then answer the questions that follow.

Where to now for ABCA Power plc?

Privatised in 2003, this profitable gas and electric power company has expanded rapidly since being freed of government controls. It has now reached a crossroads in its development as the energy market it operates in is becoming saturated and ceasing to grow. The directors are considering four growth strategies after undertaking an extensive strategic analysis. The four options are to:

- increase market share in gas and electricity in the existing countries where the firm operates – by using marketing tactics or taking over a rival firm
- enter other countries' markets for gas and electricity supply
- develop renewable forms of energy, e.g. solar and wind power, for sale in existing markets, but technological differences between renewable and non-renewable energy supplies are considerable
- develop a range of non-energy-related products, such as office equipment, for sale in new markets. One of the directors of ABCA had formerly been a senior manager for a US-based office-equipment company.

The directors had asked management consultants to estimate the potential costs and likely future revenues from these four options. The consultants had attempted this, but also reported that, as some of the options were riskier than others, the forecasts were likely to be open to a wide margin of error. The directors understood this point – but they would still have to make a decision based on as much data as possible.

26 marks, 45 minutes

1 Analyse the forms of strategic analysis the directors might have undertaken. [8]

2 Assess the degree of risk involved in each of the four strategic options. [8]

3 Discuss the factors most likely to influence the final strategic choice of ABCA management. [10]

ACTIVITY 38.6

Read the case study below and then answer the questions that follow.

Major change proposed at Buildit Construction plc

The economic recession had not been kind to construction companies. The fall in demand for houses and apartments occurred at the same time as government cutbacks on school and hospital building. The directors of Buildit Construction had achieved successful and profitable growth of the company during the good times. The question now was, would the business survive the downturn?

The directors' survival plan for the company was in two parts:

- Use existing building sites owned by the company to construct small homes for rent not for sale – this would mean operating in a new market segment of the property market, dealing with tenants renting property and not prospective house-owners.
- Make major cutbacks in administration overheads.

The second part of the plan would involve delayering of the management structure and increased multi-skilling of the administration staff to increase flexibility and productivity. The 120 administration staff were consulted, but the directors made it clear that cost savings must be made to ensure the company survived. There would be an opportunity for older staff to retire early – the managers wanted to avoid redundancies if at all possible. Staff remaining would be expected to take on more financial and accounting work as well as decision-making tasks.

22 marks, 35 minutes

1 How would you analyse part 1 of the directors' survival plan, according to Ansoff's matrix? Explain your answer. [4]

2 Using a force-field analysis diagram, identify and assess the relative strength of the forces that will drive the change in part 2 of the plan and those that will constrain it. [10]

3 Recommend to the directors ways in which they could increase the chances of this strategic choice being successful. [8]

Without successful implementation of the chosen strategies, there can be no effective change within the organisation. Implementing a major strategic change is a very important cross-functional management task. It involves ensuring that all of the following factors are in place:

- an appropriate organisational structure to deal with the change
- adequate resources to make the change happen
- well-motivated staff who want the change to happen successfully
- a leadership style and organisational culture that allow change to be implemented with wide-ranging support
- control and review systems to monitor the firm's progress towards the desired final objectives.

The processes used and the issues raised by strategic implementation have been covered in previous chapters of the book:

- Planning for changes in size:
  - methods of growth – internal or external, mergers and takeovers (see Chapter 8)
  - economies and diseconomies of scale (see Chapter 7)
  - workforce planning, flexible working and flexible organisation (see Chapter 11)
  - analysing and reviewing communication structures (see Chapter 12).
- Implementation of marketing strategies:
  - segmentation, targeting and positioning, e-commerce (see Chapter 24).
- Reviewing management/leadership styles (see Chapter 13).
- Adoptions of corporate social responsibility and ethical approaches (see Chapter 3).
- Strategies to globalise operations:
  - offshoring; outsourcing; joint ventures; decentralisation (see Chapter 7).
- Management of change:
  - developing a change culture; contingency planning and crisis management (see Chapter 17).

Source: IB Diploma Programme Business and Management guide (adapted)

CORPORATE CULTURE AND STRATEGIC IMPLEMENTATION

How does a corporation's culture affect strategic implementation?

One way is to consider how different organisations with different cultures would introduce important changes. For example, a business that has a power culture will not consult or communicate with staff affected by major strategic changes. These changes will be imposed on them – possibly with a 'take it or leave it' attitude. This approach may stir up resentment and resistance to change and the co-operation of the workforce is most unlikely to be obtained in future. In contrast, businesses that operate with task- or people-based cultures are more likely to encourage active participation in implementing major strategic change. Consultation and participation through two-way communication could lead to staff willingly accepting change – and contributing to a successful change process.

The other link between culture and strategic implementation occurs when culture is either strong or weak. Strong culture promotes and facilitates successful strategy implementation while weak culture does not. In an organisation with a strong culture there is widespread sharing of common beliefs, practices and norms within the business. Everyone – or nearly everyone – in the business has accepted what the business stands for and the 'way things are done around here'. This energises people to promote strategy implementation, because they want the new strategy to be successful. For example, if the culture of an organisation is built around people – listening to customers and empowering staff – then this promotes the implementation of a strategy that leads to an improvement in customer service. In organisations with weak cultures, employees may have no agreed set of beliefs and there is no pride in ownership of work. People may form their own groups within this type of organisation that are based around cultures that conflict with the weakly expressed business culture. Such situations provide little or no assistance to strategic implementation.

EVALUATING THE IMPORTANCE OF CORPORATE CULTURE

The significance and power of an organisation's culture to drive people's behaviour and attitudes should not be underestimated – especially during a period of strategic changes. Most of us do not want to be seen to 'do the wrong thing' within any group of people that we work with, and this feeling is particularly strong within a business environment. However, the impact of culture goes beyond the desire of most people to conform to accepted values. It can, as has been seen above, have a significant impact on how new strategies are implemented.

The following examples help to reinforce the importance of organisational culture:

- The values of a business establish the norms of behaviour of staff – what is and what is not acceptable in certain situations. For example, is it acceptable for an organisation to offer bribes to attract a large contract 'as long as we are not found out'?

- Culture determines the way in which company managers and workers treat each other. For example, if the chief executive is open and receptive to new ideas and proposals from senior managers, then this approach is likely to filter through the whole organisation – to its potential long-term benefit.
- A distinctive organisational culture can support a business's brand image and relationships with customers. For example, The Body Shop almost invented the 'ethical trading' culture. Will this approach to business now change after its takeover by L'Oréal?
- Culture determines not just how strategic decisions are made and implemented – with the participation of staff or by top managers alone – but also the type of strategic decisions that are taken. For example, the culture of a European state health service in target setting and rewards for meeting short waiting times within accident and emergency departments is, it is claimed, encouraging hospital managers to decide to leave patients in ambulances for up to two hours. How different would it be if doctors were actually taking these decisions?
- Organisational culture has been clearly linked to the economic performance and long-term success of organisations. Businesses dedicated to continuous improvement with staff involvement have been shown to be more profitable in the long term. Toyota is the prime example of success based on this principle.

ACTIVITY 38.7

Read the case study below and then answer the questions that follow.

Dell – a case study of business change

Dell Inc. is a multinational information technology business based in the USA. The company's main products include desktop and notebook computers, printers, TVs and smartphones. Founded in 1984, the company has experienced rapid growth. It currently employs 96 000 people worldwide, earned revenue of over $52 billion in 2010 and, according to the Fortune magazine, it is the fifth most admired company in the industry.

This success has not been achieved by 'standing still'. The significant changes that have occurred within Dell in recent years include:

- rapid **organic growth**
- external growth – notable mergers and acquisitions include Alienware (2006) and Perot Systems (2009)
- new marketing strategy in 2006 to start selling computers through retail stores as well as the company's traditional direct routes of telephone and internet selling
- new products featuring new technologies – a feature of the industry in which Dell operates
- a stricter environmental strategy that aims to reduce greenhouse gas emissions by 40% by 2015 (compared to 2007)
- closure of many US assembly facilities and the opening of new facilities in countries such as Mexico and India.

Making these and other key **strategic choices** is the board of directors of nine people. The founder of the company, Michael Dell, is still deeply involved in the management of the company. He has always tried to create a **corporate culture** that recognises and embraces diversity in the workplace and in the marketplace. Teamwork is encouraged. Groups offer Dell employees the opportunity to network with employees around the company, leading to many new ideas and proposals. They also provide an enhanced sense of belonging through informal mentoring, professional and community events and access to professional development. Dell's 'Winning Culture' and direct communication channels create a corporate environment based on meritocracy, personal achievement and equal access to all available opportunities. Many industry observers claim that Dell's corporate culture has allowed it to introduce and manage change more effectively than other businesses in the same industry.

50 marks, 85 minutes

1 Explain the following terms:
   a organic growth
   b strategic choice
   c corporate culture. [12]

2 Explain why almost constant change is likely to occur within businesses such as Dell. [6]

3 Outline **two** ways in which Dell can reduce resistance to change that may affect the workforce. [4]

4 Analyse how force-field analysis could help during this change. [8]

5 Discuss the advantages and disadvantages of Dell's decision to start selling computers and other equipment through retail stores. [10]

6 Evaluate the importance of corporate culture to the effective management of strategic change. [10]

THEORY OF KNOWLEDGE

Business schools across the world turn out people in their thousands who are taught to think and act strategically. This is the approach that business schools believe will deliver successful decisions and, ultimately, well-managed organisations.

Prepare a presentation which should:

a describe **two** situations where you have acted strategically
b outline **two** situations where an organisation you know about has acted strategically
c analyse the role that culture, experience, intuition and evidence play in strategic decision-making.

OVER TO YOU

REVISION ACTIVITY

Read the case study below and then answer the questions that follow.

Kraft Foods Inc.

Kraft Foods Inc. is the second largest confectionery, food and beverage corporation in the world, with sales exceeding $50 billion in 2010 – only Nestlé SA has higher sales in this industry. Kraft is a public limited company, listed on the New York Stock Exchange. Its headquarters are in Northfield, Illinois, USA, and its European base is in Zurich, Switzerland.

The company, formed in 1923, grew in its early years by taking over many smaller food businesses. It changed its name in 1969 from National Dairy to Kraftco Corporation to reflect the changing product portfolio of the business – moving away from dairy products towards higher value-added confectionery goods. The exception to this was the company's cheese division which continues to be important to this day. The name Kraft Inc. was adopted in 1976 to emphasise the importance of the company's trademark name – and, finally, Kraft Foods Inc. was the new company title after 1995.

The recent history of the company has been marked by a series of takeovers and divestments – selling off divisions. In fact, Kraft itself was taken over, at the end of 1988, by Philip Morris Companies – which led to the merger of Kraft's food division with Philip Morris's General Foods unit, which included Maxwell House coffee and Budget Gourmet frozen dinners. Nabisco Holdings – a large biscuit manufacturer – was also taken over by Philip Morris and merged with Kraft Food's operations.

Kraft regained its independent status as a listed public company when all of its shares were sold by Philip Morris (renamed Altria) in 2007. Kraft has two very well-known shareholders – Warren Buffet who owns an 8% stake and Nelson Peltz who owns 3%. It is claimed that the presence of these substantial shareholdings allows pressure to be put on Kraft's management. For example, Buffett was very opposed to the Cadbury takeover.

Since 2007 there have other acquisitions and sales:

Acquisitions	Sales
2007: Groupe Danone (France: biscuits/cookies) $7.2 billion 2010: Cadbury (UK: chocolate confectionery) $19.5 billion	2007: Kraft cereals to Ralcorp Holdings $2.6 billion 2010: Frozen pizza business to Nestlé $3.7billion

Takeover of Cadbury

'The combination of Kraft Foods and Cadbury creates a global powerhouse in snacks, confectionery and quick meals,' said Kraft's chief executive officer, Irene Rosenfeld, once the takeover had been agreed by Cadbury's shareholders. 'Together we have impressive global reach and an unrivalled portfolio of iconic brands with tremendous growth potential. I firmly believe it will deliver outstanding returns to our shareholders.' Several industry analysts believe that Kraft paid a price that was too high for Cadbury, valuing the trademarks, brands and other intangible assets of the company too generously. The $19.5 billion cost of the takeover was paid for from the sale of Kraft's pizza business, bank loans and shares in Kraft offered to Cadbury shareholders.

Many workers at Cadbury belong to the Unite trade union. The union was opposed to the takeover claiming that Kraft's debts, estimated to be $20 billion before the takeover, could lead to the need for substantial job cuts in Cadbury's UK factories to reduce costs.

The corporate culture of the two companies may cause potential conflict as Cadbury is merged into the Kraft structure and 'ways of doing things'. The founders of the 180-year-old British company had established excellent working conditions for workers and built the village of Bourneville to house them in a semi-rural environment. The tradition of prioritising workers' interests was maintained and the pre-takeover pension scheme was one of the most generous in private industry.

Here are three newspaper headlines published just after the Kraft takeover:

'One of Cadbury's UK factories to close and production outsourced to Poland'
'Cadbury workers told: accept three-year pay freeze or give up your pension scheme'
'Todd Stitzer, boss of Cadbury's, walks away with a £40 million payoff after selling the company to Kraft'

Kraft backs Cadbury café strategy

Kraft has supported the setting up of a national chain of Cadbury-branded cafés that will offer afternoon tea and a dedicated 'chocolate-making service'. The cafés will compete with a growing number of high-street cafés – the six big multiple chains increased shop numbers by 47% to 2095 in the UK in 2009. Coffee shop chains and independent cafés have been trading well in spite of the recession, suggesting that this is one market that is virtually 'recession proof'. In a form of joint venture, Kraft has now issued a 20-year licence to a group of retail entrepreneurs to set up and operate the high-street chain of cafés, to be called Cadbury Cocoa House. A spokesperson for Kraft said: 'This is a tight market dominated by the big chains but Cadbury has one of the most recognisable brand names in the world.' As well as offering beverages and food, onsite chocolatiers will make large versions of Cadbury chocolate bars such as Twirl, Curly Wurly and Flake that can then be gift wrapped. Cadbury opened a test market café in Bath several years ago, partly as a marketing tool, but the outlet was closed in 2007.

What future for chocolate?

The global market for premium branded chocolate is estimated to be worth US $13 billion in 2011. Annual growth rates average 18% as there is wider availability of premium chocolates in retail stores, especially in emerging markets, and new product development has reached high levels. Since 2003 it is estimated that 1500 new chocolate products have been launched globally by the leading companies – Mars, Nestlé, Cadbury and Hershey. Innovations include single-country-sourced chocolate bars and even chilli-flavoured dark premium chocolate.

Western Europe consumes the largest share of chocolate products – 45% of global sales – while the USA accounts for 20%. Germans consume the highest average weight of chocolate each year, at 11.1 kg per person, followed by Belgians at 11 kg. The average UK consumer eats their way through 10.2 kg, but in the USA the average is 5.6 kg. The potential for growth is greatest in emerging markets – in Russia, for example, average consumption is only 2 kg, but this is growing fast as consumers gain a taste for premium-branded chocolates and incomes rise.

In some developed economies, governments are expressing increased concern about obesity among young people. There are even some politicians, supported by consumer pressure groups, who would like to introduce strict controls over the promotion of all confectionery products to young people.

90 marks, 2 hours

1 a Define the following terms:
 i recession
 ii joint venture. [4]
 b Explain the possible advantages and disadvantages to Kraft Food Inc. of being a public limited company. [8]
 c Examine the impact of Cadbury's takeover by Kraft on any **three** stakeholder groups. [8]
 d Discuss Kraft's strategy of using mergers and takeovers to achieve growth objectives. [10]

2 a Outline **two** appropriate above-the-line and **two** below-the-line promotional activities that Kraft could employ to increase sales of Cadbury chocolate and confectionery. [4]
 b Analyse the importance of both quantitative and qualitative market research to the chances of success of the Cadbury café strategy. [8]
 c Examine whether it is ethical to advertise chocolate and confectionery products to young children. [8]
 d Prepare a SWOT analysis and use this, along with other information in the case study, to evaluate the current position of the Cadbury division of Kraft Foods. [10]

3 a Define the following terms:
 i corporate culture
 ii intangible assets. [4]
 b Analyse the problems that Kraft might experience as a result of high debt levels. [8]
 c Examine the likely reasons for outsourcing some chocolate production to Poland. [8]
 d Evaluate the opportunities and threats to Kraft Foods if it increased its operations in emerging markets such as Russia and India. [10]

EXAM PRACTICE QUESTION

Read the case study below and then answer the questions that follow.

WALMART INCHES INTO INDIA

The potential benefits to Walmart of establishing a retailing presence in India are huge. The second most highly populated country in the world with a rapidly expanding economy and a middle-income group of consumers numbering around 200 million should mean rich pickings for the world's largest retail company. Emerging economy markets – such as those of China and India – are not saturated in the way that the markets of the US and Western Europe are. For a company with the growth ambitions that Walmart has, there is really no alternative to expansion into these newly developing economies despite the potential diseconomies of scale associated with expanding operations so far from head office

Walmart set up an office in India in 2006. The company claims this was to allow for market research and strategic analysis. Critics suggested that the main aim of the office was to lobby the Indian government to change the law which currently restricts foreign retailers from owning stores directly in India. Since 2006, Walmart has begun a joint venture with a local business, Bharti Enterprises, to supply Bharti's retail stores. There are also two Walmart wholesale operations that supply shopkeepers, hotels and other businesses. This slow rate of expansion – at least when compared with Walmart's growth in other markets – is explained by three factors:

1 The legal restriction on foreign owned retailers. Walmart is hoping that, as the Indian economy becomes more open to foreign investment, this serious legal constraint will be dropped.
2 The tradition in India of consumers buying from small local stores and market traders. However, this may change as an Indian conglomerate, Reliance, is planning to invest $750m on setting up 1000 hypermarkets. The longer it takes Walmart to gain government clearance for its own stores, the better prepared the competition will be.
3 India's agricultural industry is in a poor state to supply good quality products in large quantities to a retailer as potentially huge as Walmart in India. The country has many small farmers and few big ones. Supply chains are weak and there are traditionally many middlemen in this supply chain. To try to overcome these problems the US-based retailer has been establishing good relations with farmers, paying them 5–7% above other wholesalers for top-quality produce and picking up supplies so that the farmers do not have to pay transportation costs.

Despite the market research and strategic analysis undertaken by Walmart in the emerging markets in which it has expanded, according to a senior consultant with Strategic Resource Group one of the problems for retailers, even giant ones such as Walmart, is the possible lack of a core competence, other than substantial economies of scale, that could allow them to differentiate what they offer to retail consumers.

Sources: Adapted from various sources

25 marks, 45 minutes

1 Define the following terms:
   a diseconomies of scale
   b joint venture. [4]
2 Produce a SWOT analysis for Walmart's decision to expand into India. [6]
3 Use Porter's Five Forces model to analyse the business environment Walmart will encounter in India if it is allowed to open its own retail stores. [6]
4 Evaluate Walmart's strategy of expanding into emerging economy markets. [9]

39 Examination skills

On completing this chapter you should be able to understand:

- the nature of the different aspects of Business and Management assessment
- examination technique in the Business and Management examination
- the approach to the pre-issued case study
- the way to tackle the internal assessment
- the way to approach Business and Management extended essays.

Introduction

The IB Business and Management course combines both internal and external assessment to examine your performance over the two years of the course.

Higher and standard level paper 1 includes questions based on a case study, which is provided by the IBO several weeks before the examination. You will be given the questions to the case study when you sit the examination. The case study is the same for both higher and standard level, but the questions used are different. The main aim of this paper is to assess your ability to answer questions on a given case example. You are expected to show your ability to apply business knowledge and understanding across the full range of topics covered in the syllabus.

Higher and standard level paper 2 requires you to answer structured questions based on stimulus material (short case studies). The objective of this paper is to assess your ability to use your business knowledge and understanding across a range of different case study situations.

You will also need to complete internal assessment for both higher and standard level courses. This will assess your ability to use your business knowledge and understanding in a real-world situation.

Tables 39.1 and 39.2 provide summaries of the higher level and standard level assessments.

	Paper 1	Paper 2	Internal assessment
Method	**Section A** Students must answer two from three structured questions. Each question is worth 30 marks. **Section B** Students must answer one compulsory structured question. [20 marks] **Section C** Students must answer one compulsory question based on strategic decision-making with the use of extension material. [30 marks].	**Section A** Students must answer one structured question from two based on stimulus material with a quantitative element. [25 marks] **Section B** Students must answer two out of three structured questions based on stimulus material. [50 marks]	To write a report on a business decision facing an organisation or an analysis of a business decision taken by an organisation. The report should include a separate action plan and research proposal on how the report is to be produced. Maximum 2000 words.
Total marks	80	75	25
Time	135 minutes	135 minutes	30 hours
Weighting	40%	35%	25%

***Table 39.1** Higher level assessment*

	Paper 1	Paper 2	Internal assessment
Method	**Section A**	**Section A**	To write a written commentary based on three to five supporting documents on a real issue facing a business organisation. Maximum 1500 words.
	Students must answer two from three structured questions. [Each question is worth 30 marks.]	Students must answer one structured question from two based on stimulus material with a quantitative element. [20 marks]	
	Section B	**Section B**	
	Students must answer one compulsory structured question. [20 marks]	Students must answer two out of three structured questions based on stimulus material. [40 marks]	
Total marks	50	75	25
Time	75 minutes	105 minutes	15 hours
Weighting	35%	40%	25%

Table 39.2 *Standard level assessment*

Examination technique

TIMING

It is important to get your time management right when you are approaching the Business and Management examination. In the higher level examination you should allocate just over 1.5 minutes per mark, which means spending about 10 minutes on a 6-mark question or 17 minutes on a 10-mark question.

It is possible to allocate your time in a similar way on the standard level paper, where the allocation for paper 1 is 1.5 minutes per mark and paper 2 is slightly less than this. This means a 4-mark question should take 6 minutes and a 10-mark question 15 minutes.

The 5 minutes' reading time for each of the papers will give you the opportunity to plan how to approach them. It is important to look through the questions and to decide which questions to choose based on the areas you feel most confident about. It is best to make the decision on which questions to choose based on the questions that carry the highest marks rather than choosing a question where you can do the definition for 2 marks but will struggle with the 9-mark evaluation question.

During the reading time in paper 2, to ensure you use the time effectively it is best to read the questions and not the stimulus material. Obviously, you will read the stimulus material thoroughly when you actually attempt the question.

USING THE STIMULUS MATERIAL

Once you have finished your reading and you are approaching each question, it is very important in paper 2 to read the stimulus material carefully before answering the questions. The case studies provide the foundation for your answers and should be used as a source of examples for all the points you make in your answers. For instance, in a question on the product life cycle, you should use the case study to provide examples of products at different stages in the life cycle.

ANSWERING THE QUESTIONS

Reading the question carefully and answering the question precisely are important. You should identify the key command terms in the question to determine how you should answer the question. Words such as 'explain', 'outline', 'analyse', 'evaluate' and so on carry different meanings and this should be reflected in your answers. A question that asks you to discuss requires a more detailed answer than define or outline questions.

The command terms used in IB questions are divided into four levels. The higher the level, the greater the degree of sophistication required in an answer. Table 39.3 summarises how you should use the command terms when you are answering questions and how they apply to particular questions.

SETTING OUT YOUR ANSWER

To score well in the Business and Management examinations you will need to set out your answer in a way that clearly presents itself effectively to the examiner. As we have already seen, an answer is not about making a certain number of points, it is about responding appropriately to the command terms in the question and communicating this effectively.

Effective use of paragraphs is an important style to adopt when answering questions because it allows you to express your points in a structured way and presents your ideas in a form that makes it easy for an examiner to see and understand your answers. Avoid using bullet points – they are ineffective because you cannot express yourself in

	Term	Definition	Example of application in Business and Management questions
Level 1: Knowledge [1–2 marks]	Classify	Arrange or order business ideas or data by class or categories.	Classify the products sold by a business based on the Boston Matrix.
	Comment	Description or observation of business data or information relating to a business decision or issue.	Comment on the change in XYZ's change in liquidity.
	Complete	Add information or data.	Complete the ESTs and LFTs in the critical path diagram.
	Construct	Present business data or information in the form of a diagram or table.	Construct a decision tree for Z's different options.
	Define	A clear, precise statement of the meaning of a business term, word or concept.	Define the term liquidity.
	Describe	To outline the characteristics of an object or idea.	Describe the corporate culture of company ABC.
	Identify	Recognise a feature of a business idea, observation or issue.	Identify a reason for the rise in company XYZ's costs.
	Outline	Give a brief summary of the points raised on an issue or idea.	Outline the characteristics of the democratic leadership style.
Level 2: Understanding [3–4 marks]	Compare	Examine two or more business objects or ideas in order to consider similarities and differences between them.	Compare Herzberg's and Taylor's approaches to motivating workers.
	Contrast	Consider the differences between two or more business ideas or concepts.	Contrast the TQM and traditional approaches to quality control.
	Distinguish	Show the differences between ideas or concepts.	Distinguish between democratic and autocratic leadership styles.
	Prepare	Write out data in a chart, table or diagram.	Prepare a table of coffee shop X's sales revenue over the last 5 years.
	Construct	Draw a chart or diagram.	Construct a break-even chart for retailer Y's decision to open on Sundays.
	Calculate	Give a precise numerical value.	Calculate XYZ's payback time on its new machine.
	Explain	Describe, giving reasons, a business idea, observation or issue.	Explain why XYZ Ltd's profits have fallen.
	Comment	Give an explanation of a business issue or information.	Comment on the rise in ABC plc's liquidity.
Level 3: Application [5–7 marks]	Analyse	To separate business material or information into its constituent parts and determine its essential features.	Analyse the factors that have led to a deterioration of XYZ Ltd's liquidity.
	Apply	Use a theory, principle or concept in relation to a business problem or issue.	Apply Porter's Five Forces to analyse the market ABC plc operates in.
	Examine	Consider a business decision or proposal which sets out its assumptions and interrelationships.	Examine ABC plc's decision to open a new factory in Vietnam.
	Formulate	Present a business strategy or decision in a clearly set-out form.	Formulate a marketing strategy for XYZ plc.
	Interpret	Draw out and explain information from business issues or observations.	Interpret the change in company A's profit margin.

Table 39.3 *Command terms and how they should be applied [table continues over]*

	Term	Definition	Example of application in Business and Management questions
Level 4: Opinion [8–10 marks]	Advise	A recommendation to take a particular course of action.	Based on monetary and non-monetary factors, advise the CEO of ABC Ltd on whether it should choose machine A or B.
	Discuss	By looking at all aspects of a particular business decision or proposal, consider a balanced view of the decision or proposal.	Discuss XYZ's decision to expand into an overseas market.
	Evaluate	Consider the advantages and disadvantages of a business decision or proposal.	Evaluate the use of JIT stock management by ABC Ltd.
	Justify	Provide evidence to support or defend a business decision, strategy or course of action.	Justify ABC's decision to launch a new product.
	Recommend	Suggest a course of action for a business decision based on evidence and/or argument.	Recommend a promotional strategy to Cinema XYZ.
	To what extent	Make a judgement on the success or failure of a particular course of action based on evidence and argument.	To what extent is ABC's decision to adopt profit-related pay a successful way to improve staff motivation?

Table 39.3 *Continued*

any detail and your answer will read like a list. Also avoid blocks of text which are often impenetrable to examiners.

The key thing examiners will look for is an answer to the question. If you drift from the question asked and, for example, use a pre-prepared answer that is not quite what the question is looking for, then you will not score highly. It is also important to avoid repeating the same point. Here is a useful technique to have in mind:

- Make your point.
- Use business theory to support it.
- Use an example from the case study or stimulus material.

Quantitative questions

Papers 1 and 2 for higher and standard level have quantitative questions where you will be expected to carry out simple arithmetic operations, and you will need to approach these questions in the right way to maximise your marks.

It is essential to show your working clearly so that the examiner can see where the answer has been derived from. If a question requires you to calculate the average annual rate of return, you will need to set out the figures using the formula required to calculate this value. Remember, a small calculation error will give the wrong answer, but if the method is correct your answer will still receive most of the marks.

The layout of calculations, diagrams and charts is also important. Examiners find it much easier to interpret and mark answers where, for example, the critical path diagram is drawn neatly with a ruler and is well set out on the examination paper. Things like decision trees, break-even charts and critical path diagrams need careful planning. It is advisable to draw your charts and diagrams in pencil so you can rub out mistakes.

SAMPLE QUESTIONS AND ANSWERS

Below are two example questions for you to practise your examination technique. The answers provided are model top grade 7 responses.

Question 1: standard level example

Big fall in Profits at Samsung

South Korean electronics manufacturing company Samsung revealed a big reduction in its profits when it released its trading statement earlier today. Falling profit margins on its flat screen TVs and mobile phones have led to an 11% reduction in operating profits. Samsung's net profit margins have fallen to 9.5%, down from 12% in the same period last year.

Samsung reported a 1.5 trillion won ($1.59 billion) profit in the first three months of the year, compared to a profit of 1.69 trillion won in the same period last year. The company is, however, expecting an upturn later in the year after it successfully agreed a **joint venture** with Sony. In a deal said to be worth $1.9 billion, Samsung will make LCD displays for Sony's new 50 inch flat-screen TVs.

Despite a big increase in demand for flat-screen TVs, Samsung has been struggling because the market has become increasingly saturated with many manufacturers entering this increasingly congested sector. Its mobile phone business, which faces competition from Motorola, Nokia and Apple, has fared no better.

Source: www.bbc.co.uk/news (adapted)

a Define the term 'joint venture' highlighted in the text. **[2]**

b (i) Explain how Samsung would calculate its net profit margin. **[3]**

(ii) Outline one factor that could have caused the fall in Samsung's net profit margin. **[3]**

c Examine the possible reasons for the 'significant' increase in demand for flat-screen TVs. **[5]**

d Evaluate Samsung's decision to enter into a joint venture with Sony. **[7]**

[Total: 20]

Answers to question 1

a A joint venture is where two or more businesses join together in a business activity. In this case Sony and Samsung have embarked on a joint venture where Samsung is producing flat-screen TVs for Sony.

b (i) Samsung's profit margin is calculated using the equation:

$$\frac{\text{net profit}}{\text{sales}} \times 100$$

Samsung needs to use its sales revenue figure and its net profit which is calculated as: sales – direct + indirect cost = net profit

(ii) The price of flat-screen TVs has fallen due to intense competition and this would have reduced Samsung's profit margin.

c There may have been a significant increase in the demand for flat-screen TVs because their price has fallen which makes them cheaper for consumers who are more able to afford them. As the flat-screen TVs have improved in quality because of better technology they have become more attractive to consumers. Increased promotion of flat-screen TVs by businesses like Samsung and Sony could have increased the demand for them. As global incomes rise, particularly in LCDs, more people can now afford flat-screen TVs.

d Samsung will gain the following benefits from its joint venture with Sony. It will be able to pool the costs of developing flat-screen TVs which makes it easier to afford the costs of developing the necessary technology. Samsung will be able to share Sony's expertise in consumer electronics products which will help it to manufacture and sell better TVs. Selling TVs under the Sony brand name will enable it to access the Japanese market and enter markets where the Sony brand is highly regarded.

The joint venture may have the following problems. There could be conflict between different corporate cultures and management styles which leads to poor decision-making. For example, the design of the TV may be compromised by conflict on what the best design is. If Samsung's product is sold under the Sony name it will not enhance the Samsung brand, people will know the product as a Sony TV. The profit generated by the TV sold has to be split between Sony and Samsung; it may be more profitable for Samsung to sell the TVs itself under the Samsung name.

The joint venture will be the right decision here because of the access Samsung will get to new markets by selling under the Sony brand name.

Question 2: higher level example

It's a record for Nissan Sunderland

World Markets Automotive released its annual European Automotive Productivity Index yesterday. The Nissan plant at Sunderland has, once again, gained the number one position in Europe, beating the rest of the field by almost 20%. The Sunderland plant saw productivity rise dramatically last year, with a 7% increase in output of vehicles per employee. Nissan achieved a ratio of 101 cars per employee, which is a new European productivity record. The plant's total output of cars increased from 271,157 to 327,701.

The company claims it achieved higher levels of output by using young, highly motivated staff, who are extremely well trained. It also sees the successful application of lean Japanese manufacturing methods, just in time stock control and the established practice of continuous improvement ('Kaizen') as key to its achievements.

The dominance of the Japanese car manufacturers was confirmed by Toyota's Burnaston plant, which came in second behind Nissan Sunderland. It achieved 86 cars per employee. Japanese manufacturers' belief in the efficiency of UK workers was further highlighted when Toyota announced its intention of moving production of the 3-door Corolla from Japan to the UK.

Source: www.prnewswire.co.uk (adapted)

a Define the following terms highlighted in the text:
(i) productivity
(ii) just in time. **[4]**

b Outline three ways the management at Nissan could measure how motivated its workforce is. **[6]**

c Analyse how improvements in Nissan's productivity could lead to a rise in its profits. **[6]**

d Discuss the advantages and disadvantages of Nissan's use of just-in-time stock control. **[9]**

[Total: 25]

Answers to question 2

a (i) Productivity is a business's output of goods per unit of input resource input. In Nissan Sunderland's case it is measured by the number of cars produced in one year per employee; in 2008 it achieved 122 cars per employee.

(ii) Just in time is a stock-management system where stock holding is minimised and only enough stock is kept to meet current consumer demand. Nissan uses JIT and only keeps enough cars in stock to meet current consumer demand.

b Three ways the management at Nissan could measure how motivated their employees would be, first, to look at absenteeism rates; the lower the absenteeism rates, the more motivated the labour force is. Secondly, they could look at the labour turnover; the lower the turnover figure, the more motivated staff are. Finally, managers could look at productivity figures; the more motivated workers are, the more productive they will be.

c If Nissan's productivity rises, then it will produce more cars per unit of labour and capital employed. This means that the costs of the business are being divided by a higher level of output which reduces the unit costs of producing each car. In Nissan Sunderland, for example, the plant has increased output from 271 157 in 2007 to 327 701 in 2008; if total costs do not change, then the cost per car will fall. If Nissan sells the same number of cars at the same price in 2008 compared with 2007, then the profit figure will rise. Alternatively, Nissan could reduce the price of its cars because of the lower unit costs and increase its sales revenue.

d If Nissan uses JIT it will gain the following benefits. It will be able to reduce stock levels, which means it can reduce the factory space needed to keep its stock of cars and use this to produce more cars and generate more sales and profits from this. It will see costs such as insurance and cost of maintaining the stored cars fall. It means cash will not be tied up unprofitably in stock and this will improve Nissan's liquidity. Using JIT is all part of the Japanese practice of continuous improvement which allows Nissan to achieve the high levels of productivity it has reached.

The JIT approach does, however, come with disadvantages. It needs reliable suppliers who can meet Nissan's demand for components and if one supplier lets Nissan down, the production line may have to be slowed down or stopped. It also relies on accurate forecasts for demand and this is always something which is open to error. If demand is forecasted inaccurately, Nissan may not be able to meet demand or it risks building up stock. JIT also relies on a flexible, well-trained labour force which will cost a lot of money. Wages will need to be high to attract and retain staff good enough to apply JIT. The final, crucial problem is stock-out costs which come because of holding such low levels of stock. Customers who cannot get the cars they want may well go to other suppliers, which will mean lower current and future sales.

The evidence of the case material is that JIT is working well at Nissan Sunderland and is a stock-management system which is delivering a high level of efficiency.

The pre-issued case study

APPROACHING THE CASE STUDY

Once you have received the pre-issued case study it is important for you to spend some time with your teacher and on your own preparing for it. Here are some important tips on how to approach the case study.

- Read through the case study carefully to understand fully the issues it raises. This can be done using a highlighter pen to indicate key points; another useful approach is to write a short summary by each paragraph to sum up what it is about. In the Millennium Sports case study which is provided as an example below, the first part is: *background to the business, partnership, sports and leisure market, high quality product targeting specialist consumers.* Repeat this approach for the whole case study and you will develop a good understanding of the story it tells.
- Draw up a time line for the case study organisation that summarises the changes it has gone through in a chronological order. This will help you to understand the case study.
- Consider the syllabus area covered by the case study to focus your revision for the paper. In the example case study below, Nils Marks's management style could be a clue to a possible question about leadership and management style and its appropriateness. The cash-flow data on the surfing machine could be a clue for an investment appraisal question. Remember, more information can be added to the case study on the day of the examination, so you will need to have done broad-based revision for the paper.
- Do some reading about the market the case study company is involved in. In the Millennium Sports example, you could do some research about the nature of the sports and leisure-centre market.
- Do practice questions using the case study. This will help you to familiarise yourself with the case study and the issues it raises. It will also get you into the habit of using the case study to provide examples for the points you make. However, in the actual examination make sure you answer the questions that are asked – they may not be exactly the ones you practised.
- Be careful not to over-prepare. In the end your success will depend on the way you tackle the case study on the day of the examination – if your head is filled with too much extra information on the business and market you may not be able to respond to the questions you are asked.

CASE STUDY EXAMPLE

Below is an example of the type of pre-issued case study you will get in the Business and Management examination. Try to approach it in the same way you would if it was the real thing.

MILLENNIUM SPORT

Background

Millennium Sport was started in 2001 by a partnership of Anders Rikard and Erik Brolyn. The two founders were ex-professional basketball players who had a substantial amount of money saved from their long and successful careers in the NBA. The players decided to build and operate a private sports complex that would target a different market segment to the traditional 'gym'. The facility has a 50-metre Olympic-sized swimming pool, state-of-the-art gym, dance studio, indoor tennis courts and 'double' sports hall, climbing wall and glass-backed squash courts. The facility also offers physiotherapy, sports science and sports psychology on the site. Millennium Sports has subcontracted the catering to a company that operates a health-food restaurant on site. The objective of the business is to offer a world-class sports facility that:

- targets national, professional and amateur sports teams and clubs
- has its own sports academy linked to local schools and universities
- provides a gym and sports-club facility for individuals.

Millennium's mission statement is 'to give serious athletes a sporting environment where they can fully realise their potential'.

Human resources

Millennium Sport employs ten full-time staff and 50 contract staff. The full-time staff run and operate the centre and contract coaches are brought in to run the different sporting activities the centre offers. The contract coaches are paid by the clubs and individuals that use them and as part of the centre. There are, for example, four tennis coaches who use the centre regularly to give lessons and coaching sessions. The ten full-time staff are responsible for accounting, marketing, operations (maintenance and cleaning), booking and human resources.

The centre manager, Nils Marks, has been hired by Anders and Erik to run the centre in a strict, disciplined way. Nils is an autocratic leader who expects the highest standards from the centre's employees. Staff turnover is high and this is a concern to Erik and Anders. There has also been some conflict between the contract coaches and Nils.

Finance

To start Millennium Sport required an initial investment by Anders and Erik to build the sports centre. The centre cost $30 million; Anders and Erik invested $20 million of their own funds and the remaining $10 million was put in by a venture capital company, Asterix Finance, which took a 33% stake in the business in return for its investment. Asterix is concerned about the low dividend it is receiving from Millennium and this is a major source of tension in the organisation. Anders and Erik want to retain profit to improve the centre facilities along with the quality of the service they offer and Asterix is concerned with cost efficiency. Asterix is also concerned about the number of members of Millennium Sports who are behind with their membership payments and it wants to introduce penalty charges to members who do not pay on time. Tension between Asterix's directors and Anders and Erik has become so intense that they have considered trying to buy Asterix's 33% shareholding using borrowed funds.

Millennium Sport's final accounts for 2009 and 2010 are set out below.

$m	2009	2010
Fixed assets		
Tangible	32.4	33.4
Intangible	3.1	3.1
	35.5	36.5
Current assets		
Stock	0.2	0.2
Debtors	0.2	0.5
Cash	0.8	1.5
	1.2	2.2
Current liabilities	0.8	0.8
Working capital	0.4	1.4
Net assets	35.9	37.9
Share capital	30.0	30.0
Retained profit	5.9	7.9
Capital employed	35.9	37.9

Millenium Sport's balance sheet for the year ending 31.03.2010

$m	2009	2010
Sales	6.5	6.8
Cost of sales	1.4	1.5
Gross profit	5.1	5.3
Expenses	2.1	2.1
Net profit	3.0	3.2
Tax	0.5	0.6
Dividends	0.8	0.6
Retained profit	1.7	2.0

Millennium Sport's profit and loss account, 31.03.2010

Marketing

Millennium Sport has aimed its service at a particular market segment of the sports and recreation market. The facilities are state of the art and the business is looking to attract individuals and sports clubs that play sports at a high level. Marketing is Erik's particular area of interest and he has set up a project team to develop a new promotion strategy for Millennium. Another area of concern for Millennium is pricing. Currently, the business uses a cost-based pricing strategy for its memberships and charges to teams and individuals using the facility. The key aspect of pricing is to set a price that gives Millennium enough contribution to pay the fixed costs of operation while remaining competitive in the sports and recreation market.

To develop the range of sports Millennium offers it is currently looking at surfing. This is a big growth area and something Erik feels the business ought to develop. Millennium has been approached by XTC Surf Ltd who has developed an artificial surf machine. The machine is expensive and will cost $1.2 million. The projected cash inflows and outflows are set out in the table below. Anders and Erik look favourably at projects that pay back within four years and have an average annual rate of return of over 20%.

$000	2011	2012	2013	2014	2015
Cash inflow	200	300	400	400	400
Cash outflow	50	60	70	70	70

Asterix Finance does not want this project to go ahead because it believes that it will not be sufficiently profitable. Erik, however, feels that Millennium needs to offer a range of services that other sport clubs and gyms do not offer to keep it ahead of the competition.

Operations management

One of Anders's key strategic objectives for Millennium Sport since the organisation started was to achieve the highest quality of operation possible from every aspect of its business. To achieve this Anders has relied on the following principles:

- Invest in the highest-quality equipment.
- Recruit and retain the best staff and invest extensively in training.
- Delegate responsibility for quality assurance to every employee.
- Use quality circles to continuously review and improve operations.

This approach has been one of the reasons behind Millennium Sport's success since it started in 2001. Asterix Finance has, however, raised concerns about the cost of this approach and believes that using less-expensive equipment could improve Millennium's profits.

Higher level questions

Section A

Answer two questions.

1 **a** (i) Define the term 'mission statement'. **[2]**
(ii) Describe a key feature of Millennium's mission statement. **[2]**
b Explain how Anders Rikard's approach to operations management helps Millennium Sport achieve its mission. **[4]**
c Analyse the costs and benefits of Anders Rikard's approach to operations management. **[7]**
[Total: 15]

2 **a** (i) Define the term 'market segment'. **[2]**
(ii) Describe the market segment Millennium Sport is targeting. **[2]**
b Explain two benefits to Millennium Sport of segmenting its market so precisely. **[4]**
c Examine the marketing mix that would be appropriate to attract its target market segment. **[7]**
[Total: 15]

3 **a** (i) Define the term 'working capital'. **[2]**
(ii) Identify two possible sources of working capital to Millennium Sport. **[2]**
b Explain the effect the late payment of membership fees will have on Millennium Sport's current ratio. **[4]**
c Analyse the costs and benefits to Millennium Sport of introducing penalty charges to members who do not pay their membership fees on time. **[7]**
Total [15]

Section B

Answer the compulsory question in this section.
Using the balance sheet and profit and loss accounts produced for Millennium Sport answer the following questions.

4 **a** (i) Define the term 'tangible fixed asset'. **[2]**
(ii) Describe the intangible fixed assets Millennium Sport might have. **[2]**
b (i) Calculate Millennium Sport's net profit margin for 2009 and 2010. **[4]**
(ii) Explain what the change in Millennium Sport's profit margin from 2009 to 2010 tells you about its performance over the period. **[4]**
c Discuss the usefulness of ratio analysis to judge the performance of Millennium Sport. **[8]**
[Total: 20]

Section C

Answer the compulsory question in this section.

5 Millennium Sport has been approached by a regional hotel chain, Merx Hotels, to enter into a joint venture to provide accommodation to sports teams and individuals who travel long distances to use Millennium's facilities. The joint venture would involve Merx Hotels building a 50-room hotel on Millennium Sport's site. Merx has carried out market research which suggests a sports hotel would open up Millennium's market to a national and international level. This could be particularly important for the success of the new surf machine. Merx would build the hotel and would pay Millenium Sport 10% of the hotel's revenue each year. Asterix finance is a strong driver behind the joint venture.
a Identify two driving and two restraining forces for Millennium Sport from its joint venture with Merx Hotels. **[4]**

b Use Ansoff's matrix to assess the risk of Millennium's decision to enter the joint venture with Merx Hotels. **[8]**

c Analyse the two conflict issues between different stakeholders in Millennium Sport. **[8]**

d Evaluate the advantages and disadvantages of Anders's and Erik's proposal to buy Asterix's 33% ownership in Millennium Sport. **[10]**

[Total: 30]

Standard level questions

Section A

Answer two questions.

1 a (i) Define the term 'staff turnover'. **[2]**

(ii) Describe what is happening to the staff turnover at Millennium Sport. **[2]**

b Explain one advantage and one disadvantage to Millennium Sport of high staff turnover. **[4]**

c Analyse the ways Nils Marks could change his management style to improve staff turnover. **[7]**

[Total: 15]

2 a (i) Define the term 'cost-based pricing'. **[2]**

(ii) State two types of cost Millennium Sport would base its prices on. **[2]**

b Explain why fixed costs are the most significant part of Millennium Sport's total costs. **[4]**

c Analyse two other factors Millennium Sport would take into account when setting its prices. **[7]**

[Total: 15]

3 a (i) Define the term 'strategic objective'. **[2]**

(ii) Describe an example of a strategic objective Millennium Sport would make. **[2]**

b Explain two tactical objectives Millennium Sport would take to achieve its strategic objectives. **[4]**

c Analyse the differences between the strategic objectives of Asterix Finance and Millennium's founders Anders Rikard and Erik Brolyn. **[7]**

[Total: 15]

Section B

Answer the compulsory question in this section.

4 a (i) Define the term 'cash inflow'. **[2]**

(ii) State the initial cash outflow figure for the surf machine. **[2]**

b For the surf machine project calculate the project's:

(i) payback

(ii) average annual rate of return. **[8]**

c Using monetary and non-monetary factors evaluate Millennium Sport's decision to invest in the new surf machine. **[8]**

[Total: 20]

Sample answers

The case study paper is marked in the same way as paper 1 and the sample answers below can also be used to understand the approach to answering questions on paper 1.

Answers to higher level question 4

a (i) A tangible fixed asset is something physical Millennium Sport owns which would not be 'turned over' (sold) in the normal course of trading. Millennium's gym equipment is an example of the business's tangible fixed assets.

(ii) Millennium Sport's intangible fixed assets might include patents, copyrights, trademarks and logos. If Millennium had produced its own swimming training manuals it would own the copyright to these manuals and other companies could not copy them without paying a royalty fee.

b (i) sales/net profit × 100

2009: 3.0m/6.5m × 100 = 46%

2010: 3.2m/6.8m × 100 = 47%

(ii) Millennium Sport's net profit margin has improved by 1% from 46% to 47% which means it is making more net profit from each $1 of sales. The more net profit it makes on each membership sold or club booking, the better its performance. An increase of only 1% is, however, a negligible improvement and it would be safe to say that performance on net profit margin has not really improved over the period but remained the same.

c Ratio analysis of Millennium's final accounts is a useful tool in assessing the financial performance of the business. Stakeholders can use ratios to make judgements about the business. Erik and Anders would for example look at the business's return on net assets as a measure of its success in generating net profit from its assets employed.

Return on net assets = net profit/net assets × 100

2009: 3.0m/35.9 × 100 = 8%

2010: 3.2m/37.9 × 100 = 8%

This tells the owners that performance on this measure has not improved in the same way as the net profit margin and has remained largely unchanged.

The bank and other lenders would consider Millennium's liquidity by considering its current ratio.

current assets/current liabilities = current ratio

2009: 1.2/0.8 = 1.5

2010:2.2/0.8 = 2.75

These ratio results tell us that Millennium's liquidity position has improved and with a guide of 1.5–2.0 for this ratio as a safe liquidity position Millennium looks relatively secure on this basis.

Ratios do, however, only tell you about the financial position of the business. They tell you little about, for example, the quality of the product or service it provides. Millennium may have improved the quality of the service it offers to its members but this has yet to show in its accounts. It is also dangerous to look at ratios in isolation; Millennium may well be performing above the industry average, but without information from other firms the ratios are of limited use. You also need to consider things like the business environment before you judge a business on its ratios. In the current recession Millennium's ability to maintain its performance on the basis of profit margin and return on net assets is a good achievement.

Answers to standard level question 4

a (i) A cash inflow is the cash that comes into a business as a result of a particular event or business activity. The surf machine, for example, will generate a cash inflow as a result customers paying to use the machine.

(ii) This is the purchase price of the surf machine – $1.2m.

b (i) Payback:

$000	Year 0	1	2	3	4	5
Cash inflow		200	300	400	400	400
Cash outflow	1200	50	60	70	70	70
Net cashflow	-1200	150	240	330	330	330
Cumulative	-1200	-1,050	-810	-480	-150	180

$-150/330 \times 12 = 4$ years 5.5 months

(ii) Average annual rate of return:

$$(150+240+330+330+330-1200/5)/1200\times 100 = 3\%$$

c The payback time of the project is longer than the four years Millennium Sport wants from its projects, so on this basis the project is unfavourable. The surf machine's 3% APR is below the 20% required by Millennium's management for a viable project. So, on financial terms, the project is unfavourable.

A key non-financial factor is the image the surf machine may give Millennium as an innovative, forward-looking organisation. This may enhance it in the minds of the consumer. Surfing is, however, a different type of sport to the normal sports the business specialises in – it is perhaps an outdoor activity rather than a formal sport –and this might adversely the image Millennium wants as a place for serious athletes.

On balance, the financial and non-financial factors do support the investment in the new machine because of the innovative image Millennium is keen to develop.

Internal assessment

HIGHER LEVEL INTERNAL ASSESSMENT: RESEARCH PROJECT

Introduction

If you are taking Business and Management higher level, you will need to produce a 2000-word research project as your internal assessment. The project should be based on a real business organisation and the question you are considering must be a real one facing the organisation.

Choice of topic and organization

You should choose a topic that interests you and which you can tackle effectively within the word limit. It is a good idea to select a topic and organisation that will enable you to score well on the marking criteria. Your teacher will be able to advise you.

You will need to have a thorough understanding of the business and the market in which it operates – the more information you can obtain from the organisation, the better. Local businesses are often a good choice because you can access them easily, for example an estate agent, a small engineering firm, a garage, a computer company, a theatre.

Choosing a title

The title of your project should be in the form of a question. This will enable you to focus your research and analysis precisely and to come to an effective conclusion. One of the key aspects of the report is that it must be of practical use to management and, by following this approach, you will achieve this. It is essential for you to choose a title that allows you to apply business techniques to solve a problem.

Try to avoid backward-looking titles that lead to descriptive rather than analytical projects. For example, 'What is the most effective form of marketing at fast-food retailer Z?' would be better phrased as 'How could the promotional mix of retailer Z be improved?' Your title should also allow you to come to a conclusion and make a recommendation to the business.

Here are some examples of sample titles:

- Should XYZ estate agents invest in a new computer system?
- How could staff efficiency at ABC retailer be improved?
- How could the stock-management system employed by Z and Sons Engineering be improved?
- Should ARS financial services sell their products on the internet?
- What would be the most effective way for LNM leisure to promote its new range of sports clothing?
- What would be the most effective promotional strategy for the XYZ Theatre to use to market its productions?
- Should LNM Bank provide its own catering service or use an outside contractor?

- What would be the best way for ABC Retailers to motivate its sales staff?
- How can customer service at the ABC Hardware Centre be improved?
- How could XYZ Sports improve its cash flow?

The research proposal

Part of the internal assessment involves writing a research proposal that outlines how you are going to produce your report. It should be written as a plan and set out in the following way:

1. The research question
2. The rationale for study – why you have chosen this topic
3. Areas of the syllabus to be covered
4. Possible sources of information
5. Organisations and individuals to be approached
6. Methods to be used to collect and analyse data, and the reason for choosing them
7. Anticipated difficulties
8. Action plan that sets out the order of activities and time scale of the project.

The research proposal is part of the assessment criteria, so it should be included as a separate document with your report.

Setting out your report

Presentation

You report needs to be of practical value to management, so it must be meticulously presented. The formal layout should be:

1. Title page
2. Acknowledgments
3. Contents page
4. Executive summary (abstract)
5. Introduction
6. Research question
7. Procedure or method
8. Main results and findings
9. Analysis and discussion
10. Conclusions and recommendations
11. Bibliography and references
12. Appendices

Introduction

This includes a background to the business and should cover:

- who the business's customers are
- how big the business is
- where it is located
- the business's basic legal structure (whether it is a partnership, private limited company, plc, etc.)
- the market within which the business operates
- the context of the problem – how the decision you are looking at will affect the business.

Try to keep this section fairly brief (around 200–300 words as a guideline) – avoid long descriptions of the company's history or its market(s).

Procedure or method

This is a short section that is structured around how you are going to research and then answer the question. For example:

'What would be the best way for ABC Retailers to motivate its sales staff?'
The procedure for this could be to use primary research techniques to ascertain the views of the staff.

Main results and findings

This section includes the results of your primary and secondary research. You could use tables, pie charts, bar charts and so on.

Analysis and discussion

This section gives you the opportunity to analyse your data by applying the business techniques you have used in the course. It is the substance of the project and needs to be focused precisely on the project's title. There is a huge variety of techniques you could use – some will be quantitative, such as discounted cash flow and decision trees, but they could also be qualitative, such as applying the promotional mix or the work of behavioural theorists.

Table 39.4 lists some example titles and identifies appropriate analytical techniques.

When business tools are used in the analysis they need to be briefly introduced and there must be an explanation of why they have been chosen. It is important not to copy out sections from the textbook. Any weaknesses of the methods used and their assumptions should be made clear, particularly in the way they affect the final outcome of the project.

Conclusions and recommendations

The conclusion of the project should be based on the evidence and analysis included in your report and should answer the question set in the title. Your recommendation to the business should be based on the conclusions you have drawn. In the project 'Should XYZ Industrial invest in a new cutting machine?', for example, the recommendation should state whether XZY should buy the new machine or not.

Example titles	Appropriate analytical techniques
Should ABC estate agents invest in a new computer system?	Cash-flow forecasting, investment appraisal
How could staff efficiency at retailer X be improved?	Work study, motivation theory, leadership theory, group theory
Should ABC Sons Engineering introduce JIT stock management?	Ratio analysis, stock theory, just-in-time stock management
Should ABC financial services market its products on the internet?	Marketing strategy, marketing mix, SWOT analysis
How can customer service at the Hardware Centre be improved?	TQM, motivational theory

Table 39.4 *Appropriate analytical techniques*

HIGHER LEVEL MARKING CRITERIA

Table 39.5 sets out the marking criteria used to assess your research project and how to achieve the top mark for each of the criteria.

Criteria	Nature	Marks available	What is needed to achieve the top mark for each of the criteria
A	Research proposal and action plan	4	The research proposal and action plan must: • be appropriate, clear and focused • have a clearly identified and explained methodology and theoretical framework.
B	Use of theoretical concepts, sources and data (written report)	5	The use of concepts, sources and data must show: • in-depth understanding of relevant theoretical concepts • consistent evidence of the theoretical concepts' effective application • effective application of relevant sources and data • clear integration of sources and data with the theoretical framework.
C	Analysis and evaluation (written report)	7	The analysis and evaluation must: • be appropriate • show sound integration of ideas and issues in a coherent order • show consistent evidence of critical, reflective thinking.
D	Conclusions and recommendations (written report)	5	The conclusions and recommendations must: • be consistent with the evidence presented in the report and with the research question • be well developed • suggest future action to address limitations of the research.
E	Value to management (written report)	4	To be of value to management the report must: • be well presented, • be forward-looking • follow the required written report format • have an appropriate bibliography and references.
	Total	25	

Table 39.5 *Higher level marking criteria for internal assessment*

STANDARD LEVEL INTERNAL ASSESSMENT: WRITTEN COMMENTARY

Introduction

The standard level internal assessment requires you to write a commentary on a real business issue or problem of your choice. It gives you the opportunity to demonstrate how you would apply business and management tools, techniques and theories. The commentary has a 1500-word limit.

Choosing a topic

You will need to choose a topic that interests you and which you can tackle effectively within the word limit. It is a good idea to select a topic that will enable you to score well on the marking criteria. Your teacher will be able to advise you.

Setting a question

The title of the commentary should be in the form of a question which faces a single business organisation, or a market/industry-wide issue that could affect an organisation. For example:

- Should restaurant ABC introduce a line of healthy options to its menu?
- Could an improvement in working conditions at supermarket X improve the motivation of its staff?
- Should company Y purchase new machinery to increase output and improve product quality?
- Where should retailer ABC locate a new outlet to maximise sales?

Supporting documents and additional sources

Your commentary should be based on primary and/or secondary data that you have obtained. You will need to select three to five supporting documents which will be attached to your commentary and will form part of your assessment. The best commentaries will use a range of different types of sources to support them.

Here are some examples of the secondary sources you could use as supporting documents:

- final accounts
- market research reports
- newspaper articles
- market research surveys
- business plans
- extracts from web-based articles.

You could also use primary sources such as:

- responses to questionnaires
- transcripts of interviews you have conducted.

The supporting documents must have been written within two years of the date the commentary is submitted. You may find it helpful to highlight the relevant parts of the document you have used to support your commentary.

You are not limited to using the supporting documents as sources of information – you may also use textbooks, class notes and DVDs/videos. Remember to include supporting documents and additional sources in your bibliography.

Use of business tools and techniques

A good commentary will use suitable business tools to answer the question in the title. In the example 'Should restaurant ABC introduce a line of healthy options to its menu?' it would be useful to carry out a PEST analysis that looks at changes in the business environment and how this affects consumer choice. Ansoff's matrix could also be used to consider the strategic change in the products the restaurant is offering.

Analysis and synthesis of data

You will need to demonstrate that you can use appropriate analytical skills in your commentary. In the question 'Could an improvement in working conditions at supermarket X improve the motivation of its staff?' for example, it would be important to analyse the impact working conditions have on staff motivation by using the data you have collected and secondary sources such as the work of a theorist like Herzberg. To analyse information effectively you need to refer to source material and show how it contributes to the title of your commentary.

Evaluative and critical thinking

To show effective evaluative and critical thinking you should question the evidence you have used in your commentary. For example, you could evaluate the question of staff motivation by saying how the impact of working conditions varies from worker to worker and so it is difficult to draw precise conclusions that apply to all workers.

Writing a conclusion

Your commentary should conclude with a judgement about the decision that the business should take. The question 'Where should retailer ABC locate a new outlet to maximise sales?' for example, would need to say where, based on your evidence, the retailer should locate.

Presentation

Good commentaries are clearly structured and well presented. As mentioned earlier, you should also reference your work accurately in a bibliography.

There is no required format for the commentary but an effective layout might be:

1. Title
2. Introduction
3. Research using supporting documents
4. Research findings
5. Analysis and evaluation of the findings
6. Conclusion
7. Bibliography
8. Appendices (the supporting documents).

STANDARD LEVEL MARKING CRITERIA

Your commentary is marked internally based on the marking criteria set out in Table 39.6.

Criteria	Nature	Marks available	What is needed to achieve the top mark for each of the criteria
A	Supporting documents	4	The supporting documents must be: • relevant • sufficiently in depth • provide a range of ideas and views.
B	Choice and application of business tools, techniques and theory	6	The business tools, techniques and theory used in the commentary must be: • appropriate • broad in range • skilfully applied.
C	Use, analysis and synthesis of data	6	The selection of data from the supporting documents must: • be appropriate • contain detailed analysis • show coherent integration of ideas.
D	Conclusions	3	The conclusion to the commentary must: • be consistent with the evidence presented • answer the commentary question.
E	Evaluation and critical thinking	3	The commentary must: • show evidence of evaluation • substantiate any judgements • demonstrate critical and reflective thinking.
F	Presentation	3	The commentary: • is well organised • consistently uses appropriate business terminology • sources are referenced.
	Total	25	

Table 39.6 *Standard level marking criteria for internal assessment*

Extended essay in Business and Management

The extended essay in Business and Management gives you the opportunity to study an area of the subject that particularly interests you. It is a 4000-word, research-based essay that will allow you to:

- develop your research skills
- understand how business theory, concepts and principles are used in the real world
- collect business information from a wide range of sources
- critically analyse real business information
- develop your report-writing skills
- manage your own piece of original academic work.

CHOOSING A TITLE

Choosing the title of the extended essay is probably the most important part of the whole process. The title is the factor that will enable you to produce work which is manageable within the 4000-word limit and allows you to meet the extended essay marking criteria. Make sure your title is:

- a question
- easy to understand
- focused
- accessible to primary and secondary research
- accessible to analysis and evaluation using business techniques
- manageable within the 4000-word limit.

Poor titles are ones that are too broad and unfocused to give you the opportunity to answer them well. A title such as 'Analysis of motivation in the workplace' is too open-ended and imprecise to allow you to answer it effectively. A better title would be 'How can staff motivation at ABC hairdressers be improved?'

Unlike the higher level internal assessment, the extended essay can be backward-looking as well as forward-looking.

SUGGESTED TITLES

- How could ABC Bookshop promote itself more effectively to increase sales revenue?
- Should Pizza Restaurant X change its product portfolio?
- Should Solicitor K and Partner invest in a new computer system?
- How could staff motivation at Supermarket ABC be improved?
- Has the introduction of TQM at XYZ Ltd improved product quality?
- How has the economic recession affected estate agent LMN and Co?
- Should XZZ, a consumer electronics retailer, open a new branch in town Y?
- How can the pricing strategy at Theatre X be changed to increase profitability?
- How has the increased use of e-commerce benefited XYZ Retailers in the town of Y?
- How could ABC Farm develop its outbuildings most profitably?
- Should LMN Insurance manage its own catering service or use an outside contractor?

PLANNING THE ESSAY

The basic plan sets out the order of your essay starting with the title and finishing with the conclusion. Table 39.7 can be used as guide to an extended essay plan.

1 Research question	Should Pizza Company X expand its product portfolio?
2 Research method	• Interview with the managers and staff at company X. • Questionnaires to customers. • Books on product portfolio management. • Mintel survey of pizza industry. • Articles in pizza industry. • Research paper on product portfolio management.
3 Theory to be used	• SWOT • PEST • Porter's Five Forces • Product portfolio analysis • Product life cycle • Boston Matrix • Ansoff's matrix
4 Action steps	• 21.10.10 Initial topic research. • 22.10.10 Background reading. • 23.10.10 Interview manager. • 25.10.10 Draw up questionnaire. • 27.10.10 Conduct questionnaire. • Etc.

Table 39.7 *Extended essay plan – a suggested guide*

THE INTRODUCTION

You should write an introduction that sets out the context of the essay and why it is worth studying. In your essay you will need to include:

- some background about the organisation
- the research question
- the importance of the research question.

In the essay 'Should Pizza Company X expand its product portfolio?', you would need to discuss the nature of Pizza Company X – the size of the organisation, how long it has been operating in town Y, its customers and what type of legal structure the firm has. You would then state how and why it would want to expand its product portfolio and what this would mean to the organisation and its customers. You could finish by explaining how important the product portfolio is to its restaurants.

RESEARCH METHODOLOGY

You will need to include both primary and secondary research. Sources of secondary research include:

- books
- newspapers
- periodicals
- government reports
- market reports, e.g. Mintel
- the internet.

In the essay 'What human resources strategy should GHI Printing employ to improve its efficiency?', you could obtain your information from business textbooks and business periodicals on human resources theory.

Primary research is important for good essays on organisation-based topics. For example, you could use:

- questionnaires
- interviews
- observations.

In the essay 'How could XYZ Bookshop promote itself more effectively to increase sales revenue?', you could interview the managers of the shop and use questionnaires with the customers; perhaps even set up a focus group to gain qualitative research and quantitative research. You would also need to complete extensive secondary research by using marketing texts, government research on the book retailing market, academic research on promotion and articles from newspapers and periodicals.

RESEARCH ANALYSIS

Once you have completed your research, your next task will be to analyse the results. This will involve presenting your results in a form that can be interpreted effectively such as tables and charts. In the essay 'How can the pricing strategy at the ABC Cinema be changed to increase profitability?', you could use pie charts and bar charts to illustrate the results of your primary research. This might show that a high percentage of people would go to the theatre if discounts were offered at various times. If your research also showed that more people would buy tickets in the afternoon, you could analyse this using price-elasticity theory and how demand tends to be more price elastic in off-peak periods. You could then evaluate this by considering the problems of measuring price elasticity.

DEVELOPING A BUSINESS ARGUMENT

The nature of a Business and Management extended essay means you should be developing each point of your argument to answer the research question. This will involve business theory and techniques to give your essay academic rigour.

In the essay 'Should Solicitors Y invest in a new computer system to improve their profitability?', investment appraisal can be used to highlight the monetary costs and benefits of a new computer system. You could focus on how the decision will lead to lower operational costs and higher revenues because they will offer a better service. Once again you should be analysing and evaluating your points as you make them. A new computer system may lead to redundancies and reduced staff motivation, and you may need to discuss how this would this be managed.

WRITING A CONCLUSION

Your conclusion must focus on the research question set at the start of your essay. For the essay 'What would an effective marketing strategy for a new furniture shop ABC in town Y be?', your conclusion could include:

- a summary statement of your market research findings
- the marketing objective(s) of the new shop
- how the marketing mix can be used to meet the objective(s) set
- a time scale for the marketing strategy
- a budget for the strategy
- how the strategy will be managed
- how the effectiveness of the strategy can be measured.

You must also consider any unanswered questions you may have, for example discussing how the marketing strategy would be adjusted once the firm became established.

PRESENTATION

Your essay must include:

- a title page
- a table of contents
- page numbers
- labels on all tables, charts and graphs
- clear sub-titles
- a full, clearly set-out bibliography using footnotes.

Try to keep the presentation simple. Print it in font size 12 and use a normal font style such as Times New Roman or Calibri. Do not make presentation errors such as getting the numbering wrong in your table of contents.

Criteria		Marks available	What is needed to achieve the top mark for each of criteria
A	Research question	2	The research question should be: • clearly stated in the introduction • sharply focused • effectively addressed within the word limit.
B	Introduction	2	The introduction should clearly: • state the context of the research question • explain the significance of the topic and why it is worthy of investigation.
C	Investigation	4	The data and sources should: • be appropriate • have an imaginative range • be carefully selected • be well planned.
D	Knowledge and understanding of the topic studied	4	The essay should show: • a very good knowledge and understanding of the topic studied • clearly and precisely the essay in an academic context.
E	Reasoned argument	4	The argument should be: • presented in a clear, logical and coherent manner • a reasoned and convincing argument to the research question.

Table 39.8 *Extended essay marking criteria (table continues over)*

Criteria		Marks available	What is needed to achieve the top mark for each of criteria
F	Application of analytical and evaluative skills appropriate to the subject	4	The essay should show the: • appropriate use of analytical and evaluative skills • effective and sophisticated application of them.
G	Use of language appropriate to the subject	4	The language used should: • communicate information clearly and precisely • use terminology appropriate to the subject accurately • be used with skill and understanding.
H	Conclusion	2	The conclusion should: • be clearly stated • be relevant to the research question • be consistent with the evidence presented in the essay • include unresolved questions.
I	Formal presentation	4	Excellent presentation must achieve the highest standard of layout, organisation and appearance in terms of its: • title page • table of contents • page numbers • text • illustrative material • quotations • references • bibliography • appendices.
J	Abstract	2	The abstract must clearly state: • the research question • how the investigation was undertaken • the conclusion(s) of the essay.
K	Holistic judgement	4	This is a holistic judgement of the essay; an excellent essay should show: • intellectual initiative • deep understanding • insight.
	Total	36	

Table 39.8 *Continued*

You can include appendices for related material that is not part of your essay, but anything that contributes to your argument should be in the main body. If you use appendices, then refer to them accurately.

THE ABSTRACT

This is a 300-word summary of the essay. It must clearly state:

- the title of the essay
- how you researched the question and developed an argument
- your final conclusion.

WHAT IS IT WORTH?

The extended essay is marked out of 36 and is based on the set marking criteria. The way these criteria are applied is set out in Table 39.8.

VIVA VOCE

This is an interview where you may need to explain your extended essay to your supervisor. This is optional and your school or college may not require you to attend a viva voce. There are no marks awarded for it, but it will help your supervisor to write his or her report on your essay. This will then be sent to the external examiner who will consider the report when he or she is awarding criterion K: Holistic judgement.

THE GRADE BOUNDARIES

Table 39.9 sets out the approximate grade boundaries for the extended essay.

Grade:	A	B	C	D	E
Mark range	29–36	23–28	16–22	8–15	0–7

Table 39.9 Approximate grade boundaries for the extended essay

Remember, the final bonus points you receive for your extended essay are based on a combination of grades with your theory of knowledge essay. Table 39.10 sets out the combination of extended essay and theory of knowledge grades needed to achieve bonus points.

Theory of knowledge	A	B	C	D	E
EE					
A	3	3	2	2	0
B	3	2	1	1	0
C	2	1	1	0	0
D	2	1	0	0	0
E	0	0	0	0	0

Table 39.10 Combination of extended essay and theory of knowledge grades needed to achieve bonus points

A FINAL THOUGHT

It is very easy to get wrapped up in the marking criteria, grades and bonus points associated with the extended essay and obviously these things are important. In the end, however, the extended essay should be an intellectually challenging, enjoyable experience. It is your chance to write something really original, so go ahead and embrace this part of the IB programme.

Glossary

above-the-line promotion a form of promotion that is undertaken by a business by paying for communication with consumers, e.g. advertising

acid test ratio $= \frac{\text{liquid assets}}{\text{current liabilities}}$

accountability the obligation of an individual to account for his or her activities and to disclose results in a transparent way

adverse variance exists when the difference between the budgeted and actual figure leads to a lower than expected profit

advertising elasticity measures the responsiveness of demand for a product following a change in the advertising spending on it

agent business with the authority to act on behalf of another firm, e.g. to market its products

annual forecasted net cash flow forecasted cash inflow – forecasted cash outflows

Ansoff's matrix a model used to show the degree of risk associated with the four growth strategies of market penetration, market development, product development and diversification

arbitration resolving an industrial dispute by using an independent third party to judge and recommend an appropriate solution

asset-led marketing an approach to marketing that bases strategy on the firm's existing strengths and assets instead of purely on what the customer wants

assets items of monetary value that are owned by a business

autocratic leadership a style of leadership that keeps all decision-making at the centre of the oganisation

average rate of return (ARR) measures the annual profitability of an investment as a percentage of the initial investment

backward vertical integration integration with a business in the same industry but a supplier of the existing business

bad debt unpaid customers' bills that are now very unlikely to ever be paid

balance sheet an accounting statement that records the values of a business's assets, liabilities and shareholders' equity at one point in time

batch production producing a limited number of identical products – each item in the batch passes through one stage of production before passing on to the next stage

below-the-line promotion promotion that is not a directly paid-for means of communication but based on short-term incentives to purchase, e.g. sales promotion techniques

benchmarking comparing the performance – including quality – of a business with performance standards throughout the industry

Boston Matrix a method of analysing the product portfolio of a business in terms of market share and market growth

brand an identifying symbol, name, image or trademark that distinguishes a product from its competitors

brand awareness extent to which a brand is recognised by potential customers and is correctly associated with a particular product – can be expressed as a percentage of the target market

brand development measures the infiltration of a product's sales, usually per thousand population. If 100 people in 1000 buy a product, it has a brand development of 10

brand loyalty the faithfulness of consumers to a particular brand as shown by their repeat purchases irrespective of the marketing pressure from competing brands

break-even point of production the level of output at which total costs equal total revenue

break-even revenue the amount of revenue needed to cover both fixed and variable costs so that the business breaks even

budget a detailed financial plan for the future

budget holder individual responsible for the initial setting and achievement of a budget

buffer stocks the minimum stocks that should be held to ensure that production could still take place should a delay in delivery occur or production rates increase

bureaucracy an organisational system with standardised procedures and rules

business plan a written document that describes a business, its objectives and its strategies, the market it is in and its financial forecasts

business process outsourcing (BPO) a form of outsourcing which uses a third party to take responsibility for certain business functions, such as human resources and finance

business process re-engineering fundamentally rethinking and redesigning the processes of a business to achieve a dramatic improvement in performance

business strategy a long-term plan of action for the whole organisation, designed to meet the needs of markets and to fulfil stakeholder expectations

capacity shortage when the demand for a business's products exceeds production capacity

capacity utilisation the proportion of maximum output capacity currently being achieved

capital employed = (non-current assets + current assets) – current liabilities OR non-current liabilities + shareholders equity

capital goods physical goods that are used by industry to aid in the production of other goods and services, such as machines and commercial vehicles

cash flow the sum of cash payments to a business (inflows) less the sum of cash payments made by it (outflows)

cash inflows payments in cash received by a business, such as those from customers (debtors) or from the bank, e.g. receiving a loan

cash-flow forecast estimate of a firm's future cash inflows and outflows

cell production splitting flow production into self-contained groups that are responsible for whole work units

centralisation keeping all of the important decision-making powers within head office or the centre of the organisation

chain of command this is the route through which authority is passed down an organisation – from the chief executive and the board of directors

change management planning, implementing, controlling and reviewing the movement of an organisation from its current state to a new one

channel of distribution this refers to the chain of intermediaries a product passes through from producer to final consumer

closing cash balance cash held at the end of the month becomes next month's opening balance

cluster sampling using one or a number of specific groups to draw samples from and not selecting from the whole population, e.g. using one town or region

collective bargaining the negotiations between employees' representatives (trade unions) and employers and their representatives on issues of common interest such as pay and conditions of work

command economy economic resources are owned, planned and controlled by the state

commission a payment to a sales person for each sale made

communication barriers reasons why communication fails

communication media the methods used to communicate a message

company or corporate branding the company name is applied to products and this becomes the brand name

competition-based pricing a firm will base its price upon the price set by its competitors

computer-aided design using computers and IT when designing products

computer-aided manufacturing the use of computers and computer-controlled machinery to speed up the production process and make it more flexible

conciliation the use of a third party in industrial disputes to encourage both employer and union to discuss an acceptable compromise solution

conglomerate integration merger with or takeover of a business in a different industry

consumer durables manufactured products that can be re-used and are expected to have a reasonably long life, such as cars and washing machines

consumer goods the physical and tangible goods sold to the general public. They include cars and washing machines, which are referred to as durable consumer goods. Non-durable consumer goods include food, drinks and sweets that can only be used once

consumer markets markets for goods and services bought by the final user of them

consumer profile a quantified picture of consumers of a firm's products, showing proportions of age groups, income levels, location, gender and social class

consumer services non-tangible products that are sold to the general public and include hotel accommodation, insurance services and train journeys

contingency planning preparing the immediate steps to be taken by an organisation in the event of a crisis or emergency

contract of employment a legal document that sets out the terms and conditions governing a worker's job

contribution costing costing method that only allocates direct costs to cost/profit centres not overhead costs

contribution-cost pricing setting prices based on the variable costs of making a product in order to make a contribution towards fixed costs and profit

contribution per unit selling price of a product less variable costs per unit

co-ordinated marketing mix key marketing decisions complement each other and work together to give customers a consistent message about the product

copyright legal right to protect and be the sole beneficiary from artistic and literary works

core competence an important business capability that gives it a competitive advantage

core product product made from a business's core competencies, but not for final consumer or 'end' user

corporate image consumer perception of the company behind a brand

corporate or strategic objectives important, broadly defined targets that a business must reach to achieve its overall aim

corporate plan a methodical plan containing details of the organisation's central objectives and the strategies to be followed to achieve them

corporate social responsibility this concept applies to those businesses that consider the interests of society by taking responsibility for the impact of their decisions and activities on customers, employees, communities and the environment

cost centre a section of a business, such as a department, to which costs can be allocated or charged

cost of sales (or cost of goods sold) this is the direct cost of purchasing the goods that were sold during the financial year

cost-plus pricing adding a fixed mark-up for profit to the unit price of a product

cost-push inflation caused by rising costs forcing businesses to increase prices

credit control monitoring of debts to ensure that credit periods are not exceeded

creditor days ratio $= \dfrac{\text{trade creditors}}{\text{credit purchases}} \times 365$

creditors suppliers who have agreed to supply products or services on credit and who have not yet been paid

crisis management steps taken by an organisation to limit the damage from a crisis by handling, retaining and resolving it

criterion rate or level the minimum level (maximum for payback period) set by management for investment appraisal results for a project to be accepted

critical path the sequence of activities that must be completed on time for the whole project to be completed by the agreed date

critical path analysis planning technique that identifies all tasks in a project, puts them in the correct sequence and allows for the identification of the critical path

cross elasticity measures the responsiveness of demand for a product following the change in the price of another product

current ratio $= \dfrac{\text{current assets}}{\text{current liabilities}}$

cyclical variations variations in sales occurring over periods of time of much more than a year – they are related to the business cycle

debentures or long-term bonds bonds issued by companies to raise debt finance, often with a fixed rate of interest

debtor days (days' sales in receivables)

$$= \frac{\text{trade debtors (accounts receivable)}}{\text{sales turnover}} \times 365 \text{ (days)}$$

debtors customers who have bought products on credit and will pay cash at an agreed date in the future

decentralisation decision-making powers are passed down the organisation to empower subordinates and regional/product managers

decision tree a diagram that sets out the options connected with a decision and the outcomes and economic returns that may result

delayering removal of one or more of the levels of hierarchy from an organisational structure

delegated budgets control over budgets is given to less senior management

delegation passing authority down the organisational hierarchy

demand-pull inflation caused by excess demand in an economy, e.g. an economic boom, allowing businesses to raise prices

democratic leadership a leadership style that promotes the active participation of workers in taking decisions

depreciation the decline in the estimated value of a non-current asset over time

direct costs these costs can be clearly identified with each unit of production and can be allocated to a cost centre

diseconomies of scale factors that cause average costs of production to rise when the scale of operation is increased

dismissal being removed or 'sacked' from a job due to incompetence or breach of discipline

diversification the process of selling different, unrelated goods or services in new markets

dividends the share of the profits paid to shareholders as a return for investing in the company

dividend per share $= \dfrac{\text{total annual dividends}}{\text{total number of issued shares}}$

dividend yield ratio (%) $= \dfrac{\text{dividend per share}}{\text{current share price}} \times 100$

earnings per share profit earned per share in the company

$$\frac{\text{profit after tax}}{\text{total number of ordinary shares}}$$

e-commerce the buying and selling of goods and services on the internet

economic growth increases in the level of a country's Gross Domestic Product (total value of output)

economic order quantity (EOQ) the optimum or least-cost quantity of stock to re-order taking into account delivery costs and stock-holding costs

economies of scale reductions in a firm's unit (average) costs of production that result from an increase in the scale of operations

effective communication the exchange of information between people or groups, with feedback

entrepreneur someone who takes the financial risk of starting and managing a new venture

entrepreneurial culture encourages management and workers to take risks, to come up with new ideas and test out new business ventures

environmental audit assesses the impact of a business's impact on the environment

equity finance permanent finance raised by companies through the sale of shares

ethical code (code of conduct) a document detailing a company's rules and guidelines on staff behaviour that must be followed by all employees

ethics moral guidelines that determine decision-making

excess capacity exists when the current levels of demand are less than the full capacity output of a business – also known as spare capacity

exchange rate the value of one currency in terms of another currency

expected value the likely financial result of an outcome obtained by multiplying the probability of an event occurring by the forecast economic return if it does occur

extension strategies marketing plans that extend the maturity stage of the product before a brand new one is needed

external constraints limiting factors in decision-making that are beyond the organisation's control

external growth business expansion achieved by means of merging with or taking over another business, from either the same or a different industry

extrinsic motivation comes from external rewards associated with working on a task, for example pay and other benefits

factoring selling of claims over debtors to a debt factor in exchange for immediate liquidity – only a proportion of the value of the debts will be received as cash

family branding a marketing strategy that involves selling several related products under one brand name (also known as umbrella branding)

favourable variance exists when the difference between the budgeted and actual figure leads to a higher than expected profit

first in first out (FIFO) valuing stocks by assuming that the first ones bought in were sold first

fiscal policy changes in government spending levels and tax rates

fishbone diagram a visual identification of many potential causes of a problem

fixed costs costs that do not vary with output in the short run

flexi-time contract employment contract that allows staff to be called in at times most convenient to employers and employees, e.g. at busy times of day

flow production producing items in a continually moving process – also known as line production

focus groups a group of people who are asked about their attitude towards a product, service, advertisement or new style of packaging

force-field analysis an analytical process used to map the opposing forces within an environment (such as a business) where change is taking place

formal communication networks the official communication channels and routes used within an organisation

forward vertical integration integration with a business in the same industry but a customer of the existing business

franchise a business that uses the name, logo and trading systems of an existing successful business

free international trade international trade that is allowed to take place without restrictions such as 'protectionist' tariffs and quotas

free-market economy economic resources are owned largely by the private sector with very little state intervention

full capacity when a business produces at maximum output

full-cost/absorption-cost pricing setting a price by calculating a unit cost for the product (allocated fixed and variable costs) and then adding a fixed profit mark-up

gearing ratio (%) $= \dfrac{\text{long-term loans}}{\text{capital employed}} \times 100$

geographical mobility of labour extent to which workers are willing and able to move geographical region to take up new jobs

global localisation adapting the marketing mix, including differentiated products, to meet national and regional tastes and cultures

globalisation the growing trend towards worldwide markets in products, capital and labour, unrestricted by barriers

going-rate pricing the price charged is based upon a study of the conditions that prevail in a certain market and the prices charged by major competitors

goodwill arises when a business is valued at or sold for more than the balance sheet values of its assets

gross profit equal to sales revenue less cost of sales

gross profit margin (%) $= \dfrac{\text{gross profit}}{\text{sales revenue}} \times 100$

high-quality profit profit that can be repeated and sustained

hire purchase an asset is sold to a company which agrees to pay fixed repayments over an agreed time period – the asset belongs to the company

horizontal integration integration with firm in the same industry and at same stage of production

hourly wage rate payment to a worker made for each hour worked

human resource management (HRM) the strategic approach to the effective management of an organisation's workers so that they help the business gain a competitive advantage

human resource or workforce planning analysing and forecasting the numbers of workers and the skills of those workers that will be required by the organisation to achieve its objectives

hygiene factors aspects of a worker's job that have the potential to cause dissatisfaction such as pay, working conditions, status and over-supervision by managers

income elasticity measures the responsiveness of demand for a product following a change in consumers' incomes

income statement records the revenue, costs and profit (or loss) of a business over a given period of time

incremental budgeting uses last year's budget as a basis and an adjustment is made for the coming year

indirect costs costs which cannot be identified with a unit of production or allocated accurately to a cost centre – also known as overhead costs

induction training introductory training programme to familiarise new recruits with the systems used in the business and the layout of the business site

industrial action measures taken by the workforce or trade union to put pressure on management to settle an industrial dispute in favour of employees

industrial markets markets for goods and services bought by businesses to be used in the production process of other products

inflation the rate of change in the average level of prices

informal communication unofficial channels of communication that exist between informal groups within an organisation

informal organisation the network of personal and social relations that develop between people within an organisation

information overload so much information and so many messages are received that the most important ones cannot be easily identified and quickly acted on – most likely to occur with electronic media

information technology the use of electronic technology to gather, store, process and communicate information

innovation the practical application of new inventions into marketable products

insolvent when a business cannot meet its short-term debts

intellectual property an intangible asset – e.g. inventions, literary and artistic works and symbols, names, images and designs used in business – that has been developed from human ideas and knowledge

intellectual property rights legal property rights over the possession and use of intellectual property

internal constraints limiting factors in decision-making that can be controlled by the organisation

internal customers people within the organisation who depend upon the quality of work being done by others

internal growth expansion of a business by means of opening new branches, shops or factories (also known as organic growth)

international marketing selling products in markets other than the original domestic market

internet the worldwide web of communication links between computers

intrinsic motivation comes from the satisfaction derived from working on and completing a task

intuitive decision-making involves making decisions based on instinct or 'gut feeling' (perhaps based on the manager's experience) for a situation and the options available

invention the formulation or discovery of new ideas for products or processes

investment appraisal evaluating the profitability or desirability of an investment project

ISO 9000 internationally recognised certificate that acknowledges the existence of a quality procedure that meets certain conditions

job description a detailed list of the key points about the job to be filled, stating all the key tasks and responsibilities of it

job enlargement attempting to increase the scope of a job by broadening or deepening the tasks undertaken

job enrichment aims to use the full capabilities of workers by giving them the opportunity to do more challenging and fulfilling work

job production producing a one-off item specially designed for the customer

job redesign involves the restructuring of a job – usually with employees' involvement and agreement – to make work more interesting, satisfying and challenging

joint venture two or more businesses agree to work closely together on a particular project and create a separate business division to do so

just in case (JIC) holding high stock levels 'just in case' there is a production problem or an unexpected upsurge in demand

just in time (JIT) a stock control method that aims to avoid holding stocks by requiring supplies to arrive just as they are needed in production and completed products are produced to order

Kaizen Japanese term meaning continuous improvement

laissez-faire leadership a leadership style that leaves much of the business decision-making to the workforce – a 'hands-off' approach and the reverse of the autocratic style

last in first out (LIFO) valuing closing stocks by assuming that the last one purchased was sold first

lead time the normal time taken between ordering new stocks and their delivery

leadership the art of motivating a group of people towards achieving a common objective

lean production producing goods and services with the minimum of wasted resources while maintaining high quality

leasing obtaining the use of equipment or vehicles and paying a rental or leasing charge over a fixed period. This avoids the need for the business to raise long-term capital to buy the asset. Ownership remains with the leasing company

level of hierarchy a stage of the organisational structure at which the personnel on it have equal status and authority

liabilities a financial obligation of a business that it is required to pay in the future

limited liability the only liability – or potential loss – a shareholder has if the company fails is the amount invested in the company, not the total wealth of the shareholder

liquid assets = current assets – stocks

liquidation when a firm ceases trading and its assets are sold for cash, usually to pay its suppliers

liquidity the ability of a firm to be able to pay its short-term debts

long-term bonds or debentures bonds issued by companies to raise debt finance, often with a fixed rate of interest

long-term loans loans that do not have to be repaid for at least one year

loss leader product sold at a very low price to encourage consumers to buy other products

low-quality profit one-off profit that cannot easily be repeated or sustained

manager responsible for setting objectives, organising resources and motivating staff so that the organisation's aims are met

manufacturers' brands producers establish the brand image of a product or a family of products, often under the company's name

margin of safety the amount by which the sales level exceeds the break-even level of output

marginal-cost price basing the price on the extra cost of making one additional unit of output

marginal costs the extra cost of producing one more unit of output

market development the strategy of selling existing products in new markets

market growth the percentage change in the total size of a market (volume or value) over a period of time

market orientation an outward-looking approach basing product decisions on consumer demand, as established by market research

market penetration the objective of achieving higher market shares in existing markets with existing products

market research process of collecting, recording and analysing data about customers, competitors and the market

market segment a sub-group of a whole market in which consumers have similar characteristics

market segmentation identifying different segments within a market and targeting different products or services to them

market share the percentage of sales in the total market sold by one business

market size the total level of sales of all producers within a market

market skimming setting a high price for a new product when a firm has a unique or highly differentiated product with low price elasticity of demand

market value the estimated total value of a company if it were taken over

marketing the management task that links the business to the customer by identifying and meeting the needs of customers profitably – it does this by getting the right product at the right price to the right place at the right time

marketing audit a regular review of the cost and effectiveness of a marketing plan including an analysis of internal and external influences

marketing mix the key decisions that must be taken in the effective marketing of a product

marketing objectives the goals set for the marketing department to help the business achieve its overall objectives

marketing plan a detailed report on an organisation's marketing strategy

marketing planning the process of formulating appropriate strategies and preparing marketing activities to meet marketing objectives

marketing strategy long-term plan established for achieving marketing objectives

mass customisation the use of flexible computer-aided production systems to produce items to meet individual customers' requirements at mass production cost levels

mass production producing large quantities of a standardised product

matrix structure an organisational structure that creates project teams that cut across traditional functional departments

merger an agreement by shareholders and managers of two businesses to bring both firms together under a common board of directors with shareholders in both businesses owning shares in the newly merged business

mission statement a statement of the business's core aims, phrased in a way to motivate employees and to stimulate interest by outside groups

mixed economy economic resources are owned and controlled by both private and public sectors

monetary policy changes in the level of interest rates which make loan capital more or less expensive

motivating factors (motivators) aspects of a worker's job that can lead to positive job satisfaction such as achievement, recognition, meaningful and interesting work and advancement at work

motivation the intrinsic and extrinsic factors that stimulate people to take actions that lead to achieving a goal

multinational a business with operations or production bases in more than one country

multinational companies business organisations that have their headquarters in one country, but with operating branches, factories and assembly plants in other countries

net book value the current balance sheet value of a non-current asset = original cost – accumulated depreciation

net monthly cash flow estimated difference between monthly cash inflows and outflows

net present value (NPV) today's value of the estimated cash flows resulting from an investment

net profit margin (%) $= \frac{\text{net profit}}{\text{sales revenue}} \times 100$

network diagram the diagram used in critical path analysis that shows the logical sequence of activities and the logical dependencies between them – and the critical path can be identified

non-governmental organisation (NGO) a legally constituted body with no participation or representation of any government

non-profit organisation any organisation that has aims other than making and distributing profit and which is usually governed by a voluntary board

non-verbal communication messages sent and received without verbal information such as facial expressions, eye contact, tone of voice, body posture and gestures and position within a group

no-strike agreement unions agree to sign an agreement with employers not to strike in exchange for greater involvement in decisions that affect the workforce

occupational mobility of labour extent to which workers are willing and able to move to different jobs requiring different skills

offshoring the relocation of a business process done in one country to the same or another company in another country

off-the-job training all training undertaken away from the business, e.g. work-related college courses

on-the-job training instruction at the place of work on how a job should be carried out

opening cash balance cash held by the business at the start of the month

operating profit (net profit) gross profit minus overhead expenses

optimal location a business location that gives the best combination of quantitative and qualitative factors

organisational culture the values, attitudes and beliefs of the people working in an organisation that control the way they interact with each other and with external stakeholder groups

organisational structure the internal, formal framework of a business that shows the way in which management is organised and linked together and how authority is passed through the organisation

outflows payments in cash made by a business, such as those to suppliers and workers

outsourcing (or subcontracting) using an outside agency or organisation (a 'third party') to to carry out some business functions rather than doing it within the business using the firm's own employees. When this is done by firms in another country it is called 'offshoring'

overdraft bank agrees to a business borrowing up to an agreed limit as and when required

overtrading expanding a business rapidly without obtaining all of the necessary finance so that a cash-flow shortage develops

own-label branding retailers create their own brand name and identity for a range of products

pan-global marketing adopting a standardised product across the globe as if the whole world were a single market – selling the same goods in the same way everywhere

partnership a business formed by two or more people to carry on a business together, with shared capital investment and, usually, shared responsibilities

part-time employment contract employment contract that is for less than the normal full working week of, say, 40 hours, e.g. eight hours per week

patent legal right to be the sole producer and seller of an invention for a certain period of time

payback period length of time it takes for the net cash inflows to pay back the original capital cost of the investment

penetration pricing setting a relatively low price often supported by strong promotion in order to achieve a high volume of sales

performance-related pay a bonus scheme to reward staff for above-average work performance

person culture when individuals are given the freedom to express themselves and make decisions

person specification a detailed list of the qualities, skills and qualifications that a successful applicant will need to have

PEST analysis – an acronym standing for political, economic, social, technological that refers to an analytical framework for external environmental factors affecting business objectives and strategies. PEST is sometimes rearranged as STEP and has also been extended to STEEPLE (social, technological, economic, environmental, political, legal and ethical) and PESTLE (same categories as STEEPLE but without ethical considerations)

piece rate a payment to a worker for each unit produced

portfolio working the working pattern of following several simultaneous employments at any one time

power culture concentrating power among a few people

predatory pricing deliberately undercutting competitors' prices in order to try to force them out of the market

pressure group an organisation created by people with a common interest or objective who lobby businesses and governments to change policies so that the objective is reached

price elasticity of demand measures the responsiveness of demand following a change in price

price leadership one dominant firm in a market sets a price and other firms simply charge a price based upon that set by the market leader

primary research the collection of first-hand data that is directly related to a firm's needs

primary sector business activity firms engaged in farming, fishing, oil extraction and all other industries that extract natural resources so that they can be used and processed by other firms

Private Finance Initiative (PFI) investment by private sector organisations in public sector projects

private limited company a small to medium-sized business that is owned by shareholders who are often members of the same family. This company cannot sell shares to the general public

private sector comprises businesses owned and controlled by individuals or groups of individuals

privatisation the sale of public sector organisations to the private sector

process innovation new methods of manufacturing or service provision that offers important benefits, e.g. Pilkington's float-glass process

product the end result of the production process sold on the market to satisfy a customer need

product branding each individual product in a portfolio is given its own unique identity and brand image (also known as individual branding)

product development the development and sale of new products or new developments of existing products in existing markets

product innovation new, marketable products such as the Apple iPad

product life cycle the pattern of sales recorded by a product from launch to withdrawal from the market

product line a set of related products sold by a business

product mix the variety of product lines that a business produces or a retailer stocks

product orientation an inward-looking approach that focuses on making products that can be made – or have been made for a long time – and then trying to sell them

product range all of the types of products made by a business

profit after tax operating profit minus interest costs and corporation tax

profit centre a section of a business to which both costs and revenues can be allocated

profit-related pay a bonus for staff based on the profits of the business – usually paid as a proportion of basic salary

project a specific and temporary activity with a start and end date, clear goals, defined responsibilities and a budget

project champion a person assigned to support and drive a project forward. Their role is to explain the benefits of change and assist and support the team putting change into practice

project groups created by an organisation to address a problem that requires input from different specialists

project management using modern management techniques to carry out and complete a project from start to finish in order to achieve pre-set targets of quality, time and cost

promotion the use of advertising, sales promotion, personal selling, direct mail, trade fairs, sponsorship and public relations to inform consumers and persuade consumers to buy

promotion mix the combination of promotional techniques that a firm uses to communicate the benefits of its products to customers

promotional pricing special low prices to gain market share or sell off excess stock – includes 'buy one get one free'

psychological pricing setting prices that take account of customers' perception of value of the product

public corporation a business enterprise owned and controlled by the state – also known as nationalised industry

public limited company (plc) a limited company, often a large business, with the legal right to sell shares to the general public. Its share price is quoted on the national stock exchange

public sector comprises organisations accountable to and controlled by central or local government (the state)

public–private partnership (PPP) involvement of the private sector, in the form of management expertise and/or financial investment, in public sector projects aimed at benefiting the public

qualitative factors non-measurable factors that may influence business decisions

qualitative research research into the in-depth motivations behind consumer buying behaviour or opinions

quality assurance this is a system of agreeing and meeting quality standards at each stage of production to ensure consumer satisfaction

quality control this is based on inspection of the product or a sample of products

quality product a good or service that meets customers' expectations and is therefore 'fit for purpose'

quality standards the expectations of customers expressed in terms of the minimum acceptable production or service standards

quantitative factors these are measurable in financial terms and will have a direct impact on either the costs of a site or the revenues from it and its profitability

quantitative research research that leads to numerical results that can be presented and analysed

quota a physical limit placed on the quantity of imports of certain products

quota sampling gathering data from a group chosen out of a specific sub-group, e.g. a researcher might ask 100 individuals between the ages of 20 and 30 years

random sampling every member of the target population has an equal chance of being selected

random variations may occur at any time and will cause unusual and unpredictable sales figures, e.g. exceptionally poor weather, or negative public image following a high-profile product failure

recession six months (two quarters) of falling GDP (negative growth)

recruitment the process of identifying the need for a new employee, defining the job to be filled and the type of person needed to fill it, attracting suitable candidates for the job and selecting the best one

reducing balance method calculates depreciation by subtracting a fixed percentage from the previous year's net book value

redundancy when a job is no longer required so the employee doing this job becomes redundant through no fault of his or her own

re-order quantity the number of units ordered each time

re-order stock level the level of stocks that will trigger a new order to be sent to the supplier

research and development the scientific research and technical development of new products and processes

retained profit the profit left after all deductions, including dividends, have been made. This is 'ploughed back' into the company as a source of finance

return on capital employed (%) $= \frac{\text{net profit}}{\text{capital employed}} \times 100$

revenue the income received from the sale of a product

rights issue existing shareholders are given the right to buy additional shares at a discounted price

role culture each member of staff has a clearly defined job title and role

salary annual income that is usually paid on a monthly basis

sales forecasting predicting future sales levels and sales trends

sales promotion incentives such as special offers or special deals directed at consumers or retailers to achieve short-term sales increases and repeat purchases by consumers

sales revenue (or sales turnover) the total value of sales made during the trading period = selling price × quantity sold

sample group of people taking part in a market research survey selected to be representative of the target market overall

sampling error errors in research caused by using a sample for data collection rather than the whole target population

scale of operation the maximum output that can be achieved using the available inputs (resources) – this scale can only be increased in the long term by employing more of all inputs

scientific decision-making involves basing decisions on a formal framework and a data analysis of both the problem and the options available

seasonal variations regular and repeated variations that occur in sales data within a period of 12 months or less

secondary research collection of data from second-hand sources

secondary sector business activity firms that manufacture and process products from natural resources, including computers, brewing, baking, clothing and construction

self-actualisation a sense of self-fulfilment reached by feeling enriched and developed by what one has learned and achieved

semi-variable costs costs that have both a fixed cost and a variable cost element

share a certificate confirming part ownership of a company and entitling the shareholder to dividends and certain shareholder rights

share capital the total value of capital raised from shareholders by the issue of shares

share price the quoted price of one share on the stock exchange

shareholder a person or institution owning shares in a limited company

shareholders' equity total value of assets less total value of liabilities

single-union agreement an employer recognises just one union for purposes of collective bargaining

situational leadership effective leadership varies with the task in hand and situational leaders adapt their leadership style to each situation

snowball sampling using existing members of a sample study group to recruit further participants through their acquaintances

social audit an independent report on the impact a business has on society. This can cover pollution levels, health and safety record, sources of supplies, customer satisfaction and contribution to the community

social enterprise a business with mainly social objectives that reinvests most of its profits into benefiting society rather than maximising returns to owners

social (societal) marketing this approach considers not only the demands of consumers but also the effects on all members of the public ('society') involved in some way when firms meet these demands

sole trader a business in which one person provides the permanent finance and, in return, has full control of the business and is able to keep all of the profits

span of control the number of subordinates reporting directly to a manager

staff appraisal the process of assessing the effectiveness of an employee judged against pre-set objectives

stakeholder concept the view that businesses and their managers have responsibilities to a wide range of groups, not just shareholders

stakeholders people or groups of people who can be affected by, and therefore have an interest in, any action by an organisation

start-up capital capital needed by an entrepreneur to set up a business

stock (inventory) materials and goods required to allow for the production of and supply of products to the customer

stock (inventory) turnover ratio

$$= \frac{\text{cost of goods sold}}{\text{value of stock (average)}}$$

straight-line depreciation a constant amount of depreciation is subtracted from the value of the asset each year

strategic alliances agreements between firms in which each agrees to commit resources to achieve an agreed set of objectives

strategic analysis the process of conducting research on the business environment within which a business operates and on the organisation itself in order to develop strategy

strategic choice identifying strategic options, evaluating them and then choosing between them

strategic implementation the process of allocating and controlling resources to support the chosen strategies

strategic management the role of management when setting long-term goals and implementing cross-functional decisions that should enable a business to reach these goals

stratified sampling this draws a sample from a specified sub-group or segment of the population and uses random sampling to select an appropriate number from each stratum

subcontracting see **outsourcing**

supply chain management (SCM) managing the network of businesses that are involved in the provision of products to the final consumers

SWOT analysis a form of strategic analysis that identifies and analyses the main internal strengths and weaknesses and external opportunities and threats that will influence the future direction and success of a business

tactic short-term policy or decision aimed at resolving a particular problem or meeting a specific part of the overall strategy

tactical or operational objectives short- or medium-term goals or targets which must be achieved for an organisation to attain its corporate objectives

takeover when a company buys over 50% of the shares of another company and becomes the controlling owner – often referred to as 'acquisition'

target market the market segment that a particular product is aimed at

tariff tax imposed on an imported product

task culture based on co-operation and team work

team working production is organised so that groups of workers undertake complete units of work

teleworking staff working from home but keeping contact with the office by means of modern IT communications

temporary employment contract employment contract that lasts for a fixed time period, e.g. six months

tertiary sector business activity firms that provide services to consumers and other businesses, such as retailing, transport, insurance, banking, hotels, tourism and telecommunications

test marketing marketing a new product in a geographical region before a full-scale launch

total contribution total revenue from sale of a product less total variable costs of producing it

total quality management (TQM) an approach to quality that aims to involve all employees in the quality improvement process

total revenue total income from the sale of all units of the product = quantity × price

trade barriers taxes (tariffs) or other limitations on the free international movement of goods and services

trade union an organisation of working people with the objective of improving the pay and working conditions of its members and providing them with support and legal services

trade union recognition when an employer formally agrees to conduct negotiations on pay and working conditions with a trade union rather than bargaining individually with each worker

trademark a distinctive name, symbol, motto or design that identifies a business or its products – can be legally registered and cannot be copied

training work-related education to increase workforce skills and efficiency

trend underlying movement of the data in a time series

triple bottom line the three objectives of social enterprises: economic, social and environmental

unemployment the numbers of people in an economy willing and able to work who cannot find employment

unfair dismissal ending a worker's employment contract for a reason that the law regards as being unfair

unique selling point/proposition (USP) differentiating factor that makes a company's product unique, designed to motivate customers to buy

variable costs costs that vary with output

variance analysis the process of investigating any differences between budgeted figures and actual figures (performance) and analysing reasons for such differences

venture capital risk capital invested in business start-ups or expanding small businesses, that have good profit potential, but do not find it easy to gain finance from other sources

viral marketing the use of social networking sites or SMS text messages to increase brand awareness or sell products

vision statement a statement of what the organisation would like to achieve or accomplish in the long term

workforce audit a check on the skills and qualifications of all existing employees

workforce plan thinking ahead and establishing the number and skills of the workforce required by the business to meets its objectives

working capital the capital needed to pay for raw materials, day-to-day running costs and credit offered to customers. In accounting terms: making capital = current – current liabilities

working capital cycle the period of time between spending cash on the production process and receiving cash payments from customers

zero budgeting setting budgets to zero each year and budget holders have to argue their case to receive any finance

zero defects the aim of achieving perfect products every time

Index

Acknowledgements

The authors and publishers are grateful for the permissions granted to reproduce materials in either the original or adapted form. While every effort has been made, it has not always been possible to identify the sources of all the materials used, or to trace all copyright holders. If any omissions are brought to our notice, we will be happy to include the appropriate acknowledgements on reprinting.

pp. 39, 281 © The Times 11.01.2008 and 28.08.2009/nisyndication.com; p. 44 Nick Mathiason, Copyright Guardian News & Media Ltd 2008; p. 290 © Telegraph Media Group Limited 2001; pp. 292, 366 Financial Times, January 2001 and May 2010; p. 323 Mind your business (9 Feb 2004): production methods, teamwork, motivation and change management: the news – www.bized.co.uk by permission of Cengage Learning EMEA

Photos

p. 1 Henry Nowick/Shutterstock; pp. 4*tl*, 8 imagebroker.net/SuperStock; p. 4*tr* F. Bettex – Mysterra.org/Alamy; p. 4*b* Amanda Hall/Robert Harding; p. 22 Asia Images/Photolibrary; p. 29*t* imagebroker.net/Photolibrary; p. 29*b* WR Publishing/Alamy; p. 33 Colin Barratt, Milepost 92½ / Corbis; pp. 37, 241 Getty Images; p. 39 Tata; pp. 44, 68, 166, 318*r*, 393 AFP/Getty Images; p. 45 OSO Media/Alamy; p. 51 Kevin Foy/Alamy; p. 52 Jonathan Player/Rex Features; p. 57 Bill Varie/Alamy; p. 71 © The Body Shop International plc; pp. 73, 163 dbimages/Alamy; p. 76 Sipa Press/Rex Features; p. 80 N Elder/CITY AM/Rex Features; p. 82 Jim West/Alamy; p. 90 IslemountImages/Alamy; p. 97 fstop/Photolibrary; p. 99 Electrolux; p. 108 Charles Platiau/Reuters/Corbis; p. 112 Neil Setchfield/Alamy; p. 120 Anglian Water; p. 129 Fresh Food Images/Photolibrary; p. 132 Urban Zone/Alamy; p. 141 Juice Images/Alamy; p. 142 Ford Motor Company; p. 155 Radius Images/Alamy; p. 156 B. O'Kane/Alamy; p. 159*l* Transtock Inc./Alamy; p. 159*r* Linda Matlow/Rex Features; p. 165 David Pearson/Alamy; p. 171 Reuters/Corbis; p. 174 Rob Walls/Alamy; p. 176 Eye Ubiquitous/Alamy; p. 180 Micheline Pelletier/Corbis; p. 186 Images of Africa Photobank/Alamy; p. 188 Anthony Kay/Flight/Alamy; p. 190 View Stock/Alamy; p. 195 Chris Cooper-Smith/Alamy; p. 206 Deco/Alamy; p. 212 Imagebroker/Alamy; p. 220 Gallo Images – Neil Overy/Getty Images; p. 227 Jeff Greenberg/Alamy; p. 233 Drimi/Shutterstock; p. 242 Top Photo Group/Rex Features; p. 244 Dan Vincent/Alamy; p. 246 Scott J. Ferrell/Congressional Quarterly/Alamy; p. 250 Detail Nottingham/Alamy; p. 259 Ulrich Research Services Inc; p. 264 Iain Masterton/Alamy; p. 271 Eric Vidal/Rex Features; p. 275 Gunnar Larsen/Getty Images; p. 281 Steve Skjold/Alamy; p. 293 Nikon; pp. 295*l*, 295*r*, 303 Advertising Archives; p. 299 Jeremy Selwyn/Associated Newspapers/Rex Features; p. 307 Lou Linwei/Alamy; p. 310 Ryan Pyle/Corbis; p. 312 allOver photography/Alamy; p. 316 Ben Molyneux Retail/Alamy; p. 317 Oleskie Maksyenko/Alamy; p. 318*l* Michael Rosenfeld/Science Faction/Corbis; p. 324 Kumar Sriskandan/Alamy; p. 326 Joe Fox Cypress/Alamy; p. 329 Hugh MacDougall/iStock; p. 335 Jose Fuste Raga/Corbis; p. 342 Everett Kennedy Brown/epa/Corbis; p. 343 Bernhard Ciassen/Alamy; p. 347 Simon Clay/Auto Express/Rex Features; p. 354 TriniGourmet.com; p. 357 Bloomberg via Getty Images; p. 361 Paul Prescott/Shutterstock; p. 364 Monica M. Davey/epa/Corbis; p. 366 Howard Harrison/Alamy; p. 369 Don Couch/Alamy; p. 381 Jeffrey Salter/Redux/Eyevine; p. 384 David Madison/Corbis; p. 387 redmal/iStock

l = left, *r* = right, *t* = top of page, *b* = bottom of page